"*Season of the Witch* is an enthralling—and harrowing—account of how the 1967 Summer of Love gave way to 20 or so winters of discontent. An undercurrent of rock music runs through the book . . . Some of the artists, such as the Dead and the Jefferson Airplane, still get airplay. Others enjoyed fleeting fame. *Season of the Witch*, however, is good enough to last."

—*The Washington Post*

"A gritty corrective to our rosy memories . . . enthralling, news-driven history . . . [a] smart and briskly paced tale . . . I found it hard to put down."

—*San Francisco Chronicle*

"A sprawling, ambitious history . . . Talbot's energetic, highly entertaining storytelling conveys the exhilaration of '60s counterculture as well as the gathering ugliness that would mark the city in the '70s."

—*The Boston Globe*

"Talbot's book is a gritty, poetic Valentine to the city by the bay as it emerged as a fantasia of ethnic, cultural, sexual, intellectual and social liberation. Talbot doesn't back off from having literary flowers in his hair recounting some of the halcyon days of the summer of love, but he also chronicles the city's many problems with a heavy dose of hardboiled reporter noir."

—*The Huffington Post*

"Exhaustive research yields penetrating character studies . . . In exhilarating fashion, Talbot clears the rainbow mist and brings San Francisco into sharp focus."

—*Publishers Weekly* (starred review)

"An ambitious, labor-of-love illumination of a city's soul, celebrating the uniqueness of San Francisco without minimizing the price paid for the city's free-spiritedness . . . the author encompasses the city's essence . . . Talbot loves his city deeply and knows it well, making the pieces of the puzzle fit together, letting the reader understand . . . [He] takes the reader much deeper than cliché, exploring a San Francisco that tourists never discover."

—*Kirkus Reviews* (starred review)

"Talbot presents gripping accounts of both crime sprees and football show-downs. Even people who were there might take away something new, and for others, the book offers a comprehensive introduction to the era."

—*Booklist*

"Fascinating . . . [the] absorbing, breakneck story of how the City by the Bay fought off its demons in the 1970s and '80s and emerged with enlightened values intact."

—*The Oregonian*

"Excellent . . . Talbot's account of the rise of Jim Jones and his Peoples Temple religious movement is absolutely masterful, allowing the reader to see just how and why this unstable preacher achieved such prominence. Talbot not only gives us a nuanced account of the city that he clearly loves, but he also gives us a cultural history of late-twentieth-century America."

—*Shepard Express*, Milwaukee

"Talbot's new book delves to impressive depths in tracing the city's transfor-mation from parochial backwater to countercultural beacon . . . the Salon founder deftly sketches portraits of hippies, politicos, and rights activists who forged our 'San Francisco values' and in the process rescues some old icons from obscurity . . . a compulsively entertaining page-turner . . . A use-ful lesson for our Occupied times: Change is hard, but it's possible."

—*San Francisco* magazine

"A sprawling, lurid, dishy, and electric history . . . Talbot musters magnifi-cent details from new interviews and old news reports. . . . Talbot's chap-ter on the Zebra killings is genuinely harrowing, as are his accounts of Altamont, the SLA, and miscellaneous madness in a Haight flooded with junk-addicted veterans . . . always finding fresh anecdotes to savor even in familiar stories . . . this wild, thrilling, deeply reported book is a choice guide to all of those San Franciscos—cities nobody yet has managed to reconcile in a coherent whole, so kudos to Talbot for matching subject to form."

—*SF Weekly*

"Few cities experienced a more tumultuous history throughout the 1960's and 1970's than the 'city by the bay,' San Francisco. Author David Talbot gives a tremendously engaging, accessible, informative look at the life and times of the Northern California peninsula in *Season of the Witch*, focusing on the period beginning with the 'Summer of Love' and culminating with the surprise success of the football 49ers in the 1982 Super Bowl . . . Talbot equally divides his chapters between the cultural evolution of the city and the explosive political upheavals that would directly impact the citizens and their surroundings . . . [His] book is a sociological triumph."

—*Edge*, Fort Lauderdale

"An exhilarating ride through the cultural and political history of San Francisco. Talbot weaves a magnificent narrative that incorporates key players such as Janis Joplin, the Cockettes, and Harvey Milk."

—*The Advocate*

"A fresh, fun, vigorous look at a strange American city David Talbot knows well and loves with irony."

—Oliver Stone

"As a phenomenally intuitive journalist, editor, and culture critic, David Talbot has not only channeled the Zeitgeist but helped make it."

—Camille Paglia, bestselling author and culture critic

"David Talbot is a great storyteller. He writes like an angel and has a reporter's passion for the truth. Describing people I knew, I can say that Talbot has perfect pitch, but he has also introduced me to others, as thrilling as sin. He got it all just right and gets closer to describing the lusty, languorous, glamorous, and sometimes lethal Saint named Francisco than anyone I know. The book overflows with gifts. I'm in awe of it."

—Peter Coyote, author of *Sleeping Where I Fall*

"In this wonderful book, David Talbot tells the stories deep in San Francisco's loric landscape, from its cultural greatness to the slides into madness. Talbot explores its volcanic originality with awe and respect. An unforgettable history."

—Tom Hayden, author of *The Long Sixties*

ALSO BY DAVID TALBOT

Brothers: The Hidden History of the Kennedy Years

Devil Dog: The Amazing True Story of the Man Who Saved America

SEASON OF THE WITCH

Enchantment, Terror, and Deliverance
in the City of Love

DAVID TALBOT

FREE PRESS
New York   London   Toronto   Sydney   New Delhi

Free Press
A Division of Simon & Schuster, Inc.
1230 Avenue of the Americas
New York, NY 10020

First Free Press trade paperback edition March 2013

FREE PRESS and colophon are trademarks of Simon & Schuster, Inc.

For information about special discounts for bulk purchases, please contact Simon & Schuster Special Sales at 1-866-506-1949 or business@simonandschuster.com.

The Simon & Schuster Speakers Bureau can bring authors to your live event. For more information or to book an event, contact the Simon & Schuster Speakers Bureau at 1-866-248-3049 or visit our website at www.simonspeakers.com.

Manufactured in the United States of America

19 20 18

The Library of Congress has cataloged the hardcover edition as follows:

Talbot, David
Season of the witch : enchantment, terror, and deliverance in the city of love / David Talbot. — 1st Free Press hardcover ed.
p. cm.
1. San Francisco (Calif.)—Social conditions—20th century. 2. San Francisco (Calif.)—History—20th century. 3. San Francisco (Calif.)—Biography. 4. San Francisco (Calif.)—Social life and customs—20th century. 5. City and town life—California—San Francisco—History—20th century. 6. Culture conflict—California—San Francisco—History—20th century. 7. Social problems—California—San Francisco—History—20th century. 8. Social change—California—San Francisco—History—20th century. 9. Political culture—California—San Francisco—History—20th century. 10. Countercul-ture—California—San Francisco—History—20th century. I. Title.

HN80.S4T35 2012

306.09794'610904—dc23   2011032082

ISBN 978-1-4391-0821-5
ISBN 978-1-4391-0824-6 (pbk)
ISBN 978-1-4391-2787-2 (ebook)

To Camille, who helped me finally and fully love San Francisco, while I was falling in love with her. And to the entire Peri family, the Italian-Irish-Greek clan that brought the city's history to life for me. And to my sons, Joseph and Nathaniel, who are making their own San Francisco history.

ACKNOWLEDGMENTS

B OOKS ARE FEATS OF enterprise as well as creativity. As always, I was mightily assisted in this endeavor by my work partner, Karen Croft, who brainstormed editorial strategies, managed the project's finances, arranged difficult interviews, helped me go spelunking through library caverns, read early drafts of the manuscript, and performed numerous other essential tasks.

Public libraries, like all institutions by and for the people in America these days, are endangered treasures. I relied enormously in my research on the dedicated and deeply informed staff of the San Francisco Public Library's History Center. Library archivist Susan Goldstein and her staff have a hidden empire of San Francisco history at their fingertips, and they bring it to life each day for numerous scholars and curious citizens. The serene and well-run History Center, on the sixth floor of the San Francisco Public Library's main branch, is the critical first stop for anyone trying to get a feel for this city's kaleidoscopic past.

The most vital way of touching this past, of course, is by speaking with the men and women who lived it. I am grateful to the more than 120 people who shared their stories with me, reliving the traumas and triumphs and the jaw-dropping wildness that was San Francisco.

For the chapters on Jim Jones and Jonestown, I am particularly indebted to Fielding McGehee III and the Jonestown Institute research project sponsored by the Department of Religious Studies at San Diego State University, as well as to the California Historical Society, the repository for the important and extensive files known as the Peoples Temple collection.

I was inspired throughout my toil by the energetic interest of my two sons, Joe and Nat, who kept wanting to know more, and more, about the unique city of their birth. Joe also helped with interview transcriptions, and with his usual pointed questions about his father's views and assumptions. I was also able to draw on the sharp editorial skills of my wife, Camille Peri, whose instincts are always true. My brother-in-law Don Peri—a collector of San Francisco memorabilia and also an eyewitness to some of the events chronicled here—was generous with his research materials and insights. And my brother Stephen Talbot and sister Margaret Talbot—fellow Talbot Players and sparkling siblings—were, as usual, sources of encouragement and wisdom.

Martha Levin and Dominick Anfuso of the Free Press have been the allies that every writer yearns for, but too seldom finds, in the book world. As the publishing industry goes through its convulsions, the Free Press has been a trustworthy partner for me on two books. I deeply appreciated working with talented editors Martin Beiser and Alessandra Bastagli, as well as publicity director Carisa Hays and her staff.

My fellow lover of ink and paper, Kelly Frankeny, brought her fine eye and hand to the book cover design, as she did on my previous book, *Brothers*.

Finally, my agent, Sloan Harris at International Creative Management, has always been a tough and astute defender of my forever-embattled realm.

CONTENTS

Author's Note   xiii

Introduction   xv

Prologue: Wild Irish Rogues   1

       PART ONE: Enchantment   19

1. Saturday Afternoon   21

2. Dead Men Dancing   26

3. The Walled City   32

4. The Free City   36

5. The Lost Children of Windy Feet   42

6. Street Medicine   51

7. Murder on Shakedown Street   60

8. The Napoleon of Rock   68

9. The Daily Circus   76

10. San Francisco's Morning Kiss   84

11. Radio Free America   90

12. The Palace of Golden Cocks   98

       PART TWO: Terror   109

13. A Death in the Family   111

14. Lucifer Rising   123

15. A Knife Down Your Throat   134

16. Benevolent Dictator   144

17. Love's Last Stand   156

18. Dungeons and Dragons   169

19. The Revolution Will Be Televised   180

20. Black and White and Red All Over   204

21. The Empress of Chinatown   224

22. San Francisco Satyricon   233

23. Civic War   248

24. Inside Man   267

25. Slouching Toward San Francisco   275

26. Prophet of Doom   284

27. Exodus   290

28. Rapture in the Jungle   298

29. The Reckoning   305

30. A Tale of Two Cities   311

31. Day of the Gun   322

        PART THREE: Deliverance   337

32. Fire by Trial   339

33. The Center Holds   350

34. Strange Angels   358

35. Playing Against God   376

36. The City of Saint Francis   387

Epilogue   405

Season of the Witch Playlist   407

Sources   409

Index   429

"It's the freedom of the city that keeps it alive."

—Geoffrey West, physicist

AUTHOR'S NOTE

I WAS BORN AND RAISED in Los Angeles, but even when I was growing up, I knew that I belonged in San Francisco. My father, Lyle Talbot, was a Hollywood actor, but he too loved San Francisco. In the early 1930s, while working for Warner Bros., he costarred with Bette Davis in *Fog over Frisco,* a snappy thriller about high-society types who fall into the violent grip of the underworld. The film brought my father on location to San Francisco, and he returned often to the city for business and pleasure. Years later, he regaled me and my brother and sisters with colorful stories about lavish parties at the Sheraton Palace Hotel; intimate soirees at a Nob Hill apartment where a female Chinese-American doctor raised money for the flying aces who were resisting Japan's invasion of China; and drinking escapades with Marion Davies, the fun-loving mistress of William Randolph Hearst. His tales conjured a city that was far more atmospheric and cosmopolitan than the sun-bleached Los Angeles suburb where I grew up.

During the 1960s, my father brought us to San Francisco when he performed in long runs at the Geary Theater, the city's grand old lady of pleasure. Setting out from the St. Francis Hotel in the middle of downtown, my siblings and I would trek the wind-whipped hills, wander through Chinatown and North Beach, and take the ferryboat to Sausalito. I knew—listening to some older, long-haired teenagers dressed like Moroccan tribesmen, as they played guitars and flutes in a Sausalito square—that I would make San Francisco my home one day. By then, San Francisco had come to stand for something far different than it had for my father; it was my generation's wild shore of freedom. The city held layers of allure for me that descended deeply through time.

By the time I moved to San Francisco in the 1970s, the city was at war with itself, beset by grisly crime and political violence. My city of peace and love and music, and my father's city of evening dress elegance, was being obliterated by a daily barrage of gruesome headlines. In the end, San Francisco not only survived this bloody turmoil, it emerged as a beacon of enlightenment and experimentation for the entire world.

As the years went by, San Francisco became not only my city but also my way of life. From the time I was a boy, I wanted to live in a place like my father's theater world, a magic box filled with lavishly made-up women, extravagant gay men, and other larger-than-life characters. I wanted a world that could encompass all worlds. I found something close to it in this soft-lit city in the ocean mists. I found myself here, got married here, raised my two sons here, started my own version of a theater company here—an eccentric web magazine called *Salon* that could have been born only in San Francisco, city of outcasts.

And now it's time to repay the debt. This is my love letter to San Francisco. But if it's a valentine, it's a bloody valentine, filled with the raw truth as well as the glory about the city that has been my home for more than three decades now. The story I'm about to tell is an epic one, filled with personalities and events. But in the end, this is what it is all about. It's the story of a city that changed itself, and then changed the world.

INTRODUCTION

S AN FRANCISCO WAS BUILT on a dare. The city was tossed up overnight on the shimmying, heaving, mischievous crust of the Pacific rim. A gold rush city of fortune seekers, gamblers, desperadoes and the flesh-peddling circus that caters to such men, San Francisco defied the laws of nature. It was a wide-open town, its thighs splayed wantonly for every vice damned in the Bible and more than a few that were left out. San Francisco was the Last Chance Saloon for outcasts from every corner of the globe. If the earth didn't swallow them first, hell soon enough would.

Great cities have usually been founded by wealthy burghers and craftsmen—their spires and monuments a testament to the holiness of the work ethic. But San Francisco high society was a devil's dinner party, a rogue's crew of robber barons, saloon keepers, and shrewd harlots. When the town's painted ladies went to the theater, gentlemen would rise until they were seated. By 1866, there were thirty-one saloons for every place of worship.

After the great earthquake struck in 1906, a wandering Pentecostal preacher who found himself among San Francisco's smoking ruins inevitably declared the disaster God's vengeance on Sodom. In the emotional aftershocks of the catastrophe, the Holy Roller's hellfire preaching attracted a flock of dazed souls. But the size of his congregation was dwarfed by the crowds that thronged the last theater left standing in the city, where San Franciscans lustily cheered their beloved burlesques.

San Francisco's Barbary Coast district—with its black-stocking bars, live sex shows, and opium dens—rose again from the earthquake's ashes. And well into the new century—long before Las Vegas assured tourists that it knew how to keep their secrets—San Francisco aggressively marketed its libertine image. During the Prohibition era, the local board of supervisors passed legislation forbidding San Francisco police from enforcing the dry law. Drag queen shows were written up in the tourist guides alongside the ferryboat rides and Fisherman's Wharf dining spots.

By the 1930s, however, another San Francisco emerged: Catholic, working class, family oriented. The Church's influence could be felt throughout the town, particularly in city hall and the police department, where an old-boy's network of Irish Catholic—and later Italian Catholic—officials held sway.

Catholic San Francisco had its own wild heart: tough stevedores and cable car operators who fought bloody battles for labor rights; and immigrant kids who learned to love Puccini and Dante, and collected nickels for the Irish Volunteers back home. These working-class heroes eventually turned San Francisco into a pro-labor, arts-loving stronghold of the Democratic Party.

But as the Catholic hierarchy solidified its control of the city during and after World War II, it imposed a traditional social order on San Francisco, driving the city's Barbary outlaws underground. For years, the two San Franciscos waged a clandestine civil war. Gays and lesbians would be swept up in midnight police raids on bars. (Dykes had to wear at least one article of women's clothing—usually lacy panties—to avoid arrest.) Mixed-race couples were quietly blocked by real estate covenants from renting apartments in the city. Only occasionally did the city's culture war erupt onto the front pages of the metro newspapers—as it did in 1957 when poet Lawrence Ferlinghetti, owner of City Lights Books, was put on trial for publishing "Howl," Allen Ginsberg's declaration of war on the American Moloch, and the opening salvo in the 1960s' epic struggle for cultural freedom.

A decade later, San Francisco's culture war was in full fury, as the city absorbed a wave of runaway children—refugees from America's broken family—and transformed itself overnight into the capital of the 1960s counterculture. In the 1970s, San Francisco was overrun by another army of American runaways, as it became the Emerald City of gay liberation.

No other American city has undergone such an earth-shaking cultural shift in such a short span. Today San Francisco is seen as the "Left Coast City"—the wild, frontier outpost of the American Dream. Conservatives have declared war on "San Francisco values" and are bitterly fighting to stop the spread of those values. But long before the culture war went nationwide, San Francisco was torn apart by its own uncivil war. San Francisco values did not come into the world with flowers in their hair; they were born howling, in blood and strife. It took years of frantic and often violent conflict—including political assassinations, riots, bombings, kidnappings, serial race murders, antigay street mayhem, the biggest mass suicide in history, and a panic-inducing epidemic—before San Francisco finally made peace with itself and its new identity.

In the end, San Francisco healed itself by learning how to take care of its sick and dying. And it came together to celebrate itself with the help of an unlikely football dynasty and a team that mirrored the city's eccentric personality.

San Francisco's battles are no longer with itself but with the outside world, as it exports the European-style social ideas that drive Republican leaders and Fox News commentators into a frenzy: gay marriage, medical marijuana, universal health care, immigrant sanctuary, "living" minimum wage, bicycle-friendly streets, stricter environmental and consumer regulations. Conservatives see these San Francisco values as examples of social engineering gone mad. But in San Francisco, they're seen as the bedrock of a decent society, one that is based on a live-and-let-live tolerance, shared sense of humanity, and openness to change.

One of San Francisco's more flowery laureates anointed it "the cool gray city of love." But the people who cling to its hills and hollows and know its mercurial temperament—the sudden juggernaut of sea fog and wind that can shroud the sun and chill the soul—recognize San Francisco as a rougher beast. The people who radically changed San Francisco in the 1960s and 1970s—and thus, the world—have been ridiculed and trivialized for so long that we've forgotten who they really were. But it took a frontier breed of men and women to conquer a town like San Francisco—a town that was still more Dashiell Hammett than Oz. Ginsberg called them "seekers," which gives them their due. This is the story of their quest, and how they triumphed over the machinery of night.

SEASON OF THE WITCH

PROLOGUE

Wild Irish Rogues

San Francisco, June 1932

THE CITY WAS in a frenzy. Frank Egan—the once popular public defender, a man widely considered to be a future mayor—was on the run, accused of hiring two ex-cons to murder a fifty-nine-year-old widow named Jessie Hughes.

Before he disappeared, Egan emotionally insisted on his innocence. "Mrs. Hughes has been like a mother to me," he tearfully told reporters. But it did not look good for the public defender. He was the widow's executor, as well as the beneficiary of both her will and several insurance policies—and before her murder, she had been shrilly accusing him of looting her finances. When one of the ex-cons confessed his role in the brutal murder, naming the public defender as the mastermind, Egan decided to pull a vanishing act.

By the time he made himself scarce, Egan was San Francisco's most notorious criminal, even though he had yet to be formally charged with a crime. The newspapers were filled with grisly details about the widow's murder. The two ex-cons, one of whom bore a striking resemblance to George Raft and the other to Humphrey Bogart, had talked their way into the unfortunate Mrs. Hughes's Lakewood Drive home, knocked her out with several blows to the jaw, lugged her into her basement garage, put her under the wheel of a blue Lincoln sedan once owned

1

by a gangster, and crushed the life out of her by running the heavy car back and forth over her body. Then they drove a couple blocks away and dumped the lifeless woman in the gutter, hoping she'd be mistaken for a hit-and-run victim.

The local papers also indicated that Mrs. Hughes was not Egan's only victim, that he had made a racket of bilking lonely and aging women out of their nest eggs. One of these sad victims—referred to as "a little hunchback" in the press—had fallen into Egan's clutches through the unsavory auspices of a female spiritualist, who recognized an easy mark when she saw one. Another victim was lured away from her loving husband by the George Raft look-alike accomplice, who was masquerading at the time as a debonair dancing instructor. While the woman's husband was away on business, the distraught man later recounted, his wife went "dance mad" and fell into a life of dissolution. She ended up in a gloomy Tenderloin flat, where she was kept in a permanent state of inebriation while Egan raided her savings and otherwise exploited her fallen condition. Finally, her husband charged, she was dispatched altogether with a poison powder by yet another sordid partner of Egan's—a thoroughly corrupt surgeon named Dr. Nathan S. Housman who made a living by patching up bullet-riddled hoodlums when not running criminal errands for Egan.

Hammett would have blushed to create villains as florid as Egan and his henchmen. Fortunately for Egan, he was represented by a lawyer who was well on his way to becoming a San Francisco legend: Vincent Hallinan, a brawling young Irishman with thick, wavy hair and the battered good looks of a prizefighter. Hallinan was a rising thirty-four-year-old defense attorney when he took the Egan case. He was also a confirmed bachelor and notorious ladies' man, having sloughed off his Jesuit schooling and, in his words, "the daffy theology of the Roman Catholic Church" and "embraced a pagan hedonism."

But young Vince Hallinan seemed to have finally met his match with his current romantic partner: a twenty-year-old, green-eyed, half-Irish, half-Genovese beauty named Vivian Moore. They were a true-life Nick and Nora—a young, stylish, dazzling couple who consorted with mugs and crooks and were always one step ahead of the cops.

If Hallinan drew a bad hand with Egan, those were the breaks of the game. He never bothered to ask Egan if he was guilty. A criminal lawyer can't concern himself "with the guilt or innocence of a client," he would say years later, looking back on the notorious case. "He can't. The whole thing is a racket. The prosecution puts on its case not for justice but for conviction, and you put on yours only to acquit. If you are unwilling to do all that is possible to obtain your client's acquittal, you are allowing a vicious system to grind him up, and you have no business on the defense side of the court. And you won't be there very long, either."

Later in his life, Hallinan would put his formidable courtroom skills at the service of labor leaders, Cold War dissidents, civil rights activists, and antiwar protesters. The legal victories that he and his colleagues won helped create a new San Francisco, and a new America. But there were few heroes in his life in those days. Hallinan learned his rough trade in the slimy trenches of the San Francisco courts—where the defendants were often morally depraved, and the cops and prosecutors were something worse.

Now Hallinan's biggest challenge was to bring Frank Egan safely to jail before he could commit suicide—an outcome that the newspapers were loudly suggesting the cops preferred so that the public defender couldn't make good on his threat to "blow the lid off the police department." What did Egan have on the notoriously crooked San Francisco Police Department? Hallinan didn't know. But he knew he had to find a way to safely convey Egan to the authorities—with a crowd of reporters to witness his surrender.

Each day that Egan remained at large, the city grew more frantic. The wanted man was last seen in a car with Hallinan and the lawyer's "more than attractive girlfriend," as the *San Francisco Chronicle* called Viv, while the trio drove away from Hallinan's summer cottage on Emerald Lake, south of the city. So now cops and sheriffs were combing the hills in San Mateo, and even dragging the lake. One wild rumor had Egan taking off from the lake in an amphibian plane to the open sea, where a speedboat whooshed him to a rum ship outside the twelve-mile limit.

How could the SFPD have let Egan slip through its fingers? The press smelled a rat. "What is the matter with the city's police department?" the *Chronicle* demanded to know in a front-page editorial.

"Here is a man indicted for one of the most appalling murders in the city's history . . . and the police did not even have their eye on him."

Mayor Angelo Rossi, who had ascended to his city hall suite courtesy of the all-powerful Irish political machine, knew he had to tread lightly with Police Chief William Quinn and his boys if he wanted to keep his job. But at long last, even Rossi's patience wore thin. While reporters listened outside his door, the mayor bellowed over the phone at Quinn that he wanted Egan in custody, and he wanted him now. Later, an agitated Rossi threatened to "clean house" at the police department if there was any more bungling.

With the flame turned high under his ass, the police chief knew he could no longer wait for Egan to turn up stiff—he had to go find him. And Quinn knew exactly where to look first: Vince Hallinan's various habitats. After secreting his client away in a safe place while he figured out a strategy, Hallinan drove to his house, where he was immediately greeted by four burly plainclothes cops. The top dog flashed his badge.

"We have orders to take you down to headquarters."

Hallinan was unfazed. He knew the dance. "Do you have a warrant?"

"No."

"Then you're not taking me anywhere."

The detective looked stymied. "Do you mind if we go in and call the chief on your phone?"

Hallinan normally got along with Quinn, who was an easygoing sort of man for a cop. But when Vince got on the phone with him, the chief sounded hysterical. "Listen, Hallinan, this town's in an uproar!" Quinn shouted. "You get Egan here right now, or I'm going to charge you with complicity in the murder of Jessie Hughes!"

Vince Hallinan was not the type who was easily intimidated. He grew up in a miserably poor family. Back in the old country, his father Patrick belonged to the Irish Invincibles, the terrorist fringe of the Irish Republican Brotherhood. After assassinating the agent of a rent-gouging landlord, Patrick was forced to flee to America—and to a lifetime of regrets and raw deals. Young Vince had been attracted to the law not only by the money but also as a way to fight bullies without using your fists—though he never forswore that more direct method of dealing with thugs, even if they wore three-piece suits. Hallinan took on poor Irish clients who were being evicted from their homes or had been maimed in streetcar accidents, whether or not a big payday seemed likely. And along the way, he stood up to brutal cops, corrupt court officials, ruthless corporate executives—even the powerful Catholic Church, which he always resented for robbing him and other Irish-Americans of their childhood with mysticism and fear.

So Quinn didn't scare him. Speaking firmly into the phone, Hallinan informed the chief that Frank Egan would appear only if he were indicted. Until then, if the police interfered with Hallinan in any way, he would sue them for false arrest. "You'd better simmer down and realize that you're an officer of the law, and stop letting your office be run by the newspapers," the young lawyer lectured the spluttering chief. Then he handed the phone back to the detective.

After a few minutes of "Yeahs" and "Uh-huhs," the detective hung up and turned to Hallinan.

"The chief says that you don't have to come down to headquarters . . . but we're going to stay right here with you, and we're not supposed to let you out of our sight until Egan comes in and surrenders."

"Make yourselves at home," Hallinan replied graciously. "I'll cook us up a pot of coffee."

Then Hallinan walked into the kitchen—and promptly went out the back door. He climbed over the fence into the alley, hurried to the home of a friend, and borrowed his car.

Hallinan was free, but he was in a jam. He wanted to arrange for Egan's well-publicized surrender—which he knew would not only be safer for his client but also look better in court. To do that, he needed to communicate with Egan. But with half the city's police force now looking for Hallinan, whose face had been splashed across the front pages for weeks, that wouldn't be easy. He had to find a messenger—and the first person who came to mind was his free-spirited girlfriend.

During their brief romance, Vivian Moore had already made a strong impression on Hallinan with her adventurous—some might call it reckless—exploits. The product of a broken marriage, and shuttled as a girl from one unpredictable home to another in her mother's sprawling family, Viv learned early on to take care of herself. One day she terrified Vince by plunging into the icy surf in Monterey Bay and swimming halfway to the Orient. "When she made it back to shore, I didn't know whether to slap her or kiss her."

Hallinan hated to bring his young lover into the Egan mess. But when he laid out the proposition to her, she immediately agreed to act as the go-between with his notorious client. "Of course, I was delighted," Viv recalled later. "Such excitement, and everything about the case all over the front pages!"

Soon after Vivian returned to her apartment on Fourteenth Avenue, however, the doorbell rang, and when she opened the door, two flatfoots barged inside.

"We're here to see Vincent Hallinan," growled one, a gruff old gray bear named Sergeant Mike Desmond.

"He isn't here," she shot back.

"Well, he will be," retorted Desmond. "You're his girl. He'll turn up."

Vivian sat down and began reading a book. She knew she had to think fast. Suddenly she stood up and walked across the room.

The bulky Desmond jumped up and got in her way.

She played the one card she had—the only one that would work on a tough Mick like Desmond. "I suppose that a person might be permitted to go to the bathroom," she said archly, looking the cop dead in the eye.

Desmond blushed as crimson as a cardinal's robe. "All right," he stammered, "but I'll have to stand right outside that bedroom door. I'm not supposed to let you out of my sight."

Shutting the bathroom door behind her, Vivian opened the window and shimmied through it feetfirst. Her apartment was on the second floor, and she needed to grope for the water pipe on the side of the building, but she finally grabbed on to it and slid down like a fireman to the landing below. After descending the stairs to the backyard, she took off her shoes, tipped over three large flowerpots, and stood on top of the rocky platform so that she could climb over the fence. Now she was on a sidewalk to the rear of her building, and the wild and sheltering canopy of Golden Gate Park beckoned to her, just blocks away. She sprinted for it, taking a secret path into its thick foliage that she had known from childhood.

Viv was supposed to rendezvous with Vince at the Great Highway, on the ocean end of the park, about two miles away. She had no money for a cab, so she took off on foot for her destination as the first cold gusts of afternoon began blowing in from the Pacific. Ten or fifteen minutes later, she heard the wails of police sirens, and she dropped to the ground and crawled inside the prickly shrubbery along the path, waiting there until they faded. Then she got up, brushed herself off, and headed west again.

By the time she reached Vince's car, parked near the beach, Viv was as flushed and wild eyed as an animal that had outrun a hunting party. Vince was flabbergasted. "I'm sorry I put you in this position," he told her.

She waved off his concern. "Listen," she said, still a little breathless, "I love it! Where's the message and where do I take it?"

After Viv delivered Vince's message to the strange, sallow-faced Egan at his hideout, the young couple lay low. They drove out to the country for the rest of the afternoon, and in the early evening they returned to the city and ducked inside a movie palace. The whole city was looking for them, but they were snuggled together in the theater's dark cocoon, watching a movie. At intermission, the orchestra leader turned around and cracked, "Is Frank Egan or Vincent Hallinan in the house?" The audience broke into laughter, and Vince and Viv laughed too.

IT WAS AROUND THIS time that Vincent Hallinan, bachelor for life, realized that he was going to spend the rest of his life with this woman. It had taken him awhile to arrive at this conclusion. But Viv had known all along that "the Mastodon," as she liked to call him, would finally be brought down. She knew from the moment she met him, with his blue, blue eyes and crooked smile, that this was the man who would fulfill her girlhood dream—the man who would be the father of her six children, all boys.

But before they could begin work on their brood, Vince and Viv had to navigate the mucky shoals of the Egan case. When they returned to their respective homes that night after the movies, their living rooms were occupied by armies of shotgun-wielding men in blue, who served each of them with a grand jury subpoena. When she showed up for her court appearance, Vivian, already a press sweetheart, was greeted with a fireworks of flashbulbs by the newshounds. Sweeping into the grand jury room in a jaunty flapper's cap, silky striped blouse, hip-hugging skirt, fur-lined jacket, and tight black leather gloves, Viv quickly seduced the dour-faced grand jurors. "Miss Moore told her version of [Egan's escape] fully to the jurors, who succumbed as one man to her charms and kept her in the grand jury room three-quarters of an hour—not that they thought she could give them any more information of value, but because she is such a delightful girl to talk to," the *Chronicle* reported the next day.

As for Vince, his "charms did not prove so effective," the newspaper dryly recounted, as one by one, the tough lawyer batted away the grand jury's questions and was quickly dismissed.

Soon after, the wild saga of Egan's flight finally came to an end, when Hallinan staged the public defender's surrender. Accompanied by a swarm of reporters, Egan strolled into the Golden Gate Park station and breezily greeted the cops behind the desk, a number of whom he had pounded the beat with back in his youth. "Good morning, boys."

"Good morning, Frank. How do you like our new jail?"

"I'd like to take a look at it," Egan replied—and he was given an extended opportunity to do just that.

The Egan trial enthralled San Francisco for several weeks more. Crowds jostled in the predawn damp and chill before the hall of justice opened to grab seats in the courtroom, where they marveled at Hallinan's unique blend of flowery and combative oratory. The details of the crime that emerged during the trial only darkened Egan's already villainous portrait. One of the ex-cons testified that all he got from Egan for carrying out his vile murder plan was a new hat; the public defender had threatened him with a return trip to San Quentin State Prison if he didn't comply. What sort of man offers a hat for a woman's life, the ex-con's teary mother asked? And all of San Francisco wondered the same. Only an attorney with the pugilistic artistry of Vincent Hallinan could have kept Egan from the gas chamber.

In the end, Frank Egan got life. By the time he slithered off to the penitentiary, Egan was such a reviled character that the press also turned its fury on his skillful young attorney for mounting such an aggressive defense. But the city's outrage soon found a new target: the SFPD. No sooner had Egan been convicted than a top police official confessed to the press that the cops knew in advance about Egan's murder plan but had done nothing to stop it. For months, the police department had been monitoring the phone calls between Egan and his accomplice, the nefarious Dr. Housman—which explained why the police seemed so certain of Egan's guilt from the very beginning.

Why didn't the cops rescue poor Jessie Hughes from a violent end? Their explanations seemed weak and slippery, and quickly raised new suspicions about the city's murky police bureaucracy. Was the brass somehow involved in Egan's criminal enterprise? Or were they sitting on evidence of his dark plots so they could blackmail him and secretly control the public defender's office?

The police bombshell confirmed what Hallinan knew all along: San Francisco justice was a contradiction in terms. The municipal corridors were awash in graft and vice. And the cops were some of the biggest offenders of all. The SFPD liked to boast that gangsters could never get a foothold in San Francisco, unlike mob-ridden cities such as New York, Chicago, and Philadelphia. "Good reason: the cops do their own 'protecting' in San Francisco and keep the payoffs in the family," Hallinan was quick to explain.

These unvarnished opinions didn't win Vince friends on the force. Nor did his combative courtroom style make him a beloved figure in the judges' chambers. If a defendant was to enjoy any rights at all in a judicial system as deeply putrid as San Francisco's, his lawyer had to be willing to wade in with both fists. But this style of rough justice had its costs.

Judges were in the habit of jailing Hallinan for disrespect. When one jurist asked the pugnacious lawyer if he meant to show contempt for his court, Vince replied, "No, Your Honor, I'm trying to conceal it."

Hallinan was particularly contemptuous of the judge who presided over the Egan trial, an aging courtroom despot with an obvious bias for the prosecution. The judge made sure that Hallinan would pay for his defiance.

Shortly after the Egan trial concluded, Vince finally embraced the inevitable and proposed to Viv. But as the young couple prepared to drive off on their honeymoon, a meaty paw suddenly reached into Hallinan's car and turned off the ignition. The paw, and the gruff voice, belonged to the old bear, Sergeant Desmond.

"Sorry, Vince, we have a warrant for your arrest, and we're taking you in."

"Listen, Mike," pleaded the bridegroom, "we're going on our honeymoon. Can't you hold it up for a week?"

"We held it up for a week already," growled Desmond. "We have positive orders to bring you up today."

"All right," Hallinan sighed. "Viv, this is Detective Sergeant Desmond."

The old bear looked at the young woman who some weeks earlier had slipped his grasp and bowed deeply. "I have had the pleasure."

Now Vivian Hallinan stood on the sidewalk in front of her mother's apartment as her freshly minted husband was hustled into a squad car. She was twenty years old and full of self-confidence. She had thrown herself into her new life with this "wild Irish rogue" with the same reckless abandon that she had plunged into the choppy surf of Monterey Bay. "Yet, as I stood there and watched the dark blue patrol car vanish down the street, a feeling of panic gripped me. Maybe I had bargained for more than I could handle."

In the years to come, all San Francisco would be seized by the same feeling, as the city leaped into the thrashing unknown.

DESPITE HIS PRINCIPLED OPPOSITION to married life, Vince turned out to be an enthusiastic father, energetically applying himself to the physical, intellectual, and moral development of his six children—all boys, just as Vivian had always dreamed. The most important piece of fatherly wisdom he imparted to his sons boiled down to, "Question everything in life."

"I'll always give you the best advice I can, but make up your own minds," the courtroom lion told his boys. "No matter how firmly I believe something, it might be one hundred percent false; everything I know may be wrong."

Hallinan further enforced this independent spirit in his offspring by teaching them all to box, swim, dive, ride horseback, and play a maniacal style of football and rugby at a tender age. Each boy was given a prize-fighter's nickname—Butch, Kayo, Tuffy, Dynamite, Flash, Dangerous—in hopes that he would live up to their tough monikers.

It must have occurred on a frequent basis to Hallinan that he had created a monster, or rather six of them. Visitors to the Hallinan home were often shocked to hear the old lion roaring at the top of his lungs at one of his wild cubs. But the thunderous paternal blasts never seemed to faze their intended target, who would shrug, "All right, all right, don't blow your top."

Fortunately, Vivian turned out to be a resilient parent, weathering the crises of motherhood six times over—including a broken skull (Kayo) and a life-threatening case of polio (Butch). Somehow she also found time to teach herself the real estate game. Vivian proved to have the sharp business acumen associated with her Genovese ancestors. Her dazzling beauty didn't hurt, either. "She was just gorgeous. She would sit on the bankers' laps, and she would get the deals," her firstborn son, Patrick (Butch), would recall. By the time her growing brood was in knee pants, she had amassed a small empire of downtown apartment buildings, making the family rich in the process.

Despite the family's new prosperity, Vivian also became increasingly active in left-wing causes during the Cold War years, when they were least fashionable. And she dragged Vince along with her into the maelstrom of radical politics, away from his Democratic party-line comfort zone, where he had been content to throw his vote to "any Irishmen who were on the ballot." After the death of President Franklin Delano Roosevelt, the country seemed to take a sharp wrong turn toward empire expansion and militarism, and with six boys coming of age, Vivian wasn't about to let them die on some bleak, radioactive battleground.

It was the Harry Bridges trial that really turned Vince's head around. Bridges was an undereducated, beak-nosed Aussie immigrant who electrified San Francisco, and the entire West Coast, by organizing the city's deeply abused longshoremen. In 1934, when he shut down the San Francisco port—and along with it, the entire city—Bridges earned the undying hatred of the big business elite. One corporate conclave met in a boardroom to discuss hiring a hit man to get rid of the troublesome labor leader, but voted narrowly against it. Bridges's corporate enemies lobbied feverishly to have him deported as a radical subversive. In 1945 the Supreme Court ruled that Bridges was not a Communist and therefore should not be deported. But this only momentarily stymied the anti-Bridges conspirators. By 1949, Bridges was again on trial, facing federal perjury charges for denying he was a Communist—and Vince Hallinan was defending him.

Hallinan convinced Bridges that this time he had to take the offense. They would put the US government on trial for persecuting a genuine hero of American labor. Hallinan's aggressive strategy succeeded in exposing the parade of government witnesses as a scurrilous pack of conmen and liars. And he made the federal prosecutor—a fellow Irishman named F. Joseph "Jiggs" Donohue who struck him as the sort of slick traitor that his father, Patrick, would have assassinated back in the old country—a special target of his tart rhetoric. "He tells how he has been sent here as a special attorney for the United States government," Hallinan told the court, "and I submit, Your Honor, that I have not seen such inferior qualities better rewarded since Caligula made a consul of his horse and Charles II knighted a beefsteak."

But Hallinan misjudged the country's strange mood, and the clammy atmosphere of Cold War fear and obedience. The jury convicted Bridges—and the judge cited Hallinan for contempt and immediately dispatched him to the federal penitentiary on McNeil Island, in the cold waters of Puget Sound.

These were dark days for America, a scoundrel time when a man could be put on trial for his labor activism, or jailed for defending the wrong client. The Hallinan family—blessed with good fortune and everything America offered—was now banished to the shadows. Red paint was splashed on the gateposts at their Marin County estate, and a hammer and sickle scrawled on their driveway. The older boys, now teenagers, were jumped by thugs who screamed "Commie son of a bitch!" as they beat them.

A group of marines, just back from Korea, recognized sixteen-year-old Patrick Hallinan at a Marin drive-in and felt it was their patriotic duty to assault him savagely. Patrick fought back, but by the time they were through with him, several of his bones were broken, and the bone of his right arm flapped through his flesh. The Marin County district attorney apologetically told Vivian that he wouldn't be able to bring charges against Patrick's assailants. No jury in the county would rule in favor of a Hallinan, he explained.

When Vince returned home from McNeil Island, he made sure that his family's tormentors would think twice before going after his boys again. He renewed their boxing lessons, in earnest this time, bringing in professional boxers to hone his sons' martial arts technique in the family's basement gym. The Hallinans became accomplished fighters, especially second-born Terence (Kayo), who would emerge as a middleweight contender in the 1960 Olympic trials. Boxing also took young Terry Hallinan out of his sheltered Marin life and introduced him to San Francisco's rowdy nightlife. When not teaching him to bob and weave and jab, Terry's coach, Tommy Egan, a West Coast pro-circuit mug who had grown up on the tough streets of San Francisco's Potrero Hill, would take him to hooker bars in the Mission district and teach him to drink.

Vivian had qualms about teaching the boys how to solve their problems with their fists. It seemed a violation of the family's pro-peace principles. But Vince was adamant. "The chief trouble with liberals," he told her, "is that they hope to accomplish everything by talk."

The Hallinans' fearsome boxing regimen succeeded in deterring bullies, who soon found out that they themselves would end up bloodied on the ground if they challenged the brothers. If the world was against the Hallinans, now they had a way to fight back. Terry, in particular, became a tempest. His dad would be in and out of prison during the 1950s, and he was full of adolescent rage. With his growing physical prowess, Terry began striking out at the world, even when it wasn't necessary. By age seventeen, he was made a ward of Marin Juvenile Court after he ran three taunting coastguardsmen off the road and beat up all of them.

ONE NIGHT, THE VIOLENCE swirling around the Hallinans reached a new level of terror when three drunken men, including one of the marines who had beaten Patrick at the drive-in years earlier, broke into the Ross mansion and tried to rape Vivian. She was home alone—Vince was in New York, and the boys were out celebrating graduation night—when she heard the front door open. Thinking that Vince had come home early, she ran out of her bedroom, shouting, "Vin, Vin!" One of the men jumped out from the shadows and grabbed her, while the others tore off her nightgown. Vivian stood naked in front of them, her mind racing.

She had just been operated on for uterine cancer, and the incision was still red raw. Pointing to her wound, she said, "Look, boys, this scar here is from cancer, and cancer is contagious. You don't want to get cancer. You're young boys." To her amazement, they seemed to believe her.

The drunken men stood there, trying to gather their thoughts. "Why don't you go downstairs," she told them, "and help yourselves to some liquor?" They hesitated. Vivian was still stripped bare, and in middle age she was still a striking woman. But finally they left her bedroom.

She locked the door, dashed for the telephone, and began to call the police. But one of the men was listening at the door, and he kicked it open before the call went through.

Now the men were determined to go through with their plan. They tore the mattresses off Vivian's bed and lay them in the back of their pickup truck, and they dragged her downstairs. But Vivian kept talking to them. She kept it up for forty-five minutes. Finally, miraculously, they decided to leave her unmolested, though they would attack two other less fortunate women that night.

Patrick was camping in the Sierras when he heard on the TV news that the marine who had assaulted him was now a suspect in the attempted rape of his mother. "I got a .38, and I went to kill the bastard. I didn't even go home," he later recalled. But by the time Patrick got to Marin, the marine was in police custody. He eventually was sentenced to just one year in jail.

Outcasts and targets in their own community, the Hallinans refused to give in and withdraw from public life. Vince and Viv redoubled their political efforts, joining civil rights campaigns and enlisting in the Progressive Party, the anti–Cold War coalition started by Henry A. Wallace, FDR's onetime vice president. To the shock and horror of their neighbors in the smugly prosperous and Republican enclave of Ross, the Hallinans frequently threw house parties for their growing circle of subversive friends, including blacklisted Hollywood filmmakers, labor leaders, peace activists, and black leaders high on the FBI watch list such as Paul Robeson and W. E. B. DuBois. The Hallinans' Olympic-size swimming pool was often a churning froth of children of all races.

When Wallace gave in to the mounting Cold War hysteria and left the Progressive Party, Vince allowed himself to be drafted as the party's presidential candidate in 1952. The Progressives selected Charlotta Bass, an African-American newspaperwoman, as his running mate— the first time a black, let alone a woman, had run for vice president in America. Hallinan and Bass crisscrossed the country, calling for an end to the Korean War, denouncing the rise of McCarthyism as "the open face of fascism in American political life," and demanding a halt to racial injustice.

Hallinan turned out to be an effective campaigner, but the media largely blacked him out, halls canceled his speaking engagements, and apartheid laws in some parts of the country (including the nation's capital) even prevented the mixed-race ticket from dining together in the same restaurant. On election night, Hallinan and Bass scraped together only 140,000 votes.

If Hallinan couldn't get the media's attention, he certainly got the FBI's. J. Edgar Hoover, the bureau's Grand Inquisitor, put him on the list for "custodial detention" in the event of a national "emergency"— a Kafkaesque measure authorized by the controversial McCarran Act, also known as the Internal Security Act of 1950. Hoover's secret policemen tapped the Hallinans' phones, opened their mail, revoked their passports, and followed their comings and goings. The FBI couldn't determine which one—Vince or Viv—was more vile. Their union "was a case of one warped personality marrying another," concluded one report in the couple's security file.

The year after the presidential race, the government decided it couldn't wait for a national emergency. Hallinan was again sent to McNeil Island, this time on flimsy tax evasion charges. This latest blow nearly broke the family. While he was gone, the IRS brought them to the brink of financial ruin by putting a lien on their property and income. "We were all proud as punch that Vin was in jail for principle, but our strength was gone," remembered Patrick. "We needed a father. My brothers were going through puberty and learning to be men, and he was gone. The burden fell on my mother."

Prison didn't slow down Vince. He used his jail time to lead a movement to desegregate McNeil Island, in accordance with President Dwight Eisenhower's executive order. He sat with black prisoners in the dining room to make his point, and after desegregation allowed them to mingle, he pushed his black friends to sit with other white inmates.

WHEN VINCE FINALLY RETURNED home in 1956, the family's momentum was restored. He and Viv plunged back into political activities. By the end of the fifties, it seemed the Bay Area was mellowing toward their family.

The Hallinans were convinced a new day was arriving in May 1960, when the House Un-American Activities Committee came to San Francisco—and was quickly run out of town. HUAC was an aging but still pernicious tool of the Cold War inquisition. The congressional panel would show up in cities across the country, like a diabolical traveling circus, and subpoena suspected subversives. If a witness did not comply with the committee and betray friends and associates, his life could be ruined instantly. HUAC left behind a trail of job terminations, broken families and friendships, and even suicides. But not this time.

The committee, which came to San Francisco City Hall to turn the public school system upside down in search of disloyal teachers, was greeted by a flock of student protesters, still wearing the crew cuts and sport coats of the fifties, including Patrick and Terry Hallinan. While the Hallinans' parents looked on, the protesters noisily picketed the HUAC hearings. The young demonstrators were finally driven out of the building's Beaux Arts rotunda by police, who flushed them down a flight of marble steps with roaring fire hoses. Vince, now age sixty-two, couldn't help himself: when he saw cops fall upon a student with their clubs, he intervened and got manhandled himself.

The city hall melee was a turning point. Unable to create its normal atmosphere of cringing supplication, HUAC fled San Francisco and soon faded into history. "We said, 'No way, not this time.' And HUAC stopped," said Terry.

It was no longer just the Hallinans against the world—not in San Francisco. The demonstrations for a new society spread throughout the city during the early 1960s. And while the Hallinans were often leading or participating in them, hundreds of others now joined them. Civil rights protests broke out all along the city's exclusive Auto Row on Van Ness Boulevard, at the elegant Sheraton Palace Hotel, and at the more plebeian Mel's Diner, where blacks could never find jobs. Led by Vivian, the pack of Hallinan boys all began sitting in.

During one rowdy demonstration outside an auto showroom, SFPD chief Thomas J. Cahill—a ruddy-faced, blue-eyed peace officer who still had the brogue of his native County Kilkenny—watched in amazement as the elegantly dressed Marin matron was hauled away by his men. What was the world coming to? While Vivian was being loaded into the paddy wagon, Vince, struggling to maintain his reserve as the protesters' lawyer, rooted hoarsely on the sidelines for his wife. "Attagirl, Vivian!

If all the Irish stuck together like they used to, we could still run San Francisco!"

In fact, the Irish still did run San Francisco, but Cahill got the point. To militants like Vince Hallinan, he was a sellout.

By 1967, San Francisco's year of love, the old Irish Catholic order was holding on by its fingertips. Tom Cahill was in charge of the police department, Jack Shelley occupied the mayor's office, and Judge Raymond O'Connor was responsible for juvenile justice—a key position in the bulwark against the youthful army that was besieging San Francisco.

But because of the Hallinan family—and the growing number of activists and young lawyers who had been caught up in their brawling enterprise—the seeds had been sown in San Francisco. It all came back to the Hallinans.

PART ONE

ENCHANTMENT

Listen, my friends . . .

I

SATURDAY AFTERNOON

M ICHAEL STEPANIAN LOOKED up from the blood and muck of his rugby game at a dazzling vision in the sky. A parachutist came drifting slowly through the wisps of fog over Golden Gate Park, his billowing, paisley chute aglow in the afternoon's soft winter light. The skydiver landed in the midst of a sprawling festival that was being held at the opposite end of the Polo Field, and the crowd instantly swallowed him.

Stepanian was a tough young Armenian-American from New York who had recently graduated from Stanford Law School and was now working in Vincent Hallinan's legendary law office. On weekends, Stepanian played rugby for the Olympic Club, the same athletic organization where old man Hallinan played rugby and football and boxed, long after men his age were supposed to quit. All through the afternoon, as the Olympic Club rolled to lopsided 23–3 victory over visiting Oregon State University, the burly rugby players snarled at the long-locked festivalgoers whenever they trespassed on their side of the field. But Stepanian, intrigued by the waves of music and good cheer, strolled over to the festival after the game and wandered around in his battle-torn jersey and muddy cleats. "I looked like I was from a different planet, but nobody seemed to give a shit. The sun was shining, the kids were beautiful, the music was magic. That was the beginning of my education."

It was the Human Be-In, the January 14, 1967, celebration that was billed as a coming together of every tribe in the new, emerging America: from legendary beats, to Berkeley radicals, to the San Francisco love generation. "For ten years a new nation has grown inside the robot flesh of the old," proclaimed the event's starry-eyed press release. "The night of bruted fear of the American eagle-beast-body is over. Hang your fear at the door and join the future. If you do not believe, please wipe your eyes and see."

Years later, some would call this event the true—if belated—beginning of the sixties. More than twenty thousand people poured into the Polo Field that sun-dappled Saturday, on the wild west side of Golden Gate Park, where a swaying curtain of eucalyptus and Monterey pine trees shielded the tribal gathering from the raw ocean winds. Onstage, Allen Ginsberg—wearing white Indian pyjamas and garlands of beads and flowers—looked out over the vast human dynamo that he had helped ignite and turned to his friend, Lawrence Ferlinghetti: "What if we're wrong?"

It was a typical Ginsberg remark, and its whimsy and self-doubt reflected the better angels of the growing counterculture movement. The radical Berkeley component among the Be-In organizers, led by antiwar leader Jerry Rubin, was more certain about things. They sought to enlist the crowd in their political mission. But San Francisco's more ethereal ethos prevailed that day.

The leading icons of the emerging counterculture were all gathered onstage: Ginsberg, Ferlinghetti, and fellow poet-shaman Gary Snyder; psychedelic carnival barker Timothy Leary; the Grateful Dead, Jefferson Airplane, Janis Joplin and Big Brother and the Holding Company. But the more enlightened among them knew that the crowd itself was the center stage—no one was really listening to the speakers and singers.

The Jefferson Airplane's Paul Kantner—San Francisco homeboy, and a shrewd product of Bay Area Catholic schools—got it. "The difference between San Francisco and Berkeley was that Berkeley complained about a lot of things. Rather than complaining about things, we San Franciscans formed an alternative reality to live in. And for some reason, we got away with it. San Francisco became somewhere you did things rather than protesting about them. We knew we didn't have to speechify about what we should and shouldn't do. We just *did*."

The Airplane's "White Rabbit" and "Somebody to Love" would soon become part of the cultural revolution's soundtrack and make the band world-famous. But Kantner knew at heart they would always be a Haight-Ashbury house band, just like the Dead. He later memorialized the Be-In festival in song: "Saturday afternoon / Yellow clouds rising in the noon / Acid, incense, and balloons."

Young people sprawled on the grass, playing pennywhistles, harmonicas, guitars, and flutes. Naked toddlers chased their shadows in the sun. Only two mounted policemen patrolled the grounds; one came trotting through the crowd on his horse, cradling a small child in his arms. The loudspeaker announced, "A lost child has been delivered to the stage and is now being cared for by the Hell's Angels." It was a time when that made sense.

As the sun slipped into the Pacific, Ginsberg blew on a conch shell and beckoned everyone to turn to the west and watch the final sparks of daylight. Then he asked everyone to clean up the trash, so that they would leave the Polo Field—which he and Snyder had blessed at the beginning of the festival—just as they found it. Ginsberg, a cross between holy man and Jewish mother, was precisely the beneficent figure that the infant movement needed.

Rev. Edward "Larry" Beggs, a thirty-four-year-old Congregational youth minister who had come to the Be-In out of curiosity with his wife, Nina, was surprised to see the people all around him do as Ginsberg suggested. "Because I had seen how my fellow Americans could trash out even a sacred space like Yosemite National Park," he recalled, "I was amazed to see the people around me picking up not only their own discarded items but other people's paper cups, bottle caps, orange peels, and cigarette butts. The entire Polo Field, where thousands had sat and munched longer than a baseball double-header, was now restored to its pristine green."

The tousle-haired, bespectacled Beggs—who looked like one of John Kennedy's young Peace Corps volunteers—felt like Bob Dylan's Mr. Jones: he knew something was happening here, but didn't know what it was. Within a few months, the quiet lives of Ed and Nina Beggs would be turned upside down. Ed would be jailed for running a teenage shelter, the nation's first haven for the growing swarm of boys and girls who were fleeing homes seemingly everywhere in America. And Nina would find herself on the witness stand, testifying for the defense in the obscenity trial of Lenore Kandel, an erotic poet who roared around town on the back of a motorcycle driven by her lover, a ruggedly beautiful Hell's Angel known as Sweet William.

Kandel—a curvy, sloe-eyed, olive-skinned goddess who wore her hair in Pocahontas braids—set off a tempest when she published *The Love Book*. Her poetry collection was an orgasmic celebration of carnal love, filled with rising cocks, honeycomb cunts, and "thick sweet juices running wild." Kandel made a strong impression onstage at the Human Be-In, reading her passion poems from a clipboard and then tearing off each one as she finished, crumpling it in her fist, and tossing it into the crowd. But it wasn't until a few months later, when copies of *The Love Book* were confiscated at a Haight Street bookstore by San Francisco police, that she became another infamous counterculture name. Kandel's obscenity trial would become one of Catholic San Francisco's last stands against the onrushing cultural revolution.

On the witness stand, Nina Beggs made a strong impression for the defense. She was no dark-banged folksinger type; she was a pretty, blond, pageboy-coiffed clergyman's wife. But she too found salvation in Kandel's ecstatic poetry. Nina testified that she had devoured *The Love Book* in one gulp at the Psychedelic Shop, after dining with her husband at a nearby Haight-Ashbury restaurant. After finishing the poetry in the bookstore, she turned to her husband and urged him to read it. "This is the way it is for a woman," she told Ed. "This is what making love does for me." Then, speaking in a slow, clear voice, Nina shared her joy with the packed courtroom. "The oceanic" sexual feeling expressed in *The Love Book,* she said, is "one of the greatest proofs you have of your connection with God."

THE HUMAN BE-IN WAS the beginning of the story for thousands of people, many of whom would go on to take primary roles in San Francisco's revolution. In the crowd that day were Margo St. James, a big-hearted cocktail waitress and occasional hooker who would later found the prostitute rights movement; Stewart Brand, an army veteran and aspiring artist who jumped on Ken Kesey's bus and later launched the *Whole Earth Catalog* and linked the counterculture to the digital future;

Peter Coyote, cofounder of the Diggers, the "heavy hippie" anarchists who turned San Francisco into one big stage for their radical theater.

And there was Michael Stepanian, in his rugby battle gear. It was Stepanian who would defend dozens of Be-In celebrants when they were rounded up by police later that evening on Haight Street. He would go on to represent the Grateful Dead when their Haight-Ashbury house was raided by the drug squad, and cartoonist Robert Crumb when he was charged with obscenity. Like *The Love Book* trial, these legal battles would help widen the circle of light in San Francisco.

"When we started out, the city was antiblack, antigay, antiwoman. It was a very uptight Irish Catholic city," said Brian Rohan, Stepanian's legal sidekick and another brawling protégé of Vincent Hallinan. "We took on the cops, city hall, the Catholic Church. Vince Hallinan taught us never to be afraid of bullies."

By taking on the bullies, the new forces of freedom began to liberate San Francisco, neighborhood by neighborhood. They began with the Haight-Ashbury.

2

DEAD MEN DANCING

IN THE MID-1960s, San Francisco was still a city of tribal villages. The Castro district and the Noe Valley neighborhood were working-class Irish, though the Irish in the adjacent Mission district were giving way to Latino immigrants. The Fillmore section still clung to its reputation as the Harlem of the West, though the redevelopers' wrecking ball was reducing its former glory block by block. The Italians in North Beach lived in uneasy proximity to Chinatown. At one time, the Chinese could cross over Broadway—the boulevard that divided the two communities—only at their own peril.

The cultural revolution first came to North Beach, where cheap saloons and fleabag hotels and old Barbary Coast bohemianism beckoned the beats in the 1950s. Ferlinghetti was among the first. He was a World War II navy veteran and an aspiring poet and painter when he disembarked at the ferry building in 1951, wandering into North Beach with his sea bag slung over his shoulder. "It was a small city, nestled into the hills," he recalled. "All the buildings were white, there were no skyscrapers. It felt Mediterranean. It was beautiful."

A couple of years later, Ferlinghetti opened up City Lights Books with partner Peter Martin, son of the assassinated anarchist Carlo Tresca. Italian garbage truck drivers would roar up to the curb and run inside to buy the anarchist newspapers that the store got directly from Italy. It was a cramped one-room establishment in those days; they didn't even own the basement, which is where the Chinese New Year Parade's endless, red and gold dragon was tucked away the other 364 days of the year. But City Lights became a beacon to the poets, wanderers, and angel-headed hipsters who were making their way to San Francisco. You could browse forever, and nobody would bother you. It was here that Ferlinghetti first met Ginsberg, who entered the store one day trailed by his usual crowd of young men, looking more like a horn-rimmed Columbia University intellectual than the wild Whitman of Cold War America. Ginsberg would pound out "Howl" on his typewriter a few blocks away in his railroad apartment at 1010 Montgomery Street.

North Beach's Little Italy coexisted happily with the beat underground and the new folk and jazz clubs, topless bars, and gay caverns that began popping up in the neighborhood. But it was not North Beach where counterculture history would be made in the 1960s. It was across town in the Haight-Ashbury, a neighborhood of once ornate Victorian "painted ladies" that had seen better days. By the early sixties, the old Irish and Russian neighborhood had become so dilapidated that, like the Fillmore district, it was slated for demolition, to make room for a freeway extension along the Panhandle—the strip of greenery that led to Golden Gate Park. But the Haight was now populated by a feisty mix that included black home owners who had already been pushed out of one neighborhood, the Fillmore; artists and bohemians squeezed out of North Beach by tourists and rising rents; gays, who appreciated the neighborhood's live-and-let-live atmosphere; and San Francisco State College students, who desperately needed the cheap living quarters they found in the neighborhood's subdivided Victorian flats. San Francisco State was the launch pad for many of the young civil rights activists who headed to the Deep South each summer—including Terry Hallinan—and they came back to San Francisco a battle-hardened corps. The Haight's residents knew how to fight city hall. This time the redevelopment agency's bulldozers were stopped.

THE HAIGHT WAS NOW safe to become a haven for the young, broke, and visionary. Among them was a beautiful, dark-haired elementary schoolteacher named Marilyn Harris, who moved into a Victorian flat on Ashbury Street in the summer of 1965. Two years earlier, Harris had walked out on her marriage to an Arizona lawyer and hopped on a Greyhound bus to San Francisco. She knew she belonged there ever since she and her husband had visited the city in 1960, taking in slashing comedy acts like Lenny Bruce, Mort Sahl, and Dick Gregory at the hungry i and other North Beach clubs and reveling in the city's breezy sense of freedom.

"Oh my God, this is where I'm supposed to live," Marilyn excitedly told her husband. Would he start over with her in San Francisco?

"Ah, no," he replied.

She arrived alone at the Greyhound station in downtown San Francisco, with $10 in her purse. She walked to a nearby motel and phoned her parents in New Jersey, asking them for enough money to start her new life, but they refused. So she walked into a Bank of America office. Based on her word that she was lining up a job as an elementary schoolteacher, the bank extended her a $400 loan. This is when the bank was still a local institution, and its corporate culture still held traces of its founder, Amadeo Pietro Giannini, who began the bank in a North Beach saloon and became known for extending loans to working people and not just high rollers.

The Haight was still just a scruffy, fog-bound neighborhood when Marilyn moved there, with Russian bakeries where you could buy piroshkis. But the fairy dust was already floating overhead. The year after she settled in the Haight, a young band called the Grateful Dead moved into a big Victorian across the street at 710 Ashbury. Janis Joplin rambled around the neighborhood in her scarves and boas, swigging from a bottle of Ripple with her bandmates, and Marilyn would bump into her at Peggy Caserta's clothes store on Haight. They all became friends. Nobody was a celebrity in those days. The neighborhood thought it owned the bands. Everyone took care of one another.

Marilyn was careful about whom she slept with, even in those less discriminating days. But at one point, she took up with a Hell's Angel, one of the Haight's irresistible bad boys, who gave her the clap. She didn't want to go to her ob-gyn, who had made her feel creepy the last time she saw him. So she went to the city VD clinic. It was 1967. Everyone was making love with everyone. And Marilyn knew at least thirty of the young people sitting in the waiting room's rows of pews. "Phil Lesh from the Dead was there. When I walked in, everyone just burst out laughing."

In the crush of patients, the city clinic was not taking the time to thoroughly sterilize needles, so Marilyn's blood sample that day was taken with a dirty needle. She came down with hepatitis C and became so sick that her doctor wanted to put her in the hospital. But she didn't want to go. Instead she went home, collapsed into bed, and phoned the Dead house and told Ron "Pigpen" McKernan, her closest friend in the band.

Pigpen might have looked like a greasy, badass biker, but he had a heart of gold. He tacked a signup sheet on Marilyn's front door, and various members of the band and its entourage would take turns bringing her meals and caring for her. Some nights Pigpen slept on her couch. She would wake up from a feverish nap, and there at the foot of her bed would be Pigpen or Lesh or Jerry Garcia, a couple of Hell's Angels, and the principal from her elementary school, all chatting amiably and watching over her like Auntie Em, Uncle Henry, and the farmhands hovering over Dorothy.

"The Dead were special," she later said. "They had a real devotion to friendship and care." She would soon have occasion to repay their generosity.

It took nearly three weeks for Marilyn to feel strong enough to get up from bed. One afternoon in October 1967, she was sitting in a wing chair in her third-floor bay window, soaking up the sun, when she saw a small army of grim-looking men sweep into the Dead house. The neighborhood knew the band as the sweetest of its minstrels, always plugging in and playing for free down on the Panhandle. But to the state and city drug agents who raided the band's Ashbury Street house that day, the thirteen-room Victorian was the center of a sinister narcotics ring. Boyish and spacey Bob Weir, who was meditating in the attic as the narcs invaded the house, and Pigpen were both dragged off to the hall of justice—though, as it happened, they were the nonsmokers in the band. As she saw the musicians and members of their extended family being escorted into unmarked police cars, Marilyn suddenly spotted Garcia and his girlfriend, Mountain Girl, ambling up the street carrying bags of groceries, unaware of the fate that awaited them. She leaned out her window and yelled to them, "I'm so glad you got my groceries. Come up *right now!*" Garcia and Mountain Girl immediately understood. They weren't arrested that day.

Michael Stepanian and Brian Rohan rushed to bail out Pigpen, Weir, and the others. By day, the two young lawyers worked in Vincent Hallinan's law office on Franklin Street. In the evenings, they toiled downstairs in the Dead house, doing free legal work for the Haight runaways, draft dodgers, and pot smokers who were constantly being snared in police dragnets. Stepanian and Rohan called their street practice the Haight-Ashbury Legal Organization (HALO), and it was kept afloat by benefit concerts, courtesy of the Dead and its friends. Now the band needed its own charity.

At the hall of justice, one of the narcs was dancing a victory jig. "I got 'em, I got 'em!" he taunted his prisoners, even though the task force had netted only a pound of marijuana and a little hashish.

After Stepanian sprang his clients, it was his turn to roar. Hallinan had taught his young colleagues to take the offensive, particularly in cases of police overkill, and the rugby bruiser now did exactly that. The Grateful Dead bust was a case of selective police enforcement, Stepanian told the press: "The Dead live in the Haight-Ashbury. If they lived on Russian Hill, they wouldn't be busted. If they lived on Pacific Heights, no officer would go near the house."

The next day, the band and its lawyers continued to take the offensive, holding a press conference to condemn marijuana laws as "seriously out of touch with reality," in the words of the Dead's press statement. To his young fans, Jerry Garcia, the band's spiritual leader, was Captain Trips. But he was no hippie dandelion. He was raised in the tough Outer Mission by his grandmother, a no-bullshit organizer for the local Laundry Workers Union. His free-spirited mother ran a bar near the Embarcadero, where young Jerry was regaled by hard-drinking sailors and longshoremen with tales of labor leader Harry Bridges and other working-class heroes. When city officials and cops growled about the long-haired outsiders who were turning the city upside down, Garcia thought they were talking out of their asses. His family had been here since the gold rush—Irish and Swedish and Spanish pioneers. San Francisco was as much his city as anyone else's. And Garcia, like the others in the Haight who were plugged into the city's electric current, knew that San Francisco was about to burst from its chrysalis.

———————

IN THE EARLY MONTHS of 1967, after the Human Be-In, the national media spread the message: San Francisco was the open-armed mecca of the new consciousness. And young people from all over the world were planning to arrive in time for the resplendent Summer of Love that year. It was the residents of the "little village of Haight-Ashbury," as Marilyn called it, who were the most concerned about the coming transformation. They were the ones who would bear its brunt, with swarms of homeless kids on the streets and only the city's angry, strained police force poised to handle them, or, perhaps, manhandle them. As the summer approached, the Haight dispatched a delegation—including neighborhood activists, head shop merchants, concerned clergymen, and physicians—to city hall to ask for help. Marilyn was among them. "I always got included in these things because I was respectable; I was a schoolteacher." The delegation was granted an audience with Mayor Shelley.

Another neighborhood group met with Police Chief Cahill. The chief, a big, thin-lipped man with a crown of closely cropped red curls, was known as a tough but fair cop. Cahill made a point of addressing school assemblies and youth groups. He wanted to feel in touch with the next generation. Now he listened patiently as two Haight store owners described how LSD had blown open their doors of perception. One of the merchants felt certain that Chief Cahill was "turning on" while they talked with him. That might not have been an accurate reading, but the top cop clearly did want to understand. "You're sort of the Love Generation, aren't you?" Cahill asked.

In the end, however, nothing came from the meetings with Shelley and Cahill. "All they did for the neighborhood was teargas us," Marilyn said. "You'd go down to shop on Haight Street, and suddenly some kids would go flying past you chased by cops, and you'd be choking on gas."

The old Irish Catholic brotherhood was not willing to cede control of its city. San Francisco was still a town of blue-collar family values, its public life ordered largely around the Church. People still identified themselves not by which college they attended but by their parochial schools: St. Ignatius High School, the breeding ground of the city's legal and political elites, or Sacred Heart, the funnel for the upwardly mobile children of the city's working class. As traditional San Francisco braced for the youth invasion, the city's guardians rushed to close its gates.

3

THE WALLED CITY

Mayor John Francis "Jack" Shelley was a true son of Irish San Francisco. Growing up in the Mission, Shelley would be shoved into a chair at the kitchen table by his father, Dennis—a longshoreman from County Cork—and told the way of the world. Nobody wanted to hire the Irish when he first came to America, Dennis told his son. To be Irish was to fight for every scrap, every ounce of dignity. "Jack," said the old man, in his thick brogue, "the day you forget where you came from, you won't belong where you are."

Shelley broke into politics through the labor movement, where he rose to become president of the San Francisco Labor Council and then the California State Federation of Labor. After serving a couple terms in the state legislature, he was elected to Congress in 1949, becoming friends with fellow Irishman Jack Kennedy. Shelley was not a skirt chaser, but he enjoyed his drink, and he loved the sea. The two young Democrats would go sailing on Shelley's thirty-eighty-foot Chris-Craft cruiser.

As he rose in politics, Shelley did not forget where he came from. He remembered his labor friends, and even during the height of the Cold War, he refused to join the rest of the San Francisco Labor Council in condemning Harry Bridges for his "subversive" beliefs. He was an early supporter of the civil rights movement, rising on the floor of Congress to denounce all discrimination based on race and religion, and linking the sufferings of black families to those of his Irish forebears.

Shelley loved Congress and life in Washington, even more after JFK moved into the White House in 1961. But Kennedy's election had unleashed new forces in San Francisco, and in 1963, Phil Burton, a rising Young Turk in the city's Democratic Party, maneuvered Shelley into vacating his congressional seat, which Burton coveted, and running for mayor. In November—shortly before the assassination of his good friend, the president—Shelley won the San Francisco mayoral election over conservative businessman Harold Dobbs.

Shelley was only fifty-eight when he took office. But with his sloped shoulders, receding white hair, horn-rim glasses, gray suits, and homburg, he seemed like a man from the past. He reacted with exasperated dudgeon when his first crisis exploded: a controversy over his decision to eliminate birth control funding from the city's public health budget. Planned Parenthood officials accused him of bending to pressure from his friends in the Catholic hierarchy, which Shelley heatedly denied. But, in truth, he ran all major issues by San Francisco archbishop Joseph McGucken—especially ones like this, on which the Church had strong doctrinal positions. Jack Shelley was typical of the old San Francisco breed. When it came to labor and civil rights, he was a man of progress. When it came to family and moral issues, he was a son of the Church.

The crises came fast and thick. The city was hit by a wave of social disruptions, including a strike by nurses at San Francisco General, the big public hospital, and a series of bawdy trials involving the owners of topless bars in North Beach. In September 1966 the city's simmering racial tensions erupted in Bayview–Hunters Point, the black ghetto that white San Franciscans saw only when they took backstreets to Giants baseball games at Candlestick Park. When a white cop shot and killed a black teenager, the city's first riot since World War II broke out, forcing Shelley to declare a state of emergency for six days.

Then things got weird. In March 1967 an unemployed circus clown was arrested for calling the FBI and threatening to kill the mayor. The police swept into Shelley's home, placing him and his family under around-the-clock surveillance. For Shelley, who had deeply felt the assassination in Dallas, it was history repeating itself as farce. He begged the press not to make a circus of the story. "It's creating havoc in my home, and it may give some other screwball ideas."

By the time the hippie revolution began shaking San Francisco, Shelley felt that he no longer recognized the city where he had grown up. A cartoon in the *Chronicle* showed a cranky Shelley telling a beaded and bell-bottomed young couple, "Stay off the grass—both kinds!" He kept coming down with colds and bronchial infections, and his drinking got more serious. Shelley was forced to defend his liquor habit in the press, insisting that he had cut out his "noontime belt." One friend explained to the *San Francisco Examiner* that the Shelley drinking stories only cropped up because "after three drinks his voice gets loud and he tends to slur his words"—which did little to reassure the public.

As the Summer of Love inexorably approached, like a Pacific tsunami, Shelley lacked the energy or imagination to figure out how San Francisco could absorb the enormous shock to its psyche and infrastructure. He was being talked about as a one-term mayor. The only reason that Shelley might hang on, speculated one newspaper article, was because the mayor—who supported a wife and two kids on his $38,000 salary—was "broke and he needs the job."

To solve the growing youth crisis, Shelley simply turned to his friend Tom Cahill and the San Francisco Police Department.

CAHILL WAS A FELLOW son of Eire who had emigrated to the United States on his own at the age of nineteen. The two men came of age together in San Francisco's blue-collar South of the Slot. While Shelley was leading the bakery drivers union, the broad-shouldered Cahill was hefting one-hundred-pound blocks of ice and representing the Ice Wagon Drivers' Union. After joining the San Francisco police force in 1942, Cahill made a name for himself as an expert on the Mafia, and after being loaned out as an investigator to Tennessee senator Estes Kefauver's organized crime committee, he quickly rose through the SFPD ranks. He became chief in 1958, and he prided himself on being a modern lawman with a grasp of crime's underlying social causes. But Cahill was the product of a strong Catholic upbringing in rural Ireland. "I grew up respecting the authority of my parents, and I had the wisdom of our parish priest, Father Carrigan, to guide me—and these teachings have stayed to this day," Cahill told an Irish journal early in his term as chief. And though he made an effort to understand the 1960s generation, the truth is he never could really fathom it.

Cahill bemoaned society's changing mores: "The swift kick in the buttocks by the old Irish policeman in the old days immediately becomes a violation of civil rights today." If cops were held in check, Cahill warned, juvenile problems would continue to increase. He urged fathers to use the rod on their children—and their wives.

Now, in the spring of 1967, Tom Cahill was facing the nightmare he had long predicted: an invasion of unruly children from all over the country, the progeny of America's failing family structure. And he made clear that he would greet them with the rod.

Alerted by the Diggers to the looming specter of homeless hordes on the San Francisco streets, some Protestant clergymen urged the city to allow camping in Golden Gate Park. But Chief Cahill would hear none of that. The laws would not be modified to accommodate youthful vagabonds, not on his watch. There would be no tents in any park after nightfall, and no playing of musical instruments. The radio was urging America's children to flock to San Francisco with garlands in their hair. But Cahill's message was blunt: Stay home or face "possible arrest and even injury."

"Law, order, and health regulations must prevail," the chief declared.

But the village of Haight-Ashbury knew that young people in Iowa, Texas, and Ohio were not listening to San Francisco police officials. They were listening to the music—and the music was telling them to fly "Translove Airways" and "Jefferson Airplane" nonstop, as Donovan sang, to San Francisco.

As the summer approached, it became increasingly clear to the people of the Haight that city hall would not help them. There would be no municipal resources for the new city about to be built on the old: no teenage shelters, food and clothing donations, health-care assistance, family mediation, or drug counseling. The Haight would have to do it all on its own.

4

THE FREE CITY

WITH SAN FRANCISCO'S city government abandoning its obligations, a haphazard collection of clergymen, philanthropists, and activists tried to fill the void. But none of these do-gooders did it with the flair and imagination of a troupe of political provocateurs known as the Diggers. Taking their name from a group of agrarian radicals in Oliver Cromwell's England who seized vacant land and tilled it for the poor, the Diggers created a variety of services for the army of young castaways that began pouring into the Haight, including food giveaways in the Panhandle, a network of crash pads, free clothing stores, street theater, and "ticketless" concerts in the park. But the Diggers were not simply a hippie Salvation Army, they were psychic inciters with much wilder ambitions. They wanted to liberate San Francisco's consciousness. Imagine a life, urged the Diggers, that was not bought and sold in eight-hour increments but was your own. Imagine a life where everything was free: food, music, love, but most important, you.

With the Diggers, it was not about the free food and clothes, it was about the *act* of giving away the free food and clothes. So they not only served their nutritious whole wheat bread and turkey stew to vagabonds in the park, they organized a "feed-in" at city hall, handing out picnic plates of spaghetti and meat sauce to municipal employees and even trying to serve Mayor Shelley in his office. The Diggers made sure the press got the point: their city hall action was meant to "affirm responsibility." They were simply doing what the city government should be. What do you want city hall to do? reporters asked the Diggers that day. "Eat," they replied. The menu for tomorrow would be fried rice.

Everything the Diggers did was a provocation. "You can't steal here," they told baffled shoplifters in their Free Store, "because everything is free. You can have the whole fucking store if you feel like it." The Diggers organized a bizarre procession in the Haight to celebrate the "death of money," with a group of masked mourners—made up to look like the animal gods in Egyptian funerary art—holding high a coffin stuffed with bills and coins. On another occasion, they set up an elegant dining table, including crystal glasses, linen, and champagne, on the side of a freeway during rush hour and invited the speeding commuters to take a break from their madly regimented lives and enjoy some downtime.

The Diggers did not see the Summer of Love as a catastrophe but as a welcome opportunity to free minds—not only those of San Franciscans but also of the estimated seventy-five thousand young Americans who were crowding into the Haight-Ashbury that season. "Our city has become the momentary focus of a worldwide spiritual awakening," read one Diggers street sheet. "The reasons for this do not matter. It is a gift from God which we may take, nourish and treasure . . . Recall that Saint Francis of Assisi is the patron saint of the city of San Francisco, and that therefore Saint Francis is the patron saint of the Summer of Love."

The Diggers' street manifestos were among the earliest and most passionate expressions of what would later be called San Francisco values. The leaflets' "free" ethos—which challenged the public to think of food, shelter, health care, and even entertainment as fundamental human rights, not commodities—began to shape the consciousness of the emerging new San Francisco. Decades later, echoes of the Diggers philosophy could still be heard in web mantras such as "Information wants to be free" and other slogans of the digital age.

The Diggers published a steady flow of such street communiqués, greeting San Francisco's young visitors with a barrage of news, advice, poetry, and philosophy on their street pole newsletters. Some of the Diggers street literature offered concrete legal counsel, such as the best way to be arrested if you fell into the hands of the police: "Don't resist . . . go limp . . . shout out your name while being dumped in the wagon so that bystanders can alert the bondsman." Some lit up the readers' day with flares of erotic poetry, like one by Haight homeboy Richard Brautigan, who became a counterculture literary sensation with his 1967 novel *Trout Fishing in America*. ("Pissing a few moments ago / I looked down at my penis affectionately / Knowing it has been inside / you twice today makes me / feel beautiful.") And some bemoaned the growing strains between white hippies and black residents of the Haight and Fillmore districts. "The spades, dear my brothers, are our spiritual fathers," explained a communiqué titled "Two-page Racial Rap." "They turned us on. They gave us jazz & grass & rock & roll, in the early beat days they provided a community for us, from the beginning they were our brothers deeper than blood, & now we & they don't like each other. If it weren't for the spades, we would all have short hair, neat suits, glazed eyes, steady jobs, and gastric ulcers, all be dying of unnamable frustration."

Diggers put everyone on notice. The hip merchants who were changing the face of Haight Street with their emporia of incense, beads, chimes, rolling papers, posters, LPs, and underground comics were "prettified monsters of moneylust"; radicals like Jerry Rubin and Abbie Hoffman (who took to calling himself a Digger) were "creep commies" on power trips; and counterculture gurus like Timothy Leary, who had lured America's children to San Francisco and then abandoned them to their own devices, were psychedelic charlatans.

"Have you been raped?" read one savage street sheet titled "Uncle Tim'$ Children." "Take acid and everything'll be groovy. Are you ill? Take acid and find inner health. Are you cold, sleeping in doorways at night? Take acid & discover your own inner warmth. Are you hungry? Take acid & transcend these mundane needs. You can't afford acid? Pardon me, I think I hear somebody calling me."

The Diggers attacked the commodification of hippie mantras like love and peace. "Love, by all means, but love People, not money." When a group of promoters calling themselves the Love Conspiracy Commune (who were rumored to be Mob connected) staged a "First Annual Love Circus" at the Winterland Ballroom, the old cavernous skating rink turned rock arena, the Diggers couldn't resist commenting on the absurdity of it all. The provocateurs greeted the show with picket signs reading, "Suckers buy what lovers get for free," and handed out broadsides declaring, "It's yours. You want to dance—dance in the street. You don't need to buy it back."

The Grateful Dead, the neighborhood's most beloved minstrels, were the headliners that night. And the band's manager—a red-diaper baby and University of California at Berkeley dropout named Danny Rifkin—took the irony even higher by getting into an argument with Digger Peter Coyote, spluttering at one point, "Money is sacred!" Which no doubt sounded as weird to Rifkin, son of a Communist printer, as it did to Coyote, son of a Wall Street stockbroker and later a well-known actor.

Reacting against the celebrity mania that was already infecting the counterculture, the Diggers tried to cloak themselves in anonymity. The media wanted photogenic spokesmen. But the Diggers led them in circles. When two eager magazine journalists showed up separately at the Free Store—one from *Time,* the other from *Life*—looking for the group's Mr. Big to interview, the Diggers convinced each reporter that the other one was the Diggers' mysterious leader.

"Beware of leaders, heroes, organizers: watch that stuff," the Diggers warned in one street sheet titled "Sheep? Baa." "Any man who wants to lead you is The Man. Think: why would anyone *want* to lead *me* . . . Fuck leaders."

BUT DESPITE THEIR ANARCHIC rejection of leaders and "structure freaks," the Diggers were, in fact, led by a cabal of handsome, charismatic rogues. They had met in the San Francisco Mime Troupe, the radical street theater group, and they knew how to command a stage. They called themselves "life actors." Emmett Grogan was a former Brooklyn Irish choirboy turned junkie and hustler. With his chiseled features, wavy red-brown hair, gold ear stud, and street swagger, he knew his effect on men and women alike, and he used it all the way. Peter Berg, the only one who actually had read all the anarchist and situationist literature underlying the Diggers philosophy, had a glowering intelligence that didn't let people off the hook. A transplanted "nigger-loving New York Jew" who had grown up in Florida, Berg liked to call himself a "heavy hippie." Now San Francisco was his stage, and revolution was his theater piece. And Peter Coyote, who had grown up Peter Cohon in New York, was a Grinnell College graduate with lanky, leading-man good looks and a rampant lust for women, adventure, and *the new.*

Both Peters were a little in love with Grogan. Everybody was. "Emmett was one of the most charismatic people I ever met—and I'm used to charismatic people," Berg said. "He really had it. He played dangerous, but he was a little bit sociopathic toward other people. He even stole stuff from me."

While the Diggers' men staged the spectacles that built the group's reputation, the Diggers' women did the grunt work that kept it all going. The women were the ones who woke up at five in the morning, got the old truck running, stole or charmed meat and vegetables from grocers, cooked up the hearty stews, lugged the steaming food out to the Panhandle in massive steel milk containers, and ladled it out to the hungry flocks.

Meanwhile, the Diggers' bad boys were becoming Haight-Ashbury stars. With their charisma and street cred, Grogan and his mates could amble easily from one scene to the next. They hung out with Hell's Angels and rock stars, the Black Panthers and Hollywood actors. Grogan and Coyote began spending time with Janis Joplin, in San Francisco and New York. They took her to clubs to see jazz and blues legends whom she had never heard. Coyote and Joplin became occasional bedmates in each other's passing parade of lovers, as well as dope partners. She liked Grogan and Coyote because to them she was just Janis, not a rock 'n' roll queen. "The money people, the managers, were pushing and pulling on her, and her psyche couldn't tolerate it," Coyote said. "Janis was not an icon. She was sad. She was confused and used and fucked over. She was an ugly girl with bad skin that came out of backwater Port Arthur with this gift, and she flayed herself to death in front of a crowd."

While hanging out with rock stars, the Diggers made fun of them. The rock star, they sneered, "is a man who can sing about the evils of the world while margining profits into war economies and maintaining his comfort on a consumer level of luxury." But the Diggers had their own growing contradictions, and they couldn't maintain them for long. In the summer of 1967—at the height of their fame, with people all over claiming to be Diggers—the group gave away its last worldly possession: its name. By the time the Summer of Love was over, the Diggers leaders had all drifted off to country communes, celebrity entourages, hard drugs, the Hell's Angels, or all the above.

"The Diggers were not very good at [running] institutions," Coyote said. The day-to-day assembly line of feeding and clothing people soon "got to be a drag. It's not like you were doing it because you felt sorry for poor people or something. It was a challenge: could you feed fifteen hundred people, or five hundred people?"

But as the Diggers dispersed, their "free" virus spread. Now San Francisco had free poetry readings, free concerts, free legal aid, free medical clinics, free shelters. And the city's next wave of "life actors" proved more adept at running institutions than the Diggers.

5

THE LOST CHILDREN
OF WINDY FEET

A FTER EDWARD BEGGS and his wife, Nina, experienced the "Bethlehem miracle" of a new world being born at the Human Be-In, the reverend began feeling like a prisoner of his own life. None of his daily routine measured up to the skyrocket splendor and purpose of that afternoon in the park. The youth minister enjoyed his rambling conversations with teenage worshippers at First Congregational Church in San Mateo. But the elders at his suburban church were growing concerned about the frank subject matter of those discussions, which included sex, drugs, and adolescents' rights. Even his habit of wearing corduroy coats and driving around in a red sports car began to annoy the church board. Beggs, in turn, felt the church was on "life support" and was increasingly irrelevant to young people.

Churches throughout the Bay Area were grappling with the upheavals of the sixties. Glide Memorial, a venerable Methodist church in San Francisco's seedy Tenderloin, had been taken over by a group of young clerical reformers who took down the cross and turned the church over to community free-for-alls like the Diggers' Invisible Circus, which featured billowing clouds of dope, a pulsating light show, belly dancers, and writhing naked bodies in the basement game room. Meanwhile, clerical San Francisco renegades like James Pike, the Episcopal bishop of California, compared the passion of Christ to the revolutionary struggles of the Vietcong and the martyrdom of Martin Luther King, denounced antihomosexuality laws, and challenged church orthodoxy so flagrantly that his fellow bishops charged him with heresy.

Pike was an electrifying figure to young clergymen like Beggs. He made religion seem urgently personal as well as political. And he turned his private agonies into public dramas. When his twenty-two-year-old son, James Jr.—distraught over his growing realization that he was gay—blew his head off with a rifle in a New York hotel room, Pike claimed he communicated with him during a séance that was televised in Toronto. Fellow church leaders expressed outrage, but Pike boldly defended himself. "If Christ was resurrected, then we are all resurrected. If Christ talked to his disciples after his death, then why can't we do the same?"

In this febrile environment, no minister with Edward Beggs's restless spirit could sit in suburban stupor for long. When Beggs heard that Glide Church was establishing a shelter for the growing teenage runaway population in San Francisco, he knew this was his pastoral calling. He left his life in the church and became the founding director of Huckleberry House. The name was Beggs's idea; his homage to American literature's most famous young runaway. Beggs saw Huck Finn as a "revolutionary" who hit the road with his black friend Jim rather than bow to the cultural values of the day, just like the young people pouring into San Francisco. When Huck decided, "All right, then, I'll *go* to hell," rather than condemn Jim to a life of slavery, Beggs believed it was one of the great moral epiphanies in the American odyssey. Had Huck and Jim been living in 1960s America, he surmised, they would have kept heading west, directly for the Haight-Ashbury.

Emmett Grogan thought Huckleberry House "was as lame as its name," calling it a "nice, mild, safe, responsible way for the church to become involved in 'hippiedom.'" The Diggers made an effort to take care of the boys and girls washing up on the shores of the Haight. "The city was telling all these kids—our age, a lot of them younger—to get lost," Coyote recalled. "And our feeling was that they were our kids. You know? This was America; these were our kids."

But the Diggers were never very good at housing children on the run. The communal havens in the Haight where the Diggers tried to stash runaways were nervous about sheltering the kids because they knew it increased their risk of being raided by the cops. Running away from home was a crime in 1967 if you were a teenager, and every agency—from Travelers Aid to the YMCA—and every individual, including family friends and schoolteachers, was legally obligated to turn over runaways to the police.

But Huckleberry House was something new. It was founded on the idea that runaways were family problems, not police problems. And if the kids refused to let Huckleberry House contact their parents, the shelter would not hand them over to the cops. They had the right to keep running. Grogan might sneer at Huckleberry's fresh-scrubbed piety, but in the end, Beggs and company had more guts and staying power than the Diggers. At the very first Huckleberry House meeting, Beggs and his staff discussed how to raise bail money in case they were dragged off to jail. They were right to be concerned. The police were constantly hovering around the Huckleberry House shelter, which was housed in a two-story brown Victorian at One Broderick Street, a few blocks from the tumult of Haight-Ashbury.

In the early 1960s, running away from home was depicted as a quaint American rite of passage. A 1964 article in the *New York Times Magazine* titled "Why They Run Away from Home" was illustrated with a picture of a boy toting an overstuffed bag peering longingly into the kitchen, as his mother—oblivious to his brief fling with freedom—cooks a delicious dinner. But by 1967, running away had become a more deeply disturbing cultural phenomenon. For one thing, girls were doing it, not just boys. And kids were not just hitting the road for a day or two and quickly returning home. They were running *somewhere*: into a mysterious new world that baffled and terrified their parents.

THE UNDERGROUND RAILROAD OFTEN led to San Francisco. And the local press was filled with stories of frantic mothers and fathers trying to track down their missing children on the streets of the city. In January, shortly before the Human Be-In, the *Chronicle* began running a series under the blaring headline "Runaway Girls: Life with the Hippies." The newspaper followed the trail of fifteen-year-old Diana Phipps, a "pretty, slender blonde" who had vanished from her suburban home into the shadowy "Beatnik society."

The desperation of America's families was fully displayed on the Huckleberry House bulletin board, which was papered with pleading letters and photos of missing teens. "Dad promises to ease up. You can trust Aunt Lou," read one. "Until there is some contact with my daughter, my life will be miserable," read another. Some seemed certain to drive the runaways even deeper into their new world: "Rick Hoyfeld— you have received your draft notice. You've been reclassified 1-A. Contact your mother."

Beggs would try to reunite runaways with their parents, offering to hold family counseling sessions at Huckleberry House. He wasn't interested in "demonizing" fathers and mothers, "because ultimately the kids were going to go back home." But first he had to grapple with parental rage—by the time they walked in the shelter's front door, the fathers in particular were often ready to blow. "I'd disarm the son of a bitch right there," Beggs recalled, "and I'd say to him, 'I'd like to compliment you on raising a son who has the courage to oppose you, because you're one intimidating person.' I'd tear the rug out from under his ass. And pretty soon the father is telling the kid his frustrations, and the kid is explaining why he wants to keep his hair long. And by the end of the session, the father might be saying, 'You know, our relationship is more important to me than your hair.'"

But the roots of family agony were sometimes so deep and twisted that Beggs had no chance of making it right. He heard it all: abusive fathers, alcoholic mothers, suicidal children; tendrils of incest and other worms of corruption that had thoroughly rotted the foundations of the family home. He wasn't going to send kids back to these nightmares against their will. And the boys and girls loved him and Huckleberry House for that.

There was something childlike about Beggs himself. He still looked boyish in his early thirties, and he spoke in teen-type bursts of wonder and feeling. If the runaway adolescents were struggling to find themselves in this new world, so was he.

Kids poured out their souls to Beggs in letters. They wrote to him from wrecked homes, juvenile halls, mental hospitals. Some of them had crashed at Huckleberry House, some of them longed to. Their hand-scrawled notes were a window into the bleeding heart of the American family in the 1960s.

In early September 1967, just before school started, a thirteen-year-old girl who called herself Deveron showed up at Huckleberry House. She was dressed all in black and was carrying a tiny black kitten and a battered five-string guitar. The counselor who took down her information noted that she was "obsessed with a desire to make it on her own": to enroll herself in school and get a job, a new ID, and an apartment. But at her age, there was no way she could be emancipated. She talked about a boy named Danny, but he never showed up. While walking the city, Deveron was picked up by the cops, who immediately took her to the old, city-run Youth Guidance Center on the slopes of Twin Peaks. She had no more tears left, but she cried for the kitten that the cops took away from her—she had named it after her sister.

Despite its name, the YGC didn't offer much in the way of guidance. It was a bleak, overcrowded warehouse for boys and girls who had fallen into the hands of the law, and there were more and more of them every day. Later, Deveron wrote the Huckleberry House staff to tell them what her life at YGC had been like.

"San Francisco juvenile hall cannot afford to be nice," she wrote. "It is two story's [sic] up. The rooms are steaming hot twenty-four hours a day. The windows are half an inch thick and through the tiny crack at the top you can maybe see a few lights at night outside of the barbed wire. There are no people there. Only animals. If it wasn't time to be let out they had to wet their floors. The only sounds are 'Be quiet!' 'Alright, girl—you're on tray!' and the sound of rattling trays and doors and keys."

One day, some girls stood on their cots, broke the windows of their cells, and squeezed out through the barbed wire. They were torn and bleeding, but for the moment they were free, running through the cool mists of Twin Peaks. Deveron looked out through the crack of her window at the bloodstained girls and began singing "The Star-Spangled Banner."

Now Deveron was back home. But she couldn't stop thinking about her days in San Francisco. "I worry about the children of Haight Street," she wrote Huckleberry House. "Haight Street is not dead, it never will be. But it will always be dying, so will its children. If someone doesn't help them to help themselves to live."

"You're helping them," she told Beggs and company. "You helped me . . . and mothers and fathers of lost children with windy feet. Just by being there and trying; if nothing more. Please never give up as long as children follow illusions and cities . . . And if Danny comes back, I love him."

Beggs was amazed by the heart and courage of these "lost children with windy feet." He knew what it took for them to leave everything behind and end up on his doorstep. Running away, he realized, was "an SOS—a flare in the dark"—for someone to step in and help resolve an agonizing family situation. The former minister was a godsend to the kids who found shelter at Huckleberry House. But to San Francisco's youth justice establishment, Beggs was a dangerous Pied Piper: a threat to the family structure that the city's heavily Catholic law enforcement hierarchy believed was the moral linchpin of society.

THE CHIEF ANTAGONIST OF Huckleberry House was Juvenile Court Judge Raymond J. O'Connor, who ran San Francisco's youth justice system with an iron hand and saw the upstart shelter as a challenge to his authority. Like Mayor Shelley and much of the city's hierarchy, O'Connor was a San Francisco native and a product of local parochial schools. After a long career in private practice, he was appointed to the bench by his old friend, California governor Edmund "Pat" Brown, the big-government Democrat whose political career was ended by Ronald Reagan in 1966. But despite his Democratic Party affiliation, Judge O'Connor was a crusty opponent of the decade's social activism. In 1964 the Superior Court Judge summoned newspaper reporters into his chambers to denounce the civil rights sit-ins sweeping the city as a criminal conspiracy. After he was named chief of the juvenile court the following year, O'Connor quickly made it clear that he was going to crack down on the youthful rebellion and lawlessness he saw spinning out of control in San Francisco. O'Connor began throwing teens and even preteens into the grim YGC citadel at a much higher rate and keeping them under lock and key much longer. He was particularly hard on black youths, and even jailed their parents when he felt they were lying to him. About two-thirds of the San Francisco kids behind bars at YGC were black.

In 1966 the judge ignited a furor when he tossed a twelve-year-old boy into jail for purse snatching, along with several other older boys— none of whom had ever been in trouble before. Family groups and civil liberties attorneys called for O'Connor's ouster. But police and business groups rallied to the youth czar's defense, and he held on to his post.

The following year, as San Francisco became a youth magnet, O'Connor scooped up thousands of young vagabonds and locked them up in his juvenile prison. The judge became a notorious villain in the Haight, denounced in one underground newspaper as a "sham . . . mentally and morally unqualified to sit in judgment on the young." O'Connor stuffed so many kids into his barbed-wire warehouse that they were forced to sleep in their own piss and shit on the floors of their cells and fight to defend their space. At an "emergency conference" on runaways held in the Straight Theater, a favorite Grateful Dead venue in the Haight, one boy explained bluntly what teens on the run could expect when they fell into O'Connor's net: "They get beaten up in the paddy wagon, then they get beaten up in jail . . . and then they get beaten up again when they get home."

O'Connor was determined to track down all of San Francisco's windy-feet children. In his eyes, storefront operations like Huckleberry House were a public nuisance, encouraging kids to defy parental authority and flee home. "Raymond O'Connor was a son of a bitch, and he wanted us closed," said Beggs. "This hippie minister was threatening his juvenile justice monopoly. That's how he saw it. 'Throttle the bastard!' In those years, you had complete control as a parent to force your kid to do many things. And judges like O'Connor were complicit in this. These brutal, alcoholic parents could be shit-faced drunk all week long, and then put on a suit and appear in O'Connor's court, and the judge would always take their side. He was sending these kids back home to be abused mentally and sometimes sexually."

The fifty-seven-year-old, gray-haired O'Connor was a father himself. He and his wife, Mary, had seven children. After one of O'Connor's own teenage sons ran away from the family's home in West Portal—a quiet mom-and-pop neighborhood that even today seems preserved from an earlier era—the boy ended up at Huckleberry House. The youth revolution had literally come home for Raymond O'Connor. It was only a matter of time before the judge slammed down his fist on the shelter.

The police raid took place on the night of October 19, 1967, several months after Huckleberry House opened its doors. An inexperienced night manager gave the cops their opening when she failed to make the obligatory phone call to the parents of a fifteen-year-old runaway, to get permission to shelter their son for the night. Suddenly there was a crying mother on the Huckleberry House doorsteps and a swarm of cops. The SFPD arrested everyone on the premises, including the runaways, for being without parental supervision; and the adult caretakers, for contributing to the delinquency of minors. Beggs, who was home at the time, turned himself in the next morning at county jail. Kissing his two young boys good-bye, he had to explain to them why "daddy is going to go to jail now."

Sitting in his cell, Beggs reflected gloomily on the fate of Huckleberry House, the nation's first alternative runaway shelter and, he thought, perhaps the last. But San Francisco in the sixties was not simply a bastion of Catholic law and order. There were other shifting forces at work, and it turned out that Beggs's sponsors at the activist Glide Church had some connections of their own. A young, politically ambitious, African-American attorney from the Fillmore named Willie Brown was retained to represent Huckleberry House. And within hours, Judge Joseph Kennedy—a black jurist who strongly supported Glide's social programs—released Beggs on his own recognizance. A couple of months later, the case was dismissed.

The raid on Huckleberry House was traumatic for its young staff. But it had a galvanizing effect on the community surrounding the shelter. "The overall effect of the bust," Beggs said, "was to dramatically communicate to the Haight that if we're being attacked by the police and the juvenile justice system and Judge O'Connor, that we were now legitimized as an authentic, counterculture operation." High school students went door to door to collect canned goods for Huckleberry. A printing company ran off several thousand promotional pamphlets for the shelter at no cost. An elderly woman in the Glide congregation gathered small soap bars from her residential hotel to donate to the shelter. Parents and former Huckleberry runaways mailed in small cash donations. As word spread about Huckleberry's resilience in the face of official harassment, more and more teenagers showed up on the shelter's doorsteps.

When Huckleberry House stood its ground and survived, it was a major victory for the new city growing within the old. The city's establishment didn't give a damn about the children on its streets. As an outraged editorial in the *Haight Ashbury Tribune* fumed, "If an individual treated a child with the [same] disregard for his health, safety, and welfare" that San Francisco displayed toward minors, "our law would punish that individual as a felon." But in the end, the community took care of its own.

They had flocked to San Francisco from all over the world, but they were now the city's children. And you take care of your children, particularly when they are lost and broken. That was the philosophy that took root in the new city during the Summer of Love.

6

STREET MEDICINE

As San Francisco braced itself for the Summer of Love tidal wave, a twenty-eight-year-old intern named David Smith was working as chief of the alcohol and drug abuse screening unit at San Francisco General Hospital. At night Smith drove across town to his apartment on Frederick Street in the Haight, near a donut store that sold LSD under the counter. The young doctor knew he lived and worked at ground zero. And he knew the city's public health system was woefully unprepared for the waves of drug-experimenting kids already washing up on its streets. In fact, Public Health Director Ellis Sox was openly hostile to the growing youth population, mirroring the attitude of Mayor Shelley's administration, which wanted to post "Hippies Not Welcome" signs on the bridge approaches to San Francisco.

If food and shelter were the most urgent needs in the Haight's rapidly expanding refugee encampment, health care was close behind. None of the medical facilities in the neighborhood wanted to treat hippies. St. Mary's, the big Catholic-run hospital on Stanyan Street, had a policy of turning away drug overdose victims. The Diggers once again tried to address the crisis but fell far short. They rounded up a few interns from Kaiser Hospital and an ex-mental patient named Doc, who served as a "witch doctor" to the Hell's Angels, to care for people at their free stores. But their makeshift emergency rooms were soon swamped with patients and quickly ran out of medical supplies. Grogan and his cohorts began ferrying young people who were hallucinating wildly on LSD and other chemical cocktails to Dr. Smith's small detox center. Smith would try to talk them through their nightmares, or if necessary, administer a sedative or a more potent antipsychotic like Thorazine.

But Smith's unit was open only during weekday work hours, and when high-flying kids were brought to General Hospital at other times, they were dumped across the street at Mission Emergency Hospital, where they were thrown in with alcoholics or gunshot victims, or locked in padded isolation cells. What began as a mildly bad trip could erupt into full-blown psychosis by the time a hallucinating patient made his way through the city's harrowing public health labyrinth.

Hippies who fell into the hands of public health doctors and nurses at Park Emergency Hospital, on the edge of Golden Gate Park, fared the worst. The hospital staff seemed to take pleasure in tormenting the young, disoriented patients, ignoring them or making them suffer through a long registration process. In the end, many of them were shoved into the back of ambulances and, sirens screaming, deposited on Smith's doorstep at SF General.

Like Rev. Beggs, David Smith felt estranged from his own profession. The truth was, Smith had never seemed at home in his surroundings. He had grown up "a jock and a square" in Bakersfield, the son of Okies whose families had fled the Dust Bowl for the oil fields and farms of California's Central Valley. Smith's father, Elvin, became a clerk for Southern Pacific Railroad, and his mother, Dorothy, grew up to become a nurse. But she always remembered the humiliations of working in the fields with her mother and sister during the Depression. When the farm boss would ask her mother what kind of work she would do, she answered, "Anything." Never say you will do anything, his mother told young David. She urged him to become a doctor.

In high school, David never tried to date "good girls" because he felt ashamed by his humble roots and his sickly mother, who was diagnosed with Hodgkin's disease when he was three. He was a good student and worked hard to make the varsity basketball team. But he always felt like an outsider. When his mother finally died of her illness during his senior year, David and his father, who both liked to drink, began to apply themselves to the bottle more seriously. Within a couple of years, his father had drunk himself to death, leaving David an orphan at nineteen.

Smith continued to drink heavily during the early 1960s as an undergraduate at Berkeley and as a medical student at the University of California campus in San Francisco. But he developed an interest in psychedelics while taking pharmacology courses in medical school, and after experimenting with LSD, he gave up alcohol for acid, mescaline, and marijuana. He would spend most of his professional life studying and treating the powerful effects of drugs. But he would never entirely condemn their dark magic. "It started as clinical, but it turned into a religious experience," Smith recalled. "I don't want to bad-mouth LSD, because I'd never have done what I did in my life had I not had that spiritual experience on LSD. I was the grandson of farm workers, and all I wanted was academic and financial success. The idea that I would leave the lab and risk everything to help these street kids was so foreign. But I broke on through to the other side. And it seemed to me like not only *should* I do it, but I *had* to do it."

Smith began feeling like he belonged for the first time in his life. He was a few years older than most of the ragged young people who roamed the streets of his neighborhood or found their way into his hospital office. But they were his tribe; his tribe of outsiders. The authorities had tried to block the Okies at the California border too.

As horror stories about the San Francisco public health system spread in the Haight, more and more young people refrained from going to city medical facilities, even though health-care problems in the community were reaching the crisis point. Smith knew he had to do something. Thanks to the Diggers, the idea of free medical service was blowing in the wind. A former girlfriend named Florence Martin, an African-American nurse, had also told Smith about her work at the Watts Clinic in Los Angeles, a community clinic established after the 1965 Watts riots. Before the clinic was built, neighborhood residents had to drive miles for medical care. Now they had a sense that their health-care system belonged to them. Smith was also intrigued by the stories that his Haight-Ashbury neighbor Terry Hallinan brought back from the South, where he had worked with the Student Nonviolent Coordinating Committee (SNCC) to set up free health clinics.

Brainstorming with a man named Robert Conrich—a physician turned private investigator who had dropped out of the professional world after becoming an LSD initiate—Smith developed the idea for a free clinic in the Haight. "I was pretty naïve about health politics then," he recalled. "But the concept of 'free' was all around me. I became the architect of the slogan 'Health care is a right, not a privilege.' That was the founding philosophy of the Haight-Ashbury Free Clinic. It was a very radical idea then. Now it's being debated in the mainstream. And it all came out of this area, the street university known as the Haight-Ashbury. I was learning more every day walking around in my neighborhood than I ever learned in the lab."

Smith and Conrich recruited doctors, nurses, and hippie volunteers to staff the clinic. They found an abandoned dental office on the second floor of a faded yellow Victorian at 558 Clayton Street, near the corner of Haight. Smith paid the lease out of his own pocket, with a $100 lecture fee and a $500 donation from Rev. Leon Smith, an activist Episcopal minister in the Haight. Smith and his crew then outfitted the office with scavenged furniture and medical equipment, including an X-ray machine so ancient that Smith thought it belonged in the Smithsonian.

Despite his growing emotional attachment to the hippie community, Smith was still an ambitious young medical professional who kept his curly hair closely cropped. He tried to keep one foot in the mainstream world while dipping his other into the crosscurrent. He thought he could be a bridge between the two realities. But it soon became clear to Smith that he was crossing a Rubicon. City authorities immediately resented the Haight-Ashbury Free Clinic because it was outside their domain. So bitter was city hall opposition that it seemed to Smith as if public health czar Sox "wanted to isolate the Haight-Ashbury and let its young residents die." Smith's former medical school mentors and colleagues urged him to abandon the free clinic project, warning him that he was ruining his promising career by treating drug takers and other undesirables. He was even told that someone would try to kill him.

But when the Haight-Ashbury Free Clinic opened its doors on June 7, 1967, it became instantly clear why the storefront emergency room was essential. A long line of patients in granny dresses, buckskins, and other light clothing stretched around the corner, shivering miserably in the wet fog. Eric Burdon and the Animals might have fantasized about warm San Franciscan nights, but only newcomers to the city expected to be greeted with summer sunshine. As the patients made their way up the hallway stairs to the clinic, Smith remembers, it soon turned into a "madhouse." Overdose victims clawed at phantoms in the air; runny-nosed babies wailed frantically, unappeased by their hippie mothers' bare breasts. A fever-flushed woman wrapped only in a pink blanket and racked with deep, bronchial coughs insisted that she could not be hospitalized because she had to hitchhike to Big Sur the next morning. The air was thick with marijuana, incense, and a rank mix of body odor and patchouli. Patients not utterly depleted by illness rattled tambourines and blew on wooden flutes. The cacophony went on and on.

The clinic treated more than 250 patients the first day, and more than 350 the next. By the third day, its stockpiles of bandages, antibiotics, and penicillin were depleted. When clinic doctors ran out of tranquilizers, all they could do was encourage patients freaking out on drugs to concentrate on flickering candles. The clinic's small detox room—wishfully called its "calm center"—was soon an overcrowded bedlam. An eighteen-year-old girl freaking out on acid was trying to hurl her body through the calm center wall. Another drug patient was prancing nude through the waiting room. Smith's volunteer staff—including some doctors who had served in the military—were already on the brink of burnout and comparing the beleaguered clinic to a field hospital in a combat zone.

The Haight was actually more like Calcutta, with its hordes of beggars in brightly colored rags and its stew of human misery. The Free Clinic staff treated a bizarre spectrum of infections and aggravations that Summer of Love, many of them more commonly associated with Third World slums than prosperous American tourist destinations. The young patients who came through the clinic doors were suffering from pneumonia, hepatitis, venereal disease, illegal abortion complications, skin infections, gum diseases, malnourishment, and intestinal disorders from eating rotten food.

Smith couldn't understand why the public authorities had turned their backs on the young people flooding his clinic. "Many of these kids came from traditional backgrounds," he recalled. "They were the establishment's own sons and daughters. They didn't come to Haight-Ashbury to go to the Free Clinic. They came for the music, for the freedom. And if you didn't take care of them, they'd get sick and clog up hospital emergency rooms. They certainly wouldn't go home."

When David Perlman, the science reporter for the *San Francisco Chronicle,* showed up to interview Smith for a story on the clinic, he was so stunned by the spectacle of suffering that he put down his notebook and began helping out, taking patient histories for several hours. His story, "A Medical Mission in the Haight Ashbury," ran on the front page, and it produced an outpouring of public support. Checks ranging from $5 to $100 came in through the mail. People arrived at the clinic hauling furniture, food, and medication. Celebrities volunteered to work in the clinic, including Bing Crosby's wife, Kathryn, who drove up from the family home in Hillsborough.

The *Chronicle* coverage put pressure on city authorities to support the clinic. But city hall responded only with smoke and mirrors. Public Health Director Sox vaguely promised to open a more "proper" health center in the Haight before the summer was over. And Mayor Shelley announced that in the meantime, the city was funding the Free Clinic. Both statements were untrue, and whether boneheaded or malicious, they had the effect of instantly drying up public contributions to the clinic and pushing it to the brink of financial ruin.

Meanwhile, other dark forces preyed on the struggling clinic. The police were a constant, harassing presence. Beat cops periodically roamed through the clinic's five rooms, hunting for runaways. And narcotics officers came around sniffing for illegal drugs. A sign posted in the clinic tried to avert police raids, pleading, "No dealing, no holding, no using dope—any of these can close the clinic." It concluded with a cheery, flower-decorated "We love you," because the clinic tried hard not to alienate its wary, young patients. But the sign was a reminder that everyone in the Haight was under surveillance, even in relatively safe zones like the Free Clinic.

Even more troubling to Smith and his staff were the street strongmen who tried to muscle their way into the clinic as it became established in the neighborhood. One such sketchy character called himself Papa Al. A successful speed dealer who lived in a Berkeley mansion, Papa Al roamed the streets of the Haight with a .38 revolver and a burly companion known as Teddybear. The two men began volunteering at the Free

Clinic soon after it opened up, passing themselves off as Good Samaritans. But it soon became clear that they intended to take over the clinic and use it as the base of their drug operation. When Smith confronted Papa Al and ordered him to leave, the drug dealer responded by putting out a contract on the lives of Smith and the clinic administrator, Donald Reddick. The word spread quickly on the street: any methamphetamine freak who knocked off Smith or Reddick would get $100 worth of speed.

"I freaked out," Smith said. "The neighborhood was so crazy then that if you put out the word like that, it could easily happen."

Smith went to the cops at Park Police Station, but they told him they couldn't do anything until Papa Al made a move. "So I learned the police were no protection. If Papa Al moved, I'd be dead. The cops' attitude was, Here's this insane asylum in the Haight, and whatever you crazed animals do in there to each other, we don't give a damn—just don't let it spill out into the rest of the city."

Reddick gave Smith a gun and holster, but his only experience with firearms was taking potshots at bottles on the banks of the Kern River as a kid. In desperation, Smith turned to the Hell's Angels: the hard guys in leather who brought a kind of rough justice to the neighborhood. Everyone was afraid of the Angels, including the police. But the bikers had their uses. The Haight had made a devil's bargain with the Angels. In return for protecting them from violent cops, bad drug dealers, and other rogue elements, the neighborhood turned a blind eye to the Angels' own bare-knuckled behavior. Heavy hippies like the Diggers admired the Angels for their outlaw integrity, the Dead and Janis liked their swagger and style. But people knew that bringing the bikers into the equation was like bringing a jungle cat on a leash into a party. It could all be cool—or not.

This time it all worked out. Smith phoned Hell's Angels leader Sonny Barger and told him his plight. The next day, two Angels visited Papa Al and told him how things stood. "You're David Smith's insurance policy," they said. "If anything happens to him—if he's hit by a car walking across the street—you're dead." The contract on Smith and Reddick was lifted. Papa Al disappeared from the Haight.

Smith knows everything that has been said about Barger and his gang. He knows that historians of the 1960s will have the final say. But for him, it's not complicated: "If you ask me, they saved my life."

IF SONNY BARGER SAVED Smith's life, it was another community icon—rock concert promoter Bill Graham—who saved his clinic. By July, the clinic was mired in debt. With the city still withholding financial support, the frontline medical facility was on the verge of closing its doors. But after reading about the clinic's crisis in the *Chronicle*, Graham phoned Smith, who invited him over to 558 Clayton. They were an unlikely pair: the Okie from Bakersfield and the Holocaust orphan who had raised himself on the streets of the Bronx. In the Haight's "free" circles, Graham was reviled as a moneygrubbing opportunist who was taking the neighborhood's free-floating music and selling it back to the people. But Smith saw the "heart of gold," as he put it, under Graham's snarly exterior. "He could be extremely tough, but if he decided you were one of his people, he loved you." Graham quickly sized up the young doctor as one of his people.

While talking with Smith in the clinic, Graham looked out the window and saw a phalanx of cops sweeping hippies off the street. "These kids have made my business possible," he told the doctor. "They don't deserve this treatment. Now I want to do something for them . . . We need the clinic. It's humanity—and the least I can do." Graham organized a benefit at the Fillmore Auditorium on July 13 headlined by Big Brother and the Holding Company that raised $5,000 for the clinic—a hefty sum in those days. "Without Bill Graham, the clinic would not have survived its fragile infancy that summer," said Smith. In October Graham followed up with a second benefit, this one featuring the Jefferson Airplane, that funneled another $5,000 to the clinic. Graham's largesse inspired a wave of other benefits for the clinic, including a free concert in a San Jose park again headlined by Big Brother.

"We literally built this clinic on rock 'n' roll," Smith said. It was a circular system. Many of the rock musicians who raised money for the Free Clinic were also its patients. Smith even saved some of their lives. He would get calls in the dead of night, sometimes from Graham, sometimes from friends, lovers, or bandmates. A beloved musician had collapsed and was turning a morgue-like pallor. Smith was needed right away. Years later, watching the movie *Pulp Fiction*, he instantly identified with the Harvey Keitel character—the man called in to clean up disasters.

No one required more emergency attention than Janis Joplin, whose dark romance with liquor and drugs long preceded her musical stardom. She was using up all her lives, one by one. Late one night, Smith got a frantic call from a girlfriend of Janis: the singer had overdosed on heroin and could not be revived. Smith rushed to Janis's house in the Haight and injected her with Narcan. This time Janis came back. When she opened her eyes and saw Doc Smith, she smiled and said, "Thank you."

Most of Janis Joplin's soul-wrenching music was ahead of her. Smith kept her going long enough so she could give the world those pieces of her heart. He was no miracle worker. But the young doctor built a haven that summer where America's lost children—from ragged panhandlers to rock stars—were made to feel that their lives were not disposable and that someone cared about them.

7

MURDER ON
SHAKEDOWN STREET

Before Bill Graham, there was Charles Sullivan. The king of black music promoters on the West Coast, Sullivan signed up the biggest African-American headliners for his concert circuit, which stretched from Vancouver to San Diego. He presented them all: Louis Armstrong, Duke Ellington, Count Basie, Billie Holliday, and, later, Ray Charles, Ike and Tina Turner, Little Richard, James Brown, the Temptations. His long reign as a promoter began during World War II, when he opened a joint in San Mateo, south of San Francisco, called Club Sullivan, and extended into the 1950s and 1960s, when he moved into San Francisco and took over the lease on an old dance hall originally called the Majestic Ballroom, renaming it the Fillmore Auditorium.

The Fillmore district was a hopping music scene in those years, with jazz, blues, bebop, and rhythm and blues blasting out of dozens of clubs, bars, and lounges all night long. Fillmore Street became "Swing Street." And Sullivan was the ringmaster of it all: staging big shows at the Fillmore, running a hotel where black musicians felt welcome and a bar where they jammed until dawn, and making another small fortune on the side from liquor, jukeboxes, and gambling. He was the man to see; they called him "the mayor of Fillmore Street."

In 1965 Sullivan launched Bill Graham in the concert business, loaning him his dance license—that essential city document—and subleasing the Fillmore to Graham on the auditorium's dark nights. Without Sullivan, Graham might never have cracked San Francisco's tightly controlled entertainment racket. Then Sullivan was suddenly, violently, torn out of the picture. And Graham made his move, taking over the Fillmore lease and turning the old dance hall into a hallowed name in musical history. "Behind every beautiful thing, there is some kind of pain": That's how Bob Dylan sings it. And, in the case of the Fillmore, it rings true.

Music was at the heart of San Francisco's magical transformation in the 1960s. And at the beginning of the decade, the Fillmore was the music's hot center. They called the Fillmore "the Harlem of the West." The streets were filled until the early morning hours with a parade of peacocks: men with diamond stickpins, satin ties, and long coats; women in slit dresses and furs. Adventurous white kids like Jerry Garcia would sneak into the Fillmore clubs and dance halls, this forbidden empire of cool, to hear the music they couldn't find on Top 40 radio.

And then it was all gone, destroyed block by block by the wrecking balls and bulldozers of the San Francisco Redevelopment Agency. As Jerry Garcia later sang, "Nothin' shakin' on Shakedown Street, used to be the heart of town." The agency launched the first phase of its massive urban renewal project in 1953, erasing stores, nightclubs, and churches and more than twenty-five thousand residents from hundreds of city blocks. Geary Street, a bustling commercial center, was turned into an eight-lane expressway, so that cars and buses carrying commuters downtown from the predominantly white west-side neighborhoods could hurtle directly through the Fillmore without stopping. Ten years later, the agency kicked off the second phase of its Fillmore blitzkrieg, uprooting an additional thirteen thousand people and shuttering thousands of more businesses over sixty square blocks.

The city called it urban renewal. But to residents of the Fillmore, it was "Negro removal." Redevelopment officials promised that dislocated residents would be moved back into the neighborhood. But those who were forced to sell their houses soon found that they were priced out of the Fillmore's rising real estate market.

The Fillmore was the heart of black San Francisco, and redevelopment tore it out. The Harlem of the West now looked like a war-ravaged city, pockmarked with empty, rubble-strewn lots, shuttered storefronts, and dreary street corners inhabited by lost and wasted men. After the middle-class home owners and business operators were forced out, all that was left was a crime-ridden ghetto.

As the wrecking balls turned the Fillmore into a wasteland, an ugly spirit began sweeping the streets. Cab drivers refused to take white tourists there anymore. White teenagers like John Goddard had crossed the Golden Gate Bridge from Marin County to see Little Richard (backed by a scrawny young guitarist named Jimi Hendrix) and other marvels at the Fillmore Auditorium. But now the neighborhood seemed forbidding. "It got to the point, around 1965, where I didn't feel safe coming to Fillmore Street anymore . . . people were angry—rightly so. But I didn't feel comfortable. Nothing ever happened, but it was a different vibe."

THEN, NEAR THE END of that year, Charles Sullivan loaned Bill Graham his Fillmore Auditorium dance permit. White kids began flocking to the desolated neighborhood to hear a whole new breed of musicians: the Airplane, the Dead, Quicksilver Messenger Service, Big Brother, Sopwith Camel, the Grassroots, Love, Velvet Underground, Frank Zappa and the Mothers of Invention, Van Morrison and his band Them. They all played the Fillmore in the first half of 1966. And suddenly the corner of Fillmore and Geary, the heart of the neighborhood, was jolted back to life with a surge of electric music.

The cops were not happy. They had written off the Fillmore as a no-man's-land. Now they suddenly had security headaches. More and more children of the white suburbs were venturing into the Fillmore after nightfall, which meant that the police had to patrol the neighborhood again.

Like all operators of liquor stores and late-night entertainment joints, Sullivan liked to keep everyone happy, particularly the authorities. Some of his enterprises required licenses from the city and the state. Others, like his after-hours speakeasies, depended on the look-the-other-way leniency of beat cops. Sullivan knew how to spread around the gravy. He always carried a roll of cash in his pants pocket, and he would take it out and peel off the bills whenever he needed to take care of somebody.

But this time, Sullivan couldn't smooth it over with the cops. They wanted him to pull his dance permit from Graham. They wanted the rock shows shut down. Or else they would shut *him* down: no more booze peddling, no more backroom gambling, no more vending machines. Sullivan caved. The next day he called Graham into his office and gave him the bad news. "They're leaning on me hard, and I got a business to run, and I got a wife and kids, and I have to pull my permit," Sullivan grimly informed the rock promoter.

Graham went home that night and told his wife, Bonnie: it was all over. The next morning, Graham returned to the Fillmore to pack up his office. When he arrived, Sullivan was sitting on the steps. The fifty-seven-year-old Sullivan always dressed like a gentleman, in suit and tie. And he would insist that his performers always look their best on stage too, picking up their suits after every show to make sure they were cleaned and pressed. But today Sullivan looked worse for wear. He was a big man—more than six feet tall, and close to two hundred fifty pounds—but now he seemed like a beat-down field worker. He was wearing the same suit, shirt, and tie from the day before, and it looked to Graham like he'd been up all night. "Bill," said the older man, "I want to talk to you."

They went upstairs to Graham's cubbyhole of an office. And Sullivan began pouring out his life story to him. How he had grown up on a farm in Monroe County, Alabama, raised by illiterate parents. How he had left home as a teenager and made his way out to the West Coast, washing cars in Los Angeles and then going to night school to become a machinist. How he had moved to San Francisco in search of work during the Depression, but was barred from the all-white machinists union and was forced to take a job as a chauffeur for a San Mateo socialite. It was only after years of tormented hustle that Sullivan finally began to get a leg up, saving a little money and opening a suburban hamburger stand, then adding a restaurant and a bar. Then, during World War II, as the Fillmore district began to boom, he saw his big chance to move into the city. All those black defense workers with cash in their pockets—and few places to spend it. He would become the king of swing.

All during his long trek to the top, Sullivan told Graham, the white man had messed with him. Finally, he thought, he had found his place in the sun: he was a wealthy pillar of his community with a booming entertainment business; a pretty, young wife; and a comfortable two-story house with Japanese décor near Alamo Square. But now the men downtown were messing with him all over again, making threats and telling him what to do. "Yesterday they really got to me," Sullivan said, and the big man began to shake.

"Bill, it's my life," he went on. "After I saw you last night, I started thinking about myself and what I been through and what they're making you do now." His eyes, red from lack of sleep, were fixed on Graham. "I can't do it. I can't. I just can't back off. I can't pull that permit from you."

Then Sullivan leaned forward. His voice was choked with pain and rage. "No, no, no. I just ain't going to let this happen now. You just go back downtown, man. And you beat those white motherfuckers."

Graham did just that. With typical sharp-elbows drive, the rock promoter finally finagled his own dance license out of city hall, lining up support from the *Chronicle,* neighborhood merchants, and even the rabbi of the temple next door to the Fillmore, who had complained about inebriated rock fans relieving themselves on his holy walls.

The smartest move Graham made was reaching out to San Francisco power attorney William Coblentz, who thought that the promoter was getting a raw deal and agreed to represent him for free. Coblentz hired a private eye, who snapped pictures of cops going in and out of a whorehouse across the street from the auditorium. The lawyer shared the revealing photos with the city board of permit appeals. He pointed out that the beat cops were in no position to charge that Graham was bad for the neighborhood. The board found this a convincing argument, and Graham was back in business.

But without Sullivan, nothing would have happened. "He was the guy, Charles," Graham said later. "He was *it.* I don't know if I could have *ever* found another place. Why would I have even tried? That *was* the place."

It should have been a triumphant time for Charles Sullivan too. He had stood up to the downtown bullies and won. He was at the top of his game, overseeing the West Coast tours for the top Motown Records acts and expanding into Los Angeles. But the Fillmore district, his base of operation since the 1940s, was becoming a dangerous ghost town. He was one of the few major business figures who stood in the way of the neighborhood's elimination. His turf was crowded by enemies and predators. Sullivan took to carrying a chrome-plated .38 in his briefcase.

IT WAS A .38 that took Charles Sullivan's life. Sometime after midnight in the early morning darkness of August 2, 1966, someone stuck the gun's snub nose right against his heart and pulled the trigger. He was dead before he hit the ground. The homicide cops found him sprawled on his back at the scruffy corner of Fifth and Bluxome Streets, lying next to his rented car, a tan Chevy, with the gun inches away from his outstretched right hand.

From the very start, the cops seemed strangely confused about the murder. At first they put out the word that there was "a strong possibility of suicide"—until the coroner's inquest pointed out that it would be very "awkward" for a man to shoot himself in the heart this way. Testifying at the inquest, lead homicide inspector Ken Manley, a sixteen-year veteran of the force, could not be certain whether the gun found at the scene even belonged to Sullivan. And he was at a loss to explain why no fingerprints or gun smoke odor were found on the revolver.

The story that finally went down was that Sullivan was killed while being robbed. The promoter was reported to be carrying several thousand dollars in his briefcase after having staged a James Brown show in Los Angeles and a Temptations concert in Phoenix that weekend, and the empty briefcase was found in the trunk of his car.

But the SFPD never arrested a suspect, and—like the suicide theory—the robbery story never smelled right to the Sullivan family. After the murder, Charles's wife, Fanny, and his younger brother, Marion, found that the promoter had already stashed most of the weekend's receipts—some $25,000—in the safe at his Grove Street home.

Marion Sullivan, who had been raised by Charles during much of his adolescence and later went to work for him in his jukebox business, was convinced that his brother was killed by someone he knew. "Charles was involved with some shady people," he said.

Sullivan's family and the cops were quickly able to retrace his steps that night. He had taken a flight from LA after the James Brown show and landed after nine o'clock at San Francisco International Airport, where he rented the Chevy. Sullivan's wife was out of town, and, unsurprisingly, he was accompanied by an attractive young woman. "He loved women; there was no question about it. He'd always find a broad to take with him on his trips," said Marion.

Sullivan drove into the city, dropped off the cash at his home, and then checked in at the cocktail lounge he ran, inside the Booker T. Washington Hotel on Ellis Street. Later that night, he drove his female companion, a schoolteacher who lived in Oakland, across the Bay Bridge to her home on Twenty-third Street. They enjoyed each other's company for about forty-five minutes. She later testified that she had served Sullivan watermelon. And then, after midnight, he left. On the street outside her house, he shouted out, and she came rushing outside to see what was wrong. He told her that he had seen a "kid going down the street, and it had scared him for a minute." He was worried that the kid might have snatched his briefcase, which was on the front seat of his locked car. But nothing had been taken, and he drove off. That was the last she ever saw him, said the schoolteacher.

After that, Sullivan's trajectory became murky. For some reason, he apparently exited the freeway in San Francisco on Fifth Street, rather than taking the Fell Street exit closer to his home, and he turned left into the freight district. He was miles from the Fillmore, and he had no business in the neighborhood. But that's where they found him, splayed on the street between the Chevy and a wire fence, his body silhouetted in the macabre glow of his car's headlights.

The newspapers got excited for a day or two about the murder. The African-American paper, the *Sun-Reporter,* kept the story going a bit longer, with a two-page spread on Sullivan's lavish funeral. Belva Davis, a writer for the *Sun-Reporter* who later became a prominent local TV journalist, began digging into the mystery but was suddenly pulled off the story. There were powerful interests behind Sullivan's murder, she was told. Charles Sullivan, despite all his wealth and show business glamour, soon disappeared forever. He was dropped down whatever well there was in those days for colored people, prominent or otherwise, who got themselves shot.

Homicide inspector Jack Cleary, Ken Manley's junior partner on the case, always clung to the suicide theory. And he thought that Sullivan's schoolteacher girlfriend ("a broad who had legs eight feet long; could've been a model") knew a lot more than she revealed at the coroner's inquest. Cleary suspected that she was with Sullivan when he shot himself—maybe accidentally, during a lovers' quarrel—and then took off.

Cleary confronted the "witch"—that's how he saw her—after she stepped down from the witness stand. "Come here," he said. "You know what? I'm going down to the DA's, and I'm going to get a warrant on you for perjury. You were there when Charley killed himself, and you left him there to die and should've got him some help. And you just got up on the stand and lied. You raised your right hand under oath—"

"No, I didn't," the leggy schoolteacher broke in, cool as diamonds. "I raised my left hand."

Neither Cleary nor the coroner had caught that sly move. "We were pretty good, but she was better."

But the lover's suicide theory, which seemed right out of a B movie, did not find many believers—even in Cleary's own department. There was a lingering scent around Sullivan's murder, something hidden and rank.

Some prominent San Franciscans, including a rising young political leader named Dianne Feinstein, took an interest in the Sullivan case. Feinstein, a clean government crusader married to a Pacific Heights neurosurgeon, already had her eye on the mayor's office, and she liked to poke around the city's dark corners. Always intrigued by police affairs, Feinstein collared Cleary at the hall of justice one day. "Look, Jack, this is a murder," she told him. "Murder, my foot," he shot back at her, insisting on his suicide explanation.

Some time later, after the case was filed away, Marion Sullivan was running an after-hours speakeasy when it got raided by the police. One of the cops recognized him and brought up his dead brother. "He told me that he knew who killed Charles," said Marion. "But I wasn't crazy enough to ask him to tell me who."

There was always a seamy underside to San Francisco, even during the enchanted sixties. But Sullivan's murder did not stop the music. In his place came an even bigger showman: bruising, belligerent, bighearted Bill Graham.

8

THE NAPOLEON OF ROCK

BILL GRAHAM ALWAYS seemed everywhere. Zooming around town on a motorbike and stapling concert posters to telephone poles. Mopping up spilled drinks on the dance floor. Struggling with a pack of roadies to heave an amplifier into place. Screaming at a band's hapless manager backstage. Now he was prowling the perimeter of the Fillmore Auditorium, his rock 'n' roll bastion in the heart of San Francisco's shrinking black ghetto. The line of ticket holders snaked down Geary Street and around the corner onto Fillmore: bearded young men with tie-dyed headbands and teenage girls in peacoats and bell-bottoms, carrying the bedrolls they had slept in to secure a good place in line.

Graham wasn't young, but he wasn't old. He wasn't big, and he walked with his shoulders slightly hunched. But he always seemed coiled and ready for anything that came his way. He had a brute handsomeness: with his thick, wavy ducktail spilling over his shirt collar and his sideburns, he looked like a guy who'd be cast as one of the Sharks in *West Side Story* if all the parts hadn't been claimed by gay dancers.

Now Graham was patrolling the Fillmore ticket line, counting heads—clipboard in hand; always a clipboard—when a kid with long, matted blond hair piped up, "Greedy fucking pig." Graham spun on his heels, like he was ready for it. "Who said that? Who *the fuck* said that?" With some weird street radar, the promoter instantly identified where the verbal assault had come from and was in the kid's face. "Do you know how much it costs to put on a show like this? Do you have any idea how many people have to be paid: the musicians, the roadies, the truck drivers, the sound people, the light shows? You don't have a *fuck-ing* clue." The kid wilted under the harangue. Graham knew how to use his voice like a *New Yawk* jackhammer, and it was particularly effective against soft Californian ears.

Born Wolfgang Grajonca to Russian-Polish Jewish emigrants in Berlin, Graham was a refugee from European history. His mother and one of his five sisters were gassed to death by Nazis in Germany; another sister survived Auschwitz. Sent to an orphanage outside Paris, Graham escaped from the growing inferno at age nine by walking across Europe with his thirteen-year-old sister, Tolla. When she came down with pneumonia during the trek, he was forced to leave her in a hospital in Lyon, France, and he never saw her again. It haunted Graham for the rest of his life. He was put on an ocean liner in Lisbon, Portugal, and after a torturous voyage to Casablanca and Dakar, in Africa, he finally landed in New York. There he was plucked from an adoption agency by a couple, "as though they were going to a pet shop," he said. Of the sixty-four kids who'd set out on foot from the French orphanage three months earlier, only eleven made it to New York.

At age eighteen, Graham was drafted and sent to war in Korea. He hated the army and never figured out why we were fighting, but he did his duty, killed a man in combat, and won the Bronze Star and Purple Heart. By going to war, Graham finally gained his US citizenship, enabling him to bring two of his three surviving sisters to America from Israel. After his discharge, he worked as a New York cab driver and as a waiter in the Catskills. Graham first came to San Francisco to visit his oldest sister, Rita, who had settled there with her husband after arriving in America. Right away, San Francisco made him feel different. The hills, the Golden Gate Bridge, the soft sea light. There were horizons; there were opportunities. He breathed easier. "What I liked was that the game was not always on the goal line out there. It wasn't always life and death. There were time-out signs. It was a *nicer* game."

Graham had fantasized about a show business career ever since waiting tables on the likes of Marlon Brando, Eddie Fisher, and Jerry Lewis. But New York and Los Angeles were unassailable towns without the right connections. In 1964 he finally found his opening, in San Francisco's more freewheeling atmosphere, after he became the San Francisco Mime Troupe's business manager. When the actor-provocateurs were busted in the park by censorious cops, Graham organized a benefit at the troupe's South of Market loft to raise money for legal fees. The benefit was a runaway success: Graham crammed so many people into the loft that night, it was raided by fire officials. Seeing a new world open before him, Graham held two more Mime Troupe benefits, this time at the Fillmore Auditorium. He wanted to be the next Sol Hurok. But he would become the P. T. Barnum of the greatest show on earth, San Francisco's rock 'n' roll circus.

From the very beginning, Graham sparked wildly opposite reactions in San Francisco, where music was still regarded as a public resource. "He was a pure business guy out to make a buck," said Peter Berg, who worked with him in the Mime Troupe. "A total square. He didn't even like rock music; he was into Latin dance music."

But Berg's Mime Troupe–Diggers comrade Peter Coyote saw Graham very differently. It was Graham who repeatedly came to the troupe's rescue when the performers fell into legal trouble, Coyote pointed out. And it was Graham who let the Diggers take over the Fillmore for a "Stone Your Neighbor" night in 1967, an event that could have put everyone in jail. The crowd filing into the auditorium that night was funneled between two rows of Diggers who were blowing huge clouds of marijuana smoke from giant cardboard tubes into everyone's faces. "Bill walks into the hall," Coyote recalled, "looks at this big bong show, and goes, 'What the fuck!' But then he started to laugh. This was a guy who walked from the gas chambers as a kid. Nothing scared him. He was just authentic. I don't care if he wasn't San Francisco. He was just a great man—a huge-hearted, brass-balled man. I loved him dearly."

Graham had the blustery swagger of a man who didn't give a shit what anyone thought of him. But it wounded him when he was called a bloodsucker. The Grateful Dead's drummer Mickey Hart is among those who always thought it was a bad rap. Hart remembered the night after a show at the Fillmore East, the concert hall he opened in Manhattan in 1968, when Graham walked block after block in the rain-splattered city, handing out $100 bills to the homeless.

Graham wanted to be known as a consummate showman: the impresario who harnessed the uncontrollable musical furies of stoned-out San Francisco and created rock 'n' roll's most magical evenings, from the moment the doors opened and the crowds were greeted with baskets of red apples, to closing time, when they exited the hall to the auld strains of "Greensleeves." Instead he was widely seen as the music scene's "evil necessity," Graham once ruefully observed. "Many times, someone would tap me and say, 'Great show, Bill.' Then he'd give me a dig in the ribs: 'You really made a killing tonight, huh?' It was almost as if saying, 'I wish we didn't need you, but thank God there is a you to put this on.'"

Good Times, the San Francisco underground newspaper, once attacked Graham as "the Napoleon of the rock revolution," ruthlessly driving out competition and staging concerts that "were airtight, like a prison recreation yard." *Good Times* editors prepared for the inevitable Graham eruption and lifelong ban from the Fillmore premises. Instead he sat down for a long interview with the newspaper, talking about his "maniacal" drive to serve the music-loving public, how his marriage had become a casualty of that drive, his disenchantment with the growing corporatization of live music, and how he was the only San Francisco counterculture merchant willing to comply with a Diggers plan to donate 1 percent of his gross revenue to fund community projects. By the end of the cathartic interview, the underground reporters were thoroughly disarmed, telling their readers that Graham was not "the raging tyrant we had come to expect" but a worn-out and thoughtful man trying to do his best in a "monstrous industry."

THE ROCK JOURNALISTS WHO covered the San Francisco music scene over time had to endure the full Bill Graham treatment: the charm offensives, the tirades, the extravagant gestures of generosity, the threats to end their careers. The thin-skinned Graham had a long running feud with *Rolling Stone* magazine's Jann Wenner, once holding the publisher hostage in his South of Market warehouse office for nearly seven hours while he went line by agonizing line over an article he found objectionable. Throughout the siege, magazine staffers would periodically hear explosions of Graham fury reverberating through Wenner's brick walls.

Chronicle rock critic Joel Selvin, who also found himself on the receiving end of Graham's tantrums, discovered a way to plug the volcano one day: "I looked at him, and I said, 'Oh, Bill, don't be disingenuous.' He suddenly stopped ranting. There were these moments in dealing with Bill when I suddenly remembered, 'Oh yeah, English is this guy's second or third language.' And he's looking at me, trying to figure out, 'Hey, was I just insulted or not?'"

Graham could be a vicious business operator, double-crossing partners and bullying music managers, lawyers, and vendors into submission. But he respected the ones who pushed back. One day Graham blew up at Brian Rohan, who had built his early association with HALO and the Grateful Dead into a thriving practice as an entertainment lawyer. "He was screaming at me," Rohan recalled, "and I grabbed him by the throat. I said, 'Look, I don't work for you, and I'm not your child. Don't ever talk to me that way!'" The two men grew to become frequent business collaborators and close friends.

Rohan's law partner, Michael Stepanian, also was fond of Graham, calling him the grown-up that the San Francisco music scene urgently needed. "Bill was a fabulous character," said Stepanian. "He superimposed order on this chaotic world. Yes, he was tough. Yes, he wanted to make money. But the fact of the matter is that his concerts were magnificent. The shows started on time, the sound system was great, the musicians got paid, the kids had a good time. Nobody was beat up or stabbed, everyone felt safe. He was almost like a father figure of the counterculture. Everyone was drawn to him."

Graham could be an especially intimidating figure to musicians. He expected them to adhere to basic professional standards: to show up for concerts on time, to be sober enough to play, to do encores when the crowds demanded it. He was a self-proclaimed stickler for show business principles. But the musicians he promoted were often unpredictable children, and when booze or drugs were involved, which was often, things could get even more erratic.

One night Graham fumed backstage, waiting and waiting for Jim Morrison to lead the Doors onstage. The singer never showed. The next afternoon, Morrison sauntered into Graham's cramped quarters upstairs at the Fillmore and explained that while on his way to the concert, he passed a movie theater playing *Casablanca*. He couldn't help it; he went to see the movie instead. "I'm a big Humphrey Bogart fan myself,"

Graham told him, "but you should've called." Morrison thought this over. "Yeah, I *could* have called. But I saw it *three* times."

Musicians quickly learned that excuses didn't cut it with Graham. "Bill was great unless you were late," remembered guitarist Jerry Miller of Moby Grape, San Francisco's most talented but most star-crossed band. "If you fucked up business, he didn't go for that shit. I was waiting backstage at Fillmore East when the rest of the band got bogged down in a blizzard. And Bill was coming apart. He felt you should've told it not to blizzard."

Graham was the father figure that many rock musicians needed. "I thought he was a strong, good man," said Peter Lewis, Miller's bandmate. "He'd have football games on the hardwood floors at the Fillmore on weekend days. You'd have to play him and his beefy security guys. He wasn't a hippie."

"We were hippies, and we were pissed off at him for being a businessman," said David Freiberg of Quicksilver Messenger Service. "That is, until we got paid. He showed us you have to take care of business. Everything wasn't going to be free, not when you have to pay people who work for you."

Graham would become closest to the Grateful Dead, even though the band's barrel-of-monkeys ethos seemed diametrically opposed to his clipboard efficiency. He liked their dedication, the way Jerry Garcia would show up at eleven in the morning on the day of a gig to rehearse and check the sound. With their expansive and generous spirit, the Dead came closest to rock 'n' roll "utopia," in Graham's mind. Garcia, in particular, was, in Graham's words, "the big papa bear" of what the new music should be all about, but was often grubbily not.

Graham thought of the band as his children; particularly mischievous children. Garcia and Hart were always trying to dose him with acid, but the promoter was a control freak—someone had to stay sober to keep the party in bounds—and he was always on guard against the Dead's antics.

"He wouldn't take cookies from my grandma," said Hart. "But one day Jerry and me were standing backstage watching Janis rip up the crowd. We had a couple cans of Coke. Bill went rushing by with his clipboard and, without thinking, grabbed the Coke out of my hand and took a gulp. Jerry and I had anointed the lips of the cans. We had him. I yelled, 'Bill!' over the roar of Big Brother. He yelled back, 'What?' I said, 'The road you now travel will not be a familiar one.' Later that night, he started taking off his clothes, and he was wrapped around the gong onstage singing 'Death Don't Have No Mercy' with the rest of us."

Mickey Hart and Bill Graham went way back, to the days when they worked together as waiters in a nightclub in Atlantic City. Hart came to consider him one of his best friends. He and his bandmates trusted Graham, even when they didn't trust him. "We always laughed at Bill, even when he stole from us. He did it with such class."

One night the Dead finally caught Graham skimming the proceeds at a Winterland show. The band nailed him by positioning people with counters at the doors. "He tried to make up for what he did. He put the money in a paper bag and gave it to us for years."

Hart would find more forgiveness for Graham than he did for his own father, Lenny Hart, the Grateful Dead's business manager, who went to jail for embezzling from the band. Hart never talked to his father again. "What was there to talk about?" By that point, the band was Mickey Hart's family. "And he was the enemy."

But Graham somehow received the Dead's absolution. The band members knew how important he was to the temple of sound they were all creating. "Nothing would have happened without Bill," Hart said. "He made a home for the music. We were outlaws. Nobody trusted us. We were all crazies, and he was the responsible one. He was our big brother."

THE ADVOCATES OF "FREE" wanted the music to stay in the parks and streets. And it was there. Paul Kantner's favorite place for Jefferson Airplane to take wing would always be the sprawling greenery of Speedway Meadow in Golden Gate Park. Those "sunny day afternoons, acid, incense, and balloons" would forever be part of the San Francisco mystique. But the music also needed its sacred chamber, its magical proscenium of swirling lights and sounds, in order to resonate most deeply in the city's soul. And that was Bill Graham's Fillmore.

Graham was the radio tower that pulled in the sound from the crackling universe. There was a reason that the young crowd's eyes turned to him when he walked the ticket line, as if he were a Garcia or Clapton or Hendrix. He had the power to make it all happen. Without him, the exquisite notes would have drifted away in the fog. The crowds resented and adored him for it. But they never forgot the miraculous evenings he staged for them.

Graham shows had a special alchemy. The bills mixed English rock stars and American blues masters. He tried to revive Lenny Bruce's career, as it was nodding off into oblivion, by exposing a new generation to his hipster riffs. He once opened a Jefferson Airplane show with Ferlinghetti and Russian poet Andrei Voznesensky. He combined the sweet folk-rock harmonies of the Byrds with a production of *Dutchman,* playwright LeRoi Jones's screed on America's racial tempest. In the Summer of Love alone, Graham lit up San Francisco with a dazzling galaxy, including Jimi Hendrix, Otis Redding, the Who, Cream, Chuck Berry, Eric Burdon and the Animals, the Yardbirds, the Byrds, Buffalo Springfield, the Doors, Howlin' Wolf, Bo Diddley, Sam and Dave, the Paul Butterfield Blues Band, the Charles Lloyd Quartet, and the Count Basie Orchestra—in addition to all the best San Francisco bands.

Graham turned the Fillmore into holy ground. It was the core of what the city was becoming. For the young men and women who assembled under the old ballroom's chandeliers, it was sanctuary and salvation. This was why they'd trekked to San Francisco. It all came down to the music. They weathered the cold, the cops, the scruff of the streets just to stand inside the sacred walls of sound.

9

THE DAILY CIRCUS

S AN FRANCISCO'S CULTURAL revolution was not popular in city hall or the hall of justice fortress at 850 Bryant Street. But it did find some surprising allies downtown, inside the clock tower–topped bunker at Fifth and Mission Streets that housed the *San Francisco Chronicle*. The city's reigning daily was owned by a Republican clan that traced its dynasty back to the gold rush founders of the paper. Yet readers opened the *Chronicle* on many mornings to find the newspaper championing the Haight-Ashbury Free Clinic or Huckleberry House, supporting the legal rights of North Beach topless clubs, defending hippies' pursuit of happiness, and denouncing President Lyndon Johnson's deepening quagmire in Vietnam. All of this serious business came wrapped in a candy box of gossip, carny barker promotion stunts, cheesecake photographs, and eccentric musings that San Francisco readers found irresistible. To browse the *Chronicle* each morning was to enter the portals of an enchanted city that was more than slightly cracked. Fun was the paper's first order of business, and any stuffed-shirt official who picked on the city's clowns and misfits or otherwise rained on its cockeyed parade was to be shunned and ridiculed.

The brilliant showman behind the *Chronicle*'s daily circus was executive editor Scott Newhall. His buttoned-down boss, publisher Charles de Young Thieriot, might not have always seen eye to eye with his editorial antics. But the Thieriot family could not argue with the financial results. After taking over the *Chronicle* in 1952, when it was a gray *New York Times* wannabe, languishing far behind the Hearst Corporation–owned *Examiner* in the circulation race, Newhall promptly began winning over San Francisco with his reinvigorated product and wild promotion campaigns. He made it his personal mission to defeat the Hearst newspaper empire, which he regarded as "something evil," preying on the ignorance and fear of the "Catholic, lunchbox San Francisco working man" with its "yellow peril" sensationalism, right-wing demagoguery, and shameless stories about "ghosts clanking their chains in English castles." Newhall would offer San Francisco something different: a progressive-minded and witty fish wrap that would appeal to the city's cosmopolitan aspirations and libertine tastes. His aim proved true: the *Chronicle*'s circulation soared, finally surging past the *Examiner* in 1960.

Scott Newhall's *Chronicle* was the perfect match between city and newspaper. The *Chronicle* did not just give voice to San Francisco; it invented the city. Newhall, who was born and raised in San Francisco, never got over his love affair with his hometown, and the paper was giddy with his passion. He thought of San Francisco as a "fairyland," and his newspaper spun what he frankly called "fairy tales" that added new layers of mythology to the city.

Newhall's *Chronicle* turned San Francisco into a city of fizz and fun. The cool clink of ice in a chrome shaker could always be heard in its pages. There was actor David Niven, spotted in his suite at the Stanford Court Hotel, raising his glass of Cristal to a full moon and murmuring to himself, "The moon's a balloon." There was Bobby Kennedy, at a rooftop party in the Haight with the Grateful Dead. It was the kind of city where anything could happen. Low-rent glamour girls were reborn as high-society hostesses. Square-jawed yachtsmen were inconveniently netted in raids on all-male nightspots.

When there was no fun to be found, Newhall simply made his own. He ran a story about an eccentric millionaire who was campaigning to clothe "naked" animals, which turned out to be a hoax. He ginned up an international incident when he launched a crusade to liberate Anguilla, a spit of sand in the Lesser Antilles, from the British Empire.

The mischievous editor's most famous stunt—an investigative series on the dismal quality of the coffee that was being served in San Francisco establishments—was actually his most legitimate. Newhall could remember when San Francisco was a coffee town, and the air was filled with the earthy aroma of roasting beans. "When I was a child, this was a huge shipping port. The ships came in from all over the world. As a small boy, going along the waterfront you could smell the coffee roasting: Hills Brothers, MJB, Alta Coffee, Folgers Coffee. And oh, it smelled so good, the coffee roasting. You could smell the spices in the old tramp freighters that were tied up along the waterfront—the copra, and jute, and teakwood logs and all that stuff." But things had gone downhill in San Francisco, and now its citizens were being served watery and rancid brews that were a disgrace to the city's richly fragrant heritage. So Newhall ordered a young reporter to investigate "what the hell San Franciscans were drinking today. [He] went up and down Market Street, he went to the hotels, and, my God, he found coffee urns with dead rats in them and everything else, or the coffee was three or four days old. And the stuff they were selling here was totally junk."

Newhall splashed the series across the front page under this opening cymbal crash of a headline: "A Great City's People Forced to Drink Swill." The coffee exposé became infamous in journalism circles, forever branding the *Chronicle* as a frivolous waste of newsprint. Berkeley media professors took to fulminating about Newhall's antics. Meanwhile, the sad-sack *Examiner,* now consigned to a distant second in the circulation race, scurried around trying to expose *Chronicle* "exclusives" as fakes—which, of course, they sometimes were.

Scott Newhall could be gravely serious when he had to. But he clearly preferred to live his life in an amusement park of his own making. And much of San Francisco wanted to join him there. "This guy was a complete wacko," remarked William German, who succeeded Newhall as editor of the *Chronicle.* "But a very talented wacko. And probably right for the time."

NEWHALL'S ESCAPADES SEEMED TO be his bulwark against life's inevitable vale of sorrows. By the time he made it to the top of San Francisco's newspaper racket, the miseries had piled up around him. Newhall was born into a pioneer ranching family that had multiplied its wealth in real estate and finance. He knocked around various California prep schools but didn't manage to graduate from any of them. He got himself into UC Berkeley, but, again, found it more amusing to drink and play than study. In search of adventure, he sailed out the Golden Gate with a friend on a forty-two-foot ketch called the *Mermaid*. They had 14 cents between them, but Newhall was a budding photographer, and he planned to underwrite the trip by selling freelance shots to the *Chronicle,* where he had been employed briefly. While tramping through Mexico, he was kicked by a horse (he kicked it first) and developed a bone infection in his leg. The rot went so deep that he nearly died, and he had to have the leg amputated when he returned to San Francisco. "Oh, well," Newhall thought to himself, he didn't want to be a photographer anyway.

The *Chronicle* took pity on him and gave him a job in the newspaper morgue, filing news clippings. It proved to be a resurrection of sorts. Hobbling around on crutches and filing stories about the city and the world he lived in gave Newhall the education he lacked. And deconstructing the newspaper each day with his pair of scissors taught him something about how to put one together.

From there, during the early 1940s, he began his relentless climb up the *Chronicle*'s editorial masthead. Newhall's ascent at the newspaper was interrupted only by a stint as a war correspondent with the Royal Navy. He found it harrowing on board the motorboat flotillas in the English Channel, running the gauntlet of Nazi submarines, and it made him question his own courage.

When he took over the *Chronicle* in 1952, Newhall surrounded himself with other young men from his generation. After the Depression and the war, newspapering seemed like a game. He was a ruggedly handsome, blue-eyed man, and, stalking the newsroom on his artificial leg, he had the swagger of a peg-legged pirate. Even after he got married and had four children—three boys (including a pair of twins) and a girl—Newhall still treated life like a party. His wife, Ruth, whom he had met at Berkeley, was a game sort with her own newspaper career. And the two of them would throw big parties at their *ranchito* in the Berkeley hills with a dazzling view of the Bay. Newhall loved jazz music and musicians, and his friend Earl "Fatha" Hines would often show up to play piano. Sometimes the parties lasted for days. Jon Newhall, one of the twins, woke up his parents one morning with this sober report: "The dean is asleep under the oleander."

One evening in 1955, during the Christmas season, Newhall's twelve-year-old daughter was caroling with some friends in the neighborhood. Suddenly a tow truck, its brakes having snapped, came roaring down a hill, crushing the girl against a house and instantly killing her. "It was the worst day of our lives," recalled Jon Newhall many years later. Ruth was devastated. Scott kept pushing forward. Sometime after that, he survived a heart attack. He and Ruth stopped going out much after that.

Readers of Scott Newhall's *Chronicle* were not protected from the world's daily onslaught of mayhem and grief. It was all there in easy-to-read packages, with bold-faced leads, surrounded by lots of white space. But embedded in the paper each morning was an absurdist sensibility that said, *You'd better find a way to laugh at life, because it will certainly make you cry.*

NEWHALL WAS A REGISTERED Republican, but it didn't mean much to him. He hated politics, and he thought religion was for pious hypocrites. He liked cutting against the grain. He called the *Chronicle* the country's only mainstream underground newspaper. It was the first major daily to come out against the Vietnam War. Grand newspapers like the *New York Times* and *Washington Post* liked to snicker at the *Chronicle*'s lack of gravitas, Newhall observed. But at least his paper got it right on the big issues. Year after year, the *Times* and *Post* kept toeing the government line on Vietnam, he pointed out, "braying about the communists or the domino theory and all this crap." The gullibility of the journalistic establishment never ceased to amaze him.

Like all lifelong San Franciscans, Newhall was deeply protective of his town. There was nothing about the hippie invasion of his beloved city that he found particularly endearing. He was strictly a jazz and martini kind of guy. But he knew that he didn't like to see the kids given shabby treatment. San Francisco was supposed to welcome "free souls" and "kooks," he thought. And so, as much to stick a finger in the eye of the civic establishment as anything else, Newhall made sure that the *Chronicle* rolled out the welcome mat for the young pioneers flocking into the city. The paper adopted an affectionate, even solicitous, tone toward the hippies. "Editorially, I have always felt that everyone should be free to express himself without any particular restraint as long as he doesn't bother the neighbors," the newspaper editor remarked. "Or, as they say, you can do it in the streets, as long as you don't frighten the horses."

The old expression was as succinct an expression of San Francisco's gold rush philosophy as you could find. *Just don't frighten the horses*. The *Chronicle* was the city's "water well" as Newhall put it, where everyone in town converged. By setting a tone of tolerance toward the hippies, the newspaper played a critical role in shaping the broader community's views. If long-haired boys and girls dancing beneath the diamond sky with one hand waving free was the kind of spectacle that ruined your day, the *Chronicle* told its readers, well, maybe you weren't a true San Franciscan. Curmudgeons, blowhards, and bullies were regularly treated to a good swift kick in the pants in Newhall's paper.

It was Ralph J. Gleason, the *Chronicle*'s legendary jazz and pop music critic, who brought the newspaper into the rock 'n' roll age. Newhall and Gleason were kindred souls. They roamed the streets of San Francisco together in the 1950s and 1960s, sampling the sweet sounds of the night. Gleason introduced his boss to jazz pals like Duke Ellington and Miles Davis. The music critic was a diabetic, and Newhall was trying to lay off the elixir, so they would drink tumblers of branch water on the rocks. One night Louis Armstrong—who was maintaining his own strict health regimen at the time, drinking a concoction that made him empty his bowels at regular intervals—received the two newspapermen in his backstage dressing room at Chez Paree, "a Mason Street G-string maisonette," in Newhall's words, while perched on his porcelain throne.

As the youth wave came rolling in during the sixties, Gleason immediately recognized that something shimmering was happening in the city. The music columnist was pushing fifty when the revolution hit, but he had the spirit of a man who "kept bathing his soul in the fountain of youth," said a friend. Gleason was there in 1965 when the Jefferson Airplane made its debut at a small club in the Marina district called the Matrix, and later that year when the Family Dog collective held its historic dance concert at Longshoremen's Hall, where he met a young fan of his column named Jann Wenner. Gleason used his daily column as a platform to champion the kids' right to dance in Golden Gate Park, and he talked Newhall and the *Chronicle* editorial board into siding with Bill Graham against the cops. He never indulged in drugs, but he cultivated his own unique personality, with his Sherlock Holmes hat, tweed coat, pipe and handlebar mustache. He was the patron saint of San Francisco's emerging rock scene. "There would have been no Jefferson Airplane without Ralph Gleason," said singer Marty Balin. There would have been no "San Francisco Sound" at all, added the Airplane's manager, a former *Chronicle* copy boy named Bill Thompson. "He was the grown-up who got it," said Wenner, whom Gleason affectionately called Yanno. The ambitious Wenner and his mentor would later co-found *Rolling Stone* magazine.

The *Chronicle* of the 1960s—witty, offbeat, bemused—was a Scott Newhall production. But Newhall preferred to stay behind the curtain, relying on his colorful menagerie of columnists to vocalize the *Chronicle* point of view. If he was the impresario, the columnists were his players, and he cast them as carefully as a Broadway producer. Trawling for a sports columnist, he found rewrite man Charles McCabe, who didn't like sports. Exactly what Newhall was looking for. Billed as "the Fearless Spectator," McCabe would become a *Chronicle* institution. He was pictured above the column in a bowler hat, like a member of the London Stock Exchange. But he churned out his copy each afternoon from his perch at jovial Gino and Carlo's saloon in North Beach. McCabe's column offered up an eccentric goulash of opinion—sometimes royalist, sometimes radical—on public affairs, the human heart, or any other damned thing that crossed his mind between scotch and sodas at the bar.

For the women's page, Newhall hired a former hairdresser named Marc Spinelli, rechristening him Count Marco, a bitch queen columnist who scolded women for being too fat and whiny, and instructed them how to emerge from a bathtub without looking like a cow. "It was weird," even Newhall had to admit. Female readers were outraged, but they couldn't seem to get enough of the count's acid-tongued Bette Davis routine.

Newhall's biggest star by far was three-dot columnist Herb Caen, San Francisco's beloved deadline bard. Every day but Saturday for more than a half century, Caen spun a yarn about San Francisco and its peculiar denizens that was so enchanting, the city still remains in its thrall years after his death. He called the town "Baghdad by the Bay" in his column, conjuring the exotic wonders of ancient Babylon. But his San Francisco was more like Oz, Wonderland, and Gotham City all rolled together. If much of it was Caen's own creation, it's the city that San Franciscans wanted to live in.

The columnist concocted a fizzy drink of a city, full of witty and beautiful people and equally amusing scoundrels. It was a shining metropolis with enlightened values and wide-open sensibilities, where Chinese waiters and black cable car bell ringers were as fascinating as Nob Hill playboys. Most of his columns were bird-cage ephemera: Pacific Heights marriages on the rocks, celebrity sightings, and punch lines too good to be true, like the 1962 item about San Francisco's most famous madam. ("Sally Stanford is off tomorrow for a month in Europe. 'Have you ever been abroad?' she was asked. 'Always,' she replied tartly.") But in between the bold names and the patter, there was an epic poem about San Francisco.

John Steinbeck got it. "Herb's city is the one that will be remembered," he said.

10

SAN FRANCISCO'S
MORNING KISS

H ERB CAEN WAS born in Sacramento, California, a town that combined all the glamour of a farm fair with the dazzle of a state franchise board hearing. But he carried a different story in his genes. His father was a Jew from the Alsace-Lorraine region of France whose American dream turned into a liquor wholesale business. His mother had been an opera singer in Germany. They moved to Sacramento to give their children an all-American upbringing. But even as a boy, Caen knew he didn't belong there. He subscribed to the *San Francisco Call-Bulletin* just to read Walter Winchell's column, that staccato drumbeat of metropolitan energy.

San Francisco was a revelation whenever his family visited. Known to everyone in the surrounding hinterlands simply as the City, it rose up on the hills, some of it white and gleaming, the rest wrapped in fog and mystery. Every time Caen came back to San Francisco, it was like he was arriving for the first time. Throughout his life, he carried the arriviste's desperate love for the city. It always seemed to loom slightly above him, beyond his grasp. Summoned as a young man by the *Chronicle* for a job interview in 1938, he bought a new suit and hat for the occasion. But as his big, white ferryboat steamed toward the city, while Caen once again marveled at the skyline, his hat was blown into the choppy bay. Caen would always worry whether he was sophisticated enough to fit in.

The "Sackamenna Kid," as he humbly anointed himself, found it rough going in the early years. One day the young columnist, playing the suave host, tried to introduce an heiress from the de Young family, owners of the *Chronicle,* to an heiress from the Spreckels family, the wealthy sugar barons. "Oh, we know each other," sniffed the de Young heiress. "It's just that we haven't spoken since her daddy shot my daddy." Caen was beaten up twice, both times in the lobby of the Mark Hopkins Hotel, by wealthy playboys who objected to his snappy items on their romantic peccadillos. On another occasion, he was nearly killed by a Mickey Finn heavily laced with horse laxative. The knockout punch was slipped to him by the owner of a secret Turk Street gambling joint—one of the few night spot operators whose business was hurt by a mention in Caen's column. The columnist managed to crawl out of the dive and get home before collapsing on his floor.

But Caen ultimately found his groove, working the city more tire-lessly each night than Sally Stanford's girls—who, coincidentally, often appeared in the column, in the prim Junior League dresses and corsages that the madam insisted they wear as they greeted clients in her Russian Hill mansion. The columnist's nightly circuit changed over the years. In the beginning, he trawled for items at the city's swanky Nob Hill hotels and the more colorful watering holes down below, like Shanty Malone's—whose massive floor was marked out with white lines like a football field—and the Black Cat, where drag diva José Sarria would lead patrons each night in a rousing version of "God Save Us Nelly Queens" sung to the stately tune of the British anthem. In later years, Caen preferred North Beach jazz clubs like El Matador, the hungry i, and Enrico's, where sometimes he sat in on drums.

Caen lived and breathed the city. He was so devoted to it, that his first wife, Bea, a bright-eyed showgirl with a blond bubble, threatened to name San Francisco as a co-respondent when she sued him for divorce. In his columns, he was always trying to find the city's heart. His three-dot patter had the swinging rhythm of his friend big-band drummer Gene Krupa. He was cool enough to be thrown out of Tosca in North Beach with a barefoot Allen Ginsberg. "You can't throw out Allen Ginsberg!" Caen objected. "He's a famous poet." To the Italian proprietors, however, he was just another filthy beatnik. Caen might run with a 'round-midnight crowd, but he always imagined he was writing the column for a simple housewife out on the city's westerly, windswept avenues. "Effie Zilch," he called her, and she would read his column after getting her husband off to work and making herself a pot of coffee, as she rested her slippered feet on the breakfast table.

Caen gave the tourists' San Francisco its due, with nods to sourdough aromas, the crab pots of Fisherman's Wharf, and the "ceaseless click-clacking of the cables in their slots." But he never stopped looking for some deeper truth about the city. Maybe he came close late one night in the spring of 1961.

"The other midnight, in a Chinatown bar," he wrote, "I met a real San Franciscan. He was a middle-aged longshoreman from the Mission, and he wore a zipper jacket and open shirt. While he quietly sipped a Scotch, he talked of Harry Bridges, Bill Saroyan, and Shanty Malone. He was curious about Leontyne Price and Herbert Gold. He wondered if the Duke of Bedford's paintings were any good, he missed Brubeck, and he discussed Willie Mays down to his last spike. He seemed to know everybody in town, by first names—and it was only after he'd left that we discovered he'd bought a round of drinks for the house. For want of a better phrase, he had that touch of class—the touch of a San Franciscan."

Caen found his full stride in the sixties, the decade that began with the jazzy energy of Lenny Bruce and Miles Davis and swung seamlessly into the glorious, furious wails of Janis and Grace. San Francisco's bard made the transition to the new, psychedelic city in smooth style. His column pulsed with everything San Francisco was becoming. He welcomed in New Year 1967 at the Fillmore, showing up in a tuxedo with some high-society friends to dance to the Jefferson Airplane. Despite his stiff, black-tie attire, he was warmly welcomed by the young crowd. "They think you're in costume," said his friend, novelist Herb Gold.

Caen genuinely loved the kaleidoscope scenes at the Fillmore and Winterland. And he was a big fan of the Airplane, even after an unfortunate incident at the band's Fulton Street mansion, across from Golden Gate Park. Caen and his young third wife, Maria Theresa, were among the guests one night in the fall of 1968 for a decadent banquet at the Airplane's black-painted Greek Revival mansion. The feast included a roast suckling pig (complete with apple in mouth) and a punchbowl liberally spiked with LSD. During the evening, as psychedelic wizard Owsley Stanley repeatedly blared the Beatles' new release, "Hey Jude," throughout the wired mansion's multitude of speakers, a blissfully unaware Maria Theresa dipped her cup into the punch bowl several times and was soon weeping uncontrollably about the radiant beauty she felt all around her.

Maria Theresa remained fond of rock musicians, despite her nonconsensual LSD initiation. A number of them visited the Caen residence, which by then was a Pacific Heights house big enough for the columnist's voluminous book and record collection as well as his wife and son, Christopher. "When I was growing up, Jim Morrison would drop by," recalled the younger Caen. "He'd drink all of our cognac."

Sixties San Francisco, as portrayed in Caen's column, was a room full of balloons. There was golden Julie Christie, in town to film *Petulia*, adrift in her rainwater pool in Sausalito and dancing to the Grateful Dead on a ferryboat in the bay . . . there was Paul McCartney wandering Haight-Ashbury with girlfriend Jane Asher, carefree and unbothered, and sitting in with the Jefferson Airplane . . . there were Marshall McLuhan, Tom Wolfe, and Caen doing some sociological research at a topless bar in North Beach, where the esteemed professor observed that the blushing newspaperman couldn't bring himself to look at the waitresses' bare breasts . . . and there was ballet dancer Rudolf Nureyev, swanning around the SFPD's Park Station, after being rounded up in a pot party raid, serenading the cops with "San Francisco" in the flamboyant old MGM style of Jeanette MacDonald.

But it wasn't all incense and peppermints. The decade also brought out a political edge in Caen that gave his column a new sharpness. He fulminated against the Vietnam War and picketed with Marlon Brando outside San Quentin to protest the gas chamber execution of a thirty-nine-year-old rapist and thief named Caryl Chessman. "Why isn't Caryl Chessman gassed in the middle of Union Square at high noon?" wrote an unusually bitter Caen, who as a young reporter had witnessed a hanging at Folsom State Prison. "But no, that would be an indecent spectacle, abhorrent to those who prefer to live by euphemisms. He must be done away with in a gloomy little room surrounded by a protective nest of walls—as though the act itself, the final demonstration of the majesty of law, were some dark and dreadful thing. And a dark and dreadful thing it is."

He scolded the San Francisco snoots who turned up their noses at hippies—"Goldie Locks and the Three Bores," he called them—and the cops who cracked open kids' heads on Haight Street. And, to the dismay of many of his high-society friends, he raised a ruckus over the massive high-rise developments that were beginning to overshadow the gleaming white skyline he fell in love with as a boy.

Caen had a complicated relationship with blue-blood San Francisco. He was a union man at heart, and he had a weak spot for the underdog, walking the picket line during the 1966 newspaper strike and giving Harry Bridges some of the only good press he got in town. But the Sackamenna Kid also longed to be embraced by the swell set. He certainly dressed and acted the part, gliding (not walking) about town in his Wilkes Bashford suits, and smoothly tipping two light fingers to the brim of his hat to passing ladies. But the WASP types never could fully accept a wise-cracking Jew from the Central Valley. And Jewish society was perplexed by an atheist who never went to temple, married only shiksas, and christened his son "Christopher."

When Caen joined the first anti–high rise campaign in 1968, aimed at blocking a U.S. Steel office tower on the waterfront, he helped terminate the project but also gained some powerful enemies. Sometimes it's necessary to shame the city's business class, the columnist later remarked, to remind them that a city like San Francisco is more than just a real estate opportunity—it's "a precious, special, fragile place." Walter Shorenstein, the wealthy San Francisco developer, was one of those who took strenuous exception to being labeled a money-grubber by Caen. The real estate magnate's equilibrium was not improved by the fact that he lost $5 million when the city board of supervisors voted down the U.S. Steel project. It was not the first time, and would not be the last, that Caen seemed to wield more power than the city's mayor.

A couple of nights after the board decision, Shorenstein—a distinguished-looking gentleman with thinning, silver hair—spotted Caen at a gala event and came charging across the room to throttle him. "I'm gonna run you out of town, you sonofabitch!" screamed Shorenstein, while his political sidekick, newly elected mayor Joe Alioto, tried desperately to peel him off Caen. Throughout the tempest, Caen couldn't stop laughing, which only made Shorenstein more berserk.

Caen was no muckraker, and when he vented too much steam about Vietnam or the changing San Francisco skyline, he worried about being a bore—one of the worst sins the three-dot columnist could imagine. He knew his job was to gently tickle the morning reader as his caffeine juiced him awake. But every now and then, the column performed a different duty. Amidst the daily assembly line of amusements came an important reminder of what San Francisco was all about. Caen was the city's convivial conscience, and the chatty, shameless *San Francisco Chronicle* was the perfect platform for his disposable, indispensable wisdom.

II

RADIO FREE AMERICA

THE 1960S WAS essentially a cultural dialogue between San Francisco and London. The music, art, fashions, comics, drug experimentation, sexual innovation—it was all driven by the creative interplay between the two cities (with some heavy assistance from Detroit, in the music department). In America, if you were young and longing for more, if you felt like a vagrant in your own hometown, if your life seemed elsewhere, then you headed for "Gold Mountain," as Chinese fortune seekers once called the city by the bay. Otis Redding condensed all this longing in "(Sittin' On) The Dock of the Bay," which he began writing on a Sausalito houseboat in the Summer of Love, with the city gleaming in the distance. San Francisco beckoned to dreamers and losers everywhere. Many of them found the paradise they were seeking, free of the small voices that had hobbled them. Stewart Brand, Chet Helms, Janis Joplin, Jann Wenner, Hunter S. Thompson, Robert Crumb. More and more rebels arrived every day. They found one another, they formed bands, they started underground enterprises, they made history. San Francisco was Radio Free America, beaming its message of liberation around the world and summoning an endless army of outcasts.

Crumb's exodus from the Midwest was fairly typical. His father, a twenty-year veteran of the marine corps, never got over the fact that he had produced three awkward, arty sons. To escape his old man's anger and bafflement, young Crumb moved in with a friend in Cleveland and went to work doing color separations for a greeting card company. Month after month, he woke up every morning in blank, wintry Cleveland and punched the time clock. In June 1965 deliverance finally arrived in the form of a little blue vial of Sandoz pills that his wife, Dana, brought home one day, courtesy of her psychiatrist.

"LSD knocked me on my ass," said Crumb. "It was my road to Damascus. The next day I had to go to work, but it all seemed like a cardboard world to me; people seemed like they were just going through the motions. After a couple years, I fled to San Francisco. I remember showing up in Golden Gate Park—some guy dressed like Peter Pan was flitting around dropping strange pills in people's mouths."

Crumb abandoned his old life—"deserted my job, deserted my wife. I was not a good man. I ran away from it all." And he never looked back. In the fall of 1967, a broke Crumb, sitting in his Haight-Ashbury apartment, drew *Zap No. 0* and *Zap No. 1* and sold the underground comic books out of a baby carriage on the street. It was the beginning of Mr. Natural, Angelfood McSpade, Fritz the Cat, and other warped creations of Crumb's brilliant, drug-assisted imagination. The legend had begun.

Wes "Scoop" Nisker showed up in San Francisco after coming west in June 1967 to cover the Monterey Pop Festival for a student magazine at the University of Minnesota, where he was enrolled in graduate school. The festival was a celebration of the West Coast and UK musical renaissance, with historic performances by Jimi Hendrix (who was introduced onstage by the Rolling Stones' Brian Jones), Janis and Big Brother, Otis Redding, and the Who. An eight-foot statue of the Buddha greeted festivalgoers as they entered the luminous grounds. Nisker was utterly transformed by the "colorful, joyous, quasi-spiritual explosion." Afterward, he and some Minnesota friends drove up to the city, along the winding, rocky coast studded with cypress and pines, with the Pacific crashing below. In San Francisco, he ambled through the labyrinthine greenery of Golden Gate Park and, as a young devotee of beat culture, made a trek to one of his meccas, City Lights Bookstore. Nisker quickly realized that San Francisco was where he belonged. "I knew I'd found my family. I wanted to be part of this tribe."

Nisker moved into a coffee baron's old mansion at the corner of California and Franklin Streets that had been subdivided into a hippie warren. He felt he was living in a storybook castle, with a sweeping, polished redwood staircase and majestic bay windows. The Victorian house crackled with youthful creativity. "We were remaking culture," he recalled. "The revolution was weeks away." Nisker could hear it when he tuned in to San Francisco's FM radio.

San Francisco was the center of the underground radio revolution. Until the late sixties, American radio was dominated by Top 40 AM radio—a tightly formatted Wall of Sound that allowed only the occasional Beatles or Stones song to break through with hints of the musical revolution outside. But then Tom Donahue—the gargantuan, bearded DJ and music promoter—lumbered into the San Francisco radio world.

The big man came west from Philadelphia's pioneering WIBG in 1961, on the run from the radio payola investigations that had destroyed the careers of Alan Freed and other celebrated DJs. In San Francisco, his ears quickly picked up the new hum and thrum in the universe. Listening to the Doors' first album at home late one night, Donahue wondered why the hell radio was not playing this kind of music. In 1967 he issued his revolutionary manifesto in the pages of a new San Francisco magazine called *Rolling Stone*: "AM Radio Is Dead and Its Rotting Corpse Is Stinking Up the Airwaves." Donahue convinced the owner of KMPX, a backwater FM station, to allow him to take over its programming. At that time, FM radio was lunar terrain, a rarely tuned-in world of AM station simulcasts and educational broadcasts. But when Donahue took control of the KMPX airwaves, free-form, alternative radio was born, with the DJ promising "no jingles, no talkovers, no time and temp, no pop singles."

Tuning in to KMPX in his room in the coffee mansion, Nisker knew immediately that he wanted to enlist in Donahue's revolution. For Nisker and his friends, underground FM radio was like the dawn of the web for a future generation: a hardwire connection to the essential sounds and secret ideas swirling around the globe.

One day in late 1967, Nisker got up the nerve to march down to the KMPX office at Sutter and Montgomery Streets. He talked Donahue into letting him launch an experimental news program on the station. Nisker began creating news collages, cutting up politicians' fatuous pronouncements and laying appropriately ironic music underneath them. He brought counterculture guests into the studio—like Allen Ginsberg,

Abbie Hoffman, and Alan Watts—and gave them the kind of media platform they never had before. He drew on his own unique blend of Marxist (Karl *and* Groucho) and Buddhist philosophy to create a wacky, spiritually enlightened, politically engaged news program that was a perfect fit for San Francisco's rock audience. He told his listeners, "If you don't like the news, go out and make some of your own."

For a brief and glorious moment, the inmates were in charge of the asylum at KMPX, voting on which ads to run and rejecting military recruiting spots. When the station owner suddenly tried to tighten the reins in early 1968, even instituting a staff dress code, Donahue promptly resigned. His DJs began picketing the station, with local bands like the Grateful Dead and Blue Cheer rallying around them. Soon afterward, Donahue, Nisker, and their merry band took their act to rival station KSAN-FM, which recognized the commercial potential in San Francisco's underground sound.

NURTURED BY FM RADIO and concert promoters Bill Graham and Chet Helms, San Francisco bands proliferated like fungi in the deep, wet woods. *Rolling Stone* later estimated that there were about five hundred rock groups playing in the San Francisco area during the sixties golden days. "We felt the city was the center of the universe," said Jann Wenner. "It was one great big ball."

Most of these San Francisco bands have long since faded into the mists of time—even some of the great ones, like Moby Grape, a group that many rock fans thought would soar the highest of all. But it's important to conjure the sense of *excitement* and *importance* that once swirled around these young musicians.

Moby Grape married the sweet folk-rock harmonies of the Byrds with the ballsy rage of the Rolling Stones. They were musicians' musicians: five men who, after honing their craft in various musical incarnations, created a perfect chemistry when they came together. The quintet began rehearsing together in the fall of 1966 at the Ark, a Sausalito club that had been converted from an old paddleboat. Working all night long, they perfected a slashing, symphonic sound composed of intricate, five-part harmonies and three distinctive guitar styles. The band members knew from the very start how good they were. "There was something about this particular combination of people, coupled with this magical San Francisco environment," recalled singer and guitarist Jerry Miller, who had knocked around Seattle with a young Jimi Hendrix and had played the Southwest circuit with the Bobby Fuller Four ("I Fought the Law") before joining Moby Grape. "We knew right away. Everybody in the band knew they'd better start playing better, writing better. We had to pick up our game. Each guy was better than the other guy."

The word immediately began to spread in the Bay Area's febrile music environment. Something phenomenal was happening at the Ark. Other musicians began dropping in to hear what Moby Grape was assembling: David Crosby from the Byrds, Steve Stills and Neil Young from Buffalo Springfield, Janis Joplin and Sam Andrew from Big Brother. They had never heard anything like it. Tightly constructed two-and-a-half-minute songs that came roaring through the billowing psychedelic haze of the day. "Listen my friends!" Moby Grape demanded in its swooping, breathtaking anthem "Omaha"—a song written by the group's mad genius, Skip Spence, former drummer for the Jefferson Airplane. And the entire San Francisco music scene *did* listen. "You guys are better than the Beatles," gushed a bedazzled Andrew after taking in one of the band's rehearsals.

Right here, right now—there was no other place to be for a young musician in the late sixties. That's how Peter Lewis, the son of screen legend Loretta Young, felt. The feeling came rushing into his heart as the Moby Grape singer-guitarist sat with his bandmates and other musicians on a deck in Sausalito late one afternoon, watching the fog cascade over Mount Tamalpais. He loved the fog; it was certainly more bracing than LA's suffocating smog. He loved that he was no longer "Loretta Young Jr." He loved listening to Stills and Young as they sat there playing "Mr. Soul" and "Bluebird" and other new songs from their unreleased second album.

Like Big Brother, Moby Grape was scooped up by Columbia Records. The band was going to be the Next Big Thing. The young musicians were feted at Columbia parties like dauphin princes. Columbia president Goddard Lieberson entertained the San Francisco rockers at his home, but the host and his guests didn't know what to make of one another. Lieberson, who sported a Caesar haircut and a gold chain with the letters G-O-D around his neck, was known for his cast recordings

of Broadway musicals. Joplin felt discombobulated by the glittery surroundings. She went into Lieberson's bathroom, piled all his expensive
toiletries on the floor, and pissed on them. "Go in there and check it
out," she told Peter Lewis and the other musicians when she came out.
"I really got this guy good."

"It was disgusting," said Lewis. But he understood. "Janis had been
kicked around all her life." And now the court minstrels were suddenly,
inexplicably, in command. "She knew she could put her cigarette out on
the king's rug and get away with it."

THE MUSIC HAD THE power. The music was the signal. It called out to
young people everywhere. It lured them to San Francisco—if not to the
city itself, then to its empire of dreams. San Francisco was a youth fantasy, not just a seven-mile-by-seven-mile metropolis on the tip of a peninsula. The city of dreams even called out to Ronald Reagan's children.

Reagan was the leader of the 1960s' political backlash—a backlash
that came whipping into existence almost simultaneously with the cultural revolution itself. The conservative movement's new hero was the
product of a dreary Midwestern upbringing, the son of an alcoholic
father and a pious mother. He had learned early on to create a fantasy
life, a skill that was put to good use in his Hollywood career, but even
more so in his political one. In Reagan's storybook America, San Francisco was a freakish outpost. He mocked the young people who idealized
the San Francisco way of life. Hippies, he sneered, "dress like Tarzan,
have hair like Jane, and smell like Cheetah." And yet Ronald and Nancy
Reagan's own children, Patti and Ron, were among those disaffected
teens. Raised in the lush suburb of Pacific Palisades, Los Angeles—in
a model home outfitted with the latest gadgets from General Electric,
one of their father's perks for working as the company pitchman—the
Reagan children fantasized about escaping to the Haight.

"My father became governor of California in 1966, when I was
fourteen—just as I was longing to be older and run off to the Haight
and plait flowers in my hair," recalled Patti Reagan Davis. "When he
got elected, I felt humiliated, devastated; I felt more trapped than ever.
I never did get the chance to run off to the Haight during its glory
years. Everything I believed in and wanted in those days was just out

of reach because of my age. And then my father was elected governor, and in such splintered times."

Reagan was swept into office in Sacramento on a tide of resentment against Berkeley student protests and other youthful rebellion. He threatened student radicals with a violent crackdown: "If it takes a bloodbath, let's get it over with." In later years, as president, he was known for putting a genial face on his callous policies. But the 1960s brought out Reagan's mean streak. "He was a lot more mellow as president than he was as governor," Patti said. "He was such an angry Republican in those years—he had that hard set to his mouth that you saw on the antiwar posters at the time."

It was Patti who brought the sixties home to the Reagan household. She felt suffocated in the family home's quiet, immaculate "glass atmosphere" and was constantly trying to crash through to something real. In her memoir, Patti recalled that she and her mother, Nancy, fought constantly—volcanic clashes that frequently ended with Patti being smacked across the face. Patti sought emotional solace from her father, but there was nothing there. His "presence felt like an absence."

Nancy, the future "Just Say No" antidrug crusader, used a string of mother's little helpers to get her through each day. Through the years, her medicine chest was stocked with vials of Miltown, Librium, Valium, Seconal, and Quaalude. Reagan blamed his wife's frayed nerves on his daughter. "Do you think a child can be born evil?" he once asked Ron. He was talking about Patti.

Patti was the outcast. She felt that her own parents treated her like a "trespasser." She was the daughter who probed the family lies and secrets, who questioned her father's political opinions, who stood up to her mother's bullying. And the Reagans—like so many American families at the time—were utterly incapable of dealing with her. Before Patti could run off to San Francisco, like thousands of other kids, the family packed her off to a boarding school.

Ron, the younger child, worked out a different stratagem for handling his parents. He avoided the "operatic" confrontations, and tried to finesse the conflicts instead. One day he put the *Woodstock* album on the family's state-of-the-art GE sound system, with speakers throughout the house. But he made a mad dash to the living room turntable from his bedroom before Country Joe and the Fish could give its "F-U-C-K" cheer, to spare his parents the aggravation. Ron saw his father in a more forgiving light, observing, "My dad did not have a mean bone in his body. He was just completely baffled by the sixties."

Both Reagan children found sanctuary in the San Francisco of their dreams. Exiled to a prep school on an Arizona ranch, Patti daydreamed about running off to the Haight, where she would fall in love with a musician or poet and wander the streets, handing out flowers to tourists. Meanwhile, at home in Pacific Palisades, Ron grew his hair longer, to his parents' dismay, and borrowed his sister's Jefferson Airplane albums. The music set you free.

When the truth is found to be lies, and all the joy within you dies, don't you want somebody to love.

12

THE PALACE OF GOLDEN COCKS

ONE SPRING MORNING in 1969, a doll-faced teenager named Pam Tent found herself lolling in the grass next to a pond in a remote green cove of Golden Gate Park surrounded by palm fronds and ferns. She had just hitchhiked to the city from Boulder, Colorado, and was dreamily mulling over her next move. The Haight seemed more raunchy than it was during her first trip to San Francisco the year before, and this overgrown corner of the park was an oasis of peace and quiet.

Suddenly her reverie was interrupted.

"We're having a heat wave . . ." Pam recognized the song right away. It was the Marilyn Monroe tropical dance number from *There's No Business Like Show Business*. Pam knew her show tunes. As a kid, after abandoning her original ambition of becoming a nun, she decided to become a showgirl. Now she cracked open an eye and gazed across the pond. Three young men were folded into the crook of a gnarled cypress tree, making like they were Marilyn's Caribbean chorus boys. One of the men wore lipstick.

"Yoo-hoo!" he called out to her. And Pam Tent's life changed forever.

"HE WAS A STUNNING apparition: half child, half temptress," Pam recalled. "He giggled through glamour-girl lips. His blond hair was a tousled mane, crowned with a garland of wild flowers. Coquettish in dark eyeliner, bare feet, and a white muslin caftan, he looked like a cross between Marlene Dietrich and Puck from *A Midsummer Night's Dream.*"

As Pam approached the tree, the man danced along one of the branches in his bare feet like a wood faerie, sprinkling gold glitter in his wake. She was dazzled by his radiance. He called himself Hibiscus, and he invited her home—which turned out to be a commune in a three-story Sutter Street Victorian mansion on the edge of Japantown that was slated for destruction by the city's redevelopment bulldozers.

Pam quickly accepted his offer to move in. And she dropped like Alice down the hole in the earth, disappearing into a world that would grow curiouser and curiouser by the day.

Hibiscus was the "divine dictator" of this world. Born George Edgerly Harris III to a theater family in Bronxville, New York, he began displaying a dramatic flair at an early age, staging backyard musicals and Hollywood epics. "We knew he was gay even as a kid, when he started to give our Barbie dolls transsexual makeovers," said his sister Mary Lou. After a brief romp in the New York experimental theater world, Harris headed west in 1967. He took a detour through Washington, DC, for the big antiwar demonstration outside the Pentagon, where he was captured in an iconic sixties photo, placing a carnation in the barrel of a soldier's gun. Shortly after arriving in San Francisco, he reinvented himself as Hibiscus, a vision in sequins, glitter, flowers, and diaphanous robes. "He came out of the closet wearing the entire closet," said his friend Nicky Nichols.

Hibiscus's Sutter Street commune was led by a short, severe rabbinical figure named Irving Rosenthal, who had dedicated himself to following the Diggers' free philosophy. Nicknamed the Kaliflower commune, after the weekly newsletter published every Thursday in its Free Print shop and distributed to other San Francisco communes, Rosenthal's group led a disciplined, ascetic existence. Once Pam brought home a sweet indulgence—a can of lemon pie filling—only to later discover that the Kaliflower chef had redistributed the luxury item among the commune's entire, ravenous membership while she was gone.

"If you could live communally and cheaper," thought Rosenthal, "you didn't have to bore yourself to death working in an office job."

The author of a homoerotic novel, *Sheeper,* and the sometime publisher of Ginsberg and onetime lover of William S. Burroughs, Rosenthal enjoyed a cultish cachet and was able to bend his hippie communards to his stern will. Everyone, that is, except Hibiscus. Rosenthal agreed to take in Hibiscus as a favor to a good friend—a lover of the hothouse creature who begged Rosenthal to take him off his hands. Rosenthal the disciplinarian soon fell before Hibiscus's anarchic charms. He began to indulge Hibiscus as the commune's "delicato" and allowed him to opt out of Kaliflower's strict regimen of household chores and meetings. "I don't scrub floors," Hibiscus announced merrily as he skipped in and out of the house, collecting colorful rags and trinkets from thrift stores and flea markets and assembling a wardrobe big enough for the cast of *Scheherazade*.

Hibiscus created a circle of magic wherever he went in San Francisco. He dressed like Isadora Duncan and danced in Golden Gate Park. One day a concerned young man came up to him and warned him that he should move deeper into the park because the police were beating up freaks like him. Hibiscus batted his long, false eyelashes at him. "They would do that to *me*?" he trilled in a voice as sweet and delicate as a nymph.

Hibiscus staged free kiddie shows in the park with Pam, whom he rechristened Sweet Pam. Together they sang "Tender Shepherd" from the musical *Peter Pan* and tunes from *The Wizard of Oz* and made flower headdresses for the children.

He was an angel of light. Wherever he went, he dusted the world with glitter and sequins. His lovers, including Ginsberg, had to accustom themselves to being glitter encrusted after spending a night with him. "It was difficult to sleep on [his] sheets because there was this sort of like difficult glitter stuff there," recalled the poet. "And it was always in our lips and in our buttholes . . . You couldn't quite get it out."

Hibiscus kept an enchanted scrapbook, filled with glittery scenarios for future musicals that were taking shape in his florid imagination. He pasted old publicity shots of Hollywood idols in its pages, alongside images of Eastern and Western deities. Many of the pictures were torn out of books from the San Francisco Public Library.

Over dinner at Kaliflower on New Year's Eve 1970, Hibiscus shared his vision with Fayette Hauser, a curvy and creamy young artist from New Jersey, and his other guests. It was time to put on a show. "A new theater for a new decade!" he gushed to "Fayett-ah," as he operatically pronounced her name. In fact, he wanted to do a dry run that very evening at a late-night movie house in North Beach called the Palace. They would play dress-up, jump onstage, and see what happened.

Rosenthal kept a large, locked room in the Kaliflower attic that was stuffed with feather boas, petticoats, wigs, and other drag paraphernalia—costumes for an underground film he was producing. Since Rosenthal was conveniently out of town at the time, Hibiscus quickly convinced the commune's keeper of the keys to unlock the door. The drag queens fell on the lacy frills like jackals on a fallen zebra. What would they call their troupe? The keeper of the keys pulled Hibiscus aside and whispered, "How about the Cockettes?"

Dolled up like Dorothy Lamour on acid, Hibiscus and his colorful crew piled into their motley fleet of vehicles and headed for the Palace. There was no better venue for the Cockettes' debut. The post-earthquake relic was a collision of visual fantasies. The old Italian opera house still featured its original gold leaf designs, art deco chandeliers, and curved staircases. But overlaid on all this Italian brocade were Oriental design themes that fit the theater's current role as a Chinese-language movie house. In the auditorium, a gilded lotus fresco was splashed across the ceiling, and golden dragons roared fire on the lobby walls. Around midnight, after the Chinese patrons filed out of the final show, the Palace was taken over by a very different crowd for the screening of campy Hollywood classics and experimental films. This late-night audience was part of San Francisco's emerging underground culture—hippies with a taste for more glamour than a Dead concert could provide, sexually flamboyant men and women searching for others like themselves, renegade artists looking for brave new ways of communicating. They were all hungry for something like the Cockettes.

Hibiscus and his dazzling coconspirators took the stage in a mad rush, aided by the ample hallucinogens coursing through their bodies. Someone put on a record—the exact tune is a matter of hazy dispute, either the Stones' "Honky Tonk Women" or "Jumping Jack Flash," or an old 78 rpm of a French burlesque song. And the Cockettes formed a rowdy cancan line, kicking up their heels and swishing their skirts. As the troupe finished its performance, the crowd shot to its feet, erupting in cheers and wolf whistles. "Now what?" the Cockettes wondered. Hibiscus and Fayette stared at each other. But Hibiscus knew instantly. He put on the record again, and the Cockettes began shedding their glittery costumes. A whole new galaxy of San Francisco stars was born that night.

DRAG QUEEN SHOWS HAD a long, luxurious history in San Francisco, dating back to the 1860s and 1870s, when vaudevillians like Paul Vernon, wearing lacy gowns and Goldilocks wigs, wowed local audiences—made up largely of lonely frontiersmen. At the turn of the century, the city's first openly gay bar, the Dash, featured female impersonators. The club, in the Barbary Coast, managed to stay open until 1908, when city officials shut it down as the "most notorious and disreputable establishment" in San Francisco. In the 1930s drag broke into the city's thriving sex tourism market when an Italian immigrant and former speakeasy owner named Joe Finocchio opened a dazzling female impersonator show on Stockton Street, which he later moved to a bigger venue on Broadway. Finocchio's became a major tourist attraction, drawing suburban thrill seekers as well as Hollywood celebrities such as Frank Sinatra, Bob Hope, Bette Davis, and Tallulah Bankhead. In the 1940s nightspots like Mona's Club 440 in North Beach, the city's first lesbian club, flipped the Finocchio's formula, billing itself as the place "Where Girls Will Be Boys." Mona's biggest star, in more ways than one, was a 250-pound African-American singer-pianist named Gladys Bentley. Advertised as the "Brown Bomber of Sophisticated Songs," Bentley packed her voluminous figure into white tails and top hat, flirted with women in the audience, and dedicated songs to her female paramour.

José Sarria, a hometown boy who plucked his eyebrows, slipped into a basic black dress and a pair of Capezio stilettos, and began singing torch songs at the bohemian Black Cat in the 1950s, was the first to politicize the drag world. In between songs, he started preaching that "gay is good," and at the end of each performance, he had the audience stand and belt out a parody of "God Save the Queen"—"as a kind of anthem," he later recalled, "to get them realizing that we had to work together, that . . . we could change the laws if we weren't always hiding." In 1961 Sarria took his campaign public, running for the city's board of supervisors with an early gay pride message. The campaign fell short of victory, but the gay genie was released from San Francisco's bottle.

During the 1950s and early 1960s, San Francisco had a blossoming but largely secret gay life. Indeed, the song that would become the city's anthem, "I Left My Heart in San Francisco," was written in 1954 by two gay lovers who were pining for "the city by the bay" after moving to Brooklyn Heights. Tony Bennett made the song famous, singing it for the first time at the Fairmont Hotel's Venetian Room in December 1961, with future mayor Joe Alioto in the audience. By then, the songwriters—Douglass Cross and George Cory—had moved back to the Bay Area, where Cross died of a heart attack and a grief-stricken Cory later took his own life.

By the midsixties, gay liberation was busting out in San Francisco, with picketers circling the downtown Macy's in 1964 to protest the police entrapment of men in the store's restrooms and demonstrators rallying outside the Federal Building in 1966 against the exclusion of homosexuals from the armed services. That same year, drag queens ignited a violent blowup at a Tenderloin eatery called Compton's Cafeteria— three years before the Stonewall riots in New York that are credited with launching the gay rights movement. The Compton's tempest began when a cop tried to arrest one of the queens who frequented the cafeteria, and, sick of the constant harassment, he resisted by throwing a cup of coffee in the policeman's face. In the ensuing melee, angry queens flung dishes and trays at the police, smashed the cafeteria's plate glass windows, and burned down a nearby newsstand.

Despite this colorful history, San Francisco had never seen anything quite like the Cockettes. Hibiscus and company broke down all the drag queen traditions. They were not clean-shaven men costumed as women, but all sorts of imaginative—and often furry—creatures. Hibiscus liked to resurrect Jayne Mansfield, with enormous golden balloon breasts, and a glitter-sparkled beard. Fayette once turned herself into a singing vagina. They were pirates and nuns, Betty Boops and motorcycle greasers, dominatrixes and harlequins. The audience at Cockettes shows "couldn't tell if it was a man or a woman" onstage, marveled filmmaker John Waters, who rode the drag troupe's long, sequined train to notoriety in San Francisco. "It was complete sexual anarchy—which is always a wonderful thing."

"We're not queer," explained one Cockette to the press. "We're just chicks with cocks." Which made all the sense in the world once you went through the looking glass.

AFTER THE COCKETTES' IMPROMPTU debut at the dawn of the 1970s, the troupe plunged into a frenzy of creativity, mounting sixteen different shows in two and a half years. "Hibiscus's charisma is what brought us together," recalled Rumi Missabu, a Cockette who had grown up on the edges of Hollywood show business. "Every month, he'd come up with a new theme from his jeweled scrapbook of fairy tales and fever dreams. 'We're going to do this next month—on LSD!' he would announce. The Cockettes were like the Little Rascals in drag doing Busby Berkeley on acid."

Some shows, like *Pearls Over Shanghai*—the tale of three perky, all-American sisters who fall into debauched white slavery in the Orient—featured well-crafted original scores and the makings of an actual plot. But Hibiscus, who was wedded to his wildly funky theatrical vision, made sure that the shows never could be accused of slick showmanship. He resisted rehearsals, which, in any case, often had a way of deteriorating into hissy fits and huffy walkouts. And when show business stars started to emerge from the Cockette free-for-all—like the future disco queen Sylvester—he had a way of popping their balloons. Once, as Sylvester sang a torrid solo version of "Someone to Watch Over Me," Hibiscus wandered onstage in a zebra costume. The furious diva slapped Hibiscus across the face as he stalked offstage.

There were no taboos, no politically correct inhibitions. The Cockettes did their version of *Gone With the Wind* in blackface, and *Madame Butterfly* in pidgin Cantonese. One afternoon the troupe performed *Pearls Over Shanghai* before a stunned audience on the Berkeley campus. The politically earnest young crowd grew increasingly restive as it took in the wild pageant of scheming dragon ladies, horny coolies, and virginal white victims, until one outraged woman suddenly jumped up and yelled, "This is the most sexist, racist piece of shit I've ever seen!"

The Cockettes' "nocturnal dream shows" at the Palace soon became the talk of San Francisco. Crowds whose peacockery rivaled the drag stars' themselves crammed into the 1,200-seat theater. Janis and other local rock stars began showing up. Herb Caen, a longtime fan of the North Beach drag scene, began touting the Cockettes' gender-bending chaos in his column. Denise Hale and other Pacific Heights socialites dropped by with out-of-town friends like author Truman Capote and film critic Rex Reed. "Hibiscus, we love you!" screamed the crowds as the leader of the drag queen pack made his grand entrance each night, buoyed by his shiny balloon boobs.

But as the Cockettes' star soared higher, Hibiscus resisted the siren call of commercial success. He may have dressed like Monroe and Mansfield, but he didn't want their gilded cage lives. Hibiscus had taken a vow of poverty during his days at the Kaliflower commune, and though he finally moved out of its monastic environment, he was still honoring Irving Rosenthal's "everything free" belief system.

No one was getting rich off the Cockettes' success. Sebastian, the late-night impresario at the Palace, charged only $2 a ticket. Each member of the troupe was lucky to earn a few bucks off the shows—"enough to keep us in false eyelashes," as one Cockette put it. But Hibiscus thought even this was too big a concession to Mammon. He wanted the shows to be entirely free. When Sebastian resisted, Hibiscus and his cohorts ran around the theater flinging open the exit doors to the swarming crowds.

John Waters, who would find a way to make a good living off his cultural subversion, never understood Hibiscus's "hippie Communism." As time went by, more of the Cockettes began to share Waters's view, finding their leader's free philosophy and unpredictable antics increasingly tiresome. Their frustration finally erupted in the summer of 1971, as the troupe pondered traveling east for its big New York stage debut. At an emotional meeting in the second-floor flat of the Cockettes' upper Market Street commune, several performers turned on the troupe's founder. Hibiscus was slapped and kicked and pushed down the flight of stairs.

Fayette found him there, at the bottom of the stairwell, in a puddle of tears. He had been violently ejected from his own dream. Fayette thought it was a devastating blow—not only for Hibiscus but also for the entire troupe. "Yes, he had a way-over-the-top personality," she reflected, "but they didn't get it. They didn't want anyone to mess up their makeup. My feeling was, 'Please, mess it up!' They were ego driven and uninteresting. Hibiscus wanted to do something more fantastical and revolutionary."

To make matters worse, Fayette thought, Hibiscus was the only Cockette with any real stage experience. She smelled disaster. Which is exactly what New York turned out to be.

When they landed in Manhattan, the Cockettes were greeted by the city's glamour crowd as visiting royalty. They were treated to parties with the Warhol circle, fashion magazine editor Diana Vreeland, clothing designer Oscar de la Renta, and artist Robert Rauschenberg. But when the curtains opened on the Cockettes' *Tinsel Tarts in a Hot Coma* at the Anderson Theater, a sad and tatty old barn on the Lower East Side that once featured Yiddish dramas, the celebrity-packed audience didn't know what to make of the San Francisco queens' big mess of a show. The Cockettes were accustomed to audiences that were as raucous and psychedelicized as they were—with some ardent fans even jumping up on stage and becoming part of the show. But the New York audience members expected to sit back and be entertained, and when they weren't, a snarky chill settled over the old theater. As *Tinsel Tarts* grinded on, hoots and howls echoed off the walls. By the end of their opening-night performance, the Cockettes were dead in New York. "Having no talent is not enough," sniffed Gore Vidal as he left the theater. The reviews the next day were equally merciless.

New York just wasn't the Cockettes' scene. One gay bar in Brooklyn Heights even barred Sweet Pam at the door when she tried to enter with her pack of boys—because she was a *girl*—something that never would have happened in loosey-goosey San Francisco. The troupe hung on in Gotham for another month—long enough for several members to get addicted to the cheap heroin that was all over town. Every bellhop seemed to be pushing the stuff.

By the time they got back to San Francisco, the Cockettes felt like Dorothy: that there was no place like home. "New York was nihilistic and cynical—there's a sweeter spirit here," sighed Rumi. "New York was all concrete; San Francisco is lush, plush, velvet, warm, cozy," gushed troupe member Scrumbly, who by then was expecting his first child with his new bride, Sweet Pam—a development that seemed to catch them both by surprise.

San Francisco clasped the Cockettes to its plush bosom after they returned, and they continued to perform at the Palace for several more months. But they never recovered from New York's ice-cold reality check. The pre–New York days were a topsy-turvy dream that could never be repeated.

Hibiscus went on to start a rival drag company, the Angels of Light. But it never achieved the same giddy level of phantasmagoria. He eventually drifted back to New York, where he became a high-priced rent boy in sleek Armani suits. Nothing was free anymore.

Among all the "end of the sixties" moments that would rain down on people's souls, the collapse of the Cockettes was as dreary as any. Hibiscus was the Peter Pan of Golden Gate Park. He should never have grown old or turned a trick. But there would be many more such turns of the screw.

At the end of the 1960s, Jerry Garcia was asked by a reporter to look back at everything he and his crΔowd had been through and to make some kind of sense of it. Garcia said it was too soon. For the rest of his life and longer, he predicted, America would struggle to absorb the convulsive changes of the previous five years.

No city would go through more convulsions than San Francisco as it processed the 1960s. Like the mystics who eat from strange and sacred plants to let their minds touch God, the people of San Francisco first had to know hell.

As the decade expired, the drugs became harder, the sexual freedom more rapacious, the demands on the human psyche more severe. Meanwhile, the outcasts from America—and its domestic and overseas wars—grew more damaged. They carried within them a hot and reckless lust for salvation as they showed up on the streets of San Francisco. The city was still known for its enchantments, but it would soon become notorious for its terrors.

PART TWO

TERROR

Darkness, darkness, be my pillow.

13

A DEATH IN THE FAMILY

W HAT BEGAN IN San Francisco as a celebration of life would become the opposite. Like the moon pulls on the tides, more and more young people were drawn inexorably to the darker shores of oblivion. Looking back, the death of Nancy Gurley seems an omen of all that was to come.

Born Nancy Felice Reisman in 1938, she was the second of three children in a secular Jewish family in Detroit. Her father was an ear, nose, and throat doctor, and her mother was a schoolteacher. She was at odds with the world from the very start. Dinners in the Reisman home often ended with Nancy exploding and running upstairs to her room. She began playing sexually with boys at thirteen or fourteen. One summer she was fired as a camp counselor and sent home after she was caught giving a blow job to another counselor. Dr. and Mrs. Reisman were mortified by their daughter's behavior. "My parents were so upset with Nancy that they were almost sitting shiva for her," recalled her younger brother, Alex. "They didn't trust therapy, and they didn't have the tools to deal with someone like Nancy. My mom started getting migraines because of her."

But to Alex, Nancy was an exciting, beautiful, older sister. She was an elfin five foot one and one hundred pounds, with wavy, auburn hair and deep, brown eyes that were "totally alive." And she was always turning life into an escapade. "When you were around Nancy, you always *felt*," said one of her friends. After graduating from high school, she took off for Hawaii, where she ended up marrying a Zen Buddhist poet— "a Leonard Cohen type," as Alex described him. But the marriage was quickly annulled, and she returned home, her spirit undiminished. She brought back a hula skirt and taught everyone how to shimmy like a palm tree in a tropical gale.

In Detroit, Nancy enrolled at Wayne State University, where she became a straight-A student and eventually pursued a master's degree in English literature, writing her thesis on Yiddish phrases. She had the kind of temperament that bounced between emotional extremes, and she found a philosophical home somewhere between nihilism and existentialism. "She worked hard at being positive, but she could get very down," remembered Alex.

While going to Wayne State, Nancy worked nights at a beat coffeehouse drolly named the Cup of Socrates. That's where she met James Gurley, the young man who would entrance her for the rest of her life. He was as beautiful as Nancy, a tall, lean man with a strong nose and chin, and soft, feminine eyes. His face, which had traces of his Cherokee grandmother, had the romance of a Wild West hero. James came from poor people. His father was a demolition derby driver. He worked young James into his act, tying him to the hood of his jalopy and crashing through a flaming plywood barrier at local speedways. James wore a helmet, but he would be routinely knocked out by the stunt. Once he lost his front teeth, and another time his hair was scorched to the scalp.

At age fourteen, James found sanctuary in a Detroit monastery run by the Catholic Brothers of the Holy Cross. He would live there until he was eighteen, getting up every morning at five-thirty for church and going to Mass every night before bedtime. "I was brought up in the Middle Ages," he would later say. "It may have kept me from a life of crime. I don't know what I would have gotten into."

James also found solace in music. His uncle had a guitar, and he let James play it. He taught himself chords by listening to Lightnin' Hopkins and other blues masters. One night James heard John Coltrane in a Detroit nightclub, and he tried to make his guitar wail as ecstatically as Coltrane's sax.

A man of few words, James let his music speak for him. But he was immediately drawn to Nancy, who was a cauldron of words and feelings. They moved in together in a kind of bohemian rooming house in downtown Detroit inhabited by artists, philosophy students, and drug dealers.

Nancy would return to her family's home for Friday night dinners and always leave loaded down with two bags of groceries. She was still in and out of favor with her parents, who didn't approve of James or his family. "They thought he wasn't good enough for her," Alex said. "They thought she'd come to her senses and marry a nice doctor."

But Nancy and James were paragons of cool. They tripped down the streets together, wrapped in each other's arms, the center of each other's story. She carried around a big, green, stuffed frog with her, wrapped up like it was their baby, just to see people's bug-eyed reactions. They were not made to settle down in Detroit. In 1962 they took off for San Francisco, where James eked out a living playing folk and blues in North Beach cafes.

ONE AFTERNOON IN LATE 1965, Sam Andrew and Peter Albin—the beginnings of the band that would become Big Brother and the Holding Company—were noodling on their guitars in the redwood-paneled, ballroom-sized basement of 1090 Page Street, the Victorian rooming house where Albin lived. Chet Helms—the bespectacled, soft-spoken, Texas-born rock promoter who would become the yin to Bill Graham's yang—suddenly appeared with a striking entourage in tow. The handsome young man with Helms was clad entirely in black, and he wore Indian feathers in his heroically long hair. The petite woman who accompanied him was dressed like an Elizabethan lady in waiting, in velvet and lace. She was "wild and noisy," as Sam Andrew recalled. They had a big German shepherd who seemed as untamed as a wolverine, and a baby who appeared almost as feral. The couple were James and Nancy Gurley—they were married by then—and they were about to join shining forces with San Francisco's cultural revolution.

James brought his singularly savage guitar style to Big Brother, playing at furious speed with fingerpicks, instead of the one flat pick favored by most guitar players. He soon became known as "the fastest guitar slinger in the West." The sonic explosions that James set off with his rapid-fire fingerpicking and his primitive effects, which usually involved a swift kick to his amplifier, came to define psychedelic rock. "It sounded like thunder in a Wagner opera when James shook his amplifier," said Andrew.

James was the star of the early Big Brother lineup. A photo of him taken by Bob Seidemann—staring soulfully ahead, wearing a double-breasted Civil War shirt and an Indian feather in his hair—instantly became a popular Haight Street poster, the definition of hippie masculinity. But Big Brother was incomplete until the day in June 1966 when Helms—the man who pieced together the band, player by player—brought a fellow Texan named Janis Joplin to the band's rehearsal hall in an old firehouse on Henry Street. At first look, James was not impressed with the band's new singer. "She looked like a punk or something," he recalled. "She had Levi's that had the knees turned out. She had Mexican huaraches sandals on, and her hair was pinned up in a bun. She had no makeup, and her face was really broken out. She had a bad complexion, and she had this blue sweatshirt on that was all torn and covered with paint because she had been a painter. Nobody would have looked at her and thought, 'In a few years, she's gonna be the biggest thing on the planet.'"

BUT THEN JANIS BEGAN singing, and it was unlike anything the band members had ever heard. Her voice was a wail from somewhere too deep, the saddest, most desperate orgasm ever wrenched out of a woman's body. It was as disturbing as it was exciting, equal parts sex and death. One day, while the band was rehearsing, it was interrupted by loud thumping on the firehouse door. When a man in the band's extended family opened the door, five policemen were braced to enter, straining their necks to look inside. "We have a complaint that there is a woman screaming here," said one of the cops. "That's not a woman," replied the man, "that's Janis Joplin." Men never knew what to make of Janis.

In early summer 1966, Alex Reisman moved to California. He was going to attend Stanford Law School. But he also wanted to be around his ever-dazzling sister. By then Nancy and James were living at 459 Oak Street, on the edge of the Panhandle, with their toddler, who was named Hongo Ishi Gurley, after the last of the free Indians. Nancy was an advocate of the Summerhill philosophy of child rearing and didn't want to place any constraints on Hongo. The boy roamed the house without a diaper accompanied by the family German shepherd, who also crapped on the floor whenever the need gripped him. Big Brother wasn't making any money yet, and the family seemed to get by on food stamps and various hustles.

The Big Brother orbit was becoming an exciting place to be. Nancy kept telling her brother about the volcanic new singer who had joined the band. In June 1966, Janis made her debut with the band at Chet Helms's Avalon Ballroom. It was the first time that Alex had seen Big Brother, the first time he had seen James play rock music, the first time he had seen a light show. Old Betty Boop cartoons and Harold Lloyd silent films flickered on the walls. Nancy was his magic ticket.

Before the show, Alex went backstage with his new wife, Dorothy, and smoked dope with the band in their cramped dressing room. Janis was terrified—she had never performed with a rock band before, only in coffeehouses with an acoustic guitar. Alex couldn't see what the buzz was all about. "I remember thinking Janis was not that great looking, especially compared to someone like Grace Slick. Then she went onstage and opened her mouth, and I thought, 'I get it.'"

Janis was blasted into air by the band's rocket of sound. "What a rush!" she felt. "A real drug rush. The music went boom, boom, boom, and everyone was dancing, and I stood there and clutched the mike, and I got it." There in the spotlight, that's where she belonged. It would become the only place she did belong.

JANIS NEVER STOPPED THINKING of herself as just an "ugly chick from Port Arthur with not too much talent." The girl nominated most "ugly man on campus" by her stupidly cruel fellow students at the University of Texas. She had what Big Brother drummer Dave Getz called a bottomless "hole in her gut" that she was forever trying to fill with men, women, whisky, and drugs. Her hunger swallowed the room, she wanted to suck down everything around her. "She was scary," recalled Fayette Hauser, the young artist and future Cockette who had followed Nancy to San Francisco. "She was so intense and butch. She'd come right into your face. I was shy. She was way too heavy for me."

Within weeks of joining Big Brother, not only had Janis replaced James as the star of the band but she had also claimed him as her lover. Lanky, soulful James was a magnet for women. "After shows, women would often ask me whether James would be in my room later," recalled bandmate Peter Albin. The quiet former Catholic boy was overwhelmed by the sexual attention. James's monastic adolescence had left him feeling, in his words, "shy, repressed, and screwed up." He proved an easy mark for voracious Janis. In the summer of 1966, James moved in with the band's new star, leaving Nancy and Hongo back in their Oak Street flat.

But Nancy Gurley had her own magnetic power. A couple of weeks later, she came marching into Janis's bedroom with Hongo and the German shepherd, and she took James back.

Nancy and Janis began as sexual rivals, but they quickly became a dynamic duo. They were both strong-willed, whip-smart women who loved to read. Janis always carried around her San Francisco Public Library card with her. And they both grew up feeling like angry and tormented outcasts. Janis was "very, very smart," said Getz. "And Nancy was one of the few people who was up to her caliber."

Nancy was the Big Brother tribe's mesmerizing gypsy queen. In her "long gowns of lace and velvet" and with her "many, many necklaces draped colorfully from the porcelain gracefulness of her neck," as the band's publicist, Myra Friedman, described her, Nancy set the standard for femininity in the band's circle. She took the scruffy girl from Port Arthur and made her over in her lushly romantic image.

Not long after Janis joined Big Brother, the band and its retinue of wives, girlfriends, and children all moved into an old redwood hunting lodge at the end of a road in woodsy Lagunitas. Nancy and Janis would spend hours together, talking late into the night and stringing bits of antique glass and crystal beads, which they decorated themselves with like Christmas tree lights. By this point, Nancy's natural exuberance was further amped by regular injections of speed. Janis was trying to stay away from her hard drug demons. When Chet Helms lured her back to San Francisco from Texas earlier that year, he assured her that the scene had been taken over by psychedelics, which never particularly interested her. But Nancy's speed-driven dazzle was too enticing, and during the band's Lagunitas sojourn, Janis fell back into her old meth habit.

Nancy had developed a strong affinity for speed as a girl, after her mother began freely dispensing Dexedrine capsules to all three of her children to manage their weight. The family had a cabinet that was well stocked with prescription drug samples brought home by Dr. Reisman. "We called it the drug store," Alex said. "The result was that all three of us kids developed a strong liking for uppers." For the rest of her life, Nancy would always prefer drugs that took her fast-forward rather than down.

In the beginning, San Franciscans felt they owned Janis and Big Brother. They were like the Dead, neighborhood minstrels, the Avalon house band. She was the type everyone knew from high school: the brassy bad girl rejected by the cheerleaders but beloved by losers everywhere. After shows, she would jump down from the stage and mingle with the audience. You could see her down on the Panhandle, amid all the harlequins and gypsies, smoking a cigar and swigging from a bottle of Jack. If you hadn't slept with her, you knew someone who had.

But after the Monterey Pop Festival in June 1967, when Janis stole the show along with Hendrix, Otis Redding, and the Who, everything changed. The star-making pressures grew unbearable, and the corporate sirens began wooing Janis away from the band. She couldn't walk her old neighborhood anymore. "These days Haight Street is so weird," she told San Francisco journalist David Dalton after the festival. "Remember that *Suddenly Last Summer* movie, where that guy gets eaten by cannibals? Well, that almost happened to me the last time I was there. I got out of my car. 'It's Janis Joplin, it's Janis Joplin! Hey, give me this, give me that.' Pushing, pulling on me, trying to aggravate me."

Heroin began creeping into the band's circle. Soon Janis, James, and Sam Andrew were all using. Nancy was more leery of heroin's catacomb lure, but she too started alternating speed and smack. How could people so smart put themselves at such risk? A lifetime later, Fayette Hauser could still see method in her friend Nancy's madness. Nancy and her San Francisco troupe were remaking the world by tapping into the deepest recesses of their souls. Drugs were an essential tool in the process, and each one had its own unique use. It was all about finding the right alchemy. "These were people who considered acid trips and speed as their work," she explained. "It was a serious matter with them. People had made discoveries through acid that had reshaped them. They were very consciously exploring life. The heroin was the perfect counterpart. It would put you right back to where you were on your last acid trip."

But the balancing act proved elusive. The band lost its core discipline, began to get sloppy. Janis grew crazier, becoming dangerous to herself and others. She was so desperate for a fix one time that she drew water from a toilet into her syringe. She could be equally reckless with others. One night Terry Hallinan dropped by her Noe Street apartment with Peggy Caserta, a bosomy clothing store owner with whom they were both sleeping. Janis—already high, and burning with jealousy—convinced the young lawyer to sample smack for the first time and then injected him with an extra-stiff shot. Hallinan's eyes immediately rolled upward, and he collapsed to the floor. Caserta was frantic. "Oh Jesus, Janis, he's gonna die on us!" But the singer simply began undressing Caserta and took her to bed, while Hallinan was sprawled unconscious at their feet. "Aren't we naughty girls?" Janis giggled. Only after they had finished with each other did Janis revive Hallinan with a cold towel.

Hallinan never forgave Janis. "I didn't think she was a great person," he smiled wryly many years later. "Of course, we didn't exactly get off on a good foot. She was an arrogant person. She was the Queen Bee by then." Only in San Francisco could a young man who took a near-lethal dose from Janis Joplin's needle wind up overseeing the city's criminal justice system—but that's precisely what Terry "Kayo" Hallinan did three decades later when he was elected San Francisco's district attorney.

Nancy felt that James too was disappearing into the heroin netherworld. What began as a conscious exploration of life's mysteries was becoming an endless half slumber. She was losing the love of her life to drugs and other women—there was always too many of both. It only got worse after Janis left Big Brother to form her own band in fall 1968—just as Big Brother's album, *Cheap Thrills,* was rocketing the band into the music industry heavens. Janis's abrupt departure was a betrayal that neither she nor the rest of the band ever recovered from. Now heroin was the only organizing principle in James's life.

Nancy tried leaving James. She ended up in Colorado for a while, taking up with a hippie surfer on shore leave. It was there that Fayette Hauser met her one day, while hitchhiking to Aspen. Nancy and her surfer boy picked up the young art student in their panel truck. There was a whole, exotic world in that truck. Dark velvets hung over a double mattress bed. The dashboard was covered with dried flowers and tiny bird skulls. When Fayette opened the truck door, she was greeted by Nancy with a hash pipe. "I climbed in, took the pipe, and thought, 'I'm never getting out.'"

Fayette immediately became another of Nancy's acolytes. She loved to go walking with her and listen to her discourse on literature and philosophy. "Listening to Nancy tell stories was like a walking novel. It was like taking a stroll with Jane Austen."

By the time Nancy returned to San Francisco, she had so enthralled the younger woman with stories about the Emerald City, Fayette knew she had to follow her. Nancy installed her in a Victorian flat in the Duboce Triangle neighborhood, where she became roommates with a drug dealer named Paula and a teenage groupie named Patty Cakes, who alternated between Janis and Jimi Hendrix. Nancy taught Fayette how to dress. And she showed her how to fix, warning her never to shoot up alone and always to inject herself. They were both high when they went to see Janis's final performance with Big Brother.

NANCY WAS STILL TRYING to stay away from James. "James had so many groupies that it drove Nancy crazy," Fayette said. "They were so crazy in love." At last, they fell back into each other's arms. Nancy and Hongo moved back in with James. She was euphoric; it was their destiny to be together. Their story had the inevitability of one her Austen novels. She got pregnant. She cut back on heroin. James was determined to get clean too, to start over.

On the Fourth of July weekend in 1969, James and Nancy took Hongo and drove up to the Russian River for a family outing. James loved the country; it made him feel healthy. He took along a $100 bag of heroin, but he made a junkie's bargain with himself. This would be his final trip to the underworld.

They spent the day floating lazily down the river, drinking wine. By the time they camped outside Cloverdale, James was drowsy with the day's sunny pleasures. Around ten o'clock, he drifted over to his Toyota jeep, where he had left his works, to cap off the night with a syringe full of milky sweetness. In his hazy state, he missed his vein on the first try, and, trying again, once more plunged the needle into muscle.

Nancy walked over to the jeep. She wanted to share this final journey with James. She forgot her own lesson and asked him to take care of her too. James didn't realize it—because he'd missed his own vein and hadn't felt the injection's full effect—but his heroin was more potent than Nancy was used to.

This time his needle found its mark. Nancy walked back to the campfire to read Hongo a bedtime story. Suddenly she pitched forward, in front of her little boy. When James came drifting over moments later, he found his wife sprawled in the dirt.

The rest of the night was so harrowing that, even in the clinical language of court documents, it reduces the reader to tears. James, jolted out of his haze by the sight of his wife on the ground, carried her and Hongo to the jeep and went roaring into Cloverdale. He stopped at a gas station, frantically asking where he could find a doctor in town, and was directed to the office of Dr. Lombard Sayre. The doctor, having been tipped off by the gas station attendant, arrived at his office shortly after James, who swept Nancy into his arms and took her inside. Dr. Sayre quickly realized that Nancy was beyond his help, and he quietly told James that she was dead. But James refused to believe him. He bent over his wife, put his lips to hers, and kept trying to breathe life into her. He didn't stop until two Cloverdale policemen, notified by the doctor, showed up and pulled him away from Nancy's body.

After being led into an adjacent waiting room by the policemen, James slumped into a chair, with a naked Hongo in his lap, and rocked back and forth, sobbing, "Nancy, Nancy, Nancy, no, no, no." Dr. Sayre was so concerned about James's state of mind that he urged the policemen to have him committed that night to a psychiatric ward in a nearby hospital. All during the half-hour ambulance ride to the hospital, James wept over and over to his three-year-old son, "What are we going to do? Nancy isn't here, Hongo, what are we going to do? Nancy isn't here."

The next morning, James was arrested on murder charges. Janis hired the best lawyer she could think of—the rugby-tough Vincent Hallinan–schooled drug attorney Michael Stepanian—to represent her former bandmate and fellow heroin casualty. Alex Reisman testified at the coroner's inquest where Nancy's death would be ruled either a homicide or an accident. The hearing was trying to determine whether Nancy could have given herself the fatal injection, and a key question before the court was whether she was left- or right-handed. After conferring with his family, Alex testified that his sister was ambidextrous. "We didn't want James to get pinned for giving her the shot," he said later. "We thought the worst thing for Hongo would be to have his father locked up for years."

The charges against James were later reduced to heroin possession, and he was given probation. Some regarded James Gurley as a very fortunate man. But the court didn't see it that way. "Some [life] consequences furnish greater penalties than the law can impose," read a court document in the case, a beautifully concise appraisal of the hell that James would go through after that night on the Russian River.

James never got over Nancy's death. It was a mournful note that echoed through the rest of his life. It was not the first overdose in San Francisco's hippie community, and it would not be the last. But it quickly took on a darkly mythic quality. People who knew her tried to make sense of it. Some saw it as an early feminist parable, the story of a sparkling hippie earth mother who overdosed on love for her old man.

But others simply saw a young woman who had demanded much from life and then taken her leave. There was always a brutal toughness in the beat and hippie cultures, a shrugging awareness that casualties were inevitable when you challenged life's limits. One San Francisco poet wrote a "dry-eyed" requiem for Nancy, which even suggested there was something "graceful" about her exit.

James believed that Nancy's family would never forgive him. But it was never that simple for Alex. "I never felt he was responsible. Nancy did these things on her own."

James had been a big brother to Alex. Nancy and he had been magical presences in his life, warmly welcoming him into their highly charged force field. For two or three years after Nancy's death, Alex had no contact with James. Then one day, Alex—by then a young activist lawyer—found himself at a friend's house in Marin, down the hill from where James was living with his new wife and Hongo. Alex dropped acid and found himself being drawn up the hill, where he knocked on James's door. When James opened it up, Alex told him he was tripping, and James invited him in. Alex wanted to talk about Nancy. "It was still raw," he recalled, "and his new wife was uncomfortable. But it was important for me to talk to him."

In the final years of his life, James Gurley conjured his long-lost wife in a song called "For Nancy (Elegy)." It was a sad and wispy blues-rock tune, lamenting what could have been. "In my life, you were the only one. In my life, my life had just begun." He wrote a couple of "bucket list" letters to Alex near the end, telling him how much he loved his sister. James died of a heart attack in 2009, two days before his seventieth birthday.

Nancy Gurley—this "burning star in a wild firmament," as Alex saw her—was not destined to live into a wistful old age. Nor was Janis Joplin, who, after getting word in New York about her close friend's death, said, "Well, I guess I'll go score some smack." Fuck you, death.

There's an exhilaration in that kind of recklessness. It takes a reckless kind of soul to tear down monuments and torch bridges, to shake the dead grip of the past. But by the end of the sixties, the revolution was entering its Jacobin phase, and the wreckage was growing wanton. If the revolution liberated the human imagination, it also unleashed humanity's demons. San Francisco—capital of the new world—was descending into its Season of the Witch.

14

LUCIFER RISING

ONE NIGHT IN 1969, Peter Lewis of Moby Grape peered from onstage into the cavernous darkness of the Fillmore ballroom. A sea of young faces was staring back at him. The faces were not joyous. They looked "lost and worried" to Lewis. "They looked like they were going to freak out." It unnerved Lewis; it disrupted his musical flow. "When you're trying to concentrate on a song and the crowd looks at you like they don't know what's going on, you get lost too. There was so much pain in that room." Lewis stumbled through the rest of the show, holding on until the band reached the end.

There was always a dark shadow around the San Francisco rainbow. From the very beginning, violence, desperation, and fear stalked the streets of the Haight, side by side with the euphoria. "When I hear about the Summer of Love, I say, 'Where was that?'" remarked Lewis. "It was there, but always lurking below was this seething hatred and fear from Vietnam and the Cold War. There was always this feeling that we were going to die."

As the 1960s drew to an end, and America's pain intensified, more and more of the suffering washed up in the Haight. Runaways who could never go home, strung-out Vietnam vets, draft dodgers terrified of what awaited them when they were caught, teenagers sickened by what loomed ahead of them in adult America. The war was dragging on and on, the country's most promising leaders had been mysteriously assassinated, racial divisions were growing more bitter, inner cities were smoldering.

San Francisco's cultural revolution was launched with the grandest intentions. As the Human Be-In visionaries proclaimed, they were giving birth to "a new nation . . . inside the robot flesh of the old." The great notions spawned by San Francisco's revolution—peaceful coexistence, racial harmony, sexual liberation, ecological consciousness, organic food, communal living, alternative commerce, free culture—did indeed spread throughout the country, where their green tendrils could be seen sprouting here and there in the stony ground.

But as San Francisco's revolution spread—carried by the music, the drugs, the underground railroad of wandering youth—the poison in America's soul was also billowing. You could feel it more and more on the streets of the Haight. San Francisco was no longer only a haven for the country's restless dreamers but also for its wrecked and ruined.

The 1960s turned sour in large part because of the endless bloodletting in Vietnam. The soul sickness leached everywhere as the war came home, but nowhere more than the Haight, where many ravaged veterans sought solace. The music that GIs listened to in Vietnam, and the magazine spreads of hippie revelry, promised a halcyon world far from the blood and mud. But many of them found it was not easy to leave the war behind; they brought it home with them.

Life in the Haight grew more violent and disturbing. The drugs got harder. By 1971, 15 percent of the servicemen returning from Vietnam were addicted to heroin. Smack and speed began to shove aside psychedelics. The harried staff at the Haight-Ashbury Free Clinic was seeing more and more hard-core drug abusers. The speed freaks were the most harrowing cases: amphetamines worked their dark magic on the brain with power-drill intensity.

Speed freaks were loathe to approach the health system when their bodies started breaking down. But one day a meth head named Randy ventured into the Free Clinic in search of help for an AWOL soldier who was too wasted to come in. Dr. Ernest Dernburg, a clinic psychiatrist who had won the trust of the meth addict subculture, agreed to follow Randy back to his residential hotel—a crystal palace on Haight Street. It was a mission of mercy into San Francisco's darkening drug underworld that only a doctor like the Free Clinic's Dernburg would have been willing to risk.

In the hotel lobby, Randy had to convince the heavily armed and suspicious manager at the front desk to let the doctor enter the premises. Dernburg continued to run a hostile gauntlet as he mounted the staircase to the AWOL soldier's third-floor room. "Gaunt and menacing faces peered out" from half-open doors, he later told his colleague, Dr. David Smith, and he could see "corpselike figures stretched out on the floors and the furniture in several shuttered rooms."

When Randy and Dernburg reached the third-floor landing, they were again stopped, this time by a handful of half-naked phantoms, who grilled Randy about the doctor's identity for a full ten minutes and then demanded to see his medical credentials before they were finally allowed to proceed. As Dernburg approached the GI's door, he could hear high-pitched wails. After Randy and his wraith-like companions shouted through the locked door, it was finally opened by another specter with "a thin, deathly white, female face," the doctor recalled. Dernburg entered and picked his way through a room littered with needles, piles of white powder, filthy bedsheets, sleeping bags, soft-drink cartons, and cat shit. The doctor was guided to a bed where the soldier lay. He was once a robust, six-foot-tall young man, but he had been shriveled to a twisted knot of human misery.

"He was lying in a foul pool of sweat," Dernburg recounted. "Beside him was much-used needle with a broken, rusty tip. His jaundiced face glistened with perspiration and was sunken around the eye sockets. His heart raced. His arms, visible under the shreds of a long-sleeved uniform, were covered with fresh tracks or needle punctures and swollen with abscesses the size of baseballs. Running up to one shoulder was a darkened blood vessel, the sign of septicemia, or blood poisoning. He mumbled incoherently and writhed under [my] touch. He screamed, 'Let me die! Don't bust me; I've had enough!'"

This is as good a portrait as any of what the Vietnam War did to the young men who fought in it.

Dernburg knew that somehow he had to extricate the young soldier from the meth den and get him immediately to a hospital. He sent Randy back to Clayton Street to fetch the clinic's "ambulance": an old Peugeot station wagon. He then picked up the emaciated GI, who was too weak to walk, and carried him to the third-floor landing. Here Dernburg's path was blocked by a raving young man in a greasy trench coat, who, thinking he was a narcotics agent, assaulted the doctor. Dernburg finally pacified the violent man by again fishing his medical credentials out of his pocket. He continued to run the meth hotel's grim gauntlet, with the soldier in his arms, until they finally emerged onto the street. By this time, Randy and a Free Clinic colleague had arrived with the ambulance. But before they could load the wasted man into the back of the vehicle, they were again confronted: this time by a half dozen Hell's Angels, who demanded to know what was going on. One of the Angels recognized Dernburg's colleague, who explained the emergency, and the bikers offered to escort the ambulance on their Harleys, plowing through traffic on the way to San Francisco General.

And this is as good a picture as any of how counterculture communities like the Haight took care of the war's mangled souls: a doctor from a hippie clinic carrying a dying, emaciated soldier in his arms. For decades after the war, up to this very day, right-wing politicians and pundits have spread the libel about how peace activists and hippies greeted returning Vietnam vets with gobs of spit and contempt. The truth is that many survivors of the war headed directly to havens like the Haight, where they found more comfort than they ever could in veterans' hospitals or bastions of flag-waving patriotism.

VETS AND OTHER REFUGEES from the American wasteland continued pouring into the Haight, even as its streets grew meaner. Much of the neighborhood's growing craziness was fueled by new waves of drugs. Even the psychedelics were getting more potent and exotic. Superhallucinogens like STP and PCP, which were developed and tested in military laboratories, were suddenly and inexplicably flooding the Haight. STP made a particularly insidious debut in the Haight, sending users on a three-day trip that was "like being shot out of a gun," according to one unsuspecting victim. The nightmare was intensified for those who were treated with Thorazine, the standard remedy for LSD freak-outs, which only compounded STP's effects. Some of the superpsychedelics coursing through the neighborhood were cut with poisonous additives such as strychnine and insecticide.

The Central Intelligence Agency and the military had long been fascinated with LSD and other psychedelics as potential mind control weapons. Beginning in the early 1950s, the CIA became the leading sponsor of LSD experimentation, using agency personnel and civilians as unsuspecting lab rats. The army followed in the CIA's footsteps, testing drugs at its Edgewood Arsenal and Dugway Proving Ground facilities.

The CIA and the military became unwitting birth mothers for the psychedelic revolution when they began expanding their drug test groups to include bohemians, artists, and students. One of the research scientists who administered Allen Ginsberg's first acid trip in 1959 had conducted hallucinogenic drug experiments for the US Navy. Moloch, the vast stone of war, was everywhere.

LSD's leading apostle in the 1950s and early 1960s was, in fact, a former OSS (Office of Strategic Services, predecessor to the CIA) officer with strong ties to the espionage establishment: Captain Alfred M. Hubbard. He traveled the world, introducing acid to an elite spectrum of statesmen, corporate chieftains, church leaders, and writers, including Aldous Huxley, who became another influential advocate for the drug. "They all thought it was the most marvelous thing," said Hubbard about his acid evangelism among the elite. "And I never saw a psychosis in any one of these cases."

As psychedelic drugs jumped from agency labs into the general population, the CIA had an ambivalent reaction. On the one hand, it feared that the counterculture might try to use the drugs against the political establishment, including the agency itself. Ginsberg was not the only underground figure who fantasized out loud about turning on the world's warmongering leaders and saving the human race from nuclear extinction. These pipe dreams even made their way into intelligence circles, where Mary Meyer—the ex-wife of high-ranking CIA counterespionage official Cord Meyer—sought Timothy Leary's help to conduct acid experiments in her Washington circle. Among Meyer's circle was none other than her secret lover, President John F. Kennedy.

On the other hand, as LSD consumption began spreading widely in the youth culture, the CIA welcomed it as an opportunity to test its mind control techniques. One CIA agent referred to the Haight-Ashbury as a "human guinea pig farm." As early as June 1967, the dawn of the Summer of Love, a CIA-sponsored psychiatric researcher named Dr. Louis Jolyon "Jolly" West set himself up in a safe house in the Haight to monitor the neighborhood's young drifters and their drug intake. Bearded, ruddy-cheeked Jolly West had a peculiar resumé. In the fifties and early sixties, as the head of the University of Oklahoma's department of psychiatry, he had turned the campus into a center of CIA experimentation on LSD and brainwashing. One of his more notorious stunts was injecting a circus elephant with lethal doses of LSD. In 1964, when Jack Ruby, the murderer of Lee Harvey Oswald, began intimating that President Kennedy was the victim of an ultraright conspiracy, the CIA dispatched West to examine Ruby in his jail cell. West diagnosed Ruby as "paranoid" and delusional.

In the Haight, Jolly West later wrote, he rented a "typical, large apartment, or pad" which he "cleaned, disinfected, and humbly but suitably furnished and decorated with posters, flowers, and paint. For the next six months, an ongoing program of intensive interdisciplinary study into the life and times of hippies was undertaken . . . The Haight-Ashbury district proved to be an interesting laboratory for observations concerning a wide variety of phenomena."

It is still not fully known what West's research entailed, but one visitor to his CIA "pad" recalled a bizarre, "messy" scene, with tangles of young people lying about, "blasting off" on various chemical fuels.

After his Haight experiment in the summer of 1967, West predicted the demise of the counterculture: "The very chemicals they use will inevitably enervate them as individuals and bleed the energies of the hippie movement to its death." Some counterculture figures thought the death of the movement was, in fact, a primary goal of the CIA's drug experimentation. The ever-stronger drugs, the hollowed-out zombies walking the streets, the violent psychotics. The point, they alleged, was to kill the surge of youth rebellion before it became any more of a threat to the established order. New Left activist Tom Hayden, beat writer William Burroughs, and radical White Panthers leader John Sinclair were among those who denounced the drugs cooked up in CIA labs as instruments of social control. "The new drugs were reminiscent of the distribution of alcohol for American Indians, gin for the 'gin mills' of Irish and British workers, and Britain's introduction of opium into China," Hayden later wrote.

As hard drugs took their toll on Haight-Ashbury, the neighborhood descended into crime and squalor. By 1969, most of the stores on Haight Street were boarded up and vacant. Cats were said to be hard to find on the streets, because starving junkies were hunting them for food. The neighborhood was hit by a wave of grisly drug murders. A twenty-three-year-old biker who claimed he had been high on acid for eighteen straight months was pulled over by police one day. He was driving a stolen black Volkswagen owned by an unemployed flute player turned drug dealer. The severed arm wrapped in blue suede that police found in the back of the car also turned out to belong to the flute player. "I'm very, very hazy about that arm," the biker told his lawyer after he was arrested on murder charges.

Guns were suddenly everywhere in the neighborhood that had been, until very recently, the capital of peace and love. The SFPD reported confiscating more weapons in the Haight than any other San Francisco district. One day a gunfight broke out between hippie dealers and black teenagers from the Fillmore who were trying to rob them. A long-haired dope peddler blasted away at the teenagers with a .22 pistol as they crouched behind garbage cans.

The homicide cops who worked the Haight called it "Hippieville." Most of these inspectors were born and raised in San Francisco, like Jack Cleary, a graduate of Archbishop Riordan High School. Cleary wasn't a hard-on. In the old days, when he and other cops saw burnouts and rummies on the streets, they'd put them in the back of their patrol cars and drive them home. Young Cleary's sergeant would remind him that a lot of these sad cases were World War II vets. "You gotta always remember: they fought for their country."

But the Haight was a different world. Cleary saw unspeakable things there; the sort of things a man can't tell his wife. "I had a guy who put his cowboy boots in this girl's vagina. He killed her that way. It was out there in Hippieville."

There was a carelessness about life among these young people that Cleary found stunning. One day he and his partner got a report about a body sprawled outside a big boardinghouse near Haight Street and Masonic Avenue. It turned out that a young man had plummeted to his death from a third-story window. When Cleary entered the building to investigate, he found a party in full swing. "I go into the bathroom to check it out, and here's a hippie making some kind of Kool-Aid in the bathtub—with a fucking oar! This other guy has just died, but there's a party still going on!"

MORE AND MORE LOST children kept arriving in the Haight, even as the streets grew rougher. Many were looking for the families they never had. One of those who found her way there was Susan Atkins, a sad-eyed, oval-faced teenager from the drab suburbs south of San Francisco. She had a high, sweet, wispy voice, and she sang in her church choir. But when she was fourteen, her mother died of cancer, and afterward her hard-drinking father sank deeper into alcoholism. Susan herself struggled with depression, liquor, and pills. Her family began coming apart. Her older brother went off to join the navy, and she dropped out of high school. By the time she arrived in San Francisco, Susan had survived a codeine overdose, an endless string of men—some bad, some just faceless—and a hard stretch in county jail for robbery. She was hired as the youngest topless dancer on North Beach's neon strip after her boyfriend of the moment talked her into getting onstage for an amateur show. She was girlish and full breasted, and she knew how to turn off her mind and sink her hips and ass into the music. She did whatever her nightclub boss asked her to do.

One afternoon Susan's boss brought an eerie-looking man into the bar. He was dressed all in black and had glistening, black eyes and a devil's goatee, and his shaved head gleamed a ghostly white in the shadowy bar. Her boss introduced the man as Anton LaVey and asked her to dance for him. The name meant nothing to Susan, but LaVey had achieved local notoriety as the Church of Satan's "Black Pope." A one-time crime-scene photographer and carny musician, LaVey played the calliope and Wurlitzer organ on dozens of midways and in numerous strip palaces. But he found his true showbiz calling as San Francisco's celebrity Satanist.

LaVey tooled around town in a black 1949 Citroën and bought a two-story Victorian mansion out on the windswept avenues, which he covered with a thick coat of black surplus submarine paint. A stream of devil worshippers and curiosity seekers frequented the satanic services and séances at his house, where they were greeted by dangling skeletons, a stuffed werewolf, and a mangy, roaring lion named Togare, who roamed the backyard. Among LaVey's followers were eccentric socialites, city officials, artists, and Hollywood celebrities, including the monumental blonde Jayne Mansfield. LaVey, like all violators of social convention, also found it useful to cultivate cops. One of the retired police inspectors in LaVey's thrall never forgot the night he dropped by the black mansion and saw a naked Mansfield draped on top of the grand piano. "She liked to be humiliated," LaVey said of the B-movie queen. "She longed for a stern master."

LaVey recruited Susan Atkins to perform in another of his spectacles, a topless Witches' Sabbath that he staged in the North Beach nightclub where she was working. She played a voluptuous vampire, rising out of a coffin with jet-black hair, bloodred lipstick, and bare breasts. Susan couldn't bring herself to climb into the coffin until she dropped a tab of acid. During the show, she remained motionless in the coffin, taking in every sound, the audience's footsteps, sighs, and breathing. She found that she liked playing dead. When it finally came time for her to rise up, she freaked out the men and women who were packed into the club. They gasped loudly as she stood up and pointed a long, red fingernail at them to mark them as her next victims.

To LaVey, Susan was just another hippie burnout—"perhaps a bit more drug befuddled than some," as he later recalled. LaVey had contempt for San Francisco's hippie culture, which he found "a mire of ignorance, stupidity, and egalitarianism." His Witches' Sabbath was just another carny show. But Susan felt something deeper. She liked the way the gaudy ritual made her feel each night; she liked her role's wicked power to shock and excite. Her new boyfriend thought it was all too creepy. He told her she was losing herself to LaVey, and he moved out.

After the Witches' Sabbath show closed, Susan once again found herself without a home, with no direction home. Inevitably, she ended up on the streets of the Haight, among crowds of other young drifters who shared her feelings that the world was "crooked and perverted." By now, the Diggers had scattered. There were no more street guardians to look out for the lost children. With no one to guide them, the kids fell into the hands of long-haired Fagins and worse. One day, standing in front of the Drugstore Café, a neighborhood institution, Susan was scooped up by an old girlfriend from the suburbs and taken to her communal house at the corner of Oak and Lyon Streets. She quickly fell into the house's hazy routine, binging on an endless supply of marijuana, hashish, and acid, and sitting stoned on the front balcony, listening to her next-door neighbor Janis Joplin sing blues arias.

It was in the living room of the old two-story brown house where Susan first met the scrawny, bearded little man who would change her life. He introduced himself as Charles Manson, and as they talked, Susan felt he was seeing right inside her. He took off her clothes and stood her in front of a full-length mirror. She wanted to look away, but he made her look. "Look," he whispered to her. "Look at yourself. You're beautiful."

He asked her if she ever imagined making love to her father when she was a little girl. She giggled. "Don't be silly."

He kept staring at her, unblinking. "I know you have. You must be honest. Every girl at some time wants to make love to her father."

He told her she had to break free of the inhibitions that were choking her. "Make love with me," he said, his voice getting lower. "Make love with me and imagine that you're making love to your father. You must break free from the past." Charlie would be her new father.

Even though he was a hardened, thirty-two-year-old ex-con, Manson was just as lost as the other young drifters when he arrived in the Haight after being released from McNeil Island penitentiary in March 1967. Manson, the son of a teenage prostitute, was the survivor of a childhood even more obliterated than Susan's. He had spent most of his life behind bars. "I still didn't know anything about marijuana or LSD or any kinds of drugs," he said later. "In fact, I didn't really want to come out of jail—I was frightened and didn't know where to go."

The Haight-Ashbury folded Manson into its arms. The ex-con became a well-known figure on the streets, collecting young women like Susan and becoming the father that they—and he—had never had. They created a "nest" for themselves in a two-story building at 636 Cole Street, near the Free Clinic, which he would frequent with his female tribe. Manson never seemed to require medical attention—"sickness is the product of an impure mind," he told the clinic staff. The Manson women were treated for vaginal infections, and they often asked for advice about natural childbirth.

As his reputation and strangely obedient family grew, residents of the Haight began to recoil from Manson. "I met Charlie Mason," recalled rock attorney Brian Rohan. "He was a little troll. He kept his girls on drugs all the time; they didn't know what they were doing." Susan later estimated she dropped acid at least three hundred times during her days with Manson.

Peter Lewis recalled meeting Manson at the home of Los Angeles record producer Terry Melcher "He didn't have an immediately weird vibe because there were a lot of guys like that. There were a lot of people coming back from Vietnam like him, and they headed right for the Haight. They were like the war casualties in Robert Stone's *Dog Soldiers*. So in the context of the sixties, Manson didn't really stick out. Who the hell was Manson? Maybe the CIA worked on him, you know, with one of its drug programs. I don't know who Manson was. Manson might not have known who Manson was."

Susan, though, knew who Manson was: the man she was supposed to follow. "I was eighteen but older inside. I was free. My father, brothers, and I were irreparably torn apart, it seemed. I had come close, but so far had found no substitute. Charlie had instantly seemed more of a father to me than my own father. He not only preached love, he had power. What he wanted, he could get. He often sounded like God."

As time went by, Manson was feeling less comfortable in the Haight. He thought the streets were getting "ugly and mean." He didn't feel safe in San Francisco anymore. One day in 1968, he sat down with Susan, whom he called "my right-hand man." He said, "Come on, we're going to LA." She didn't hesitate. She followed her destiny.

15

A KNIFE DOWN YOUR THROAT

A YEAR LATER, THE whole world knew Charles Manson—and Susan Atkins, too, as the giggling, witchy-eyed Sexy Sadie.

"Woman, I have no mercy for you," she told Sharon Tate as the actress begged for her life and the life of her unborn baby. Susan held down Tate as her accomplice, Tex Watson, plunged a knife into her belly sixteen times. They both had been snorting crystal meth for the past three or four days. When Susan and her Manson family accomplices showed up that night at the house off Benedict Canyon, one of Tate's houseguests asked them, "Who are you?" Watson replied, "I'm the devil, and I'm here to do the devil's business." Despite all the speed racing through her bloodstream, Susan felt strangely immobile, like "even if I had wanted to run, I couldn't." She felt "caught in something that I had no control over . . . it was like I was a tool in the hands of the devil."

The media coverage of the Manson mayhem wallowed in satanic hippie mythology. But the most horrific explanation was the one offered by Manson himself: "These children that come at you with knives, they are your children. You taught them. I didn't teach them . . . You made your children what they are."

The Manson family's gory helter-skelter in August 1969 was followed by the bloody debacle of Altamont in December. That's how the 1960s ended, with Manson and Altamont. "No more peace and love," reflected Peter Lewis. "It was stabbing people thirteen times just to see if the fourteenth time would make you feel funny."

By 1969, Lewis's own band was going to hell. Moby Grape was once the tightest, most promising rock group in San Fransisco. "For one second, they were great," said Mickey Hart. "They had chemistry. I saw them play. They were a *powerful* band, but they burned out in a second. They were just like a flash." Moby Grape began coming apart as soon as it burst on the scene—a victim of Columbia Records' overhype in a distinctly antihype environment, bad management, and perhaps most of all, the band members' own manias and drug excesses. Like the Cockettes' meltdown, the band's dissolution took place in New York, where they went to finish recording their second album. The city seemed to infect the band with poisonous spirits. While they were holed up there, the group began hanging out with the Rolling Stones and their ghoulish retinue, including a group of "sex witches," as Lewis described them, "who dabbled in black magic and various shit. The Stones didn't believe any of that. But the chicks really believed the Stones were satanic."

Skip Spence, Moby Grape's manic spark plug, fell into the sex witch darkness, and never really came back. "He went from a jolly, cool guy to a guy with a leather jacket, no shirt, and a big old dangly hanging from him," said bandmate Jerry Miller. "He looked like he'd shaved with a battleaxe. He was sweating all over the place."

After lunging at a Columbia executive with a pair of scissors and chopping through drummer Don Stevenson's hotel door with an axe in pursuit of the drummer, Spence ended up in the criminal ward of Bellevue Psychiatric Hospital and was later diagnosed with schizophrenia. Following Spence's breakdown, other members of the band also wrestled with their sanity. Moby Grape released their second album, appropriately titled *Wow,* and went on to record several other LPs over the years, mostly without Spence. But they never fulfilled the enormous expectations that swirled around them during those long, foggy nights at the Ark.

When the music scene withered, so did San Francisco's soul. Sages of dubious distinction began declaring the end of the sixties before the decade was even done. Except that it really wasn't. The 1960s would have many endings and beginnings, up to this very day. But, like the Manson bloodbath, the Altamont "festival"—if that's the right word for the macabre event—was undeniably a funeral of sorts.

The Rolling Stones, inspired by Woodstock, and sensitive to the charge that they were ripoff artists, decided to stage their very own free festival at the end of their 1969 US tour. San Francisco was the obvious location. The Stones' organization consulted with the right people: the Grateful Dead and what was left of the Diggers. At the Dead's suggestion, Stones tour manager Sam Cutler lined up the Hell's Angels to provide security. That's the way it was done in San Francisco: no cops, no professionals, just the badass bikers whom the longhairs always kept wanting to be their heroes. The free concert was supposed to take place in Golden Gate Park, as usual. But city officials knew that a Stones crowd would strain park facilities, so the venue shifted at the eleventh hour to Altamont, a speedway in the remote, tumbleweed hills of the East Bay.

Every headlining rock band in those days had its own karmic aura. San Francisco bands like the Grateful Dead and Jefferson Airplane gave off a life-celebrating shimmer that made even the Hell's Angels want to dance. The Rolling Stones cultivated a different identity. They played with the dark side. Mick Jagger became the midnight rambler, jumping your garden wall. He was in character when he screamed, "I'll put a knife right down your throat, baby, and it hurts!" He was a sinuous East End actor with a stage dagger and a crimson cape. But in America, the savage song sounded like the evening news. He had no idea what he was conjuring.

Earlier that year, the Rolling Stones had used a group of self-styled British Hell's Angels for security at a free concert in London's Hyde Park. But that crew, which simply liked strutting around in the outlaw bikers gear, was far from the real deal. The Stones were soon to find out what the real Hell's Angels were all about.

By the time the World's Greatest Rock 'n' Roll Band rolled into San Francisco on its long-awaited 1969 tour, its first in three years, Peter Coyote and Emmett Grogan were strung out on heroin, and the Diggers were fading fast. But Grogan, hanging on to his old role as ringmaster of all things free, began lining up the usual suspects for the concert, including the Angels. As the plans for Golden Gate Park began falling apart and the event began spiraling out of control, the Diggers got nervous.

"We tried to warn the Stones before Altamont," said Coyote, "but they were too rich, too powerful, and there was too much flow of multinational capital to listen to us. We warned the Dead too. They should've known better. We were the experts at bringing thousands of people together with no violence. But mainly I blame the Stones, who were planning to make a fortune off the movie rights, for trying to put on a phony free concert, with the Angels and all these kids as their extras. And I blame Mick Jagger for fucking with black magic. They reaped what they sowed. So you want to go strolling on the dark side, boys? This is what it fucking looks like."

As the helicopter carrying Jagger and drummer Charlie Watts across the bay from San Francisco hovered over the Altamont Speedway, it looked like the end of the world. More than three hundred thousand people were packed into a dust bowl ringed by scrub-covered hills. A poisonous-looking vapor blanket, combining the first wisps of tule fog from the Central Valley and the choking fumes from thousands of campfires and burning tires, hung over the bleak landscape. The copter made a bumpy landing, and Jagger—dressed like a medieval prince reviewing his battlefield, in yellow crushed-velvet pants, red silk shirt, and a leather cape—emerged into the crowd. A young, wild-eyed man immediately rushed up to him and hit him square in the face. "I hate you! I hate you!" he screamed at the rock star.

Jagger and his entourage pushed their way through the crowd to a trailer behind the low, makeshift stage. The scene already crackled with madness. Hell's Angels hovered around the trailer, binging on speed, acid, and red jug wine, and brandishing lead-weighted pool cues. Blood pulsed from the nose of a fat, naked boy. Inside the crowded trailer, guitarist Keith Richards—who had spent the previous night on the festival grounds, dropping acid and smoking opium—was sprawled on a bed, exchanging banter with a two-year-old girl.

"I'm gonna beat you up," she kept telling him.

"Don't beat me up," he pleaded.

Reports of the growing mayhem kept filtering back to the Stones' trailer—of Hell's Angels running amok in the crowd, cracking skulls and bloodying faces with fists, those pool cues, even full cans of beer. They heard that Marty Balin, the Jefferson Airplane's founder and singer, had been knocked out cold by the Angels when he jumped off the stage and tried to stop one of their gang assaults. It was the one heroic act by a performer during the entire sickening spectacle. As the Airplane broke into "Somebody to Love," Balin looked into the throng and saw the Angels—not known for their racial enlightenment—flailing away at a bare-chested black man with their pool cues.

"I saw the whole crowd, this mass, just back up and allow it to happen," Balin recalled. "I said, 'To hell with the song, this guy needs help.' So I went down there and started fighting, helping the guy out. When I woke up, I had all these boot marks tattooed all over me." Afterward, "Animal," the Angel who slugged Balin, tried to explain himself backstage to the singer. "Fuck you," spat Balin, who was promptly knocked out again.

Balin's act of courage didn't save the day, but it saved a small piece of San Francisco's soul. "That was a stand-up thing to do," Coyote said. "Brave man."

Years later, Balin's bandmate Paul Kantner resisted the idea that Altamont was a tragic watershed. "It didn't end the sixties," he insisted. "It was just a bad day with a bunch of drunken Hell's Angels who couldn't hold their liquor. I thought Marty did the right thing by jumping off."

Why didn't Kantner plunge into the melee too?

"Because Marty did."

As night fell, and the Rolling Stones finally prepared to take the stage, Sonny Barger and the Hell's Angels' high command began plowing through the crowd on their roaring Harleys to get to the front of the stage. Rock photographer Michael Zagaris never forgot their terrible entrance. "Barger was wearing a bear's head on his head. The crowd parted, people were trying to appease the Angels, offering them bottles of wine as they passed through. You could tell everyone hated them. As stoned as I was, I was thinking, 'This is like Poland when the Nazis marched in.' Everyone hated them but felt they couldn't do anything."

Once upon a time, the Angels had offered some kind of protection and rough justice on the Haight's wild streets. San Francisco bikers lived among the hippies, like wolves among lambs. But now the red-fanged realities of nature were making themselves clear. "I used to hear all the time in the Haight, 'Hey, the Angels are our brothers,'" said Zagaris. "But I thought most of these guys are killers—they could've hung with Attila the Hun, Genghis Khan. How the fuck are these guys our brothers?"

By the time the Stones took the stage, hours late, it was cold and dark, the crowd was surging toward the music's hot center, and the Angels were angry, fucked-up, and ready to pounce. As Jagger began singing and dancing in his "prissy clothes," Barger glowered at him from his corner of the stage. The top Angel was furious at the Stones' diva-like delay, while the crowd grew increasingly frantic and unpredictable. "I could no longer picture the Hell's Angels playing the part of bodyguards for a bunch of sissy, marble-mouthed prima donnas," Barger later remarked. He and his gang quickly made clear who controlled the stage.

When some Angels began manhandling a fat, drug-crazed, bare-breasted girl who kept trying to crawl onstage, Keith Richards leaned into Barger's face and said, "Man, I'm sure it doesn't take three or four great big Hell's Angels to get that bird off the stage." Barger responded by walking over to the edge of the stage and kicking her in the head. "How's that?" he asked Richards.

Then came the final descent into the jungle. Meredith Hunter, a black teenager with a flashy lime-green suit and a white girlfriend, was a target for the Angels' resentment all day long. Finally, while he was being roughed up, Hunter pulled the gun he was carrying with him—"but only to make them stop and think when they were beating him," said his girl-friend, Patty. "I know he would never have used it." An Angels desperado named Allen Pizzaro responded the way you do on the street. He spun the teenager around and knifed him in the back with his long blade in one smooth, acrobatic move. And then the other Angels of Death were flocking all over Hunter. They kicked the fallen boy in the face, they smashed him over the head with a metal garbage can, then they kicked his head some more with their heavy boots. His last words came in bloody bubbles from his mouth: "I wasn't going to shoot you."

Onstage, Jagger was the midnight rambler, he was the devil asking for sympathy. As the savage frenzy rose and fell in front of the stage, he broke character to plead for civility. "Everyone just sit down! Keep cool! Let's just relax, let's get into a groove. Come on, we can get it together, come on!" His voice was pleading, desperate. But it was his singing that weaved a deeper spell that night. "I'm called the hit-and-run raper in anger, the knife-sharpened tippy-toe." He was Charlie Manson invading a family's quiet sanctum.

The Rolling Stones were at the height of their artistic power at the time. America wasn't their native country, but they had mastered its roots music and made it uniquely their own. Their songs surged with the country's violent energy. But Altamont shook their souls. It exposed the utter artifice of their bad-boy act.

At one point during the Hell's Angels' bloody carnival, a disgusted Keith Richards walked across the stage to Barger and announced, "Either these cats cool it, man, or we don't play." But star power had no pull in that mad abyss. Barger stuck a gun in the guitarist's ribs and told him to start playing or he was a dead man. "He played like a mother-fucker," the head Angel recalled.

After it was all over, and the Stones had fled back to the safety of their San Francisco hotel rooms, they tried to make sense of it all. But they simply sounded stupefied, like English schoolboys who'd found themselves in some unspeakably barbaric outpost of the empire. Talking to a San Francisco radio station, Jagger sounded on the verge of tears: "I thought the scene here was supposed to be so groovy. I don't know what happened, it was terrible. If Jesus had been there, he would have been crucified."

SOME HEAVY HIPPIES SHRUGGED off the bloodshed at Altamont as col-lateral damage. Stewart Brand was an old Merry Prankster. He had been around the cosmic block and prided himself on being unshockable. He knew the Angels, they had partied together at Pranksters ringmaster Ken Kesey's compound in the hills above Palo Alto, they were fixtures at the early Acid Test happenings. The counterculture was always a mix of ecstasy and depravity, Brand noted. "If you're going to have a Ken Kesey, you're going to have a Charles Manson—the one basically gave permis-sion to the other. I went to Altamont and thought it was terrific. The hubris of hiring the Angels to work as security was both ballsy and bad judgment, but that's what the period was all about—exploring the limits of bad judgment. I remember a woman shrieking and humping the stars, losing herself orgiastically into Jagger's lips as the Stones bashed away onstage. It seemed entirely appropriate that there'd be people beating each other to death in the midst of all that. Dionysus leads people to being shredded and eaten. Those were the death-defying leaps we were about in those days, and some people die in the process."

But few in San Francisco's underground culture were philosophical enough—or perhaps hard souled enough—to take Altamont in stride. People were dispirited, angry, dazed. Everyone was talking about it, trying to sort through it, and figure out what it meant for the future of the counterculture movement. One of the more perceptive commentaries on Altamont popped up in the letters section of *Good Times,* the underground San Francisco newspaper that began in hippie bliss but became increasingly hard-bitten and radical as the years went by. The letter was written by a twenty-seven-year-old reader named John Peters, who had attended the festival. It's worth quoting at length, because of the way it captures the darkening mood of Hippieville.

> What's made Mick and his boys rich and famous and great is their whole fantastic trip of power and violence, and it's a very American trip by the way . . . For [the Rolling Stones], the power and violence is fantasy, something close to pornographic literature. But Americans just ain't like that. The real Americans want to get their hands and faces in the mud and the blood and the beer.
>
> The Love Generation never made it, except in a few communes way off by themselves, because it had no roots. The Pranksters and the Angels and the tough blacks, whatever their differences, they all have roots. Put any of them in a frontier town and they'd be running around with the worst motherfuckers around within a week. Their power and violence isn't a fantasy.

There was a burning desperation in the Altamont crowd, wrote Peters, like the hollow-eyed mob in *The Day of the Locust,* crowding desperately around its Hollywood idols, threatening to devour them. The young people jostling with the Hell's Angels for the prime turf around Mick Jagger's stage were the craziest of all. "At Altamont," Peters wrote, "you had to fight your way tooth and nail to the front if you wanted to be where the action was. If I were 18 instead of 27, with a sharp edge of despair in my stomach, I might have done the same." The people up front, in the killing pit, "were there because they wanted to be. In spite of what Mick says, sometimes you do get what you want. But when you do, it can hit you in the face."

Sensing the strong need of people in the Haight to discuss Altamont, Stephen Gaskin, a popular counterculture medicine man, resumed his Sunday morning gatherings at the tip of Golden Gate Park, across the highway from the ocean. Gaskin, a former semantics teaching assistant at San Francisco State College, attracted a large following that spilled out of the classroom and into the park when he began exploring the mysteries of sex, drugs, and consciousness. With his hollow cheeks, long, stringy brown hair, scraggly beard, and wiry body, Gaskin looked like a blazing-eyed Confederate cavalryman, still haunting the Tennessee woods long after the war was over. His followers hung on his every word.

San Francisco's "vibes" were seriously damaged by Altamont, Gaskin told his flock. He said the Stones' music was "sadistic," and he had stopped listening to it after it sent him spiraling downward during a frightening acid trip. Those who attended the concert were on a death trip, which inevitably ended in the human sacrifice of young Meredith Hunter.

The Stones, however, were not to blame for America's wretched state. "Let's face it, this country is weird right now." It was an empire reveling in its savage glory. During the height of the British Empire, Gaskin observed, "flagellation was a popular sport."

Gaskin announced that he would try to counter Altamont's morbid vibes on Easter Sunday in March 1970 with an enormous celebration of life in the Polo Field, where—an eternity-seeming three years earlier—the Human Be-In had ushered in a new era of higher consciousness.

But, in the end, Stephen Gaskin gave up on San Francisco, rolling out of the Haight with his congregation in October 1970 in a caravan of thirty-two rebuilt school buses and dozens of other motley vehicles. Gaskin's great exodus ended in Tennessee, where he established one of the most successful and longest-running communes in American history, the Farm.

Peace and love no longer held dominion in San Francisco, Gaskin decided. "The information we got in San Francisco was that folks were buying into violence in a wholesale lot," he said in explaining his flock's mass departure. His apocalyptic vision extended to American cities in general. They were falling into brutishness and depravity. And the only solution, according to Gaskin, was to withdraw from their destructive vortex and lead a simple, communal life in the country.

Gaskin's declaration of rural retreat marked another key turning point in the San Francisco counterculture's long, strange trip. Most of the Haight's original wave of visionary settlers were now gone. The bands were broken up or had dispersed to sunny hillside mansions in Marin. The Diggers were no more, and Grogan wound up back in New York, deeply enslaved by his heroin habit. He died on April Fool's Day 1978, nodding into the afterworld on a subway car, at the end of the Coney Island line.

Without its street-smart leaders, the Haight—capital of the counter-culture—was at the mercy of the growling packs of hustlers and thugs who began overrunning the neighborhood. Even more ominous, the same powerful redevelopment forces that had erased the Fillmore were now maneuvering to exploit the Haight's decay and do the same to that once robust district.

The Haight now found itself confronted by its most sophisticated antagonist: the new mayor of San Francisco, the brilliant dynamo Joseph L. Alioto. A bridge from San Francisco's old order to the new, Alioto was a strong defender of civil liberties and artistic freedom. But he regarded the youthful rebellion sweeping San Francisco as borderline anarchy. And he was prepared to destroy the Haight in order to save it. The struggle between Mayor Alioto and the street rebels of the Haight-Ashbury became an epic battle for the city's soul.

16

BENEVOLENT DICTATOR

J OE ALIOTO GREW up in North Beach in the 1920s and 1930s, when San Francisco was wracked by labor violence and civil turmoil. So the upheavals of the 1960s and 1970s—many of which shook the city during his eight-year mayoral reign, from 1968 to 1976—did not seem to undo him the way they did many political leaders during those years.

In 1926, when Alioto was ten years old, anarchists bombed the majestic Saints Peter and Paul Church on North Beach's Washington Square on four separate occasions, rattling the windows of his family's apartment a block away at 572 Filbert Street. To Italian Catholics in the neighborhood, the church—built in Romanesque Revival style, with twin cathedral-like spires and a massive Carrara marble altar—was a towering symbol of their faith and national heritage. But to labor militants, including the anarchists who targeted the church, the looming edifice stood for reaction and superstition. The Catholic Church was a mighty cross of gold that bent the shoulders and buckled the knees of San Francisco's immigrant working families.

During the Depression, San Francisco became even more violent a battleground. The Catholic Church and the Communist Party competed bitterly for the hearts and minds of San Francisco's Irish and Italian working class. After Harry Bridges's longshoremen's union closed down the waterfront and set off a general strike in 1934, Catholic officials condemned extremism on both sides of the bloody conflict and moved aggressively to mediate an end to it. When the eighty-three-day strike was finally settled, the church stepped up its efforts to counter labor militancy in San Francisco, organizing rival Catholic unions, staging mass rallies at Kezar Stadium, and sharing intelligence information about left-wing activists with the shipping companies, the right-wing American Legion, and the SFPD. Many of these church actions were carried out under the banner of Catholic Action, a global crusade to counter the rise of social democracy and Communism and inject traditional church values into civic life. The crusade was embraced by San Francisco archbishops Edward Hanna and John Mitty. And it was led by Sylvester Andriano, an Italian-born San Francisco attorney and a tireless soldier for the church.

Andriano, a Fascist sympathizer with close ties to both the Vatican and the Mussolini regime, was drafted to evangelize among San Francisco's Catholic youth. The Catholic activist told Archbishop Mitty that his goal was to steer young church members from "the evil influence of liberalism and laicism" and build in them "discipline, obedience, and respect for authority."

Among the young men caught up in Andriano's Catholic Action crusade was Joe Alioto, who—after graduating from Sacred Heart High School in the city—had enrolled at Saint. Mary's College in the East Bay, Andriano's alma mater. Alioto, a gifted debater, was assigned a prominent role in the church's social campaign, giving speeches against Communism, which he denounced as a "soulless philosophy [bent on] destroying Christianity, civilization, and all the sweet fruits which art and culture have bequeathed."

This would always be one side of Joe Alioto: Manichean, implacable, brutal in his opposition. You could see it on display when he became a lawyer—first as a young antitrust litigant in FDR's Justice Department, and later as a wealthy, corporate attorney for clients like the wine industry, rice growers' association, and Hollywood studios. And it was there in full fury—with his shiny, balding head radiating heat—as mayor of San Francisco, confronting the young militants in the Haight who screamed "Mussolini!" and "Pig!" at him, as well as the student radicals who shut down San Francisco State College during the longest campus strike in American history, which dragged on for five months in 1968 and 1969. Alioto's religious upbringing had instilled in him a deep sense of sin in the world, and also the will to combat it to the end.

But there was always another, big-hearted side to Alioto. He was a son of North Beach's "rich Italian peasant life," as he called it—a life centered on family, food, and the arts. Alioto came from Sicilian stock. His father, Giuseppe, sailed to America from Palermo, alone, at the age of ten. When he was eighteen, Giuseppe met his future wife, eleven-year-old Domenica Lazio, in the midst of the 1906 San Francisco earthquake. Fleeing the fiery chaos, young Giuseppe ran down to the wharf, where he saw Domenica's father shoving off the family boat into the bay. *"Salta, giovanotto, salta!"* yelled old man Lazio at Giuseppe, and the teenage boy did just that, leaping aboard the fishing boat, where he and the family floated for two days until the fires subsided. There were three Lazio daughters on board. By the time they docked, Giuseppe knew he would marry Domenica. His two brothers married the other two Lazio girls. The three young Alioto-Lazio couples moved into the same Filbert Street building, a different family in each of the three flats, and their children began arriving at regular intervals, including baby Joe in 1916.

The Aliotos and Lazios built the San Francisco fishing industry, opening wholesale fish companies and restaurants on the wharf. The families were not rich, but they were comfortable, even during the Depression. At home, the Aliotos dined on the sea's bounty—Dungeness crabs, clams, oysters, shrimp—and the red wine they made in their backyard, with the kids stomping the grapes, laughing and splattering themselves with plummy juice.

Prohibition turned many law-abiding San Franciscans into outlaw bootleggers. The Mafia was intertwined with Italian immigrant life in North Beach. "My father never forgot where he came from," said his daughter Angela, who later followed him into city politics. But this is one aspect of his North Beach background that Alioto never dwelled upon in public.

Joe Alioto grew up to become a symbol of Italian-American success in San Francisco, the political leader who represented the second-generation bridge to the American Dream. He might have risen even higher, to the nation's summit, but he could not untangle himself from his tribal past.

ALIOTO WAS A WEALTHY, fifty-one-year-old antitrust lawyer in 1967 when he was selected by a backroom group of city power brokers to replace Jack Shelley as mayor. He was the candidate of the downtown elite, but he was no shoo-in. Relatively unknown to the general public, he knew he had to win over the city's powerful unions—particularly Bridges's International Longshoremen's Workers Union (ILWU) and the Laborers' International Union of North America (LIUNA)—to rally voters. The political novice was smart enough to hire campaign staffers with strong labor ties, including press secretary Hadley Roff, a stocky, glad-handing former newspaperman who was chummy with longshoremen union officials Jimmy Herman and Dave Jenkins.

But Roff thought he had picked the wrong horse when he showed up at Alioto's elegant Presidio Terrace house one evening to accompany him to a make-or-break ILWU meeting, where the mayoral candidates were to vie for the union's endorsement. Alioto told Roff to pile into his car—to the press flack's horror, it was a shiny, brand-new Rolls-Royce.

As the two men cruised through a pea soup fog straight out of Dashiell Hammett, on their way to the Longshoremen's Hall building near Fisherman's Wharf, Roff stared glumly through the Rolls's window, which Alioto—unable to decipher his gleaming 747-like dashboard—could not defrost. Finally, Roff voiced his concerns to his new boss.

"Jesus, Joe, we're going to the ILWU!"—which, he did not need to remind Alioto, was San Francisco's toughest, most battle-scarred union. "And they'll see you in your pinstripes stepping out of a Rolls-Royce, for God's sake."

"Well, what do you wanna do—walk?" said Alioto, fumbling with the knobs on his dashboard.

Sure enough, when they pulled up in front of the building and Alioto emerged from his luxury car, he was greeted with a lusty chorus of boos from the rank-and-file stevedores filing into the building. The meeting hall inside was packed, and the air was filled with stale smoke and angry mutterings as the candidate made his way to the stage. Opposing him was Jack Morrison—a balding, bespectacled Adlai Stevenson–type—who spoke first. As the leading liberal tribune on the board of supervisors, Morrison was articulate, knew the city issues, and knew what mattered to the union. The crowd gave him a big round of applause.

Then Alioto got to his feet. He had served on the San Francisco Board of Education, but this was his first real campaign. He had never been in a position of courting hostile voters before. But he did know how to win over a jury. He quickly turned the cavernous room into his own chamber, and he took complete control of it.

"Can you guys hear me?" he yelled.

"Yeah!" came the booming response.

"Well, then, we don't need this microphone," he said. With that, Alioto jumped off the stage—looking more like a working stiff than an executive—and began prowling the hall.

"I had no idea what he was going to do," recalled Roff. "No talking points had been provided, no notes had been made. He talked for about fifteen minutes, walking down the center aisle. There must have been over a thousand people there that night, but he seemed to be talking to everybody like he was talking to them personally. He was talking to the proverbial jury. The next day, we had the endorsement of the most integrated, leftist union in town. And through the ILWU, he had access to the black community too. The number of blacks who got involved in the campaign was unheard of in San Francisco."

Putting together a formidable coalition of downtown business interests, organized labor, and black voters—along with his base in Italian North Beach—the centrist Alioto swept to victory on November 7, 1967, beating businessman Harold Dobbs on the right and Morrison on the left. Despite his political inexperience, Alioto proved to be a natural politician. He brimmed over with an infectious passion for the city of his birth, and he moved easily through crowds, touching and loving to be touched.

"Joe had an extraordinary physical electricity," Roff said, "and I say that not as an ex–press secretary who's strumming the usual violin, but as a fair observer. He was one of those guys who had an open heart to people. He had instant empathy. Once we were walking into the press club, and a couple of ambulance drivers were just coming out with somebody on a gurney, with the sheet pulled over him. The man's wife—or widow—was following behind. And Joe immediately rushed over to her and put his arms around her, so she wouldn't have to see her husband's lifeless form being clunked into the ambulance. Joe was crisp."

Shiny headed, bull shouldered, and encased in sleek suits, Alioto seemed as dynamic as a missile. His intensity was a tonic to the city after the fatigue of the Shelley administration. Charles McCabe, writing in the *Chronicle,* greeted Alioto's election as a welcome power shift to robust, Italian North Beach—away from the tired "Irish politicos who have been running this town for practically all of its history . . . It is an honored tradition to permit the Italian-Americans to take over when the harps have become bored, or otherwise rendered themselves useless."

Alioto started fast, promising to lift all boats with redevelopment dollars and federal aid. He also vowed to shower money on the arts and make San Francisco a world-class city. It was still a time when mayors could think big, and he wanted the whole city to share his gusto.

Alioto, the immigrant's son, brought a wider spectrum of people into the city's political establishment than ever before, appointing the first African American as deputy mayor and the first Latino and Chinese-American to the board of supervisors. He also paid off his big campaign debt to the unions that helped carry him into office, especially the Longshoremen's Union, giving their leaders key roles and advisory positions in his administration. Alioto named Harry Bridges to the port commission—a long overdue honor for San Francisco's legendary labor warrior, but a move that certainly sent the mayor's old Catholic Action mentor, Sylvester Andriano, twirling in his grave.

ALIOTO'S BOUNDLESS OPTIMISM ABOUT the city was immediately challenged by a series of stormy events. During his first year in office, rioters clashed repeatedly with police in the Haight and on the San Francisco State campus. A lecturer at State named George Murray, who belonged to the Black Panther Party, called publicly for the assassination of "slave-masters" Alioto and Police Chief Cahill. Three San Francisco policemen were shot after they pulled over a van filled with armed Panthers three blocks from the hall of justice. A police station in the Richmond district was bombed.

Throughout the tumultuous year, Alioto kept his cool. He affirmed protesters' right to express themselves. "Persons have the right to use the streets to say anything, no matter how unpopular," he announced in the midst of the Haight-Ashbury riots. But he just as firmly drew the line at violence. "There is no constitutional protection for throwing rocks and bottles," he pointed out.

Alioto strenuously avoided the provocative rhetoric of Governor Ronald Reagan, with his threats of a "bloodbath" and other extreme responses to youth protests. But while he tried not to demonize dissenters, the new mayor was not afraid to send the infamous tactical squad—a riot control unit whose black-helmeted, heavily padded members looked like storm troopers from an Orwellian nightmare—into the Haight or onto the San Francisco State campus when protests verged on chaos.

The mayor had a confidence about himself that allowed him to engage with protesters, even when they were enraged and foul mouthed. Some saw it as a cocky Il Duce swagger. But its true sources were his street-tough upbringing in North Beach, his finely honed skills as a Catholic school debater, and his deep love of San Francisco—which he assumed anyone of sound mind must share.

When Alioto heard about the assassination of Martin Luther King Jr. on April 4, 1968, he immediately called for a memorial service to be held on the steps of city hall the following day so that people from all over the city could grieve together in public. Police Chief Cahill was panic-stricken. A crowd could lead to a riot. But the mayor was unswerving.

The next afternoon, as thousands of people of all races crowded into the plaza in front of the city hall steps, a police official came rushing into Alioto's office. "There's a bunch of young kids from one of the high schools in Daly City, and they're all armed," he told the mayor.

"Well, invite the leaders up here right now. Right in my office," Alioto said.

When the four African-American students were ushered into the mayor's office, he told them, "I want you to march downstairs with me and sit on the platform." And that's what they did. Alioto and the students sat together on the makeshift stage on the city hall steps, next to a row of priests, ministers, rabbis, and a robed monk, as speaker after speaker offered prayers for King and pleas for the peace and racial harmony for which he had given his life.

The crowd, eerily silent, could see police snipers silhouetted on the roof of San Francisco Civic Auditorium across the plaza. The police had informed Alioto that there were many armed people in the crowd, just a few feet from the stage. Everyone seemed ready to explode. A firecracker could have set off a bloodbath. But at the end of the ceremony, people in the crowd joined hands and swayed in unison like a giant wave as they sang "We Shall Overcome." San Francisco did not blow up that day. It was one of the few major American cities that did not.

Alioto was a loyal mainstream Democrat, and he supported Lyndon Johnson's war in Vietnam. But he respected antiwar students' opinions, and he engaged in give-and-take sessions with them about the war and the limits of dissent. He arranged for KQED, the local public TV station, to host a seven-hour public forum for all sides in the San Francisco State strike to air their views. He also challenged Black Panthers leader Eldridge Cleaver to a debate on KQED. The ex-convict had become a literary sensation with his bestselling book *Soul on Ice*. And Cleaver used his badass, black-shades image, and his assaultive eloquence, to intimidate his critics into submission. But Alioto stood toe to toe with him on the studio stage.

"When everybody else was afraid to talk to this guy, I told him that I had seen tougher kids at Fisherman's Wharf," Alioto recalled years later. "He didn't bother me, and what the Black Panthers were doing was wrong. They were espousing violence, and violence was going to be met, no matter who was creating the violence."

As the 1968 Democratic Convention approached, Alioto's star was on the rise. Just a few months into his job as San Francisco's mayor, he was already being talked up as a potential running mate for presidential nominee Hubert Humphrey. He was an ethnic Catholic with impeccable labor and civil rights credentials, and he also brought a strong law-and-order reputation that could deflect Republican charges that the Democrats were soft on crime. But the vice presidential nomination went elsewhere, and the party, presiding over a disastrous war and torn by the violence-wracked Chicago convention, suffered a close defeat at the hands of Richard Nixon.

NIXON'S VICTORY IN NOVEMBER did not dampen Alioto's political ambitions. The following year, he began to position himself to challenge Ronald Reagan in the 1970 California gubernatorial race. San Francisco's tough-love mayor would have been Reagan's most formidable opponent. But in September 1969, *Look* magazine dropped a bombshell on Alioto that knocked him out of the governor's race and shadowed the rest of his political career. An investigative feature charged that Alioto was caught in a "web of relationships" with the Mafia that dated back to the days of the mayor's father, Giuseppe, who was partners with a San Francisco gangster in a Fisherman's Wharf restaurant. According to the magazine, Alioto himself had provided a variety of legal and financial services to mob figures. The most damaging charge against Alioto was that in 1965, as the board chairman of the newly opened First San Francisco Bank, he arranged a series of loans totaling $105,000 for a notorious Mafia executioner and ex-convict named Jimmy "the Weasel" Fratianno, who was trying to muscle his way into the California trucking business.

Alioto, fighting for his family's reputation and his political life, filed a $12.5 million libel suit against the magazine. The legal battle consumed nearly a decade of his life. He finally won, but it was a pyrrhic victory. His political career was finished, and his reputation carried the faint marks of a stain until his dying days. Alioto later claimed that he was a political victim of the conniving Nixon administration, which saw the mayor as a rising threat following his star turn at the Democratic Convention. Alioto said he obtained federal documents under the Freedom of Information Act showing that the Mafia allegations were leaked to *Look* by Nixon officials.

But the story grew complicated in 1981 when Mafia chronicler Ovid Demaris published Fratianno's life story, *The Last Mafioso*. In the book, the mobster declared that the *Look* exposé was "basically accurate." Alioto was not "a made guy," Fratianno told Demaris, but in the gangster's view, he "had impeccable credentials." The mobster described how he would drop into Alioto's offices at 111 Sutter Street—unannounced, to avoid FBI surveillance—where the two men would discuss various business schemes to enrich themselves.

The Weasel's confessions, which were published while he was in the federal witness protection program, became a bestseller. Alioto later dismissed him as a "notorious stool pigeon . . . who was paid more for being a stool pigeon than for any criminal activities he engaged in." But this time Alioto chose not to sue.

After the *Look* article exploded, Joe Alioto never seemed to bring the same sharp focus to his job as mayor. Throughout his life, he had wrestled with theological questions about good and evil. Now that he was accused of sin, he became obsessed with absolving himself. The strenuous attention that he devoted to his libel case went beyond the legal requirements; he was a man on a spiritual crusade to define himself.

WHILE THE MAYOR WAS distracted by his legal mission and his lingering political ambitions, his city grew more feral. The Haight, in particular—with its hard drugs, crime, and decay—was becoming a no-man's-land. Alioto's responses to the city's growing problems became less imaginative. With protesters, he began using the iron fist more than the velvet glove.

One day Alioto summoned an energetic Fillmore community activist to his office. The day before, the activist had organized a sit-in occupation of the mayor's office. Now, as he walked into the mayor's suite, he was greeted warmly by Alioto, who was flanked by two policemen.

"I like your style," said Alioto. "Do you want to come work for me?"

"No," the activist replied—his job was on the streets.

"Oh, come on, you can do a lot for those kids in the Fillmore by working for me," Alioto pressed. "You're a very bright person."

The community organizer held his ground.

"You sure?" asked Alioto, giving it one last shot. He was sure.

Alioto immediately had the organizer thrown in jail, where he spent the next ninety days for his illegal takeover of the mayor's office.

Early in his administration, Alioto attempted a balancing act with protesters, mixing force with reason. But as the civil disturbances spread, he grew more exasperated, and he gave the SFPD's fearsome tactical squad full rein to run riot, chasing down student protesters at

San Francisco State and Haight hippies and beating them at will. When riot cops roughed up Terry Hallinan, the lawyer for the SF State demonstrators, putting a gash in his head that required sixteen stitches, Alioto declared that the young attorney got what he deserved. After the Hallinans threatened to drag the mayor into court, he wisely made a conciliatory gesture toward the famously combative family, saying that he had "respect and admiration" for paterfamilias Vincent and "for the spirit of the entire family."

But Alioto continued to make war on the young settlers in the Haight, vowing that "a few thugs and malcontents are not going to turn the Haight-Ashbury into a war zone." Actually, the mayor's police department was doing exactly that. One evening, the tac squad even laid siege to the Free Clinic when a group of badly battered young longhairs sought sanctuary there. The police unit—high on its own testosterone and unhinged authority—surrounded the Clayton Street building, smashing the front door and manhandling clinic staff.

As far as Alioto was concerned, the Haight-Ashbury was enemy territory. And he was intent on occupying it. Neighborhood activists were convinced that he wanted to go further. They believed that city hall was allowing the district to sink deeper into decay, so that redevelopment officials could send in the bulldozers and erase it from the map, as they had done with the Fillmore.

The mayor took the first step toward remaking Hippieville in fall 1970, when he appointed a Mayor's Committee to Restore the Haight-Ashbury, composed of the same business, labor, clergy, and academic types who had given their blessing to the leveling of the Fillmore neighborhood. The mayor boldly decided to venture into the Haight to unveil the committee, sweeping into the Polytechnic High School auditorium across from Kezar Stadium one evening in October flanked by twenty-seven police bodyguards.

Alioto assured the hostile audience that city hall would not "shove anything down your throats." The redevelopment project would be a "grassroots" enterprise, he declared. But Haight activists—some of whom were refugees from the blasted Fillmore—had heard that before. "You wouldn't know a grassroot if you saw it, pig!" screamed one heckler.

The mayor stood on stage, peering into the crowd of some five hundred people, as the jeers and catcalls washed over him. "Motherfucker!"

"Thief!" "Mafioso!" That latter dagger found his soft spot. But he kept standing there in the sharp glare of the TV lights, with his jaw clenched and his eyes flashing. He was the one in control. His opponents seemed crazed, disorganized. At one point, a group of his loudest hecklers stormed out of the public meeting, a staged walkout that only left Alioto in more command of the battlefield.

A reporter from *Good Times* took note of Alioto's frozen smile, his self-confidence, his empty promises. "Patronizing prick," thought the underground journalist. Everyone knew where this was going to end: with the neighborhood razed, and high-rise condominiums and office buildings replacing the old Victorians. With the colorful, ragtag circus on the street replaced by white-collar commuters.

Only it didn't. Not this time.

17

LOVE'S LAST STAND

THE HAIGHT WAS a war zone by the time that Robert McCarthy found his way there on Christmas Eve 1969. But he had seen worse. McCarthy had served in Vietnam as a gunner's mate on a patrol boat on the upper Mekong River, near Cambodia. "It was the whole *Apocalpyse Now* experience," he said many years later. "I was terrified the whole time."

McCarthy lost a number of mates there. "And I killed a lot of people. I never said that until recently."

When McCarthy returned to the United States, he was stationed on Treasure Island in the San Francisco Bay. He tried faking mental illness to get a medical discharge, but it wasn't that far from the truth. One time, while way too high on white lightning acid, he considered suicide. "The reality was setting in, and it felt good to have a gun," he recalled. The truly crazy ones at Treasure Island were the guys who clutched pouches they had made from the scrotums of dead Vietnamese. The navy patched up their heads and sent them back into action.

The Haight beckoned to McCarthy from across the choppy, cold waters of the bay. On Christmas Eve, he went strolling in the hippie haven that he had read about years before in *Life* magazine. He wasn't looking for sex but for "mystical camaraderie." It was a harder connection to find in those days. As he walked down Haight Street, some ratty-looking speed freaks were hanging out in front of him, hassling anyone who went by. When a hooker passed them, the jitterbugs grabbed at her, trying to pull her into their doorway. She broke away, and the freaks started to go after her. But the navy man, high on LSD, fixed them with a look of death, and they backed off the woman. After Vietnam, it was a look that came naturally to McCarthy, and it was only enhanced by the acid.

Twenty yards past the meth head toll bridge, McCarthy heard a loud scuffle behind him and then the sharp crack of a gunshot. As he spun around, a young man stumbled past him, blurting out, "My God, they shot me!" The kid, who had ventured into the Haight from an outlying suburb to score some drugs, had been shot through the thigh. Snapping into action, McCarthy threw him over his shoulder and carried him to the corner, where his frantic girlfriend was waiting in her father's T-Bird.

McCarthy's introduction to the Haight started out as pure misery, but then he got lucky. He stumbled upon a store called the Ever Lovin' Trading Post, where a swarm of young men and women were caught up in the Christmas Eve mood of celebration, singing and dancing and exuding good cheer. He began talking with them. They had long, flowing hair, and all of them—men and women alike—looked beautiful to McCarthy. Even though he was trying to hide where he was from, they took one look at him and knew he was military. But they received him warmly. "They understood," recalled McCarthy. "They knew that I was looking . . . for . . . it."

McCarthy spent that night in a dilapidated house in the Haight—"no vibes, no love, just junkies crashing around." On Christmas morning, he woke up and went back out on the streets, still searching. He ran into Steve Kever, one of the young men he had talked to the day before at the Ever Lovin' Trading Post. Kever had a strong, compact body, and with his long blond hair and beard, he looked like Thor. "I just wanted to touch that: not his hair, his vibe. Steve had an enormous, open heart." Kever asked the sailor if he had found what he was looking for. He said no. So Kever invited McCarthy for Christmas dinner at his communal house that evening.

When he showed up at 1915 Oak Street, headquarters of the Good Earth commune, McCarthy instantly felt he was stepping into his dream of what the Haight was supposed to be. The ornate, three-story Victorian was beautifully kept, with shiny, oiled wooden floors and staircase, and heavy velvet curtains. The high-ceiling dining room was dominated by a huge table that looked like it was constructed of railroad ties that had been bolted together. The table was filled with steaming platters of food—roasts, winter vegetables, mashed potatoes—and the room was spilling over with people. Men, women, babies of all races—white, black, brown, yellow, red. McCarthy just stood there quietly in the midst of the festive chaos and took it all in. He knew that he had found home.

McCarthy began spending all his free weekends at the Good Earth commune. And when he was finally discharged from the navy on October 12, 1970, there was a blue hippie bus filled with his Good Earth mates waiting for him outside the Treasure Island Naval Base. As he left the base for the last time, McCarthy flung off his white cap and the rest of his uniform piece by piece. By the time the sailor reached the bus, he would recall, he was "butt-fucking naked." Climbing aboard, he was handed a fat joint by a commune member called Kentucky Jim. "It was the beginning and the end," said the Vietnam veteran. Robert McCarthy was gone: "killed in Vietnam." From that point on, he would be Mouseman, a nickname from his childhood days in Chicago.

The Good Earth commune was a central part of the second wave of Haight-Ashbury's hippie settlement. The commune was founded in 1968 by Kever and a fellow ex-convict named Cyril Isaacs, whom he had met in Susanville State Prison, where Kever served four and a half years for armed robbery. The idea came to Kever while he was on parole and working on the rapid-transit tunnel that was being constructed under the bay. He and his ex-con friends would pool their resources and live communally in the Haight. At first it was just a small group of Kever's and Isaacs's friends and the women who loved them. But Good Earth rapidly grew until it was a sprawling network of more than a half dozen houses in the Haight and a loose, ever-changing membership that was estimated at its height to number over seven hundred people.

The Good Earth communards took up where the Diggers left off, but in many ways they were tougher and more resilient. The core group within the commune were life-hardened young men and women— ex-cons, Vietnam veterans, streetwise runaways—who knew how to survive. They called themselves a church and claimed pot as their sacrament, and they preached the usual peace and love philosophy. Still, they were no pushovers. They loved their neighborhood, but they knew it was turning into a jungle, with violent predators and vicious cops around every corner. Good Earth made it widely known that it was prepared to defend its turf.

At first this self-defense took the form of simply escorting female commune members at night from house to house through the Haight's mean streets. But then it became a campaign to clean up the streets themselves. By 1970, the neighborhood was swimming with heroin and speed. A scruffy crew of junkies had moved into a boarded-up house directly across from the Good Earth house at 409 Cole Street. The commune decided that they had to go. Calling the police was not considered an option, since they would probably take the opportunity to raid the Good Earth house too. Besides, the police had closed down nearby Park Station and had apparently abandoned the Haight-Ashbury bestiary to the reddest in tooth and claw. So one day, a group of the commune's tougher members, including Mouseman/McCarthy, simply paid the junkies a visit and convinced them to leave. Good Earth took over the house, fixed it up, and moved in its own members.

Heroin dealers still roamed the neighborhood as if they owned it. But Good Earth began to run them out too. One afternoon, a smack pusher named Rico came roaring down the street in his flashy car, nearly running over several commune members, including Kever. The Good Earth crew loudly let the dealer know what they thought of him. Ten minutes later, Rico returned and stepped out of his car with a gun. "What are you going to do now?" he said. Kever and several other commune members began walking straight at him.

"They had no fear. Rico freaked out and raced away," said Will "Wild Bill" Huston, a commune member who was there that day. Kever and his posse knew they had backup. Huston—who had grown up in a Missouri Bible-thumping family and had served briefly in the air force—was stationed on the roof of the Good Earth house with a rifle. "I was ready to shoot if necessary," he recalled. "I knew how to use a rifle from my military and hillbilly background." Not long afterward, Rico moved out of the Haight, never to be seen again.

On another occasion, "Sag" Darel Ferguson and "Leo" Ron—known, like many Good Earth members, by their astrological nicknames—witnessed a gangster roughing up his girlfriend on the street. "We stepped in," said Ferguson. "We didn't tolerate that kind of behavior. You beat a girl, and you're going to pay for it."

The thug aimed a shotgun at the Good Earth men. "Big mistake," said Ferguson, who had learned how to handle himself on the streets after being kicked out of his family's house when he was sixteen. "We chased him like lightning down Haight Street, and he kept pointing it at me like he was going to shoot me. When we caught him, we smashed him over the head with the gun and beat the hell out of him, then dumped him in a trash can and left him for dead."

Good Earth became a solid community bulwark in a neighborhood battered by crime and decay and deserted by city authorities. Some longtime residents, like the Free Clinic's Dr. David Smith, credited the commune with saving the Haight. Smith said he knew of no other urban neighborhood that had been rescued this way once the scourge of heroin had taken hold on its streets. "Good Earth won, they beat the heroin dealers, because they were a warrior tribe," marveled Haight-Ashbury activist Calvin Welch. "They knew how to fight."

GOOD EARTH'S BIGGEST FIGHT turned out to be with Mayor Joe Alioto, whom commune leaders accused of letting the Haight decay so that he could bulldoze it and turn it over to his real estate cronies. "It was the same old story," said Larry "The Hat" Lautzker, a savvy Brooklyn-born commune member. "The government basically targets a neighborhood, they pull out the police and let the bad drugs flood the streets, they let crime go rampant, they let abandoned houses fall apart, they let the neighborhood go to hell—and then the redevelopers come in."

The commune took the lead in resisting city hall's redevelopment plans for the Haight. It was Good Earth members who had led the heckling and walkout when Alioto showed up at Polytechnic High in 1970 to announce his new citizens' committee to "restore the Haight-Ashbury." Later they infiltrated the committee and convinced it to disband. In the Fillmore, this kind of grassroots resistance had sprung up too late to save the neighborhood. But because of troublemakers like the Good Earth's "heavy hippies," this time the redevelopment juggernaut hit a wall.

Alioto was not happy with the commune's pesky interference. "He gave us thirty days to get our hairy asses out of town," recalled Mouseman. When Good Earth didn't budge, the mayor unleashed the police department on the commune, subjecting the tenacious hippies to a withering harassment campaign that would go on throughout the early 1970s. Commune members were stopped on the streets, shoved against the wall, and taken into custody on the slimmest charges. The Ever Lovin' Trading Post, the Good Earth store on Haight Street, was padlocked by the city. The commune's old vehicles were pulled over and ticketed.

The city crackdown on Good Earth culminated one evening in January 1971, when plainclothes SFPD narcotics officers raided the Oak Street house, arresting twenty-three people on charges of possessing marijuana, hashish, and LSD. Women were dragged onto the streets, and babies were torn from their arms. Men were roughed up, and some were smacked with billy clubs. The cops confiscated Good Earth property and over $1,200 in rent money from the commune treasury during the raid. They later returned the money, but by then, Good Earth members had been evicted from one of their houses for nonpayment of rent.

Good Earth leaders, increasingly frustrated by the police harassment, turned their arraignment a week and a half later into a near riot. As helmeted police tightly gripped their batons in the courtroom, Steve Kever and other commune leaders traded barbed comments with the presiding municipal court judge. Kever's heated exchange with the judge, which resulted in multiple contempt citations and jail sentences, began with this frank remark: "Fuck the court. You're a bastard and pig and fucker."

It spiraled downward from there.

Good Earth members briefly considered turning to armed resistance against the police brutality. But, they decided, that's not who they were. Instead of going down the violent path of the Weather Underground, the Black Panthers, and other armed groups on the radical left, Good Earth found a good lawyer. His name was Tony Serra, and with his long Native American–looking hair, pirate's gold tooth, and stoner aura, he seemed every bit the spacey hippie that the Good Earth hard hippies disdained. But when it came to the legal battlefield, Tony Serra was a brilliant warrior.

Serra, a San Francisco native, grew up in the outer Sunset district in an artistic, blue-collar family that also produced a younger brother, Richard, who would become a world-renowned sculptor. Their father, an immigrant from Mallorca, Spain, made jelly beans. Their mother, a Russian-Jewish bohemian aesthete, later killed herself, walking straight into the ocean at the end of Taraval Street, where she had taken her boys to the beach when they were growing up. Serra majored in philosophy at Stanford and threw himself into combative sports, joining the boxing and football teams. After graduating from law school in 1962, he tried to avoid his professional destiny, bumming around Morocco and South America and writing bad poetry.

It was Vincent Hallinan who convinced him that he had chosen the right profession. Two weeks after beginning his career as a criminal law-yer, Serra was walking past a courtroom in city hall, when the doors flew open and two men came spilling out like brawlers in a gold rush saloon. One man had the other man—a distinguished, corporate attorney type—by the throat. He slammed the unfortunate gentleman against the wall in the hallway and popped him in the mouth with a right jab.

"Who's that?" young Serra asked, staring at the pugilist wide-eyed.

"Oh, that's one of the best lawyers in town," a face in the crowd told him. "That's Vincent Hallinan."

"I'm going to like this profession," Serra thought to himself.

He brought Hallinan's combative style and poetic oratory to the courtroom on behalf of his Good Earth clients. The Haight-Ashbury communards grew fond of their legal champion, as he repeatedly suc-ceeded in getting charges against commune members thrown out of court. After the Oak Street raid, they hatched a plan with Serra to fight back against Alioto on his own turf. Good Earth would challenge the incumbent mayor in his November 1971 reelection bid, running none other than the commune's attorney on its "Platypus Party" ticket.

Alioto faced a typically colorful field of San Francisco opponents in his race for a second term, including one serious challenger: Dianne Feinstein, the ambitious president of the board of supervisors, who ran against the incumbent from the left, attacking him for his opposi-tion to school busing and courting the gay vote. But Alioto succeeded in slapping the limousine liberal label on Feinstein, who resembled a prim Snow White and was squired around town to political events in a Rolls-Royce. Once Feinstein was marginalized, the race became more entertainment than politics. Scott Newhall, the *Chronicle's* mischievous former editor, injected a weirdly honest and even literary note into the campaign when he entered the race. But the real fun in the campaign came from Tony Serra.

Good Earth campaign workers scurried around the city, tacking up Serra posters and distributing the Platypus Party's unique platform, which called for abolishing victimless crimes such as drug possession, prostitution, and all consensual sex acts, and turning San Francisco into a city-state sanctuary against the war and the draft. The party also envisioned transforming San Francisco into an eco-friendly urban model, banning cars from the downtown area and replacing paved streets with green spaces.

Good Earth held a rock 'n' roll rally outside city hall to promote its candidate, who was photographed dancing exuberantly to the music, with one hand waving free. Commune members provided security at the campaign events, decked out in long, tie-dyed underwear. The rock fund-raisers staged by the Serra campaign failed to fill the candidate's coffers, but he shrugged it off. "I've always been nonmaterialistic, and I don't give a damn," Serra told the alternative press. "Also, I represent a lot of dope dealers, and they lay many thousands of dollars on me."

Serra had no illusions of knocking off Joe Alioto in the race. "I don't expect to win. But before I entered the race, I consulted the I Ching. The Ching referred to the planting of a seed—all I want to do is to make my ideas known." And Platypus Party ideas about greening the city and decriminalizing consensual sexual behavior would indeed seep into San Francisco's political mainstream a few years later.

After Alioto was reelected, he escalated his war on Good Earth. In May 1972, the SFPD launched its biggest raid on the commune, bursting into several Good Earth houses in the Haight in a predawn raid and sweeping off eighty-seven people to jail. Dan "Spud" Moore, a Vietnam vet from Boston, opened the Cole Street door when he heard the police pounding. "I just stood there; I thought we had nothing to fear. Little did I know." A long-haired narcotics cop came rushing into the house with a small army behind him, yelling, "Let's get these hippies!" He began to beat up Moore, breaking one of his front teeth.

Serra again quickly got the charges dismissed against the incarcerated commune members. But when they returned home, they discovered that the cops had trashed their living quarters, smashing guitars and other possessions and overturning furniture. Steve Kever and Tony

Serra held a press conference to denounce the police mayhem and filed suit against the city for $240,000 in damages. Good Earth leaders also rounded up support from community organizations such as the local Catholic Social Services, which complained in a letter to Police Chief Al Nelder about the raiders' "brutality" and "wanton" destruction of property.

Good Earth's pressure campaign put Alioto and the police department on the defensive. One day Supervisor Feinstein and Richard Hongisto, the city's maverick sheriff, even showed up at the Cole Street house to inspect the damage from the raid. Wild Bill Huston was still in bed as the political dignitaries were escorted through the house. Hearing a commotion outside his door, a stark naked Wild Bill jumped up from bed and flung open the door to see what was going on, just as the starched and coiffed Feinstein went walking by. "Sorry you had to see that," Wild Bill later told Feinstein, who stayed for the commune's spaghetti dinner. "She said it was fine. She even chipped in a couple bucks for beer when we passed the hat," he recalled. "I thought that was cool."

DESPITE THE UNRELENTING POLICE harassment, Good Earth continued to thrive. The commune was built loosely around Kever's charismatic but reluctant leadership. "I never liked to call myself a leader; it was all somewhat anarchistic," Kever recalled. And yet the commune developed a strong social code and work ethic that allowed it to weather police aggression and neighborhood upheavals, while absorbing a steady influx of new members from all over the country. Everyone was expected to share household cooking and cleaning duties, while also working to help support the commune. Good Earth ran a trucking business, mechanics shop, clothes store, crafts business, recycling operation, day care center, and house-painting crew. The commune even had its own house band, Osceola, that sometimes featured ex-Monkee Peter Tork.

"The goal was to do everything ourselves," said Ferguson. "We thought, 'Screw the business world. We have to get off the grid, unplug from Babylon.'"

"I was always trying to disprove the 'lazy hippie' epithet," said Spud Moore, who took pride in his work with the paint crew, sprucing up dozens of old Victorians in the Haight. "Everybody in Good Earth had some type of skill, especially the ex-navy guys, who knew machinery, carpentry, electricity. If you didn't work hard, you'd be quickly ostracized, and you got the message. We'd call those people 'energy rip-offs.'"

Sometimes Moore's work brought unexpected benefits. When the Jefferson Airplane hired the Good Earth crew to paint their Fulton Street mansion, Moore couldn't believe his good fortune. After coming home from Vietnam, he had bought all the Airplane albums and listened to them in constant rotation. The work was hard: the crew had to strip years of paint from the mansion's big Greek columns with butane torches, sand them down, and restore the beautiful redwood underneath. But Moore still found it a joy to show up every day. "While we worked, we could hear the Airplane rehearsing inside. I thought, 'Here I am listening to Marty Balin's voice soaring out the windows.' It was something I could only dream of back in Boston."

One of Moore's fellow housepainters discovered another perk to the job. While working on the scaffold, he looked into bassist Jack Casady's second floor bedroom window and spied a big bag of weed. Climbing through the window, he helped himself to the stash.

But the work itself was surprisingly rewarding at Good Earth. "Didn't matter how laborious it was—garbage or recycling runs, moving furniture, painting, etcetera—we were doing it for ourselves," said Huston. "That in itself was a gas, and to do it with the sense of love and loyalty to one another made it much more special. Self-sufficiency running at full speed."

Despite all the hard work, Good Earth was far from a drone culture. Everyone was young, healthy, and fun loving. And all the houses were charged with sexual electricity. While sex was readily available, predatory behavior was not allowed. "Relations between the sexes were incredibly equal," said Dana Jaffe, a beautiful, self-possessed fourteen-year-old runaway who became Steve Kever's lover. "Back then, men really felt like brothers. The guys were tough—after all, some of them came out of prison, some out of the military. But there were not a lot of male conflicts and power games. It felt like a different type of society, where everything seemed possible."

The Good Earth "hippie wonderland," as one member called it, seemed robust enough to survive the 1970s, the graveyard of the 1960s.

But in the end, it was hard drugs—what else?—that brought down the saviors of the Haight.

DRUGS WERE ALWAYS CENTRAL to Good Earth's operation, since most of the commune's revenue came from dealing weed and acid. But in the early years, Good Earth banned members from using, let alone selling, anything harder. Commune members knew that smack had almost killed the community, and they were mortal enemies of the junk trade. But by 1974, cocaine was creeping into San Francisco. Good Earth vigorously debated whether "nose candy" was a hard or soft drug, but in the end, the commune's leadership made a fateful decision. "We finally decided it was a soft drug," said Jaffe.

It was a decision that she, as well as Kever, would come to deeply regret. "Drugs and money were our downfall," she said. "We became very self-indulgent; we got seduced by all the flash. There was suddenly huge amounts of money from dealing coke, and we had access to a kind of lifestyle that people can only dream of. We had been a hard-working hippie commune, and suddenly people were giving you their flashy cars when they got tired of them because they wanted something flashier."

As coke suppliers for the city's rich and famous, Good Earth's royal couple were suddenly in demand, and Kever and Jaffe began showing up at the mansions of San Francisco luminaries like celebrity lawyer Melvin Belli. Early one morning, a gaggle of Good Earthers ended up at Pam Pam's, a downtown diner favored by the late-night drug crowd. They noticed David Bowie standing in line, and one communard invited Ziggy Stardust outside for a toot, delicately putting a spoon to each one of the rock star's nostrils.

Even the grease monkeys in the Good Earth garage started snorting the stuff, and when they did, they noticed that lots of girls from the neighborhood started swarming them. "Sex turned from something intimate, from simply enjoying each other, to sex for drugs," said Huston.

One night in 1974, at an Oak Street house party, a pack of beautiful young women whom no one in the commune had ever seen before came strutting through the front door. The beauties headed straight for the long communal dining table, where a crowd was gathering around a man as he cut up generous lines of white powder on a big mirror. The glamour girls couldn't wait their turn—suddenly they began crawling over people to get to the coke. "They were like animals," said Huston. "I said to myself, 'Jesus, this is not good.'"

Along with the coke riches came even more paranoia. Even in the weed-and-acid days, there was always tension as Good Earth braced for the next raid. Commune members practiced their own version of fire drills in preparation for the police sweeps. Some of those who were assigned to the commune's pot store, which operated in a safe house behind several heavily bolted doors, cracked under the psychological pressure and asked to be reassigned. But the cocaine racket turned up the heat higher than ever. Good Earth members began walking around with guns and looking over their shoulders.

"People were afraid, burned out," said commune member Chris Wickman. "We were always fighting the cops, fighting evictions, fighting the utility companies by pouring concrete over our meters. And we were fighting more and more with each other. The Good Earth scene went from being a very mellow, gentle vibe to a hard, reality-based scene. It all had to do with drugs and money."

Wickman and other commune members began leaving the city for a more pastoral life in Oregon. Those who stayed behind in the San Francisco drug business, like Kever and Jaffe, faced a grimmer journey. Kever got caught in a US Drug Enforcement Agency coke bust in 1976 and served seventeen months in federal prison. After he was released, he became addicted to crack cocaine, and his life skidded downward until, years later, he ended up in living in a tent city in Florida. "It was disgusting," he said. "I hated to even take a shower there." He finally picked himself up, put himself through community college, graduating in 2008 on his seventieth birthday, and becoming a social worker and activist for the homeless.

Jaffe left Good Earth when she was twenty and got deeper into the cocaine trade. She was arrested for trafficking in Colombia, spending six months in prison there and another year under house arrest. She too would finally turn her life around, winding up as an executive chef at a four-star hotel in the Napa Valley wine country. And like Kever, whom she would always consider the love of her life, she looked back at the Good Earth days with a full heart.

"We saved the Haight," she reflected. "We helped create San Francisco values. We had, and still have, real convictions. We weren't nearly as laid back as we're pictured in Hollywood movies and the media. Nothing in popular culture has captured the reality of our experience. We were trying to save the world."

Kever, Jaffe, and many others from the scattered Good Earth tribe found one another decades later in an online forum, brimming over with feelings for their youthful selves. But before they could reach that serene place in their lives, they—and the utopian city they fought for—had to go into "free fall," as Jaffe put it. The freakish and the cruel, the desperate and the cracked—all of San Francisco's darker impulses began to flourish when the final community bulwarks like Good Earth came flying apart. After these neighborhood levees crumbled, anything was possible. *The blood-dimmed tide was loosed, and everywhere the ceremony of innocence was drowned.*

18

DUNGEONS AND DRAGONS

B Y THE EARLY 1970s, the revolution was over in America, and San Francisco—its fallen capital—staggered on the edge of chaos. The city was overrun with false prophets and savage messiahs, as well as double agents and police informers. Strange creeds and mysterious leaders developed overnight followings. Inexplicable communiqués were issued from the underground. The sacraments of blood and guns replaced peace and love.

A wave of bombings rocked the city, striking corporate offices, supermarkets, electrical plants, and neighborhood police stations. The front of Mayor Alioto's house was torn open by an explosive device hidden inside a box of See's candy left on his family's front steps. The anarchy Alioto had witnessed growing up in North Beach in the 1920s was back in full force.

The leading players in the bombing craze called themselves the New World Liberation Front (NWLF), and the press speculated about how many secret cells and combatants were involved. One scholarly radical journal heralded the NWLF as "the most tactically advanced guerilla group in the United States" and gushed that "its record of success . . . verges on the astonishing," with nearly fifty bombings to its credit. The underground group even boasted its own magazine, *The Urban Guerrilla* (*TUG*), which featured esoteric debates about Maoism and armed struggle, and offended gays and feminists with its reactionary positions on sexual liberation.

But the New World army turned out to be nothing more than a front after all—the work of one mad bomber and his aboveground PR man. The bomber finally fell into the hands of the law after he murdered his wife in the Santa Cruz mountains. "They believed in reincarnation, and she wanted to be reborn, so he chopped off her head with an axe," explained Tony Serra, who put his services at the bomber's disposal. His defense? Insanity, what else? But it didn't work. The mad bomber died in prison.

There was only so much a lawyer could do, even a brilliant one like Serra. By then, heroic clients were in short supply. Instead there were axe murderers, terrorists, and drug dealers.

As the broader movements for peace and social justice fell into disarray, the left-wing action in the Bay Area shifted to the dark burrows of prison reform. In the early 1970s, the California penal empire had only a fraction of the staggering inmate population—170,000 souls—it has today. But it was already on its way to becoming the nation's most dysfunctional prison system, bloated by ever more draconian sentencing laws and filled with grotesquely disproportionate numbers of black and brown men. California maximum-security dungeons like San Quentin, Folsom, and Soledad were cauldrons of prisoner rage and official brutality.

It was George Jackson who came to symbolize the desperate plight of California's black prison population. Arrested at eighteen for a gas station robbery that netted $70, he spent his entire adult life behind bars: one more intelligent young black man whom the state of California could find no other use for. Jackson ensured his lifelong incarceration when he got involved in militant prison politics. As Bob Dylan, one of the many artistic and intellectual figures who came to celebrate Jackson, later sang, "He wouldn't take shit from no one, he wouldn't bow down or kneel." Jackson saw the prison system, with its cruel conditions and forced labor programs, as a modern form of American slavery. And he refused to be a broken-back field mule.

In January 1970, Jackson and two other black Soledad inmates were charged with murdering a prison guard—a vengeance killing, authorities claimed, for the deaths of three other black prisoners who had been cut down by gunfire from a guard tower. Held in solitary confinement for twenty-three hours a day as they awaited trial, Jackson and his codefendants became internationally renowned as the Soledad Brothers. While in the hole, Jackson studied Marxist theory and black liberation philosophy, and wrote a steady flow of impassioned letters about race, injustice, and prison life that were later collected into two bestselling books, *Soledad Brother* and *Blood in My Eye*.

Jackson's life now seemed on some flaming trajectory with a preordained fiery finale. In August, his seventeen-year-old brother, Jonathan—who had grown up with the legend of his brother but not his brother—burst into a Marin County courthouse, brandishing an automatic weapon. He freed three prisoners in the courtroom and took several hostages, including the judge, who was led outside with a sawed-off shotgun taped to his neck. The younger Jackson hoped to use the hostages to force the release of his brother. But as the group tried to escape from the court building in a county van, the vehicle came under a massive hail of fire from San Quentin guards and other lawmen, who clearly had no regard for the lives of anyone in the van, including the judge. Jonathan Jackson and two of the escaping prisoners were killed, as well as the judge, whose head was blown off when the shotgun discharged.

A year later, just days before he was to go on trial, George Jackson met his own violent end when he was shot down by San Quentin guards during what prison officials claimed was an attempted escape, but which Jackson supporters such as French writer Jean Genet declared "a political assassination." Jackson's death sparked a wave of furious protests and bombings in the Bay Area, and instantly wreathed him in a romantic glow. Black intellectual, unbending political prisoner, resistance fighter. Jackson became the model for would-be revolutionaries inside and outside of California's barbed-wire empire. And he became a ghostly nightmare for state law enforcement officials, who feared that his Stagger Lee Marxism would inflame the poor, black, and angry everywhere.

Bay Area radicals began looking to rally around other eloquent black prophets in California's penal hellholes. Black prisoners were championed by many on the left as the bleeding edge of the revolution. Meanwhile, police and intelligence agencies began grooming counterfeit leaders and informers to embed inside the volatile world of the prisoner rights struggle.

The FBI had been targeting a broad range of antiwar, civil rights, and black power groups throughout the 1960s and early 1970s with its counterintelligence program, Cointelpro, infiltrating the groups and using a variety of subversive measures to disrupt them. At the extreme end, this even included assassination. A charismatic, young Black Panthers leader named Fred Hampton was murdered in his bed in 1969 by Chicago police connected to Cointelpro, and Los Angeles Black Panthers Bunchy Carter and John Huggins were shot down on the UCLA campus in 1969 by members of the rival United Slaves (US) organization, a murky black nationalist group run by Ron Karenga. The FBI had incited the murderous hostilities between Karenga's group and the Panthers, and, according to one FBI informant, the US assassins were even ferried from the scene of the crime by the bureau. It was Karenga, who ruled his turf with a mixture of Afrocentrist mumbo jumbo and thuggish violence, who went on to give black America Kwanzaa. He created the holiday after being released from California prison in 1975, after serving four years for stripping and torturing two women he accused of trying to poison him with magical crystals.

FBI director J. Edgar Hoover and his secret police clearly understood the dark powers of subversion. And his agency was not alone. In 1967 the FBI was joined in its clandestine war against American activism and radicalism by the CIA, which launched a nefarious, Bondian-sounding program called Operation Chaos. A direct violation of the CIA's charter, which forbids the spy organization from engaging in domestic activities, Operation Chaos, among other things, sought to enlist "assets" in the black movement for purposes that were left unspecified. Finally, the state of California also ran its own intelligence operation aimed at black militants, prison rights crusaders, and other activists, as did the police departments in Los Angeles and other cities.

THIS WAS THE CHURNING froth of black rage and counterrevolutionary cunning from which slithered the Symbionese Liberation Army in late 1973. The group would turn San Francisco and Berkeley upside down and hijack headlines around the globe for more than two years, pitting left-wing groups against one another, tarring the prison reform movement, and generally sucking air and light out of the progressive scene.

The fantastical group, which invented a completely imaginary world of armed revolution, seemed the hideous dream child of those overheated Berkeley communes and Washington counterintelligence offices, which were the only places where something like the SLA made sense. The true symbiosis in the Symbionese Liberation Army was not between all "the oppressed peoples" it claimed to be fighting for, but between the SLA and the police agencies that hunted it.

The SLA was born in the Black Cultural Association (BCA), a behavior modification program masquerading as an African-American consciousness-raising group in Vacaville, the California prison system's medical facility. Vacaville Prison had a controversial reputation as a center of mind control experimentation. And BCA was run by a man with a shadowy intelligence background named Colton Westbrook. A pudgy, black linguistics instructor at UC Berkeley, Westbrook had served in Asia with the US military and worked in Vietnam for Pacific Architects and Engineers, a CIA-controlled firm that built the interrogation chambers for the spy agency's notorious Operation Phoenix program, which used torture and assassination to destroy suspected Vietcong cadres.

BCA won favor with prison authorities, rejecting George Jackson–style militancy and offering black inmates classes and workshops that advocated a soothing blend of racial pride and self-help. But black prisoners distrusted Westbrook. Although he tried to keep his military and intelligence backgrounds hidden, stories circulated about the brainwashing techniques he had learned in Asia and how he was applying them at Vacaville. One of the few inmates with whom Westbrook developed a close bond was Donald DeFreeze, an armed robber and gunrunner with a history as a police informer.

DeFreeze had led the charmed life of a snitch for several years, released or paroled time and again after being arrested for stealing and selling enough guns and explosives to fill an armory. In 1968 he was recruited by the Criminal Conspiracy Section, a secret intelligence unit within the Los Angeles Police Department, to supply guns and grenades to be used against the Black Panthers. There is evidence that the guns used to kill Bunchy Carter and John Huggins on the UCLA campus were delivered to Karenga's assassins by DeFreeze.

But in 1969 the LAPD's patience with DeFreeze finally ran out when he was wounded during a gun-blazing shootout after trying to cash a stolen $1,000 check at a Los Angeles bank. By the time he was imprisoned in Vacaville in December 1969, DeFreeze felt that his life had hit rock bottom. At age twenty-six, he was deeply estranged from his wife and six children, his only skill was the black-market gun trade, and he was facing a long stretch in prison. "I was slowly becoming a nothing," DeFreeze later wrote a friend.

DeFreeze found a savior in Colton Westbrook. Under the BCA overseer's tutelage, the convict developed his own prison course, which he titled Unisight, and began teaching a bootstrap philosophy lifted directly from the seven Kwanzaa principles popularized in black circles by Ron Karenga: self-determination, production, cooperation, collective work and responsibility, faith, unity, and creativity. DeFreeze later emblazoned each principle on the seven-headed cobra that became the exotic symbol of the SLA.

At Vacaville, DeFreeze reinvented himself as Cinque, taking his new name from the legendary African slave who led the 1839 rebellion on board the *Amistad*. His fellow inmates kept the odd, self-promoting Cinque at a wary distance, and Unisight failed to attract a big following. But Cinque's work did win Westbrook's admiration. "We were a hell of a team in many ways," Westbrook remarked later. "Cinque did his job . . . He wasn't brilliant, but he was smart. He was quite methodical and thorough. He had his shit together. He was the type of brother who would take a lead."

Though Cinque touted Unisight as a mind-liberating tool for the black man, it was young white men and women who filled his prison classroom. The BCA program at Vacaville had become a magnet for white radicals from nearby Berkeley. Inspired by the legend of George Jackson, they signed up as tutors in the program, hoping to become part of the prisoner rights struggle. One of the most active group of tutors came from a Maoist commune in Berkeley called Peking House, including future SLA members Russell Little and his girlfriend Robyn Steiner, and William Wolfe. Why a virulent anti-Communist like Westbrook would allow avid young followers of Chairman Mao to hijack his program is unclear. Westbrook later explained, rather weakly, that BCA "lacked the money to draw tutors other than those people at Peking House."

After a while, Westbrook claimed to be fed up with the young "self-taught commies," as he called them, and he funneled them into the

Unisight course, where he thought Cinque would keep them firmly in check. Instead Cinque's consciousness-raising class became the seedbed for the Symbionese Liberation Army: an "army" led by a sketchy black snitch with an even murkier prison patron, and made up of earnest, middle-class firebrands suffering from deep self-loathing and white guilt.

In December 1972 Cinque was suddenly transferred to Soledad Prison, in the coastal farmlands of central California. Shortly after, Westbrook followed in the path of his favorite inmate, when he was hired to teach community relations to Soledad guards. Cinque seemed to be under the wing of prison officials, and other prisoners suspected that he was an informer. In March 1973 Cinque was given a plum job as a late-night boiler attendant in a remote, unguarded section of the prison grounds. On his first night, Cinque was dropped off by a guard at the facility. As soon as the guard drove away, Cinque sprinted to the twelve-foot fence and scaled it, making his way north up Highway 101 to the Bay Area and his date with infamy. He had escaped from the same area of the prison where Colton Westbrook taught his class. Westbrook realized this seemed to implicate him in Cinque's drama, and he claimed that he looked into the strange coincidence "to see if I was being set up."

As Cinque roamed around the Bay Area, prison authorities seemed surprisingly lax about tracking him down. He approached various radical groups and offered his services as "a hit man," which the stunned activists declined. Many of them suspected that he was a provocateur. After reuniting in Berkeley with the young white militants who had filled his Unisight class at Vacaville, Cinque soon began building his own underground liberation force, which he named the Symbionese Liberation Army. The SLA leader mesmerized his followers with his revolutionary gibberish and his prison-hardened, bull-like physique. He strutted around the SLA's various safe houses buck naked and fully erect, quickly establishing sexual dominion over the women in his flock, even lesbian lovers Patricia Soltysik (Mizmoon) and Camilla Hall. He swilled plum wine and squatted on the floor, rattling a handful of small bones, mumbling voodoo incantations, and weaving a spell over his acolytes. Cinque and his women formed the power nucleus within the group. None of the men ever challenged him; his skin color and prison credentials gave him supreme status.

"I crave the power Charlie Manson had," declared Cinque, who claimed that he had met the fellow ex-con in Los Angeles. Like Manson's followers, the SLA soldiers were disillusioned children of the sixties. But in contrast to Manson's girls, they came from solid, middle-class backgrounds. Angela Atwood (formerly DeAngelis) was a high school cheerleader from a strong Catholic Italian-American family in New Jersey. Camilla Hall, the daughter of a Lutheran minister and missionary, had worked as a social worker in Minneapolis. None of them seemed destined for lives as revolutionaries. Bill Harris, a Vietnam veteran, met his wife Emily at the University of Indiana, where she was an honors student and sorority girl. While at Indiana, Emily and Bill worked for the Indiana State Police Department, setting up drug arrests, before moving to Berkeley in the spring of 1973.

They were all raised in the bosom of Middle America, and were dutifully making their way up the chutes and ladders of life, heading toward their own versions of the suburban family dream in which they had been raised. But something snapped in each of them along the way. Sincere young Americans, they were driven crazy by the 1960s—or more precisely, by what America was becoming in the sixties. There is no other way to put it.

Joe Remiro had been a "gentle boy" and a good student at San Francisco's Sacred Heart High School, according to his father, Charles. But after Remiro served two tours of duty in Vietnam as a decorated, gung-ho rifleman with the 101st Airborne Division, he was "never the same."

Nancy Ling Perry grew up in Santa Rosa, a sun-splashed, idyllic corner of small-town America eighty miles north of San Francisco. Her family, the owners of a successful furniture store, were prominent in local business circles and supporters of conservative standard-bearer Barry Goldwater. But something cracked in Nancy at age sixteen, when she watched the national nightmare in Dallas on November 22, 1963. Later, she explained the Kennedy assassination's impact on her, in a "letter to the people" that seemed more from the heart than most of the SLA's bombastic communiqués.

"When I was in high school," Nancy wrote, "I witnessed the first military coup against we the people of this country. I saw us passively sit by our TVs and unconsciously watch as the militarily armed corporate state took over the existing government and blatantly destroyed the constitution that some of us still believed in. I listened to the people around me deny that a military coup had taken place and claim that such a thing could not happen here . . . In 1964 I witnessed these and other somewhat hidden beginnings of the military/corporate state which we now live in. And I heard my teachers and the government-controlled media spread lies about what had happened. I saw the civil rights protests, the killings and bombings of my black brothers and sisters and the conditioned reactions of extreme racism in my school and home . . . I told my teachers and family and friends that I felt that we were all being used as pawns and puppets, and that those who had taken over the government were trying to keep us asleep and in a political stupor. I asked my teachers to tell me what happened in Nazi Germany; I asked them to tell me the meaning of fascism; I asked them to tell me the meaning of genocide. And when I began to hear about a war in Vietnam, I asked them to tell me the meaning of imperialism. The answer to all my questions then was either silence, or a reply filled with confusion and lies."

This is as clear and concise a summary of the radicalization process in the 1960s as you will find. We've long been conditioned to accept this grotesque sequence of events, to put it all away in a safe time capsule labeled "the Tumultuous Sixties." But for a young person at the time, one with a searching heart and mind, these traumas—assassinations of popular leaders, imperial war, and brutal acts of government repression—were crimes against the national conscience. And the longer they went unpunished, they became, to these young people, stark proof that American democracy was a fairy tale.

Many young radicals in the early 1970s, faced with the ceaseless gore of Vietnam, as well as the police-state measures employed by the Nixon administration and the FBI against the left, felt that they were engaged in a war with the government. Groups all over the Bay Area—from Berkeley to the Santa Cruz mountains—began arms training and munitions making. The looming showdown with the militarized "corporate state" might end in a suicidal inferno, but "the revolutionary vanguard" believed that it was its duty to set an example and inspire the people to rise up. A thick air of doom and drama hung over the youth ghettos of San Francisco and Berkeley. But nowhere was this atmosphere of death and glory more pungent than in the subterranean world of the SLA.

As FALL 1973 APPROACHED, Cinque huddled with his soldiers. It was time to strike. They pored over the business sections of local newspapers and trolled through business periodicals and annual reports at the public library, searching for suitable members of the corporate state to kidnap or execute. The target selection process had an absurdly macabre quality. At one point they seriously considered killing Charles O. Finley, owner of the World Champion Oakland A's, who had enraged the baseball team's blue-collar fan base by firing popular manager Dick Williams. In the end, Cinque zeroed in on Marcus A. Foster, the superintendent of the Oakland public school system. It seemed like an equally bizarre choice.

Marcus Foster was a progressive black educator who had committed himself to turning around the city's deeply troubled public school system. Teachers and students did not feel safe going to school in Oakland. Pressures mounted on Foster to increase security after a young elementary schoolteacher was raped in her classroom in front of an eight-year-old student. In response, Foster announced that he would ask Oakland police officers to patrol campuses and would issue photo identification cards to students. To Foster, creating a safe environment in which to learn was essential for the survival of Oakland's public schools. "We are going to have to get away from the rhetoric of the 1960s, where policemen were called pigs and were viewed as enemies of the people and all of that foolishness," he told a community meeting. "We are going to have to see policemen as protectors of our society."

In response to an outcry from some activist parents and Black Panthers leaders, Foster later softened his security proposal, making it clear that the campus cops would not be armed. But either the SLA news monitors weren't following the story closely enough, or they didn't feel Foster's compromises were sufficient. Cinque issued his death warrant: "We are gonna off that nigger," he told his army. "We want to show the oppressed peoples there are black pigs just as there are white pigs."

Strong black men like Marcus Foster seemed to push Cinque's buttons. One SLA chronicler speculated that authority figures put Cinque in mind of his father, a laborer who muscled his family into the middle class but took out his violent rages on his son, whom he beat regularly with his fists, and even a baseball bat and a hammer, until the boy finally fled home at age fourteen.

Thero Wheeler, another escaped black convict, and Robyn Steiner were the only SLA members who questioned Cinque's fatal selection of Marcus Foster. "If you are talking about executing a highly positioned black man in Oakland," said Steiner, "you will defeat our objectives straight away by alienating the black population." But Cinque made Wheeler feel that his life was unsafe, and he fled the group. After the Foster assassination was carried out, Steiner also ran for her life.

Foster was ambushed on the evening of November 6, 1973, as he walked with his deputy, Robert Blackburn, to the parking lot behind the school administration building. Cinque fired first, blasting both men with a sawed-off shotgun. Then Cinque's two accomplices—his "official" bedmate Patricia Soltysik and the ever-loyal Nancy Ling Perry—joined in, firing with automatic pistols. It was Nancy, the woman who decried "the killings of my black brothers and sisters," who stepped over Foster's wounded white deputy and pumped eight cyanide-filled bullets into the chest of Marcus Foster. As the SLA assassins ran for their getaway car, she was heard giggling. When Steiner asked Nancy how she felt about killing a person, she said, "He's not a person, he's a pig."

After the Foster assassination, a cloud of fear and suspicion fell over the Bay Area. Activists puzzled over the mysterious organization that claimed credit for the killing. To many, "symbionese" conjured some exotic overseas guerilla army. When it became clear that the violent group was homegrown, some radicals immediately suspected a government plot, since Foster—despite his tough security proposals—was a progressive who had shown that he was willing to negotiate with groups like the Black Panthers. The Panthers saw the Foster murder as part of a government campaign to stir up "hatred, fear, and disunity in the black community" and to inflame white paranoia. When SLA members Russ Little and Joe Remiro were caught in a police dragnet in January 1974, many on the left breathed a sigh of relief, hoping that the bizarre drama was coming to an end. It had only just begun.

19

THE REVOLUTION WILL
BE TELEVISED

D ESPITE THE POLICE noose that seemed to be tightening around the SLA after the arrests of Little and Remiro, Cinque decided that the group needed to strike again "to prove to the world the Foster killing wasn't an isolated action." This time they would rivet the public's attention by kidnapping a high-profile target and issuing demands on behalf of the downtrodden. Cinque kept a thick, blue journal filled with names of powerful figures in politics, business, and media who were potential kidnap victims, including President Nixon and his daughter Tricia, Governor Ronald Reagan, and Senator Edward Kennedy. But in the end, the group settled on Patricia Hearst, daughter of *San Francisco Examiner* publisher Randolph Hearst and his wife, Catherine, a Reagan appointee to the University of California Board of Regents. Patty Hearst, a Berkeley undergraduate, conveniently lived, unguarded, just blocks away from the SLA hideout.

Like Marcus Foster, Patty Hearst was an indefensible target, both morally and politically. Though the nineteen-year-old coed was born into a family that presided over a vast media empire, whose newspapers were known for their reactionary editorial slants, she bore no responsibility for the Hearst Corporation's hidebound conservatism. As Robyn Steiner, who was put in charge of surveilling her, found out, Patty was no "rich bitch" but a socially conscious young woman who attended protest rallies on the Berkeley campus. She also was outspoken in her criticism of the Hearst press, including her father's own newspaper, telling him, "Dad, nobody under eighty reads the *Examiner* anymore. It has become irrelevant to the times."

For that matter, neither was Randy Hearst stamped from the same conservative mold as his father and older brothers. In fact, realizing that his daughter was right, Hearst launched an effort to liberalize and liven up the *Examiner,* hiring his young nephew Will to shake up the fusty editorial page and pushing his news editors to do a better job of covering the city's overlooked groups, including blacks, Latinos, Chinese, and the young.

But Cinque was not interested in the moral component of the kidnapping. Ever mindful of how the SLA was playing on the public stage, he was focused on the crime's potential media impact. Once the young Hearst newspaper heiress was in the SLA's hands, Cinque knew that he would become the ringmaster of a gaudy media circus. In this respect, it was a brilliant decision.

The SLA's mad dash onto the world stage began on the evening of February 4, 1974, when Cinque, Bill Harris, and Angela Atwood forced their way at gunpoint into Patty's Berkeley apartment, beat her fiancée, Steven Weed, gagged and blindfolded her, dragged her down the building's concrete stairs in her bathrobe, smashed her in the face with a rifle butt, and stuffed her in the trunk of a car. Patty was kept blindfolded in a closet in a Daly City safe house, just south of San Francisco. Her captors scorned their "prisoner of war" as "Marie Antoinette" and "a bourgeois bitch," and she was subjected to weird interrogations by Cinque, who grilled her about the stocks that her parents owned, how much money her father made, and whom he visited when he went to Washington— none of which she knew.

Later Atwood informed Patty that "Cin wants to fuck you," explaining what "a great honor" it would be for her. He entered the closet and ordered her to take off her clothes, then raped her on the floor of her stale, musty cell. "I lay there like a rag doll, my mind a million miles away," she recalled. Afterward she told herself, "Well, you're still alive." Cinque and his armed band established complete dominion over Patty's body, letting her know when she could eat and go to the bathroom, and who would rape her.

As Patty underwent her ordeal, the SLA gloried in the media explosion sparked by her kidnapping. The revolutionaries glued themselves to the TV and radio, spinning the dials and searching for the latest reports on their exploits. Cinque stoked the publicity fires with his strange, militaristic communiqués from the underground. In one taped message released in early April, he announced that "all corporate enemies of the people will be shot on sight at any time and at any place," setting off more panic in elite circles.

Colton Westbrook tried to establish contact with his former prison protégé, holding a bizarre press conference on the Berkeley campus during which he read an open letter to Cinque in "black English."

"No rich white man is going to talk to a nigga, especially a pure nigga. But maybe a bousie nigga and a pure nigga can rap a bit," declared Westbrook, standing in front of a battery of TV cameras and microphones. The portly lecturer, wearing an African cap and matching vest, then went on to compliment Cinque's "brilliant" political strategy, while cautioning restraint in handling Patty Hearst. "Dig it, Cin, I can understand your Symbionese thing and know that you will not harm Patty unless the man makes a bum move."

Westbrook then made a puzzling reference to Cinque's "leader," as if he were someone known to both men. But when asked about this by reporters, Westbrook shrugged it off, saying that he was only referring to a statement made by Cinque in one of his taped messages.

Finally, Westbrook urged Cinque to talk to him "man to man, brother to brother, nigga to nigga." He suggested that the SLA leader could relay messages to him through one of a number of convicts and ex-cons whom he listed by their "reborn," or Swahili, names.

Was it a comical sideshow in the SLA media circus, or was the former CIA spook trying to send Cinque a veiled message? If Westbrook was trying to reestablish a supervisorial role over the escaped con, it obviously didn't work. Cinque announced his break with Westbrook in typically dramatic style when he publicly called for him to be "shot on sight." On the FBI's advice, Westbrook immediately fled east with his wife and child.

As WESTBROOK NOTED IN his open letter, the most ingenious demand issued by Cinque came a week after the kidnapping, when he ordered Randy Hearst to underwrite a massive food giveaway to the poor. The demand, which came with a thinly veiled threat about Patty's "health" if it were not met, set off an extraordinary chain reaction. The food give-away would reposition the violent gang as benefactors of the poor, pit left-wing groups that cooperated with the food program against those that rejected it, drive a wedge between press mogul Hearst and his powerful friends, and create a witches' brew of political intrigue.

As Patty Hearst's desperate father scrambled to see how he could meet the SLA's food distribution scheme—which California welfare officials estimated would cost a bracing $400 million—it soon became clear that his corporate and political cronies would be of no help. Governor Reagan grimly quipped that he hoped those who took the food were stricken with botulism, and suggested in a more serious vein that anyone who did accept the handouts would have their welfare checks cut off. Ludlow Kramer, a Washington state official whom Randy Hearst appointed to direct the food effort, and the publisher's young nephew Will made an urgent call on the chairman of the Bank of America. Kramer and Will Hearst—who was long-haired, unshaven, and wearing sandals—took an elevator to the top floor of the B of A headquarters, a dark tower looming over the San Francisco financial district. "Sir," Kramer told the bank chairman, "what I want you to do is call—you're the one man who can do it that I know of—call forty of the top businessmen to meet with me for cocktails this afternoon or breakfast tomorrow morning." But instead of helping the Hearst family raise the ransom money for Patty, the Bank of America chief offered Randy Hearst a $4 million loan instead—a loan that he was in no financial position to accept.

The SLA kidnapping exposed the fact that Randy Hearst and his brothers did not have access to the vast resources of the company founded by their legendary father. In the end, he scraped together a $2 million food budget, wheedling $1.5 million from the surprisingly stingy directors of the Hearst Foundation and putting up the other $500,000— one quarter of his wealth—himself.

The Randy Hearst who emerged at regular intervals during the fifty-seven-day kidnapping drama to face the media swarm outside his home was a study in muted agony. Outside his two-story French chateau in plush, suburban Hillsborough squatted a permanent encampment of jostling TV reporters, cameramen, and newspaper scribblers from around the globe. The cacophonous scene must have struck him as some sort of hellish punishment for all those decades of Hearst yellow journalism. But in front of the cameras, tightly gripping the hand of his stricken-looking wife, he appeared resolutely composed and polite, in his thick-rimmed spectacles and tailored suits. Hearst displayed more dignified grit than one would expect from a man born into the pampered comforts of his family, with its storied castle, club memberships, and luxurious trips abroad.

Will Hearst—who went through the ordeal with his uncle, living in the Hillsborough "bunker"—pointed out that Randy had flown transport planes through enemy flak in World War II and was a "man of signature bravery." But life inside the family bunker was "a living hell for my uncle," Will recalled. "It totally devastated his life. He was never the same again. It changed what reality was to him forever. He had the strength to live through it. But it surely haunted him. Is it enough to have a quiet, comfortable life and have a bunch of sweet kids and live in a sweet place, when all that can be blown away? Maybe one has to be more armored and serious in life."

Life inside the Hillsborough mansion during the long ordeal was a nightmarish carnival. Randy and Catherine Hearst engaged in heavy drinking bouts, sometimes with Charles Bates, the FBI San Francisco bureau chief who was in charge of the SLA hunt. At the urging of Patty's four sisters, the family brought in psychics who attempted to locate the kidnap victim and her abductors with their extrasensory powers. One of the psychics—whom the Hearst girls labeled Swami Number One, Swami Number Two, and so forth—constructed a small altar on the Hearsts' dining room table to perform rituals. Meanwhile, Catherine, a devout Catholic, turned to a steady flow of priests for consolation, when she wasn't relying on the bottle. Her drinking unleashed a fiery temper, which she often directed against Patty's weaselly fiancé, whom she accused of not being man enough to die fighting her daughter's abductors.

At one point, the agile Colton Westbrook even inserted himself in the Hearst family compound, spending two late-night sessions with Randy and Catherine in Hillsborough. Hearing about Westbrook's intelligence background, the distraught parents begged him to use his connections to help track down their daughter. But Westbrook demurred, insisting, "I am no kind of a superagent." Late one night, after Catherine went to bed, Randy and Westbrook shared another round of heavy tumblers of scotch, and Randy asked the question that had long been nagging him: "Is it possible that Patty is pregnant by Cinque?" This time Westbrook could provide an answer, though it turned out to be false. "I've heard those rumors," he said with a nod.

Patty was her father's favorite daughter. He liked her feisty sense of humor and independent streak. She was known as "Randy's spoiled brat." He would do anything to save her life.

"I've never put in an honest day's work in my life," the publisher once joked. "I don't really know what it's like out there." But as the ordeal dragged on, Randy began getting a hard education about life. He drifted away from his club society and entered a world vastly different from anything he had ever known. It was a world peopled by the militants and community activists whom he recruited to implement his People in Need (PIN) food distribution program. The anguished father was convinced that somebody in this world could connect him to the underground tunnel where his daughter was hidden.

The PIN program got off to a chaotic start in February 1974. Some of the organizations that the SLA requested to coordinate the food giveaway, including the Black Panthers and the United Farm Workers union, refused to play a role, with Panthers leader Huey Newton proclaiming that he wouldn't be a party to SLA "extortion." Many of those groups that did participate used it as an opportunity to steal food and to shake down Randy Hearst for more money. Meanwhile, fewer than half of the twenty thousand people whom PIN organizers hoped to feed on the first day actually received food packages, with long lines forming outside distribution centers before daylight, made up mostly of black women, many with children in tow. The bags of food included a frozen turkey, a box of saltine crackers, a small can of tomato juice, a box of biscuit mix, and, occasionally, a quart of milk and some eggs. But as the day wore on and the food supply began running out, frustrations grew. Fights broke out at the East Oakland center, and a number of people were injured when distribution workers began throwing the frozen turkeys from the back of trucks into the crowd.

In the following days, Hearst worked frantically to improve the quality of the food and to appease the community groups involved in PIN. He ordered the *Examiner* to run flattering stories about activists who were participating in the program. He sat down for a four-hour lunch meeting at a Hilton hotel in San Francisco with suspicious American Indian Movement (AIM) leaders Russell Means and Dennis Banks, who—after first making their bodyguards taste the meal—agreed to help with PIN.

Hearst also made a series of generous gestures directly to the SLA, hiring power attorney William Coblentz to represent Little and Remiro and trying to arrange a live national telecast for the SLA's two jailed "soldiers." Hearst even contemplated turning himself into an SLA hostage to win his daughter's freedom.

The SLA drama sent Hearst tumbling down a rabbit hole into the company of vivid personalities with whom he never would have crossed paths before Cinque's gang upended his life. They circled through his executive office at the *Examiner,* with the big oil painting of his father staring down at him, Citizen Kane in his prime. He featherbedded the staff at the PIN headquarters with them; they drifted through PIN's China Basin warehouse building near the San Francisco docks, snarling at reporters, threatening the white administrators, helping themselves to food supplies, and working their shady hustles. There were ex-cons, street-tough detectives, left-wing firebrands, loopy volunteers, undercover cops, FBI informers.

Randy's most surprising new friend was Wilbert "Popeye" Jackson, the iron-pumping, forty-four-year-old black ex-con who led the radical United Prisoners' Union. Like George Jackson, who was no relation, Popeye Jackson had spent a good chunk of his life in prison for robbery, and, despite his soft Louisiana drawl, he exuded a badass charisma that white activists, especially women, found irresistible. Like Cinque, whom he had known behind bars, Popeye Jackson also had a reputation as a police snitch.

Randy brought Jackson into the PIN operation and treated him like a prized executive. He offered to underwrite a private school education for the ex-con's son. He made sure that Jackson's prison reform work got glowing coverage in the *Examiner,* and it was no surprise when the paper editorialized that Jackson should remain a free man despite a parole violation for drug selling. Two weeks later, the state parole board agreed. In return, Hearst asked that his new friend tell him anything he heard about the SLA's movements and Patty's whereabouts. They had a gentleman's agreement.

Jackson was flattered by all the attention he was getting from his Hillsborough booster. "Hearst has great respect for me as a man, and I respect him," the ex-con told friends. But the unusual relationship did nothing for Jackson's reputation on the street. When his parole was not revoked, some Bay Area militants speculated that he was an informer— not only for Hearst but, worse, also for the FBI.

In the dark, early morning of June 9, 1975, Popeye Jackson drove home from a party, pulling to the curb in front of his Albion Street apartment in the Mission. His wife, who was pregnant with his child, was inside the apartment. But Jackson, accompanied by a woman named Sally Voye, didn't want the party to end. Voye—another one of his white admirers in the United Prisoners' Union, and also an undercover narcotics agent—was burying her face in Jackson's lap when a man walked up to the car and emptied the clip of a 9-millimeter automatic pistol into the couple, killing both of them.

Popeye Jackson's murder released another poisonous plume around the SLA case. Frantic claims and counterclaims clouded the air. A letter to the underground *Berkeley Barb* speculated that he had been killed by the New World Liberation Front because he was a double agent. Jackson loyalists in the United Prisoners' Union charged that he was killed by the cops. The SFPD, in turn, zeroed in on the Tribal Thumb, yet another militant Bay Area group led by an alpha-male ex-convict, Earl Satcher. The cops arrested a Tribal Thumb member, who was tried and convicted of the murder.

ALTHOUGH IT WAS LONG kept quiet, Randy Hearst had another strange bedfellow in the PIN subculture. Her name was Sara Jane Moore. Eccentric even by the colorful standards of the SLA cast of characters, she showed up one day at the food program's warehouse headquarters and announced, "God sent me to help." The scruffy volunteers stared dumbfounded at the middle-aged woman in her preppy Peck & Peck pantsuit, pearl necklace, and tight-curled salon perm. But Moore soon wormed her way into the heart of the organization, taking over its bookkeeping duties, setting herself up as its press spokeswoman, and becoming a confidante of Randy Hearst.

Moore had led several different lives before she showed up at PIN. Born in West Virginia during the Depression, she was raised in a traditional Baptist household grimly presided over by her father, the superintendent of a DuPont chemical plant, and her spic-and-span mother. Moore rebelled, running off to join the Women's Army Corps, and burning through two unhappy military marriages. She gave birth to three children, but, clearly not the mothering type, abandoned them with her own parents and disappeared. Moore popped up for a while in Hollywood as a bookkeeper at RKO Studios, where she met and married an Academy Award–winning sound technician and became pregnant with child number four. But a month after her wedding, Moore again overturned her life and headed for the Bay Area. Here she would marry husband number five, a successful doctor, and reinvent herself yet again as a gardening housewife in Danville, an exclusive East Bay enclave. For a while, she seemed to fit into her conservative surroundings, volunteering in the reelection campaign of Republican senator George Murphy, an amiable old Hollywood song-and-dance man in the Reagan political mold. But after the inevitable conclusion of her fifth marriage in 1973, the shape-shifting Moore suddenly found herself in the middle of the SLA storm.

In April 1974, as the PIN program was winding down, Moore was approached by FBI special agent Charles Bates, who was carefully monitoring the food operation and its murky undercurrents. One afternoon Bates picked up Moore on a designated San Francisco street corner and drove her to tony Pacific Heights, where he parked the car and asked her to become an informer. In the press, the fifty-four-year-old Bates came off as a lanky, genial G-man with a lazy Texas drawl, but the FBI veteran had a deep history in some of the nation's most sensitive cases, including the assassination of President Kennedy and the Watergate investigation, which he had led for the bureau. The FBI saw the Bay Area in the early 1970s as a critical battleground in its struggle with the radical left. Sitting in their car that afternoon, Bates and fellow agent Bert Worthington convinced Moore that she could play a vital role in this battle, spying on Popeye Jackson and other activists, and finding out what they knew about the whereabouts of the SLA. "These are dangerous people," Worthington told her. "They are out to destroy the country. Many of them are dupes of foreign governments, of the KGB and the Red Chinese."

It was Moore who later helped seal Popeye Jackson's fate, circulating a letter among Bay Area radicals that accused him of being an informer for Randy Hearst. *Rolling Stone* later called it Jackson's "death warrant."

The FBI men planned to keep Moore busy. They wanted her help not only in probing the Bay Area radical underground but also in keeping tabs on Randy Hearst, whom Bates suspected was running his own private investigation of the SLA. Moore agreed to work for the FBI, throwing herself into her clandestine assignments so vigorously that the bureau was soon loaning her out to other law enforcement agencies, including the San Francisco Police Department.

But when it came to infiltrating the radical underground, the FBI's judgment was often unsound. Sara Jane Moore turned out to be one of the most embarrassing informers in the bureau's history. During her brief career as an FBI snoop, the ever-surprising Moore shifted alliances a dizzying number of times, betraying her G-men controllers, and then sweet-talking her way back into their good graces—and doing the same with her radical targets.

While reporting back to the FBI about Randy Hearst, Moore was developing a close bond with the newspaper publisher. Hearst, in fact, asked Moore to develop secret lines of communication with the SLA. Neither Hearst nor Bates knew that she was acting as an informer for both of them. Meanwhile, Moore was also reporting about Hearst and the FBI to radical friends whom she had befriended while spying on *them.* The many-lived Sara Jane Moore had finally found her ideal place in life, inside an utterly bewildering hall of mirrors.

All the conflicting forces inside Sara Jane Moore exploded on the morning of September 22, 1975, when she bought a .38-caliber Smith & Wesson revolver from a Danville gun dealer and drove across the Bay Bridge to assassinate President Gerald Ford as he was leaving the St. Francis Hotel. Feeling increasingly desperate, like a spy without a country, Moore decided to choose the antigovernment side in the end, and to prove her allegiance with a dramatic act of violence.

Jerry Ford was a bland Washington hack, but he had somehow set off a perplexing firestorm of madness. Two weeks earlier, Charles Manson devotee Lynette "Squeaky" Fromme, had waved a gun in the air in a Sacramento park where Ford was speaking. Moore proved more of a threat, squeezing off a shot that ricocheted off a wall just behind Ford's head. If her revolver's sight had not been faulty, as she pointed out later, Moore might have found her target.

As she tried to adjust her aim and fire a second shot, a Vietnam veteran named Oliver Sipple knocked down Moore's arm, and a San Francisco cop pried the gun from her hand. Sipple was hailed as a national hero, but when Herb Caen revealed that he was gay, it tore apart the ex-marine's closeted life. Sometimes, when he was drinking heavily—which happened more and more frequently in his later years—Sipple would wish out loud that he'd never saved Ford's life, because of all the torment that fame had brought him. It was one more twisted footnote in these strangest of times.

Sara Jane Moore served thirty-two years of a life sentence for the attempted assassination. In 2009, after she was released from prison, she tried to make sense of what she had done. "I thought if I didn't try to kill President Ford, someone else would . . . that was the tenor of the times," she said. "I thought it would trigger a new revolution.

"We thought San Francisco was the world—and it wasn't."

But to the SLA members, it seemed that their ratty safe houses were the center of the universe.

In early March 1974 the SLA moved from Daly City to a new hideout in San Francisco, a one-bedroom apartment at 1827 Golden Gate Avenue, in a predominantly black neighborhood north of the Panhandle. Cinque and his seven soldiers transported their captive in a large plastic garbage can. It was here—in the dreary Golden Gate safe house, with a filthy Indian bedspread covering the bay windows and old mattresses crowding the floor—that Patty Hearst was transformed into Tania, the SLA's pin-up girl, the reincarnation of Che Guevara's brave companion in the Bolivian jungle. Cinque sat down at the edge of her new closet cell and put the question to his blindfolded prisoner: did she want to be released or did she want to join their revolution? She instantly knew the right answer. "He was testing me, and I must pass the test or die."

"I want to join you," Patty said into the darkness around her. "I want to fight for the people." In return, she was finally allowed to take off her blindfold and look into her captors' faces. "Oh, God," she thought, "what a bunch of ordinary-looking, unattractive little people." Somehow, after hearing only their assaultive voices for weeks, she had expected them to look "bigger, stronger, more commanding."

"Well, now that you've seen us, what do you think of us?" burbled Angela Atwood.

"Oh," said Patty, forcing a smile, "you're all so attractive!"

Cinque told his soldiers what a stunning "propaganda coup" this would be for the SLA. They dressed up Patty like a combat doll, chopping off her hair, putting a beret on her head, sticking a sawed-off M-1 carbine in her hands—and posing her in front of the serpent-covered SLA banner, they snapped the Polaroid photo of her that would forever change her image. Then they wrote the script announcing her conversion and made her read the words into a tape recorder. It was a bitter farewell to her parents. She called her father a "corporate liar" who cared more about his wealth than his daughter's life. "One thing I learned," Patty read in a grim monotone, "is that the corporate ruling class will do anything in their power in order to maintain their position of control over the masses, even if this means the sacrifice of one of their own."

The Tania communiqué, which the SLA released on April 3, set off a new round of media convulsions. It also excited the more romantic ranks of the radical left, which posted photos of the new, gun-toting Patty all over the Berkeley campus, with the gushing salutation, "We Love You Tania." Patty herself hoped that her father would see through the tape recording's stilted language and realize that it was coerced. He did. "I don't believe it," he told the press, after listening to the tape twice. "We've had her twenty years, and they've had her only sixty days, and I don't believe she's going to change her philosophy that quickly in that time."

Meanwhile, Cinque plotted an operation that would prove to the world that Patty Hearst belonged to him, not to her family. Day after day, he put his soldiers through their commando drills in their stuffy apartment—and this time Patty was included. As they ran around with their weapons, they were soon sweating and panting in the claustro-phobic room, its windows shut tight and draped heavily for security. Cinque, who never joined in the exercises, swilled his plum wine on the sidelines and exhorted his troops. "Come on girls, it's hot—take your shirts off!" he would say. He loved to see his female soldiers bare breasted while they exercised.

On the bright, crisp morning of April 15, the SLA members unveiled their next act, leaving their safe house and piling into two cars. Patty felt dazed as she left the darkened apartment, feeling the sun and wind for the first time in two and a half months. Cinque's last words to her before they drove off were, "If you mess up, if you do anything different from what you're supposed to, you're dead." She felt like she was "walking to the gallows." Minutes later the group pulled up outside a branch of the Hibernia Bank—which, ironically, was owned by a friend of the Hearst family—in the quiet Sunset neighborhood. Bursting through its front doors, weapons drawn, they scooped up more than $10,000 in the heist and shot and wounded two older bank patrons before driving back to their hideout on Golden Gate. Caught on the bank security cameras, cradling her sawed off M-1 and wearing a wig, Patty Hearst seemed no longer a victim but a desperado.

Randy Hearst was stunned, but he remained convinced that his daughter was being coerced, and the *Examiner* reflected his conviction. "Patty a Puppet?" a headline in the newspaper suggested. But Hearst's friends in high places now abandoned him altogether. Evelle Younger, California's politically ambitious Republican attorney general, declared that the San Francisco police and FBI had been too timid because of concern for Patty Hearst's safety, but now she was fair game. "I think the moment of truth has long since passed for Patricia Hearst," the law-man intoned grimly. In Washington, President Nixon's attorney general, William Saxbe, weighed in, opining that Patty "was not a reluctant par-ticipant," and lumping her in with the other SLA "common criminals." Randy Hearst lashed back, denouncing the "irresponsible statements," and even the more buttoned-up Catherine got into the fray, pointing out the assumption of innocence at the heart of our judicial system. But after the Hibernia robbery, the blood was in the water.

As Mayor Alioto confidently predicted that law enforcement agencies would soon "wipe out the SLA completely," more than 125 federal agents combed the Sunset district and other neighborhoods, going door to door in their search for the outlaws. They waved around hundreds of thousands of dollars in reward money. One person thought to be connected to the SLA was shown an FBI briefcase stuffed with $50,000 in cash.

Despite the tightening dragnet, Cinque was feeling cocky. One day in late April 1974, he and Emily Harris showed up outside the Pacific Heights home of Angela Veronese, the married daughter of Mayor Alioto. While Cinque cased the house from across the street, Harris approached Veronese's two young children, who were playing outside while their mother gardened nearby. Harris asked the kids where their grandfather was. "Upstairs," they told her. The mayor, who was having marital difficulties at the time, was staying temporarily with Angela and her family. When Angela came over to ask what Harris wanted, the SLA soldier told her, "None of your business," and quickly walked away with Cinque. If the SLA had tried to kidnap the mayor, it certainly would have resulted in a bloody showdown. Alioto, the target of many threats, was being guarded round the clock by the SFPD's tough tac squad.

IN EARLY MAY RANDY Hearst offered $50,000 in reward money for the safe return of his daughter, prompting Cinque to finally decide that it was time to flee San Francisco. Although Cinque was forever reminding his white troops how fortunate they were to have him as their leader—and how he "could be leading a whole army of black soldiers" instead—the truth is that he could never win the allegiance of black followers. And Cinque feared that one of the SLA's cash-strapped black neighbors on Golden Gate Avenue, or later in the Hunters Point ghetto where they relocated briefly, would turn in his army for the tempting reward. On May 8 Cinque and his gang slipped out of San Francisco and headed south for Los Angeles. It was a fatal miscalculation. LA was not the Bay Area, with its underground networks of safe havens. And the Los Angeles Police Department was a more ruthless force than the SFPD.

On May 10, 1974, Lake Headley, a Los Angeles private investigator hired by author-activist Donald Freed to dig into Cinque's shadowy past, called a press conference in San Francisco. The SLA press pack, tipped off to some of Headley's startling inside information, jammed the event, and the private eye did not disappoint them. Headley, a former Las Vegas cop with good law enforcement connections, ran down Cinque's long rap sheet and the special treatment he had received from police and the courts as a multiple offender. He laid out evidence indicating that the escaped convict had worked as a snitch for the LAPD and later as a double agent for Colton Westbrook and the CIA, as well as the state prison system. Headley, whom Manson prosecutor Vincent Bugliosi once hailed as "the best private investigator on earth," concluded with a stark prediction about Cinque's fate.

"He'll be killed, probably in a shootout," the private eye told the press.

Headley was certain that Cinque had become a liability to his former sponsors. "He could not be allowed to live," he later observed, "any more than Lee Harvey Oswald could be allowed to survive and start talking."

One week later, on the evening of May 17, Headley was sitting down for Friday dinner at his Los Angeles home when his local TV news show cut away to live coverage of a police showdown in the black South Central part of the city. A massive law enforcement army—including 150 Los Angeles police officers, 100 FBI agents, 100 sheriff's deputies, and an assortment of motorcycle officers—had surrounded a squat yellow stucco bungalow where the SLA was holed up. Moments after issuing a perfunctory warning to surrender, the assault force let loose an awesome fusillade, pouring five thousand rounds into the little house, as well as a number of highly flammable tear gas projectiles. Only about fifty shots were fired from inside the bungalow, and no officer was hit. When Nancy Ling Perry, Angela Atwood, and Camilla Hall tried to surrender, they were driven back to the house by a hail of bullets. Nancy was later found dead in the backyard with a bullet in her back. When the house went up in flames, police blocked firefighters from putting out the blaze and continued to pour gunfire into the pyre. Clearly, no one inside was supposed to come out alive that day. As *Rolling Stone* remarked acidly, "It was not really a shootout at all; it was a police shoot-in."

Six SLA members died in the flames and the gunfire, including Cinque, who put a bullet through his head before he could be burned alive. After the Los Angeles inferno, there was a rash of press speculation about Cinque before he disappeared completely from media view. When he was buried in Cleveland, his hometown, the *New York Times* ran a story headlined, "Cinque: Still a Mystery." The *Times* reporter, interviewing a young black mourner outside the funeral home, was told, "Even his family didn't know him." One reason that Cinque might have been a mystery to his family was that his father's savage beatings drove him from home at a tender age. But none of his relatives dwelled on that.

Lake Headley probably came the closest to understanding Cinque. He was a "monster," Headley said, created in the dark criminal netherworld where police and government agencies manufacture their agents of chaos. And when their Frankenstein went rogue and began imagining that he truly was a revolutionary hero, he had to be put down.

Cinque had a gift for engineering public havoc, with the help of a panting press corps. Before it was finally extinguished, his army engaged in assassination, kidnapping, bank robbery, murder, and attempted bombings and executions of police officers. The SLA gave America the closest look it would get at the kind of bloody mayhem that the Red Army Faction was capable of producing on a grander scale in West German society during the 1970s.

The SLA stumbled on for over a year, kept alive by survivors Bill and Emily Harris and a few more recruits they scraped together in Berkeley. The Harrises, with Patty Hearst in tow, watched the fiery end of their comrades on a motel TV near Disneyland, sobbing and screaming at the television as the sickening spectacle unfolded live and in color. Bill Harris had triggered the chain of events that resulted in the SLA massacre when he shoplifted a bandolier at Mel's Sporting Goods store in the Inglewood neighborhood of LA and got into a scuffle with a store security guard. When police found the Harrises' abandoned getaway van, they discovered a parking ticket in the vehicle with the address of the SLA hideout. "It's all my fault!" wailed Harris as they watched the inferno in their Magic Kingdom hideout. "If it weren't for Mel's . . . I killed them . . . Oh, I should have been there with them, shooting it out to the end . . . I wish I were dead too."

Patty couldn't stand listening to the TV news cacophony and the Harrises' loud lamentations anymore. She crawled into the bathroom and shut the door behind her. All she could think was that she was glad Cinque and the others were dead. "They deserved to die for what they did to me," she reflected later.

She hated the Harrises too but felt that she was stuck with them. Throughout that weekend, as the press speculated about her whereabouts, Patty sobbed until her chest ached, thinking about her fate. The trigger-happy army that surrounded the SLA bungalow assumed that she was also inside, but that had not stopped the cops from torching it to the ground. She felt that her family and her old life were lost to her forever. As soon as she was spotted, she would be gunned down. "My fear of the police outweighed my hatred for the SLA," she later remarked.

Patty and the Harrises soon made their way back to the Bay Area, which they agreed was their "true territory," and the safe place they never should have left. The threesome made for an odd group marriage. They bickered constantly—arguments that would frequently end with Bill Harris slugging the women in the face and blackening their eyes. The short, vain, hot-tempered Harris was forever trying to assert his masculinity, turning whiny and wheedling when his wife denied him sex.

Rejected, he would turn to Patty, who didn't have the will to stand up to him. "There was nothing loving, romantic, or even affectionate in this," she recalled. "I had no feelings whatever. In fact, much of the time I was half drunk, feeling no pain, on mountain red wine."

The remnants of the SLA spent their first night back in San Francisco huddled in the crawl space under a dilapidated Victorian. Later they made their way to Berkeley, where they found a resurgence of support for their cause in the wake of the horrific police bonfire in LA. At a memorial rally for the SLA dead in a Berkeley park, a disguised Emily Harris heard a woman named Kathy Soliah mourn the brutal death of her friend Angela Atwood. And then Soliah bitterly announced to the crowd, "I am a soldier of the SLA." Afterward, Emily approached Soliah, who agreed to help the hotly pursued outlaws.

Soliah connected the fugitives to sports author and activist Jack Scott, who saw a bestselling book in the SLA story and agreed to find them a safe haven. Scott and his wife, Micki, transported the Harrises and Patty to a farmhouse in the rolling hills of Pennsylvania, where they spent a quiet summer. After Scott grew disillusioned with the SLA, he dropped the book project, but he arranged for the fugitives' safe passage back to Berkeley before he parted company with them. In Berkeley, the SLA trio reconnected with Soliah, who decided to join their battle, bringing several new recruits with her, including her sister, brother, and boyfriend. The group began plotting a new wave of bombings and robberies that would prove to be the last stand of the SLA.

All during this time, Patty Hearst's family continued to explore every avenue they could to find their daughter. When *Rolling Stone* reporters Howard Kohn and David Weir began digging up exclusive information about the SLA's subterranean journey, using their contacts in the radical underground, the Hearsts regarded them warily, fearing that they would portray Patty as a true convert to the SLA. But in the course of their investigation, the reporters developed a relationship with Will Hearst, swapping information with him, and they got to know Randy as well.

Weir saw how the ordeal was turning Randy Hearst's life upside down, alienating him from the authorities, who in their blood lust had been willing to incinerate his daughter along with her kidnappers—and, in the process, turning the SLA "dingbats," as he scornfully called them, into "martyrs." The Hearst family had grown deeply estranged from law enforcement officials and no longer counted on them for protection. On his lawyer's advice, Will Hearst hired a private eye to guard him, explaining, "Neither I nor my family have any faith in the FBI or the local police."

The ordeal was also driving a wedge between Randy and his more conservative wife, who infuriated him by agreeing to let Governor Reagan reappoint her to the University of California Board of Regents, even though the announcement was certain to inflame the SLA. As their torment dragged on, Randy and Catherine went increasingly separate ways.

At one point, Randy reached out to Jack Scott, asking him to dinner at a house in San Francisco, where they ate roast beef and drank vodka late into the night while the publisher pumped him for information about Patty. On another occasion, Scott met Randy and Catherine at a Mexican restaurant in Ghirardelli Square near San Francisco's Fisherman's Wharf, where he reported to them that Patty was growing increasingly disenchanted with the Harrises' macho style as she developed a feminist consciousness and was talking of secretly visiting her parents. Randy wondered if Patty might agree to return if Catherine resigned from the UC Board of Regents, but again his wife refused adamantly, saying that she didn't trust "that little weasel Scott." She was growing increasingly fed up with her husband's dalliances with the radical underground.

"Randy would meet with anybody who might help find Patty," recalled

Weir. "He struck me as a very uptight, traditional person, but sincere. When I look back at him through older eyes, the eyes of a father, I feel sorry for what he went through. He would have given away his whole fortune to get her back safely. I think the whole thing broke his heart."

THE NEW SLA TEAM was cut from the same all-American cloth as the original members. The Soliahs grew up in a Southern California high-desert town where their father, an ardent Nixon supporter, was a teacher-coach at the local high school. Their friend and fellow recruit Michael Bortin was the product of a typically liberal San Francisco family, half Jewish and half Unitarian, and he graduated from the city's most elite public high school, Lowell. Bortin grew up during simpler times in San Francisco, playing baseball day and night, and hanging around Candlestick Park to talk to his favorite Giants. Willie Mays used to give Bortin and his friends rides in his pink Thunderbird.

But Bortin was raised with a strong social conscience, accompanying his father, a capital punishment lawyer, to San Quentin as a kid. And the events of the sixties only deepened his sense of estrangement from American society. After dropping out of UC Berkeley, he hung around the Haight for a year, taking acid and working a "shitty job" at Western Union.

"I started seeing these telegrams that said, 'Your son so-and-so,' and underneath there'd be three or four boxes saying, 'You can see his remains at the airport' or 'It's a closed coffin,'" he recalled. "One of the boxes would be checked. And I thought, 'What a hell of a way to tell people that their kid has been killed in Vietnam.' I just tore them up. That's just no way to find out."

Later Bortin volunteered in Bobby Kennedy's 1968 presidential campaign, going door to door in black neighborhoods in Oakland. "The people were supernice," he said. "It seemed like half of the homes had statues of JFK. That had a big impact on me."

The night Bobby was assassinated, Bortin was celebrating his victory in the California Democratic primary by dropping acid. "You don't want to get bad news like that on acid," he said later. His fury grew in the following weeks as the Democratic Party tried to go about business as usual. "Watching the convention in Chicago just kept turning the knife in you more because Bobby wasn't there. Those assholes were trying to substitute for him."

Soon after, Bortin walked up to a Students for a Democratic Society (SDS) table on the Berkeley campus, declaring, "I'm willing to burn down ROTC buildings." It was a rage that would take him all the way to the SLA.

"After Bobby was killed, something grew inside me that has been with me ever since—it was the realization that I really hate this country. I hate it totally."

When he joined the SLA, Bortin took an immediate dislike to the Harrises. "They were like Patty's evil stepparents. One time she had a black eye. We put a stop to that. Bill was treating her like a prisoner. I think he had manhood problems. She made the SLA what it was. Everybody respected Patty. Everybody liked her. She didn't play games like the Harrises. She was a pretty together person, in my opinion."

Despite his antipathy toward the Harrises, Bortin was willing to work with them, plotting bank robberies, cop killings, and other SLA missions. In the end, the SLA was responsible for only one more death, but it haunted Bortin the rest of his life. On the morning of April 21, 1975, the SLA gang walked into a bank in a Sacramento suburb, pulled out their guns, and ordered the patrons to hit the floor. When a forty-two-year-old woman named Myrna Opsahl did not move fast enough for Emily Harris, who was leading the heist, she thrust her shotgun at her to speed her up. The gun, which Harris was warned had a hair trigger, went off, killing Opsahl instantly. The mother of four had come to the bank to deposit a collection from her church. Her husband, a surgeon, was later called to his hospital emergency room, where he found his wife dead on the table.

"It doesn't really matter," shrugged Emily Harris when she heard about Opsahl's death. "She was a bourgeois pig anyway."

Patty, who had driven the getaway van, felt sick. "I loathed the Harrises more than ever before. They were violent, evil, unpredictable, incompetent people," she later remarked. She would soon find a way to get away from them forever, moving into a second-floor apartment at 625 Morse Street in San Francisco's Outer Mission with Wendy Yoshimura, a fellow SLA feminist who shared her disgust for the Harrises.

Bortin too pulled away from the group after the bloody bank robbery.

"I still have dreams about that day," he said. "It was a sunny morning. As we were going inside the bank, there were these three women behind us. I didn't want them to get hurt, so I slowed down and held the door for these ladies. And one of them turns to me with this real nice, warm smile, like, 'Finally, a young person who has manners.' And she looked at me and said, 'Thank you.'"

He was running to the bank counter when he heard the roar of Emily Harris's shotgun. Spinning around, Bortin saw instantly that the blood-ied woman on the floor was the same one who had complimented his good manners.

Bortin eventually served three years for the second-degree murder of Opsahl. At his sentencing, he took shared responsibility for the murder, even though he hadn't pulled the trigger. "By our recklessness," Bortin told the Opsahl family members gathered in the courtroom, "we killed a woman. Whatever consequences we suffer is of no consequence. I can offer nothing but apologies. I'm sorry."

ON THE AFTERNOON OF September 18, 1975, San Francisco police and the FBI finally swooped down on the Harrises, as they returned from jogging in nearby Precita Park. The couple were arrested in front of their safe house at 288 Precita Avenue, in the funky, lefty Bernal Heights neighborhood. An hour later, a San Francisco police intelligence officer named Tim Casey and an FBI agent broke through the glass-windowed back door of the house on Morse Street, and, with guns drawn, charged inside to arrest Patty Hearst and Wendy Yoshimura. Patty froze in terror, wetting her pants. She couldn't believe it when they didn't shoot her, the end she'd always expected.

"Why . . . Patty," said Casey, who was just as surprised to have finally found her. "What are you doing here?"

Returning to San Francisco from Los Angeles turned out to be one of the SLA survivors' few smart decisions. Their long run did not have a fiery finale.

Randy Hearst, now comfortable with San Francisco's left-wing milieu, hired Vincent Hallinan and his two-fisted son Terry "Kayo" Hal-linan to represent his daughter. When she was driven to county jail in the police car, she was photographed raising her handcuffed right fist in a power-to-the-people salute, and when she was booked, she stated "urban guerilla" as her occupation. Reunited with her elated parents and sisters in jail, Patty felt oddly removed from them, as if she were a different person. She was exhausted and just wanted to sleep all the time.

But Patty bonded with the curly-haired, roguishly handsome Terry Hallinan. And after Yoshimura told Terry about the ordeal that Patty had undergone in the SLA closet, he began to peel away the Tania layers. Terry and his father thought that Cinque had subjected Patty to some kind of drug-induced mind control program that he had learned in Vacaville. The Hallinans wanted to build their case on an "involuntary intoxication" defense of Patty. But her parents didn't want drugs to be brought up in the trial. And Catherine in particular developed a strong repugnance to the left-wing Hallinans. "She thought of me as some kind of Russian agent," Terry said later with a smile. The Hearsts decided to replace the Hallinans with one of the biggest brand names in the legal profession, Boston criminal attorney F. Lee Bailey.

Ironically, Bailey wound up presenting a defense similar to the one proposed by the Hallinans, arguing that Patty had been "brainwashed" by the SLA. But he gave the argument a different twist, ignoring the drug and sensory deprivation methods that Cinque might have learned at Vacaville, and contending instead that the SLA leader's mind control program was modeled on insidious techniques developed in Mao's China. The author of this line of defense was none other than Dr. Louis Jolyon "Jolly" West, the CIA-sponsored psychiatrist who had studied mind-altering drugs in the Haight in the 1960s. At first Patty was repelled by the "too smooth" Jolly West, with his "creepy, hypnotic voice." But she finally opened up to him, and West became Bailey's leading expert witness. It was another strange intrusion by the psychiatrist into San Francisco's saga.

In the end, however, the jury believed the prosecution's key witness more, Harvard-trained forensic psychiatrist Harry Kozol. He looked like a "fuddy-duddy Kewpie doll," according to one court chronicler, and had a high-pitched squeak. But his testimony had a ring of truth. After interviewing Patty five times in jail, Kozol told the court, he concluded that she was a genuine convert to the SLA. Why else would she have sprayed gunfire at the windows of Mel's Sporting Goods to free Bill Harris after he was apprehended for shoplifting, he pointed out, and why else would she stay with the Harrises on their long underground journey, when she had numerous opportunities for escape? "In a sense," he testified, "she was a member of the SLA in spirit, without knowing it, for a long, long time": a "rebel in search of a cause" at the time of her kidnapping, who had grown deeply alienated from her suffocating family and fiancé. "She was ripe for the plucking," he declared, in his most memorable turn of phrase.

As Kozol testified, Patty "turned the dead white color of a fish's belly," according to an observer.

The truth about Patty Hearst was probably a complex mix of the psychiatrists' opinions. Some type of conversion did occur, but she accepted the SLA's subterranean existence only under extreme duress. At the time of her trial, the Stockholm syndrome—named after the 1973 Swedish bank robbery during which the hostages became emotionally attached to their captors—was not yet a widely accepted concept. But that explanation probably comes closest to getting at the dramatic transformation of Patty Hearst.

After a two-month trial, she was convicted of bank robbery and sentenced to seven years in prison. However, her sentence was commuted by President Jimmy Carter in 1979 after she had served nearly two years. Looking back, Patty felt that she had been victimized twice: once by the SLA and then by the court of public opinion, where she became a convenient scapegoat in the increasingly conservative pre-Reagan climate. "So much anger was directed at me," said Patty, "because of the whole sixties generation that had disappointed their parents so badly."

Patty married her bodyguard, a San Francisco cop named Bernard Shaw, after she was released, and they moved to Connecticut, where they raised two daughters. "Marrying her bodyguard? I don't think that requires Dr. Freud to figure out," remarked her cousin Will. "But I think they like each other, and they have a good relationship." Shaw found a new line of work as a Hearst Corporation security executive. And Patty ended up creating the kind of comfortable suburban family life that she had shunned as a teenager, though her irreverent, wild streak came out at times, as when she popped up in John Waters movies and other campy cameos.

Randy and Catherine Hearst divorced after the SLA ordeal. He too fled San Francisco, moving back to New York, where at the age of seventy-two he married forty-two-year-old socialite Veronica Beracasa.

Hearst resumed his life as a media tycoon, splitting his time between a Fifth Avenue penthouse apartment and a mansion in Palm Beach, Florida. The days of late-night meetings with ex-cons and left-wing militants and CIA spooks were long behind him. He led a more cautious life, surrounding himself with bodyguards until his death in 2000.

While the Hearsts found calmer lives elsewhere, San Francisco continued to be racked by demons. Contemplating the Symbionese Liberation Army's morbid legacy years later, sociologist Todd Gitlin observed that the SLA was the "graveyard" of the 1960s New Left. But after the SLA, the city continued to be haunted by ghouls and gravediggers.

20

BLACK AND WHITE
AND RED ALL OVER

O N THE EVENING of December 13, 1973, Art Agnos, an administrative aide to California assemblyman Leo McCarthy, was leaving a community meeting near his home on Potrero Hill, a racially mixed, blue-collar neighborhood overlooking the downtown San Francisco skyline. At thirty-five, Agnos retained the sense of Kennedy-era optimism that had drawn him into public service in the 1960s, first as a social worker and later as a Democratic political operative. San Francisco was still his dream city. After growing up in tradition-bound Springfield, Massachusetts, where his Greek immigrant father toiled as a shoeshine man, Agnos was eager to fill his lungs with San Francisco's bracing sea drafts when he disembarked from a Greyhound bus at Seventh and Mission Streets in 1967. The clean, chill wind smelled like freedom to him. "It immediately felt like the kind of city where you could be whatever you wanted to be," he recalled.

Agnos felt good that night as he left the meeting of predominantly black activists. He had come to reassure the neighborhood, which was a few blocks away from the bleak housing project where football star O. J. Simpson had grown up, that a long-anticipated community health clinic was finally making its way through legislative channels in Sacramento.

It was one of those golden moments when the system seemed to be working.

As he walked down the 900 block of Wisconsin Street to his parked car, Agnos was stopped by a couple of women from the meeting who wanted to follow up on an item of business. While they were chatting, Agnos suddenly saw their eyes grow wide. A split-second later, he felt two deep, dull thumps to his back, as if a boxer had delivered a one-two kidney punch. Agnos spun around to face his attacker and saw a tall, handsome, well-groomed young black man with a smoking .32 automatic pistol in his hand, and he knew that he hadn't been punched. The gunman gazed directly at Agnos, as if in a trance, and then turned and ran into the night.

The women were running in the opposite direction, screaming. Agnos, strangely calm, hurried after them, to reassure them that they would be all right. "It's not us—it's you!" they shouted, pointing at the widening red splotch on his shirt. Now Agnos was surrounded by a cluster of people from the meeting, who helped him across the street to a house, where he knocked on the front door.

"Excuse me," he told the startled middle-aged African-American man who answered, "I've been shot—can you call an ambulance?" By now Agnos was having trouble breathing, so he lay down on the man's floor. "Hey, man," said the home owner, staring down at the gravely wounded Agnos, "you're bleeding all over my rug."

Agnos was fortunate to be shot near San Francisco General Hospital, with the city's most skilled trauma unit at treating gunshot victims. The emergency medical team was waiting for him on the ambulance dock. It immediately began cutting off his suit coat and shirt. A young female resident surgeon was straddling Agnos, her dress riding up her thighs. "For someone I just met, you're getting to know me really well," said Agnos, slipping into shock. The resident laughed and told Agnos she was just trying to identify his wounds.

The bullets had ripped through his insides, damaging his spleen, kidney, lungs, and colon. But the SF General trauma team saved his life that night on the operating table. After surfacing from his chemical slumber, Agnos realized how fortunate he was. He learned that he was the sixth victim in a mysterious carnival of blood that was rolling through the city, and only the second survivor.

As Agnos recovered from surgery at Kaiser Hospital, where he was transferred, his room was guarded by San Francisco cops. One day two homicide detectives showed up to see the shooting victim: fellow Greek-Americans named Gus Coreris and John Fotinos. The inspectors, who'd been friends ever since they played football against each other in high school, were a tight team: two ethnic outsiders in a department filled with multigenerational Irish and Italian cops. "It was all Gaelic and garlic—no Greek," said Coreris. "We had to prove ourselves."

Standing over Agnos's bed, the detectives began speaking to him in Greek. What they told him was so explosive, they didn't want it to be overheard by any nurses or hospital orderlies. They informed Agnos that he was the victim of a Black Muslim death cult that was randomly shooting and slashing white men and women in the city. Agnos couldn't believe his ears. Ever the good liberal, he immediately thought that they were overplaying the race angle. "You cops are all the same," he told them. The detectives were flabbergasted by Agnos's uncooperative attitude.

But in the months to come, as the soon to be nicknamed "Zebra killers" claimed a total of twenty-three victims in 179 days, Agnos realized that Coreris and Fotinos were right. San Francisco was in the grip of a bloody nightmare that tested the very threads holding it together. Cities are frighteningly fragile social enterprises, built on the tacit compact that one racial or religious group or neighborhood won't start warring on another. Gang violence within the same community is generally shrugged off by the civic establishment as an unpleasant fact of urban life. But when blood is spilled across turf lines, an electric charge of alarm surges through a city—particularly within urban boundaries as tight as seven-mile-by-seven-mile San Francisco, where racial, class, and ethnic tribes are crowded elbow to elbow. One racially charged murder, or even hit-and-run accident, can set off a prickly panic: a flushed foreboding that the whole tinderbox could blow.

The Zebra murders—named after the Z police radio frequency that was assigned to the case—struck a drumbeat of terror, inexplicable and unrelenting, that threatened to drive the city mad. The bloodletting went on day after day. And each explosion of gunfire or grisly discovery of butchered remains took San Francisco closer to the brink of civic breakdown.

San Francisco was already on the edge. In the early months of 1974, the city was reeling from two other unsolved crime sprees in addition to the Zebra murders. While combing the city for Zebra clues, the overburdened SFPD was also fanning out in search of Patty Hearst and the SLA, who were still hunkered down in their Spartan hideout on Golden Gate Avenue. And in January, the Zodiac serial killer—the publicity-mad psychopath who killed at least seven people in the sixties and early seventies—suddenly resurfaced after a silence of nearly three years. Zodiac again began tormenting the city with cryptic letters that he sent to the *San Francisco Chronicle*. One of the killer's creepiest mailings was a 408-symbol cryptogram that, when decoded, sent shivers throughout the city. It was a misspelled, upper-case, unpunctuated howl from some rank cave deep in the human soul:

I LIKE KILLING PEOPLE BECAUSE IT IS SO MUCH FUN IT IS MORE FUN THAN KILLING WILD GAME IN THE FORREST BECAUSE MAN IS THE MOST DANGEROUE ANAMAL OF ALL TO KILL SOMETHING GIVES ME THE MOST THRILLING EXPERIENCE IT IS EVEN BETTER THAN GETTING YOUR ROCKS OFF WITH A GIRL THE BEST PART OF IT IS THAE WHEN I DIE I WILL BE REBORN IN PARADICE AND THEI HAVE KILLED WILL BECOME MY SLAVES

By 1974, the Zodiac killer seemed more interested in staging macabre theater and toying with the police and press than in taking any more lives. In one handwritten postcard to the *Chronicle*, he engaged in some twisted humor with the newspaper's editors, complaining about the newspaper's "poor taste" in deciding to run ads for *Badlands,* Terrence Malick's controversial movie about a couple of sexy, young serial killers. "In light of recent events," Zodiac wrote, with tongue grotesquely in cheek, "this kind of murder-glorification can only be deplorable at best."

Despite the Zodiac's media antics, it was the Zebra murders that unnerved San Francisco deepest of all—particularly after it became clear to the public what the police already knew: that the savagery was racially motivated. The "Zebra" code name might not have been intended to convey a racial meaning, but the city soon realized that the slaughter was a black-on-white thing. The killings were a direct assault on the city's sense of itself as an oasis of racial harmony and civility. In reality, that image was largely false, masking a city of raw racial divisions—between whites and Chinese, whites and Latinos, and especially between whites and blacks.

Prentice Earl Sanders, a black homicide cop who was forced to break down one color barrier after the next within the Irish-dominated SFPD, was keenly aware of the city's racial codes. The racism he experienced in San Francisco was not like what he encountered growing up in Jim Crow–era East Texas. But for all its softer edges, it was still deeply humiliating. "There wasn't some scowling cracker on the other end of the whip," Sanders observed. "In San Francisco, racism came at you with a smile. Like they were doing you a favor when they told you that they didn't have any jobs open after you'd seen a half dozen white guys fill out applications; or that you couldn't buy a house, when they'd just sold one to a white guy who made less money."

Rev. Amos Brown, who became a pillar of San Francisco's black community in the 1970s after moving from Mississippi to take over the Third Baptist Church in the heart of the Fillmore, was astonished by the stories he heard from older members of his congregation about the liberal Bay Area. He was told that even baseball star Willie Mays had trouble overcoming the race ban when he and his wife went looking for a house near posh St. Francis Wood in 1957, even though the Giants' move from New York after the '57 season had electrified San Francisco.

"It was a strange place back then, in the fifties and early sixties," said Rev. Brown. "There were certain areas that were off-limits, certain restaurants where if you went to eat, after you finished, the waiters would break the dish in front of you. San Francisco was only truly liberal when it came to sex. As far as race, it was a microcosm of the United States."

The demolition of the Fillmore district was the greatest source of poison in the city's black-white relations. The uprooting of the neighborhood's population not only stirred a simmering rage among those black residents who clung on but also wiped out much of the community's business bedrock and stable leadership. The subsequent vacuum—a social and economic void as desolate as the neighborhood's weed-choked vacant lots—would attract various types of mischief and madness for years to come.

Among the perverse saviors who worked their way into the Fillmore's carved-out heart in the 1970s were the Black Muslims, Elijah Muhammad's occult, white-hating sect that spread its tentacles from its Chicago headquarters into prisons, ghettos, drug dens, and other pits of African-American misery. In one of the sorrier developments of the times, the Black Muslims took over the old Fillmore Auditorium at the corner of Geary and Fillmore—the scene of so much ecstatic, black-and-white harmonic convergence—after it was abandoned by Bill Graham in 1971, and they turned the venerable building into a mosque known as Muhammad's Temple no. 26. It was this mosque that gave rise to the Zebra murder cult that terrorized San Francisco from the fall of 1973 to the spring of 1974.

The core group of killers came together at the Black Self-Help Moving & Storage Company, one of the enterprises that operated under the Nation of Islam's umbrella. Two of the Zebra murderers were college dropouts from comfortable middle-class backgrounds: Larry Green and J. C. Simon. Two were prison-hardened ex-convicts recently released from San Quentin: Jesse Lee Cooks and Manuel Moore. The moving and storage company on Market Street was owned by Tom Manney, another son of relative privilege. A graduate of elite St. Ignatius High School, Manney starred on the football field at San Francisco State College and was drafted by the Pittsburgh Steelers. But the team cut him before the start of the season, and he drifted back to San Francisco. The ex-convicts and other Black Muslim converts who found their way to Black Self-Help Moving found not only work and companionship under Manney's roof but also new meaning in their lives and an explanation for life's bitter disappointments. The machinations of the white devil—the "grafted snake"—were behind all black men's sorrows and tribulations.

A select group was invited to attend evening meetings in the second-floor loft of the moving company. They watched films about the white man's atrocities; they heard lectures about his perfidy. On special occasions, they were addressed by a distinguished official from Chicago, the Nation of Islam's "New Mecca." The white man's depraved rule was coming to an end, he told the young believers. The white devil was beyond reform or salvation. He must be killed.

"All Muslims will murder the white devil because they know he is a snake," declared the Nation of Islam official. "Each Muslim is required to kill four devils." The reward for slaying the requisite number of serpents would be admission into a rarefied knightly order of "Death Angels" and free transportation to New Mecca to see Brother Elijah Muhammad himself. Led by the minister from Chicago, the meetings climaxed in a chorus of martial chants: "Kill the grafted snakes!" "Kill the blue-eyed devils!"

Pumped up by the bloodthirsty rhetoric, the Zebra killers cruised San Francisco in search of white victims, riding in a Black Self-Help Moving van and a black Cadillac borrowed from Manney. The bloodshed began one balmy evening in October 1973 following a meeting in the loft, when Green, Cooks, and Anthony Harris, another ex-con recently released from San Quentin, began prowling the streets of the Excelsior, a drab neighborhood of stucco bungalows and lowered expectations.

They were on the lookout for white children, because killing women and kids was the quickest way to become a Death Angel. Cooks, who as a boy had tried to smother his dozing mother with a pillow, had particularly savage fantasies about white kids, telling his Muslim brothers that he wanted to pick them up by their feet and smash their brains out against a wall. On Francis Street, Cooks and Green pulled a gun on two young girls and a teenage boy and tried to hustle them into their van, but the kids broke away and saved their lives by dashing down the street.

Not to be denied their first kill, the aspiring Death Angels fled and headed north on the freeway, exiting on gaudy Broadway in North Beach. It was here they found Quita Hague, a pixie-faced twenty-eight-year-old reporter for a business newspaper, and her thirty-year-old husband, Richard, a mining engineer, as the newlyweds strolled down Telegraph Hill from their Chestnut Street apartment. The Hagues were forced at gunpoint into the back of the van, where their hands were bound behind their backs and they were pushed facedown on the floor. As Green drove back onto the freeway, heading south, Cooks and Harris began molesting Quita. When Richard objected, Cooks smashed him repeatedly in the face with a straight lug wrench, shattering his jaw and knocking him out.

Green pulled off the freeway at Pennsylvania Avenue and drove to a desolate warehouse area at the base of Potrero Hill. Here, hissing, "The white devil is mine," Green dragged Quita out of the van by her thick dark hair to a stretch of railroad tracks. Then, as she begged for her life,

Green raised a sixteen-inch machete high over her head and swooshed the blade downward against her throat with all his might, nearly decapitating her. Afterward, the elated Green snapped Polaroid pictures of his mangled victim, to make sure he got credit for his kill.

Meanwhile, as the flashbulbs ignited the darkness, Cooks pulled the unconscious Richard out of the van and, after dumping him across the tracks from his wife's body, began hacking at his face with the same long blade that had taken her life. After finishing their butchery, the men jumped back in the van and drove off.

Later that night, a married couple driving near the dark intersection of Twenty-fifth and Minnesota Streets saw a figure come stumbling out of the gloom. At first the couple thought it was a drunken tramp, but then they looked closer at the horrible specter. It was Richard Hague. The flesh on his face had been hacked into bloody strips, the wounds so deep that they exposed his skull. The couple drove Richard to a nearby police station, where he frantically told the cops about his wife. Rushed to San Francisco General, Richard miraculously survived his ordeal. But as soon as the police found Quita's body, crumpled near the train tracks, they knew she had not.

Earl Sanders, who later inspected Quita Hague's body at the morgue, thought he was prepared for anything after nearly ten years on the force. But what he saw in the autopsy room took his breath away. The deep gashes in the woman's face, head, and upper body "screamed out hate," Sanders later recalled. "Whoever cut her didn't just cut through flesh, they cut through bone. They cut *deep*." Sanders thought it was like looking at a beautiful painting that had been slashed to shreds by a madman.

Ten days later, Cooks—whose victim had not died—was eager to go out again with his devil-hating accomplices, but they told him it was too soon: the cops were on high alert after what they did to the Hagues. Cooks could not wait; the walls of his dingy little apartment off Market Street seemed to be closing in on him. That evening he began walking the streets. The University of California extension campus was only a block from where he lived. He was lurking in the shrubbery near the front gates of the campus when a twenty-eight-year-old student named Frances Rose rolled slowly up the driveway in her gold Ford Mustang, on her way to class. Cooks suddenly emerged from his lair, threw open the car's passenger door, and jumped inside. Rose had no time to even scream before he began firing point blank at her, hitting her four times in the face and chest.

Jack Cleary and his partner Frank Falzon, who were patrolling nearby when the call came in, went racing to the campus. When the detectives got there, they saw the young woman hanging out the side of her car. She died in Cleary's arms. After getting a description of the shooter from a witness, the cops jumped back into their car and began prowling the neighborhood. On Steiner Street, they spotted a muscular black man with a shaved head. It was Cooks. Cleary jumped out and cornered him in a doorway. The shooter's right hand made a twitching movement for his belt. The cops drew their service revolvers. "Just freeze, mister!" When they patted down Cooks, they found the automatic stuffed in his belt.

After he was handcuffed and installed in the backseat of the patrol car, Cooks became surprisingly cooperative. "Before I could even read him his Miranda, he was confessing," Cleary said. "He said, 'Oh yeah, I shot her, I shot her.' He had raped a woman a few days before, and he didn't want to get caught for that because he was Muslim." Killing a white devil would look much better in the eyes of his Nation of Islam death cult.

Cooks's arrest was a swift piece of police work, but it didn't stop the Zebra onslaught. A few weeks after the vicious murderer was taken off the streets, the Zebra killers' ranks were reinforced by two new recruits: a handsome, ambitious, true believer from Houston named J. C. Simon, who had found sanctuary in the Black Muslims from his failing marriage and career; and a big, genial, dull-witted ex-con named Manuel Moore, who had been taken under the Muslim wing at San Quentin. The killing resumed with a new fervor.

THE DEATH ANGELS FLOATED through San Francisco, striking randomly by day and night, shooting down the young and old, women and men, all of them white, or at least white looking. One rainy Sunday morning, Simon walked into a corner grocery store in the Civic Center area owned by a Jordanian Muslim with whom he had a friendly relationship. "Peace be with you," the two men would tell each other in Arabic when Simon went there to buy his daily apples. But this morning,

Simon pulled out a .32 after exchanging greetings, took the man into the back of the store, and shot him in the head. The store owner was a fellow Muslim. But to Simon, his lighter skin color still made him a white devil.

Some of the savagery that came out of the Black Self-Help Moving Company rivaled the baroque barbarity of the Spanish Inquisition. One night a young white man was kidnapped near Ghirardelli Square and taken back to the warehouse loft, where he was stripped naked, tied to a chair, and gagged with a dirty cloth. A line of devil slayers then took turns on him while he screamed into his gag. Using a hideous assortment of instruments—including knives, meat cleavers, and metal cutters—they clipped off parts of his body, starting with his fingers and toes, until he was disassembled like a hog in a butcher's shop.

Anthony Harris, who by then was feeling estranged from his blood-mad Black Muslim brothers, was summoned to participate in the depraved ceremony, but he arrived after it was over. "You too late," said Larry Green—a former Berkeley High School basketball star who once dreamed of playing in the NBA, a young man who had kissed his mother every day when he was growing up. "All the fun done through." Green and the others ordered Harris to dispose of the body, or at least a large chunk of it, which was wrapped in canvas and plastic. Harris drove the grisly package out to Sutro Heights, where he lugged it to the edge of the cliff and heaved it into the sea. It washed up nearby on Ocean Beach on a foggy Christmas Eve morning, where it was discovered by a woman whose dog picked up the deep biological scent.

Once again Earl Sanders had the duty of inspecting the body. The odor hit him first, and then he saw the bundle: it reminded him of the frozen turkeys the department handed out each Christmas. "It was like a fever hit me. I felt dizzy. Like there was no up or down, just gray everywhere I looked—clouds, sea, fog, everything. And right in the middle was this thing that had once been a man."

The body's head, hands, and feet had been chopped off, even its penis and scrotum. A deep hole had been gouged in the stomach, from which spilled ribbons of intestine as the plastic was peeled away. Sanders knew immediately that the same zealous rage that had taken the life of Quita Hague was responsible for the butchery before him. The police had no way of identifying the deconstructed human on the beach. They simply labeled him Unknown Body #169. Some cops called him the Christmas Turkey.

The biggest night of mayhem in the Zebra gore fest took place after Muhammad Ali's dramatic comeback victory over Joe Frazier on January 28, 1974, in the second of their three legendary heavyweight bouts. After watching the bout on closed-circuit TV at the Winterland Ballroom, Simon and Moore, high on their Black Muslim hero's triumph, pressed Harris into joining them on an extended killing spree. Gliding through the city in their black Cadillac of death with the big shark fins, the trio shot down a young woman on her way to a fabric store, a retiree whistling as he strolled home celebrating his sixty-ninth birthday, an eighty-four-year-old homeless man rummaging through a trash bin, a middle-aged woman doing her weekly load of clothes in a Laundromat, and, finally, a twenty-three-year-old mother carrying a box into her family's new apartment. She was the only one who survived, but she was paralyzed from the waist down.

The eruptions of unspeakable violence made this most beloved of cities seem like hostile territory. Suddenly Herb Caen's lovely jeweled city became strange and ominous—the way one's house feels after it's been broken into and ransacked. Whites saw blood in the eye of every able-bodied black male, and every black man saw fear and rage in white faces. Everyone scanned the streets as if on combat patrol, even when walking to the corner store. The city's very identity began to dissolve.

That cruel night in January was the final tipping point for the nerve-racked city. Panic shot through its neighborhoods before the killing was even done, while police sirens were still wailing in the distance. A young gay couple was dining at a Potrero Hill restaurant that evening when their black waiter suddenly interrupted their meal with a distraught look on his face. "You have to go home," he said. "They're killing white people."

The scream that San Francisco had been choking back for weeks finally burst from its throat. The next day's newspapers echoed with the horror. "A Night of Killing in SF." "Madmen Slay Four on City Streets." "SF Killing Spree—5 Shot on Streets." Gun applications soared. Hotels were hit by a wave of room cancellations. For the first time in San Francisco's history, the police officially warned citizens not to venture outdoors after nightfall. The streets were soon deserted, the city's raucous nightlife grew ghostly. Even Caen couldn't muster his usual moxie. "After reading about the latest wave of San Francisco killings yesterday morning," he wrote, "I walked out into the foggy street and looked both ways. Nobody was in sight. Was I the only person left alive in the city? 'The Last Time I Saw Paranoia' is not my favorite song, but I felt a chill."

Caen was not the only one on edge. Others who emerged from their homes darted their eyes nervously over their shoulders. The yellow chalk outlines on the sidewalks reminded them of the mayhem that had left its mark on nearly every district in the city. People got off the streets as quickly as they could. Shades were drawn. Kids were kept home from school. "We are very frightened," one woman told a reporter. "We do not know who they are or when they will come back."

In their agony over what their city was becoming, three women wrote a letter to Jack Valenti, president of the Motion Picture Association of America, to complain about how Hollywood had turned San Francisco into a "crime mecca," with blood-soaked movies like Clint Eastwood's *Dirty Harry* and *Magnum Force,* as well as *The Laughing Policeman,* whose deranged killer opens up with a machine gun on a crowded San Francisco bus. Meanwhile, Karl Malden and Michael Douglas were closing off city blocks so that they could be filmed shooting it out with gunmen on TV's *The Streets of San Francisco.* It was just all too much for some local residents. The gore was everywhere, on the screen as well as the streets.

Even in the midst of the madness, some San Franciscans managed to display grace and civility. While Art Agnos was recuperating from his wounds, fourteen black men of varying ages who were involved with the community health clinic campaign met to vent their anger about his shooting. They decided to take some positive action to reduce the racial tensions in their neighborhood. When Agnos returned to the block on Potrero Hill a month after he was shot to take part in another clinic meeting, he was startled to see four sturdily built black men waiting for him as he parked his car on the street. As they began to cross the street toward him, Agnos struggled to control a rising feeling of panic, telling himself that not every black man in the city was out to shoot him. One of the men walked directly up to Agnos and introduced himself. "Mr. Agnos," he said, "we're your escort."

"My escort?" stammered Agnos.

"That's right. We're going to walk around with you tonight. We want to show anybody who's looking that when you come into this neighborhood, you come as a friend. And that nobody better *ever* mess with you again . . . The hate has got to stop someplace. Maybe this will be the place."

But elsewhere in the city, tensions were rising. Sanders and his partner Rotea Gilford could feel it when they showed up at the latest Zebra murder scene—this one in the racially mixed Ingleside neighborhood, where a twenty-three-year-old man had been shot down while helping a friend move a rug. As Sanders and Gilford worked with the Greek detectives to secure the crime scene and gather evidence, the African-American inspectors noticed that white and black neighbors were standing in separate groups, eyeing each other across an eerily quiet chasm.

"I don't think either Gil or I slept that night," remembered Sanders. "We kept talking about it after we left the scene. If things were like that in Ingleside, what would happen if a crowd formed in the Fillmore, or Hunters [Point], and someone did make a move, white against black or black against white? The whole place could go up in smoke."

The specter of a race war was already looming over the city. After the mayhem on Muhammad Ali's victory night, Herb Caen got a phone call in his office at the *Chronicle* while he was sorting through items for his next day's column.

"Five white people are dead, right?" the caller asked. "I just want you to know that tonight some of us are going out and get ten blacks in trade."

"That's not very smart," replied Caen, trying to keep his voice calm.

"Smart or not, we're going to do it. Two for one is about right, don't you think?"

THE POLICE WERE UNDER withering pressure from Mayor Alioto, the press, and the public to crack the case. The SFPD Zebra unit, which was eventually put under the command of Coreris and Fotinos, worked around the clock. The Greeks staggered through the long days and nights, rarely seeing their families, fueled by cop-house coffee and late-night diner food. They took the case personally. This was their city, they were San Franciscans born and bred. And they could see what the murder wave was doing to it. The cops flooded neighborhoods with patrol cars, they slipped money to informants, they tracked every lead. But nothing paid off.

The police department was hobbled by its own racial troubles. The SFPD had few blacks in its ranks, so it had limited access to the black community. In 1973, black police officers—with Gilford and Sanders taking a leading role—filed a civil rights lawsuit in federal court against the SFPD to end age-old discriminatory practices in the department. The lawsuit triggered a savage backlash from the old-boy network of Irish cops, one of whom shouted out as Gilford and Sanders passed by, "Somebody ought to take a contract out on those two niggers!"

Coreris and Fotinos were seen by black officers as the most unbiased white detectives in homicide. "I'm not white," Fotinos used to laugh, "I'm Greek." But even the Greek partners felt frustrated as they tried to get inside information on the black community, particularly on the Black Muslim temple at Fillmore and Geary that they suspected was the sanctuary for the Zebra killers.

Coreris complained that the Nation of Islam, which had a few converts on the police force (at least one of whom seemed to take an inappropriate interest in the investigation), had more success infiltrating the SFPD than the other way around. The detective liked to drive by the Fillmore mosque at night; it made him feel he was homing in on the killers. But he knew that was as close as he would get to the temple. The Black Muslims were too careful about screening strangers to let a police informant get inside. Coreris wanted to put Temple no. 26 under full photographic surveillance, but city law prevented him from subjecting a house of worship to this type of police scrutiny. After the Zebra executioners claimed their eighteenth victim in San Francisco, state investigators finally helped Coreris circumvent the local law by putting the mosque under their own surveillance.

By the time that the Zebra victim count hit number twenty-three on April 16, 1974, city hall was frantic. Alioto made clear that he would clean house if the police department didn't come up with something fast. But Coreris and his team had no firm suspects or even strong leads. In desperation, he and Fotinos went to a police artist and had him draw a composite sketch of one Zebra shooter, based on witness descriptions. The artist came up with a generic-looking portrait of an African-

American man with a pencil mustache that vaguely resembled a significant percentage of the Bay Area's black male population. On April 17,
Alioto announced that police would resort to an "extreme" measure to
stop the reign of terror: stopping anyone they saw who resembled the
composite drawing.

The mayor knew that this kind of dragnet, the country's first official
racial profiling operation, might spark an uproar. "I want the people of
San Francisco to understand that this is not a racial issue," he told a
packed press conference, "but it is a blunt fact that the victims are white
and our description says the suspect is black."

The mayor used all his political influence, drawing on his admirable
record of minority appointments, to line up support for the police sweep.
Alioto was the first San Francisco mayor to open city hall to minorities,
naming African Americans to head the police commission, public utili-
ties commission, and BART (Bay Area Rapid Transit) board, as well as
appointing a black deputy mayor. "So there wasn't any question about
our credentials," he later remarked.

But Police Chief Donald Scott lacked the mayor's deft touch. "We're
not going to stop very young blacks or big, fat blacks," he announced
ham-handedly. "We're not going to stop seven-foot blacks or four-foot
blacks." Even worse, police officials announced that they would be
handing out a "Zebra card" to those black men who were searched and
cleared—a document, as Earl Sanders angrily declared, that brought
to mind the pass books that blacks were required to carry in apartheid
South Africa. Sanders and Gilford were so outraged by the police measure that they stood up and walked out of the department meeting where
it was explained.

Despite Alioto's best efforts, the reaction from black community leaders was equally furious. Rev. Cecil Williams accused the city of imposing
a "police state" on the black community, which he direly predicted could
set off "a racial war." Black Panther Bobby Seale charged that the SFPD
would never target white people this way, stopping "every white girl," for
instance, who resembled Patty Hearst. But as Alioto pointed out later,
San Francisco cops were doing precisely that. Even Cinque, who was
still in hiding in San Francisco at the time, waded into the Zebra storm,
denouncing the operation in a taped message as the white man's attempt
to "remove as many black males from the community as possible."

The city seemed to crackle with madness. A combustible jumble of civil rights groups and militant left-wing sects convened on the steps of city hall to protest the Zebra operation, carrying signs that read "Stop Alioto Storm Troopers" and "Smash Racism—The Rich Man's Tool to Divide and Rule." As the crowd, estimated at over one thousand, worked itself up, Alioto and two aides suddenly emerged from the building and began walking down the steps to his limousine at the curb. It was a typical act of Alioto bravado: he refused to flinch when confronting a hostile force. As the mayor and his aides made their way through the crowd, demonstrators began jostling him and spitting on him. One began whacking him on the head with a picket sign before his aides could clear a path to his car. Then the crowd surrounded the limousine, pounding on it and rocking it back and forth until the mayor's driver could finally speed away.

As the protests against Operation Zebra grew, helmeted Nazis and other white-supremacy groups mounted counterdemonstrations outside city hall, volunteering to help police round up black suspects and exchanging loud insults with the other demonstrators.

Meanwhile, the police dragnet seemed to be spiraling out of control. Within three days of its announcement, the Zebra operation had swept up more than five hundred black men of all ages, shapes, and sizes, including doctors, lawyers, and other pillars of the community. On the fourth night, the city came perilously close to the long-feared inferno when an elderly black man was accosted on a street in the Fillmore by a plainclothes cop. Instead of stopping, the pedestrian—who in the city's fetid climate of fear thought that he was being attacked by a crazed racist—pulled out a pistol and began firing at the cop. The street was thick with undercover policemen, who all pulled out their Dirty Harry .357 Magnums and unleashed a hail of fire, bringing down the old man, who, miraculously, lived despite being tattooed with six bullets.

That same night, a brawl broke out south of Market between white cops and several blacks who refused to stop. Gilford and Sanders were able to cool the situation when they arrived on the scene, but then two more white cops came roaring up in their squad car and began lashing into the subdued blacks with their billy clubs. "Gil lost it," said Sanders. The black detective began to go at it with the white patrolmen. Sanders threw himself between the fuming cops to stop the confrontation from turning even uglier. But Sanders knew how close that the highly pressurized San Francisco police force, with all its bubbling racial tensions, came to blowing up that night.

Less than a week after Operation Zebra began, a federal judge pulled the plug on it, ruling that widespread profiling of African Americans was a violation of the Constitution's Fourth Amendment ban on unfair search and seizure. The ruling left the city in a strange state of suspended animation, shamed by what it had done to many of its citizens but afraid that there now appeared to be no other options. Everyone seemed to be holding his breath, waiting for the next spasm of gunfire to crack the city's psyche.

IN THE END, IT was a kind of fluke that pulled San Francisco back from the fiery abyss. When the composite Zebra drawing was splashed across the Bay Area's front pages and TV screens, many young black men undoubtedly saw their own faces in its generic features. Among these men was Anthony Harris, who by then was deeply alienated from his fellow Death Angels. At the time, Harris was lying low in Oakland with his wife and baby, trying to pull away from his Muslim brothers without rousing their murderous ire. It was a delicate dance, and Harris knew his days might be numbered. When he saw the police sketch, he thought that the noose was tightening around his neck. Harris decided his only option was to turn himself in to the San Francisco cops and seek immunity as the prosecution's star witness.

As soon as Harris sat down in the hall of justice interrogation room on the evening of April 22 and began telling the gory tale, Coreris and Fotinos knew their long hunt was finally coming to an end. Harris provided the kind of details that only someone who had gone on the death rides could supply. But the detectives weren't done yet. They needed to keep Harris and his family safe from harm until they could negotiate a formal confession with him. Harris, his wife, and baby were checked into a Holiday Inn near the hall of justice. The next morning, a black Cadillac pulled up to the motel, and five well-groomed black men strode into the lobby, asking for Anthony Harris. The Black Muslims had found out Harris's whereabouts when his wife, lonely and distraught in police custody, phoned the wife of a minister at the Fillmore mosque. Coreris blocked the men's passage long enough to allow Fotinos, with gun drawn, to hustle Harris and his family down a fire stairwell. They escaped just as the Muslims came flying up the motel stairs.

The Black Muslims didn't give up their search for Harris. They made the rounds of other San Francisco hotels and motels, politely asking desk clerks if a man fitting Harris's description had checked in. But the most brazen attempt to locate Harris came when a black officer approached Coreris in his office and asked about the witness's whereabouts on behalf of "some friends of mine."

"Are your friends Muslims?" Coreris asked the cop.

"Yes, as a matter of fact," he replied, taken aback.

Coreris bluntly informed the cop that he would report him to Chief Scott.

Harris finally agreed to make a formal confession, but only if he could give it directly to Mayor Alioto. "He wants his promise of immunity to come straight from the horse's mouth," Harris's lawyer told Coreris. "He wants to meet with Mayor Alioto."

The cops tracked down the mayor in Los Angeles, where he was campaigning for governor, and explained the urgency of the situation. Alioto flew home after midnight and rushed to his office at city hall. It was here—after three in the morning, in the morgue-like silence of the high-domed building—that Anthony Harris brought the Angels of Death crashing down.

In the predawn hours of May 1, 1974, an army of more than one hundred law enforcement officers led by Coreris and Fotinos swept down on apartments on Fillmore Street and Grove Street, as well as the Black Self-Help Moving and Storage Company on Market, arresting seven men named by Harris, including J. C. Simon, Manuel Moore, Larry Green, and Tom Manney. An eighth suspect, Jesse Lee Cooks, was already behind bars at Folsom. In the end, they went with a whimper. "Don't shoot, don't shoot!" Simon pleaded, shivering with fear in his bed as Coreris and Fotinos burst through the door with their guns drawn.

The Zebra arrests came at the final hour, as the poison was dangerously leaching. Two nights before, an eighteen-year-old black student named Theodore Gooden was driving through the Broadway Tunnel in North Beach with his friend, James Cook, an army medic stationed at Letterman Hospital on the nearby Presidio base. Suddenly a pickup raced up alongside Gooden's car. A long-haired white man leaned out the truck's passenger window, aimed a gun at Gooden and Cook, and fired three times before the truck roared away. Gooden was wounded in the hand. His friend crumpled onto the seat beside him, where he died.

At a press conference following the arrests, Alioto fanned public fears when he announced that the seven Zebra suspects were part of a nationwide Black Muslim cult "dedicated to the murder and mutilation of whites and dissident blacks," and insisted that unless law enforcement continued to crack down on the shadowy organization, there would be more bloodshed. Alioto said that the total Zebra victim count throughout the state might exceed eighty, not the twenty-three officially listed in San Francisco, and suggested that the mysterious disappearance of numerous hitchhikers on California roads might be tied to the group that he identified as "the Death Angels."

The information about a wider Muslim conspiracy was fed to the mayor not only by Harris but also by state investigators. There was a lurking suspicion in law enforcement circles that not all the Zebra conspirators had been rounded up. In the end, only Green, Simon, and Moore were positively identified by witnesses at the police lineup and only they, in addition to the already incarcerated Cooks, stood trial for the Zebra mayhem. The other suspects, including former local gridiron hero Manney, went free.

The SFPD continued to stake out the Black Self-Help building. Many in the department believed that the four Zebra defendants must have had accomplices in the Muslim organization, since they had borrowed vehicles from Manney and carried out some of their goriest butchery in his moving company loft. Some frustrated cops even slashed tires on the company's trucks and torched one of the vehicles, to provoke Manney and his employees into doing something rash. But the Zebra killings stopped after the arrests, and Earl Sanders was among those who came to believe that Harris had exaggerated the dimensions of the Zebra plot and even its official connection to the Black Muslims.

Still, it was the Nation of Islam that paid for the defense of all the Zebra suspects, except for Cooks. Mosque officials cut him loose after he confessed to the murder of Frances Rose—a violation of Black Muslim code, which forbade cooperating with white authorities. The other three defendants remained defiant throughout their trial, which took longer than a year, making it the longest courtroom drama in California at the time. Gus Coreris stationed himself at the prosecution table throughout the lengthy proceedings, to make sure justice was done. Finally, on March 9, 1976, the jury found the defendants guilty of all counts. The death penalty had been suspended temporarily in California. All four Zebra killers were sentenced to life in prison, where they remain today.

After the Zebra case was cracked, San Francisco enjoyed a respite from the carnage and terror that bedeviled the city in the early seventies. The city was buoyed by a new wave of progressive activism—young men and women of all races and sexual preferences who took their fever for change into the city's cultural and political mainstream instead of underground cells. One of the new leaders who rode this ebullient groundswell was named Art Agnos. In 1987, long after the horror of Zebra had faded, Agnos won an overwhelming victory in the San Francisco mayoral race, gathering 70 percent of the vote. In 1989 his leadership of the city would be severely tested when the Bay Area was slammed by the Loma Prieta earthquake, killing sixty-three people, setting the Marina district aflame, and leaving thousands homeless. Throughout the crisis, Mayor Agnos showed the same calm serenity and self-command he had displayed on that night when a stranger walked up to him and pumped two bullets into him at point-blank range.

21

THE EMPRESS OF CHINATOWN

Like WILLIE BROWN, her longtime political comrade, Rose Pak mastered San Francisco by walking it. Young Willie, a transplant from the sleepy East Texas railroad junction of Mineola, strolled the streets of San Francisco all day long in the early 1950s after moving in with his flashy, high-rolling uncle, Itsie Collins, in the Fillmore. Uncle Itsie, who gave his nephew some pocket change every morning, advised him to talk to as many people as he could during his daily wanderings— a stiff challenge for a seventeen-year-old black kid from Texas, particularly in some less than hospitable neighborhoods. But it turned out to be good training for the man who became San Francisco's most successful African-American politician, and the city's first black mayor.

Rose Pak learned much about San Francisco politics from watching its master, Willie Brown, at work. Pak would turn herself into Chinatown's top power broker. In the process, she was able to protect her own community from suffering the same fate as the Fillmore district.

Pak arrived in the city as a teenager in 1967 to study at the Catholic-run San Francisco College for Women. It was evening when she landed at the airport after a long flight from Hong Kong. She was alone and had no family or friends to greet her. But Pak was used to relying on herself.

In 1951, when she was three, her family fled China after the Communist takeover, but only Rose, her younger sister, and her mother made it to Hong Kong. Her father, a wealthy businessman on the Communists' blacklist, disappeared during their escape and was never seen again. At age nine, Pak was sent to a Portuguese Catholic boarding school for girls in Macao that was run by Italian nuns. There were only a few other Chinese students. She had to learn Portuguese, as well as Italian and English. The nuns liked to make her stand in front of the class and read from Western classics while the other girls roared with laughter at her accent. But Pak had a strong will. By the second year, she was running the school's boarding company.

After Hong Kong's neon blaze and hustle and bustle, the streets of San Francisco seemed so quiet and dark to Pak. She was staying with a doctor in Pacific Heights, where she received room and board in return for being his wife's companion. When Pak looked out her window, she couldn't see one person on the street. But she was enchanted by the city's fairy-tale beauty. The painted lady Victorians looked like dollhouses to her.

Chinatown had a special allure for Pak. It seemed like an old movie set, with its green pagoda buildings, strings of red lanterns, and ferocious lion statue guarding the entrance gate on Grant Avenue. But the neighborhood's quaint exterior masked a social tempest. Following the immigration reform law of 1965, which eased the longtime anti-Chinese quotas, a new wave of immigrants came flooding into San Francisco's Chinatown, West Coast capital of the Chinese diaspora. The neighborhood's dreary tenement buildings, welfare hotels, and public housing barracks were soon stuffed with families from Guangdong Province and other Asian regions that were the chief exporters of human capital to America.

By the time Pak arrived in Gold Mountain in the late sixties, the disenchantment of Chinatown's youth was spilling into the streets. "Keep Grant Avenue Narrow, Dirty, and Quaint for Tourists," read a sign carried by a droll, young protester at one Chinatown demonstration. "Preserve Chinatown's Uniqueness—Highest TB Rates, Most Suicides, Lowest Wages," read another.

The youthful rebellion in Chinatown mirrored the turmoil in the rest of the pulsating city. Like Willie Brown a decade earlier, Rose Pak trekked the hills and valleys of San Francisco, sampling all its strange and wondrous offerings. In college, she had to wear pumps and curtsy to the reverend mother. When she went downtown with her classmates, they had to wear white gloves. But in her free time, Pak was an intrepid explorer. In the Haight, she would follow hippies down the street and into their homes, as intrigued as a jungle anthropologist. They were warm and welcoming, but she was mortified by the jiggling, braless girls, and she thought that the hippies' habit of sharing wet joints was grossly unsanitary. When she began to experiment with magical smoke, she used glass water pipes.

In the Fillmore, Pak walked into churches and talked to worshippers. "I was interested in everything having to do with African Americans," she recalled. "I wanted to find out why they were rioting."

One day Pak—a lover of English poetry, particularly Keats and Shelley—saw a flyer announcing a women's poetry reading. She showed up at the address, which turned out to be a house in the Mission. There were a dozen women gathered in the living room, in jeans and flannel shirts. The women told Pak they were there to make poetry that expressed their love. "If you're expressing love, why aren't there any men here?" Pak inquired innocently.

"They looked at me like I was from Mars," she later recalled. "I had never heard the word *gay* before. Lesbianism? I mean how would you do it? I had no clue."

Rose was a crusader; she wanted to save the world. She was studying to be a journalist because she felt that would give her the best platform to speak to people. But she was a political operator at heart.

Pak started out in city politics by volunteering for Dianne Feinstein's first campaign for the board of supervisors in 1969. Feinstein was an attractive young Pacific Heights housewife with strong political ambitions, and, like Pak, the strict discipline of someone raised by nuns: in Feinstein's case, the sisters of the Convent of the Sacred Heart High School.

Pak, Feinstein, and the candidate's second husband—Dr. Bert Feinstein, a wealthy surgeon utterly devoted to his younger wife—drove all over town, climbing up ladders and nailing campaign posters to telephone poles.

"Dianne never climbed up those ladders," remembered Pak. "She was the same person she is today: very proper, never swore. The madams taught us well. If she had gone to a cocktail party, and a button had popped off her dress and it fell down to around her knees, she wouldn't have blinked an eye. She would've simply reached down, picked it up, and pinned it perfectly in place."

Pak took her growing political expertise back to Chinatown. She loved everything about the neighborhood: the strings of ducks in the store windows, the gambling joints in the back, the wheeling and dealing at the smoky Empress of China bar. It was a pushing, shoving throng of humanity—a steaming urban teapot filled with the type of people who had the moxie to uproot themselves and travel halfway around the globe so that their children could have better lives.

Pak dedicated her life to giving the Chinese of San Francisco a voice in city affairs. As late as the 1970s, Chinatown was still an insular world. She knew that its immigrant population arrived with a heavy baggage of fears and inhibitions. "We come from countries where there are no free elections. So politics is a dirty word." It wasn't until 1977 that San Francisco elected an Asian-American to the board of supervisors, and he could not manage to get reelected.

Rose Pak would become a one-woman Tammany Hall for her community, building political connections downtown, pulling strings, arranging favors, scratching for a place at San Francisco's table. She had the devotion of a nun. "It was a choice that I did not get married, that I did not have children," she said. "It would have taken time from the work I do."

By rousing Chinatown, the sleeping dragon, Pak tapped into a new vein of human energy that helped revitalize the entire city. The Chinese, confined for years in a forbidden city surrounded by downtown skyscrapers, Nob Hill hotels, and North Beach Italian hostility, began to break out and redefine San Francisco.

PAK WAS JOINED BY a rising generation of young activists. Ed Lee, a Rhodes Scholarship finalist and UC Berkeley Law School graduate, could have joined his classmates who went to work for elite corporate law firms. Most of the Chinese kids he knew in professional schools were practical; they went for the money. But Lee was too angry and rebellious to go down that path. Growing up in Seattle, one of six kids

in a household that spoke Toisanese and Cantonese, he always resented
the way that his father was treated. Lee's father worked as a cook in a
restaurant, and toiling alongside him as a dishwasher, he saw his dad
get yelled at and insulted day after day. They treated him like a coolie.
The older man had to take the abuse; the family came first. But the
stress took its toll, and he died too young of a heart attack. Lee, who
was fifteen at the time, told himself that when he got into a position to
do something about it, he would make sure that the Chinese didn't get
pushed around like his father.

While still in law school in the mid-1970s, Ed Lee went to work
for the Asian Law Caucus and began to organize tenants in Ping Yuen,
a forbidding-looking public housing fortress that towered over Chinatown. The San Francisco Housing Authority officials who ran Ping
Yuen—which means "Tranquil Garden"—treated the immigrant families stuffed into its boxy rooms like caged chickens. It was just clucking
to them when the tenants complained that they had gone without heat
or hot water for months, that the elevators didn't run, the lights were
out in the hallways, and their families were preyed upon by thugs and
thieves. Lee and the other law crusaders told the tenants that they had
the right to withhold rental payments until the building was brought up
to code. But a rent strike at Ping Yuen would never succeed, the activists
were warned. Chinese immigrants were too quiet and submissive to put
up a fight.

Then late one night in 1978, Julia Wong, a seventeen-year-old girl
who worked as a seamstress in a Chinatown sweatshop, came home
to Ping Yuen after her long shift. As usual, the elevator was out, and
Wong began climbing the dark stairwell to her apartment. On the fifth
floor, somebody tried to rape Wong and then threw her screaming off the
balcony onto the pavement below. Miraculously, she survived. But her
attacker was persistent. He dragged her back upstairs and again hurled
her to the ground, this time killing her.

Julia Wong's hideous murder galvanized the Tranquil Garden's long-
abused tenants. They told Ed Lee and his legal warriors that they were
ready to fight back. Ping Yuen's outraged residents unfurled a banner
over an upper-floor balcony announcing a rent strike. Housing authority
bureaucrats were stunned. Chinese residents were the most dependable
renters in the city's public housing system; they always paid on time.

When they started withholding their monthly payments, the housing authority immediately felt the financial pinch. After six months, housing officials caved, agreeing to make a long list of improvements at Ping Yuen.

The successful Chinatown rent strike was the beginning of Ed Lee's career as a community organizer. "You can go to law school to make money, or you can go to help the community," Lee said. "I fought landlord-tenant battles where I would face off against people I went to law school with. They were working for corporations trying to evict people, and I was trying to stop them. Landlords—many of whom were absentee, and many were Chinese—hated my guts. They saw me coming and said, 'There's that Communist Ed Lee!'"

The housing battles of the 1970s were the crucible for an entire generation of new activists in San Francisco. The city was a finite peninsula of competing dreams and ambitions. Was it to become a Manhattan of the West, whose office towers and high-rise apartment buildings overshadowed everything else, or remain an affordable, human-scale city of light nestled into the hills and hollows? The land-use war sparked a full-blown identity crisis for San Francisco, forcing the city to grapple with a range of social, economic, and aesthetic dilemmas.

Tensions exploded in 1977 during a dramatic showdown over the International Hotel, a decrepit brick building squeezed between Chinatown and the financial district that was home to nearly two hundred elderly Filipino and Chinese tenants. The residential hotel at the corner of Kearny and Jackson Streets became a symbol of resistance for a new generation of Asian activists, community organizers, and student radicals—including Ed Lee—when it was bought by developer Walter Shorenstein, who planned to raze it and build a parking lot. After Shorenstein was stymied by lawsuits and public opposition, he dumped the property, selling it to a mysterious Bangkok tycoon known as "the Godfather." The tycoon's company announced plans to build a commercial tower on the I-Hotel site and finally succeeded in ramming an eviction order through the courts.

Late one summer night, as the rest of the city slept, an army of helmeted riot cops, some on horseback, began marching on the I-Hotel. Some three thousand protesters formed a human barricade around the building and sang "We Shall Overcome," as they were eerily lit up by the midnight sun of countless TV lights. "It was like the Roman Legions coming after the Christians," one young Asian protester said later. "I could almost hear drumbeats; their batons looked like swords drawn." The riot cops bulldozed their way through the crowd, scaled the hotel's fire escapes, and began smashing through the windows with sledgehammers. Once inside, they dragged the terrified old tenants out of their rooms and began trashing the building, breaking toilets into pieces and knocking down walls to make sure that the I-Hotel would never again be inhabited.

The demolition of the I-Hotel was the last stand of old Manilatown, once home to thousands of Filipino farmworkers, cannery workers, houseboys, and sailors—like the hotel's elderly tenants, most of whom never married because of antimiscegenation laws and restrictive immigration policies. But the hotel residents' plucky fight, and their rough treatment at the hands of police, galvanized neighborhood activists throughout the city. Determined to clamp limits on the runaway corporate real estate machine that was plowing through the city during the Alioto era—fueled by powerful downtown business interests and labor unions—organizers put anti–high rise initiatives on city ballots and campaigned for sympathetic local candidates. Nowhere was this battle more urgent than in Chinatown, where some thirty thousand people—mostly Asian immigrants—were crammed into twenty-four square blocks, all in the growing shadow of a steadily encroaching financial district.

GORDON CHIN WAS ONE of the young Chinatown crusaders lit up by the I-Hotel fireworks. Chinatown was his native ground, the richly storied turf that he would dedicate his life to protecting and revitalizing. Chin was born in Chinese Hospital in the heart of Chinatown. His parents waited tables by day, but at night they went out gambling, a Chinatown passion. When his mother was young, she and her friends would dress up and go out dancing at Forbidden City, the nightclub that featured leggy Chinese showgirls and singers who belted out Broadway show tunes. The club, which opened in 1938, also advertised its "exotic Oriental dancers," nude performers who hid their female charms with nothing more than balloons and fans. Forbidden City attracted celebrities like Bob Hope, Duke Ellington, and Gene Kelly—the latter of whom cruised through the club searching for entertainers to cast in *Flower Drum Song,* the Rodgers and Hammerstein musical he was directing on Broadway. Behind the red door at 363 Sutter was a world that remained, well into the 1940s, truly forbidden, where white men and Asian women danced together on the ballroom floor—and sometimes, in defiance of race-mixing prohibitions, fell in love.

Chin came of age in a different San Francisco, haunting the city's jazz and soul music clubs, where he heard Miles Davis and Smokey Robinson perform. In his day, cool Chinese kids took their lead from black musicians and militants. At Merritt College in Oakland and later at San Francisco State College in the late sixties, Chin got caught up in the black power confrontations, listening to Huey Newton and Bobby Seale speak on campus and taking inspiration from their defiant swagger. But Chin and his friends were not into burning down the system, they wanted to pry it open. He interned in the San Francisco office of Congressman Phil Burton, the city's powerful Washington operator, watching rising young stars like Nancy Pelosi and Willie Brown glide past. "Willie had charisma and style," Chin recalled. "Everyone wanted to be like him; he was cool. If Miles Davis had gone into politics, he would've been Willie Brown."

When the city was convulsed by the SLA and Zebra, Chin and his fellow activists just kept their heads down. "We knew all that stuff was just a passing circus," he reflected. "We were committed activists who were in it for the long haul. We weren't out to overthrow the American government or even city hall. But we did want to force fundamental change in the system."

The long march of San Francisco crusaders such as Rose Pak, Ed Lee, and Gordon Chin eventually paid off. Years later, they could look back and marvel at what they had accomplished. There, one evening in February 2011, ensconced at a window table at North Beach Restaurant, were the two political veterans whom the *San Francisco Chronicle* anointed as the city's reigning "power couple": Willie Brown and Rose Pak. At ages seventy-six and sixty-two, respectively, they might have simply been reminiscing about old times over their Italian dinners. Instead they were feting San Francisco's new mayor: none other than Ed Lee, the man they craftily maneuvered into office after it was vacated a year early by Gavin Newsom, who won California's lieutenant governorship in 2010. Lee, the former public housing agitator, was now in charge of the city bureaucrats with whom he once clashed. Lee made history in November 2011 when he secured the office in the municipal election, becoming the first Asian American to be elected mayor in San Francisco.

Meanwhile, Gordon Chin was finishing a long and successful career as the founding executive director of the Chinatown Community Development Center, a nonprofit organization that has built more than two thousand affordable housing units in the neighborhood and rehabilitated many more. As he looked back over his accomplishments, Chin was proudest of the sixteen-floor residential hotel he built on the corner of Kearny and Jackson. The building's views of the Bay Bridge and downtown skyline were the kinds usually enjoyed by owners of luxury condos and lofts, but these hotel rooms were reserved for seniors on fixed incomes. Chin's organization built the hotel on a vacant lot; a hole in the ground that had remained an ugly scar in San Francisco for more than two decades. When the building opened in 2005, it was given the name of the old brick structure that once stood there: the International Hotel.

But all this was decades in the future. Before San Francisco could congratulate itself on its inclusive civic climate, the city had to withstand other shock waves. The biggest tremor shook San Francisco even more powerfully than the city's bulging Asian immigrant population. It was triggered by a cultural invasion as momentous as the hippie migration of the sixties.

Ever since its earliest Barbary Coast days, San Francisco had, with varying degrees of hospitality, made room for its dandy men and masculine ladies. But the gay carnival that rolled into town in the 1970s was like nothing the city had ever seen, or any other city for that matter. Like the hippies, gays arrived in San Francisco from all corners of the country and planet, on the run from brutality, boredom, and the daily tyranny of clenched minds. Once they arrived, they had no intention of leaving. They promptly began giving San Francisco a makeover in their own image. It was the closest thing to a hometown they had ever experienced. The resulting identity war embroiled the city for years to come. There would be blood, rioting, and plague before San Francisco was finally liberated.

22

SAN FRANCISCO
SATYRICON

JOE ALIOTO WAS a complex man. A lover of poetry and the arts, he could rise to defend the authority-bedeviled Allen Ginsberg, as he did at the Spoleto Arts Festival in July 1967, when Italian police arrested the poet after local authorities read "Who Be Kind To," his paean to the "orgy of our flesh." The carabinieri questioned Ginsberg, never one to make a secret of his homoerotic appetites, about the exact nature of some of his orgiastic verse. Perhaps the following words got lost in translation: "Desire given with meat hand and cock, desire taken with mouth and ass, desire returned to the last sigh!" Alioto, who was on the festival's board, introduced himself to the police as Ginsberg's $1-a-year lawyer—certainly the lowest rate ever charged by the millionaire attorney—and quickly managed to spring the poet.

As a poetry enthusiast, Alioto could champion the bard who wrote lines like these:

> *Come beautiful boys with breasts bright gold*
> *Lie down in bed with me ere ye grow old,*
> *Take down your blue jeans, we'll have some raw fun*
> *Lie down on your bellies I'll fuck your soft bun.*

But as mayor of San Francisco, Joe Alioto was no friend of queers. In his official role, he was true to his traditional Italian upbringing when it came to policing the city's sexual frontiers. Playing to his Catholic base, Alioto oversaw one of the most severe crackdowns on gays in San Francisco history. Driven from bars by unrelenting police raids, gays were forced into city parks, but the cops pursued them there as well. By 1971, San Francisco police were busting an average of nearly three thousand gay men a year on public sex charges. The same year, by contrast, New York City police made only about sixty such arrests.

The SFPD was not as perversely clever as it was in the 1930s: when staking out one notorious Market Street theater, some undercover cops painted their cocks with Mercurochrome before allowing gay cruisers to suck them. The unsuspecting cruisers, their lips aflame with telltale red, would then be arrested as they exited through the lobby. But police entrapment was still in widespread use under Alioto. And San Francisco courts could not be counted on for leniency. In 1971 alone, over one hundred local men were sentenced to a stunning fifteen years to life for the crime of "sodomy and oral copulation."

"To tell you the truth, I don't think my father knew many gay men," said Alioto's daughter, Angela. "I think he was sheltered at the time. I was raised in a house where the word *sex* was never mentioned."

Joe Alioto's police sweeps would be the last hurrah in San Francisco City Hall's century-old, hot and cold war on homosexual freedom. By his second term, Alioto faced a mutiny in his own government when the board of supervisors voted in 1972 to prohibit city contractors from discriminating against homosexuals—a legal landmark in the long battle for gay rights. "Does this mean that contractors have to hire men who wear dresses?" asked a genuinely perplexed Supervisor Dianne Feinstein when lesbian activist Del Martin first suggested the law. But within five years, Feinstein, responding to the city's shifting mores, was hosting a lesbian wedding in the backyard of her Pacific Heights mansion.

As San Francisco's political climate became more welcoming, more and more gays flocked to the city. By 1976, the police chief estimated that more than 140,000 gays were living in San Francisco—more than one in five citizens—and nearly 100 homosexual settlers were arriving each week, figures widely considered to be conservative.

VINCE CALCAGNO WAS ONE of the young gay men who arrived in San Francisco that year. He had grown up in blue-collar Akron, Ohio, in an Italian Catholic family, and after graduating from college had found a John Waters–like bohemian niche for himself in Cleveland. Calcagno lived with his boyfriend Fred in a house owned by Paige Palmer, a local TV fitness queen with million-dollar gams who would demonstrate scissor kicks and jumping jacks in black fishnet stockings and pumps. Colorful personalities flowed through the house, including the young musicians who would later become the New Wave group Devo. But by 1976, Calcagno felt that he had done Ohio, and he and Fred headed west.

They arrived in February, rising up from underground on a BART escalator that deposited them at the downtown corner of Market and Montgomery. The temperature hovered around seventy, and they were bathed in a soft winter light. Strolling down Market to the cable car turnaround at Powell Street, Calcagno spotted a phone booth and called his mother in Akron. "Mom, you lied," he told her. "The grass *is* greener." She burst into tears. "It sounds like you're never coming home."

He never did.

That first evening, Calcagno and Fred checked into a small hotel off Polk Street, picked up a gay tourist guide, and went looking for the Castro district. Riding on a bus near the corner of Market and Duboce Streets, they knew that Oz was near when a stark naked man scampered merrily across the street, and the entire bus erupted into cheers. On Castro Street, the couple were surrounded by more gay men than they had ever seen in one place. Calcagno had a feminine halo of hair and big disco shades. But these men had a macho swagger, dressed in tight Pendleton wool plaid shirts and ass-hugging jeans or army fatigues and leather bomber jackets. "I just didn't know if I could do this," remembered Calcagno. "I grabbed on to Fred and thought, 'I'm probably going to lose my boyfriend here.' The whole thing seemed scary to me." He paused. "I got over that quick."

San Francisco in the mid-1970s was a never-ending party for gay men. Calcagno went to work in a Castro store that made T-shirts and processed film—including gay customers' X-rated pictures. He and his coworkers pored over the photos when they came back from the developer, wide eyed at the infinite ways that men could find to pleasure each other. One of the most popular T-shirts on sale in Castro shops showed Judy Garland from *The Wizard of Oz* and read, "Toto, we're not in Kansas anymore." It was a feeling that Calcagno had nearly every day.

On their first Halloween in San Francisco, he and Fred put on sailor suits and dance shoes, and tapped their way up and down Castro Street like Frank Sinatra and Gene Kelly in *Anchors Aweigh*. Halloween—the one night that San Francisco cops traditionally ceded to gays, allowing even the most dazzling creatures to flutter around town—was a high holiday in the Castro and up and down Polk Street.

Their first Gay Freedom Day Parade was even more unforgettable. Crisscrossing the city on foot and bus, they felt like they were part of a moveable orgy. "There were people having sex on the MUNI [municipal] trolleys, there were people having sex in broad daylight in the park," said Calcagno. "There were bands and music all over. It was ninety-six degrees, and everyone was stripped down and sweaty."

Gays were changing the face of San Francisco in countless ways. They bought ramshackle Victorians in the Castro from Irish-American families fleeing the homosexual invasion and turned them into postcard gems. They edged into drug- and crime-infested neighborhoods in the Mission and the Duboce Triangle and spruced them up too, opening cafes and flower shops and clothing stores.

The food revolution that is still sweeping the nation—based on locally grown organic ingredients, seasonal cycles, and the age-old wisdom of the Mediterranean—was largely the creation of female and gay foodies in the Bay Area during the 1970s. Like Alice Waters and her dashing gay chef, Jeremiah Tower—founders of Chez Panisse in Berkeley—this new culinary wave simply expected a more sensual experience than the local dining world provided.

"When I began cooking at Chez Panisse in the early seventies," recalled Tower, "I'd go to the meat markets in Oakland and see all these boxes of frozen meat marked 'Ernie's' and the names of other top San Francisco restaurants. It's hard to imagine, but you couldn't find fresh herbs, very few fresh vegetables. In California! I had to go to an Italian deli to buy good olive oil; it was the only place in the Bay Area that carried it. After we got things going, people began showing up at the back door of the restaurant with fresh mushrooms they had gathered. And it was, 'Here we go!'"

In San Francisco, the first gay-owned restaurants in the 1970s were known for their floor shows more than their food. Hamburger Mary's, at the corner of Folsom and Twelfth Streets in the heart of the leather district, was opened by a man nicknamed Trixie and his hippie friends. It was a truck-stop diner on poppers, catering to the gays and gay-friendly who worked up powerful appetites on the dance floors and in the back rooms of nearby clubs like the Stud, Febe's, and the Eagle Tavern. The carb-heavy menu was known for its greasy burgers and pillowy omelettes, but Trixie's hippie roots could be found in the mound of green sprouts atop his salads. The service, provided by distracted bare-chested men with nipple rings, was chaotic. And the décor was loopy, with a giant ruby slipper doubling as a planter, rubber-nippled baby bottles serving as creamers, and anything-goes unisex bathrooms. But Hamburger Mary's was the perfect blend of 1960s and 1970s San Francisco, an only-in-SF mix of nine-grain wholesomeness and disco mania.

It was the Zuni Café that took San Francisco cuisine to a new level. The restaurant was opened in 1979 by Billy West, a boyishly charming sprite who learned about the joys of food while traveling the world as a navy "wife" with his sailor boyfriend. Inspired by the Southwest themes popular at the time, West took over a Market Street storefront next to a cactus store, hand plastered the walls to give it an adobe look, and began serving dishes inspired by cookbook author Diana Kennedy's Mexican sojourns. Later, with the help of former Chez Panisse chef Judy Rodgers, West began working French and Italian influences into the menu, all the while developing bonds with local farmers and ranchers, and introducing diners to the new splendors of California cuisine. Succulent Tomales Bay oysters, grass-fed beef from the Niemann-Schell ranch in Bolinas, cheeses from organic Point Reyes dairy farms, arugula and escarole from Green Gulch gardens that were sprinkled by the wet sea breezes off Muir Beach. These were the ingredients of the San Francisco food revolution that would challenge the rest of the country to eat local, fresh, and organic.

Zuni quickly became the most popular watering hole for the new San Francisco, drawing a democratic clientele that included rakish gay men, Pacific Heights socialites, city hall politicos, and struggling writers and artists with their last freelance checks in their pockets. It was Jeremiah Tower's favorite late-night escape, inspiring him to open his own legendary San Francisco restaurant, Stars, in 1984. "I once figured I spent over three hundred thousand dollars eating and drinking in Zuni's," Tower said. "I'd nip over there, and if they didn't have a table, I'd just stand at the bar and have a glass of champagne and a soppressata sandwich. It had the best bar in town."

The restaurant drew the town's luminaries and those just passing through. Robin Williams, Julia Child, Mick Jagger, Hunter Thompson, Phillip Roth, Ted Kennedy. No one bothered them while they were eating. There were no celebrity photos on the walls. That was for the Fisherman's Wharf joints that served shrimp scampi.

Not long after Zuni opened, Billy West, aware of his limitations as a manager, brought in Vince Calcagno to help him run the place. "Billy was very smart, very cute, very fun—but like a lot of creative people, his head was in the clouds," said Calcagno. "He was a hippie, but he ended up with a Maserati. He liked nice things."

Calcagno, who had worked in a bank back in Ohio, proved to be a well-organized and disciplined manager. His skills were sorely tested in Zuni's early years, when he found waiters shooting up drugs and fucking in the bathroom. "In those days, even managers always had a glass of wine going; you were never stopped from drinking. So it was hard to tell the waiters they couldn't get high. It felt hypocritical."

There was a lust for life that spilled out everywhere in the city. "Everyone was sleeping with everyone, and everyone knew and no one cared," said Calcagno. "All the boundaries were being broken. It seemed there was no end to it."

The gay carnival eroticized all San Francisco. Bars like the Stud began as dark, rough-trade dens of iniquity but somehow morphed into polymorphously perverse playgrounds for men and women of all sexual tribes. Gays went carousing at the Stud with their favorite fag hags, who drew straight men into their flirtatious webs. A Freddy Mercury type shaking his ass on the dance floor would suddenly be groped from behind, and couldn't be sure if it was the man or woman dancing next to him. Most bathhouses in the city were strictly gay cruising zones, but a few—like the coed Grand Central and Sutro Baths—began catering to men and women who fantasized about public or anonymous sex.

Gay men started the party in San Francisco in the 1970s. But everyone was soon invited.

INSPIRED BY THE GAY and feminist bravado of the period, a beloved party girl named Margo St. James brought prostitution out of the closet in San Francisco, founding a hookers' liberation group in 1973 called Coyote (Call Off Your Old Tired Ethics). St. James had arrived in town in 1959, a wide-eyed farm girl from Bellingham, Washington, and soon became part of the North Beach beat scene. The parties in her upstairs apartment at the corner of Grant Avenue and Green Street, which she shared with a couple of ladies of the night, drew the likes of Lenny Bruce and Ken Kesey, as well as bartenders, 49ers football players, and off-duty cops. The colorful parade of men was drawn by the charming young women and by the fourteen-foot marijuana plant that St. James kept in a backyard shed.

Party girls like Margo St. James, with big hearts and outsized personalities, are clasped to San Francisco's bosom. Herb Caen thought San Francisco's Holly Golightly made a merry sight zooming around town in her sporty Triumph TR3 convertible, wearing an overturned salad bowl on her head for a helmet, and she popped up often in his column. St. James delighted lovers by shaving her pubic hair into a heart shape—years before actress Valerie Perrine, who played Honey Bruce in the 1974 movie *Lenny,* made headlines with her own pussy valentine.

St. James knew everyone in town. While moonlighting as a secretary at a bail bondsman's office, to pay off her own bond on a prostitution bust, St. James ate lunch across the street at the hall of justice. Her lunch companion was often a rising young attorney named Willie Brown. "Willie took a lot of hooker cases back then. We used to eat together in the cafeteria because he's black and I'm a whore, and nobody would sit with us, so we sat together."

One evening at a party in her home in woodsy Marin County, where she had moved in the early seventies, St. James accosted guest Richard Hongisto, the iconoclastic San Francisco sheriff. Hongisto, who was known as "Big Dick" by St. James's hooker friends, was a favorite of every liberal group in San Francisco. St. James thought it was time for prostitutes, still preyed upon by SFPD vice squad zealots and often abused by pimps, to stand up for their rights. She asked Sheriff Hongisto what it would take for a union of whores to win the respect of the feminist and gay rights groups that supported him. Hongisto told her that a prostitute with spunk, a working woman from the "hidden victim class," needed to speak out; that was the only way the issue would be heard. After mustering her courage, St. James decided that she would be the one.

As the founder of Coyote, St. James fought for the rights of all those she described as "sex workers"—including whores, porn film actors, strippers, and massage parlor employees. She argued that women who sold their labor in the sex industry should be granted the same rights as those who worked as secretaries or nurses. Coyote offered legal advice and referrals to sex workers and lobbied city hall to decriminalize prostitution. But St. James realized that the quickest way to San Francisco's heart was to create a spectacle.

Coyote began promoting an annual Halloween Hooker's Ball: a bawdy gathering of men and women in debauched masquerade that grew more flagrant and more popular each year. By 1978, the erotic extravaganza was drawing more than eighteen thousand to the cavernous Cow Palace arena—home to epic roller derby duels and rodeos and site of the 1964 presidential nomination of Republican Barry Goldwater.

The night began with a roaring parade of tap dancers, cheerleaders, and a squadron of Harley-straddling Dykes on Bikes. Then the curtain parted, and out came the Whore Queen herself, Margo St. James, riding on an elephant and dressed like the scourge of the San Francisco sex industry, Supervisor Dianne Feinstein. Around midnight, George Carlin made a brief appearance onstage, but the comic quickly realized that the real entertainment was happening among the carousing masses down on the floor. After shouting a string of FCC-banned words into the microphone, he quickly made an exit.

WHILE MARGO ST. JAMES was trying to revolutionize the world's oldest profession, two aspiring San Francisco porn film moguls—brothers Jim and Artie Mitchell—were striving to take X-rated movies out of the seedy, sticky-floor, stag-film era and inject them with a giddy, groovy sensibility that appealed to a new generation of men and women. The Mitchell brothers, born and raised in the Okie culture of the Sacramento Delta, escaped the drudgery of the local paper and chemical mills the same way that their cardsharp father had: by learning to hustle. They proved to be shrewd carny barkers, opening a porn theater in the early seventies in an old Pontiac showroom on the edge of the Tenderloin and screening their own film productions. Mitchell Brothers movies developed a reputation for their slicker production values and their quirky, self-mocking attitude—giving them a cool buzz among the counterculture crowd. They hired hippies and college girls instead of hookers to star in their films, and the women actually seemed to be enjoying themselves, not just laboring over their partners' towering erections.

In 1972 the brothers released their underground masterpiece, *Behind the Green Door,* which, along with *Deep Throat,* took porn into the American mainstream. *Green Door* is a hazy, druggy sex fantasy, the extended wet dream of an innocent, young woman named Gloria who gives herself over to her deepest desires. Blindfolded and carried off to a secret world, Gloria is first caressed by a troop of robed women, then ravished by a beautiful black god, and, finally, taken by a group of horned satyrs in trapeze swings. As Gloria is flooded with pleasure, she is publicly displayed before a kinky mélange of masked sybarites, who—driven mad by the wanton spectacle—fall on one another in all variations of couplings and sate their lust. The film, suffused with the wild sexual imagination of 1970s San Francisco, set a variety of porn precedents that later became standard hard-core fixtures, such as interracial and bisexual coupling.

The Mitchell brothers scored a casting coup by convincing a nineteen-year-old blonde, all-American-looking actress-model named Marilyn Briggs to take the part of Gloria. Briggs, the daughter of a Madison Avenue advertising executive, had never acted in a hard-core film before. But after shrewdly negotiating a percentage of the profits, she agreed to star in the film under the name Marilyn Chambers.

In a huge stroke of luck for the filmmakers, the manufacturers of Ivory Snow detergent released a newly designed box of soap flakes just as *Behind the Green Door* premiered. Pictured on the box was a sweet-faced Marilyn Briggs—who had done the photo shoot months before her reincarnation as a porn star—cuddling a cherubic baby. The story of the pure-as-Ivory-Snow porn queen exploded around the world, helping *Behind the Green Door* set adult film box office records. The movie, which cost $60,000 to make, eventually earned $50 million, an estimate that is probably low because of all the bootleg copies that circulated.

The Mitchells' success as mainstream pornographers—and their ballsy way of flaunting it, such as staging a Hollywood-style premiere of *Behind the Green Door* at their O'Farrell Theater—inevitably aroused the ire of prudish city officials like Feinstein and the Irish Catholics who ran the police department. It didn't help win friends downtown when the brothers released *Reckless Claudia*, which featured a scene in which the horny heroine sucks an aroused priest in a confessional and is splattered with his holy fluid. The police routinely raided the O'Farrell Theater, busting one or both brothers. During one raid, a vice cop ordered the lights turned up in the theater and proceeded to scold the unfortunate patrons like a red-faced Irish priest. "You gentlemen should be ashamed! Ashamed!" he fumed as he stalked up and down the center aisle. "It's a beautiful day outside, and you pasty-faced perverts are in here abusing yourselves! Don't you care about your health?"

But unlike old-school smut peddlers, who deflected police aggression by crawling off to the city's shadows and greasing the right palms at the hall of justice, the Mitchell brothers fought back. With the help of their attorney, Michael Kennedy, another brawling San Francisco barrister in the Hallinan mold, the brothers played hardball, filing injunctions and lawsuits and demonstrating once again that the best defense is a good offense. They also courted local reporters, politicians, and hipsters like Robert Crumb and Hunter Thompson. The upstairs room at the O'Farrell—with its massive pool table, bare-breasted dancers, and congenial flow of drugs and booze—became a popular boys club for an emerging crop of San Francisco players.

The most potent factor in the Mitchell brothers' defense, however, was the changing nature of the local porn film market. Contrary to the fulminating cop, not all of the theater's customers were pasty-faced perverts. Many were couples on adventurous dates, in search of some extra, precoital stimulation. When police officials threatened to yank the Mitchells' theater permit, a healthy cross section of the local bourgeois showed up at the public hearing to protest, including an architect who

urged the police commission to grant the permit because San Franciscans needed a nice, clean place to enjoy their porn movies.

THERE WAS A NEW San Francisco being born like a chrysalis in the
crumbling shell of the old city. And no one captured the feeling of this
butterfly world better than a young gay writer named Armistead Maupin. Like many of San Francisco's homosexual refugees, Maupin had a
deeply ironic American backstory. Raised in a wealthy conservative family in Raleigh, North Carolina, that was one step removed from the Con-
federacy, he interned at the radio station owned by the rising tribune of
white southern reaction, Jesse Helms; the future senator was a "hero
figure" to the young Maupin. Later Maupin joined the navy, serving a
tour of duty in Vietnam as an aide to legendary admiral Elmo Zumwalt.
His duties consisted primarily of escorting senators and congressmen
on thirty-minute PR tours of the war. Maupin, desperate for a combat
action ribbon to impress his flag-waving father, was glad when his base
finally came under a rocket attack, which immediately qualified him for
the commendation.

After leaving the navy, Maupin was recruited by the Nixon White
House to return to Vietnam and build houses for disabled Vietnamese
sailors—a publicity stunt meant to counter the political threat posed by
a young naval lieutenant from Massachusetts named John Kerry and the
"unpatriotic" Vietnam Veterans Against the War. Maupin—looking like
a photogenic Young Republican, with his helmet of longish blond hair,
and wearing a dark blazer and tie—was ushered into the White House
to shake hands with the president.

"Nixon was trying desperately to seem like a real guy in front of us
GIs," recalled Maupin, "and he did so by saying, 'Aren't those Vietnamese girls cute with their little pouty eyes and hair flowing behind them
like butterfly wings?' It was creepy—creepy on a level that I cannot convey to you. And he's trying this out on a closet homosexual."

In 1971, when he moved to San Francisco as a twenty-seven-year-old
Associated Press reporter, Maupin was still a southern Republican and
"gentleman racist." He expected to be shunned by the city's liberal social
world. At a party in Sea Cliff—the city's windblown balcony—in a mansion later owned by Robin Williams, Maupin was introduced as a navy

veteran just back from Vietnam. There were no antiwar lectures. Instead a man looked at Maupin, wrapped his arms around him, and said, "I'm so glad you're alive. Welcome home."

"The man was certifiably straight," said Maupin. "And I came from a place where straight men didn't hug each other. They never spit on me here."

It took three more years of living in San Francisco's warm embrace before Maupin finally mustered the courage to come out. After downing three Mai Tais, he decided to announce his sexuality to a friend named Jan Fox, showing up at her apartment as she was bathing her babies. When Maupin told her that he had something urgent to tell her, the worried Fox immediately came out of the bathroom. "I made this big weeping confession, and Jan knelt in front of me, took my hand, and said, 'Big fucking deal.' That was a big discovery for me—I had landed in a place where the heterosexuals were more comfortable with homosexuality than I was."

Bottled up his entire life, Maupin suddenly was free to express himself. Encouraged by the *Chronicle*'s crusty but literary Charles McCabe during one of the columnist's ritualistic rounds of heavy drinking at the Washington Square Bar & Grill, Maupin quit AP and began freelancing, eventually creating a new column about Bay Area manners and mores for the weekly *Pacific Sun*. McCabe became a fan. At a party, McCabe confronted Chronicle owner Charles Thieriot, telling him that most of his columnists were headed for the retirement pastures at Laguna Honda. The *Chronicle* desperately needed new talent, growled McCabe—like this kid Armistead Maupin.

"McCabe was homophobic, but if he liked you individually, he'd overlook that you were a faggot, like a parent would," Maupin said.

The *San Francisco Chronicle* launched Armistead Maupin's "Tales of the City" on May 24, 1976. The daily serial gave birth to a cast of make-believe characters who summarized seventies San Francisco, including Mary Ann Singleton, a twenty-five-year-old transplant from Cleveland, and her gay sidekick, Michael Tolliver, Maupin's alter ego. After moving into a Russian Hill apartment building at mythical 28 Barbary Lane, Singleton falls into a magical world where single gals don't just drink Tab and heat up Stouffer's TV dinners at night. They explore the city with their gay pals, going to jockey shorts dance contests at the Endup and sunning themselves at Devil's Slide, the nude gay beach south of the city. Maupin's San Francisco was part Balzac's Paris, part Lewis Carroll's Wonderland, and part Federico Fellini's *Satyricon*. Society dames slummed it with Chinese delivery boys and Samoan mechanics with big tools while their husbands dallied in the bathhouses. Party girls swallowed ludes and snorted "happy dust" and praised Jesus with the drag queens at the Reverend Willie Sessums's holy rock 'n' rolling Glibb Church (read Cecil Williams's Glide Church). Meanwhile, up above in the sky over Telegraph Hill, a raucous squadron of electric-green wild parrots went jetting through the wisps of fog on their way to the eucalyptus trees that shaded Julius' Castle, the fairytale-looking restaurant that clung to one side of the hill. The part about the feral parrots was real. Maupin lovingly colored his series with real-life local flora and fauna, like Edsel Ford Fong, the abusive "warlord turned waiter" who presided over Sam Woh's in Chinatown—or the boys in their tight Pendletons "circling the floor in predatory delight" on Gay Night at the roller skate rink as the organ merrily played "I Enjoy Being a Girl."

For all the kinky and fantastical twists and turns in "Tales of the City," Maupin's San Francisco was essentially a warm-hearted hometown where people like Mary Ann and Michael could get over their Christmastime blues when everyone else was huddled with their families, by donning their gay apparel and creating their own families. That's how Maupin saw the city: it had "a small-town vibe with cosmopolitan attitudes." He couldn't imagine any other city in the world coaxing the newspaper serial out of him day after day. San Francisco was a "waking dream," thought Maupin, a place that was as much about people's self-invention as it was about the misty, movie-set scenery.

IT DID NOT TAKE long for "Tales of the City" to become a San Francisco institution, as avidly read at the exclusive Bohemian Club on Nob Hill as it was in Cafe Flore in the gay Duboce Triangle. *San Francisco* magazine declared that the city was embracing Maupin's serial "with a passion hitherto reserved for the Cockettes." Nurses at a private San Francisco health care agency became such big fans, reading each episode out loud over their brown bag lunches, that they named their modest medical library after Maupin.

But the serial almost did not survive its rocky takeoff. *Chronicle* publisher Charles Thieriot went bug-eyed when he began reading "Tales," with its Samoan-loving socialites and its drag queen nuns zipping through town on speed skates. "People don't act like this!" thundered Thieriot, who apparently led a sheltered life for a lifelong San Franciscan.

Gordon Pates, the paper's punctilious, mild-mannered managing editor, grew concerned about the proliferation of gay characters in the serial. He instituted a new rule, telling Maupin that homosexuals must never number more than one-third of the cast in "Tales of the City." Pates kept a chart labeled Heterosexual or Homosexual in his office, adding each new character that Maupin introduced to a column.

"I spent two weeks trying to find a way to queer this, so to speak," Maupin recalled. "I wrote an episode in which Frannie Halcyon, the Hillsborough matron, has an affair with her Great Dane. This was done very tastefully and subtly, of course. I suppose an affair would be an inaccurate way to put it. She had passed out drunk in the rose garden and woke up to find the dog on top of her, but didn't want to complain because she knew the dog didn't mean it. After I wrote this episode, I came into Gordon's office and told him the dog had to go in the heterosexual column." That was the end of Pates's quota system.

With his impeccable southern manners, twinkly eyed charm, and cavalry officer good looks, Maupin routinely outmaneuvered his *Chronicle* editors, who—in the post–Scott Newhall era—were not known for their dazzle. Constantly fretting that "Tales of the City" would offend subscribers in the sleepy Sunset district, the paper's overseers were poised to pull the plug on the serial. But its fan base was too damn big and loyal. "They stuck with me," Maupin said, "because the readers stuck with me."

Armistead Maupin not only chronicled the new San Francisco but also helped dream it to life. Fans of the serial started feeling like they were living out their own true-life tales of the city. Vince Calcagno—like Mary Ann Singleton, recently arrived from Cleveland—was far from alone when he had his "Mary Ann moments" as he navigated his way through his new city. The serial became a daily touchstone for the new San Francisco. As a neighbor told Mary Ann in one episode, "Nobody's from here." Everybody in San Francisco was making it up as he or she went along. And reading "Tales of the City" each morning told the city's newcomers they were no stranger than the next person—and San Francisco accepted them, even loved them, for who they were.

By the time "Tales of the City" debuted, everything seemed in flux in San Francisco, including the political establishment. Looking back long afterward at his tumultuous eight years in office, Joe Alioto said that his main task had been to "manage the revolution" that went roaring through the city. He was like the captain of a storm-tossed ship, presiding over a dining table whose glassware, wine carafes, and cutlery were constantly on the brink of being dashed to the floor. If Alioto tried to keep a rein on the turbulence, his successor rode the revolution into office. And he, George Moscone, would become a victim of its violent backlash.

23

CIVIC WAR

GEORGE MOSCONE, RUNNING hard to succeed Joe Alioto in San Francisco's 1975 mayoral race, swept into the hippie commune on Ashbury Street with a couple of young aides hustling beside him. Sue Bierman, the godmother of Haight-Ashbury neighborhood activism, had set up the meeting for the mayoral candidate. Bierman became a big fan of Moscone in 1964 after he cast the deciding vote on the board of supervisors against a freeway extension that would have bulldozed the Golden Gate Panhandle. An old-fashioned populist from a long line of Nebraska radicals and anti-slavery Republicans, Bierman midwived a new generation of San Francisco crusaders with her battles against downtown fat cats and developers' wrecking balls. Among her young protégés was Calvin Welch, one of the Haight community agitators whom Bierman had persuaded to meet with Moscone.

But despite Bierman's embrace of Moscone, Welch and his fellow commune members were skeptical of the mayoral candidate. Moscone was, after all, a career politician, a breed that Haight activists had come to disdain. Welch and his housemates decided that in order to win their support, Moscone would have to pass the ultimate Haight-Ashbury test.

Moscone and his hippie hosts were seated around a massive communal table. As they began to discuss neighborhood issues, one of Welch's comrades fired up a pillow-sized reefer. "We were going to pass it around the table and see if that motherfucker takes a hit or not," recalled Welch. As the smoldering joint came around to George Miller, Moscone's young aide and a future California congressman, the protective Miller tried to pass it over his boss to an aide on the other side of Moscone. "*Waaait* a minute!" the candidate exclaimed, deftly intercepting the contraband.

"Moscone grabs the joint and takes a huge fucking hit!" Welch laughed.

The whole room burst into applause. The candidate passed the test. The Haight was in his column.

George Moscone ran as the candidate of change in 1975. If Alioto was the embodiment of establishment power, Moscone presented himself as the people's champion. "It's time to take the decisions out of the secret rooms in the Fairmont, out of the secret rooms in Hillsborough, and the secret rooms in Marin County, and give them back to the people of San Francisco," he roared at one tumultuous campaign rally.

In some ways, Moscone and the outgoing mayor were strikingly similar. Both San Francisco natives were products of Italian families and Catholic schools. Both men were avid readers of literature and philosophy, and could quote the gospels and papal encyclicals in debates, although Moscone leaned more toward Saul Bellow and Bernard Malamud than to Dante. Both had a taste for good wine and food, and an eye for women.

But Moscone was more a man of the streets than Alioto. He was raised by a single mother in the Cow Hollow–Polk Gulch area, a colorfully scruffy neighborhood he later described as Runyonesque. His father was a movie-star-handsome drunk who careened from job to job as a garbageman, milk deliveryman, and San Quentin prison guard. When George was nine, Lee Moscone defied her Catholic upbringing and kicked out her roguish husband for good, going to work as a secretary at a car dealership and machine shop and finally at the Department of Motor Vehicles to support the two of them.

Lee Moscone's travails as a working mother made her son a lifelong battler for the underdog. "When I hear people today talking about single parents, women's rights, and tenants' rights, my mother did it all," he said years later. "I mean, she got chased out of one apartment house after another because she had a son. They always do it subtly by raising the rent. She worked all day and then on weekends as a clerk in a liquor store so I could have a good education. She just made every sacrifice in the world for me."

Young George learned about San Francisco by playing basketball in the city's parks. His talent on the court allowed him to cross turf lines and play with Irish, black, Chinese, and Latino kids. He was a high school basketball star at St. Ignatius, making the all-city team. Moscone worked his way through high school and college, taking jobs as a sports director at the parks. He helped pay his tuition at UC Hastings College of the Law in San Francisco by working as a school janitor alongside his friend and fellow law student Willie Brown, who dubbed the two of them "the Broom Brothers." While in law school, Moscone began dating Eugenia Bondanza, the sister of an elementary school classmate. Gina was small and delicately built, with big eyes that dominated her fine-boned features. Like Moscone, she was raised by a single mother, after her father died of cancer when she was eleven. While she was growing up, Gina planned on becoming a nun. But as soon as she started dating George, they both knew that they would marry.

Later, after two decades of marriage, Gina Moscone was asked if she had any regrets. Just one, she said. She wished that George had never gone into politics. A private woman, she resented the constant public demands on her husband. But she knew it was his calling.

Moscone was handsome and charming. Smoothly comfortable in his own skin, he had a gift for putting people at ease. "He was the most charismatic guy I've ever met," said Welch. "Guys loved him. Women loved him. I got to know people who went to school with him at S.I., when he was all-city. I remember this one guy telling me, 'Fourteen-year-old boys dream of having sex, but George *had* sex, and we all knew it. He was our god.'"

John Burton, his best friend since high school, opened the door to politics for Moscone when he introduced him to his older brother, Phil, the city's congressional power broker. Moscone became a rising star in the Burton machine, along with Willie Brown. The machine was pow-ered by Phil's bare-knuckled ambition. But it was more about scoring victories for Burton's liberal constituencies—labor, minorities, gays, and environmentalists—than it was about delivering patronage and graft. "The Burton machine was based on ideology and public service," said

Art Agnos, who belonged to the rival Leo McCarthy machine but still admired the Burton operation's significant accomplishments. "It was all about making a difference in people's lives."

Moscone soon made it clear that his political career was rooted in deeply held progressive values. In 1965, not long after winning his first election to the board of supervisors, he announced that he was going to Mississippi with a task force of lawyers to help blacks register to vote—a mission that took physical courage in those days of bloody civil rights struggle. "If you've got to die, it's better than dying on a freeway," Moscone declared.

The following year, he was elected to the California State Senate, where his Democratic colleagues made the popular legislator their majority leader. Moscone proved himself a master vote getter, shepherd of progressive legislation, and worthy opponent of Governor Reagan—a man he loathed. While serving in Sacramento, Moscone helped create California's school lunch program. Later, with the help of Willie Brown, then the powerful Democratic whip in the state assembly, he pushed through bills that decriminalized the possession of modest amounts of marijuana and—to the everlasting gratitude of San Francisco's gay population—sex between consenting adults. Unafraid of taking controversial stands, Moscone fought to overturn the state death penalty. "I'd rather lose the damn election than twist my views to fit popular opinion," he once said.

In the spring of 1967, Moscone invited Don Peri, a teenager interested in the workings of government, to watch him in action on the Senate floor in Sacramento. The senate was hotly debating a bill to legalize abortion in California, and Peri—a fellow Catholic—was shocked to see Moscone stand up and argue for its passage. Later Moscone came over to the teenager and said quietly, "You and I know it's wrong, but that doesn't mean we can tell other people what to do."

WHEN MOSCONE ANNOUNCED HIS campaign for mayor in December 1974, he made clear that his goal was to redistribute power in the city—from downtown suites to the neighborhoods, where families were struggling to hang on against developers and real estate speculators. He also vowed to expand the democratization process that Alioto had begun at city hall, bringing gays, women, and more minorities into the halls of power once firmly controlled by the city's old Irish-Italian network.

Moscone's populist race was helped greatly by a new city law that clamped tight limits on mayoral campaign spending. In the previous mayoral race, Alioto had spent more than $600,000 to get reelected. But now each candidate was limited to $128,000, a level playing field that made it possible for Moscone to run without big corporate money and to cap individual donations at $100. The *Examiner* declared Moscone "the poorest candidate" in the crowded field, reporting that his only assets were his family home and a modest piece of rental property in suburban Antioch valued at $10,000. But in the people's election of 1975, that was no drawback.

Dianne Feinstein, running in the center as a good government candidate, was originally considered Moscone's toughest opponent because of her high political profile and the strong support she attracted from downtown business interests. But the new campaign law rendered her wealthy backers' deep pockets irrelevant. Instead Supervisor John Barbagelata, a West Portal realtor and gadfly critic of government spending, emerged on the right as Moscone's top adversary, knocking Feinstein out of the race in the November election and forcing a December runoff with his fellow Italian.

Barbagelata was the voice of old San Francisco: a conservative Catholic who was baffled and enraged by the new social currents flowing through his city. The father of eight was so devout, he remarked that "if the pope asked me to push a peanut with my nose down the middle of the street, I'd do it." He entered city politics in the 1960s to fight the spread of moral contamination in his city, and as supervisor he succeeded in banning bottomless dancing in North Beach clubs and in covering Carol Doda's blinking neon nipples on the marquee of the legendary stripper's Condor Club. In the 1970s, Barbagelata took aim at the rising gay peril. The Gay Freedom Day Parade, spilling out of the Castro and down Market Street in all its shameless exhibitionism, filled him with revulsion on behalf of his city. And when the board of supervisors proposed that city contractors open their hiring to gay job seekers, Barbagelata fumed that city hall had no right to force companies "to hire perverts."

ALARMED BY THE PROSPECT of four more years of antihomosexual fervor at city hall, gay activists rallied around Moscone, the man who had legalized sodomy in California. Harvey Milk, a rising political star in the Castro, urged gay voters to block Barbagelata. "I think he wants to be a priest and not a mayor," said Milk.

The Moscone campaign was buoyed by strong support from gay, labor, and civil rights groups, as well as neighborhood organizations fighting the "Manhattanization" of San Francisco's skyline. But Moscone underestimated the lingering power of Barbagelata's traditional San Francisco. The surprisingly tight runoff campaign divided the city down the middle: with the older, white districts west of Twin Peaks, along with the upscale Marina and Pacific Heights firmly aligned with Barbagelata; and the poorer, nonwhite, and newcomer neighborhoods such as Bayview–Hunters Point, the Fillmore, the Castro, and Haight-Ashbury heavily supporting Moscone. The race was as much a culture war as it was a class war.

Barbagelata's campaign was fueled by a different kind of populist rage: it was a revolt of San Francisco's middle-class home owners and taxpayers, the city's financial bedrock. These families felt ripped off by the city's powerful unions and the labor-friendly Burton machine, and John Barbagelata was the voice of their resentment. San Francisco needed a "businessman mayor" to make sure that people "get their money's worth," he told voters. And a good half of the electorate agreed. With his blunt, no-nonsense manner and his lean, sharp-featured, bespectacled good looks, Barbagelata resembled a trustworthy family accountant—the kind of man who could balance the city's checkbook.

Election night on December 11 was an excruciating ordeal for George Moscone, who was stunned that a conservative realtor had taken him to the brink of defeat. It rattled his sense of San Francisco, a city whose heart he thought he knew intimately. As the evening dragged on, Moscone's early lead eroded steadily until the candidates were neck and neck. Phil Burton, the master vote counter, was monitoring the election results for Moscone in a boiler room at city hall, and the updates he phoned in were filled with grim portents. As the candidate and his circle of family, friends, and campaign aides huddled in his seventh-floor suite at the unglamorous San Franciscan Hotel on Market Street, he chain-smoked Viceroys, drank cognac, and stared at the TV while his mother rubbed the back of his neck.

Moscone was finally declared the victor late that night, squeaking by Barbagelata with a wafer-thin margin of 4,443 votes. His hotel suite erupted with cheers. "It's just like Kennedy!" one aide enthused, summoning up JFK's by-a-nose finish over Nixon in the 1960 presidential election. By then, the mayor-elect was wrung out. Minutes later, Moscone stood at the ballroom podium in front of his raucous supporters, his shirt drenched with sweat, wiping tears from his eyes.

Corey Busch, Moscone's young press aide, had been at the Ambassador Hotel in Los Angeles the night in June 1968 when Bobby Kennedy celebrated his final victory in his race for president. After Bobby was assassinated that night, Busch thought he would never work on another campaign. But Moscone breathed new life into the dispirited young politico. "He represented everything that was good about politics," said Busch.

Now, surveying the smoky, crowded ballroom at the San Franciscan, Busch marveled at the wide variety of urban energy packed into the room. "Some reporter later said it was the greatest cross section of San Franciscans ever assembled under one roof in the history of the city," he reminisced. "I was twenty-six years old, and I couldn't believe that we were actually going to be able to shape a major American city and make the changes we wanted to make."

Willie Brown had been in the political trenches much longer than Busch, but he too had a bedazzled, "pinch-me" look on his face that night. "Can you imagine George Moscone in city hall?" he kept saying out loud. "It's a whole new world."

At the victory podium, Moscone made a point of calling out to his gay supporters, who had delivered a critical block of voters in the close election. San Francisco, he proclaimed to loud cheers, is liberated territory—a haven that "allows with pleasure gay people walking the streets of the city with freedom from harassment."

But Moscone's state-of-the-art field operation could not have succeeded without two organizations that were beginning to make a major impact on San Francisco. "The two institutions that were most helpful in getting George elected were the Delancey Street Foundation and the Peoples Temple," said Richard Sklar, who became the city infrastructure's indispensable fix-it man under Moscone. "They each put hundreds of bodies on the streets during the campaign." Both organizations served society's rejects, and both were run by charismatic misfits. Delancey Street, a self-help community of addicts and ex-convicts, was founded by John Maher, a Bronx grade school dropout and ex-junkie with a Tammany Hall gift for street politics. The Peoples Temple, a renegade church that ministered to a flock of mostly black lost souls, was run by a more mysterious man, the Reverend Jim Jones.

John Maher and George Moscone had a genuine affection for each other, based on their shared values and spirited love of politics. In the end, Maher and his partner Mimi Silbert helped resurrect thousands of lives and enriched the city's soul. The only person Maher irreparably harmed was himself, when he fell back into addiction and could not pull himself back to shore. Moscone's relationship with Jim Jones was a much different story. What began as a political marriage of convenience ended in unspeakable horror.

Even in the midst of all the jubilation that election night in December, a sad note played somewhere in Moscone's heart. A physically affectionate father, Moscone clasped the face of his fourteen-year-old son Christopher in his hands and made the boy look directly at him, the way he always did when he had something important to say to his kids. "Promise me one thing," Moscone said, peering into Christopher's eyes.

"I'm thinking, 'Anything—just let me go,'" remembered Christopher Moscone years later.

"Promise me you'll never go into politics," Moscone told his son on the night of his greatest political triumph.

It wasn't until he was older that Christopher fully understood. Because for people like his father, politics demands everything. "Because you're all in. And it eventually killed him."

HERB CAEN CALLED MOSCONE'S populist victory a "bloodless civil war." Dick Nolan, the *Examiner's* political columnist, wrote that "a bell tolls for [San Francisco's] Tories," declaring the election "a turning point between the old 'in's' and the newly awakened neighborhood 'out's.'"

Moscone, caught up in the excitement of the moment, announced that he had a sweeping ambition for San Francisco: to make it a beacon of tolerance and enlightenment to the world. "I will only be satisfied," he said, "if in four—or hopefully eight—years, I can not only change the face of San Francisco, but change the soul of San Francisco, and, with its extraordinary international authority, [make it] a catalyst for conversion for the rest of the country, if not the world."

At his inauguration in the city hall rotunda—a ceremony stripped of the pomp and circumstance of Alioto's ascension—Moscone dedicated his administration to serving the public instead of private interests. "My door will be open, and, more importantly, I will be inside," he said, a line that electrified the audience but was greeted grim faced by the outgoing mayor, who was known for his back-door deals and his jaunts around the state and country in search of higher office. As if to underline the upstairs-downstairs transition, Alioto stripped the mayor's office of the Louis XIV treaty table and high-backed chair, the gold candelabrums, and other decorative finery that he had installed, leaving Moscone to scavenge for old furniture from the city hall basement.

A new era of "small is beautiful" government was dawning in California, with conservative tax revolts like Proposition 13 placing strict curbs on government spending and a rising generation of Democratic leaders led by recently elected governor Jerry Brown trying to balance social needs with fiscal realities. Moscone immediately signaled that his administration, like Brown's, would be "lean and mean."

At forty-six, the tanned, trim six-foot-one mayor projected an energetic image. He dispensed with Alioto's official limousine and chauffeur and zipped around town in his aging maroon Alfa Romeo, waving to startled citizens at stoplights. Sometimes he imposed on staff members, many of them young and long haired, to drive him to civic events in their even more battered cars. The young aides prized their time with their affable, quick-witted boss. But sometimes they prayed that it wasn't him calling when their home phones rang on Sundays.

"It was not unusual for me to get a call from George on Sunday to play some basketball on the courts at Nineteenth and Vicente," Busch recalled. "Even if I didn't want to, hey, he was the boss. He'd show up down there in a T-shirt and shorts, and we'd start playing a pickup game with some guys. He was a competitive guy, so he's backing into guys and playing hard. He was in his forties, definitely the oldest guy there, but that didn't stop him. One day this young guy looks at him and says, 'Man, you play some rough ball. And, hey, you look a lot like our mayor.' George says, 'I am.'"

Moscone always carried around "a little bit of that street thing," said Busch, even as mayor. Aides had to stop him from getting into fistfights in restaurants when drunken customers' taunting grew too personal. Before his election, Moscone got into a brawl at a party when someone called Willie Brown a "nigger." On another occasion, Moscone and his police bodyguard Jim Molinari were having drinks late one night in a North Beach restaurant when two yahoos from Los Angeles began heckling the mayor, berating him for coddling gays and accusing him of being gay himself. The mayor jumped up and, moving toward the two men, prepared to explain San Francisco values to them. "Sit down, Mayor!" Molinari barked, with visions of ugly headlines looming before him. The cop calmed the situation by telling the two men, "Keep your mouths shut or you're going to jail."

Moscone recognized that he was operating in a new era of Spartan political life, but he lacked Jerry Brown's monastic temperament. A San Francisco sensualist, he gloried in the bounties of his city, roaming the town nearly every night—seldom with his wife, who hid at home from the clatter of social functions—and often in the company of Willie Brown, who played Sammy Davis Jr. to his Frank Sinatra in their version of the Rat Pack. Moscone loved jazz, he loved scotch, he loved North Beach restaurants. There was no more satisfying meal in life, he said, than Dungeness crab with a mayonnaise-mustard dip, a plate of fettuccine, and a good bottle of chilled wine. He couldn't quit his cigarettes, and he couldn't give up the black women. And although he never managed to save any money from his public salaries, he always found a way to dress elegantly, drinking scotch in the dressing rooms at Wilkes Bashford while the exclusive clothier displayed his hand-sewn Italian wares.

"Every day of his mayorship, George told me, 'Man, you gotta be mayor. This is like being king.' And we really had a ball," recalled Willie Brown, who was a rising power in Sacramento during Moscone's city hall tenure but still found time to enjoy the San Francisco nightlife with his friend. "He loved everything about this city. He was indigenous. He *was* the city."

While Moscone immediately took to the job he called the greatest in the world—running the city he loved—his administration was embattled from the very start. John Barbagelata proved a bitter loser, charging voter fraud after his narrow defeat and sending 150 of his supporters marching into the voter registrar's office to inspect ballots. Barbagelata demanded a recount, and a stormy air hung over the city as the tedious process unfolded. The recount awarded Barbagelata only seventy-three more votes, not enough to bring him victory. But even after Moscone was sworn in as mayor, his resentful opponent refused to give up.

Barbagelata thought that Moscone was delivering San Francisco to a horde of barbarians: outsiders who did not share the city's traditional values. And his feverish suspicions focused on the heavily poor and black congregation of Peoples Temple, which was shifting its base from rural Redwood Valley to San Francisco at the time of the election. Barbagelata was convinced that the sketchy church had stolen the election for Moscone by busing in nonresidents and driving them from precinct to precinct to vote. As Peoples Temple cast a long shadow over San Francisco, it became clear that Barbagelata had good reason to be suspicious.

The Moscone administration found itself ensnared in a culture war that pitted it against not only relentless political foes like Barbagelata but also the old-boy power structure of the San Francisco Police Department. The SFPD grudge against Moscone was personal. "George and I grew up with a lot of guys who became cops," recalled John Burton, "and later on they'd say shit like, 'You two guys are nigger lovers,' or 'You two guys are fags.' They were kind of old-fashioned." The force was full of cops who thought Moscone was a traitor; that he'd sold out their city to the freaks and fairies who were driving out families like their own.

San Francisco's new mayor made it as clear as a blazing siren light that he was going to shake up the police department when he hired Charles Gain as his police chief. The soft-spoken Texan, who called himself a "sociological cop," was known as one of the most liberal law enforcement officials in the country. As chief of Oakland's historically redneck police force, he eased the city's explosive racial tensions by reaching out to the black community. Later he served as a deputy to innovative, gay-friendly San Francisco sheriff Richard Hongisto, who was more interested in rehabilitating his prisoners than breaking them.

Gain wasted no time in challenging the SFPD's rosary-and-billy-club culture. He outraged veteran cops by taking down the big American flag in the chief's office, explaining that it was an overly zealous display of patriotism, and replacing the flag with a potted plant. He banned drinking on the job, a longtime tradition on the force that reinforced its brawling Irish image. He announced his support for District Attorney Joseph Freitas Jr.'s hands-off policy on streetwalkers, effectively decriminalizing prostitution in the city—a policy that had been lobbied for by the chief's ally Margo St. James. Gain also encouraged gay cops on the force to come out, insisting that such honesty "will help everyone." And he ordered the SFPD's black-and-white patrol cars to be repainted powder blue—a move that he thought would soften the department's authoritarian image.

The police force reeled under Gain's social experimentation. Cops muttered that their new leader was a flaming queen. They called him "Gloria Gain" behind his back. They took their complaints to the *Examiner*, long known as the cops' newspaper. "It's disgusting," one anonymous officer told the paper. "First Gain called us alcoholics, and now he's calling us fruits," said another.

Gain refused to ease up, even after senior police officials began resigning in protest. "I don't look for controversy," he said, "but change has to come."

As word spread that San Francisco was a wide-open town, hookers began flooding downtown streets. Hoteliers and convention bureau officials lobbied for a police crackdown—an ironic turn of events, since it was a wide-open secret that San Francisco's tourism business was boosted greatly by the local sex trade. But the new wave of prostitutes was apparently not up to the local convention industry's standards. "If she is black or if she is garishly dressed, she is more likely to be stopped than if she is elegantly dressed," explained a local prostitute-rights activist who worked with Margo St. James.

Moscone finally caved to the downtown business pressure and ordered Gain to reverse his tolerant policy on prostitution. But for the most part, the mayor stood squarely by his beleaguered police chief. This became particularly difficult in the fall of 1977, when Gain became embroiled in another only-in-San-Francisco tempest. On the evening of October 28, Chief Gain, caught up in the festive spirit of the Hooker's

Ball, showed up at the libidinous event, which drew ten thousand people that year to the Civic Auditorium. To compound his sin, Gain—who had the long, somber face and plastered-down hair of a country undertaker—was photographed at the ball by the *Examiner*, wedged between a madly grinning St. James and a woman identified only as "Wonder Whore," who displayed a dildo instead of a laser gun on her belt.

As the police commission later determined, Chief Gain had admirably maintained "officer-like conduct" throughout the evening. But this was of little consolation to the Barbagelata crowd, which saw it as one more sign that its city was going to hell in black lace panties. Quentin Kopp, a curmudgeonly lawyer following in Barbagelata's footsteps on the board of supervisors, demanded that Moscone fire Gain. The police chief's appearance at the Hooker's Ball, Supervisor Kopp huffed, was "too much even for a tolerant city like San Francisco . . . What a spectacle for the children of San Francisco: their police chief reveling with self-professed whores and their associates." But Moscone shrugged off the sound and fury. Gain's track record as a crime fighter "is a far better barometer of the chief's performance," he said, "than a photograph at a social event."

Moscone further antagonized the police force by pushing hard for an out-of-court settlement of the long, bitter civil rights lawsuit against the department. And in February 1978 the mayor again riled the SFPD by ordering a halt to its racial profiling practices. "Stopping and frisking people because they are black in a white neighborhood is simply not going to be tolerated," he announced, calling such "police state" tactics "unconstitutional." Moscone's order followed an ugly incident in the Richmond district when police pulled over a successful realtor named Paul Sing after apparently deciding that a Chinese-American had no right to drive a Mercedes sports coupe. Sing was frisked twice, with a gun pointed to his head, before the cops finally let him go.

THE SNARLING ABOUT MOSCONE grew louder in police stations. Cops passed around eyebrow-raising stories about him. Not only was the mayor soft on crime, they said, but he himself was an outlaw. They talked about weed, cocaine, black hookers. The stories went back a long time, and they had popped up during the campaign. On the eve of his inauguration, Moscone had sat down with a *Chronicle* reporter, telling him that he was finally "ready to talk about my personal weaknesses." But all he was willing to reveal was that he had sampled pot before introducing the state bill to decriminalize it, because "I wanted to be an authority to some extent"—an explanation undoubtedly greeted with hilarity by anyone who knew Moscone's deep knowledge of cannabis. As mayor, he pledged, scotch and soda would be "good enough for me."

Moscone swerved sharply in the interview to avoid any discussion of his extramarital life. But the *Chronicle* helpfully reminded readers in a sidebar about an "unhappy incident in Moscone's past" when he collided with another car in the parking lot outside a Chinese restaurant in Sacramento called Frank Fat's. Police reported that Moscone smelled like a bar and was accompanied by a young black woman whom the politician had kindly agreed to drive home.

The restaurateurs and bartenders who presided over the city's nightlife knew that Moscone kept the party going as mayor, often sharing the fun with Willie Brown. "The two of them were with a black woman in an alley at two in the morning at some restaurant in North Beach," said Ed Moose, the legendary proprietor of the Washington Square Bar & Grill, the most popular watering hole in the city for the political and literary crowds. "That whole gang of people, when they got together, they felt pretty hip. John Burton was part of that gang too. They were all using marijuana and cocaine."

Herb Caen snickered that Moscone meant "Big Fly" in Italian, making it all a matter of ribald fun rather than career-ending tragedy. Moscone knew his city well enough to tell one press conference that rumors about his personal life "won't rattle San Francisco's teacups." As he reminded the *Chronicle* reporter, "All of us, we're all so terribly human." He was not the only good Catholic in town with a Madonna at home and whores on the side.

In the end, most San Franciscans with an opinion on the subject thought that the mayor's personal life was between him and his family. George and Gina had worked out some kind of church-and-state separation. The family was holy ground, and Moscone was utterly devoted to his four children, showing up for their games and performances, spoiling his two daughters and straightening out his two sons. The two boys, Christopher and Jonathan, never forgot the morning ritual when their father came into their room before school and brushed their unruly hair, breathing hard through his nose as he flattened the every-which-way sprouts. Once Archbishop Joe McGucken was called in to help the Moscone marriage through an especially stressful period. But the couple managed the rough strife of marriage largely on their own, behind closed doors.

What George did outside the home was his business. But Gina was adamant that it never interfere with the family. "Saying that everything about him is public is something I can't buy," she said in one of her rare interviews. "Not when the family is involved."

Moscone came to feel he was invisible in his late-night romps through the city. And he largely was—exposing and shaming was just not part of San Francisco's culture, even as city politics grew more bitterly partisan. But there was one group that kept a close eye on the mayor: the city's cops, centurions of the embattled moral order. They watched the mayor at play, and they filed it all away for the right time. Moscone's antics made some of them sick, like vice cop Joe Ryan. "He's so high and mighty," sneered Ryan, "and he's pulling these capers and getting away with it."

Some cops had urged Barbagelata to use Moscone's sexual escapades against him during the campaign, but he refused out of concern for Moscone's family. Barbagelata grew to despise Moscone, but the men's families went way back together. Barbagelata's brother attended St. Ignatius with Moscone. One of Moscone's daughters dated one of Barbagelata's sons. Barbagelata was old school, and he believed you don't do certain things to another man's family, no matter how passionate the feud.

"My dad knew everything about George Moscone: the prostitutes, the drugs," said son Paul Barbagelata, who today runs the family realty business. "And he was told to bring it out, but he didn't. He was just being a stand-up guy for Gina's sake. In his mind, George was dirty, but he would never say that in public."

WHILE HE STEERED CLEAR of Moscone's personal life, John Barbagelata remained a constant political thorn in the mayor's side, using his platform on the board of supervisors to bottle up Moscone's initiatives and frustrate his efforts to guide the city in a new direction. Moscone was worn down by the raw grind of city politics, which struck him as much pettier than the legislative give-and-take in Sacramento. "He had guys like Kopp and Barbagelata who every morning couldn't wait to figure out how to set the next bonfire," said Busch. "They harassed us on everything we did."

In the spring of 1977, Barbagelata's protracted guerilla war on the Moscone administration escalated into a bold frontal assault. Moscone's implacable foe succeeded in putting an initiative on the local ballot that would force the mayor, the DA, and the sheriff—San Francisco's liberal triumvirate—to run for office all over again in November, two years before their terms expired. It was a deft saber thrust on the part of Barbagelata, who had never accepted his defeat.

The campaign to fight Barbagelata's Proposition B, however, had an electrifying effect on the listless Moscone administration. The humiliating prospect of a recall brought the mayor to life. "Nobody cuts short my term," an infuriated Moscone told his staff, finally showing the sharp-elbowed drive he'd learned on the city's basketball courts. Moscone's activist base rallied to his side, and he stockpiled a $150,000 campaign war chest with the help of Democratic millionaires like developer Walter Shorenstein and Levi Strauss & Co. board chairman Walter Haas Jr. The solicitation of downtown support was a surprising move for the populist Moscone. But when downtown power brokers tried to extract a quid pro quo for their financial support, Moscone rebuffed them.

One day during the Proposition B campaign, Moscone was summoned to lunch in the Bank of America's downtown black tower to meet with chief executive A. W. "Tom" Clausen. Moscone brought along his young, bearded, long-haired aide Josh Getlin, who was outfitted in a rumpled sport coat and clashing tie that could only have dismayed the stylish mayor. The two were ushered into the private dining room on the top floor of the bank's headquarters, where, over drinks, Clausen and his men quickly got to the point. They knew that Moscone was on the ropes. If the bankers came to his rescue, could they count on him to block rent control in the city? It was a battle that the San Francisco business community had made a top priority.

"I could never promise you that," said Moscone, who never forgot how his mother had been treated by landlords. "There are a lot of people who have to be heard from. They're the people who rent homes and work in this city." It was the kind of stand that made young aides like Getlin fall all over again for their boss.

On August 2, 1977, Moscone rolled to a crushing victory, beating Proposition B by a two-to-one margin. It was a huge turning point in his mayoral reign. He finally cast off the shadow that had been hanging over his administration ever since his squeaky victory over Barbagelata in 1975. "I think George took that close election in '75 personally," said John Burton. "It came as a real shock to him." But now he had swamped his nemesis. Moscone celebrated that night by taking his family out to dine on roast duck at elegant Fleur de Lys: the first time he had eaten with them since the frantic recall battle started three months earlier.

The 1977 election was a major turning point for San Francisco in another key way. Voters approved a new way of electing supervisors: by district instead of citywide. District elections for supervisors—long a dream of neighborhood activists—brought in a new, more grassroots board in November, since candidates did not have to raise as much money as they did when they had to campaign throughout the city. The most dynamic player on the new board was the Castro district's new representative, Harvey Milk.

Milk, a glad-handing, New York Jewish force of nature, had turned his funky Castro Street camera store into the boiling eye of the city's gay hurricane. Until the 1977 election, Milk had lost so many campaigns for office that he joked he was the gay Harold Stassen, the sad-sack Republican who couldn't stop himself from running for president every four years. But district elections, which allowed Milk to wave his rainbow flag high, finally opened the door for him to city hall. He won office by beating a rival gay candidate—an establishment-backed goody-goody named Rick Stokes—and none other than Terry "Kayo" Hallinan.

Hallinan, whose father, Vince, had instilled in his sons enlightened views about homosexuality, found himself utterly charmed by his ebullient opponent. "Harvey wasn't easy to run against because there wasn't much we didn't agree on," recalled Hallinan. "As the campaign went on, we ended up becoming friends."

Michael Stepanian, who served as Hallinan's campaign manager, also wound up falling for Milk. "Early in the campaign, Terry and I decided we'd better check out this guy Harvey," recalled Stepanian. "So we go to this event where he and Stokes are giving speeches. Stokes is gay, but a very straight guy. He gets up and says, 'I'm very concerned about Harvey Milk. One time I was outside his camera shop, and a man and woman walked by with their child, and Harvey used a profane word.' Then Stokes says, 'I don't want to be referred to as the gay candidate for supervisor. I want to be known as the candidate who happens to be gay.' Polite clapping ensues. Then Harvey gets up. 'Fuck that shit, mother-fucker! I'm gay!' The place went wild with screaming. I looked over at Terry and said, 'How the hell we gonna beat this guy?' I loved Harvey from the start, just loved him."

Moscone, who had his political ups and downs with Milk in the past, also ended up embracing the new supervisor. The mayor and Milk—who saw his gay rights crusade as part of a much broader progressive agenda—formed a powerful duo. With Milk shaking up the board of supervisors and taking on Moscone enemies like Quentin Kopp, the mayor seemed newly energized. In April 1978 Moscone signed a land-mark gay rights law that had been pushed through the board by Milk. The two beaming men were pictured in the next day's newspapers shak-ing hands at the signing ceremony.

As Moscone settled into his new groove as mayor, he began winning over some staunch critics. *Examiner* columnist Kevin Starr sat down with Moscone at a restaurant for a three-hour interview and made the extraordinary gesture of apologizing to the mayor for being too hard on him. Moscone, in an expansive mood after a round of vodka on the rocks and Chardonnay with dinner, gave his most heartfelt defense of the changes he was bringing to city hall. "Believe me, I'm no leftish ideologue," he told Starr. "Like you, I was raised in the Catholic school system in this city. From both the Gospel and papal encyclicals on social and economic justice, weren't we both taught that people who were bit-terly antiblack or anti-Chicano or antipoor were jerks, just plain jerks? I never could stand racism or indifference to poverty. That doesn't make me a lefty ideologue. It makes me an ordinary American.

"When I first tried to break into politics in this city," he continued, "it was the dispossessed who welcomed me. They were getting short shrift from a lot of the fat cats in office. I'm not going to abandon the poor now that it has suddenly become fashionable to sound hard-line and ultrarealistic about social goals. That would make a farce of my previous beliefs.

"Sure, I brought new sorts of people into city government—blacks, Asians, Chicanos, gays. But look around you: I brought them into government because they constitute a significant portion of the people who are now here, committed to making San Francisco a decent, viable place. What would you have a mayor to do, suppress the new San Francisco to satisfy the old?"

It was a remarkable expression of Moscone's core values, and it could have served as an eloquent basis for his reelection campaign. As Moscone neared the last year of his term, it seemed liked the political momentum had shifted his way. But the forces unleashed by the Moscone and Milk revolution were waiting to devour them.

Legendary San Francisco attorney Vincent Hallinan—flanked in this 1932 news photo by his beautiful future spouse, Vivian (left), and the wife of his notorious client Frank Egan—epitomized the city's world of Hammett-like criminal intrigue and brawling politics.

By the 1960s, thanks to the pugilism of pioneering progressives like the Hallinans, San Franciso's old Irish-Catholic order began to give way to a new spirit of sublime anarchy. In January 1967, Allen Ginsberg—a combination of holy man and Jewish mother for the new cultural movement—celebrated the dawn of the future at the Human Be-In festival in Golden Gate Park. *Steve Rees/Associated Press 1967.*

Radical hippie attorney Tony Serra learned his combative courtroom style from the master, Vincent Hallinan. Floating in an acid reverie, Serra enjoyed the vibes at a city hall rally held to promote his 1971 mayoral campaign on the Platypus Party ticket. *Copyright © Michael Zagaris.*

The Diggers, fronted by the roguish Emmett Grogan (flashing the peace sign), wanted to turn San Francisco into a "free city," unplugged from the capitalist grid of 9-to-5 serfdom. *"Diggers," GAP0073, photographer Gene Anthony, © www.wolfgangsvault.com.*

While the Diggers tried to care for the runaway teens flooding the city during the 1967 Summer of Love, it was a renegade minister named Edward "Larry" Beggs (wearing eyeglasses) who defied the law by setting up a shelter for the young refugees from middle America. *Photo courtesy of Edward Beggs.*

Dr. David Smith realized that his neighborhood, the Haight-Ashbury, was becoming ground zero for the youth revolution. But until he opened a free clinic in 1967 for the street children, San Francisco's medical establishment turned a cold shoulder to their suffering. *Copyright © Liz Hafalia/San Francisco Chronicle/Corbis.*

The *San Francisco Chronicle*'s beloved columnist Herb Caen weaved a fantasy city in which all San Franciscans wanted to live. According to Caen, those locals who turned up their noses at the hippie invasion were guilty of the ultimate San Francisco sin: they were "bores." *Copyright © Brant Ward*/San Francisco Chronicle/*Corbis.*

Before she rocketed to rock stardom in 1967, Janis Joplin belonged to the Haight-Ashbury. Everyone knew her, or knew someone who had slept with her. *Photo copyright © Baron Wolman.*

Fueled by the rising power of rock music, a new San Francisco social support system emerged. In 1975, rock impresario Bill Graham (far right) called on friends like Francis Ford Coppola and Marlon Brando to stage a benefit concert for the city's after-school programs. *Copyright © Michael Zagaris.*

The wild, gender-contorting Cockettes burst onto the San Francisco stage on New Year's Eve 1970. "We're just chicks with cocks," explained one troupe member to the press. *Copyright © Fayette Hauser*

For a soaring moment, Moby Grape was San Francisco's most powerful band. The group's tumultuous decline mirrored the city's own growing turmoil. *Courtesy of Sony Music Entertainment.*

Anton LaVey, high priest of the Church of Satan (shown here in an occult ceremony with his wife, Diane), held a strange allure for women, including actress Jayne Mansfield and future Manson follower Susan "Sexy Sadie" Atkins. LaVey was just a carny showman at heart, but his gothic cult reflected the dark side of the City of Love. *Copyright © Bettmann/Corbis.*

By the mid-1970s, Lucifer was rising in San Francisco as the city fell under the spell of hard drugs, guns, and radical violence. Kidnapped in 1974 by the SLA, an underground gang with delusions of revolutionary grandeur, young socialite Patty Hearst became the eye of a boiling media storm as she seemed to join forces with her captors. After she was finally arrested, Hearst went on trial for her complicity with the group in 1976. *Associated Press.*

Mayor Joseph Alioto—who struggled to "manage the revolution" roaring through San Francisco in the 1960s and '70s—fielded questions from the press after a pre-dawn police raid on May 1, 1974, finally ended the reign of racial terror known as the Zebra murders. *Copyright © Bettmann/Corbis.*

In 1977, George Moscone (right), the city's new, progressive mayor, rewarded Peoples Temple leader Jim Jones (left) for his decisive help in winning the mayoral race by appointing him to the city's housing commission. It was a pact with the devil that would later haunt Moscone. *Copyright © Clem Albers/San Francisco Chronicle/Corbis.*

Inspired by the militancy of the black power movement, a new wave of young Chinese activists such as Rose Pak, pictured here in 1977, began to demand a place at the head table for their long ignored community. Over three decades later, Pak and Brown helped engineer the ascension of San Francisco's first Chinese-American mayor, Ed Lee. *Copyright © Joseph Rosenthal/ San Francisco Chronicle/Corbis.*

After George Moscone took over city hall, a diverse generation of new leaders began to challenge San Francisco's Irish-Catholic hierarchy. Willie Brown, who rose from the streets of the Fillmore district to become California's powerful speaker of the assembly, high-stepped it at a 1978 fashion show put on by his clothier friend Wilkes Bashford. *Copyright © John O'Hara/San Francisco Chronicle/Corbis.*

Supervisor Harvey Milk (wearing tie), the whirlwind behind the city's gay revolution, celebrated the twenty-fourth birthday of his aide Cleve Jones (wearing eyeglasses) in October 1978. Weeks later, Milk was dead. *Copyright © Rink Foto 1978.*

Supervisor Dan White is taken into custody after assassinating Mayor George Moscone and Supervisor Harvey Milk in city hall on November 27, 1978. White, a former cop who seethed with the bitter resentments felt by many traditional San Franciscans, was greeted like a hero by some members of the police department. *Copyright © John Storey/San Francisco Chronicle/Corbis.*

Dianne Feinstein (left), at a press conference following the assassinations, took over as mayor during the city's darkest days since the Great Earthquake of 1906. Though she lacked Moscone and Milk's progressive spark, Feinstein gave the shaken city the stable leadership it needed to absorb the tumultuous changes. *Copyright © Bettmann/Corbis.*

Fiery rioting erupted after Dan White received a shockingly lenient manslaughter verdict in 1979. When he was released from prison in January 1984, after serving just five years for the carnage at city hall, White again sparked angry protests like this one. *Copyright © Susan Gilbert/San Francisco Chronicle/Corbis.*

In the 1980s, the San Francisco 49ers' legendary duo—coach Bill Walsh and quarterback Joe Montana—brought a blaze of glory to a city in desperate need of resurrection. *Copyright © Michael Zagaris.*

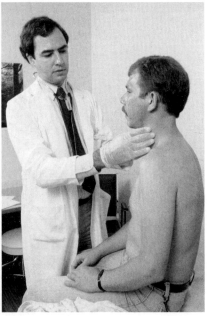

Fans poured into the streets on January 25, 1982—still celebrating the day after the 49ers won their first Super Bowl. As Mayor Feinstein rode in the raucous victory parade, she felt the shroud finally begin to lift: "I saw with my own eyes what a team can do for a city." *Copyright © John O'Hara/San Francisco Chronicle/Corbis.*

The terrifying AIDS epidemic that began scything its way through San Francisco in the early 1980s could have sparked a new wave of civic panic and fury. Instead—led by gay activists and by courageous health workers like Dr. Paul Volberding, cofounder of San Francisco General Hospital's pioneering AIDS ward—San Francisco became a model of compassion. *Copyright © Roger Ressmeyer/Corbis.*

24

INSIDE MAN

D AVID REUBEN—A SHORT, scrappy investigator with the kind of commanding beak that looked like he enjoyed sticking it in people's business—leaned back in his chair in the district attorney's office, nursing a cup of jailhouse java. Reuben listened with growing intensity as a middle-aged couple named Al and Jeannie Mills unraveled a jaw-dropping story about their lives in Jim Jones's peculiar church. The Millses were the kind of homespun, *American Gothic*–looking people you wouldn't glance at twice on the streets. But if 10 percent of what they were saying was true, Reuben figured, this case was going to rock the city—and the tremors would radiate far and wide.

Reuben had been recruited by Joe Freitas after he took over the DA's office in the 1975 liberal electoral sweep. Like Moscone, Freitas was a Kennedyesque Catholic politician with wavy-haired, Mediterranean good looks. Raised in a Portuguese family in the Central Valley, Freitas had served in all the stations of the liberal cross, including the National Urban League and Common Cause, before running for San Francisco DA at the age of thirty-six. Brimming with youthful self-confidence and political ambition, the new district attorney created a special prosecutions unit, filling it with young "red hots"—as Reuben described himself and his gung-ho colleagues. Freitas promised his mod squad a free hand in going after city corruption. "He told us there were no holds barred:

dirty cops, dirty politicians, payoffs," recalled Reuben. "Joe said, 'I don't care who it is, you go after them.'"

Freitas recruited crusading lawyers and investigators from all over the country for his new unit. Reuben and his crew came in with guns blazing, targeting the deep corruption in the San Francisco police force, including payoffs to cops by the skin trade moguls in North Beach. But Reuben soon found that the San Francisco justice establishment was more impregnable than he had imagined.

Coming from Chicago, where he had broken in as an investigator for the state attorney's office, pursuing corruption in Mayor Richard Daley's permanent regime, Reuben thought he had seen it all. But the San Francisco cop culture proved an even tougher nut to crack. "I thought that coming from Chicago, I knew old-boy's networks," he said, "but this was really something out here. It's a true old-boy's network. All the cops and prosecutors know each other, they're all friends and family, they all went to the same parochial schools. And here we all come into the DA's office: we were all in our twenties, and we're all ballbusters. I mean, I took on the Daley machine. We didn't care, we were going to investigate every-body. Well, it turns out that you don't do that in San Francisco—not unless you have the inside support. And I'm Jewish, from Chicago. So I was more outside than you can ever imagine."

By the time that Al and Jeannie Mills walked into his small office at the hall of justice in early 1977, Reuben and his team were beginning to feel demoralized. They had won some minor victories in their campaign against police corruption, but they were feeling increasingly isolated—not just within the hall of justice, where police inspectors feared and hated them, but within the DA's office itself, which was bitterly divided over Freitas's progressive reign. But the Peoples Temple investigation could make up for all the frustrations, Reuben realized. It was the kind of case that could make an investigator's career.

The Millses, who defected from the Peoples Temple in 1976, told Reuben and his team that Jim Jones was a violent, drug-crazed des-pot. They accused him of ordering the murders of disaffected members and subjecting others to savage beatings, including their sixteen-year-old daughter, who was whipped so severely, according to Al, "her butt looked like hamburger." The couple—who had changed their names from Elmer and Deanna Mertle to evade temple enforcers—told the investigators that Jones forced members to turn over their property and possessions to the church and confiscated their welfare and Social Security checks. They said Jones had also built his organization into a potent political machine, manipulating elections and politicians and working his way into the inner circles of power in San Francisco.

Reuben and his colleagues immediately recognized how explosive the Millses' charges were. "At the time, Jim Jones was an acknowledged civic leader," recalled Reuben. "I mean, he was the Second Coming in this city, bringing together black and white, rich and poor. He had presidents and governors and congressmen kissing his ring. And Joe Freitas was one of those people."

Reuben and the chief of the special prosecutions unit, a former US prosecutor named Bob Graham, girded their loins and walked into their boss's office to present the accusations against the Peoples Temple. As Reuben and Graham itemized the charges to Freitas and his number two man, Danny Weinstein, the room grew tense. "We lay it all out, and you could've heard a pin drop," Reuben said. "And then Joe looks at us and says, 'What, are you guys nuts?'"

Freitas heatedly pointed out to his special prosecutions team that people walked into the DA's office all the time with wild charges and personal grudges. "You guys can't just buy this stuff," Freitas admonished them.

Reuben and Graham were incensed. The hard-charging, windmill-tilting DA who had hired them—and told them they had carte blanche—was now suggesting that they back off what could be the hottest case they'd ever worked. They immediately knew what was going down. They'd read the newspapers and knew all about the furious allegations from the Barbagelata camp: that Jim Jones and his zombie flock had stolen the election for Moscone, and had worked hard for Freitas too.

"We were pissed," Reuben recalled later. "It was too dynamic for us not to dig into. All the names mentioned—Willie Brown, Dianne Feinstein, George Moscone—the whole gang was in there, I'm sure. And, of course, it was obvious to us—we're not idiots—Joe was in the middle of the thing. He knew that if we started doing this thing, *his* career might be affected."

Freitas was too politically savvy to simply shut down the Peoples Temple investigation. He knew that his angry investigators' suspicions could wind up in the press. So he gave his special team just enough leash to quietly look into the Millses' accusations. And to make sure that Reuben and Graham did not dig too deeply, Freitas appointed a young deputy named Tim Stoen as his liaison on the case.

REUBEN DID NOT KNOW much about Stoen. The deputy DA, who wore horn-rimmed glasses and three-piece suits, was a straitlaced loner. "He was a nerdy kind of guy," Reuben recalled. "Very bright, well spoken. We thought he was one of us, a reformer. But we joked about it, because he seemed *too* idealistic. He really wasn't friendly with anybody, just did his own thing."

As Reuben and his team dug deeper into the Millses' hair-raising stories about the Peoples Temple, the allegations were checking out. Interviewing other defectors and anxious relatives of temple members, the investigators soon learned how fearful these people were of reprisals from Jones's security guards—all of whom, Reuben discovered, had long rap sheets. Reuben promised his witnesses that he would protect their anonymity. But when he and his colleagues casually referred to their partner on the case, Deputy District Attorney Tim Stoen, the witnesses looked stunned. *"Tim Stoen?"* said one defector to Reuben, with panic in his eyes. "He's Jim Jones's top legal advisor."

A chill ran up Reuben's spine when he heard this. Afterward he and Bob Graham stumbled in a daze over to a cop bar across the street from the hall of justice, to compare notes. What the hell was going on? The question hung over them like a noose as they hunched over their drinks. "So now we're figuring, Is Stoen a plant? Does Freitas know who he is, or did this guy just weasel his way in? Does this all go back to Jones? Even before this, we didn't know who to trust in the office. But now we're really paranoid, because we don't know who's calling the shots."

The two investigators marched into Freitas's office to confront their boss. "We blew up," recalled Reuben. "We said, 'What's going on here? Are we being made patsies in this whole thing?'"

Freitas acted surprised. "He said, 'Are you guys sure?' And this and that, like he didn't know anything about Stoen." But the investigators realized that Stoen was far too cozy with their boss for him not to have known.

Joe Freitas would later tell the press he had no idea that Tim Stoen was Jones's right-hand man when he hired him; that he had simply plucked his resumé out of the slush pile. But in truth, the Peoples Temple, which had contributed money and campaigned for Freitas, engineered Stoen's insertion into the DA's office as a political reward for its efforts. And in a brazen move to cover up the voter fraud committed by the temple during the 1975 election, Freitas put the temple's lawyer in charge of the investigation. In doing so, he ensured that San Francisco would never find out who'd really won the mayoral election. Stoen brought in Peoples Temple clerical volunteers to help with his politically sensitive probe. The foxes had free run of the henhouse, and they left only feathers.

Three years later, after the name Jim Jones had gone down in infamy, state and federal investigators finally began looking into the shady election. When they asked for all the rosters showing who voted, the city's deputy registrar of voters went searching for the records in three locked vaults where they were kept. All the records were missing.

After they found out about Stoen, Reuben and Graham began taking their files home at night, no longer sure that they could protect the confidentiality of their Peoples Temple witnesses, some of whom feared for their lives. The investigators' suspicions were well founded. Stoen, it turned out, was literally a sleeper in the DA's office. He often spent the night there, though he had a residence on Page Street, giving him free access to the office's most sensitive documents for almost a year. Stoen and his wife, Grace, whom he had brought into the temple, enjoyed "a free romp through the place after hours," one source reported. Freitas later shrugged off his deputy's after-hours routine. "He was a hard worker," the DA explained, and after toiling late into the night he often needed to avail himself of his office couch.

Freitas accommodated Stoen in other ways as well. When citizen complaints about temple criminality came into the office, Freitas made sure that Jones's lieutenant was brought into the loop. Hannibal Williams, a charismatic Fillmore leader who fought a brave but losing battle against the razing of his neighborhood, was one of the few black pastors who dared to criticize Jones's operation. When Williams was threatened by Peoples Temple thugs, he went to the DA, only to be turned over to Tim Stoen.

If Tim Stoen confounded his colleagues in the DA's office, he was also a mystery to some members of Jones's inner circle. A deeply religious Republican attorney with political ambitions when he discovered Peoples Temple, Stoen soon became a true believer and a man so trusted by Jones that the temple leader delegated much of the organization's legal and financial affairs to him and his wife. Despite Stoen's middle-American upbringing and early anticommunism, he declared himself a disciple of Jones's oddball socialism. "Tim Stoen was so close to my dad; I think he was Dad's real true friend," said Jim Jones Jr., the cult leader's adopted son.

Nonetheless, Jones, easily threatened by accomplished men like the Stanford-educated lawyer, put Stoen through the same bizarre loyalty tests and sexual humiliations to which he subjected other temple members. Jones toyed perversely with the Stoens' marriage, wheedling Tim into having affairs with other women in the church and then planting doubts in Grace about her husband's loyalty and sexual orientation.

Jones—whose sexual appetites were imperial, establishing rapacious dominion over men and women alike—was of the eccentric opinion that he was the only true heterosexual male in the temple. All the other men around him secretly harbored lusts for their fellow man, Jones insisted, and he was in the habit of offering to relieve various fellows of their illicit desires by buggering them. Jones once finagled Stoen into going out shopping for a bra and panties, and then used the female frillies to convince Grace that her husband was a closet drag queen. The preacher also tried to get Tim to confess in front of a church assembly that he was gay, but the buttoned-down lawyer refused.

Other times Stoen seemed recklessly willing to prostrate himself before his master's will. In February 1972—after Grace gave birth to a baby boy named John Stoen—Tim agreed to sign a document stating, "I entreated my beloved pastor, James W. Jones, to sire a child by my wife [because I] was unable after extensive attempts to sire one myself. My reason for requesting James W. Jones to do this is that I wanted my child to be fathered, if not by me, by the most compassionate, honest, and courageous human being the world contains." This wanton act of self-abasement would come back to haunt the Stoens.

Despite the many mortifications of serving Jim Jones, Tim Stoen remained zealously steadfast. One member of the temple's inner circle was amazed to see the lawyer go along with some of Jones's most violent fantasies without objection. "Jim started turning crazier by the day in San Francisco," said the temple insider. "I knew he was going over the edge when he ordered a woman named Maria Katsaris to start taking flying lessons. He wanted her to learn how to fly so they could fill a plane with temple members and then crash it, in an act of 'revolutionary suicide,' as he called it. Maria went to flight school, but she hated it. Stoen knew about Maria's flight training. He was in the room when it was discussed. It was talked about a number of times."

On another occasion, Stoen told a temple insider to get a gun, in case Jones was harmed by outside enemies and the organization needed to strike back. The lawyer also talked about putting plutonium in the Washington, DC, water supply. One of Stoen's ideas, according to the insider, apparently surprised even Jones. "He ordered a couple of us to set up a bomb factory in San Francisco. I went to Jim and told him. He said he knew nothing about it, and he told me not to do anything."

The insider came to believe that Stoen was an agent provocateur. Later, after Jones began shifting his operation to Guyana, other members of the temple's leadership circle, including Jones himself, also concluded that Stoen was a government agent. While rummaging through Stoen's briefcase in Guyana, Jones's lieutenants found a newspaper clipping about his arrest in East Berlin when he was an overseas college student, as well as a diary from this period, full of strong anti-Communist sentiments. They also discovered a second passport. In the febrile and suspicious atmosphere of the Peoples Temple, this seemed to prove that Stoen had some sort of intelligence background.

While Stoen was working in the San Francisco District Attorney's Office, however, he did nothing to inflame Jones's paranoia. As far as Dave Reuben could tell, he was a temple loyalist, Jim Jones's man inside the hall of justice. "I didn't talk to Stoen after we found out about him," said Reuben. "I probably wanted to shoot him. We may have even tailed him at some point."

Stoen always denied he was aware of the Peoples Temple voter fraud and its coverup, despite the key positions he held within the church and the San Francisco DA's office. "Jim Jones kept a lot of things from me," he later told the *New York Times*. Years after the Peoples Temple saga, Stoen went full circle, returning to the north California coast region where he had joined Jones's church and resuming his career as a respected prosecutor and Republican Party politician in Humboldt and Mendocino counties. Stoen declined to comment for this book on his years with Jones.

Jim Jones proved a master at politically wiring San Francisco in the midseventies. Planting Stoen in the DA's office was just one of his successful maneuvers. Considering the criminal underside of his operation, it was also one of the most useful. *Sun Reporter* publisher Dr. Carlton Goodlett, one of the pillars of the black community to be seduced by Jones, marveled at his ally's manipulation of the civic power structure. "You always got a man pretty close to a law enforcement agency in a town, don't you?" Goodlett once observed.

"You're very perceptive," chuckled Jones.

Later, after Jonestown became an international symbol of mass lunacy, it was widely assumed to be one more outgrowth of "San Fransicko." But, in fact, Jim Jones was a God-fearing product of the American heartland.

25

SLOUCHING TOWARD SAN FRANCISCO

J IM JONES WAS raised by a mother whose dreams were too big for the
Indiana farm town where they lived. "Don't be nothing like your dad,"
Lynetta Jones drummed into her boy, while Big Jim rocked forlornly in
his armchair, his lungs so badly scarred by mustard gas in the First World
War that he couldn't wheeze his way through a full day's work. The boy
developed a messianic complex at an early age, killing a cat so he could
try raising it from the dead. One day he marched into the drowsy, God-
fearing town wearing a makeshift white robe to confront the sinners in
the pool hall—including his own sad, hard-drinking father. "You're all
going to hell," the boy preacher proclaimed sternly.

Jones became a rising young Pentecostal preacher in Indianapolis,
building a mixed-race congregation—a daring move in 1950s Middle
America—and starting a rainbow family of his own with his wife, Marceline. Soon after Marceline gave birth to their first son, Stephan, the
couple adopted a girl from a Korean orphanage and an African-American
infant whom Jim anointed with his own name—only the beginning of
what would become a multiracial brood.

A cloud of menace hung over Jones's racially advanced church.
The preacher and his wife received late-night crank phone calls, and

a dead cat was thrown at their house. Someone painted a swastika on the church door, and Jones once found glass in his Sunday potluck dinner. But some members of the church wondered if the hostile acts were staged by Jones himself.

In July 1965 Jones convinced 140 members of his congregation to abandon their lives in Indiana and move westward with him to the California promised land: a valley in Mendocino County where Jones said they would be safe from redneck tormentors and from the nuclear doomsday that he predicted would reduce most of America to poisonous smoke and ash. It was the first exodus engineered by Jones, who was always trying to outrun his own demons. His followers headed west in a dusty caravan of pickup trucks, vans, and cars.

As the Peoples Temple established itself in Redwood Valley— recruiting new members, many of them black and poor, from the Bay Area, Los Angeles, and other cities—Jones set about infiltrating the local power structure. Though Jones told his flock that the one true God was socialism, the church worked hard to win over the Republican establishment that controlled Ukiah, the county seat. The Peoples Temple bought tickets to local Republican fund-raisers, bombarded GOP politicians with flattering letters, and contributed to their campaigns. Jones announced that he was a registered Republican and was supporting Nixon for president in 1968, and even befriended the head of the local John Birch Society. Meanwhile, the church infiltrated members into the sheriff's department and the county social services department, and Tim Stoen went to work in the Mendocino County District Attorney's Office as the county counsel. The same political strategy that would work so effectively in liberal San Francisco was first tested in conservative Ukiah.

It did not take long for Jones, always looking for the big stage that his mother envisioned for him, to outgrow the Redwood Valley. He began extending feelers into San Francisco, leading weekly services at a junior high school auditorium in the Fillmore as early as 1970. Long before George Moscone came into their sights, temple officials wooed Mayor Alioto, buying one hundred tickets to a breakfast fund-raiser for Alioto in 1973 and sending him a box of homemade candy in 1975.

That year, the Peoples Temple moved its headquarters to San Francisco, taking over an old Jewish synagogue next to the Black Muslim mosque on Geary Boulevard once occupied by the Fillmore Auditorium. It was an eerie synchronicity—the building once a haven for the Zebra butchers sitting side by side with the temple that would become infamous as the headquarters of the deadliest cult in US history.

Using the same bag of tricks he used on politicians—including donations, bouquets of flattery, and his considerable personal charm—Jim Jones won over key black church leaders in the Bay Area, including activist pastors Cecil Williams of Glide Memorial in the Tenderloin and J. Alfred Smith of the Allen Temple Baptist Church in Oakland. With Jones's impassioned pulpit performances and his organization's social outreach programs, including a free medical clinic and food and clothing donations, the Peoples Temple soon established firm roots in the devastated Fillmore neighborhood. Traditional black churches—whose pastors "preached the sweet by-and-by," in Rev. Smith's words, and limited their social services to Christmas basket giveaways—found it hard to compete with Jones's theatrical evangelism. The white preacher began luring away hundreds of black worshippers; massive "sheep stealing" that rival black ministers grumbled about but did little to counteract.

Jones moved into the Fillmore at its most vulnerable moment. Urban renewal czar Justin Herman had "literally destroyed the neighborhood," observed neighborhood activist Hannibal Williams, "[and] people were desperate for solutions, something to follow. Jim Jones was another solution. He had a charismatic personality that won the hearts and souls of people. And people followed him to hell. That's where Jim Jones went. That's where he took the people who followed him."

In the beginning, Jones was greeted as a "godsend" in the black community, remarked Rev. Smith. Here was a white pastor who "had the gift of communicating with black people. He didn't communicate in the sterile way of the seminary. No, if you listen to Jones's sermons, you can hear him following the rhythms and cadences to match the beating of the human heart."

And his flock, ignored and scorned by society, was electrified by Jones's vision of a new Eden. Everybody was exalted in his services, even the lowliest recovering drunks and addicts. "He made us feel special, like something bigger than ourselves," said one temple member. "Total equality, no rich or poor, no races," said another. "We were alive in those services," testified one more. "They had life, soul power."

Jones—an oddball and renegade his entire life, someone who never felt at home in his own skin—had found his identity by taking on a black persona. He saw himself following in the footsteps of Malcolm and Martin, leading "his" people out of bondage and into the promised land.

In reality, Jones maintained a racial hierarchy within the organization. While church membership was primarily black, the thirty-seven-member planning commission, as Jones called his leadership council, was dominated by white women—at least six of whom were his sexual conquests and firmly under his sway. "When people talk about my father manipulating black people, that's true," said Jim Jones Jr., the preacher's black adopted son. "It was politically advantageous for him to give me his name."

There was something exhibitionistic about the way that Jones and his wife treated their black son. "I was the chosen one," he said. "I was more loved in my family than the other kids, even their biological son, Stephan. I remember Mom wiping charcoal off a dirty pot one day and rubbing it all over her face—to show that we were all black."

JONES SOON LEARNED THAT his control over a well-organized, mixed-race army of some eight thousand dedicated followers gave him major stature with San Francisco's liberal elite. Redevelopment had bulldozed the Fillmore's political power into the ground. But now this strange white man with the hipster shades, Indian-black hair, and cadences of a black Bible-thumper seemed to be erecting a new political power line into the rubble-strewn, crime-ridden no-man's-land. Jones could be counted on to deliver busloads of obedient, well-dressed disciples to demonstrations, campaign rallies, and political precincts. The city's liberal Burton machine quickly identified the Peoples Temple juggernaut as a potentially game-changing ally in its long battle to take over city hall.

It was Willie Brown who first recognized that Jones's organization could play a pivotal role in his friend George Moscone's run for mayor. A meeting was set up between Jones and Moscone in the office of Don Bradley, the candidate's veteran campaign manager. Bradley was initially cautious. "I was a little leery we were getting into something like the Moonies," he later recalled. But after he looked into the temple's campaign history in Mendocino and saw how effective it was in delivering victories there, Bradley enthusiastically embraced Jones's volunteer army. Nearly two hundred temple members showed up at Moscone headquarters, fanning out to campaign in some of the city's toughest neighborhoods, and helping the candidate finish first in the November election.

In the December runoff between Moscone and Barbagelata, Peoples Temple went even further to secure victory for its candidate. On the eve of the election, Jones filled buses with temple members in Redwood Valley and Los Angeles and shuttled them to San Francisco. Security at polling places was lax on Election Day, and many nonresidents were able to cast their ballots for Moscone, some more than once. "You could have run around to twelve hundred precincts and voted twelve hundred times," said a bitter Barbagelata later, after losing by a whisper of a margin. But he was not the only one who claimed that the Peoples Temple stole the election for George Moscone. Temple leaders also claimed credit.

"We loaded up all thirteen of our buses with maybe seventy people on each bus, and we had those buses rolling nonstop up and down the coast into San Francisco the day before the election," recalled Jim Jones Jr. "We had people going from precinct to precinct to vote. So could we have been the force that tipped the election to Moscone? Absolutely! Slam dunk. He only won by four thousand votes. I'm sorry, but I've got to give my father credit for that. I think he did the right thing. George Moscone was a good person; he wanted what was best for San Francisco."

Jim Jones made sure that George Moscone never forgot his political debt to Peoples Temple. The man who began his term in city hall with a ringing promise to make San Francisco a beacon of enlightenment would start off his administration with a wretched burden on his back. The mayor could never rid himself of the stench of contagion that Jones brought with him, and as time went by, the power-hungry preacher only sunk his fangs in deeper. The pastor was a wickedly smart reader of a politician's character, and he knew that the way to enchant Moscone was with young women, not money. When it came to bribing politicians, the temple leader had ample supplies of both. Jones bragged of supplying Moscone with black female members of his congregation. Jim Jones Jr. remembered the mayor as "a party guy. He'd always be there at temple parties with a cocktail in his hand and doing some ass grabbing."

Temple insiders talked about how Mayor Moscone was one of the politicians under the control of "Father." They gossiped about the night that the mayor had fallen into Jones's hands. "Moscone was known to be a boozer; he liked to drink at parties," recalled temple member Hue Fortson, now a pastor in Southern California. "One night there was some sort of temple event that the mayor attended. The next morning I heard that Jones phoned Moscone and told him it was a pleasure to see him the night before and to see him having such a good time. 'But I want to let you know that the young lady you went off with is underage,' Jones told him. 'Now don't worry, Mayor, we'll take care of you—because we know that you'll take care of us.'"

Jones might have made up the stories of sexual blackmail. He was known to concoct outlandish tales. "Jim was always bragging that he had sexually compromising information about politicians," remembered Terri Buford, an on-again, off-again mistress of Jones who belonged to the temple's inner circle. "But you never knew if what he said was true. He once told me that Willie Brown was sexually attracted to him. He just made stuff up."

Whether or not Moscone was sexually compromised by Jones, he was certainly politically ensnared. The mayor initially resisted the temple's efforts to insert its members throughout city government. And when Jones himself pushed for a high-level appointment, Moscone at first tried to appease him with a harmless post on the human rights commission. But the temple leader insisted on a position that had more clout, and the mayor decided he was in no position to alienate Jones. In October 1976 Moscone announced that he was naming Jones to the San Francisco Housing Authority, which oversees the operation of the city's public housing. The agency, the largest landlord in the city, was a notorious maze of corruption, and it provided Jones's organization with ample opportunity for shady self-dealing. A few months later, Moscone pulled strings to promote Jones, making him chairman.

Jones swept into the normally tedious meetings of the housing commission like a banana republic despot, surrounded by an entourage of aides and grim-faced security guards. Looking stern and inscrutable behind his aviator sunglasses, Jones ran the meetings with scripted precision while sipping a frothy white drink brought to him by a hovering retainer. The audience, packed with elderly black temple worshippers, erupted into wild cheers at his most routine pronouncements. Temple enforcers roamed through the meetings, keeping a watchful vigil, and even blocking people from entering the bathroom while Jones was inside.

Jones used his position to take possession of public housing units and install temple members in them, and he put other followers on the housing authority payroll. The preacher was building his own power base within city government. "He was using his power to recruit members and to put the hammer on people," said Dave Reuben. "He had a lot of authority."

"Jim Jones helped George Moscone run this city," said Jim Jones Jr., a chillingly matter-of-fact assessment of the temple leader's creeping encroachment in San Francisco.

Political leaders, aware of Jones's ability to deliver—or manufacture—votes, lined up to pay tribute to the preacher. He worked his way into the good graces of officials high and low—most of them Democrats, since that was the party in power in California and San Francisco in the mid-1970s. But Jones was also happy to exchange mutually complimentary correspondence with the offices of Ronald Reagan and statesman Henry Kissinger.

During the 1976 presidential campaign, Jones wangled a private meeting with Jimmy Carter's wife, Rosalynn, at the elegant Stanford Court Hotel on Nob Hill, arriving with a security contingent that was larger than her Secret Service squad. Later Jones accompanied Moscone and a group of Democratic dignitaries who climbed aboard vice presidential candidate Walter Mondale's private jet when it touched down at San Francisco International Airport.

Governor Jerry Brown sang the preacher's praises. Congressman John Burton lobbied the governor to appoint Jones to the high-profile board of regents, which oversaw California's sprawling public university system. Supervisor Dianne Feinstein accepted an invitation to lunch with Jones and to tour Peoples Temple.

But no political figures were more gushing in their praise of Jones than Harvey Milk and Willie Brown. Milk, a perennial candidate for office until he finally won a supervisor's seat in 1977, aggressively sought Jones's political blessing. "Our paths have crossed," Milk wrote Jones during an earlier campaign for supervisor, in a letter filled with the kind of awed reverence that the cult leader demanded from his followers. "They will stay crossed. It is a fight that I will walk with you into . . . The first time I heard you, you made a statement: 'Take one of us, and you must take all of us.' Please add my name."

Not content to hear dignitaries whisper flatteries into his ear, Jones staged a testimonial banquet in his own honor and demanded that politicians in his debt offer him public tribute. On the evening of September 25, 1976, the temple on Geary Boulevard was converted into a formal dining hall with linen tablecloths and floral arrangements. At the head table sat Mayor Moscone, District Attorney Freitas, and Assemblyman Willie Brown, who acted as the evening's exuberant master of ceremonies. As he introduced the man of the hour to the overflow audience, Brown reached new heights of shameless, ass-kissing puffery. "Let me present to you," Brown roared, "a combination of Martin King, Angela Davis, Albert Einstein . . . Chairman Mao." By the time Jones rose to tumultuous applause, he seemed likely to walk on water.

Privately, San Francisco political leaders expressed doubts about Jones and his strange church. One day a friend of Milk's named Tory Hartmann dropped off some boxes of campaign brochures at Peoples Temple, so that Jones's army could distribute them. Hartmann was immediately creeped out by the uptight, high-security atmosphere inside the temple, where sentries stood at attention outside each room, like the palace guards in the Wicked Witch's castle. "This is a church?" Hartmann said to herself. Later, after she sped back to the Castro and told Milk about her bizarre experience, the naturally cheery politician turned deadly serious.

"Make sure you're always nice to the Peoples Temple," he told her. "They're weird and they're dangerous, and you never want to be on their bad side."

Cleve Jones, a young Milk aide, accompanied him to Peoples Temple for a couple of Sunday services. "Harvey told me, 'Be careful, they tape everything.' Everyone knew Jim Jones was creepy, everyone knew he was a megalomaniac. But everybody also saw this church full of black and white people—black people from the Fillmore who had been subjected to apartheid-like policies and seemed to finally be getting some respect."

Members of Moscone's staff were also beginning to hear troubling reports about Peoples Temple. One day mayoral aide Dick Sklar suggested to his family maid—an African-American woman who had followed the Sklars to San Francisco from Ohio—that she attend a Sunday service at Peoples Temple. "I didn't know anything about it," Sklar said, "but she was a churchgoing woman, and I thought she might like it. Afterward she came back and said it was the scariest place she'd ever been. They searched her, asked her questions. I had no idea."

Moscone himself could not ignore how peculiar his political ally was. "I was at every meeting that Jim Jones ever attended with the mayor," said Corey Busch. "I can tell you that after every one of those meetings, the reaction was, 'This is one weird bird.' He always wore the dark glasses. You couldn't predict Jonestown, but he was definitely weird. In retrospect, maybe we should have seen that, but we didn't."

As city hall looked the other way, Jones quietly consolidated his power in San Francisco, extending his influence in political, religious, and media circles. The temple worked its mojo on dozens of community organizations, from small groups like the Telegraph Hill Neighborhood Association to higher-profile ones like the American Civil Liberties Union, the National Association for the Advancement of Colored People, and the United Farm Workers. Jones won their gratitude by donating money and flooding their rallies and events with vocal supporters.

By early 1977, it seemed that Jim Jones had conquered San Francisco. He had the mayor in his pocket and commanded the fawning loyalty of power brokers such as Willie Brown and rising stars like Harvey Milk. Using San Francisco as its power base, the Peoples Temple was ready to expand its operations in Los Angeles, Seattle, and other cities where it had already sunk roots.

There was only one politician who seemed willing to confront the powerful cult: cantankerous John Barbagelata, the fading voice of San Francisco conservatism.

26

PROPHET OF DOOM

J OHN BARBAGELATA, WHO'D never stopped fuming about his shady
mayoral defeat, kept banging the drum about Jim Jones's political
machine and its insidious influence in city hall. During the Proposition B recall campaign, the supervisor charged loudly that San Francisco
was being taken over by extremists and kooks—and the Peoples Temple
was the most dangerous element of this new coalition. Moscone angrily
rejected Barbagelata's accusation. "There's no radical plot in San Francisco," the mayor declared. "There's no one I've appointed to any city
position whom I regard as radical or extremist."

Meanwhile, Joe Freitas bluntly dismissed Barbagelata's voter fraud
charges. In March 1977 the DA wrote Barbagelata, assuring him that
his deputy Tim Stoen had investigated the fraud allegations and had
determined "that there was not sufficient evidence" to pursue the case.
An outraged Barbagelata, now finally aware of Stoen's blatant conflict
of interest, circled Tim Stoen's name in red on the Freitas letter and
scrawled, "President Peoples Temple."

By then Stoen had disappeared from the DA's office and had flown to
Guyana, where Jones was already preparing his next refuge in a remote
jungle. But Barbagelata kept after the Peoples Temple, which he suspected of getting its hands on foster children and kids deemed "incorri-
gible" by courts, and spiriting them off to Guyana, along with the public

284

funds attached to the children. The anxieties of Peoples Temple relatives were beginning to rise as members began vanishing from San Francisco and Oakland. The conservative supervisor was the only city official
who seemed to be making inquiries about the fate of children in Jones's
control. San Francisco's welfare chief reacted huffily that Barbagelata
would even propose such an investigation.

It took courage to confront Jones's maniacal organization. Barbagelata was barraged with scornful letters from a phalanx of well-positioned
Peoples Temple supporters such as the Reverend Norman E. Leach,
executive director of the San Francisco Council of Churches, who condemned the supervisor's talk of a "radical takeover" of the city as "merely
sour grapes."

Leach then went on to offer pious counsel to Barbagelata: "Have
you ever discussed with the Reverend Jim Jones your views as to his
belonging to some sort of 'coalition' which is eroding the 'balance of
power in San Francisco' and 'attempting to control everything'? I know
Jim and know him to be an independent person, a man of strong values
and convictions, and a man not beholden to any organization or group
or individual . . . Build your own coalition, if you wish. But don't find
secret coalitions in existence which are not there." Jones was sending
his number one political enemy a message: if Barbagelata sat down and
came to terms with him, maybe he too could reap the benefits enjoyed
by San Francisco's political winners.

Rev. Leach had been arrested in 1974 and convicted of "contributing to the delinquency of a minor twelve or younger" in Napa, California, but if temple officials knew about the Presbyterian minister's legal
record, they apparently did not use it to manipulate him. "They were
simply very good at co-opting people," Leach said later.

Other letters that Barbagelata received from temple members felt
more ominous. "We got letters from Jones's followers saying, 'We hear
you've been saying these things about Father, and we want you to stop
saying these things about Father.' And then there were subtle threats,"
recalled Barbagelata's son Paul.

The Peoples Temple letters came during a very disturbing period for
the Barbagelata family, which had been subjected to a terror campaign
for months, beginning during the 1975 mayoral race. To serve in San
Francisco politics during the 1970s was to sign up for war duty. Many

local officials—especially high-profile ones such as Mayor Alioto and
Supervisor Feinstein—were subjected to death threats and bombing
attempts. But Barbagelata, the city's leading conservative, was a particular obsession of the radical underground.

The Barbagelata home in quiet, leafy St. Francis Wood, was the
target of more than one bombing attempt; strangers showed up at St.
Brendan's, the family's church, saying they'd been asked to drive the
Barbagelata kids home; bricks, beer cans, and other projectiles were
thrown through Barbagelata's real estate office and campaign headquarters; and cars belonging to campaign volunteers were firebombed and
vandalized.

THE NEW WORLD LIBERATION Front, San Francisco's leading mad
bombers, were Barbagelata's principal tormentors. One day in January
1976, the underground group delivered a box of See's candy—the supervisor's favorite—to the family residence. His kids were eager to open
it, but Barbagelata's wife told them they had to wait until their father
came home. At one point, two of his daughters playfully tossed around
the unopened package. Early that evening, a frantic Supervisor Quentin
Kopp, who had received a similar package and figured out it was wired to
explode, called the Barbagelata home, warning the family in time.

The NWLF bombed dozens of targets in the Bay Area, including
corporate buildings, Pacific Gas and Electric Company power stations,
and even luxury cars and homes owned by rich businessmen. The public face for the NWLF was a tall, lean, mustachioed man in his early
thirties who called himself Jacques Rogiers (real name: Jack Rogers).
Rogiers, operating out of an Oak Street flat, churned out threatening
communiqués on his Poor People's Press. When Rogiers—the son of a
Minnesota Twins baseball scout who'd once played professionally—was
finally arrested, the group launched a campaign to release him, accusing Barbagelata of squelching his freedom of speech. Leaflets depicting
Barbagelata as a bloody-fanged rat were brazenly stuck to the marble
walls inside city hall.

Early one evening in March 1977, the mad bombers took more direct
action against Barbagelata, tossing an explosive at the family home.

The device fell short, exploding in the yard next door, minutes after the neighbor's young boy had stopped playing there. Barbagelata never liked to show that he was rattled by the radical elements trying to drive him and his family from his hometown. But this time he let his temper fly. "These people have twisted and depraved minds," he exploded in the *Examiner.* "Had their little game been played fifteen minutes earlier, they would have blown that little boy away. Here's a message for them. If that ever happens, then a few of them are going to be blown apart by people who refuse to be intimidated."

A heavy smoker who had suffered a heart attack in 1970, Barbagelata showed signs of the strain, collapsing one day on his way to mass at St. Brendan's. But the crusty conservative refused to give in. Barbagelata—not trusting the SFPD, which he felt had fallen apart under liberal Chief Gain—armed himself and his oldest son and installed floodlights in his backyard.

On some occasions, the family would be wakened by phone calls from the police in the middle of the night, warning them to leave the house immediately. Barbagelata quickly packed his family into their station wagon, and they sped away, driving to a walnut grove near Stockton where Mrs. Barbagelata's relatives lived.

In the middle of the terror campaign against the Barbagelatas, Jim Jones suddenly appeared at the supervisor's city hall office to offer him Peoples Temple security guards as protection. It was a surreal moment. Barbagelata considered Jones's organization an even bigger threat to San Francisco than Jacques Rogiers's mad bombers. He declined Jones's offer. The temple enforcers were just as likely to shoot him, thought Barbagelata, as protect him.

John Barbagelata was finally driven out of politics—not by terrorists or mad cultists, but by the voters of San Francisco, who rejected his warnings about a radical takeover and defeated his attempted recall of the city's liberal leaders by a lopsided margin. "This is the last hurrah for conservatives in San Francisco," he bitterly told an *Examiner* reporter on the night that Proposition B went down to defeat. "I've done everything I can to expose the deceit, deception, and dishonesty in city government. Maybe the people will wake up someday, but I'm going back to my family and business."

As he announced his retirement from politics, Barbagelata issued a dire prophetic warning to his fellow San Franciscans: "In the next few months, the people are going to go through an emotional experience when they find out who's running the city."

JOHN BARBAGELATA DID NOT understand the heart of San Francisco the way George Moscone did. He was so flustered by homosexuals that he choked on the word *gay*, and the city's cultural revolution just seemed coarse and offensive to the old-fashioned Italian Catholic who had a hard time pronouncing intimate body parts. San Francisco's powerful unions, he believed, were not a vehicle for middle-class prosperity and social decency, as most of the city regarded them. In Barbagelata's mind, they were leeches on the public treasury. And the city government was not a guardian of the poor, the nonwhite, and the dispossessed. It was the bully that had taken his family home under the brute authority of eminent domain when he was boy growing up on verdant Lombard Street, because the cottage stood in the way of the expanded, new thoroughfare to the Golden Gate Bridge. To Barbagelata, government would always be the enemy of decent home owners and taxpayers.

But Barbagelata was not simply a curmudgeonly skinflint. He was the kind of man who would take homeless people off the street and put them to work painting a back room at his real estate office. Some colleagues suspected that was the sole purpose of the room. Later he would bring the hard-luck fellows home for a hearty Italian dinner, just as good families took care of hoboes during the Depression.

"I would say, 'Mom, who is that guy?' and she would say, 'One of your father's friends,'" remembered Paul Barbagelata. "My father was tough, inflexible, and a hard-ass. But the other side of him was quite compassionate. As long as you were not lazy, he could like you. He truly cared about this city and its residents from all walks of life."

Barbagelata never stopped caring about San Francisco. And if he didn't understand how the city was changing, the way that Moscone and Milk did, he was more aware than his rivals were of the sinister elements in their new coalition. Barbagelata was the only one to confront the serpents in the garden. And it galled him that others didn't take the threat as seriously as he did.

As he faded from the political stage, the crusty Cassandra lit a fire under the local newspapers, which had shown little interest in the slithery maneuvers of Jim Jones as he wrapped his coils around the city. "I think the media has to get off its goddam ass and find what's going on in this city," Barbagelata growled as he made his exit.

The *Chronicle* blithely dismissed Barbagelata's fulminations. "This newspaper is accused by Barbagelata of having complacently ignored his warnings of evil doings in San Francisco politics," the newspaper editorialized in August 1977. "In truth, his theory of some gigantic conspiracy against the public interest and weal in city hall is a theory we don't understand and have never found any evidence for."

The more conservative *Examiner* fretted that Barbagelata might be on to something, but simply hoped for the best. "It's true Barbagelata's imagination is overactive," the newspaper opined, "but he was right when he said the city must not be turned over to leftists and kooks. Let's hope his prophecies of doom are off the mark."

The men who ran San Francisco's influential dailies would soon learn that Barbagelata's prophecies were hideously accurate. But by then it was too late. The city's watchdogs did nothing to alert the public to Jim Jones's growing menace. The cult leader won the local media's silence with the same artful combination of seduction and intimidation that he had used on San Francisco's political caste.

Later, after the horror of Jonestown was reverberating around the world, a reporter for a neighborhood newspaper found Barbagelata at home on a rainy afternoon, where they talked over a lunch of chicken sandwiches and beer. The retired politician was recovering from a recent stroke, and from the calamities of his service in San Francisco public life. He still seemed stunned by it all: the evil machinations of Peoples Temple, the complicity of city hall, the stubborn refusal of the press to investigate the "growing train wreck" that was San Francisco. He was not a naïve person, he had seen some dark and vicious things in his life of nearly six decades. "But that was nothing," he said, "compared to San Francisco politics."

27

EXODUS

JIM JONES'S MOST ardent supporter in San Francisco press circles was Steve Gavin, the *Chronicle*'s city editor. A Baltimore native, he joined the *Chronicle* in 1969. Life in San Francisco agreed with Gavin, a gay man in his thirties who loved theater, baseball, and a well-mixed Manhattan. The socially aware newspaperman was delighted when he discovered Peoples Temple and its racially mixed, politically energized congregation. His increasingly warm relationship with Jones made Gavin feel connected to the kind of constituency that newspapers usually overlooked: the black, poor, and religious. Jones and his slick media strategist—a handsome, former local TV newsman named Michael Prokes—made sure that Gavin felt the temple's love.

"Jones took Gavin under his wing and made a big fuss over him," said *Chronicle* reporter Marshall Kilduff. "It was very flattering. And I think there was a degree of social usefulness in the relationship. Jones handed him a chunk of the city that wasn't a big *Chronicle* franchise. Gavin liked that."

Gavin began exchanging heartfelt letters with Jones in 1976. In July the city editor wrote to the preacher, thanking him for serving him lunch and taking him on a tour of the temple. "I enjoyed our discussion," Gavin wrote. "As I told you, I look for small victories [in life]. You have accomplished major ones. I know the feeling of getting discouraged. There is so much to do. It helps, periodically, I think, to count our blessings and to look back, to see how far we've come. To this outsider's eye, you have done a tremendous job . . . Thank you for what you are contributing to my city."

A few days later, Gavin sent the cult leader a wryly charming homily from Irish writer Brendan Behan. Jones, communicating through Prokes, responded that he was "delighted" by the quote and urged the newspaper editor to call on him for assistance if he ever needed it.

That fall, Gavin did call on Jones for help, asking him to support four *Fresno Bee* reporters who had been jailed for refusing to reveal the names of confidential sources. Jones dispatched busloads of temple members to Fresno to demonstrate on their behalf.

Around the same time, the temple deluged the *Chronicle* city editor, who was suffering from a persistent cold, with a pile of get-well letters. Gavin, touched by the congregation's generosity, responded with another fervent letter, telling Jones that he wished the press could be as compassionate as the temple was toward "the multiplicity of people that make up our community . . . Caring is all."

Jones was a master at drawing liberals and idealists who yearned for a better world into his web. He could smell the feverish longing for deliverance that wafted off them, and he made them believe he was their salvation. Jones offered a vision of heaven on earth that made even the most secular suspend rational judgment and take a leap of faith. It was all for show, but people like Gavin longed to embrace the Peoples Temple pageant: black and white, rich and poor, gay and straight, all joining hands in blissful communion.

"I was always wary of being manipulated by [temple officials] and conscious of the possibility, but I don't think I was," Gavin later insisted. "I think all my decisions about Peoples Temple stories were made on a professional basis." But the record shows a newsman who was utterly in thrall to Jones.

The Peoples Temple skillfully courted other journalists too, including Herb Caen, who enjoyed two long, chatty lunches with the cult leader. "I found him appealing—soft-spoken, modest, talking earnestly of helping people," Caen wrote later. "If he was a con man, he was masterful at it." Jones continued to get good play in Caen's column even after the bloom was fading from the temple's rose.

But no one in the San Francisco media world proved more useful to Jones than Steve Gavin, who single-handedly made sure that the city's leading newspaper did not shine a harsh spotlight on the cult leader. When *Chronicle* reporter Julie Smith began working on a story about the temple in the spring of 1976, Jones somehow learned the exact contents of the story draft while it still sat in her newsroom desk. Later Marshall Kilduff, who had a prickly experience with Jones while covering his strange performance on the housing commission, decided to write a profile of him. Showing up at the temple on a Sunday in January 1977 to interview church officials, the *Chronicle* reporter was taken on a long tour that ended in the main auditorium, where a service was in progress. As Kilduff was escorted to his seat near the front of the congregation, he was stunned to see his boss, Steve Gavin, sitting among the worshippers.

The next morning, Kilduff gingerly approached Gavin in the *Chronicle* newsroom. "Quite a show," said the reporter. "Don't you think we should do a story about this guy? I hear he's powerful politically."

But the city editor cut him off. "We've already done it," said Gavin, referring to the bland, carefully managed article produced earlier by Julie Smith.

Blocked by his own newspaper, the dogged Kilduff continued to work the Peoples Temple story on his own time, while searching for a magazine to publish it. As he tracked down sources, temple members kept close watch on him, digging through his garbage and reporting his every move to Gavin, their friend at the *Chronicle*. In March, Kilduff finally got a freelance assignment from *New West*, a regional magazine owned by Rupert Murdoch. But when a temple delegation called on its editor, Kevin Starr, and explained that the article would harm its humanitarian work, he killed the piece. Only after Starr was replaced by a more enterprising editor, Rosalie Wright, did *New West* revive Kilduff's assignment.

WHEN THE STORY, "INSIDE Peoples Temple," was finally published, it marked the beginning of the end for Jones's sinister reign in San Francisco. The article, written by Kilduff and *New West* reporter Phil Tracy, was based on the disturbing accounts of many of the same defectors who had taken their complaints to the San Francisco DA's office, only to see them bottled up. They told of the beatings, the bizarre temple ceremonies, the confiscation of members' money and assets, and the political empire building throughout the state. Among the reporters' sources was Grace Stoen, who had been forced to leave behind her five-year-old son, John, when she fled the temple. To his mother's anguish, the boy had been taken away to the temple's Guyana retreat.

While the reporters were still working on their exposé of Peoples Temple, Tim Stoen also defected, disappearing from the temple's command post in Georgetown, the capital of Guyana, in June 1977. The defection of Stoen, who joined his wife in an increasingly desperate custody battle for John, was a particularly grievous blow for Jones. Stoen knew all the organization's legal and financial secrets. His betrayal sent Jones spiraling downward into a whirlpool of panic. Battle-mode fever gripped the temple.

Before the *New West* article hit the newsstands in late July, Jim Jones ran off to Guyana, leaving his stunned liberal supporters in San Francisco to make sense of it all. Moscone was privately rattled by the magazine's charges, but he and the rest of the city's liberal elite publicly closed ranks behind the temple leader. After Jones took flight, the temple officials who were still in San Francisco organized a rally in their Geary Boulevard citadel to show support for their embattled leader. Willie Brown was still willing to shill for Jones, blaming his flight on his political enemies. "When somebody like Jim Jones comes on the scene," Brown told the gathering, "that absolutely scares the hell out of most everybody occupying positions of power in the system." The assembly then listened raptly as Jones himself ranted over a long-distance radio hookup, denouncing his tormentors as "bitches" and "bastards," sounding more like a tantrum-throwing brat than an esteemed religious leader.

Assemblyman Art Agnos, another benefactor of Jones's support, was visiting the temple for the first time, sitting next to Harvey Milk in the audience. Listening to the frantic, disembodied voice from Guyana, Agnos turned to Milk and said, "Harvey, that guy is really wild."

Milk, who was still standing by Jones, replied weakly, "Yeah, he's different, all right."

As the political fallout from the *New West* article grew, some San Francisco officials began running for cover. In late August Joe Freitas ordered investigator Bob Graham to write a memo stating that the DA's office looked into the charges leveled by the magazine and found no basis for legal action. Graham's memo also gave Tim Stoen a pass, stating, "So far, no evidence has surfaced that would link Stoen with any criminal activity in San Francisco." The memo was one more humiliation for Freitas's gung-ho investigators. They had tried hard to dig to the bottom of the Peoples Temple swamp, only to be roped in by their boss. Now Freitas was making them concoct a cover story for him.

"It was an ass-covering memo," said David Reuben. "It gave Freitas the ability to talk to the press and say, 'Yes, we looked into the charges and couldn't find anything.' But the truth is, we kept investigating after that memo. Bob Graham would not have taken a dive, and I certainly wouldn't. We were too invested in the case."

The problem, however, was that Jim Jones, the chief target of their probe, was now in Guyana, far from the reach of San Francisco investigators. And no officials—federal, state, or local—seemed interested in pursuing Jones into the jungle.

Reuben and his team were stunned by Jones's sudden flight. They thought the timing of his escape was suspicious, prompted not just by the imminent publication of the *New West* exposé but also by their own investigation. Somebody in the hall of justice had clearly tipped off the temple. "We were ready for grand jury indictments; we were *this* close," said Reuben. "And Freitas would've had to go along with it, because he had no other choice. The next thing I know, I get a phone call in the middle of the night. 'Guess what, he's gone.' Jones is gone, and the temple is packing up and getting ready to join him. I remember, we had a meeting in the office, and we said, 'Somebody snitched us off.'"

IN THE FALL OF 1977, as Jim Jones hunkered down in Guyana's steaming tropical wilderness with his flock of more than one thousand souls, disturbing reports about the "utopian" community began filtering back to the Bay Area. But political supporters like Harvey Milk, newly elected to the board of supervisors, stuck by the increasingly fanatical leader, out of fear, expedience, or stubborn loyalty. In December 1977 Milk wrote to Joseph Califano, President Carter's secretary of health, education, and welfare, protesting HEW's decision to stop forwarding Social Security checks to elderly temple members in Guyana—a key financial pipeline for Jones. "Peoples Temple," Milk informed Califano, "[has] established a beautiful retirement community in Guyana, the type of which people of means would pay thousands of dollars to patronize."

In February 1978 Milk intervened on Jones's behalf in the raging custody battle over young John Stoen, writing to President Carter himself in support of the cult leader. "Rev. Jones," Milk told Carter, "is widely known in the minority communities here and elsewhere as a man of the highest character, who has undertaken constructive remedies for social problems which have been amazing in their scope and effectiveness." Milk complained that Tim and Grace Stoen were trying to get the State Department to help win the return of their son—a move, he warned, that could create an international incident. "Not only is the life of a child at stake, who presently has loving protective parents in Rev. and Mrs. Jones," Milk wrote, "but our official relations with Guyana could stand to be jeopardized."

Jones was maniacally obsessive about hanging on to little John Stoen. Keeping custody of the boy was a way to continue control over Tim Stoen, ensuring that the high-level defector kept silent about temple secrets. The long-running furor over the case was also a way for Jones to keep his followers in a constant state of fear and embattlement, always on the lookout for the helicopters carrying US agents or Guyanese soldiers that might swoop down on them to seize the boy and destroy their last refuge.

As he whipped his followers into frenzies of fear, Jones called on fellow revolutionaries back home to demonstrate their support. Radical celebrity Angela Davis—a charismatic Marxist scholar who had been tried and acquitted of aiding Jonathan Jackson in his doomed attempt to free his brother George—was a die-hard temple defender. She sent heartfelt greetings by radio to the emotionally wrung-out community, her voice booming out to a temple assembly over loudspeakers. "I know you're in a very difficult situation right now, and there is a conspiracy," Davis declared. "A very profound conspiracy designed to destroy the contributions which you have made to the struggle." But Davis assured her "brothers and sisters" in the temple that "we will do everything in our power to ensure your safety."

The temple assembly also heard Huey Newton via a crackling phone patch from Cuba, where the Black Panthers leader was in exile: "I want the Guyanese government to know that you're not to be messed around with. Keep strong, and we're pulling for you."

Longtime Black Panthers attorney Charles Garry, a lion of the Bay Area left, agreed to represent Jones in his legal battles. Garry became an aggressive mouthpiece for the temple back in the United States, telling the press, "There is a conspiracy by government agencies to destroy the Peoples Temple." Garry began to question Jones's mental stability, but he kept his doubts to himself. After visiting Jonestown in October 1977, the radical lawyer announced, "I have seen paradise."

IN REALITY, THE JONESTOWN "paradise" was a nightmarish Third World police state. Everyone but the youngest and oldest were forced to work like mules from dawn to dusk in the sweltering fields, scratching out a living from the wild jungle terrain. Chronically short of food, residents struggled to keep their weight up with starchy meals like cassava bread drenched in brown syrup and rice soaked with gravy. Families and lovers were forced to live apart, relatives were pitted against one another, neighbors were ordered to inform on each other.

After dinner, the exhausted community was forced to assemble for interminable "emergency meetings" and listen to Jones's increasingly mad ravings late into the night. Punishment was swift for those who nodded off. One evening a sixty-year-old father of five named Charlie, worn out from fieldwork, slumped to the ground. An incensed Jones commanded Charlie's son to wrap a boa constrictor around his father's neck, releasing him only after the poor man's face was turning red and he had humiliated himself by pissing his pants.

Jones and his heavily armed security team kept the community in a state of terrorized obedience. Minor infractions could send malefactors of all ages, even children, to the dreaded Box, a stuffy underground cubicle where they could be held for days. Those who dared to dissent were dispatched to the medical unit, where they were forcibly drugged and kept in a zombified state indefinitely.

While his followers lived hungry, spartan lives, Emperor Jones resided in relative splendor in a cottage well stocked with electric appliances, delicacies like hard-boiled eggs, snacks, and soft drinks, and a cache of medications that he had expropriated from his aging and feeble residents. His drug supplies were endless.

The temple leader had been dependent on amphetamines, sedatives, and other drugs for years. Jim Jones Jr. remembered that as far back as the family's days in Redwood Valley, his father kept a tray of white liquid in the refrigerator and would fix syringes with the fluid and inject himself. One time he overdosed, flailing around on the floor, and the worried kids were told that their father had suffered a heart attack. But years later, after working in a hospital, the younger Jones came to realize his father had displayed the symptoms of a speed addict.

In the glorious isolation of Jonestown, under his tropical canopy, Jones surrendered fully to his drug-fueled manias. He created an Orwellian dystopia and forced his captive followers to live in it. The nights were the worst, as the jungle's dark silence was broken by a ghastly soundtrack of howler monkeys' screechings and Jones's sudden eruptions over the loudspeakers. Father's voice was everywhere: in the huts, outhouses, fields. There was no getting away from his sleepless rants.

"White Night!" Father would yell in the deepest black of night, jolting his followers from their exhausted slumber. "White Night!" Residents were rushed toward the glaring lights of the pavilion, the elderly shuffling along in a daze, the children crying. When they were all gathered there, Jones—spazzy and hot-wired on speed—told them that the US government was about to pounce. They had to act quickly.

"Hear that sound?" Father told them. "The mercenaries are coming. The end has come. Time is up. Children . . . line up into two queues, one on either side of me."

The guards stood solemn vigil over a large vat next to Jones.

"It tastes like fruit juice, children. It will not be hard to swallow."

The White Night drill. It was terrifying but not real. Until the day it was.

28

RAPTURE IN THE JUNGLE

BACK IN THE United States, relatives of Jim Jones's terrorized flock grew increasingly desperate as they tried to arouse the interest of public officials. Democratic congressman Leo Ryan, who represented a suburban district south of San Francisco, was the only one who took their concerns seriously. The State Department shrugged off Ryan's inquiries, assuring him that all was well in Guyana. He held a hearing on Jonestown, inviting defectors and worried relatives to testify before a congressional panel, but his colleagues were distracted and uninformed, and the witnesses' testimony drew little media coverage.

Ryan was the kind of congressional lone ranger who tackled issues in dramatic ways. He once traveled to Prince Edward Island off Newfoundland to confront fur hunters who were killing baby harp seals. He decided to fly down to Guyana and inspect Jonestown firsthand. Ryan invited other members of the Bay Area congressional delegation to accompany him, but they all turned him down. The congressman knew the risk. David Reuben warned him not to go. Before he left Washington, Ryan gave his will to an aide for safekeeping.

"I think he was afraid," said his daughter Pat Ryan. "But he also believed that, goddammit, somebody's got to do something."

As Ryan walked out of the family's Bay Area home on the way to catch his plane to Guyana, his daughter hugged him for the last time. "Don't let anybody shoot you," she joked anxiously.

"Don't worry," her father assured her. "I'll be fine."

Ryan and his entourage, which included two San Francisco newspaper reporters, a *Washington Post* reporter, and an NBC news team, hoped there would be safety in numbers. Everything seemed calm during the delegation's visit to Jonestown, as the cult leader managed to shake off his drug haze and keep his congregation in line. But when the visitors prepared to leave, one resident after the next came forward nervously and begged to go with them. The defections, sixteen in all, cracked the hellish community's carefully constructed façade, and the madness began sluicing out.

As Ryan was politely taking his leave, one of Jones's loyalists rushed forward and threw his arms around the congressman. "Congressman Ryan, you motherfucker!" he spat out, jabbing at Ryan's jugular with a homemade knife. Others lunged for the attacker, and after a frantic scuffle on the ground, he was disarmed. Ryan was not hurt, but as he jumped aboard the truck taking the delegation and the defectors to the nearby landing strip, a thick air of menace hung over the group. It was suddenly, terribly clear that nothing—not Ryan's congressional status, not the presence of a media pack—protected them here in the blazing, humid middle of nowhere, in Jim Jones's remote empire.

While the group was boarding two small planes, a Peoples Temple tractor-trailer rolled onto the runway carrying several armed men. They opened fire on Ryan's delegation with rifles and shotguns. When the explosion of gunfire stopped, five people were dead, including the congressman, and ten were wounded.

As word got back to Jonestown about the massacre at the airstrip, the congregation was gathered in the pavilion, in the midst of another White Night drill. But Jones knew this was no drill, it was his final stand. A congressman had been murdered. This time they really would be coming after him.

Always looking for a wider audience, the megalomaniacal preacher taped his last sermon—a rambling, self-pitying, insidiously seductive performance that is deeply disturbing to hear. Jones addressed his distraught flock from his usual throne, a wooden garden chair on the stage. Assembled before him were over nine hundred men, women, and children who had followed him into the wilderness and would soon be told to join him in oblivion. Many had been outcasts: welfare mothers, convicts, and addicts. But most were solidly working-class people. They were former factory workers, nurses, teachers, longshoremen, and field hands. Around 70 percent were black, and women outnumbered men nearly two to one. Later they would be portrayed as figures of pathos, but there was nothing pathetic about their dreams of a better world— dreams that Jones manipulated brilliantly.

Now he played on those deep aspirations one last time, in his lulling voice, trying to convince them that the promised land could not be found in this life, it awaited them in death.

"It's all over," Jones told the assembly. "The congressman has been murdered." Troops would soon overrun Jonestown, he said, and horribly torture them; even the children and old people would not be safe. They must avoid this terrible fate by taking control of their destinies and committing "revolutionary suicide."

"My opinion is that we be kind to the children and be kind to the seniors and take the potion like they used to take in ancient Greece, and step over quietly," he explained to them, with the patience of a schoolteacher. "Because we are not committing suicide. It's a revolutionary act."

ONLY ONE MEMBER OF the assembly dared to stand up and disagree with Jones that day as the setting sun began to burn itself out and Jonestown prepared to sear itself into history. Not surprisingly, it was an outspoken, middle-aged woman from Los Angeles named Christine Miller—an African-American "church lady" who had repeatedly demonstrated that she was not afraid to speak her mind to Jim Jones, even at great risk. Miller's brave argument with death is that grotesque spectacle's only redeeming act of humanity.

Miller had fought her way through life, picking cotton in the scorching Texas fields as a young girl and eventually finding work as a county clerk in Los Angeles. "I pulled myself up by my bootstraps," she used to say. After a lifetime of hard work, Miller was able to buy a home and a Pontiac Grand Prix, and could afford some of the finer things: furs, jewelry, and travel. But she was the kind of woman who wanted to be of service. When she discovered the Peoples Temple, its social mission struck her as a truer manifestation of Christ's teachings than what she found in the sweet-by-and-by churches. She began to give away her hard-earned possessions to Jones's organization and moved to San Francisco to join a temple commune. But even after she made the trek to the Guyana wilderness, Miller kept a few articles of fancy clothing and some jewelry pieces as totems of her past accomplishments—and Jones knew well enough not to collectivize the proud woman's last items of distinction.

Miller was not happy in Jonestown, where the sweltering agricultural compound brought back harsh childhood memories of the Texas cotton fields. She wrote letters to Jones, complaining that she had worked too hard in life to be pushed so hard in Jonestown. During one pavilion assembly, Jones grew fed up with Miller's vocal independence. "Shut up, woman!" he barked at her.

"You can't talk to me that way," Miller replied.

"I'll talk to you any way that I like, I'm the leader," Jones shot back.

But Miller stood her ground. "Oh, no, you won't."

Outraged to have his authority challenged so brazenly in front of the entire congregation, Jones picked up the gun he often brought to meetings and pointed it directly at Miller. He could shoot her right there, he shouted, and have her body dragged out to the jungle, and nobody would ever find out.

The entire assembly held its breath.

"You can do that," she said, "but you are going to have to respect me first."

Jones scrambled to his feet and waded into the gathering. He walked right up to Miller and pointed the gun at her head. "Woman, I will blow your motherfucking brains out right now!"

Miller didn't flinch. She looked directly into his face with a gaze fierce enough to pierce his sunglasses. "You can do that," she repeated, "but you have to respect me first."

Hue Fortson, who was at the meeting that day, remembered the stunned silence. "We all felt he was about to shoot her. He could easily have done it and gotten away with it. But slowly he put down his gun and walked back to his chair. He tried to gloss it over, saying it showed that he was such a loving person because he didn't take her life, and what a strong leader he was. But we all knew he had backed down. Later people were afraid to talk about it. But you held it inside yourself and treasured it."

On November 18, 1978, Christine Miller lost her final argument with Jim Jones. But she put everything she could muster into the fight, combating the preacher's slippery logic with reason, using old sermons of his to counter his march toward death, and passionately defending the right of people to live, including those whose lives had just begun. Miller knew that this time it was not just her life at stake, but those of 913 people, among them more than 300 children.

It's a chilling duel. Even today, listening to recordings of Miller making her argument against mass extermination, while she is heckled by frenzied Jones loyalists, one still hopes that she can prevail. Miller's voice is clear and strong as a bell, with a slight Texas drawl. Jones's tongue is thick, and at times he seems lost in a stupor. But his powerful, dominating will is still there, and he still unleashes flashes of eloquence as he herds his flock toward its doom. Miller is the last obstacle in his way, and he alternately patronizes her ("Christine, you've always been a very good agitator . . . I personally like you very much") and heatedly rebuts her.

"I'm not afraid to die," Miller says at one point. "But I look about at the babies, and I think they deserve to live, you know."

"But don't they also deserve much more?" replies Jones sweetly, lovingly. "They deserve peace."

Miller tries a different tack, trying to appeal to the sense of defiance that Jones had instilled in his followers over the years. "When you—" she begins, catching herself before continuing. "When we destroy ourselves, we're defeated. We let them, the enemies, defeat us."

Jones responds by quoting Chief Joseph's eloquent surrender speech, after the US cavalry had tracked down the remains of his suffering Nez Perce tribe. "I am tired; my heart is sick and sad. From where the sun now stands, I will fight no more forever."

Miller lacks Jones's education and his ability to invoke history and scripture. But she has one last line of defense, and it's the most powerful of all. She has a right to choose her fate, she tells Jones, and the others do too. "As an individual, I have a right to say what I think, what I feel. And I think we all have a right to our own destiny as individuals. And I have a right to choose mine, and everybody has a right to choose theirs."

Other women in the audience seem to shift toward Miller, murmuring assent. And for once, Jones is tongue-tied.

"I have a right to my opinion," Miller insists, echoing the words of every strong black woman in American history, from nineteenth-century evangelist Sojourner Truth on. ("And ain't I a woman?") All Jones can mumble in reply is, "I'm not taking it from you."

For a brief, heart-stopping moment, it seems that Miller might win the day—as she did when she stared down the barrel of Jones's gun and made him blink. But suddenly Jim McElvane, one of the most respected black members of Jones's inner circle, jumps in. McElvane, who once had a brief relationship with Miller, silences her by reminding her that individual rights are not relevant in a socialist paradise.

"Christine, you're only standing here because *he* was here in the first place," he chides his former lover, reminding her of their leader's sacrifices. "So I don't know what you're talking about, having an individual life. Your life has been extended to the day that you're standing there, because of him."

Then the tide rushes back against Christine Miller, as the anguished and tormented congregants bow and scrape once more to Father. "You've saved so many people!" shouts a female worshipper. Once again, collective madness reigns.

Jones regains his morbid rhythm. "I've saved them, I've saved them," he agrees. But now "the best testimony we can make is to leave this goddam world."

No one can stop Jim Jones now. The big aluminum vat is brought out. This time, the grape Flavor Aid is laced with potassium cyanide. In his eerie singsong voice, Jones urges his flock to take their final communion—babies and children first. Ghostly church music plays in the background.

It scars the soul to listen to the infants' screaming and crying. As the children begin their death throes—vomiting and bleeding through their noses and gasping for breath—Jones urges them to stay quiet. "Look children, it's just something to put you to rest."

Many parents are now hysterical, watching their children die, and

Jones scolds them. "We must die with some dignity." But one mother can't stop wailing.

"Mother, Mother, Mother, Mother, Mother, please," croons Jones, whose own hysteria seems held down only by sedatives. "Mother, please, please, please. Don't—don't do this. Lay down your life with your child. But don't do this."

Jones seems offended that people are not dying according to his choreography. "Keep your emotions down," he commands. "I don't care how many screams you hear, I don't care how many anguished cries, death is a million times preferable to ten more days of this life."

Many Jonestown residents did not agree with their raving leader that day. But there was no escape. The pavilion was surrounded by armed security guards, including some of the murderers who had returned from the airstrip. One survivor saw dozens of people being dragged to the tub of purple-colored poison and estimated that about sixty adults were forcibly injected with the potion. By some accounts, one of those who went down resisting was Christine Miller.

Jonestown has become widely known as the biggest mass suicide in history. But with so many adult members of the community strong-armed to their doom, hundreds of children murdered, and many parents so anguished that they could not help but join their little ones in death, it is more appropriate to call Jonestown a slaughter. Even those who went to their deaths singing Jones's praises were victims of his con. Incarcerated in a jungle concentration camp and robbed of their free will, they were programmed to follow their leader to the gates of hell.

"Free at last," moans Jim Jones near the end, before someone puts a bullet in his head, his preferred method of exit. The invocation of Martin Luther King was one last sacrilege by the man who had wrapped himself in the glorious rhetoric of suffering and resistance.

When Jones staged his grand escape, he did not simply destroy over nine hundred lives and plunge thousands more into bottomless grief. He poisoned a language of social justice. Everyone who had joined hands with his crusade, whether for opportunistic or idealistic reasons, was now contaminated by Jonestown. As the news images of bloated corpses sprawled in the dust were beamed back to San Francisco, the city shuddered. The same free air that had nurtured the beats, hippies, gays, and a growing garden of the imagination had given birth to a monster.

29

THE RECKONING

As THE GRISLY spectacle in Guyana was revealed, the Fillmore neighborhood was filled with wailing and tears. Ravaged by redevelopment, poverty, drugs, and crime, San Francisco's black heartland reeled once more. Nearly every family in the neighborhood was touched by the loss of someone in Jonestown.

Shrieking relatives and frenzied reporters and TV crews besieged the Peoples Temple building on Geary. Family members, uncertain about the fates of their loved ones, demanded information. Inside the barricaded church, the remnants of Jones's holy army—the ones who had been left behind to take care of temple business in San Francisco—wandered in a daze, trying to figure out what to do. A few spluttered with rage, frustrated that they had not been included in Jones's Rapture. Others railed against the enemy: the faceless government agents whom they were convinced had wiped out Jonestown.

Rev. Norman Leach, Jim Jones's outspoken defender in the local National Council of Churches chapter, slipped into the back of the temple on a rainy night to console the survivors. As people wept and crowded around the shortwave radio for information from Guyana, Leach walked into another room, where Angela Davis and some cohorts were holding an intense strategy meeting. Davis was using the occasion to politically vent—"her usual anti-American shtick"—and Leach couldn't take it. "These people need to be comforted, not agitated," he told her. When the Davis contingent reacted heatedly, Leach got up and left. "I was not there to argue politics," he said.

Jonestown was a hideous stain on all those in the Bay Area left who had been taken in by Jim Jones, including attorney Charles Garry. The aging lawyer was forced to flee for his life during the Jonestown blood-bath, huffing and puffing through the Guyanese jungle alongside Mark Lane—another celebrity attorney who had shared Garry's rosy view of Jones's "paradise." Garry forced Lane to carry his suitcase as they sweated their way through the thick, tropical greenery. Lane griped about his burden, but suspecting that the heavy case was stuffed with money, he kept carrying it. The suitcase was actually filled with the toiletries and grooming equipment that the notoriously vain Garry found indispensable, including the hair blower he used to perfect his comb-over. Back home in San Francisco, Garry struggled to make sense of the debacle. "Jim Jones created one of the most beautiful dreams in the world and then destroyed it," said the still-confused attorney.

Jonestown struck George Moscone in the gut. He vomited and broke down crying when he heard the news. The mayor spent much of the next few days—what turned out be the last days of his life—consoling those who had lost loved ones in Guyana, including the family of Leo Ryan.

Moscone knew that Ryan, who had risen with him in local Democratic politics, was one of the few heroes in the grotesque Jim Jones drama: the only political leader who had the courage to investigate the demonic preacher in his jungle lair. Ryan's death was particularly troubling to him. "I don't know how to cope with anyone being killed or assassinated," the mayor said mournfully after he was told about Ryan. Moscone wrote a heartfelt letter to Ryan's ex-wife Margaret, the mother of his five children, adding in his own handwriting, "He was a very good friend of mine, and I am without words to express my grief."

At Ryan's funeral ceremony in All Souls Church in South San Francisco, Moscone again broke down in tears. House Majority Leader Jim Wright's eulogy must have been particularly painful for Moscone, the progressive politician who prided himself on comforting the poor and afflicted. Ryan, Wright told the overflowing church, had a "readiness to go where suffering was. When relatives and friends came to him with a story of abounding horror, inhumanity, and bizarre brutalities, Leo Ryan went to see and serve. And it was while helping to free captives that he met his death. Greater love has no man than this."

Moscone and San Francisco's liberal leadership had aided and abetted Jones's reign of "horror, inhumanity, and bizarre brutalities." And the press immediately clamored for an explanation. The mayor was the only political ally of Jones to admit any error of judgment, conceding that he had been "taken in" by the powerful preacher. The *Examiner* gave Moscone credit for his admission: "At least Mayor George Moscone is willing to admit he made a mistake in sizing up the charismatic leader of the Peoples Temple . . . He had the decency to admit it. Not so with some of our other politicians in this city and in the state."

While Moscone was clearly deeply shaken by Jonestown, however, he couldn't bring himself to fully acknowledge his role in empowering the cult leader. "It's clear that if there was a sinister plan, then we were taken in," he told reporters. "But I'm not taking any responsibility. It's not mine to shoulder." When a reporter pressed him, asking the mayor if he felt "culpable" for helping to politically legitimize Jones, a distraught Moscone responded heatedly, "I deeply resent that. You're reaching far out." Then he shuddered visibly and added, "It's all too bizarre for me."

Willie Brown was even more defiant, proclaiming nervily that he had no "regrets" about his close political alliance with Jones and scorching other politicians who were now running for cover. "They all like to say, 'Forgive me, I was wrong,' but that's bullshit. It doesn't mean a thing now, it just isn't relevant."

Some of Jones's useful acolytes never stopped justifying their promotion of Peoples Temple, even many years later. Norman Leach is now retired from the church and living in Nebraska, after again being convicted of pederasty, this time with a member of a Boy Scout troop he started. The judge at Leach's trial called him "dangerous" and said that he had "sexually assaulted juvenile males in every area of the country he has lived in during the last forty years of his life." Looking back at his days in San Francisco, the former reverend denied sharing any guilt

for Jim Jones's reign of horror. "I feel no remorse or responsibility," said
Leach, whom Jones continued to court even after fleeing to Guyana,
bombarding him with dozens of obviously scripted letters from temple
children inviting him to visit Jonestown. "I turned him down—it made
me uneasy," he declared.

Leach concedes there were many "red flags" about the Peoples Temple. "But there's no way that I could've had insight into the depth of his
evil," he insisted. "I still think the goal of Peoples Temple was beautiful:
black and white, gay and straight, rich and poor, all coming together.
That's Christianity right there—or Judaism, or whatever great faith you
name."

The San Francisco press was as reluctant as local political and religious leaders to take responsibility for Jones's ascension. The *Chronicle*,
which had chastised John Barbagelata for his strident warnings about
Jones and shut down its own enterprising reporter, never acknowledged
its mistakes in covering the media-savvy preacher. Herb Caen could not
bring himself to do anything more than offer the city bland condolences
in his daily column: "Gray skies dripped sadness and sorrow over San
Francisco yesterday," wrote Jones's former booster. "Headlines told of
tragedy and madness in steaming jungles . . . how to judge the insanity
surrounding the end of Rev. Jim Jones . . . Who would have expected
this?"

David Reuben, for one. The DA's investigator saw the nightmare
coming, but, hobbled by city politics, could not stop it in time. After the
news flashes from Guyana, a disgusted Reuben accosted his boss. "*Now*
do you think we had something there, Joe?" he asked Freitas.

The district attorney, still in ass-covering mode, dodged any responsibility for bringing Peoples Temple agents into his office and imped-
ing his own investigators' inquiry. "In the period I had contact," Freitas
lamely told the press, "it was an activist church, and Jim Jones seemed
a pretty okay fellow."

Reuben, one of the few people in San Francisco city government
who tried to bring down Jones, still feels guilty that he failed. "Peoples
Temple was the highlight and lowlight of my career. I kind of peaked and
died with that investigation," said Reuben, who left government service
after Jonestown and is now a private eye.

Jonestown released a poison cloud over San Francisco. There was blood and terror in the air. Even those who loudly denied any guilt were running scared. City leaders were convinced that Jonestown hit squads were on the loose and were gunning for them. The district attorney's office fielded panicky phone calls from politicians who had been entangled with Jones, even taking a call from the White House. One call came from a hysterical Willie Brown, who tearfully pleaded, "What do I do?"

The Jonestown survivors who trickled back to the Bay Area had more reason to fear for their lives than the politicians did. The survivors had to confront the turbulent grief and rage of people who lost relatives in Guyana.

On the final White Night, Jim Jones Jr. was in Georgetown, where he, his brother Stephan, and the rest of the Jonestown basketball team had gone to play in a tournament. Over the radio, Jones Sr. ordered his two sons to get knives, scissors, and wire and kill themselves too, but they didn't comply with their father's final command. Others in the Guyana capital did obey, however. Jim Jr. was in the temple headquarters in Georgetown when Sharon Amos, one of his father's most zealous lieutenants, unleashed an orgy of blood. Taking her three young children into the bathroom, she began slicing their throats with a butcher knife before ordering another child to cut her own jugular. One of Jim Jr.'s teammates, Calvin Douglas, raced down the hall, threw open the door, and was able to rescue one of Amos's daughters. Jim Jr. can still remember the torrent of blood pouring out of the bathroom.

After he was flown back to the Bay Area, Jim Jr., who was eighteen at the time, moved into his sister Suzanne's house in Daly City. Everywhere he went in San Francisco, he saw the ghosts of people he once knew. He attended memorial services for people who died in Jonestown—there were many of them. One day, after the service for a woman named Valerie, Jim Jr. was sitting with the bereaved relatives and friends in the living room of Valerie's mother. Suddenly the mother appeared in the room with a gun, which she pointed directly at Jim Jr., the Peoples Temple's chosen one. "Why are you alive and my daughter is gone?" the woman asked young Jones. He looked at her and said simply, "I'm already dead."

Other mourners quickly took the gun away. Jones stopped going to the family memorials.

San Francisco crackled with a strange electricity, as if a massive thunderstorm was building offshore, out beyond the fog bank, and it was all about to burst. "Earthquake weather," they called it in San Francisco. Political leaders were hunkering down, frantically heading off investigations. But there was a powerful feeling in the city that there would be a reckoning, a growing sense that there must be blood.

30

A TALE OF TWO CITIES

EVEN BEFORE JONESTOWN, San Francisco seemed headed for a violent cataclysm. By the late 1970s, the sexual revolution centered in San Francisco had sparked a vehement backlash from defenders of traditional morality, in the city itself and throughout the country. Family values demagogues like politically ambitious California state senator John Briggs and Anita Bryant—a former beauty queen and singer who was the pitchwoman for the Florida orange juice industry—tapped into a growing pool of antigay fear and revulsion. San Francisco, which in the blink of an eye had become the ballroom for America's coming out party, was targeted by conservative crusaders as a modern Sodom.

Briggs, denouncing San Francisco as "the moral garbage dump of homosexuality in this country," kicked off a carnivalesque, moral-revival campaign for governor. The obscure politician grabbed the media spotlight by scapegoating gay teachers. Portraying them in the same lurid ways that McCarthyites once vilified Communists in the classroom—as vicious predators threatening the purity of America's children—Briggs campaigned for a 1978 state initiative to ban homosexual teachers from California schools.

Bryant also cast her holy march as a battle to "save our children," leading a successful campaign in 1977 to repeal a gay rights law in

Florida's Dade County, which inspired a wave of similar antihomosexual uprisings around the country.

Meanwhile, in San Francisco's Visitacion Valley—a secluded hollow of white, Catholic, working-class families fighting a losing battle against the encroaching black Sunnydale housing project—a former altar boy and cop named Dan White was kicking off his own moral restoration campaign. In 1977 White announced his bid for the board of supervisors in the new district elections, declaring himself the champion of all those frustrated, longtime San Franciscans who no longer recognized their city. Echoing Briggs, White lashed out at the "social malignancies" and "cesspool of perversion" that were contaminating his hometown. "I am not going to be forced out of San Francisco by splinter groups of radicals, social deviates, and incorrigibles," vowed White. "Believe me, there are tens of thousands who are just as determined to legally fight to protect and defend our conservative values." White struck a chord in his embattled district, sweeping into office along with Harvey Milk, the flag bearer for the city's "social deviates."

The escalating culture war inflamed the city's humors. Violent attacks on gays spiked in San Francisco. Roaming packs of teenagers and young men sprang on gays with fists and knives. Many of the attackers were from the heavily Latino Mission district that abutted the Castro—a neighborhood that had shared the Mission's Catholic family values until gays displaced the Irish. Some of the young thugs were wrestling with their own sexual confusions. In June 1977, on the first warm night of summer, Robert Hillsborough, a thirty-one-year-old city gardener known as Mr. Greenjeans to the kids at the park where he worked, was jumped by four young men as he walked to his apartment with his boyfriend. A nineteen-year-old Latino named John Cordova pinned Hillsborough to the ground and plunged a fishing knife repeatedly into his chest and face, screaming, "Faggot, faggot, faggot!" It was an intensely personal and physical way to kill a man. Cordova, it was later revealed, led his own secret homosexual life.

The savage murder of Robert Hillsborough set off new emotional eruptions in the city. The victim's mother blamed antigay crusaders like Anita Bryant, who was busy telling America that one homosexual act should land offenders in prison for at least twenty years—as a grim warning to young men who were contemplating the gay lifestyle. "My son's blood is on her hands," said Hillsborough's grieving mother.

Mayor Moscone agreed, attributing the rise of antigay violence in San Francisco to the "climate of hate and bigotry" fomented by Bryant and Briggs. Moscone ordered flags at city hall and other municipal buildings to be flown at half staff in honor of the murdered city gardener. The mayor's decision set off a backlash of complaints from citizens who thought it was an improper civic display.

Feeling unsafe in their own neighborhood, gays in the Castro began carrying whistles to sound the alarm if they came under attack. Some of the district's more butch residents formed street patrols, surrounding neighborhood invaders until the police showed up. An editorial in the police-oriented *Examiner* denounced the "semi-vigilante" tactic and admonished gays not to "get hysterical" and interfere with police business. But when cops did respond to attacks on gays, they often ended up arresting the victims instead of the assailants.

One evening Harvey Milk and a friend heard a whistle and ran to the scene of the crime. Milk, a navy veteran who believed in aggressive self-defense, chased down and tackled the thug, who begged Milk not to beat him. When the victim, more afraid of the police than he was of the attacker, said he wouldn't press charges, Milk was forced to let the gay basher go. But as he released the thug, Milk warned, "Tell all your friends we're down here waiting for them."

HARVEY MILK, THE STREET-SMART ex–New Yorker, often drew historical comparisons between the treatment of Jews and gays. He vowed that homosexuals would fight back against their tormentors to their dying breath. "Do you think gay people are going to go with their heads bowed into the gas chambers?" he asked an *Examiner* reporter one day, in an impassioned tone that made clear his answer. "I mean, I'll go kicking and screaming before I go with my head bowed."

As a San Francisco supervisor, Milk brought the same combative spirit to city hall. But he was also a master at the sweet and gentle art of politics, reaching out to groups that normally had no use for faggots and sodomites, from teamsters to black church groups.

"Get a load of this fruit. He ain't half bad," growled a tough old labor guy in a union hall where Milk had gone for a meeting. That's when Cleve Jones, Milk's political protégé, began to realize it: *Everybody* liked Harvey. And the feeling was mutual.

"He really loved lots of people; he was a natural politician," Jones said. "He wasn't just deploying the significant eye contact. And it was more than simply caring about people—he *enjoyed* them. The best evidence of that is the kids. At a time when gays were being demonized as child molesters, kids just *adored* him, they flocked to his camera store. He was always surrounded by gay kids, straight kids, boys, girls. I was hardly the only young person he mentored. He just had a gift for making people feel good. He would hear that a woman in the neighborhood had a miscarriage, and he would go out and buy a bouquet of flowers and go visit her. I had been bullied all through my childhood, and I hated straight people out of fear. But to see Harvey fearlessly crossing all these boundaries, going into union halls and all these ethnic and racial communities—it made us all braver."

"Milk has something for everybody." That was Harvey's first campaign slogan, lifted from the dairy industry's billboards. The sentiment was a sharp contrast to White's rallying cry of resentment, "Unite and fight with Dan White." But Milk believed that he could even win over White. After both men won seats on the board of supervisors, the odd couple began making joint appearances on local talk shows, warmly praising each other. White claimed that he was referring to junkies, not gays, when he condemned "social deviates." The two men began having coffee every Thursday morning at a café in the Castro.

A friend of Milk said it sickened him to see the two political opposites schmoozing that way. "Harvey, that guy's a pig," he said. "He's never gonna be different. He's a cop." But Milk strongly disagreed. "Dan White is just stupid. He's working class, a Catholic, been brought up with all those prejudices. I'm gonna sit next to him every day and let him know we're not all those bad things he thinks we are . . . Everyone can be reached. *You* think people are hopeless—not me."

Milk's attitude—ebullient, embracing, and more than a little patronizing—both charmed and enraged White. The gay leader would come to realize how tough a challenge Dan White was, even for someone with his dazzling political and personal skills.

Warm, wickedly funny, and flirtatious, Harvey Milk was the opposite of Dan White in more ways than one. White was the son of heroic fireman Charlie White, who worked himself into an early grave trying to feed ten hungry mouths. Grim and devout, White spent his entire life trying to live up to his father's life of service. In Catholic school, Danny White became known for being good with his fists, mixing it up with the black kids whose families were pressing in on the old Irish neighborhoods. He was also good at sports, captaining his high school football and baseball teams, and heading for the New York Yankees farm system until an injury ruined his playing career.

White's life never measured up. He served in Vietnam but saw no action, and army officials called his record undistinguished. A self-described "romantic," he grew a beard and ran off to Alaska to write stories like Jack London, but he had no literary talent. He joined the SFPD, but, disappointed that it did not offer the heroic opportunities in his imagination, he quit and became a fireman. He finally matched his father's heroism one day, rescuing a mother and baby from the seventeenth floor of a blazing fire at Geneva Towers—ironically, the crime-infested housing project in Visitacion Valley that symbolized to many in White's neighborhood the end of their way of life. It was a daring act, rushing through the flames and out onto the balcony where the woman was screaming, with her baby cradled in her arms, and then sweeping them both to safety. But the next morning, the *Chronicle* buried the story about the courageous fireman who was also running for supervisor on page six. His late father's heroics had made the front page.

The handsome, square-jawed White married the woman he was supposed to: a pretty Catholic-reared schoolteacher named Mary Ann Burns, whose father was the commander of White's firehouse. Mary Ann reminded White of his own sainted mother. In the beginning, the young couple seemed happy enough, and Mary Ann bore Dan a son. But the passion seemed to leak from the marriage too soon. White seemed happiest when playing shortstop on the police softball team, where he attacked every game with the spikes-flying zeal of Pete Rose. He stayed in athletic condition into his thirties, sculpting his body with weight lifting and exercise.

One day the board of supervisors organized a softball game against Mayor Moscone's staff. Milk asked White what he should wear on the field, and White told him whatever he wanted to. "Well, I've got a brand-new print dress," flounced Harvey. "Would that be okay?"

"Dan went nuts," Moscone aide Dick Sklar recalled. "He hated being taunted. And Harvey was always taunting Dan."

White was flustered by the witty and nimble Milk. He found his gay colleague alternately captivating and exasperating. Milk thought his political opposite was just as vexing. White invited Milk to his son's christening—an invitation he extended to only one other colleague on the board of supervisors. But while fraternizing with the country's only openly gay elected official, White also railed against the disgusting carnival of male flesh he saw on display whenever he drove through the Castro. "They're screwing around right out in the streets," White fumed to his equally censorious friend, a Visitacion Valley parish priest named Father Tom Lacey. White was also disturbed when he squeezed among the throngs lining Market Street to watch the raucous and shameless Gay Freedom Day Parade go strutting by.

Milk told Cleve Jones that he thought White was secretly gay. And the more he got to know White, he became convinced that the former altar boy was a cauldron of bubbling emotions that could boil over at any time. "Dan White is a closet case," Milk confided to a boyfriend one day. "And he's dangerous."

HARVEY MILK AND GEORGE Moscone were everything that Dan White was not: charming, politically shrewd, sexually rambunctious, and comfortable in their own skins. The cool, athletic Moscone sometimes acted like a suave father for White, who had lost his own workhorse dad at age seventeen. And Milk was like a wild older brother to White: sometimes adorable, often maddening. But in truth, Dan White was a stranger, utterly lost in these two men's world.

Moscone and Milk were the dynamic duo of San Francisco's progressive revolution. They never forgot what they were elected to do: to fight for the burdened and afflicted, for those whose voices were never heard in the halls of power. They fought for the rights of workers, minorities, gays, and renters. And they made the same enemies: the chamber of commerce, developers, realtors, the SFPD.

Moscone and Milk both loved politics, and they loved the city they served. They roamed its streets, savoring its rich brew, always ready to plunge in. Christopher Moscone remembers going with his family to a North Beach restaurant, and when they emerged after dinner, his father spotted some people down the street picketing and chanting for higher wages. "My dad just joined right in, walking the picket line. We all stood there waiting for him, and my mom's like, 'Any time now, George.'"

Harvey Milk liked to ride the MUNI to city hall so that he could overhear San Francisco talking. He never got over the ornate beauty of his workplace, the temple of gold, marble, and carved wood dedicated to the people of San Francisco. He liked to give friends tours of the building, explaining the intricate friezes that illuminated the interior of the grand rotunda and urging them to pretend they were stars of a Cecil B. DeMille spectacle and go sweeping down the epic marble staircase in the colonnaded lobby. "Never take the elevator when you're in city hall," Milk advised. "Always take that stairway. You can make such an entrance—take it slowly." In his own dreams, Milk wasn't Gloria Swanson but the mayor of San Francisco. He had dreamed of becoming mayor from the time he first set foot in this jewel box of a city. There were some city hall observers who believed that Milk was indeed Moscone's logical successor. He would make history again when he was elected as the country's first openly gay mayor.

In the meantime, the city's current mayor was already championing gay liberation. George Moscone was as much a product of the San Francisco parishes and parochial school sports as Dan White. But he embraced all of San Francisco. He looked as comfortable in Amelia's, the divey lesbian bar on Valencia Street, as he did in the dining room at North Beach Restaurant.

Moscone shared Milk's mischievous sense of humor. One day Milk told the mayor that he had been picked up on a Castro street corner that morning while waiting for a bus by fellow supervisor Quentin Kopp, who gave him a ride to city hall in his official car. Kopp was the perfect foil for the two fun-loving liberals: a tall, gawky, balding, bespectacled bean counter. "You've got to do me a favor," Moscone told Milk. "Next time

Kopp picks you up, reach over and grab the inside of his thigh." Milk exploded in laughter and promised the mayor he would do just that.

IN THE FALL OF 1978, Moscone joined Milk in the campaign to defeat Proposition 6, the antigay Briggs initiative. The two men made regular Saturday morning visits to the San Franciscans Against Prop 6 head-quarters. In the closing days of the campaign, the momentum swung against Briggs as a phalanx of political leaders took a stand against the nasty piece of legislative intolerance, including President Carter and Governor Jerry Brown.

Desperate to create a media spectacle to turn the tide in his favor, Briggs—a dreary little man with thinning hair and baggy, brown suits from an equally dreary Southern California suburb—phoned the SFPD and announced that he would be showing up that night at the Hallow-een festival on Polk Street. Anything could happen if Briggs waded into the annual street carnival, which had long been a gay high holiday in San Francisco. The ruthless politician was clearly hoping for the worst. As Briggs headed for Polk Street, surrounded by a media swarm eager to capture his confrontation with San Francisco's leather boys, he pro-claimed righteously, "I'm going because this is a children's night, and I'm interested in children."

But San Francisco was Moscone's and Milk's town, not John Briggs's—and they had a surprise for him. The police car carrying Briggs did not stop at Polk Street but instead dropped him a few blocks away, where an official delegation including Moscone, Milk, and pro-gay police chief Gain welcomed him to San Francisco. Moscone then informed the trou-blemaking state senator that it would not be in the best interests of law and order for him to roam Polk Street that night, which was choked with some eighty thousand party maniacs. Chief Gain, flanked by twenty-five cops, firmly agreed. Briggs spluttered with rage, but he had no choice. Outwitted by San Francisco's politicians, he was packed into his car and driven back to Sacramento.

Just a few years before, the SFPD happily billy-clubbed any flagrantly costumed Halloween revelers who made the mistake of wandering off Polk Street. But with Moscone and Milk in city hall, times had changed.

Now the cops were being used on Halloween to run the state's leading gay basher out of town.

The following week, Briggs's attempted pogrom against California's gay teachers was crushed by a two-to-one landslide at the polls. In San Francisco, the vote was even more lopsided, with Proposition 6 losing by a three-to-one margin. At the ecstatic celebration in the Castro that night, a brass band marched into the hall blaring "San Francisco," the Judy Garland show tune that gays had revived as the city anthem ("San Francisco, open your golden gate / You let no stranger wait outside your door"). Joining Milk onstage, Moscone was greeted by a thunderous ovation. The exuberant mayor declared the night a Waterloo for all those bigots and blowhards who'd tried "to make political advances on the backs of those who are at the bottom of the spectrum."

"This is your night!" Moscone shouted to the crowd of activists who had appealed to California's better angels and won big. "No-on-six will be emblazoned upon the principles of San Francisco—liberty and freedom for all, forever!"

But not all of San Francisco was celebrating. The Briggs initiative won a majority vote in Dan White's District 8, where crucifixes and saints under glass protected homes from the devilry over the hills. And the same old values held sway at the hall of justice and the precinct stations. Most San Francisco cops would have preferred to run Moscone and Milk out of town that Halloween night instead of Briggs.

By NOVEMBER 1978, THE rage in police ranks against the mayor and his liberal police chief was white hot. Moscone was close to winning the board of supervisors' approval for a resolution to the civil rights lawsuit against the SFPD that would make the department's old-boy culture extinct. Meanwhile, Chief Gain was continuing to reengineer the force, recruiting gays, promoting women and minorities, and driving out the drunks, burnouts, and bullies long coddled by the department.

The veterans felt betrayed by Moscone. When he was running for mayor in 1975, he'd met with the bureau of inspectors, the core group of detectives that traditionally provided the SFPD's leadership. As he looked at the stone-faced cops gathered in the fifth-floor auditorium at

the hall of justice, the liberal candidate knew what he needed to promise them to get their support.

"Let me tell you something: when I'm mayor, the chief of police will
come from this room," Moscone declared. "In fact, I'm looking right at
the man I'm going to appoint: Captain Ray Canepa."

"Boom—that's what we wanted to hear," recalled veteran homicide
inspector Frank Falzon. "Canepa was the most popular guy in the room,
liked by all the cops. So when George Moscone leaves the room that day,
every inspector stood up and gave him a round of applause."

But after he was elected, Moscone picked maverick outsider Charley
Gain instead. "He was our worst nightmare," said Falzon. The veteran
cops felt stabbed in the back by Moscone.

It got worse as the police watched Moscone and Gain preside over
what they saw as a morally lax regime. "We had some serious problems,
and now they're not being dealt with correctly," said Falzon. "Things
you were told were against the law were suddenly no longer against the
law." Gay bathhouses, for instance, were off-limits to the cops in the
new San Francisco. And the permissive climate only seemed to draw
more homosexuals. "They were migrating from everywhere," Falzon
remarked. "A lot of cops felt it was the liberal attitudes—the anything-
goes atmosphere—that was attracting them here." Soon there would be
nothing left of the San Francisco that they had grown up in, the San
Francisco that Dan White kept warning was dying.

The resentment in the ranks was so palpable that a police beat
reporter wasn't surprised when he saw this graffiti on a police station
bathroom wall one day: "Who's going to get the mayor?"

Rumors began flying around the city in 1978. The cops were going
to kill Moscone, or Gain, or both. As San Francisco's most high-profile
hooker, Margo St. James heard a lot of the murderous chatter, passed
along from cops she knew. One day a cop who was one of her clients
phoned her, and, knowing that she was friendly with the police chief,
warned her to stop Gain from going out at night. St. James tracked down
the chief at a local college where he was giving a speech and told him to
go home. "The cops are going to bump you off," she said.

The cops messed with Gain. One time officers showed up at the
chief's house and told him that his car in the driveway had a bomb

planted in it. "It was a lie," said St. James. "They just hated him. They thought he was handing the city to the dogs."

The streets buzzed with assassination talk. One day an ex-con who had served in Vietnam and was known for his lethal skills was approached by someone claiming to represent a prominent San Franciscan. He promised the ex-con a big reward for killing Mayor Moscone.

Milk also received death threats, including a flurry in advance of the 1978 Gay Freedom Day Parade, where he was scheduled to speak. "You get the first bullet the minute you stand at the microphone," read one neatly typed postcard.

Milk spoke often about his premonitions of a violent death. "I'll get it from a closet queen," he predicted. Cleve Jones grew tired of his mentor's morbid talk. "Who do you think you are?" mocked Jones. "Martin Luther King? Gandhi? You're not on anybody's radar, you're just a gay shopkeeper."

"I was wrong," Jones said years later.

31

DAY OF THE GUN

I T WAS DAN White who became the missile of old San Francisco's rage. The pressures had been building inside him ever since he took his supervisor's seat at city hall. John Barbagelata had warned White not to get involved in San Francisco politics when the young fireman came to the retired supervisor for his blessing. Barbagelata, whose health was still damaged by his municipal battles, didn't think that White had the temperament for the San Francisco arena. Some of White's old friends on the police force, such as Frank Falzon and Jack Cleary, also worried about him. They thought he was too much of a Boy Scout for the city hall snake pit. "Why do you want to go down to city hall and get caught up in all that bullshit?" Cleary remarked to him. "You're a good fireman."

After White took his seat on the board—at age thirty-two, the city's youngest supervisor—it soon became clear he was out of his depth. He was outmaneuvered by his nimble adversaries on the left, Milk and Carol Ruth Silver. And even allies like Quentin Kopp seemed more interested in manipulating the political novice for their own purposes than in grooming him as a civic leader. The only supervisor who seemed to take White under her wing was Dianne Feinstein, but she was often distracted by her own personal and political burdens, including the wrenching illness of her beloved husband, neurosurgeon Bert Feinstein, who died in 1978 after a long bout with cancer.

Meanwhile, White was under growing financial pressures at home, having given up his $18,000 fireman's salary for a role in city government that paid only $9,600 a year. To supplement the family's income, he put in long hours with Mary Ann at the Hot Potato, a struggling French fry and baked potato concession that the couple had opened on touristy Pier 39. Ever since he was a boy, White daydreamed of being the kind of man, like his dad, who would take care of his loved ones and rescue people. But now—sinking in debt and flailing to support his family and take care of his constituents—it was Dan White who needed to be rescued.

On November 10, 1978, White stunned the San Francisco political community—including his own supporters—by announcing that he was resigning from the board of supervisors, explaining, "I didn't have any time to be both a good husband, father, and supervisor."

Moscone, long troubled by the toll that politics had taken on his own family life, responded with feeling to White's announcement. Expressing sympathy for White's decision, the mayor told reporters, "I've always harbored strong admiration for someone who can push aside the vanity of public service and gauge his life accordingly."

But White's biggest backers were not as understanding. The cops and the downtown business establishment were increasingly frantic about San Francisco's leftward direction. They knew that political control of the board of supervisors was hanging in the balance. As soon as Moscone filled White's seat with a political ally, the mayor would finally have a liberal six-to-five margin on the board, and there would be no stopping his progressive legislative agenda. The board of realtors was particularly concerned, because Harvey Milk had already announced his plan to slap controls on soaring rents in the city. And the police union knew that by replacing White on the board, Moscone could finally settle the civil rights lawsuit and repaint the heavily white SFPD with all the colors of the San Francisco rainbow.

White's supporters descended on him and began twisting his arms. They told him he needed to be a man and do his job; they worked on his fears of being a quitter. They reminded him that San Francisco was becoming a cesspool, and he was the only one who could rescue the city. And they sweetened the deal: real estate developers offered to bail out the cash-strapped family man with long-term, low-interest loans.

Five days later, White reversed himself, telling the mayor that he was taking back his resignation letter. At a press conference outside his old city hall office, White made no attempt to camouflage the powerful interests behind his change of heart. Addressing reporters, he was flanked by police union officials and representatives of the real estate industry.

Once again, Moscone responded to White's flip-flop with fatherly forgiveness, telling the press, "As far as I'm concerned Dan White is the supervisor from District Eight . . . A man has a right to change his mind."

But now it was Moscone's turn to feel the political heat. Liberal supporters, including Milk, began working the mayor hard, telling him that this was a golden opportunity to finally achieve his legislative goals; that he would be crazy to throw it away. Dan White had to go, they told him.

As the backroom drama over White embroiled city hall, spilling into the weekend of November 18, the chilling reports from Guyana began filtering back home. Now there was a grisly and surreal backdrop to all the political machinations in San Francisco. Moscone's enemies quickly made it clear that they were going to hang Jonestown around his neck, with Quentin Kopp charging that the mayor had rebuffed his demands for an investigation into Peoples Temple.

Meanwhile, Harvey Milk began using Jonestown to pressure Moscone from the left, telling the mayor that he was now going to need the gay vote more than ever to get reelected the following year. "You reappoint Dan White to the board, and you won't get elected dogcatcher," Milk told Moscone—a political threat loaded with chutzpah, considering Milk's own Jonestown vulnerabilities. On Monday, November 21, Moscone signaled that he was backing away from reappointing White.

THAT WEEK, AS THE maneuvers over San Francisco's political future grew more heated, politicians also wrestled with their guilt and fear about Jonestown. Responding to the rumors about Peoples Temple hit squads, Moscone ordered tightened security at city hall. Police guards were added at both main doors to the building, where all visitors were required to walk through metal detectors. More officers were assigned to the mayor's security team.

Moscone was worried not just about fallout from Jonestown. Dan

White, whose efforts to reclaim his job were growing increasingly frantic, was also adding to the strange and jumpy atmosphere at city hall. White continued to haunt the corridors of city hall, a phantom of increasing pathos, even after it became painfully clear that he was not going to get back his old office. He began threatening the mayor with legal action, and he huddled over the city hall copy machines, cranking out "unsolicited" letters of support for his crusade that were obviously written by himself.

"I'm worried about Dan White," Moscone confided to his wife, Gina. "He's taking this hard. He's acting sort of flakey."

It was no secret to White who was working against him: the same liberal cabal that was turning his hometown into a freak show. And Harvey Milk was at the center of all the intrigue. Wandering around city hall one day, White overheard Milk on the phone, vigorously lobbying the city attorney to reject White's legal bid for his old office. Milk had pretended to be his friend, but now he was showing his true colors. He was the enemy.

On Monday, November 27, Moscone was scheduled to make it official, announcing his replacement for Dan White on the board of supervisors: a liberal federal housing official who would give the mayor his swing vote. White had spent another sleepless night in the basement of his stucco bungalow in the Outer Mission, pacing back and forth, and poring over a scrapbook filled with family clippings and photos. There was nothing in the book of mementoes about his own achievements: his heroic feat at blazing Geneva Towers, or the state softball championship that he and Frank Falzon had helped win for their police all-stars team. The scrapbook was all about his dad's bravery; about the time Charlie White had rescued a minister's suicidal son off a high tower. Dan White had made up his mind. This was the day he was going to rescue San Francisco. He showered and shaved and dressed for his mission.

An aide dropped off White at city hall around ten thirty that morning. He told her he was going to give Moscone and Milk "a piece of his mind." His .38 Smith & Wesson police revolver was tucked into a soft leather holster clipped onto the back of his belt, hidden by his suit jacket. He had loaded the gun with hollow-point bullets, to make sure the physical damage would be explosive. In order to avoid the metal detector at the front door, White went around to the side of the building and crawled through an open basement window. He then climbed the back stairs, heading for room 200, the mayor's second-floor suite.

White knew that Jim Molinari, the mayor's police bodyguard, would be in the reception area, so he entered the mayor's suite through a side door. As White walked into Moscone's office, Willie Brown was leaving. Brown had been shooting the breeze with his old friend about football, politics, and their annual plans to go Christmas shopping in the Wolf's Den, a lingerie shop where women modeled silky garments for male customers. As Brown left Moscone's office, White went gliding past him. "He always had the same blank look on his face," Brown said later.

Moscone was not happy to hear that Dan White was waiting to see him that morning. "Shit," he told his secretary when she announced that White was outside. "How come he's doing this?" But Moscone greeted White graciously, closing the door behind them so that he could give White the bad news in private. The mayor wrapped a consoling arm around his shoulders, and took the distraught young man into a private nook in the back of his office, where he kept a bottle of White Horse whisky. That's the way men like Moscone did these things. "What're you gonna do now? You thinking about being a fireman again? Maybe we can help out." Moscone was all sympathy, but his words just sounded slick and syrupy to White, who was exploding inside.

Suddenly White reached behind his back, ripped the .38 out of his holster, and began firing point-blank at Moscone. As the first two hollow-points tore through Moscone's chest and shoulder, he toppled onto the floor, blood drenching his white shirt. White was not finished. He stood over the mayor's body like an executioner, and, sticking the barrel of his gun almost directly against his victim's ear, pumped two more exploding bullets into Moscone's brain.

Jim Molinari, the mayor's thin blue line, heard nothing as White carried out his mission. While the gunfire erupted in the mayor's office, his bodyguard sat in the reception area, reading the Green Sheet—the *Chronicle* sports section—and chatting with a city hall official. "You don't hear anything in city hall, with all the marble and woodwork," Molinari explained later.

Meanwhile, White reloaded his gun with five more hollow-points and headed for Harvey Milk's office. Dianne Feinstein—who was on the lookout for White that day, worried that he would cause a scene when the new supervisor was sworn in—cried out to him as he passed her office. "Dan!" She knew that she was the only one who might be able to talk some sense into him.

"It'll have to wait, Dianne," White told her, moving with a laser intensity to his next target.

White found Milk in his office. "Harvey, can I see you for a minute?" Milk was surprised to see White. But he agreed to follow the man whom he had called "dangerous," as White led him into his old office, now nearly bare of furniture and equipment.

"What the hell are you doing to me?" White began shouting at Milk after closing the door behind them. "Why do you want to hurt my name, my family? You *cheated* me!" It was the pleading voice of a boy who had never grown up, who had never lived up to his own standards of manhood. And then he was firing his gun at Milk, one, two, three, four times. The fourth bullet slammed into Milk's skull, spraying blood and brain tissue all over the wall. But White wanted to make sure that his tormentor was obliterated. He stood directly over him and fired one more time at point-blank range into Milk's already shattered skull.

Feinstein heard the shots from her office, and immediately thought Dan White had killed himself. She moved toward White's office as if in a trance, shoved open the door, and saw Milk's body splayed on the floor in a glistening pool of blood. Feinstein, whose father and second husband had been doctors, immediately went into emergency mode, kneeling next to Milk and picking up his wrist to feel for a pulse. Her finger slipped into a bullet hole, and was coated with blood and slime when she pulled it out.

One of Milk's aides had followed Feinstein into the room, and she told him to call the police chief's office. But he was sobbing so uncontrollably that he couldn't dial the number. "Here, let me," said Feinstein, gently taking the phone out of his hand. The aide ran out of the room to a water fountain and gulped down two Valiums.

As frantic whispers about the shootings floated through city hall, the cavernous building grew small and quiet. But when word reached the hall of justice, the reaction was different. Scattered cheers broke out on the fourth floor, among the police inspectors who had felt betrayed by Moscone. The jubilation soon spread throughout the SFPD network. Moscone and Milk were dead, and a member of the cops' family, Danny

White, had done the job. The Notre Dame Fighting Irish song crackled on the police radio, then "Danny Boy." The jokes immediately began making the rounds of the precincts. "What did Mary Ann tell Dan after she heard about the shootings? 'No, Dan, I said to get milk and macaroni, not Milk and Moscone.'"

The San Francisco police force was deeply implicated in the murders of Moscone and Milk. Dan White was not carrying out SFPD orders that morning in city hall, but he was carrying out the department's will. He was no longer on the force, but he was one of them: their star ballplayer, their political representative, their brother. He knew all about the cops' murderous feelings toward the city's liberal leadership. He felt the same way. They had the will, he had the willpower.

All the cops knew Danny White. Jim Molinari grew up in the same neighborhood with him, and Molinari's brother was a close friend. Frank Falzon was a few years ahead of White at St. Elizabeth's Grammar School. Danny used to shag balls for Falzon at the park as a kid and later became the star player on Falzon's police softball team. White played shortstop, Falzon was on second. They were wizards at turning a double play. He was like a kid brother to Falzon.

When the alert went out from city hall that morning, Falzon and Jack Cleary rushed to city hall. It was Molinari who told them that Dan White was the shooter. "I felt sucker-punched," said Falzon. "He was one of my best friends." Cleary said, "Check the shithouse. Dan's gonna blow his brains out."

Instead White had slipped out of city hall just as easily as he had entered and gone to St. Mary's, the nearby cathedral that soared, gleaming and white, like a giant sailboat in the San Francisco sky. He met Mary Ann inside. He wanted to make her understand. Mary Ann convinced her husband to turn himself in, and as they walked down Cathedral Hill to Northern Station, she clutched him tightly so that he couldn't use the gun on himself. When he entered the police station, White nodded toward the .38 in his holster and held his hands away from his body to show he was going easy. But when he was led into the cramped interrogation room, the assassin had nothing to say about the mayhem he had left behind in city hall.

It was Frank Falzon who got White talking. When the homicide cop walked into the room, he played it exactly the way he felt it: like Dan

White's stunned, outraged older brother. "It hit me in the fucking throat, seeing him there," Falzon said later.

"Why?" Falzon shouted at his friend. "What's wrong with you?"

Tears were streaming down White's face. "I want to tell you about it," he told Falzon. And he began to talk. He was under so much pressure, said White. "They put a lot of pressure on me and my family." As White mentioned his family, he began sobbing, and Falzon reached out and squeezed his forearm. "Can you relate these pressures you've been under, Dan?" the cop asked softly. And then the floodgates opened: how he was trying to take care of his family and serve the people of his district and keep the potato stand going. "My wife's got to work, long hours, fifty and sixty hours, never see my family." He was crying so hard he was choking on the words now. How he was forced to give up his job as supervisor for the good of his family. How supporters rallied around him and he tried to get his job back and Moscone promised the seat was still his. But then they betrayed him: Moscone, Milk, and the others. When the mayor told him he was going back on his word, was not going to reappoint him, "I got kind of fuzzy . . . my head didn't feel right." He didn't go to city hall that morning intending to kill anyone. But something just cracked inside him, and he shot the mayor. After that, he walked down the hall to talk to Harvey. "Maybe he'll be honest with me," White thought. He told Harvey what the supervisor's job meant to him and his family, and how important his reputation as a hard-working public servant was. But "he just kind of smirked at me, as if to say, 'Too bad,' and then I just got all flushed, an', an' hot, and I shot him." Then he phoned Mary Ann and met her at the cathedral. He wanted her to understand "how the pressure hit me, just, my head's all flushed, and it's like my skull's gonna crack." She slumped when he told her—another crushing blow to the woman who was so good-hearted and giving. Mary Ann begged him not to harm himself, promised that she would stand by him, and they walked down the hill together, arm in arm to Northern Station.

It felt good to tell Falzon everything. Confession was good for the soul. But Falzon felt like hell when he walked out of the room. "I thought I was sending my friend to the gas chamber. I had a confession on two murders, had the murder weapon, had witnesses. To me it was an open-and-shut first-degree-murder case."

Jack Cleary had a different feeling when he listened to the tape recording of White's confession. "When I heard that confession, I said, 'This better be tried right in the courtroom, because if not, he'll walk.'" Cleary knew that White's emotional narrative, the story of a good family man who was finally pushed beyond his limits, could make a jury of Dan White's peers weep for his mortifications. Falzon's gentle questioning had produced the ideal psychological defense.

Later Falzon would be widely excoriated for his kid-gloves handling of White. Critics said that the veteran homicide cop should never have interrogated him—the men were too close, it was a glaring conflict of interest. Falzon strongly denied that he had compromised his professionalism. "They would say, 'You were Dan White's friend, you buddied up.' And I'd say, 'Bullshit, I did my job. I got a confession.'" But looking back on it years later, Falzon wished he never had done it. "Because I had a remarkable career." The kind of career a cop could always be proud of, could tell his grandkids about. All of it except Dan White.

White, exquisitely in touch with his own pain, showed no remorse or sympathy for his victims or their loved ones. After his interrogation, the assassin was driven to the hall of justice to be jailed. Jack Cleary rode in the elevator with White to the jailhouse floor. "As we're riding in the elevator, Dan says, 'Wasn't that a bad ball game between USC and Notre Dame?' I said, 'Holy Christ, Dan, you just killed a couple people, and you're telling me about a ball game!'"

But White knew he was among his people at the hall of justice. As he was being fingerprinted, a crowd of sheriff's deputies gathered around him. A few had fury in their eyes, but most were smiling at him. One deputy walked over to White and patted him on the ass, like a coach in the dugout greeting a player who'd just scored.

WHILE SAN FRANCISCO'S MEN in uniform greeted their hero, the citizenry was informed of the latest calamities to strike their city. It fell to Dianne Feinstein to deliver the unspeakable news. A horde of city hall reporters surged around her as she stood at the top of the marble staircase that Milk loved to sweep up and down. Feinstein's face was gaunt, and her eyes shimmered with tears. She was flanked closely by Chief Gain and by one of her aides, who seemed to be holding up her tall frame as she spoke. She later said that she had stopped herself from breaking down by focusing on a familiar face, *Chronicle* reporter Duffy Jennings.

"As president of the board of supervisors, it is my duty to make this announcement," she began with a trembling voice. Then, pausing for a deep breath, she continued. "Both Mayor Moscone and Supervisor Harvey Milk have been shot and killed." The press pack gasped and cried out, and visibly recoiled—"as if to pull away from the story," one newspaper reporter later recalled, "as if it were too much, as if this couldn't be true or that they didn't want it to be true. We're human beings first." Then came the final blow. "The suspect . . . is Supervisor Dan White."

City hall was a small world, and the reporters who covered the mayor took it hard. Jennings, born and raised a few blocks from where Moscone grew up, couldn't help but like the guy. He enjoyed being around him. Moscone was always smiling, but he didn't seem like a phony. He was streetwise and politically shrewd, and fun to chew the fat with. At the end of the day, the mayor would sometimes invite Jennings and other city hall reporters for drinks in his private back room—the dark, intimate chamber where his life had just ended.

Harvey was always good copy too, a rubber-faced clown one minute and the city's conscience the next. He turned city hall into his opera house. Even tedious supervisor meetings seemed stage-lit when Milk took the floor.

Now the enormous and beautiful old building suddenly felt like a mausoleum.

As the news sped around the city, reaching those who knew and loved the two men, the ripples of pain widened. Cleve Jones was putting in a few minutes on a hotel workers union picket line in the Castro when a bus wheezed to a stop and someone shouted that the mayor had been shot. Jones had a frantic feeling about Milk and grabbed a taxi to city hall, arriving in time to see a dazed Feinstein walk by, her hands stained with Milk's blood. There was a gaggle of cops gathered around Dan White's old office. Jones saw a pair of feet in scuffed-up wingtips sticking out the door, and he knew it was Harvey. It was the only pair of shoes Milk owned. Jones pushed his way into the room and saw Harvey's blue face and his thick, blood-clotted hair. "I had never seen a dead person before," he recalled. "I think I was in shock for a long time after that."

Milk was the first person other than his parents who had seen something in Jones. Recognizing his potential as a leader, Milk had given the young man one of his most prized possessions: his bullhorn. Jones promptly put it to good use, rallying dozens of protest marches around the city. But now, Jones thought, that was all finished.

"When I saw his body there on the floor, I said to myself, 'It's all over now.' I felt it was the end of the gay liberation movement, the end of the city. I couldn't imagine how San Francisco could ever come back from this."

It also seemed like the end of days for the Moscone family. A fireman picked up Christopher, then sixteen, and Jonathan, fourteen, at St. Ignatius and drove them home. The boys knew something terrible had happened but didn't know what until Christopher finally asked. "Your father has expired," the fireman told them. Everything seemed wavy to Christopher. He barely made it to his room. He remembers a "numbness" settling over him for a long time after that. "My mom let us do what we wanted for a while. If we wanted to go to school, we did. If we wanted to watch television until three in the morning, we could. I became very introverted."

Rebecca Moscone, an eighteen-year-old student at UC Berkeley, was pulled out of class by campus policemen the day her father was killed. Her boyfriend gave her the news. "I flipped out, started sobbing. I kind of collapsed," Rebecca recalled. "Up until then, life was great. After that was a big emptiness . . . My father taught me to play basketball. I remember driving to Tahoe with my dad in his Alfa Romeo . . . Afterward I was in this fog for a year, trapped."

Gina Moscone withdrew entirely from her husband's world, the arena that had taken so much of him and now had taken all of him. She never spoke in public about his murder. A newspaper photo of the mourning family captured Gina Moscone's fathomless grief, picturing her bent over, with her face buried in her hands, as her children tried desperately to comfort her. "I felt pretty helpless," said Christopher years later. "What could I do? She's alone, she doesn't have her partner, and nothing can replace that."

When Moscone and Milk died, they were both nearly broke. Milk was deeply in debt, and Moscone had only a few hundred dollars in his savings account. They left nothing for their families and friends. But the two men bequeathed something invaluable to San Francisco. They presided over the modernization of the city. Under their leadership, city hall was finally opened to all of those who made San Francisco their home. Milk said in his final days that San Francisco was the home that he and thousands of other gay men had been searching for their entire lives. It was a haven for dreamers and outcasts and wandering souls. Both men gave their lives for this oasis of freedom; the city where no stranger was kept outside its golden gate.

In the days after Jonestown and the city hall assassinations, San Francisco sleepwalked under a dark canopy of clouds that seemed like it would never lift. The city was racked with despair. The San Francisco Suicide Prevention center received twice its normal number of phone calls. Rev. Cecil Williams fielded a flood of calls at his Tenderloin church from distraught people who feared that they, and the city itself, would never recover from the multiple traumas. The *Examiner*'s Washington, DC, bureau reported that San Franciscans visiting the nation's capital were bombarded by questions about their dark-starred city. "There must be something evil out there," one San Francisco visitor was told. "It's crazy, it's sick . . . I'm glad I'm here," another San Franciscan was informed.

Some media commentators in the local press picked up the "sick San Francisco theme," conveniently overlooking that Dan White was no denizen of the city's wacky fringe but a wholesome-looking product of the Catholic Church, US Army, and San Francisco police and fire departments. San Francisco had become "Aberration City," wrote conservative *Examiner* columnist Guy Wright, sounding like White himself. "A fermentation vat for oddball notions. A haven for all sorts of kook cults . . . A city where tolerance deteriorates into license. A town without a norm."

The defenders of a wide-open San Francisco rallied around their wounded city. Lawrence Ferlinghetti published "An Elegy to Dispel Gloom" in the *Examiner,* writing, "It's poor vanity / to think that all humanity / is bathed in red / because one young mad man / one so bad man / lost his head." Meanwhile, Reverend Williams held a special evening service at Glide Memorial Church to soothe his suffering rainbow

flock. Williams reminded worshippers why San Francisco—their spar-
kling, sea-glass city that now seemed so damned—was actually blessed.
"San Francisco is the most tolerant city in the world. Harvey Milk and
George Moscone gave their lives for that idea."

Cleve Jones soon realized that he was wrong: that it was not all over,
that George's and Harvey's San Francisco lived on. He saw it that Monday evening, just hours after the assassinations. Jones was an expert
at working phone trees whenever Harvey and he decided that people
needed to be mobilized in the streets. But that evening, it wasn't necessary. "People just knew, everybody knew what to do," said Jones.

As the sun dipped below Twin Peaks, Jones wandered toward Castro and Market and saw the huge crowd starting to gather. "It was the
most amazingly beautiful, heart-wrenchingly sad, magnificent example
of what San Francisco is. It was gay people, straight people, white people, Filipinos, Chinese, African Americans, men and women of all ages,
children, the poor and well dressed, people in fur coats next to people in
rags. We estimated there were between thirty thousand and forty thousand people. We marched in almost total silence down Market Street to
city hall and filled Civic Center Plaza, a sea of people holding candles.
I remember standing there and thinking, 'This isn't the end of anything.
This is the beginning.' And I was right.

"I think every city has a soul, every city is unique and special. But
for San Franciscans, I don't think there could ever be another place to
call home. And a lot of it has to do with what I saw that night: with this
ability to suffer horrible and dreadful events, earthquakes, civil turmoil,
assassinations, and to not only endure but to create something beautiful
from it."

Crowding into the plaza, people listened in a church-like hush as
Joan Baez sang "Amazing Grace" on the city hall steps. After she finished, Dianne Feinstein stood up and began to address the vast throng.
Hours earlier, her arms were bathed in Harvey Milk's blood. Facing the
press, she could barely choke out the announcement about the city hall
murders. The explosion of violence had caught Feinstein in a delicate
midlife moment. At forty-five, the recently widowed mother of a teenage
daughter was grappling with her future. Before Dan White overturned
San Francisco's political order, Feinstein's political career was all but
finished. She had been rejected twice by the city's voters in her quest

for the mayor's office. It seemed clear to her that she was not the leader that San Francisco wanted—too starched, too middle of the road, too goody-goody.

In the weeks before the assassinations, Feinstein had gone trekking in the mountains of Nepal to ponder her next steps. "I need to get my life together," she had said. While hiking in the Himalayas, she came down with an intestinal illness. By the time she recovered from her nausea and fever, she had decided to announce her resignation from politics when she returned home.

But now Dianne Feinstein was acting mayor. And as the tall, lean, attractive woman with the bonnet of dark hair and piercing green eyes stood before her fellow San Franciscans that candlelit evening, there was something different about her. In the course of that terrible day, Feinstein had become the leader that the city needed. As she began to speak, she found the right words to express San Francisco's howling pain and to make people believe that the broken city could be put back together. As long as she had anything to say about it, Feinstein told the crowd, she would make sure that San Francisco continued to follow the path of human rights, love, and understanding. No bullets could stop that forward march. The people gave her the kind of heartfelt ovation she had never heard in her political career.

Two days later, at the city hall memorial service for Moscone and Milk, Feinstein was even more eloquent. Standing once again on the city halls steps, on a stage draped with black bunting, the acting mayor pledged to honor the two men's sacrifice by bringing together the deeply divided city. "Neither of the two men we mourn today were bitter or vengeful. Their deaths should not engender feeling alien to their natures or to the nature of this beautiful city . . . If there has been rancor between the neighborhoods and downtown, between our different races, and between our different lifestyles, let us put it aside. Let us join together in a spirit of unity and reconciliation. Let us take pride in the memory of George Moscone and Harvey Milk, for the San Francisco we all love."

It has become fashionable in recent decades to disparage public service. The political profession is widely scorned and reviled. But there are times when political leadership seems like a blessing. San Francisco in November 1978 was a broken vessel on a dark sea. The city had endured so many blows and afflictions that it seemed cursed. When deliverance finally came, San Francisco owed it in large part to an unlikely leader. Though she was a homegrown native, she seemed miscast for the role. San Franciscans had a fondness for lovable rogues and other colorful characters. But in a city of Marx brothers, Feinstein was Margaret Dumont, forever distressed and befuddled by the antics around her. Not only was she the grownup in the room, it seemed like she had always been a grownup.

Feinstein was well grounded, resolute, firm, managerial. Even her eccentricities, like her love of uniforms and ceremonial displays of military power, seemed weirdly un–San Franciscan. Yet she turned out to be precisely the right leader for the time. While she shifted the city back toward the center, she stabilized it enough to allow many of the revolutionary changes that preceded her to become fully absorbed by the body politic. Though she herself was not in harmony with all of these "San Francisco values," they became enshrined under her leadership.

PART THREE

DELIVERANCE

One way or another, this darkness got to give.

32

FIRE BY TRIAL

LOOKING BACK AT the harrowing period when she became mayor of San Francisco, Dianne Feinstein said, "I found out one thing about myself. When I am really in crisis, things are much clearer to me. I move in a regular way and can just sustain myself through the crisis. And it's always been that way in my life. I just can't explain it, but it is. I needed that ability when I became mayor, because the city was falling apart."

Feinstein developed the ability to navigate her way through traumas at an early age. The oldest of three daughters, she was raised in an elegantly appointed San Francisco home that from the outside looked picture perfect. Her beloved father, Dr. Leon Goldman, was a highly respected surgeon and professor at the University of California, San Francisco, medical complex. Her mother, Betty, was a beautiful and exotic Russian émigré, the daughter of a czarist general forced to flee the Bolshevik Revolution. But Betty Goldman, who was later revealed to have been brain damaged by a childhood case of encephalitis, was prone to terrifying and unpredictable rages. She once chased Dianne around the dining room with a knife, and she often locked her out of the house at night. Dianne was forced to study for her high-stakes Scholastic Aptitude Test in the shelter of her parents' car. Feinstein idolized her father but discovered early on that he could not protect his children from their volatile mother.

Feinstein said later that she learned leadership at home by figuring out how to manage her mother's eruptions and to shield her younger sisters. "It is fair to say we lived in a great deal of fear," Feinstein recalled. "The part that was hard was the unpredictability. My mother was capable of great hostility. I mean terrible things . . . It was brutal."

Young Dianne found comfort in the clubby, male world of San Francisco politics, following her colorful uncle, Morris Goldman, a coat manufacturer and Democratic Party wheeler-dealer, as he made his rounds through the city. In 1945, when she was twelve, Dianne was taken to her first city hall meeting by Uncle Morris, who offered running commentary on "the board of stupidvisors" and pointed out how the flick of a portly city boss's stogie could change the vote count.

Feinstein, who was raised Jewish, also gained insight into the Catholic core of San Francisco politics by going to high school at the exclusive Convent of the Sacred Heart. The school, housed in the historic, white-marble Flood Mansion overlooking the San Francisco Bay, imbued in Feinstein a lifelong respect for Catholic ritual and order. Sometimes she would slip into a nun's habit when the sisters weren't looking. But when the young woman saw some of the church's deeper reactionary principles on unvarnished display during a trip to Spain, she decided she could never convert.

After studying political science at Stanford in the 1950s, Feinstein was selected as a Coro Fellow, a program started by two wealthy San Franciscans to train future government leaders. She entered city politics reeking of squeaky-clean, good-government elitism instead of the usual smoky, backroom funk. She won her first race for the board of supervisors in 1969 as a moderate Democrat without the help of any of the local machines. At thirty-six, she was the mother of a twelve-year-old girl and married to her second husband, brain surgeon Bert Feinstein, and living happily with her family in a Pacific Heights mansion. But, compelled by a restless ambition, she already had her eye on the mayor's office. And Dr. Feinstein, two decades older, was wholeheartedly dedicated to his wife's happiness, helping with all the campaign chores, the way her father had when she ran for student office in high school.

Though she had grown up in the city and had reaped the benefits of her uncle's street-savvy wisdom, Feinstein seemed painfully cloistered when she first jumped into San Francisco politics. To her credit, she felt a need to venture into pockets of the city that had always been terra incognita to her. "I wasn't ever afraid of going places or looking at new things or opening my mind," she said.

But Feinstein's fact-finding missions often verged on the ludicrous. An ardent opponent of the city's growing porn industry, Feinstein decided she should go to an adult movie to see for herself what she was up against, dragging along another nice Jewish girl, *Chronicle* society columnist Merla Zellerbach, to a seedy theater. Predictably, Feinstein and her friend were horrified. On another occasion, Feinstein—determined to clean up the Tenderloin, the city's drugged-out red-light district—put on a blond wig and stood on a street corner for three hours to learn more about the raunchy neighborhood.

The earnest supervisor once stood in front of a Glide Memorial Church congregation and lectured the downtrodden Tenderloin worshippers about the importance of good hygiene and hard work. "Good citizens," she enlightened them, "are people who keep themselves clean." Her perky sermon was met with scattered boos. Cecil Williams, sitting behind Feinstein, was tempted to pull on her coattails to stop her. "Dianne," the minister later scolded her, "you don't talk that way to these folks. If they had a place to get cleaned up, most of them would get cleaned up. If they could get a job, they'd get a job."

But over time, as Feinstein explored her city, she grew more understanding about San Francisco's changing social currents. She still tended to be stiff—as if "her feelings were wrapped in wax," as one reporter put it. And she never would be the kind of rakish politician who'd take a deep hit off a joint if it were offered. But she became more comfortable with the city's colorful cast of characters. And when Pacific Heights residents lobbied the board of supervisors to evict the Delancey Street halfway house from their tony neighborhood, Feinstein broke with her own neighbors and supported the ex-cons and recovering addicts.

"Quentin Kopp led the campaign against us," said Bill Maher, the Delancey Street founder's younger brother and political sidekick. "Kopp suggested that we move to a neighborhood more appropriate to our social stature. Dianne was our main supporter, even though she lived nearby. She was great—vibrant and young, and very progressive. She has always worn sensible shoes, and she has always been a formidable woman."

Despite the hands-on intensity that she brought to her job as a supervisor and her keen intelligence, Feinstein hit a political ceiling after losing her second bid for mayor in 1975. San Francisco respected her but didn't love her. She simply seemed too sensible, too measured for a city that fell for brawling, brash, leading men.

By the time she returned to San Francisco in November 1978—after a life-challenging trek through the Himalayas with her new friend, investment banker Dick Blum—Feinstein thought her political career was over. "I was firmly convinced that I was not electable as mayor," she said in hindsight.

Feinstein's life had been racked by grief and turmoil. Her husband Bert—the love of her life, the man who had filled her with the confidence to pursue her ambitions—had died after a long and agonizing battle with colon cancer. While he was dying, Feinstein became a target of the New World Liberation Front. One night after her deeply ill husband was brought back from the hospital, the terrorists planted a bomb on the windowsill of their Pacific Heights home, immediately underneath her daughter's bedroom. If the bomb had not misfired, the house—which was being painted at the time and was surrounded by scaffolding—could have exploded in flames. On another occasion, the underground radicals shot out the windows of her weekend beach house in Pajaro Dunes, on Monterey Bay, which Feinstein thought of as her only refuge. "It was a terrible, terrible time."

IN SPITE OF ALL this, Feinstein did not hesitate when duty called on the morning of November 27, 1978. The job that she had pursued for nearly a decade was suddenly hers, under the most hideous of circumstances. San Francisco was torn and bleeding. Her predecessor and one of her colleagues lay dead in city hall, and another colleague was under arrest for the murders. Rage and suspicion ruled the city of love. Already the target of political violence herself, Feinstein knew that her new position would make her even more vulnerable to the dangerous passions swirling through the city. But like a nun or nurse in a battlefield hospital, it never occurred to Feinstein to turn down the job when it was presented to her.

The morning following the assassinations, Feinstein awoke after a restless night in the same state of shock as the rest of the city. "I had hoped to wake up and find it was a nightmare," she said. But then she simply drove to city hall and went to work. "This will not be a rudderless city," she told the shell-shocked public. As the president of the board of supervisors, Feinstein automatically had become San Francisco's acting mayor. A week later, she outmaneuvered rival Quentin Kopp and was elected by her fellow supervisors to officially fill out the remaining year of Moscone's term.

The traumatic events surrounding her political ascension filled her with "a feeling of destiny." She had been groomed for the embattled leadership role ever since her childhood. Feinstein always steeled herself for the worst, from the time she was a bobbed-hair little girl, smiling gamely for a family photo while her demon-possessed mother looked on balefully. And now, in the worst of times, Dianne Feinstein was mayor of San Francisco.

She wisely chose to retain Moscone's staff—even his controversial police chief, Charles Gain—and to steer a similar administrative course during her first few months in office. This was primarily smart politics. Quentin Kopp had already made it clear that he would be challenging her from the right in the mayoral election the following year. Keeping the Moscone constituency happy was a matter of political survival.

Just to make sure that Feinstein realized this, Willie Brown spelled it out for her in a *New York Times* interview: "If she starts making all those changes, maybe some of us liberals—either Phil or John Burton, now in Congress, or myself—will have to take her on in the election next year. Kopp's got the right, and there is no middle. If one of us enters the race, she'll run third. One way or another, we're going to fight to keep the gains we made under George." Feinstein had already seen the way this campaign movie turned out, and she did not care to repeat it.

But honoring the Moscone and Milk legacy for the remainder of these slain officials' terms was also a matter of principle to Dianne Feinstein. This became clear as she pondered her choice to fill Milk's seat on the board of supervisors. The establishment gay Democrats in the Alice B. Toklas Democratic Club—whom Milk had reviled—were lobbying strongly for one of their own to be chosen. Feinstein, closely aligned with these mainstream activists, could have ensured that the board would be more manageable by doing so. But she had listened to the tape-recorded will that Milk had left behind in the full expectation that he would be assassinated, naming four potential successors whom he trusted to carry on his progressive mission. Feinstein simply couldn't violate her former colleague's dying wishes. She filled Milk's seat with one of the left-wing gay activists on his list: Harry Britt, a former Methodist minister and Milk protégé.

Britt, painfully shy and a novice in the world of city politics, at first resisted the call to duty. But feeling that he owed it to Harvey and the liberation politics they both espoused, the soft-spoken Texan finally agreed. It was the beginning of an often prickly relationship between Britt and Feinstein. But Harvey Milk's successor always respected the courage and integrity that Feinstein showed by appointing him.

"Dianne never had a good relationship with Harvey Milk—they weren't kindred spirits," Britt recalled. "*Her* homosexuals were not *his* homosexuals. But very much to her credit, she put all that aside when she appointed me. Because she really, passionately did not want Dan White's bullets to be the end of the Harvey Milk story. She took Harvey's will extraordinarily seriously. She deeply *hated* what Dan White had done."

The new mayor, who was concerned about rebuilding police department morale, hoped that Britt would vote her way on his first major test as a supervisor: the hotly debated settlement of the civil rights lawsuit against the SFPD. Feinstein wanted to block the settlement that Moscone had worked out. But instead Britt joined with the black police officers group and other minority plaintiffs against the department and voted for the settlement. The affirmative action deal that was finally brokered by the supervisors began to open up the white, tradition-bound force.

Feinstein's driving goal as the city's new mayor was to restore a sense of civic normality. In March 1979 she pep-talked the San Francisco business community at a luncheon held in the Sheraton Palace, the ornate grande dame of San Francisco hotels. "San Francisco is now in the process of rising once again," she assured the downtown crowd. "It's not the kook capital of the world; it's a beautiful, diverse, open, tolerant city." To help restore the corporate diners' confidence in San Francisco, the mayor announced that she was increasing the police department budget and putting more cops on the streets than ever before.

It was a balancing act that defined San Francisco's new leader: celebrate the city's bright galaxy of queer and colorful planets, and simultaneously affirm the primacy of law and order. "I believe safety is the first thing you need to guarantee as mayor," she said, looking back at her years in city hall.

The problem for Feinstein was that many San Franciscans—particularly its "diverse" citizenry—felt threatened, not protected, by the city's police force. There were strong suspicions in the Castro that the city hall assassinations were an inside job, and that Moscone and Milk were both victims of "law and order." The outrage in the gay community was stoked hotter when it was reported that police and firemen had raised $100,000 for Dan White's defense fund, and that White's jailers were allowing him special privileges behind bars, including meals from his favorite restaurants and chocolate cakes baked by admirers. These churning feelings of rancor and distrust exploded on the night of May 21, 1979.

THE WHITE TRIAL, WHICH sparked the first major crisis of Feinstein's administration, was a pageant tableaux of San Francisco's civil war. The city's deepest discords were on vivid display in department 21, the third-floor courtroom in the hall of justice.

In his opening argument, White's lawyer—a rising young criminal attorney named Doug Schmidt, who zoomed around town in a Corvette and owned six hundred acres in Mendocino County—made it clear that he was putting San Francisco values on trial. The jury, which Schmidt carefully cleansed of gays and other new San Franciscans, was told that White was "an idealistic, young, working-class man—the voice of the family" in city hall. White had been taken advantage of by scheming politicians, the same ones responsible for bringing Peoples Temple and other alien elements into a city once known for its hard-working, family values. Overwhelmed by the growing pressures in his life, and binging on Twinkies and other junk food as he fell deeper into depression, Dan White finally cracked. The story that Schmidt unfolded clearly struck a nerve with the jury, which was dominated by working-class Catholics.

Several jurors wept openly when the recording of White's teary confession was played in the courtroom.

Frank Falzon, still the chief investigator for the prosecution despite his longtime friendship with the defendant, reinforced the sympathetic portrait of White when he took the witness stand. The "shattered" figure of a man who faced him in the police interrogation room that terrible day was "totally unlike" the Dan White he had known nearly his entire life. *That* Dan White, testified Falzon, "was a man among men."

Prosecutor Tommy Norman was caught flat-footed by his investigator's testimony. Falzon was supposed to be *his* witness, but instead he came across as Dan White's most effective character witness. Falzon, who was sharply criticized for his performance on the stand, still defends himself. "I played it straight," said Falzon. "Do you deny your friendship? All I said to the jury was the man I knew was a man's man. The man fought for his country. He was a good police officer. Up until the day he walked into city hall with a gun, Dan White was my friend. All his other friends—Quentin Kopp, Dianne Feinstein—they all turned their backs on him after the shooting. I couldn't do that. This kid was too close to me."

It was Tommy Norman, a smooth hall of justice veteran who waltzed into the courtroom in sleek suits and a twinkle in his eye, who was primarily to blame for the inept prosecution of White. He and his boss in the DA's office, Joe Freitas, were utterly unprepared for Schmidt's aggressive political strategy. Because Freitas, facing reelection that year, had been deeply tainted by the Peoples Temple scandal, his prosecutors were tongue-tied when it came to countering Schmidt's charges that White was a victim of the city's snake-pit politics. Freitas and Norman made no effort to explore the hate-filled culture of the San Francisco Police Department that had spawned Dan White.

The prosecution had a slam-dunk case. The defendant was a scheming killer who cold-bloodedly plotted the assassinations of his political enemies, equipped himself with enough extralethal ammunition to do the job, and crawled through a basement window to avoid detection. But by the end of his trial, White had emerged as a broken-winged angel. And on the afternoon of May 21, the jury delivered a stunningly sympathetic verdict, finding the double assassin guilty not of murder but of manslaughter.

The rumblings began rolling through the city as soon as the verdict was announced, like the roar from a distant flash flood. City leaders, fearing the worst, rushed to denounce the jury's decision. She had found Harvey Milk's body, Mayor Feinstein told the press with tears in her eyes. She knew what the verdict should have been: "These were two murders . . . We've gone through a physical bloodbath, and now we are going through a mental one." Supervisor Carol Ruth Silver, one of White's intended victims, remarked bitterly, "Dan White has gotten away with murder. It's as simple as that."

Gina Moscone, grieving once again in private, remained silent about the verdict. But her children were in turmoil. "I remember thinking I had to go the trial because I was the oldest man in the family," recalled Christopher, who was still a teenager at the time. "I told my mom, and she talked me down from that. I wanted revenge."

The Castro did exact its revenge that night. "This means that in America, it's all right to kill faggots," a furious Cleve Jones told a radio reporter. Minutes later, Jones ran into the streets, carrying the banged-up bullhorn that Harvey had given him, and began to rally the crowd that was already forming at the corner of Castro and Market. This time there would be no candles or mournful gospel songs. This time there would be fire and rage.

By the time the crowd reached city hall, it was more than five thousand strong and screaming for blood. "Dan White was a cop!" "Avenge Harvey Milk!" "Kill Dan White!" The thin blue line on the city hall steps, shocked by the fury of men they'd long dismissed as pansies, quickly retreated inside the building. As the night wore on, the protesters lay wild siege to city hall, smashing windows and torching a row of police cars. Meanwhile, Police Chief Gain—hunkered down inside the mayor's glass-strewn second-floor office with Feinstein and her fiancée, Dick Blum—tried to keep a rein on his notoriously violent riot squad. Christopher Moscone, watching the mayhem at home on TV, was lit up with the rioters' burning rage. "I was like, 'Yeah, I get it.' I was with the rioters in spirit."

As the police tac squad finally drove away the army of night from city

hall, many cops broke free from their chief's control and pursued protesters all the way back to the Castro. Now it was time for a police riot.
Roving bands of cops hunted down gays on the street and invaded bars,
cracking skulls with their nightsticks and screaming, "Sick cocksuck-
ers!" Not until Gain and Harry Britt appeared on the scene and ordered
a stop to the violence did the cops finally withdraw.

The poisonous feelings between cops and gays lingered long after
"White Night," as the night of flames came to be called, eerily echoing
Jim Jones's death drills. In the post–Dan White period, antigay street
violence spiked again. And gays accused the police of standing by and
letting the blood flow in their neighborhoods.

ONE OF THE STRANGER crimes involving a gay victim occurred in July
1979, when a gay artist-propagandist named Robert Opel was shot and
killed in his erotic gallery in the SOMA leather district. Opel, who was
known for his provocative stunts, achieved fleeting notoriety during the
1974 Academy Awards ceremony when he streaked naked past Oscar
presenter David Niven. Opel later moved from Los Angeles to San Francisco, where he plunged into the sadomasochistic underground, hosting
fist-fucking parties and gallery openings featuring the notoriously butch
art of Tom of Finland and the early work of a young photographer named
Robert Mapplethorpe.

Opel became increasingly involved in gay politics in San Francisco,
investigating the Milk assassination and staging a mock execution of
Dan White near the Civic Center. During the execution ceremony, Opel
handed out pamphlets that read: "What would happen if a gay cock-
sucking faggot killed an ex-cop? Would *he* get away with murder?" Robert Opel was precisely the kind of perverse troublemaker San Francisco
cops wanted out of their city.

Ten days after Opel acted out his Dan White "execution," the artist's
Fey-Way Studio on Howard Street was invaded by a couple of thugs
demanding money and drugs. These were not the boys in leather masks
who came to Opel's parties, but *real* rough trade. One of the bandits,
a scruffy, twenty-eight-year-old hustler named Maurice Keenan, stuck
an automatic pistol at Opel's head and said, "I'm gonna blow your head
off." The artist replied, "You're going to have to. There's no money here."

They were Robert Opel's last words. Keenan made good on this threat and blew his brains out. The thugs fled with $5 in cash, a camera, and a backpack.

When Opel's sister went to the hall of justice to meet with homicide detectives, she saw that someone had written *Homocide* on her dead brother's evidence box. After he was arrested, Keenan walked out of his unlocked jail cell at the hall of justice and disappeared. Jail officials were at a loss to explain the bizarre getaway. Recaptured, the murderer repeated his disappearing act until officials finally found a way to keep him behind bars.

Opel's friends and family speculated that he might have been set up by drug dealers or other sleazy elements connected to the police force. After his murder, other gay agitprop artists went into hiding, fearing that brazen performance pieces like Opel's execution of Dan White could put a man's life in danger in San Francisco's volatile climate.

In the raw-nerved period after the White verdict, San Francisco could have easily spun violently off its axis. But Feinstein became increasingly assertive, shedding any lingering feelings that she was merely a caretaker mayor, and taking command of the city. "This city has to be managed," Feinstein reflected later. "If you don't manage, it falls apart."

33

THE CENTER HOLDS

As the November 1979 mayoral election loomed, Dianne Feinstein hit the streets, popping up all over town—from a Tenderloin residential hotel, where she was photographed laying hands on the crippled leg of an eighty-nine-year-old tenant, to a streetcar in the Sunset, where she discussed the finer points of MUNI commuting with the vocal passengers. If she seemed painfully earnest at times, she also came across as being thoroughly on top of the city's operations.

In September the city was forced to shut down its storied but aging cable car system for long-overdue repairs. It was a potential public relations disaster, with the *New York Times* announcing, "No longer do 'little cable cars climb halfway to the stars' over San Francisco's hills." But Feinstein pushed repair crews to work eighteen-hour days and began raising a $10 million private fund to upgrade the quaint transit system, shaking down wealthy supporters and visiting celebrities such as Mick Jagger. The day before the election, the sound of clanging cable car bells was heard once more on Nob Hill.

As she threw herself into the campaign, Feinstein exposed herself to the madness that still crackled in San Francisco. While going door to door in the rough and unpredictable Fillmore district, the mayor was suddenly approached by a man who pointed a silver pistol directly at her head. The mayor and her entourage froze as the man pulled the trigger.

A butane flame came hissing from the gun instead of a bullet. "There was no time to duck or react. Sure, I was scared," Feinstein later told reporters. But she immediately gathered herself and continued campaigning.

Feinstein was no shoo-in. Her main opponent, Quentin Kopp, rallied John Barbagelata's angry taxpayer crowd, running as a fiscally responsible fix-it man, and painting Feinstein as a captive of the downtown elite and limousine liberals. Kopp tried to broaden the Barbagelata coalition by making a strong appeal to gay voters, promising them equal police protection and freedom from harassment. Feinstein's challenger won the endorsement of the *Chronicle* and the support of key political establishment figures like Joe Alioto as well as neighborhood activists such as Calvin Welch, who appreciated Kopp's endorsement of a ballot initiative to limit high-rise construction in the city.

Forced into a runoff, Feinstein fought back hard, drawing on Moscone's campaign staff and his grassroots playbook. In the end, she won a decisive victory over Kopp by holding on to much of Moscone's coalition of gays, union members, and progressives. Embracing Gina Moscone onstage at her victory party, Feinstein paid tribute to the man whose shoes she was filling. "We carry with us the heritage of a fallen leader," she told the emotional crowd. "We will not forsake that heritage."

The Moscone team never warmed up to Feinstein's centrist, downtown-oriented politics or her Big Nurse personality. As Moscone himself had put it coarsely in his Rat Pack way, Feinstein was a "stiff bitch. Her problem is that she needs a good fuck." But they knew that she was a better option than Kopp. "All of George's people helped her get elected," said Dick Sklar. "Kopp would have desecrated George's chair."

Finally elected mayor by the people of San Francisco, Feinstein quickly began putting her own moderate stamp on city hall. While keeping some of Moscone's former aides and making sure that the Moscone family was taken care of financially, the new mayor made it clear that she would lead San Francisco in her own way.

Feinstein appeased police department veterans by firing Chief Gain and by fighting the establishment of a civilian review board that would have investigated the gay community's charges of police brutality. But she also made it clear to the SFPD that the old days of fraternity mayhem were over. Under Feinstein, the department became more professional and diverse. Stories about the new police force began appearing in the newspapers, with headlines like "A Gay Cop Talks" and "Changing Times for S.F. Police"—an article featuring Heather Fong, a Chinese-American female patrol cop who years later would become chief of the SFPD. The gay cop, Woody Tennant, insisted that attitudes were rapidly changing inside the force: "You end up boring straight officers out of being uptight. Once they find out you don't want to have sex in the patrol car and that you're as boring as they are, everything's fine."

The mayor also pulled off the same balancing act with the gay community, making it clear that antigay violence was not going to be tolerated and appointing gays to prominent city hall positions, while at the same time clamping firm limits on the gay revolution in the city.

Even though she had hosted the wedding of lesbian friends in her own backyard, Feinstein vetoed a law introduced by Supervisor Britt that would have extended health insurance benefits to the live-in partners of gay city employees. Her veto of the domestic partners legislation set off a round of angry "Dump Dianne" protests, but she weathered the storm. For the rest of her days in city hall, Feinstein and San Francisco's gay community endured a rocky marriage, in which bitter recriminations alternated with outbursts of genuine affection. Feinstein could lecture gays one day about their wanton exhibitionism at Gay Freedom Day Parades, and the next day approve S&M sex safety workshops taught by the city coroner.

The mayor had a more consistently adversarial relationship with neighborhood activists, who—enraged by the downtown building boom she green-lighted—accused her of selling out the city to big developers and construction unions. She countered that in a Reagan era of diminishing public resources, she was doing what she must to bring revenue and jobs to the city. The surviving Moscone appointees on the city planning commission fought a rearguard battle with Feinstein against the high-rise proliferation, forcing developers to contribute funds for parks, sewage facilities, public transportation, and housing. In the end, the mayor succeeded in massively changing the San Francisco skyline, but her progressive opponents forced the city to concede that there were social costs to development and to take steps to help address them.

Feinstein and progressive activists also fought a seesaw battle throughout her tenure over rent control, with Harry Britt championing the city's hard-squeezed tenants. Feinstein, who herself was a landlord, would veto rent control bills passed by the board of supervisors, only to have persistent housing activists rebound by placing pro-renter initiatives on the ballot.

Despite her running battles with San Francisco activists, many progressives harbored a grudging respect for Feinstein's managerial skills. With her firm hand on the city's rudder, she managed to steer a middle course that gradually brought stability back to the city. "She ran the city with an iron fist," recalled Mike Hennessy, a former prisoner rights lawyer whose long reign as San Francisco's sheriff began the year that Feinstein was elected mayor. "Of all the mayors I've worked with, she was the best," he said. "That's because she took responsibility for this city. San Francisco is a very hard city to run. It's very politically fractious. It takes a lot of work to hold it together. And that's what Feinstein did."

EVERY MONDAY MORNING, MAYOR Feinstein briskly presided over a meeting of elected officials and department heads that evaluated the state of the city. If an official did not seem on top of his fiefdom, the mayor could be merciless. She was particularly tough on her new police chief, Cornelius Murphy, if crime stats were up in any part of the city. At one meeting, the mayor—who was in the habit of listening in on the police radio as she was driven around town in her limousine—badgered Murphy about a crime spike that she had heard about over the radio. "What do you propose I do about this, Chief?" she pressed Murphy. "Stop listening to the radio," the exasperated cop told her.

Feinstein became known as the most hands-on manager in San Francisco's history. One day, while being driven to city hall, she saw an elderly man collapse on the sidewalk. Ordering her chauffeur to stop, the mayor jumped out and rushed to the man. Rose Pak, who was riding with her at the time, was amazed to see the mayor kneel over the man, wipe foam from his lips, and give him mouth-to-mouth resuscitation.

"People later pointed to this and said, 'See, she's not a cold fish, she has a heart.' But I didn't see it that way," said Pak. "I saw her as a doctor's daughter and a doctor's widow, doing the proper clinical thing."

Jim Molinari, the police bodyguard whom Feinstein inherited from Mayor Moscone, learned that riding through the streets of San Francisco with her could be an adventure. One day Molinari saw someone burglarizing a car. Feinstein ordered Molinari to cut off the thief's escape with her limousine while she radioed for police backup. Another time, the mayor overheard a report about a Hunters Point fire on her limousine radio and ordered Molinari to race to the scene of the blaze. When they arrived, Feinstein threw on a fire coat and helped lug a fire hose toward the flames.

Hadley Roff—the lovable bear who had helped guide the Alioto administration through the political shoals and was brought back to city hall by Feinstein as her deputy mayor—thought she was the "perfect mayor for the time. She was a nurturing, tough, thoughtful person, which is exactly what the city needed. She hated to leave the city, even for important political trips, for fear that something would happen, like a mother."

Feinstein once flew home early from Washington, DC, after a gas pipe ruptured near the Embarcadero, spewing a fine mist over the city. On another occasion, she took the next flight home from Los Angeles when a fireworks factory in the Bayview exploded. Deeply sensitive about the traumas that had ravaged her city, Feinstein was on constant alert against any new calamities.

Despite Roff's respect for his boss's managerial skills, there was not a lot of fun to be found in the Feinstein administration for the roly-poly politico. The mayor seemed as constitutionally barren of a sense of humor as an undertaker. One day Feinstein and Roff met with her gay task force at a restaurant in the Castro. Among the diners was Jim Foster, Feinstein's longtime gay ally, a nattily dressed, balding man with a twitching mustache who put Roff in mind of the old Andy Gump cartoon character. During the meeting, Feinstein—a big fan of military displays and ceremonies—brought up a subject near to her heart. "By the way," she told the group, "next week is Fleet Week, and the bay is going to be filled with aircraft carriers, and there are going to be at least fifteen thousand sailors in town. I hope they're going to be given a warm welcome."

Foster wiggled his brushy upper lip and replied with queenly certitude, "Oh, they will be."

"The whole table broke out in laughter—except for one person," recalled Roff. "She just didn't get it."

Feinstein had a way of bringing out the naughty side of the men around her. Some of it was obvious sexism, the resentful response of politicos whose all-male club was finally invaded by a formidable woman. But much of it was due to her prim and proper attitude. In her role as San Francisco's straight woman, she was simply too tempting a target. At the Monday morning meetings in city hall, as Feinstein drilled down on civic issues, the Irish old boys would roll their eyes while her head was turned and make obscene gestures. Gays loved to slip into Dianne drag on Halloween, wearing Snow White wigs and her trademark suits with floppy bows.

Sister Boom Boom—a half-Catholic, half-Jewish drag queen named Jack Fertig, who wore a whore's makeup and a nun's habit and vamped it up with the other political pranksters in the Sisters of Perpetual Indulgence—was an especially aggravating thorn in Feinstein's side. Boom Boom ran a remarkably aggressive campaign against Feinstein during her 1983 reelection bid, under the slogan "Nun of the Above," eventually winning twenty-three thousand votes.

During the campaign, Boom Boom would pop up in full nun's regalia at Feinstein events—to the obvious annoyance of the Catholic-educated mayor. "Haven't we met before?" Feinstein asked Boom Boom at one function, trying to remain polite as the media gathered around. "No, darling, that was Sister Vicious Power Hungry Bitch," Boom Boom replied, taking the opportunity to pin a "Dump Dianne" campaign pin on her blouse as news photographers' snapped away.

At his own rallies, Boom Boom would provoke howls of laughter by cat-fighting with a Dianne-look-alike drag queen, finally overcoming the lioness mayor by throwing her kicking and screaming over his shoulder and hauling her offstage.

Feinstein was forever being bedeviled and bewildered by San Francisco's more colorful elements. During her mayoral campaign four years earlier, she was challenged by Dennis Peron, the city's leading crusader for legal marijuana, and Jello Biafra, the politically rambunctious lead singer of the San Francisco punk band the Dead Kennedys. Peron, a pixie-like Vietnam veteran and former Milk activist, argued that San Francisco was indeed the kook capital, and that all the kooks should vote for him. Biafra enlivened the campaign by calling for the erection of Dan White statues all over the city, from which the parks and rec department would generate revenue by selling eggs and tomatoes to hurl at them.

The shameless antics of the Mitchell brothers drove Feinstein to distraction, provoking her to launch a ceaseless wave of police assaults on the porn nickelodeon. The brothers responded in typical ballsy style by slapping a big, bold message on their marquee: "Want a Good Time? Call Dianne," followed by the mayor's unlisted home phone number. No sooner would Feinstein switch numbers than her new number would pop up on the theater sign. It turned out that the Mitchell brothers had moles inside the phone company, who in return for supplying Feinstein's private numbers were rewarded with free passes to the nudie theater.

Warren Hinckle—who was keeping alive the old Scott Newhall tradition of provocative, carny-barker journalism as a *Chronicle* columnist— also had a knack for irritating the mayor. Hinckle, a crony of the Mitchells, regularly lampooned her porn obsession. But it was a Hinckle column about rent gouging at the Hotel Carlton, the residential hotel owned by Feinstein, that finally tipped her over the edge. Spying the portly, eye-patched, often sodden scribe at a party in the decorum-conscious Presidio Officers' Club, as he predictably perched himself at the bar, the mayor strode briskly over and tried to dump a drink on top of Hinckle's head. Herb Caen, delighted by the rare flash of mayoral intemperance, later saluted Feinstein in his column. "According to less than reliable two-eyed witnesses, the drink was an Old Fashioned, that being the kind of girl Dianne Feinstein is. Or was."

By making herself the target of the city's demonic energy, Feinstein rendered it fun and largely harmless. She was the firm but fair mother figure that the city ridiculed but needed. She was unable to grab all of the city's wildness and slam it through the swinging saloon doors. But she let everyone know—cops, queers, clowns, con artists—that the party had its limits, and that the city had to get up in the morning and go to work.

In any other city in America, Dianne Feinstein would have been considered a raving liberal. She pushed through the toughest antigun ordinance in the country, banning nearly all residents from owning handguns. She supported gay rights, labor unions, strong environmental protections, and the feminist Equal Rights Amendment. She believed that government should play a nurturing role in the lives of its citizens.

Nationally, her governmental philosophy was distinctly out of step in the era of Ronald Reagan, the man who had ridden the backlash against Bay Area utopianism all the way to the White House.

But in San Francisco, it was a different story. In San Francisco, after the short-lived reign of progressive hero George Moscone and the joyful radicalism of Harvey Milk, the Feinstein administration struck the city's surging left as a false interregnum. The dreamers and firebrands driving San Francisco politics in the late 1970s and 1980s would forever have gnarled and complicated feelings about Dianne Feinstein.

"Dianne was a very gracious person," said Harry Britt, her frequent foe and sometimes admirer. "My grandmother in Georgia was gracious. But when graciousness is a central part of your philosophy, it's limiting. Because grassroots politics ain't gracious, there's a roughness about it. And the gays and lefties in San Francisco—my people—are not always well behaved. Dianne was very much in favor of good behavior.

"She wasn't a social-change person. She didn't want to be the trail-blazer on city ordinances. Her attitude was, 'Don't ask me to do something that nobody has done anywhere else before.' Still, she was a very compassionate human being, on a lot of issues. She was extremely liberal in that old-fashioned sense, meaning giving. And in a world of Ronald Reagan—or Glenn Beck—that is a very welcome sort of decency."

Feinstein gave San Francisco back its solid center, without sacrificing its core values of tolerance and adventure. She made life in the city seem normal again—a significant accomplishment after the macabre events that preceded her rule. But there was something she could never bring to the city: a sense of ecstatic communion. She was smart enough, however, to realize that a sports team could. Feinstein's efforts to bring together San Francisco were about to be boosted greatly by that magical, unifying force that only a championship team can bring to the daily chaos of a city.

34

STRANGE ANGELS

I N THE FALL of 1978, during San Francisco's darkest days, the city's lowly spirit was matched by the dismal play of its beloved football team, the 49ers. Despite their gold rush name, the Niners had never struck fortune. Each year brought their long-suffering fans new heartaches. But by the late seventies, the 49ers had sunk to the most wretched state in team history. And still the 49er Faithful—as the team's largely blue-collar diehards were known—clung on. "Wait 'til next year" became 49ers fans' increasingly worn-out mantra.

The Faithful tried to keep up their spirits with bitter jokes: "Why do they call them '49ers?' Because they never cross the forty-nine-yard line." "What do the 49ers and Billy Graham have in common? They can both fill a stadium and within two minutes have everyone throwing their hands in the air and screaming 'Jesus Christ!'"

The Niners had deep roots in the loam and life of the city. Founded in 1946 by Tony Morabito, a local Italian-American lumber salesman, the 49ers were the only homegrown professional team in San Francisco. Willie Mays and the Giants were imported from New York in 1958, while basketball star Wilt Chamberlain and the Warriors came from Philadelphia in 1962.

Until 1971, the 49ers played in the heart of the city in rough and rowdy Kezar Stadium, a neighborhood arena squeezed between Golden

Gate Park and the Haight. Going to games at Kezar was not for the faint of heart. Fans often arrived drunk and braced themselves further against the sobering ocean drafts by continuing to drink throughout the afternoon. By the end of the game, the crowd was generally in a foul mood, its temper frayed by yet another 49ers loss, the raw weather, and the steady intake of alcohol. As the Niners fled the field into the dark, dirt-floored tunnel that led to their locker rooms, they were often bombarded with beer and whisky—some of it still in cans and bottles. Visiting teams could expect the same salutation. Wise players kept their helmets on as they headed toward the tunnel of doom.

Life in the Kezar bleachers was nasty, brutish, and not short enough. The wood benches were hard on the ass—and since it was easy to sneak into the stadium, there were usually too many asses jammed together. Screeching seagulls swooped overhead, splattering fans below with their foul white glop. Over the years, the benches became so saturated with seagull droppings that you couldn't help but take the stench home with you on the seat of your pants. It was impossible to buy a hotdog without a dozen other grubby hands passing it down the row to you, and the change from vendors often disappeared on the way back. Brawls were a common occurrence, making the stands more dangerous than the field.

There were fleeting glory days for the 49ers. In the 1950s, legendary players like Y. A. Tittle, Joe Perry, and Hugh McElhenny brought the team tantalizingly close to a championship. A 49ers team led by quarterback John Brodie took another run at the gold ring in the early seventies. But Niners hopes were always dashed by rival teams during the playoffs—especially by the hated Dallas Cowboys, who scored three consecutive, dagger-in-the-heart victories over San Francisco in 1970, '71, and '72. When beloved team owner Tony Morabito dropped dead of a heart attack during a game at Kezar, it seemed to sum up the fate of his team.

In 1977 the Morabito family sold the 49ers for $17 million to Edward DeBartolo Sr., a self-made billionaire in Youngstown, Ohio, who had amassed his fortune from building shopping malls. DeBartolo, whose real estate empire included three racetracks, had long wanted to buy a major league baseball team, but he was blocked by league officials, who explained that the horse racing connection would bring an unsavory odor to America's national pastime. The DeBartolo family knew what that was code for. "Mr. DeBartolo happens to be of Italian descent," a family spokesman observed dryly. But the Morabito family had no problem with the Italian heritage of the DeBartolos, who edged out comedian Bob Hope and real estate mogul and future San Diego Chargers owner Alex Spanos for the Niners.

DeBartolo bought the 49ers for his son, Eddie Jr., who at thirty years old became the youngest owner of an NFL team. The short, brash junior DeBartolo immediately alienated the San Francisco sports press and 49ers fan base, coming off as a cocky outsider from a fading smokestack town who had been given a shiny new toy by his daddy. DeBartolo Jr. breezed in and out of San Francisco, commuting from Ohio in the family Learjet, and casually referring to the Niners' hometown as "Frisco"— a violation of local custom that, as Herb Caen had impatiently explained for many years, was committed only by clueless rubes.

Fans grew increasingly sour on the team's new ownership, as Joe Thomas, the general manager installed by DeBartolo, began running the franchise into the ground. Thomas cut stars in their prime such as quarterback Jim Plunkett, who went on to become the most valuable player in the Oakland Raiders' 1981 Super Bowl victory, and traded away valuable draft picks for broken-down veterans like gimpy running back O. J. Simpson.

As the losses piled up and team attendance plummeted, Thomas grew increasingly unhinged. He would show up in the locker room to give the players' rambling pep talks after their defeats, fortified by a drink or three. As the team spiraled downward, the general manager's postgame speeches grew more threatening than inspirational. "If I go down the fucking tubes," he railed at players after another demoralizing loss, "I'm going to take all of you with me!"

The team's thoroughly fed-up fans took out their frustration on DeBartolo whenever he showed up for games at Candlestick Park—the cavernous stadium on a bleak, wind-whipped stretch of the bay where the 49ers had moved after finally abandoning Kezar. DeBartolo took his life into his hands whenever he left the security of his private box to relieve himself in the stadium's public urinals. The young owner was subjected to fusillades of verbal abuse and occasionally to censure of a blunter variety. He was once plunked by a full can of beer.

"I began wondering what I had got myself into," said DeBartolo years later. "I was very happy in my little cocoon doing real estate in a large family company in Youngstown, Ohio. And here I am suddenly in the public eye, getting spit on and battered by cans of beer. That was a tough time."

The lowest point for the 49ers came late in their 1978 season. "We were so bad it was embarrassing," recalled guard Randy Cross. "We were about to go 2–14, and I'll tell you, we weren't nearly that good. I was surprised we won any games at all." On the night of November 27, the Niners were scheduled to play the fearsome Pittsburgh Steelers—the team of the 1970s—in a nationally televised *Monday Night Football* game in Candlestick Park. That morning Dan White crawled through the basement window at city hall with his Smith & Wesson.

A panicky Joe Thomas begged NFL commissioner Pete Rozelle to cancel the game. Thomas was not thinking about the grieving citizens of San Francisco. He was worried about himself, convinced that the killings weren't over yet, and someone might be gunning for him.

"Joe just totally lost it," remembered Carmen Policy, DeBartolo's lawyer, and later president of the team. "He thought there might be some sort of conspiracy. Joe was doing all sorts of crazy things by the end. Eddie was fed up. He told Joe, 'I'm going to the game. If you don't want to come, Joe, stay home.' It was just a terrible situation."

After the 49ers were predictably humiliated by the Steelers, 24–7, DeBartolo finally fired Thomas. It was at this dark hour for San Francisco and its football franchise that DeBartolo began seeking a savior for the team.

THE YOUNG OWNER ZEROED in on Stanford University's maverick coach, forty-seven-year-old Bill Walsh, who had knocked around college and professional football for decades without ever winning a top coaching spot in the NFL. Among the old guard of owners and head coaches who dominated the NFL, Walsh had a reputation as a brilliant but emotionally fragile offensive strategist—a man not built for a commanding role in the brutally competitive world of professional football. He was too sensitive, he became too entwined with his players. He broke down after losing games, he even choked up before every kickoff when "The Star-Spangled Banner" was played. He was a poet in a Stone Age world. Only an NFL owner as young and frantic as DeBartolo would have taken a risk on someone as intriguingly eccentric as Walsh.

Bill Walsh grew up in Southern California and later the Bay Area, the son of a hard-drinking, hard-working man who juggled a job on a Chrysler assembly line with his own auto body shop. Walsh was a moody, indifferent student. "He didn't see the benefit of being a great student, so he wasn't," said Craig Walsh, his son. "He didn't fit into any of the high school cliques; he was always an outsider."

But Walsh had a passion for sports, particularly football and boxing. He began his football career as a high school coach in blue-collar Fremont, California, turning around a losing team with a sophisticated passing game that left opponents dumbstruck. He developed a mathematician's love of diagramming plays, sometimes absentmindedly tracing Xs and Os on the back of his wife Geri when his arm was wrapped around her.

"Everyone [else] was running three yards and a cloud of dust," one of Walsh's high school players recalled. "Under him we ran three wide receivers, a lot of motion and sprint-out pass patterns. Most teams we played only had two receivers in the pass patterns. We had three to five in every play. He'd say [to the quarterback], 'This is your primary receiver, then I want you to look here, then here.' At that time, everybody played a three-deep zone defense. He really attacked that area. He'd flood the zones with two or three receivers."

It was the beginning of Bill Walsh's "West Coast offense," a delicate and brutal ballet whose intricacy would revolutionize professional football. Walsh began to perfect his multidimensional attack while working as an offensive coach for Paul Brown, the legendary head coach of the Cincinnati Bengals. Brown was a stern traditionalist whose teams were noted, as Walsh later observed, for "their almost mechanical, error-free precision." But Walsh was not afraid to challenge his boss, and gradually he began working a more complex architecture into the Bengals' game, with increasingly successful results.

Brown and Walsh had a complicated and troubled relationship. A remote father figure, Brown appreciated his protégé's brilliance while at the same time resenting how he was modernizing the game. Brown dropped hints to Walsh that he was his heir, while doing the same to another assistant coach, Bill Johnson.

But when the day arrived for the aging Brown to hand over the reins of the team, at the end of the 1975 season, the coach devastated Walsh by choosing Johnson instead. Walsh, who learned of Brown's decision from a sports reporter, immediately told his wife, "We've got to get out of here." Walsh uprooted his family from Cincinnati, where Geri and the kids had made a happy life for themselves, and began wandering around the football world in search of a new job—as his itinerant father had done when he was growing up. He was a dazzling football tactician who had devoted his life to the game, but in middle age, he found himself jobless, starting all over again.

Though Paul Brown had bequeathed his estate to someone else, like a spiteful father, he expected Walsh to stick around and still work on it. Walsh applied for head coaching positions with the Seattle Seahawks and the New York Jets, but neither team hired him. He later found out that Brown was poisoning the waters for him, spreading word throughout the league that he was "too soft" to lead an NFL team.

Finally, Walsh managed to land an assistant coach position with the Chargers, despite Brown's efforts to sabotage that opportunity as well. A year later he accepted an offer to coach football at Stanford, leaping at the chance to finally run a team himself. It was here—after working his magic for the Stanford Cardinal, capped by a dramatic comeback victory over Georgia in the 1978 Bluebonnet Bowl—that Walsh came to Eddie DeBartolo's attention.

DeBartolo and Walsh met in the 49ers owner's suite at the Fairmont Hotel to complete the deal. DeBartolo's father was skeptical about Walsh after having phoned around the league and hearing the negative, Brown-inspired chatter about him. Eddie Jr. was not inclined to listen to the old guard's take on Walsh. But before the Fairmont meeting, the elder DeBartolo took aside family attorney Carmen Policy and instructed him to sign Walsh at the lowest possible salary, "so that when we fire him, he won't cost us that much."

The tall, white-haired, professorial Walsh and the squat, dark-mopped, ebullient DeBartolo made an odd pair. But the young owner sensed within the first ten minutes of the meeting that Walsh was his man. Walsh proved to be a shrewd negotiator, wrangling out of DeBartolo an impressive $160,000 starting salary and a generous array of benefits, including a membership in the local country club—a princely package that left Policy to face the old man's wrath back in Youngstown. But in return, the younger DeBartolo made his own stiff demand. "I want a championship," he told Walsh flatly. "Don't take the job if you can't deliver that." There was a long pause. At last, Walsh said softly, "You have my word."

Bill Walsh faced a deeply discouraging task when he took over the 49ers in January 1979. Not only was the team widely considered the worst in the NFL—with less talent and experience than any other franchise—it also had the dimmest prospects for improvement, since Joe Thomas had traded away many of its future draft picks. "It was like raising the *Titanic*. I thought it might be impossible," the coach said later.

Walsh, who had felt disrespected by his colleagues throughout his career, constantly worried that DeBartolo would run out of patience before he could complete the Niners' turnaround. During Walsh's first season, the team ended with the same abysmal 2–14 record that it had the year before. His second season began more brightly, with the team winning three games in a row. But then the Niners went into a tailspin, losing eight straight games, including a spirit-crushing 59–14 blowout by their longtime tormentors, the Cowboys.

After a frustrating loss to the Dolphins, Walsh broke down sobbing on the long flight home from Miami. His assistant coaches formed a circle around him, eating peanuts and pretending to be chatting with the head coach, so the players couldn't witness his breakdown. Walsh was "an emotional basket case," he confessed later. "I felt like a casualty of war being airlifted away from the battlefield."

He had poured all of himself into rebuilding the team, working around the clock, abandoning his family, and drawing on all of his hard-won wisdom to revitalize the lowly Niners. But nothing seemed to be working. Maybe his critics were right; he lacked what it took to succeed in the NFL. He decided to quit when he got home. It took him the rest of the flight, sitting alone in the dark cabin, to pull himself back from the brink.

Throughout his years with the 49ers, Bill Walsh was a tormented soul, constantly racked by self-doubts. He carried within him a Platonic ideal of athletic achievement, a standard of physical and intellectual perfection that always loomed maddeningly beyond his reach. Everything had to be just right; he even carefully selected the paint colors for the Niners' new training facility. He would wander the hallways of the building straightening pictures. DeBartolo used to plague him by tipping them to the side. "He never knew who did it," said the team owner years later.

DeBartolo's mercurial temperament did little to reassure the fragile Walsh. During the decadelong partnership between the owner and coach, Eddie Jr. ordered Policy to fire Walsh "about four or five times," according to the team executive. "Part of my job was to keep those two stable when things were bad, so as not to cause irreparable harm."

Walsh frequently broke down in tears after team setbacks. He would lock himself in his office and listen to mournful Willie Nelson tunes. He asked the team's trainer for medication to help him sleep. "Bill was sensitive about everything," said Policy. "In some way, he was a terrible pain in the neck, a deeply insecure man. He measured everything in terms of money, and he wondered why a star player like Joe Montana made more than him. I'm not saying it was motivated by greed. I think it was a sense of insecurity. How am I viewed, how am I valued? But all this sensitivity was tied to his genius; this almost artistic way that he managed the football field."

ALTHOUGH NO ONE KNEW it at the time, the turning point for Walsh and the 49ers had come in a New York City hotel ballroom in May 1979, when the coach, brilliantly working the NFL draft, selected two players who would change the dark-starred team's history: Notre Dame quarterback Joe Montana, and a little-known Clemson University wide end named Dwight Clark, who would become Montana's favorite receiver.

Joe Montana, the eighty-second choice in that year's draft, did not strike most NFL experts as starting quarterback material. Coltish and spindly legged, at six feet two and 185 pounds, he seemed too fragile for pro football's clash of behemoths. The buzz on Montana was that he was a big-play QB but also erratic and weak armed.

Like Walsh, Joe Montana had to fight his whole life for the top spot. From age eight, when he played midget football in Monongahela—a blue-collar town in western Pennsylvania, cradle of legendary quarterbacks—Montana always started out on teams as the unappreciated backup. The scrawny athlete began his college career at Notre Dame lost in a pack of quarterbacks. He seemed destined to never break out, hobbled by injuries and disregarded by coach Dan Devine. Even after leading the team to the greatest comeback victory in Fighting Irish history, in a game with the University of North Carolina during his sophomore season, Montana continued to ride the bench.

At the start of his junior year, Montana was still listed as Notre Dame's third quarterback. "If I ever thought sincerely about quitting football, it was then," he said later. It was not until the third game of his season, against Purdue, when Montana finally secured the starting position. With just eleven minutes left in the game and Notre Dame trailing, 24–14, Devine inserted him out of desperation. Montana led three scoring drives, and Notre Dame stunned Purdue, 31–24.

It was the beginning of Joe Montana's "Comeback Kid" legend. Again and again, for the rest of his football career, the skinny-legged quarterback would demonstrate a gift for winning under the direst of circumstances. When all seemed lost, when fans were heading for the gates, the Comeback Kid would begin to work his magic, guiding his team to victory through all the mayhem swirling around him with a trance-like calm.

Montana capped his college career with his greatest comeback of all, on a freakishly cold and snowy day at the 1979 Cotton Bowl in Dallas. Suffering from flu and hypothermia, he was pumped full of bouillon at halftime. When Montana ran back onto the field in the third quarter, he had no feeling in his hands, and his team had fallen behind the University of Houston, 34–12. But Montana brought his team back to within striking distance, and with two seconds left in the game, he threw a miracle pass—a low bullet to the right corner of the end zone—and Notre Dame won, 35–34.

During their rookie years as 49ers, Montana and his friendly, shaggily handsome southern roommate, Dwight Clark, seemed dazzled just to be in the NFL. Montana, taking the field during training camp, couldn't believe that he was handing off the ball to O. J. Simpson. Clark, fully expecting to be cut, never unpacked his bags.

Walsh took his time with his young QB, slowly working him into action behind starting quarterback Steve DeBerg. During the 49ers' punishing, lopsided loss to Dallas in Montana's second year, the coach periodically turned toward the bench, as if to decide whether he should throw his young QB into the meat grinder. "I must admit, I was scared," Montana said later. "I didn't want to go in, so every time he looked around, I turned my back on him."

The coach knew that the Niners' offensive line was weak and Montana would be vulnerable, so he took pity on him. Walsh realized that a rookie could be physically and mentally scarred by being thrown too early against the speed and force of NFL opponents.

But by the end of Montana's second season, the coach—certain that his young second-string QB had learned his labyrinthine system—made it clear that he was the franchise's future. Before the start of the 1981 season, Walsh traded DeBerg. It was a major confidence booster for Montana, who had been pitted against rivals throughout his career. Now everything was on the young quarterback's shoulders.

THE 49ERS BEGAN THE 1981 season with low expectations. Ira Miller, the *Chronicle*'s 49ers beat reporter, told fans that "the most they should hope for is a .500 finish, but they shouldn't expect it." Miller predicted that the Atlanta Falcons would win the 49ers' conference and quite possibly the Super Bowl as well. When Atlanta blew the Niners off the field, 34–17, early in the season, it confirmed for many in the local sports media that San Francisco was simply not in the same league as its top rivals.

After the 49ers lost two of their first three games, fans were gripped by the same old sinking feeling. Walsh became obsessed with the idea that the press was out for his scalp, and he later claimed that one publication began running a series on the imminent demise of his 49ers career, although no such articles ever appeared in print. Offensive tackle Keith Fahnhorst, who had weathered the grim Joe Thomas years, decided he couldn't take it anymore and asked the team to trade him. "'Oh hell, here we go again'—that's what I was thinking after those first few games," recalled Fahnhorst. "Thank God the front office didn't listen to me."

Finally, in week four, all of Bill Walsh's sweat and inspiration started to pay off, as the 49ers beat New Orleans and went on to win eleven of their twelve remaining games. The elegant game that he had been designing in his head ever since he was a boy began to materialize on the field. It was a game that relied as much on mental nimbleness as it did on brute force.

"Bill didn't see football as a contest over who was the tougher man," said 49ers linebacker Keena Turner. "His game had to do with quickness of mind and body, and outthinking the opponent. It was more of a chess game than a wrestling match. That's the way he approached it, and he always wanted to be two moves ahead."

Walsh used clever strategies to mask the team's weaknesses, developing a short passing attack to augment the Niners' mediocre running game. He carefully choreographed the opening twenty-five plays of each game, hoping to seize the momentum early and control the direction of the contest. Opponents dismissed the Walsh style as "finesse football" or "swish and sway," stopping just short of calling San Francisco's team "flaming queers."

The coach did not believe in punishing practices. He was not a screamer. He came across more as a professor than a drill sergeant, teaching rather than terrorizing, and invoking epic battles and heroic feats from history to inspire his players. He told the team to call him Bill instead of Coach. But he had learned to keep his emotional distance from players, steeling himself for the day when they would inevitably break down and be cut. He was neither a friend nor a fatherly figure, but players worked hard for his respect. A smile from Walsh on the sidelines was a cherished trophy.

On paper, the 49ers were not a team that should have gone to the playoffs that year. It was a grab bag of promising but still green players, NFL castoffs, and battered veterans. "We were a no-name team," said Turner. But Walsh identified each player's potential before he himself saw it. And he made each of them believe that if they embraced his system, the 49ers could go all the way to the top. Under his leadership, the team at last found that rare chemistry that distinguishes champions, becoming more than the sum of its parts.

The 1981 team was an eccentric collection of athletes. The defense was anchored by two oddball veterans, maniacal linebacker Jack "Hacksaw" Reynolds and future Hall of Fame defensive end Fred Dean. Hacksaw Reynolds set a level of intensity for the team that lit a fire under the younger players. At the beginning of every season, Reynolds dispatched his wife to the Bahamas, knowing that he was not fit to be around while he was in warrior mode. On Sunday mornings, Reynolds rose early, dressed in full battle gear—including his pads and black eye-glare war paint—and ate breakfast in the hotel restaurant, already exuding a game-ready ferocity.

Fred Dean, who was picked up from San Diego midway through the 1981 season, was immediately credited with giving the 49ers the final spark they needed. Dean, a lightning-quick pass rusher, could create chaos in an opponent's backfield. The Pro Bowl player was stung when he found out that the Chargers were paying him less than his brother-in-law made as a truck driver, and he threatened to sit out the next two seasons if he wasn't given a raise. The Chargers decided to dump their disgruntled player instead, and Walsh was only too happy to grab him.

Dean had suffered from crippling migraine headaches after running into a massive TV camera cart on the sidelines during a 1976 game, hitting the metal cart so hard with his head that his helmet cracked. He showed up for his first 49ers meeting pulling a canister of oxygen and sucking from it with a mask. A country boy from Louisiana, where he developed an impressively muscular build in the hay fields, Dean was convinced that he did not need to work out. "Whenever I feel like exercising," he told reporters, "I lie down until the feeling goes away." Dean walked through the 49ers locker room puffing on menthol cigarettes. Walsh finally told him that if he was going to keep on smoking, he had to do it in a training room closet, away from the rest of the team.

The son of a dairy farmworker, Dean was raised to appreciate the rich language of the Bible and Shakespeare. "My parents always read us stories," he explained. "Finding the true meaning of Shakespeare under all those flowery words was always a mind twister for me." Dean was fond of quoting inspirational lines from Shakespeare in the 49ers locker room. One of his favorites was, "Cowards die many times before their deaths. The valiant never taste of death but once." He also recited his own poetry.

Walsh was well equipped to work with idiosyncratic personalities because he was one of them. Out of step his whole career with the NFL mainstream, he knew how to handle the peculiarities of his players. Differences didn't threaten him; he didn't see rebelliousness as an affront.

AFTER TAKING OVER THE Niners, Walsh hired a head athletic trainer named Lindsy McLean, whom he later discovered was gay when McLean brought his partner to a 49ers Christmas party. "I was forty, and I wasn't a player, so I couldn't understand why I had to hide," said McLean. The revelation did nothing to affect Walsh's attitude toward McLean, whom the coach deeply respected for his professional skill. When players learned that McLean was gay, however, a few freaked out. One defensive back refused to let the trainer tape a pulled groin muscle. But most players continued to treat McLean like one of the 49ers family.

Joe Montana, who brought a playground sense of fun to the game, didn't seem to give a damn about McLean's sexuality. "I never heard anything bad from Joe," McLean recalled. "He was just there to play football." Some of the toughest stars on the team, like future Hall of Fame defensive back Ronnie Lott, developed a particularly trusting relationship with McLean. Lott, who subjected his body and those of his opponents to severe punishment, relied on McLean's healing powers.

Even permanently cranky Hacksaw Reynolds warmed up to the Tennessee-born McLean, who shared Reynolds's affection for the player's college team, the University of Tennessee Volunteers.

Despite the occasional ugly remark in the locker room, the trainer continued to care for his players' battered and bruised bodies throughout the Walsh years and beyond. "On the road, I'd go to their rooms and give them their pillow fluff, and I'd give them a little massage or something." If anyone had insulted McLean in his presence, star running back Roger Craig said years later, he or Lott would've "kicked his ass."

When he finally retired from the San Francisco 49ers in 2004 after his sixth-fifth birthday, Lindsy McLean was still the only openly gay trainer in the NFL.

Bill Walsh was also ahead of his time when it came to race relations in the NFL. Concerned about the lack of coaching opportunities for African Americans, he created a Minority Coaches Fellowship Program and invited talented minority coaches to the 49ers headquarters to observe him at work. The league eventually modeled its own minority program on the coach's initiative. Walsh, the perennial outsider, knew what it felt like to be rebuffed and ignored.

The coach also brought in UC Berkeley sociologist Harry Edwards, a black liberation firebrand in the 1960s, to serve as a mentor to African-American athletes on the team. No other NFL coach would have inserted a man with Edwards's outspoken reputation into his organization, and some of Walsh's own staff expressed grave doubts about the decision.

Harry Edwards had drawn the violent wrath of the FBI and white supremacists when he tried to organize a black athlete boycott of the 1968 Summer Olympics. He was denounced by politicians like Ronald Reagan and sports broadcasters like Brent Musburger, who compared him to Hitler; his classes at San Jose State College, where he worked as a sociology instructor, were infiltrated by undercover FBI agents, and he was later fired by the administration; his off-campus apartment was broken into and his dogs were killed; his car was vandalized and repeatedly ticketed by policemen; he was warned by CBS news producer Louis Lomax that he would be targeted by government authorities for assassination if he attended the Olympic Games in Mexico City.

When track star Tommie Smith, who had taken classes from Edwards at San Jose State, raised his clenched fist along with John Carlos on the victory stand in Mexico City, they created an iconic image of black power defiance. Smith, and his mentor Edwards, also won the lasting enmity of the athletic establishment.

By the time Smith returned home with his gold medal, he was an outcast. Nobody would hire him, callers threatened to kill him. "One rock came through our front window in our living room, where we had the crib," Smith recalled. "It seemed like everybody hated me. I had no food. My baby was hungry. My wife had no dresses."

Only one coach in the country was willing to hire Tommie Smith: Bill Walsh. When he was coaching for the Bengals, Walsh tried out Smith as a wide receiver—"just to give Tommie an NFL payday," said Harry Edwards. Smith stayed with the team for three seasons, but never really succeeded in football.

Walsh brought Edwards to the 49ers as an advisor after the two men exchanged a series of letters on race, drugs, and other social aspects of professional sports. Invited to lunch at the 49ers training facility, Edwards ended up spending the night and signing on with the team. It was the beginning of a long conversation about sports, society, and life that did not end until Walsh died in 2007.

"Bill was not just a reader and a thinker," said Edwards, still an imposing edifice of a man at a solid six foot eight and wearing the wraparound shades of his Black Panthers days. "He was the greatest teacher that I had ever been around. He was analytical to the point of understanding how the flap of a butterfly's wing can cause a hurricane. In other words, he understood details and how everything mattered. He was always looking for the missing piece that would put his world together.

"He understood that the demographics of the locker room were changing. He told me that with the exception of Montana, who as the quarterback was really more like a coach, all his leaders on the team were black: Ronnie Lott, Jerry Rice, Roger Craig. He understood that these young black athletes needed to be integrated into the 49ers system. He knew what it was like to be excluded. It was written in his Irish soul. He understood what it meant as a boy when he heard the jokes— you know, like God was kind, he invented wheelbarrows and the Irish to push them."

Walsh knew that his eclectic team mirrored San Francisco itself. And he was well aware that the rest of the league regarded both the team and the city as somehow deviant. The coach used this us-against-the-world feeling to motivate the team. No one in the sports establishment believed in them, he told his players, so they had to believe in themselves.

In the sixth game of the 1981 season, a matchup with the dreaded Cowboys, the 49ers exploded on the field, avenging their lopsided defeat a year earlier and crushing Dallas, 45–14. But on ABC's *Monday Night Football* the following evening, the network did not include any footage of the overwhelming Niners victory in its halftime highlights reel. Walsh, suspecting that ABC was protecting "America's Team" from national humiliation at his own team's expense, erupted at his weekly press conference. "We're not accepted nationally, obviously," he fumed to reporters. "The jockstrap elitists don't consider us in their comfort zone. There are power sources, influence sources in the National Football League, forty-five-year-old men who are football groupies who prefer that we not exist so they can hold on to their football contracts and associations or power groups."

BUT IF THE NATIONAL sports establishment still snubbed the surging 49ers, the team's hometown was starting to glow with the unfamiliar sensation of victory. As the 49ers vanquished one team after the next, including powerhouses like the Steelers and longtime rivals like the Los Angeles Rams, the excitement steadily mounted in the city. It was too soon for euphoria. Wounded by one civic trauma after the next—and long used to the dreariness of defeat on its athletic fields—San Francisco was not quite ready to give itself over to 49ers fever. But the numbness from all those years of grisly headlines slowly began to lift from the city. The glow was spreading, like the first fingers of light over Twin Peaks, after an endless shroud of gloom.

The 49er Faithful in blue-collar San Francisco grew more celebratory each week. Even Eddie Jr. was now greeted warmly in the Candlestick bathrooms as he stood in line to take a piss. Hard-core fans were starting to love the young owner for the passion he brought to the team. "To me, the 49ers is not just a job, it's very personal," he told the press that season. "The team has become my wife." And the Faithful knew exactly what he meant.

After games at Candlestick, George Seifert, the 49ers' up-and-coming defensive coach, would drive to his in-laws' house in the working-class Mission-Geneva district to pick up his kids. As the Niners inched closer to the playoffs, the cheering and car-horn blasting that greeted him in his family's neighborhood grew louder each week.

But the 49ers were no longer the exclusive property of the Faithful. The team was starting to be embraced in every corner of the city. There was something about brainy, brooding Coach Walsh and his band of misfits that struck a chord with the city. Walsh's 49ers seemed like an only-in-San-Francisco phenomenon, but in the best possible way.

The crowds started to squeeze into bars all over the city on Sunday afternoons—from Ed Moose's Washington Square watering hole for literary folk, politicos, and Pacific Heights party drinkers, to Maud's, a flannel-and-blue-jeans lesbian bar in the Haight where the bartender wore a "Don't Fuck with the 49ers" T-shirt.

San Francisco desperately needed to enjoy itself again, and even in the Castro, the suddenly victorious 49ers seemed as good an excuse as any. "You couldn't help get caught up in the excitement even if you weren't a sports fan," said Tom Ammiano, a gay schoolteacher inspired by Harvey Milk to go into city politics. "The team began to bring the city together. I think there was a nude photo of Joe Montana that was being secreted around the Castro. Of course, there was a lot of photo trickery then, so who knows."

"There were a lot of gay folk who knew they should be happy, but weren't quite sure why," said Harry Britt, a hard-core football fan ever since his Texas childhood. "It was more like, 'Why don't they have boy cheerleaders too?'"

San Francisco cineastes were flocking that season to the War Memorial Opera House to watch Abel Gance's *Napoleon,* the 1927 silent classic lovingly restored by director Francis Ford Coppola. At one Sunday screening of the movie, the elegant Beaux Arts temple suddenly erupted in raucous cheers. Touchdown, 49ers! Dozens of the movie fans had come equipped with transistor radios and earphones.

Celebrities began gracing the beer-soaked aisles of Candlestick, where a recently freed Patty Hearst and her bodyguard husband were seen making their way through the crowds. Ferlinghetti pronounced the Niners the city's new gods, while San Francisco old gods Jerry Garcia and Bob Weir paid homage to the football deities at Candlestick. Michael Zagaris, the wild and woolly team photographer better known as "Z-Man," began bringing friends from his other life as a rock 'n' roll shooter to 49ers games, and suddenly psychedelic cowboys like Ramrod—a legendary Grateful Dead roadie and former Merry Prankster—began wandering the sidelines. When a young band from Ireland called U2 showed up in San Francisco on its first tour of America, the four members wisely took the stage at the Old Waldorf wearing Niners' red and gold.

Mayor Feinstein, who didn't know a tight end from a tight ass, suddenly developed a case of 49er fever, demanding that Willie Brown return the mayoral box seats at Candlestick that she had given him in return for securing a $25 million state bailout for the city.

Herb Caen spotted Gina Moscone at Candlestick late in the '81 season. Three years had passed since her husband's murder. The late mayor's widow was still rarely seen in public. But there she was in the stands as the home team trotted off the field to a chorus of cheers after defeating the New York Giants. "We won! We won!" she shouted, her big eyes glimmering in the late afternoon light.

As the excitement grew, San Francisco seemed closer and closer to exorcising its demons—at least those that could be expelled by dancing in the streets and kissing strangers on the lips. All that stood in the way of the city's deliverance was the grim-faced executioner Tom Landry and his horsemen of the apocalypse known as the Dallas Cowboys.

35

PLAYING AGAINST GOD

THE DALLAS COWBOYS organization was the brutal antithesis of San Francisco finesse. The team had become an NFL juggernaut under the ownership of right-wing oilman Clint Murchison Jr. and coach Tom Landry, a God-fearing evangelical from deep in the heart of the Rio Grande Valley who turned the Cowboys into a religion in Texas. Under Landry, the Cowboys became not only America's Team but God's team. Along with two or three other dynasties like the Green Bay Packers and Pittsburgh Steelers, Landry's Cowboys seemed to have a divine calling to rule the NFL year in and year out.

Landry carved out his iconic position in pro football—alongside the likes of Vince Lombardi, George Halas, and Paul Brown—in an era when coaches ruled their empires with omnipotent authority. A chill fear filled the locker room whenever he entered. He stalked the sidelines every Sunday with a stone face, wearing a G-man's brimmed hat and overcoat. He never seemed to flinch under the pressure of combat, not even during the Cowboys' Super Bowl showdowns. "Once you commit yourself to Christ," he explained, "it's in God's hands."

When it came to religion and football, Landry believed in the fundamentals. "The best offense," his NFL mentor taught him, "can be built around ten basic plays, the best defense on two. All the rest is razzle-dazzle, egomania, and box office." The Dallas coach clearly thought that

Bill Walsh's West Coast offense was nothing but fancy-pants gimmickry, as sinuous and vaguely sinister as San Francisco itself.

Walsh and Landry were a clashing contrast in nearly every way. The former approached football like an artistic challenge, the latter like the World War II bombardier that he once was. While Walsh followed a frustrating, circuitous route to the top, Landry had marched up football's chain of command with a military-like precision. Starting as a cocaptain on the University of Texas team, he went on to become a Pro Bowl player and then coach with the New York Giants before finally coming home to take over the new expansion team in Dallas in 1960.

The Cowboys' corporate culture was light years removed from San Francisco values. Clint Murchison, a crony of reactionary FBI czar J. Edgar Hoover and a business partner of Mafia godfathers such as Carlos Marcello, was Richard Nixon's biggest financial supporter during the 1960 presidential race. Some Kennedy assassination researchers have alleged that Murchison played a key role in the plot against JFK. On the afternoon of November 22, 1963, after he was told about the president's assassination, Landry kept on running the Cowboys' practice drills as if nothing had happened just miles away in Dealey Plaza.

Many black players on the Cowboys felt the team was run like a plantation, with white athletes getting preferential treatment. Duane Thomas, a Cowboys running back in the early seventies, later wrote an exposé of the team, lambasting Landry as a "plastic man [with] a John Bircher . . . white supremacist mentality. His philosophy was intimidation, intimidation, intimidation, of the mind and body."

As the 49ers swept to a miraculous 13–3 record in 1981, they headed for the inevitable showdown with the Cowboys, the last obstacle between San Francisco and the Super Bowl. Bitterness and humiliation were built into these Cowboys playoff contests for Niners fans. The feelings were buried as gloomily in San Franciscans' genes as Jews' revulsion for Cossacks. Every time the 49ers seemed to be soaring toward a Super Bowl, the Cowboys would crush their hopes. The fact that Dallas seemed to take a holy warrior's joy in vanquishing "Sin Funcisco," as Herb Caen tongue-in-cheeked it, made the chronic defeats all the more bitter. Caen insisted that he actually didn't mind Dallas calling itself America's Team—but the God's Team business sent him, and the rest of San Francisco, screaming around the bend.

As if there weren't enough reasons to hate the Cowboys, Caen deadpanned as the hour of doom approached, "They have a quarterback named Dan White and a running back named Jim Jones." And QB Danny White was in a typically swaggering Cowboy mood despite the 49ers' upset victory over Dallas earlier in the season. "We don't have much fear of them," White drawled to the press.

Ed "Too Tall" Jones, the giant pass rusher who anchored Dallas's "Doomsday Defense," was even more dismissive. The earlier 49ers victory was a fluke, he informed reporters. "I didn't have a whole lot of respect for the 49ers before that game—I didn't know half the names of the team." And, Jones made clear, his opinion had not improved much since.

Caen, always quick to comfort and tickle his city through its bleak days, tried to prepare San Francisco for the worst. "If Dallas wins today," he wrote on the morning of the epic battle, "it will not be the end of the world—just the end of a very successful season—and San Francisco will continue to be the greatest city in the world, and don't you forget it, buddy."

But the whole city knew how devastating another loss would be. "It would be Jim Jones and the purple Kool-Aid all over again," thought 49ers team photographer Michael Zagaris.

A few days before the Dallas game, Mayor Feinstein invited DeBartolo, Walsh, and a few 49ers executives to dinner at Ernie's, one of the city's most illustrious dining spots, though it looked like a classy Barbary Coast whorehouse. "I don't know if you realize it," Feinstein told the men who held the morale of her city in their hands, "but San Francisco needs this team."

As the 49ers practiced for the big game, Walsh tried to fire up his players with the same underdog resentment he had employed earlier in the season. It was not simply a coaching ploy. He felt it in his guts. Walsh told his men how he felt about the Cowboys. "Their press releases are all about how they are going to kick ass. They're so arrogant down there in the sports empire of the world . . . I'm sick of them. I hope you guys feel the same way I do."

Throughout his career, the Tom Landrys of the league had regarded him with contempt. Now, on the eve of the biggest game of Walsh's life, he still didn't command any respect. Giants coach Ray Perkins, defeated

by Walsh in the previous playoff round, summed up the prevailing sentiment in the NFL when he predicted a decisive Dallas victory over San
Francisco, flatly declaring the Cowboys the "better football team."

WHEN GAME DAY ARRIVED on January 10, 1982, Walsh was in a meditative frame of mind. There were no pep talks in the locker room. He
simply made his way around the room, shaking hands with his players
and offering each man a few words of personal encouragement.

By this stage of the season, the 49ers were a wounded and weary
army. Fred Dean's sternum was so badly bruised that it hurt him to bend
over. Trainers heavily padded his chest to protect it, but Dean knew that
the first hit he took would be torment. Keena Turner had come down
with chicken pox, and the maddening sores had erupted all over his
body, including his mouth and his ass crack. He was slathered in cala-
mine lotion and wrapped in plastic in hopes that the pustules would not
burst in the heat and friction of the game. "I was completely miserable,"
Turner recalled. "But come on, how do you not play in a game like that?"

Many of the players had come down with the flu during the week
before the game—some with a respiratory virus, others with a stomach infection. Keith Fahnhorst, who was hacking and coughing during
practice, remembered being harnessed to an experimental device in
the training room that was supposed to loosen up the congestion in his
chest. "There were these strange prods, like a sci-fi movie. It was bizarre.
I'm not sure if it had any scientific backing." When they ran onto the
field, some players—including Dwight Clark and Randy Cross—already
felt depleted. Cross was puking on the sidelines before the game even
began.

Candlestick Park, crammed to capacity with more than sixty-five
thousand fans, was humming with an unbearable tension. Fans had
lined up for days in the stadium ticket line, braving howling wind and
rain and even hail. They wrapped themselves in plastic, they huddled
together drinking whisky and smoking weed, they slept in soggy sleeping bags. Nothing was going to stop the Faithful from witnessing this
moment of truth.

On the Thursday before the game, the storm that had been besieging
the Bay Area all week became so savage that President Reagan declared

Northern California a disaster area—which is exactly the way he had viewed the San Francisco area ever since he was governor. There were no good wishes extended to the home state team from the White House. San Franciscans assumed that the president would be rooting for Dallas.

On Sunday the clouds finally parted, and as the game began, Candlestick Park was bathed in a cathedral light. Guided by Walsh's opening script, the 49ers got off to a fast start. Driving down the field, Montana threw a fake on Too Tall Jones that sent the monster hurtling into the turf, allowing the QB to hit his favorite receiver, Dwight Clark, with a 30-yard pass that set up a touchdown. As Jones picked himself off the ground, a pumped-up Montana, losing his famous cool, screamed at him, "Respect *that,* motherfucker!"

But the Cowboys quickly responded with their own touchdown, and the game turned into one of the most excruciating seesaw battles ever played on the gridiron. Too Tall Jones and the other Doomsday Defenders subjected Montana to withering pressure throughout the afternoon, forcing the quarterback to constantly dance out of trouble. Montana seemed to play most of the game with one or two defenders hanging on to his arms and legs. Off balance much of the day, he threw three interceptions.

As the teams trotted off the field at halftime, Dallas led, 17–14 and Montana felt lucky the game was that close. In the locker room, Walsh maintained his meditative calm. The 49ers were on a level of combat where a coach's rah-rah rhetoric made no difference anymore. It was now a matter of how deeply the players could plumb their exhausted bodies and spirits.

The game continued to swing back and forth in the second half. The Niners, not used to the high-wire tension of a playoff game, seemed wound too tight, and they kept turning over the ball. As the fourth quarter began, San Francisco was clinging by its fingertips to a 21–20 lead. Then the 49ers fumbled away the ball again near the 50-yard line. Danny White drove the Cowboys for a touchdown, and Dallas retook the lead, 27–21. At that point, as Charle Young—the Niners' eloquent tight end—observed, "A big hush came over the crowd, as if a coffin had closed on our season."

The conclusion seemed preordained. San Francisco fans had suffered through this familiar ending again and again. "You can almost close your eyes and see what happens [next]," CBS football announcer Pat Summerall told the TV audience. "The Cowboys have done it so many times."

When they got the ball back on their own 11-yard line, Montana and the 49ers had less than five minutes to reach the distant goal line. As the young quarterback huddled with his team to begin the most important drive of his career, he went into that deeply calm place where his greatest gifts always awaited him. "I felt numb," Montana said later. "I heard no noise. I didn't know where I was or who I was playing. All I saw was eighty-nine yards between us and the end zone."

Montana immediately recognized that Dallas had dropped into a pass-stopping defense, with six defensive backs and only one linebacker. He knew this left the Cowboys vulnerable to a running game, and he knew that Walsh would grasp this immediately too.

At the most demanding moment in his career, Walsh abandoned his pass-centered West Coast offense and began "shoving the ball down Doomsday's throat," as Montana later put it. Walsh turned to his no-name running back, Lenvil Elliott, who had just been activated for the game after missing the entire season with a damaged knee. Elliot carried the 49ers' season on his back as he ran four of the first eight plays of the drive, baffling the pass-prevent Dallas defense and chewing up the yardage.

With Dallas on its heels from the surprise running attack, Walsh knew that he could now go back to the pass. Montana began to pepper the field with passes to Dwight Clark and Freddie Solomon, another NFL reject who had found new life in Walsh's offense.

As they fought their way down the field, the 49ers were on their last legs. Randy Cross kept vomiting in the huddle, forcing his teammates to move a few yards away to escape the mess. "Aw, man, R.C.," they recoiled, "what's wrong with you?" With 1:15 left in the game, Montana had driven the 49ers to the Dallas doorstep, on their opponents' 13-yard line. As Walsh called a time-out, the ailing Clark fell to one knee, utterly drained.

When action resumed, Elliot took the ball again, grinding his way to the Dallas 6-yard line. Now it was third down and three. San Francisco was tantalizingly close to the end zone, with less than a minute remaining in the game. Walsh took advantage of a Dallas time-out to confer with Montana one last time on the sidelines. The coach chose a play that required his QB to roll to his right and hit Solomon in the end zone, with Clark as a secondary target if his first receiver was covered.

"Joe, be very cautious," Walsh told him. "It's only third down. If we miss on this one, we still have another shot at putting it in."

"Bill, don't worry," replied Montana, still in his deeply tranquil zone. "If it's not there, I'll put it up so no one will catch the ball."

WHEN MONTANA RAN BACK onto the field, it was twilight. The crowd seemed lost in a dream that was sure to end terribly.

Montana's teammates were deeply familiar with the play that he called in the huddle. They had rehearsed it so often in practice that they were sick of it. But as soon as the ball was snapped, the team's choreography began to break down. Solomon slipped and fell on the soggy Candlestick turf, and as Montana rolled to his right, there was no receiver to hit in the end zone. Too Tall Jones and a couple of other Dallas defenders were now in hot pursuit of the quarterback, and Montana pump-faked the ball twice to slow them down. Colors—each player a bright and vivid shape—and silence. That's what it was like for Montana in these moments of frenzied urgency on the field. Suddenly Clark emerged in the end zone, running along the back line toward the right corner. By now, Jones—Montana's brutal shadow all day long—was nearly on top of him. There was no more time. Backpedaling awkwardly, Montana threw off-balance in Clark's direction.

As the high, soft pass arced into the air, it looked like a prayer. Montana himself thought it was uncatchable. "I thought it was an arm's length above his head." But Clark was in the air, soaring higher than he had ever been, his body at full extension. With his fingertips, the receiver somehow gripped the ball in midflight, juggled it briefly, and then brought it with him to the ground.

The moment Clark's feet hit the turf, the crowd exploded as if it had been holding its breath for years. Montana, sprawled on the ground and surrounded by huge bodies, couldn't see anything, but his silent bell jar was suddenly shattered by the cacophonous roar, and he knew that Clark had completed the miracle. Michael Zagaris, crouched in the far corner of the end zone with his camera, took a shot of the euphoric moment as the referees flung their arms in the air to signal touchdown, and a sea of fans leaped into the air, nearly as high as Clark. This was the exact instant of San Francisco's salvation.

The terror was not quite over for San Francisco. Cornerback Eric Wright, part of the 49ers' brilliant young defensive backfield, had to save the day by making a desperate, clawing tackle from behind on Dallas receiver Drew Pearson as the Cowboys tried their own comeback in the final seconds of the game. Then Danny White fumbled away the ball, and the game at last belonged to San Francisco by a wafer-thin 28–27.

The 49ers-Cowboy game would be immortalized as one of the greatest battles in NFL history, and Dwight Clark's heroic leap into the ages would forever be known as "The Catch." The game marked the beginning of one sports dynasty and the fall of another.

A bitter Tom Landry insisted that Dallas was still the better team, except for Joe Montana's black magic. "Montana has to be the key," brooded the Cowboys coach after the game. "There's nothing else there except him." Landry, whose coaching fortunes went into decline, later said that he never recovered from the defeat.

After leaving every ounce of himself on the field, Montana stumbled off in "a dazed dream" and immediately collapsed in the locker room. Eddie DeBartolo, whose view of the Catch had been blocked by the ass of a police horse on the sidelines, came bursting into the locker room to share his effusive joy. "I'm so proud," he said, throwing his arms around the giants who towered over him. "I don't think anything can top this in my life. I love you all."

Thousands of ecstatic fans stormed the field, cutting squares out of Candlestick's sodden turf for souvenirs. But many of the Faithful simply remained in their seats long after the game was over, some in tears, letting all the tragedies of the past come spilling out of them.

Meanwhile, bedlam reigned in the city. As he drove home from Candlestick, through Hunters Point, down Army Street, and into Noe Valley, one long-suffering fan screamed out the window of his car the whole way—and every neighborhood answered his wail. It reminded him of the day that the Japanese surrendered and the whole city went mad, in anguished celebration.

Back in the Haight, the dykes at Maud's came careening out of the bar and into the street. They cheered as a trio of middle-aged black women, who had slipped into their old high-school cheerleader skirts and sweaters, paid hip-shaking tribute to the triumphant Niners. Hordes of other fans—including long-haired veterans of Haight-Ashbury's glory days and the tough Irish families who had long been the neighborhood's backbone—snarled traffic, embracing one another in the street like survivors of a terrible siege. Some particularly nimble celebrants climbed onto the roofs of stalled buses and dazzled the crowd below with acrobatic cartwheels.

"It was like somebody had sprinkled fairy dust on the whole city," said Cheryl Bertelli, one of Maud's delirious patrons. "People were hugging strangers, laughing, singing. It was the Summer of Love all over again."

The next morning, Herb Caen spoke for the entire city, as usual, when he wrote: "Oh, I wanted the Niners to win! I especially wanted them to beat Dallas, which exalts itself as 'God's Team.' Lordy knows the God-fearing folk in that sector have long derided Sin Funcisco as Sodom West, overdue for obliteration by fire, brimstone, and earthquake. One wonders what tortures they are now going through, now that 'America's Team' is God-forsaken and the scarlet-clad representatives of Babylon by the Bay are on their way to the Super Bowl."

After the emotional whirligig of the Dallas game, the 49ers' Super Bowl battle with the Cincinnati Bengals two weeks later seemed almost anticlimactic. It was enlivened, however, by the underlying Oedipal drama pitting Bill Walsh against his former Bengals' mentor Paul Brown, who was now president of the team. Though Walsh insisted that revenge was not a motivating factor for him, his players knew how sweet the victory was for their coach when they beat the Bengals, 26–21. For the first time in football history, the San Francisco 49ers were champions.

TWO DAYS LATER, THE 49ers returned home from the Silverdome in Pontiac, Michigan, for a Super Bowl victory parade through downtown San Francisco. As the team set out along the Embarcadero on its way to Civic Center, riding in motorized cable cars and vintage convertibles festooned with red and gold balloons, the city seemed strangely empty. Mayor Feinstein, squeezed between Walsh and DeBartolo in an open car, voiced the fear that was starting to grip all three of them. "What do we do if nobody comes?" she said. A familiar gloom was creeping over

Walsh. He was certain that the parade would be a terrible humiliation for his team.

Then the fleet of vehicles turned onto Market Street, the city's main commercial artery, and the team was greeted by an explosion of cheering, screaming, horn-blowing humanity. The boulevard was jammed with more than a half million ecstatic 49ers lovers, the biggest celebration in San Francisco's history since the end of World War II. People were clinging to light poles, jumping up and down on top of cars, and hanging out of office tower windows. The sky was a blizzard of confetti.

Tears flooded Walsh's eyes. It was at that moment when he finally felt in his heart what his team's amazing odyssey had done for the beleaguered people of San Francisco. "I saw every cross section of people, all standing in unison, from the executives who came out of the office buildings to the people who clean the streets, right next to each other, screaming. It was just the most electrifying moment I've ever had.

"Seeing that outpouring of emotion that day, I realized what an historic moment it was, not just for the team, but for the entire city. We were salving wounds and lifting spirits that had been very low for a long time."

Feinstein too felt the veil begin to finally lift that afternoon. "I saw with my own eyes what a team can do for a city."

The parade was a uniquely San Franciscan celebration. As the players chugged along on the cable cars, swarmed by fans reaching out to touch them, Eric Wright, one of the heroes of the Dallas game, turned to Zagaris. "Hey, Z-man, some motherfucker's been chasing the car yelling your name." Zagaris scanned the vast throng and saw a familiar face: Dennis Peron, the city's pixie-ish pied piper of marijuana. Peron had decided that grass could save humanity ever since it helped him survive the war in Vietnam, where he was forced to bag dead soldiers as punishment after refusing to leave his job as an air force postal clerk and shoot at Vietcong soldiers during the Tet offensive of 1968.

Zagaris, who had once been busted during a raid on Peron's marijuana supermarket, peered down at the Johnny Appleseed of cannabis as he ran alongside the cable cars. "Thank you, thank you for winning the Super Bowl!" Peron trilled, digging into a shopping bag filled with joints and flinging them to the players.

"Actually, they weren't just joints, they were bombers," recalled

Zagaris. "Ronnie Lott was saying, 'Hey, Z, I got three under my foot.' Wright was going, 'I got two!' The players wanted to know if the weed was any good. I said, 'Trust me, it's good.'"

Games are just games. No team, no matter how heroic, can undo tragedies or erase history. Life is what it is. And yet there are moments when a team seems to come to the salvation of its wounded fans. When *their* victories seem *our* victories. Victories that we can savor for a lifetime, whenever we need to be reminded that life is not just a losing battle against disappointment and defeat.

Walsh himself, the chronic worrier and self-doubter, would, in the end, psyche himself out of his job. In 1989, after winning his third Super Bowl victory, an emotionally exhausted Walsh called it quits. But by then, the 49ers had done their job for San Francisco, helping reverse the city's fate.

Cities, like people, have souls. And they can be broken by terrible events, but they can also be healed. It was just a game. It was just one catch. But sometimes that's enough.

36

THE CITY OF
SAINT FRANCIS

I N JANUARY 1984 San Francisco suffered a disturbing flashback when Dan White was released from Soledad Prison after serving little more than five years for the carnage at city hall. His release reignited a spasm of fury, with protests breaking out in the Castro—where nine thousand gathered and chanted "Kill Dan White"—and Union Square, where some demonstrators wore buttons declaring themselves members of the "Dan White Hit Squad."

To avoid violence, authorities paroled White to Los Angeles, where he changed his name, grew a beard, and worked out obsessively. One day White invited his old friend Frank Falzon to visit him. White, barred from driving, took the San Francisco cop on a long trek through the San Fernando Valley, where he lived. While they were walking, White made a second confession to his friend that left Falzon feeling "like I had been hit by a sledgehammer."

"I was on a mission," White told Falzon. "I wanted four of them. Carol Ruth Silver, she was the biggest snake of the bunch. And Willie Brown, he was masterminding the whole thing."

White's eruption that day in November 1978 had not been temporary insanity, Falzon realized. It was premeditated murder. The enraged former supervisor had planned to decapitate San Francisco's liberal leadership.

He was trying to rescue San Francisco, the city he loved, White told Falzon. He expected his old friend to sympathize. But Falzon was already starting to realize that the San Francisco that White was trying to protect—the one where they had both grown up—was just make-believe. "What did we really know?" said Falzon years later. "Afterward we found out that Catholic priests were having sex with boys. We were living in a fantasy world." White was trying to save a world that never existed.

After finishing his yearlong parole, White headed back to San Francisco in 1985, despite Mayor Feinstein's pleas for him to stay away from the city. He moved back into his old Excelsior home with his wife and two young sons, one of whom had been born with Down syndrome while White was in prison. Death threats were slipped under White's door. But Dan White was already a ghost. He rarely went outside; the front yard was choked with weeds. He grew estranged from Mary Ann, who was forced to support the family with her schoolteacher's salary.

One day John Barbagelata, long retired from San Francisco's political wars, was walking in St. Francis Wood. As he passed the Moscone family home, he was shocked to see Dan White come riding by on a bicycle. White had never expressed remorse or apologized to the families of his victims. But that day the assassin was clearly wrestling with a need for absolution. White stopped to talk with Barbagelata, but he found little comfort there. He had warned him, Barbagelata reminded White, not to get involved in San Francisco politics. "But you didn't listen," said Barbagelata.

On the afternoon of October 21, 1985, Dan White's body was found by his brother inside a white Buick sedan parked inside his garage. White, whose lifeless hands were clutching photographs of his family, had run a garden hose from the exhaust pipe into a partially opened car window. He left four suicide notes to family members. None of the letters mentioned George Moscone or Harvey Milk.

There was no celebration in the gay community over White's suicide. Newspaper reporters searching for searing quotes in the Castro found only weary emotions. "I'm glad his conscience caught up with him," one

Castro resident told the *Los Angeles Times*. It was the strongest feeling anyone seemed capable of mustering.

By the time White died, a phantom from another era slipping into the gray mists, the Castro itself seemed like a ghost town.

"The whole [Dan White] story had dangled like a sentence without a period. And now we have that period," said the *San Francisco Chronicle*'s Randy Shilts, the only daily newspaper reporter in the country assigned to cover gay issues. Shilts's coverage of the Harvey Milk political drama had become a compelling book, *The Mayor of Castro Street*. Now Shilts was deeply immersed in another epic story—about a scourge that threatened to destroy the gay community.

The AIDS (acquired immunodeficiency syndrome) virus slipped stealthily into San Francisco's bloodstream during the wild bacchanalia of the late 1970s. By the time the epidemic reached its fever pitch in the mideighties, more than half of the city's gay population was infected. So many young men were suffering and dying, it seemed like San Francisco was at war. Men in the prime of life crept through the city streets with sunken faces and withered legs, hobbling along on canes and walkers. Men hideously disfigured by florid lesions all over their faces, necks, and arms were greeted by appalled and awestruck reactions everywhere they ventured. The first case of Kaposi's sarcoma (KS) in San Francisco, a rare skin cancer that usually struck middle-aged men of Mediterranean and Jewish descent, was reported in April 1981. By then young gay men were also falling sick with a virulent type of pneumonia and exotic afflictions found only in people with ravaged immune systems.

Bobbi Campbell—a boyishly handsome hospital nurse who led a second life as a drag queen nun (Sister Florence Nightmare) in the Sisters of Perpetual Indulgence—was one of the first people diagnosed with KS. He noticed the purple blotches on his feet after hiking with his boyfriend in Big Sur, and at first he assumed they were blood blisters. But when they got bigger, Campbell went to Dr. Marcus Conant, a dermatologist at the UC San Francisco medical complex overlooking Golden Gate Park, and Conant recognized it as one more strange occurrence of KS. Campbell immediately went public with his diagnosis, writing a story about his "gay cancer" in the *Sentinel,* a local gay newspaper, and persuading a drugstore in the Castro to post photos of Kaposi victims in its window as a warning to the community.

A political comrade of Cleve Jones's urged the activist to meet with Campbell, who showed him the lesions on his feet and told him about his plans to start a gay cancer support group. Later, over dinner, Marc Conant filled Jones in on what he was learning about the mysterious new plague. Jones turned pale and ordered a stiff drink. He was thinking about all the young men with whom he had juicily joined flesh, and about how the Castro had turned itself into one big bed. "We're all dead," Jones muttered.

THE NONSTOP PARTY THAT was San Francisco seemed to end almost overnight. Paul Volberding, a young oncology doctor from the Midwest who worked late hours at the San Francisco campus of the University of California, used to peer wide-eyed at the wild celebrations that poured out of the bars and bathhouses in the Castro no matter what hour he drove through the neighborhood on his way to work or back home. "Suddenly it just all disappeared," he recalled.

Joel Selvin, the night-crawling rock critic for the *Chronicle,* immediately noticed the change. "In the old days, fully a third of every restaurant crowd, every nightclub, every parking lot was homosexuals. They spent more, they yelled more, they had more fun—and they were the best dressed. They were the cheerleaders of our culture. Then, poof, they were gone. The restaurants were half-empty, the clubs weren't as jammed. A light was turned off in this town. Because if you left the straights to handle the party, it just wasn't going to happen. One day it was just, 'Hey, where did the gay guys go?' You'd walk around town and see all these garage sales on the street. They were gone—only their stuff was left behind."

In the early days of the plague, when nobody knew for certain how the infection was spread, a shudder went through the entire city. Customers avoided restaurants run by gays and even shunned Castro clothing stores, not wanting to try on shirts or pants that might have been worn by a victim of the disease. When Zuni Café founder Billy West fell sick, his business partners decided to keep his illness quiet. "No one knew anything—there wasn't even a name for AIDS then," said Vince Calcagno. "We kept Billy's condition a secret for a good five years. We knew it would ruin the restaurant. People thought it could be foodborne."

As the panic spread, sick men were fired from their jobs and evicted from their apartments—sometimes by fellow gay employers and landlords. Once, after Dr. Volberding and an AIDS patient were invited to appear on a local TV show, the sound technician refused to put a microphone on the sick man.

The medical workers on the front lines of fighting the epidemic were not immune to the rising panic. Volberding, who had begun treating the first wave of AIDS patients at San Francisco General Hospital, was starting a family with his wife, Molly, around the same time. In the early days of the epidemic, he frequently woke up in a cold sweat after having nightmares that he had infected his two young children. One day Molly, also a physician, noticed a little red mark on the ear of their son Alex. "Anybody else—a grandmother in Iowa—would've said, 'That's just a stork bite.' But I remember looking at that and saying, 'Could that be Kaposi's?'" Volberding and his wife were so frightened of what the plague could do to their family, they had to agree not to talk about it with each other.

Volberding, who cofounded the world's first AIDS clinic at San Francisco General in January 1983, sometimes had difficulty staffing ward 5B. Once he hired a data processor to work in the clinic's computer room, but when he showed up for work, the new employee insisted that the room be disinfected from top to bottom with bleach. "We told him, 'This job is not for you,'" said Volberding. On other occasions, new employees would disappear after their first or second day on the job, when their spouses became hysterical about where they were working.

But ward 5B soon developed a highly dedicated core team of doctors, nurses, and orderlies. Dr. Constance Wofsy, a cofounder of the clinic, had a simple reply for anyone who questioned her choice of workplaces. It was a doctor's job to take care of the sick, even if that put you at risk. Period.

Volberding knew that frontline AIDS work was above and beyond the call of duty for most health workers. But the ward 5B staff was an unusual crew. As a boy, Volberding—who grew up on a dairy farm near Rochester, Minnesota, the son of German-American Lutherans—often heard about people who had "a calling" in life. "The people who worked in ward 5B clearly had that sense of calling. We worked long hours and took the job home with us. We became friends with the patients. They were our same age, they listened to the same music, they ate at the same restaurants. Some of the clinic workers' friends and lovers were patients. And some of the clinic workers became patients themselves. You're trained as a doctor to separate yourself from those whom you're treating. But we couldn't possibly do that."

One day, Lisa Capaldini, a young intern in the AIDS ward, was saying good-bye to a patient named Gordon with whom she had grown close. Gordon was about to be discharged, but he was blind and dying, and Capaldini knew that she would never see him again. While she hovered over his bed, the intern began to cry. "And I thought, 'That's okay, he won't know.' Then I realized that my tears were dropping on his face. And I thought, 'Busted.'"

Gordon reversed roles with Capaldini and began to comfort the young doctor. By the time she fled the room, Capaldini was sobbing uncontrollably. A nurse named Diane Jones, one of the tough angels who were the clinic's heart and soul, took Capaldini aside and told her she should be proud of everything she had done for Gordon. "That was one of the best moments in my medical training," recalled Capaldini years later. "To have a medical professional say it's okay to have feelings. It made me a better doctor and, I think, a better person."

San Francisco General's ward 5B became a model for AIDS care throughout the world. The clinic staff quickly realized that it had to adapt to the harrowing new medical world in which it found itself, battling an incurable and lethal disease that was devastating a unique part of the population. Ward 5B pioneered the development of what later became known as patient-centered care.

"Back then it meant that a lot of hospital rules just had to go out the window," said Diane Jones. "Such as visiting hours. People were sick and many were dying. They needed people with them, and they needed to decide who was going to be with them. Not just a father or mother or legal spouse. We said patient-centered care means you get to decide who comes into your room and who gets to be with you when you're dying."

The AIDS ward began to take on the flavor of the predominantly gay patient base that it was serving. Volunteers began flocking to the clinic, bringing bouquets and toiletries and fashionable-looking bathrobes, because no patient still in his right mind wanted to be caught dead in a hospital gown. Gay nightclub diva Sharon McNight rolled her piano into the ward and belted out songs like "Stand By Your Man" as the patients sipped champagne and screamed encouragement. For many in the audience, it would be the last show they ever saw. Rita Rockett brought her tap-dancing act, along with baskets of food, to the hospital so often that a lounge in ward 5B was named after her.

Meanwhile, another beloved San Francisco institution, Mary Jane Rathbun—aka Brownie Mary—dispensed her magical cannabis-laced cookies and brownies to ward 5B patients. The elderly Brownie Mary, a former pancake house waitress forced into retirement by a back injury, had turned to the marijuana bakery business after finding that smoking weed helped alleviate her pain. Brownie Mary was convinced it could do the same for AIDS patients, and she inspired one clinic researcher to undertake his own scientific studies of medical marijuana.

THE AIDS PLAGUE COULD have tipped San Francisco back into the bubbling cauldron from which it had just emerged. Terror and hatred could have torn apart the city, with opponents of the gay revolution condemning it for breeding the contagion and using it to inflame anti-homosexual passions. In fact, this was happening at the national level, as conservative crusaders like Patrick Buchanan flayed the suffering gay population with their hellfire rhetoric. "The poor homosexuals," remarked Buchanan, his voice dripping with scorn. "They have declared war upon nature, and now nature is exacting an awful retribution."

Instead the epidemic brought out the best in San Francisco. The city's response became a model for the nation. Inspired by the heroic efforts of the staff and volunteers at the AIDS clinic—who calmed San Francisco by talking openly and rationally about the epidemic in the media and public forums—the city as a whole began to rally around its stricken brothers.

In 1985 a retired grandmother named Ruth Brinker, alarmed to hear that AIDS patients were dying at home of malnutrition, began cooking hot meals in her kitchen and delivering them to the sick. Brinker had little money, and her only business experience was running her own antique shop. But she knew how to cook, and within three years she was serving five hundred nutritious meals a day to AIDS patients. Project

Open Hand, whose motto was "Meals with Love for People with AIDS," outgrew Brinker's kitchen, moving into a church basement, and then into its own headquarters, where it inspired similar groups all over the world.

Other volunteer groups also sprang into action, like community firefighters rushing to the scene of a blaze or people filling sandbags on a crumbling levee. "I look back on those days," said Tom Nolan, executive director of Project Open Hand, "and if you were a gay man or almost anybody [living in San Francisco] and you're seeing the suffering on the streets, the KS lesions all over people's faces, and you saw all that, how could you *not* do something . . . There was something for everybody to do."

The San Francisco AIDS Foundation, jump-started by Cleve Jones, lobbied for government funding for research and education. Project Inform educated those infected with HIV (human immunodeficiency virus), the virus that causes AIDS, about the latest medical therapies. Shanti Project offered emotional solace and practical support to people with AIDS, and the Coming Home Hospice was founded to help those who were dying. The Sisters of Perpetual Indulgence began working like real nuns, raising money for the sick at church bingos and organizing a charity dog show featuring Shirley MacLaine as emcee.

The Sisters, long estranged from the Catholic Church, began to find a surprising amount of sympathy in church circles. For a long time, the Most Holy Redeemer parish in the heart of the Castro provided the San Francisco police force with many of its toughest Irish cops. The church was a target for gay protesters after the Anita Bryant ordinance passed in Florida and after the Milk and Moscone assassinations. But the parish began to change with the times, and in 1985 some church members started an AIDS support group. John Quinn, San Francisco's enlightened archbishop, regularly visited Most Holy Redeemer throughout the 1980s to demonstrate his support for AIDS patients and their caregivers. When the church began reaching out to suffering gay men, it was the clearest sign that the savage epidemic also had a strange power to heal. These acts of human grace, in the midst of unspeakable anguish, began to help close San Francisco's deepest wounds.

Even the Mitchell brothers jumped into the AIDS battle, producing a safe-sex remake of *Behind the Green Door*. The film's leading lady—

Elisa Florez, aka Missy Manners—had grown up in a conservative Catholic family and was a former intern for Utah Republican senator Orrin Hatch and the daughter of a Reagan administration official. But the buxom, golden-skinned Florez saw her porn debut as God's work. "This film is putting an important message out there. You have to have a social conscience when it comes to having sex. We made condoms exciting. After this film, I can put condoms on a man better than anybody. I can slip them on with my mouth, and a man would never even know it."

Early in the epidemic, members of ACT-UP—the militant group formed by gay playwright Larry Kramer to agitate for a stronger government response to AIDS—showed up at the opulent opening night of the San Francisco Opera season to disrupt the festivities. As the activists ran screaming up and down the aisles of the opera house, some wealthy patrons groused that they should be arrested. But Angela Alioto—who was in the audience with her father, whom she would follow into city politics—cheered on the activists. "I thought it was pretty cool," she recalled. "I'm thinking these are human beings who want to be treated like human beings."

ACT-UP played an important role in focusing public attention on the epidemic, particularly in New York and Washington, DC. But in San Francisco, the group seemed largely unnecessary.

Under Mayor Feinstein, San Francisco mounted the most aggressive campaign in the country to confront the health crisis. In 1984 alone, San Francisco poured $7.6 million of scarce city funds into AIDS programs, while New York, with triple the caseload, was spending little over $1 million. In the mid-1980s, San Francisco spent more on AIDS than the entire federal government under President Reagan. When Supervisor Harry Britt brought Feinstein the first AIDS funding proposal in 1982, the mayor simply told him, "Fund everything."

Feinstein was not only familiar with medical crises and protocol, she had friends who were sick with the virus. She proved to be the best possible civic leader for the crisis. "Dianne spent more time visiting AIDS patients in hospitals than I did," said Britt. "She was a giver, she was a very compassionate person. I don't want to say 'queenly,' because that sounds negative, but she was a good queen."

"My staff and budget at the AIDS clinic doubled every year," recalled

Volberding, "and Feinstein didn't blink an eye. She was completely responsive to whatever I asked from her."

Other metropolitan areas with big gay populations lagged far behind San Francisco. Some cities tried to dump their AIDS patients on San Francisco. In one notorious incident in 1983, a hospital in Gainesville, Florida, put a seriously ill patient on a plane and deposited him at San Francisco General—a maneuver that Feinstein denounced as "outrageous and inhumane." When the twenty-seven-year-old AIDS patient died in ward 5B two weeks later, thousands of miles from home, Feinstein commented, "It is sad that a young man had to spend his final days as a medical outcast." Florida health officials admitted that they were having difficulty finding medical professionals who were willing to treat AIDS patients. "We are seeing people take any opportunity within the law to avoid providing care," said a Florida Health Department spokesman.

FEINSTEIN TRIED TO SPARK a nationally coordinated response to the epidemic, pushing the US Conference of Mayors to establish an AIDS task force in 1984. The federal government should have played that role. But the Reagan administration turned a blind eye to the rapidly spreading disease. The White House was under the sway of its Christian right supporters—many of whom, like Moral Majority leader Rev. Jerry Falwell, viewed the plague as "the wrath of God upon homosexuals." Even though the Reagans were friends with a number of Hollywood entertainers afflicted by AIDS, including actor Rock Hudson, the president refused to even utter the name of the disease in public. In 1985, as the contagion spread like wildfire across America and around the globe, Reagan slashed AIDS funding in his annual health budget, at the same time his health secretary was calling the disease her "number one health priority."

If Dianne Feinstein was the best possible local leader in the war on AIDS, Ronald Reagan was the most disastrous leader for the country to have sitting in the Oval Office. The demon virus took root in the population at the worst possible political moment. "The AIDS story is the purest illustration of how this administration deals with health concerns," said Stanley Matek, former president of the American Public Health

Association, during the height of the plague. "They tend to see health in the same way that John Calvin saw wealth: it's your own responsibility, and you should damn well take care of yourself. This epidemic, however, has tested the limits of that philosophy."

At a time when the American public desperately needed reliable medical straight talk about AIDS, Reagan blocked his widely respected surgeon general, Dr. C. Everett Koop, from delivering speeches or talking with the media about the disease. "For an astonishing five and a half years," Koop recalled later, "I was completely cut off from AIDS." White House advisors, he said, dismissed the epidemic as a problem for gays, junkies, and other social undesirables. The president's aides, according to Koop, "took the stand, 'They are only getting what they justly deserve.'"

Ron Reagan became so upset with his father's lack of leadership on AIDS that he intervened with his parents. "I went to my mom, because I knew she was ahead of him on that curve. She was a doctor's daughter, and all that. And I knew they had gay friends. I remember parties at our house when I was growing up where at least one gay couple was there. Patti's godmothers were a lesbian couple. And Cesar Romero was one of my mom's gay escorts when my dad was out of town. Patti would get all mad about it, like my mom was cheating on my dad somehow. But *hello!* Later, in the White House, [gay New York society fixture] Jerry Zipkin was one of my mom's walkers."

Young Reagan pleaded with his mother to get the White House moving on AIDS. "I just knew that people were suffering and dying," he said, "and the government had to move more quickly. If for no other reason than it was terrible PR to just stand there. When people they knew started dying, like Rock Hudson, it finally came home for them."

But President Reagan waited nearly two years after Hudson died before he at long last addressed the raging epidemic in public, speaking at the Third International AIDS Conference in Washington, DC, in May 1987, with actress Elizabeth Taylor urging him on from the wing of the stage. Reagan's public remarks, which came near the end of his presidency, did not lead to a late-hour burst of leadership on AIDS. To the very end, his administration remained politically incapable of mounting a full public health campaign. "In the history of the AIDS epidemic, President Reagan's legacy is one of silence," later remarked Michael Cover, the former public affairs director of the capital's leading AIDS clinic—a facility just a few blocks from the White House that was never visited by the president or first lady.

THE PEOPLE OF SAN Francisco realized early in the plague that Washington was not going to help them. They had to look out for themselves. So San Francisco took care of its own sick and dying, its own scorned brothers. The city had learned to embrace these men when they were young and wild, fleeing Kansas and Wyoming and Alabama for San Francisco's frontier freedom. Now, as they lay in sweat-soaked sheets, closer to death than life, these young men were once again wrapped in San Francisco's arms.

By taking care of these suffering men, San Francisco finally became a united city. "The city learned to behave like one organism, to fight against the disease," observed Volberding. This was the true birth of San Francisco values. The plague burned down to the city's core, where one simple truth was revealed: we must take care of each other. No matter how sick or helpless or untouchable people are.

Some said that this fundamental sense of human solidarity was wired into the very origins of the city, into San Francisco's namesake, Saint Francis—the wandering friar who renounced his family's wealth for a life of humble service, calling all creatures his brothers and sisters, and devoting himself to the poor and wretched. But it was not until the epidemic invaded the city that San Francisco truly became worthy of the saint's name.

As the years went by and AIDS researchers still struggled to find a cure, the disease came closer to home for many San Franciscans. In 1988 Bill Walsh's oldest son, Steve, was diagnosed with the infection. The coach, who had long neglected his family for football, was overcome with feelings of guilt. He tried to reach out to his son, but it was difficult. Steve Walsh, who had left home early and made a separate life for himself in Colorado as a TV and radio reporter, had been estranged from his father for so long that conversation did not come easily.

A deeply private man, Bill Walsh couldn't bring himself to talk about his son's disease in public, always referring to it as "leukemia." But after

Steve died in 2002, Walsh finally spoke the truth in a conversation with the veteran 49ers trainer Lindsy McLean.

At McLean's retirement party in 2004, Walsh told the trainer that he wanted to give a gift to him and his "pal," as he always called McLean's longtime lover, George Paiva: a trip for two to Hawaii. It was a poignant gesture. Back in 1983, Walsh had sent his staff and their spouses to Hawaii as a reward for their hard work that season. But Walsh made it clear that it would be impolitic for McLean to bring George.

"It wasn't meant to condemn me," said McLean. "Bill was only concerned with the image of the 49ers in the eyes of the rest of the league . . . Bill was accepting of my lifestyle. I never felt judged by him . . . There was no homophobic bone in his body."

Still, Walsh knew that excluding McLean's partner was wrong. Now, more than twenty years later, he was making amends. As Walsh and McLean discussed logistics for the Hawaii vacation at the party, the trainer mentioned that George was not always up for the hardships of travel. His partner had been infected with HIV years before, McLean told Walsh, and he had his good days and bad days. "Well," said Walsh, "we'd better schedule it now, while he can enjoy it."

Then Walsh stunned McLean by talking about his late son. "You know, Lindsy, my son had AIDS." McLean had heard the rumors but was too respectful of the coach's privacy to ever bring it up. Now Walsh was telling his gay colleague, a man who had shared so much of his warrior life, that they shared this wound too.

The plague kept scything through San Francisco's gay population well into the 1990s. Some of the city's brightest lights were snuffed out. Men who had breathed new life into local democracy with their passionate activism; men who had enriched the city with their artistic, theatrical, culinary, fashion, and design skills. Hibiscus, the glorious ringleader of the Cockettes, was among the first wave to die, in 1982. As the years went by, other members of the legendary troupe succumbed, one by one. Sylvester, the fabulous disco diva who had debuted with the Cockettes, fell ill in 1988. He was too sick to attend that year's Castro Street Fair, where he had performed nearly every year, a black goddess in sequins and feathers. But as he lay dying in the bedroom of his Collingwood Street apartment, the beloved entertainer could hear the crowd chanting his name two blocks away: "Sylvester! Sylvester! Sylvester!"

So many of his friends died, recalled Armistead Maupin, that he threw away an entire address book. The obituary columns grew engorged with the names of the young and vital. Award-winning documentary filmmakers Peter Adair and Marlon Riggs. Gay politico Bill Kraus, a leading crusader in the battle for more AIDS funding. Intrepid journalist Randy Shilts, whose book *And the Band Played On* would stand as the epic chronicle of the plague years, and the era's heroes and villains. Shilts, suffering from both KS and pneumocystis pneumonia, told the *New York Times* in the final months of his life, "HIV is certainly character-building. It's made me see all of the shallow things we cling to, like ego and vanity. Of course I'd rather have a few more T-cells and a little less character."

Bobbi Campbell's death came as a particularly strong blow. Sister Florence Nightmare had turned himself into the "AIDS Poster Boy," charming and agitating his way into the public's heart. Campbell was a force of inextinguishable life. Adopting Gloria Gaynor's disco masterpiece as his theme song, he wore a button proclaiming "I Will Survive" and vowed to outlive the epidemic. At a rally in front of San Francisco's Moscone Center, where the Democratic National Convention was being held in July 1984, a thin but still impassioned Campbell told the country, "We're not victims—we are your children, and your mothers and fathers, and your sisters and brothers . . . It's still business as usual in Reagan's Washington while we are dying."

Soon after, Bobbi Campbell was admitted to ward 5B, where he continued to fight his illness until his last breath. "I was at his bedside when he died," recalled Paul Volberding. "I don't know many people who accept death easily, and Bobbi certainly did not. A young body is an amazingly vigorous thing. It does not want to die. People go through amazing ordeals and still cling to life. Those scenes in movies where people die gently and nobly sure don't ring true for me."

Cleve Jones organized a memorial rally for Bobbi. Jones knew how to close down Castro Street, he knew where to plug in the sound equipment: in the ever-amenable neighborhood pizza joint the Sausage Factory. Bobbi's father, a graying man in a three-piece suit, spoke to the crowd. He had struggled with his son's homosexuality, and now he struggled with his emotions. "We didn't see eye to eye," Bobbi's father told the mourners. "But my advice to parents is to give your kids support. They want your love and understanding."

CLEVE JONES HAD BEEN a human rights agitator for nearly his entire life, but these days his activism seemed to be mainly on behalf of the dead and dying. On a cold, wet Thanksgiving night in November 1985, as Jones led the annual parade to commemorate the deaths of Milk and Moscone, the gay leader asked marchers to take Magic Marker pens and posters and write down the names of friends and lovers who had died of AIDS. When the marchers arrived at the old federal building near Civic Center, Jones—addressing them with the same bullhorn that Harvey Milk gave him years before—told the demonstrators to tape the posters to the wall of the building. Soon the peeling, gray wall was covered with a blanket of colorfully drawn names.

A hush fell over the crowd as people stared at the wall of death. "I went to school with him," somebody said, pointing at one poster. "I used to dance with him every Sunday at the I-Beam," said another marcher. As he looked at their collective handiwork, Jones said to himself, 'It looks like a quilt.' It was the genesis of the AIDS Memorial Quilt, Jones's brilliant brainstorm to turn the private pain felt by thousands upon thousands of Americans into a stunning national tapestry of remembrance.

That night's march gave Jones the courage to finally take the HIV-antibody test, which he had been putting off for more than a year. He knew all along what the results would be. When he was told, he felt "absolute nothingness." The words of the lab social worker kept repeating in his head: "Sorry, Mr. Jones."

It took several years for the virus to start making him sick. During that shadowy period, he kept up a frantic pace, overseeing the AIDS Quilt as it continued to grow and displaying the billowing expanse of hand-sewn folk art all over the country. But by the spring of 1993, Jones's body was breaking down. After collapsing in the San Francisco airport on his way back home from a quilt event, he checked into a hospital suffering from pneumocystis pneumonia. He quickly went downhill after that, running fevers, fighting nausea and diarrhea, and losing so much weight that he had to sit on cushions to protect his increasingly bony ass.

There was something particularly sad about Cleve Jones falling sick. Everyone in San Francisco who knew his name, gay and straight, felt a special attachment to him. For many, he was the living spirit of Harvey Milk, and now that spirit was dying all over again.

Jones began to teeter around the Castro on a cane, like all the other wasted men he had seen over the years. Once upon a time, they had fought with cops and danced in the streets. Now they were shadows. One day he saw someone collapse and die on the sidewalk in front of Cafe Flore. Jones thought he was an old man. He turned out to be thirty.

Jones didn't want to die that way. His family scraped together $10,000, and he bought a bungalow in a hamlet on the Russian River, north of the city. He was getting sicker by the day, and he didn't want anyone to see him. He was going there to die. His aging parents came from Phoenix now and then to look after him. But it hurt Jones to see his seventy-five-year-old mother take on one more burden. He had never seen such deep sadness in her eyes.

Jones was losing his fingernails, his eyesight. He was afflicted with rashes in his throat and mouth. He couldn't keep any food in his stomach. He spent so much time emptying himself into the toilet bowl that he kept a pile of blankets and pillows in the bathroom. One day his neighbor Marigold found Jones in a half-conscious stupor. "Cleve, you've given up," she told him in her deep, firm voice. "You got to change and fight back."

Not long after that, in October 1993, Marcus Conant phoned Jones from the city. The doctor had seen encouraging results from a new combination of drugs. Jones, loath to add to his suffering with any more painful side effects, was worried about trying this latest pharmaceutical cocktail, but Conant persuaded him. An old friend named Shep, who had lost his partner to the plague, showed up to help, knowing Jones was worried about a negative reaction to the experimental drugs.

When Jones took the first handful of antiviral pills, he began puking his guts out late that night. Shep rushed into the bathroom, rolling a joint. "Smoke this," he told Jones. The sick man waved him away—he hadn't smoked pot in years and, in his miserable state, wasn't remotely interested in getting high now.

But Shep was insistent. "Smoke this or you're dead," he said. He knew it was the only way that Jones could keep down the pills.

Jones took one puff and stopped vomiting. He took a few more, and his stomach settled down enough for him to pick himself off the floor and walk out of the bathroom.

Over the next few days, Conant's elixir began to work its magic on Jones. "About a week later," he recalled, "I woke up one morning, [and] I could feel the coolness of the sheets, hear the birds out the window. To my astonishment, I had an erection. I hadn't seen one of those in a year. And I was hungry."

Cleve Jones got out of bed, put on his bathrobe and rubber boots, and stepped outside, where a light rain washed over his face. There was a small market a block and a half away. He couldn't remember the last time he had felt strong enough to walk there. He began to make his way down the winding lane to the store. He could smell the wet redwoods and ferns. When he got to the village market, he bought eggs and bacon and bread and butter and marmalade. Back home, he made himself a greasy feast and devoured it all.

Later he sat in his cottage and watched as a pale light broke through the clouds and glittered on the river.

I'm going to live, thought Cleve Jones.

I'm going to live.

EPILOGUE

WHEN VINCENT HALLINAN DIED in October 1992 at the venerable age of ninety-five, he was not memorialized in the Catholic Church, which he reviled until the end as a citadel of medieval values. He was sent off into the great unknown by a thousand mourners who gathered, appropriately, at the Longshoremen's Hall, where they sang the labor anthem "Joe Hill" and told fond stories of the invincible warrior. The audience was filled with many of the San Francisco liberation fighters whose causes Hallinan had championed during his seventy-three-year courtroom career, including labor, civil rights, antiwar, and AIDS activists. But perhaps the most eloquent tribute came from one of his old foes, former mayor Joe Alioto.

"If his duels and tilts were with God, at least he was picking on someone his own size," eulogized Alioto. "Vincent Hallinan was the social conscience of San Francisco. He was in many respects the heart of San Francisco."

Vince left behind five of his six sons and the love of his life, Vivian. Terry Hallinan had visited with his father the night he died. By then the younger Hallinan was a San Francisco supervisor, on his way to becoming the city's district attorney. The old man couldn't believe that his second son had become a member of the political establishment, but Vince heartily approved. Kayo still had the brawling, underdog instincts that his father and mother had instilled in him.

"My father was lying in his bed with a wide smile on his face," Terry recalled. "He said all his old friends 'are waiting outside for me.' Then

405

he sang 'The Best Things in Life Are Free.' I kissed him on the forehead, and then I left."

Two hours later, Vivian called her sons to tell them their father had died in his sleep. "There were many ups, and there were many downs, but it was exciting all the way," she told the memorial gathering at Long-shoremen's Hall.

Before the decade was over, Viv joined her husband, as did Joe Ali-oto. Many other San Francisco legends also died during the decade, including Herb Caen, Bill Graham, Allen Ginsberg, Jerry Garcia, Scott Newhall, and Artie Mitchell. It was the end of a rough and gaudy and fearless epoch. San Francisco was the greater for these knights' mighty exertions. They had tilted with God, and sometimes they had won.

SEASON OF THE WITCH PLAYLIST

The Best Songs Recorded by San Francisco Bands, 1965–1985

The Ace of Cups
"Circles"

The Beau Brummels
"Just a Little"
"Laugh Laugh"
"Sometime at Night"

Big Brother and the Holding Company
"Call on Me"
"Combination of the Two"
"Farewell Song"
"Piece of My Heart"

Creedence Clearwater Revival
"As Long as I Can See the Light"
"Fortunate Son"
"Walk on the Water"

The Dead Kennedys
"Holiday in Cambodia"

The Flamin' Groovies
"Shake Some Action"
"Slow Death"

The Grateful Dead
"Box of Rain"
"The Golden Road (To Unlimited Devotion)"
"New Speedway Boogie"
"Ripple"
"Uncle John's Band"

The Great Society
"Grimly Forming"

Kak
"Trieulogy"

The Jefferson Airplane
"It's No Secret"
"Lather"
"Law Man"
"Somebody to Love"
"Today"
"White Rabbit"

Jorma Kaukonen
"Genesis"

Lee Michaels
"Heighty Hi"
"What Now America"

Moby Grape
"8:05"
"Going Nowhere"
"I Am Not Willing"
"Naked, If I Want To"
"Omaha"
"Sitting by the Window"

The Mojo Men
"Sit Down, I Think I Love You"

Romeo Void
"Never Say Never"

Santana
"Samba Pa Ti"

Skip Spence
"Diana"

Tracy Nelson and Mother Earth
"Down So Low"
"Seven Bridges Road"

Translator
"Everywhere That I'm Not"

The Vejtables
"I Still Love You"

The Youngbloods
"Darkness, Darkness"
"Get Together"

For more about San Francisco history and music, go to www.talbotplayers.com

SOURCES

INTRODUCTION

Books:

Asbury, Herbert, *The Barbary Coast: An Informal History of the San Francisco Underworld*. New York: Thunder's Mouth Press, 2002.

Boyd, Nan Alamilla, *Wide Open Town: A History of Queer San Francisco to 1965*. Berkeley, CA: University of California Press, Berkeley, 2003.

Brechin, Gray, *Imperial San Francisco: Urban Power, Earthly Ruin*. Berkeley, CA: University of California Press, Berkeley, 2006.

Hammett, Dashiell, *Nightmare Town: Stories*. New York: Vintage Books, 1999.

Layman, Richard, *Discovering the Maltese Falcon and Sam Spade: The Evolution of Dashiell Hammett's Masterpiece*. San Francisco: Vince Emery Productions, 2005.

Layman, Richard, *Shadow Man: The Life of Dashiell Hammett*. San Diego: Harvest/HBJ, 1981.

Maravelis, Peter, editor, *San Francisco Noir 2: The Classics*. New York: Akashic Books, 2009.

Hammett, Dashiell, "The Scorched Face"

London, Jack, "South of the Slot"

Norris, Frank "The Third Circle."

Morgan, Bill, editor, *Howl on Trial: The Battle for Free Expression*. San Francisco: City Lights Publishers, 2006.

Sides, Josh, *Erotic City: Sexual Revolutions and the Making of Modern San Francisco*. New York: Oxford University Press, 2009.

Solnit, Rebecca, *A Paradise Built in Hell: The Extraordinary Communities That Arise in Disaster*. New York: Viking, 2009.

PROLOGUE: WILD IRISH ROGUES

Interviews:

Hallinan, Patrick

Hallinan, Terence

Newspapers and Magazines:

San Francisco Chronicle, May–June 1932; Oct. 3,1992; Dec. 6, 1995; May 13,1996; Mar. 2, 2003, Mar. 9, 2003.

San Francisco Examiner Image magazine, Feb. 22, 1987, "Hallinans Against the World," Steve Chapple.

San Francisco magazine, Nov. 1997, "Sex, Drugs and Political Paranoia," Nina Schuyler.

Books:

Hallinan, Vincent, *A Lion in Court*. New York: G.P. Putnam's Sons, 1963.
Hallinan, Vivian, *My Wild Irish Rogues*. Garden City, NY: Doubleday and Co., 1952.
Walsh, James P., *San Francisco's Hallinan: Toughest Lawyer in Town*. Novato, CA: Presidio Press, 1982.

PART ONE: ENCHANTMENT
1: SATURDAY AFTERNOON

Interviews:

Beggs, Edward   Rohan, Brian
Ferlinghetti, Lawrence   Stepanian, Michael
Kantner, Paul

Documents:

Human Be-In press release, Jan. 12, 1967, "Hippie Collection," San Francisco Public Library History Center.
"Huckleberry House and the Summer of Love," essay, courtesy Edward Beggs.

Newspapers and Magazines:

San Francisco Chronicle, Jan. 16, 1967, May 13, 1967.

Books:

Kandel, Lenore, *The Love Book*. San Francisco: Superstition Street Press, 2003.
Morgan, Bill, *I Celebrate Myself: The Somewhat Private Life of Allen Ginsberg*. New York: Penguin Books, 2006.
Perry, Charles, *The Haight Ashbury*. New York: Wenner Books, 2005.

2: DEAD MEN DANCING

Interviews:

Ferlinghetti, Lawrence   Stepanian, Michael
Hart, Mickey   Valentino, Sal
Kriegel, Marilyn (Harris) Welch, Calvin

Newspapers and Magazines:

San Francisco Chronicle, October 3 and 4, 1967.

Books:

Boyd, Dick, *Broadway-North Beach: The Golden Years*. San Francisco: Cape Foundation Publications, 2006.
McNally, Dennis, *A Long Strange Trip: The Inside History of the Grateful Dead*. New York: Broadway Books, 2002.
Perry, *The Haight Ashbury*.
Selvin, Joel, *Summer of Love: The Inside Story of LSD, Rock & Roll, Free Love and High Times in the Wild West*. New York: Dutton, 1994.
Tamarkin, Jeff, *Got a Revolution: The Turbulent Flight of the Jefferson Airplane*. New York: Atria Books, 2003.

3: THE WALLED CITY

Documents:

Speech by Thomas Cahill, Dec. 3, 1958, SFPL History Center files.
Program for Thomas Cahill Testimonial Dinner, June 23, 1967, SFPL History Center.

Newspapers and Magazines:

San Francisco Chronicle, Sept. 5, 1958; Apr. 11, 1964; Mar. 23, 27, 29, 30, 1967; Sept.
  9, 10, 1967; Nov. 8, 1967, Feb. 28, 1968, Sept. 2, 1974.
San Francisco Examiner California Living Magazine, Apr. 30, 1967.
San Francisco News, Sept. 20, 1958.
The Irish Digest, Apr. 1960, "San Francisco's Fighting Irish Chief of Police," Lenore
  Archuletta.

Books:

Perry, *The Haight-Ashbury.*

4: THE FREE CITY

Interviews:

  Berg, Peter
  Coyote,Peter
  Rosenthal, Irving

Documents:

Diggers street sheets, Hippie Collection, SFPL History Center.
Diggers papers, The Digger Archives, *www.diggers.org.*

Newspapers and Magazines:

San Francisco Chronicle, Jan. 23, May 5, 1967.

Books:

Coyote, Peter, *Sleeping Where I Fall: A Chronicle.* Berkeley, CA: Counterpoint, 1999.
Grogan, Emmett, *Ringolevio: A Life Played for Keeps.* New York: New York Review
  Books, 1990.
McNally, *A Long Strange Trip.*
Perry, *The Haight Ashbury.*

5: THE LOST CHILDREN OF WINDY FEET

Interviews:

  Beggs, Edward.
  Coyote, Peter.

Documents:

"Huckleberry House and the Summer of Love," Beggs.
Runaway children's correspondence, Huckleberry House files, SFPL History Center.

Newspapers and Magazines:

San Francisco Chronicle, Feb. 8, 1966; Apr. 19, 1966; Jan. 2, 3, 1967; Oct. 21, 1967; Dec. 12, 1968; Jan. 31, 1969.
San Francisco Examiner, Mar. 27, 1965; Apr. 28, 1966; Aug. 10, 1967.
New York Times, Feb. 5, 6, Oct. 11, 1966; Sept. 27, 1967; Apr. 9, 1968.
New York Times Magazine, May 10, 1964, "Why They Run Away from Home."
Wall Street Journal, Aug. 11, 1969.
Life, Nov. 3, 1967, "Runaway Kids."

Books:

Beggs, Edward (Larry), *Huckleberry's for Runaways.* New York, Ballantine Books, 1969.
Staller, Karen M., *Runaways: How the Sixties Counterculture Shaped Today's Practices and Policies.* New York: Columbia University Press, 2006.

6: STREET MEDICINE

Interviews:

Smith, Dr. David
Welch, Calvin

Newspapers and Magazines:

San Francisco Chronicle, October 8, 1967.
San Francisco Examiner, June 8, 1987.
San Francisco Medicine, Sept. 2009, "David Smith: Pioneering Community-Based Health Care."

Documents:

"We Built This Clinic on Rock 'n' Roll," essay by Dr. David Smith, *www.DrDave.org.*
"The Evolution of Addiction Medicine and Its San Francisco Roots," draft essay by Dr. David Smith, courtesy of the author.

Books:

Smith, David E., and Luce, John, *Love Needs Care: A History of San Francisco's Haight-Ashbury Free Medical Clinic and Its Pioneer Role in Treating Drug-Abuse Problems.* Boston: Little, Brown & Co., 1971.
Sturges, Clark S., *Dr. Dave.* Walnut Creek, CA: Devil Mountain Books, 1993.

7: MURDER ON SHAKEDOWN STREET

Interviews:

Brown, Willie   Hall, Harry
Cleary, Jack   Sullivan, Marion
Davis, Belva

Documents:

Proceedings of the coroner's hearing on the death of Charles Sullivan, Aug. 18, 1966, case number 1966–1545.

Newspapers and Magazines:

San Francisco Chronicle, Oct. 17, 21, 1963; Aug. 3, 1966; Aug. 31, 1971; July 21, 2008
San Francisco Examiner, Aug. 2, 1966
San Francisco Examiner Pictorial Living, Sept. 2, 1962, "The Man Who's Renewing the City," Jerry Adams.
San Francisco Sun-Reporter, Aug. 13, 1966.
National Journal, Sept. 18, 1971, "Herman Death Ends an Era."

Documentary Films:

The Fillmore, directed by Rick Butler, produced by KQED and PBS, 2000.

Books:

Graham, Bill, and Greenfield, Robert, *Bill Graham Presents: My Life Inside Rock and Out.* Cambridge, MA: Da Capo Press, 2004.
Hartman, Chester, *City for Sale: The Transformation of San Francisco.* Berkeley, CA: University of California Press, 2002.
Pepin, Elizabeth, and Watts, Lewis, *Harlem of the West: The San Francisco Fillmore Jazz Era.* San Francisco: Chronicle Books, 2006.

8: THE NAPOLEON OF ROCK

Interviews:

Berg, Peter	Selvin, Joel
Coyote, Peter	Smith, Dr. David
Hart, Mickey	Sullivan, David
Kantner, Paul	Stepanian, Michael
Lewis, Peter	Wenner, Jann
Miller, Jerry	Zagaris, Michael
Rohan, Brian	

Newspapers and Magazines:

San Francisco Chronicle, Oct. 28, 29, Nov. 3, 1991; Apr. 17, 1994.
San Francisco Examiner Image magazine, Dec. 8, 1991, "Raging Bill," Paul Kantner and Mickey Hart.
San Francisco Good Times, Dec. 10, 1971; July 9, 1973.

Books:

Glatt, John, *Rage & Roll: Bill Graham and the Selling of Rock.* New York: Birch Lane Press, 1993.
Graham and Greenfield, *Bill Graham Presents.*
Hertzberg, Hendrick, *Politics: Observations and Arguments, 1966–2004.* New York: Penguin Books, 2005.
McNally, *A Long Strange Trip.*
Selvin, *Summer of Love.*

9: THE DAILY CIRCUS

Interviews:

Newhall, Jon
Wenner, Jann

Oral Histories:

Newhall, Scott, the Bancroft Library, University of California at Berkeley, interviewed 1988–1989.

Documents:

Scott Newhall files, SFPL History Center.

Newspapers and Magazines:

American Journalism Review, Jan.–Feb. 1999, "The Battle of the Bay," Cynthia Gorney.
Old Town Newhall Gazette, Jan.–Feb. 1996, "The Life and Times of Scott Newhall," Ruth Waldo Newhall.
San Francisco Chronicle, Dec. 23, 2004; June 21, 2009.
Rolling Stone, July 17, 1975, "Ralph Gleason in Perspective," edited by Jann Wenner.
San Francisco magazine, July and August 1968, "My Search for Scott Newhall," two-part article, John Luce.

10: SAN FRANCISCO'S MORNING KISS

Interviews:

   Brown, Willie
   Caen, Christopher
   Moose, Ed

Newspapers and Magazines:

San Francisco Chronicle, Mar. 31, 1996, Feb. 3, 13, May 11, 1997; April 5, 2009.
San Francisco Chronicle, Herb Caen columns, 1967–1997.
San Francisco Examiner, Feb. 2, 1997.
Harper's Magazine, Nov. 2009, "Final Edition," Richard Rodriguez.
San Francisco City Magazine, May 14, 1975, "Herb Caen: San Francisco's All-Time Favorite Sweetheart," Burton Wolfe.
San Francisco Focus, Apr. 1986, "The Interview: Herb Caen, The 70-Year-Old Kid, " Ken Kelley.
San Francisco Focus, Dec. 1987, "The Wooing of Herb Caen," Michael Munzell.
San Francisco Focus, Dec. 1995, "Citizen Caen," Mark Powelson.
San Francisco magazine, Dec. 1978, "The World According to Caen," Wayne Warga.

Books:

Caen, Herb, *Baghdad By-the-Bay,* Garden City, NY: Doubleday & Co., 1950.
Caen, Herb, *The Best of Herb Caen, 1960–1975,* San Francisco: Chronicle Books, 1991.
Conrad, Barnaby, editor, *The World of Herb Caen: San Francisco, 1938–1997,* San Francisco: Chronicle Books, 1997.

11: RADIO FREE AMERICA

Interviews:

   Brand, Stewart   Nisker, Wes "Scoop"
   Davis, Patti Reagan   Reagan, Ron
   Hart, Mickey   Rodriguez, Spain
   Lewis, Peter   Wenner, Jann
   Miller, Jerry

Oral Histories:

"R. Crumb in Conversation with Francoise Mouly," Oct. 31, 2010, Jewish Community
  Center, San Francisco.

Documents:

"The History of Crumb," *www.RCrumb.com.*
The Very Best of Moby Grape, Sony, 1993, liner notes by David Fricke.

Newspapers and Magazines:

Austin Chronicle, Jan. 8, 2010, "Naked if I Want To: Moby Grape Now and Then," Louis
  Black.
Time, Apr. 29, 2005, "R. Crumb Speaks," Andrew D. Arnold.

Books:

Cannon, Lou, *Governor Reagan: His Rise to Power.* New York: Public Affairs, 2003.
Davis, Patti, *The Way I See It.* New York: G.P. Putnam's Sons, 1992.
Nisker, Wes "Scoop," *The Big Bang, the Buddha, and the Baby Boom.* New York: Harp-
  erOne, 2004.
Perry, *The Haight Ashbury.*
Selvin, *Summer of Love.*

12: THE PALACE OF GOLDEN COCKS

Interviews:

Hauser, Fayette   Missabu, Rumi
Koldewyn, Richard "Scrumbly"   Rosenthal, Irving

Documents:

"Before the Castro: North Beach, a Gay Mecca," essay by Dick Boyd, *www.foundsf.org*
Kreemah Ritz papers, Cockettes files, SFPL History Center.
"Kaliflower and the Dream Continues," essay by Eric Noble, *www.foundsf.org.*
"The Cockettes," essay by Sebastian, Cockettes files, SFPL History Center.

Newspapers and Magazines:

San Francisco Chronicle, Rex Reed column, Oct. 3, 1971, Dec. 2, 1971.
New York Times, Aug. 17, 2003.
Rolling Stone, Oct. 14, 1971, "Les Cockettes de San Francisco," Maitland Zane.

Documentary Films:

The Cockettes, David Weissman and Bill Weber, co-directors, Strand Releasing Home
  Video, 2002.

Books:

Boyd, *Wide Open Town.*
Sides, *Erotic City.*
Stryker, Susan, and Van Buskirk Jim, *Gay by the Bay: A History of Queer Culture in the
  San Francisco Bay Area.* San Francisco: Chronicle Books, 1996.
Tent, Pam, *Midnight at the Palace: My Life as a Fabulous Cockette.* Los Angeles: Alyson
  Books, 2004.

PART TWO: TERROR
13: A DEATH IN THE FAMILY

Interviews:

Hauser, Fayette   Reisman, Alex
Hallinan, Terence Stepanian, Michael

Documents:

"The People v. James Martin Gurley," crim. no. 9084, ruling by Court of Appeal of California, First Appellate District, Division One.

Books:

Caserta, Peggy, *Going Down with Janis*. New York: Dell Publishing, 1973.
Dalton, David, *Piece of My Heart: A Portrait of Janis Joplin*. New York: Da Capo, 1991.
Echols, Alice, *Scars of Sweet Paradise: The Life and Times of Janis Joplin*. New York: Holt Paperbacks, 1999.
Friedman, Myra, *Buried Alive: The Biography of Janis Joplin*. New York: Three Rivers Press, 1992.
Joplin, Laura, *Love, Janis*. New York: Harper, 2005.
Selvin, *Summer of Love*.
Sporke, Michael, *Living with the Myth of Janis Joplin: The History of Big Brother and the Holding Company, 1965–2005*, Books on Demand, Norderstedt, Germany, 2003.

14: LUCIFER RISING

Interviews:

Cleary, Jack   Smith, Dr. David
Lewis, Peter   Welch, Calvin
Rohan, Brian

Documents:

"The Green Rebellion: Notes on the Life and Times of American Hippies," essay by Dr. Louis Jolyon West and Dr. James R. Allen, University of Oklahoma digital libraries.

Newspapers and Magazines:

San Francisco Chronicle, Jan. 27, Mar. 15, June 7, Aug. 8, Aug. 17, Dec. 12, 1967.
San Francisco Examiner, Nov. 7, 1997.
Washington Post Magazine, Feb. 23, 1986, "Anton LaVey: America's Satanic Master of Devils, Magic, Music and Madness," Walt Harrington.

Books:

Atkins, Susan, *Child of Satan, Child of God*. New York: Bantam, 1978.
Emmons, Nuel, *Manson in His Own Words*. New York: Grove Press, 1986.
Hayden, Tom, *The Long Sixties: From 1960 to Barack Obama*. Boulder, CO: Paradigm Publishers, 2009.
Lee, Martin A., and Shlain, Bruce, *Acid Dreams: The Complete Social History of LSD— The CIA, the Sixties, and Beyond*. New York: Grove Weidenfeld, 1992.
Perry, *The Haight-Ashbury*.
Sanders, Ed, *The Family*. New York, Thunder's Mouth Press, 2002.
Smith and Luce, *Love Needs Care*.

15: A KNIFE DOWN YOUR THROAT

Interviews:

Brand, Stewart	Lewis, Peter
Coyote, Peter	Wenner, Jann
Hart, Mickey	Zagaris, Michael
Kantner, Paul	

Newspapers and Magazines:

San Francisco Chronicle, Dec. 8, 1969.
San Francisco Examiner, Dec. 7, 1969.
Good Times, Jan. 7, Oct. 16, 1970.
Mademoiselle, Mar. 1971, "A Talk with Stephen Gaskin," Mary Cantwell and Amy Gross.
Rolling Stone, Jan. 21, 1970, "Let It Bleed," Lester Bangs et al.
San Francisco magazine, Aug. 1970, "The Rainbow Maker," Geoffrey Link.

Documentary Films:

Gimme Shelter, 1970, directed by Albert and David Maysles, Criterion Pictures.

Books:

Barger, Ralph "Sonny," *Hell's Angel: The Life and Times of Sonny Barger and the Hell's Angels Motorcycle Club.* New York: William Morrow, 2000.
Booth, Stanley, *The True Adventures of the Rolling Stones.* New York: Vintage Books, 1985.
McNally, *A Long Strange Trip.*
Selvin, *Summer of Love.*
Tamarkin, *Got a Revolution.*

16: BENEVOLENT DICTATOR

Interviews:

Alioto, Angela	Roff, Hadley
Feinstein, Dianne	Welch, Calvin
Moose, Ed	

Oral Histories:

Alioto, Joseph, Bancroft Library, UC-Berkeley, interviewed 1991–92

Documents:

"Mayor Alioto and the Haight," excerpt from lecture by Calvin Welch, *www.FoundSF.org.*

Newspapers and Magazines:

San Francisco Chronicle, Jan. 23, Feb. 20, Mar. 9, Mar. 14, July 18, July 30, Aug. 13, Oct. 28, Nov. 9, Nov. 20, Nov. 26, 1968; Nov. 18, 1969; Oct. 21, 1970; Feb. 1, 1998.
San Francisco Examiner California Living, Mar. 24, 1968.
San Francisco Examiner Magazine, Mar. 17, 1996, "King of the City," Kandace Bender.
The Bay Guardian, Oct. 31, 1967, "Shelley, Alioto—It's a Deal!" Bruce Brugmann.
Look magazine, Sept. 23, 1969, "The Web That Links San Francisco's Mayor Alioto and the Mafia," Richard Carlson and Lance Brisson.

Books:

Alioto, Angela, *Straight to the Heart*. San Francisco: Russian Hill Press, 1997.
Hartman, *City for Sale*.
Issel, William, *For Both Cross and Flag: Catholic Action, Anti-Catholicism, and National Security Politics in World War II San Francisco*. Philadelphia: Temple University Press, 2010.
Demaris, Ovid, *The Last Mafioso: The Treacherous World of Jimmy Fratianno*. New York: Bantam Books, 1981.

17: LOVE'S LAST STAND

Interviews:

Ferguson, "Sag" Darel
Huston, Will "Wild Bill"
Jaffe, Dana
Kever, Steve
Lautzker, Larry "The Hat"

McCarthy, Robert "Mouseman"
Moore, Dan "Spud"
Serra, Tony
Welch, Calvin
Wickman, Chris

Documents:

"Communes and Housing," essay by Calvin Welch, *www.FoundSF.org*.
Goddam Independent commune newspaper and other Good Earth documents and memorabilia, courtesy of Robert McCarthy.
The Good Earth conversation thread, *www.hipforums.com*.
The People v. Steven Kever, Municipal Court of the City and County of San Francisco, Jan. 18, 1971, Minute Order Holding Person in Contempt and Commitment.

Newspapers and Magazines:

San Francisco Chronicle, Jan. 19, 27, 1971.
Good Times, Jan. 6, 1971; June 2, 1972.

18: DUNGEONS AND DRAGONS

Interviews:

Hanlon, Stuart
Serra, Tony

Documents:

"A Letter to the People," by Nancy Ling Perry and other documents from the Symbionese Liberation Army files, SFPL History Center.

Newspapers and Magazines:

The Bay Guardian, Feb. 27, 1974.
The Black Panther, Nov. 17, 1973.
Daily Californian, Feb. 9, 1974.
Montclarion, Nov. 8, 14, 24, 1973.
New York Times, Nov. 20, 1973.
Oakland Tribune, Mar. 21, 1973.

San Francisco Chronicle, Nov. 7, 9, 1973; Jan. 19, Feb. 11, Apr. 8, 1974; Nov. 28. 1979.
San Francisco Examiner, Jan. 20, 1974.
Village Voice, Feb. 28, 1974.

Books:

Headley, Lake, *Vegas P.I.: The Life and Times of America's Greatest Detective.* New York: Thunder's Mouth Press, 1993.
Jackson, George, *Blood in My Eye.* Baltimore: Black Classic Press, 1996.
Jackson, George, *Soledad Brother: The Prison Letters of George Jackson.* Chicago: Lawrence Hill Books, 1994.
Mitford, Jessica, *Kind and Usual Punishment: The Prison Business.* New York: Vintage, 1974.
Payne, Les, and Findley, Tim, *The Life and Death of the SLA.* New York: Ballantine, 1976.

19: THE REVOLUTION WILL BE TELEVISED

Interviews:

Bortin, Michael   Molinari, Jim
Hallinan, Terence   Weir, David
Hearst, Will

Documents:

Symbionese Liberation Army files, SFPL History Center.

Newspapers and Magazines:

Berkeley Barb, Feb. 14, 22, 1974.
Daily Californian, Mar. 5, 1974.
Detroit Sun, Jan. 22, 1976, "Who Ran the SLA?," Dick Russell.
Los Angeles Times, Feb. 15, Mar. 20, Apr. 7, 17, May 18, 1974.
New York Times, Feb. 15, Apr. 14, May 24, 1974.
Oakland Tribune, Feb. 23, 1974.
Ramparts, May 1974, "Terrorism and the Left."
Rolling Stone, June 20, 1974, "The Revolution Was Televised," Tim Findley.
Rolling Stone, Oct. 23, 1975, "The Inside Story," Howard Kohn and David Weir.
Rolling Stone, Apr. 22, 1976, "The Lost Year of the SLA," Kohn and Weir.
San Francisco Bay Guardian, Feb. 13, May 11, 1974.
San Francisco Chronicle, Feb.19, 23, Mar. 5, 7, 12, 26, Apr. 4, 10, 16, 17, 1974; Nov. 29, 1979.
San Francisco Examiner, Apr. 16, 1974.
Washington Post, Dec. 31, 2006.

Books:

Alexander, Shana, *Anyone's Daughter: The Times and Trials of Patty Hearst.* New York: Viking Press, 1979.
Graebner, William, *Patty's Got a Gun: Patricia Hearst in 1970s America.* Chicago: University of Chicago Press, 2008.
Hearst, Patricia Campbell, *Every Secret Thing.* New York: Doubleday & Co., 1982.
Headley, *Vegas P.I.*
Payne and Findley, *The Life and Death of the SLA.*
Spieler, Geri, *Taking Aim at the President: The Remarkable Story of the Woman Who Shot at Gerald Ford.* New York: Palgrave MacMillan, 2009.

20: BLACK AND WHITE AND RED ALL OVER

Interviews:

Agnos, Art   Coreris, Gus
Brown, Rev. Amos   Jennings, Duffy
Cleary, Jack

Oral Histories:

Alioto, Joseph, Bancroft Library UC-Berkeley

Documents:

www.thezebraproject.blogspot.com.

Newspapers and Magazines:

San Francisco Chronicle, Jan. 30, Apr. 18, May 2, July 10, 1974; Feb. 25, 2007.
People magazine, May 6, 1974, "San Francisco's Alioto: Snarled in a Zebra Dragnet."

Books:

Graysmith, Robert, *Zodiac,* Berkley, New York, 2007.
Howard, Clark, *Zebra: The True Account of the 179 Days of Terror in San Francisco.* New
    York: Richard Marek Publishers, 1979.
Sanders, Earl Prentice, and Cohen, Bennett, *The Zebra Murders: A Season of Killing,*
    Racial Madness and Civil Rights. New York: Arcade Publishing, 2006.

21: THE EMPRESS OF CHINATOWN

Interviews:

Chin, Gordon   Moose, Ed
Lee, Ed   Pak, Rose

Documents:

"Overview of Chinese American-Asian American Political Power in San Francisco,"
    essay by Gordon Chin, Oct. 14, 2008, courtesy of author.

Newspapers and Magazines:

Asian Week, July, 22, 2005.
San Francisco Chronicle, Aug. 4, 1997; Sept. 3, 2000; June 8, 2001; July 7, 2005; Dec.
    2, 2007; Sept. 19, 2010; Jan. 8, 11, 24, Feb. 21, 2011.
San Francisco Examiner, Jan. 31, 1996.

Books:

Chang, Iris, *The Chinese in America: A Narrative History.* New York: Viking, 2003.
Hartman, *City for Sale.*
Robbins, Trina, *Forbidden City: The Golden Age of Chinese Nightclubs.* Cresskill, NJ:
    Hampton Press, 2010.
Tsui, Bonnie, *American Chinatown: A People's History of Five Neighborhoods.* New York:
    Free Press, 2009.

22: SAN FRANCISCO SATYRICON

Interviews:

Alioto, Angela   St. James, Margo
Calcagno, Vince   Tower, Jeremiah
Maupin, Armistead

Documents:

"Ivory Snow Girl, R.I.P.," by Warren Hinckle, *www.counterpunch.org.*

Newspapers and Magazines:

San Francisco Chronicle, July 21 2007.
San Francisco Focus, Oct. 1992, "The Outsider: Interview with Armistead Maupin,"
    Amy Rennert.
San Francisco magazine, Dec. 1977, "The Tale Behind Tales of the City," Nora Gallagher.
San Francisco magazine, June 1979, "The Greening of Margo St. James," Jennifer
    Thompson.
Smithsonian magazine, July 2007, "Mad, Stark Mad," Armistead Maupin.
Washington Post, Apr. 14, 2009.

Books:

Boyd, Nan Alamilla, *Wide Open Town.*
Hubner, John, *Bottom Feeders: From Free Love to Hard Core—The Rise and Fall of Coun-
    terculture Heroes Jim and Artie Mitchell.* New York: Doubleday, 1993.
Maupin, Armistead, *Tales of the City.* New York: Harper, 1994.
Morgan, *I Celebrate Myself.*
Shilts, Randy, *The Mayor of Castro Street: The Life and Times of Harvey Milk.* New York:
    St. Martin's Press, 2008.
Sides, *Erotic City.*
Tower, Jeremiah, *California Dish: What I Saw (and Cooked) at the American Culinary
    Revolution.* New York: Free Press 2004.

23: CIVIC WAR

Interviews:

Barbagelata, Paul   Moose, Ed
Brown, Willie   Moscone, Christopher
Burton, John   Peri, Don
Busch, Corey   Sklar, Richard
Hallinan, Terence   St. James, Margo
Maher, Bill   Stepanian, Michael
Molinari, Jim   Welch, Calvin

Documents:

Mayoral campaign literature, 1975, George Moscone files, SFPL History Center.
Personal files of John Barbagelata, courtesy of Paul Barbagelata.

Newspapers and Magazines:

City magazine, Dec. 9, 1975, "The Phenomenal John Barbagelata," Warren Hinckle and Marjorie Leland.

Los Angeles Times, Nov. 27. 1998.

New West magazine, Mar. 28, 1977, "The Broken Promises of Mayor Moscone," Phil Tracy.

Santa Barbara Independent, Dec. 11, 2008.

San Francisco Chronicle, Dec. 12, 1975; Jan. 8, 9, 1976; Jan. 8, 1977; Nov. 18, 1978; Nov. 26, 1998; Dec. 5, 2008.

San Francisco Examiner, May 25, Oct. 6, 24, Nov. 5, 10, Dec. 6, 7, 12, 14, 17, 18, 25, 26, 29, 1975; Jan 9, 20, July 8, Nov. 27, 1976; Apr. 30, May 9, Aug. 3, Oct. 26, Nov. 3, 1977; Feb. 1, Apr. 11, May 14, 1978.

San Francisco magazine, Jan. 1976, "Moscone: What's in Store for the City?" Lawrence Fanning.

Books:

Brown, Willie, *Basic Brown: My Life and Our Times.* New York: Simon & Schuster, 2008.

Jacobs, John, *A Rage for Justice: The Passion and Politics of Phillip Burton.* Berkeley, CA: University of California Press, 1997.

Richardson, James, *Willie Brown: A Biography.* Berkeley, CA: University of California Press, 1996.

Shilts, *The Mayor of Castro Street.*

Sides, *Erotic City.*

24: INSIDE MAN

Interviews:

Barbagelata, Paul   Jones, Jim Jr.
Buford, Terri   Reuben, David

Documents:

Personal files of John Barbagelata.

"Madman in Our Midst: Jim Jones and the California Cover Up," essay by Kathleen and Tom Kinsolving, *www.rickross.com.*

Newspapers and Magazines:

New York Times, Dec. 17, 1978.

San Francisco Chronicle, June 25, 1976; Jan. 20, July 31, Aug. 1, 1979; Nov. 12. 1998.

San Francisco Examiner, Jan. 21, 1979.

Books:

Klineman, George, and Butler, Sherman, *The Cult That Died: The Tragedy of Jim Jones and the Peoples Temple.* New York: Putnam Publishing Group, 1980.

Layton, Deborah, *Seductive Poison: A Jonestown Survivor's Story of Life and Death in the Peoples Temple.* New York: Anchor Books, 1998.

Reiterman, Tim, *Raven: The Untold Story of the Rev. Jim Jones and His People,* New York: Penguin Group, 2008.

25: SLOUCHING TOWARD SAN FRANCISCO

Interviews:

Brown, Rev. Amos	Jones, Cleve
Buford, Terri	Reuben, David
Busch, Corey	Sklar, Richard
Fortson, Hue	Williams, Rev. Cecil
Jones Jr., Jim	

Documents:

Election Special, Nov. 1979, published by Barbagelata, "Peoples Temple and Joe Freitas."
Jonestown Institute files, courtesy of Fielding McGehee III, *www.jonestown.sdsu.edu.*
Peoples Temple collection, California Historical Society, San Francisco.

Newspapers and Magazines:

New West, Aug. 1, 1977, "Inside Peoples Temple," Marshall Kilduff and Phil Tracy.
San Francisco Chronicle, Nov. 23, 2003.
San Francisco Examiner, Aug. 7, 1977; Nov. 20, 1978.

Documentary Films:

The Fillmore, Butler, KQED.
Jonestown: The Life and Death of Peoples Temple, "American Experience," PBS, 2006.

Books:

Klineman, *The Cult That Died.*
Layton, *Seductive Poison.*
Moore, Rebecca, ed., *Peoples Temple and Black Religion in America,* Bloomington, IN:
    Indiana University Press, 2004.
Reiterman, *Raven.*
Shilts, Randy, *The Mayor of Castro Street.*
Williams, Cecil, *I'm Alive: An Autobiography,* San Francisco: Harper & Row, 1980.

26: PROPHET OF DOOM

Interviews:

Barbagelata, Paul
Leach, Norman

Documents:

Personal files of John Barbagelata.

Newspapers and Magazines:

City magazine, Dec. 9, 1975, Hinckle and Leland.
San Francisco Chronicle, Jan. 12, Feb. 9, 1976; Mar. 7, July 18, Aug. 3, 4, 1977.
San Francisco Examiner, Jan. 12, 1976; Jan. 25, Mar. 3, Aug. 3, 4, 1977.
San Francisco Today, Sept. 21, 1977; Jan. 17, 1978.
San Francisco Weekly, Nov. 18, 1998.

27: EXODUS

Interviews:

Agnos, Art   Kilduff, Marshall
Jones Jr., Jim   Reuben, David

Documents:

Internal SF District Attorney's office memo from Bob Graham to Joe Freitas and Danny Weinstein, Aug. 28, 1977.
Peoples Temple collection, California Historical Society.

Books:

Layton, *Seductive Poison.*
Reiterman, *Raven.*

28: RAPTURE IN THE JUNGLE

Interviews:

Fortson, Hue
McGehee III, Fielding

Documents:

"The Death Tape," Jonestown Audiotape Project, transcript prepared by McGehee, *www.jonestown.sdsu.edu.*
"Christine Miller: A Voice of Independence," essay by Michael Bellefountaine, Jonestown Institute, *www.jonestown.sdsu.edu.*

Newspapers and Magazines:

San Francisco Chronicle, Nov. 17, 1998.

Books:

Layton, *Seductive Poison.*
Reiterman, *Raven.*

29: THE RECKONING

Interviews:

Brown, Willie   Leach, Norman
Jones Jr., Jim   Reuben, David

Documents:

George Moscone files, SFPL History Center.

Newspapers and Magazines:

Lincoln (NE) Journal Star, Mar. 12, Aug. 24, 2004, "Leach Gets One Year in Assault."
San Francisco Chronicle, Nov. 17, 2008.
San Francisco Examiner, Nov. 19, 20, 1978.

30: A TALE OF TWO CITIES

Interviews:

Busch, Corey   Moscone, Christopher
Falzon, Frank   Sklar, Richard
Jones, Cleve   St. James, Margo
Kopp, Quentin

Documents:

Harvey Milk, George Moscone files, SFPL History Center.

Newspapers and Magazines:

San Francisco Chronicle, June 24, 1977; April 11, Sept. 16, 1978.
San Francisco Examiner, Nov. 28, 1978.

Books:

Shilts, *The Mayor of Castro Street.*
Weiss, Mike, *Double Play: The Hidden Passions Behind the Double Assassination of George Moscone and Harvey Milk.* San Francisco: Vince Emery Productions, 2010.

31: DAY OF THE GUN

Interviews:

Brown, Willie   Jennings, Duffy
Cleary, Jack   Jones, Cleve
Falzon, Frank   Molinari, Jim
Feinstein, Dianne   Moscone, Christopher

Documents:

Harvey Milk, George Moscone files, SFPL History Center.

Newspapers and Magazines:

Los Angeles Times, Nov. 21, 1993; Nov. 23, 1998.
San Francisco Chronicle, Nov. 10, 16, 21, 28, 29, 1978; Feb. 1, 1979; Nov. 18, 26, 2008.
San Francisco Examiner, Nov. 27, 28, 29, Dec. 2, 3, 1978; Nov. 9, 1998.
San Francisco Focus, Nov. 1988, "New Revelations About the City Hall Assassinations," edited by Amy Rennert.

Books:

Brown, *Basic Brown.*
Shilts, *The Mayor of Castro Street.*
Weiss, *Double Play.*

PART THREE: DELIVERANCE
32: FIRE BY TRIAL

Interviews:

Britt, Harry	Moscone, Christopher
Falzon, Frank	Roff, Hadley
Feinstein, Dianne	Sklar, Richard
Kopp, Quentin	Williams, Cecil
Maher, Bill	

Documents:

Dianne Feinstein files, SFPL History Center.

Newspapers and Magazines:

Los Angeles Times, July 9, 1979.
New York Times, Dec. 3, 11, 1978; Jan. 27, Feb. 10, 16, 1979.
San Francisco Chronicle, Dec. 12, 1978; Feb. 23, 1979.
San Francisco Examiner, Nov. 28, 29, Dec. 4, 5, 1978; Mar. 4, 1979.
San Francisco Examiner California Living, Apr. 29, 1984, "Bucking That White Bow Image," Carol Pogash.
Bay Views, Apr. 1981, "San Francisco's First Lady," Betsy Foster.
People, Oct. 8, 1990, "Dianne Feinstein," J.D. Reed.
San Francisco magazine, July 1975, "What Makes Feinstein Tick?," Mavis Groza.
San Francisco magazine, Dec. 1981, "Feinstein in the Middle," Jeff Gillenkirk.

Documentary Films:

Uncle Bob, 2010, directed by Robert Oppel, *www.unclebobmovie.com.*

Books:

Shilts, *The Mayor of Castro Street.*
Weiss, *Double Play.*

33: THE CENTER HOLDS

Interviews:

Britt, Harry	Molinari, Jim
Feinstein, Dianne	Nothenberg, Rudy
Fertig, Jack "Sister Boom Boom"	Pak, Rose
Hennessy, Mike	Sklar, Richard

Documents:

Dianne Feinstein files, SFPL History Center.

Newspapers and Magazines:

New York Times, May 23, 24, July 6, Sept. 5, 8, 27, Oct. 8, Nov. 1, 6, Dec. 24, 1979; June 29, July 29, Dec. 10, 1982; Sept. 9, 1984.
San Francisco Chronicle, Mar. 1, Apr. 6, May 3, 22, 23, July 9, 13, Oct. 8, 26, Dec. 10, 11, 12, 1979; Jan. 24, Mar. 13, Dec. 14, 1981.

34: STRANGE ANGELS

Interviews:

Ammiano, Tom   Hicks, Dwight
Britt, Harry   McLean, Lindsy
Dean, Fred   Policy, Carmen
DeBartolo Jr., Eddie   Seifert, George
Dickey, Glenn   Turner, Keena
Edwards, Harry   Walsh, Craig
Fahnhorst, Keith   Zagaris, Michael

Newspapers and Magazines:

San Francisco Chronicle, Sept. 2, 4, Oct. 12, 14, 15, 26, 27, Nov. 2, 10, 23, Dec. 2, 8,
    23, 29, 31, 1981; Jan. 15, 18, 19, 20, 22, 1982; Apr. 22, 2008.
San Francisco Examiner, Sept. 21, Dec 27, 1981; Jan. 3, 4, 5,10, 1982.
San Francisco Examiner Image, Oct. 6, 1985, "Eddie D.," Burr Snider.

Documentary Films:

Distant Replay: Kezar Stadium, YouTube.

Books:

Barber, Phil and Zagaris, Michael, *We Were Champions: The 49ers' Dynasty in Their Own
    Words.* Chicago: Triumph Books, 2002.
Dickey, Glenn, *Glenn Dickey's 49ers: The Rise, Fall and Rebirth of the NFL's Greatest
    Dynasty.* Roseville, CA: Prima Publishing, 2000.
Harris, David, *The Genius: How Bill Walsh Reinvented Football and Created an NFL
    Dynasty.* New York: Random House, 2008.
Montana, Joe, and Raissman, Bob, *Audibles: My Life in Football.* New York: William
    Morrow & Co., 1986.
Walsh, Bill, *Building a Champion: On Football and the Making of the 49ers.* New York:
    St. Martin's Press, 1990.
Walsh, Bill, *The Score Takes Care of Itself: My Philosophy of Leadership.* New York: Port-
    folio Penguin Group, USA, 2009.

35: PLAYING AGAINST GOD

Interviews:

Bertelli, Cheryl   Hicks, Dwight
Dean,Fred   Policy, Carmen
DeBartolo Jr., Eddie   Seifert, George
Fahnhorst, Keith   Turner, Keena
Feinstein, Dianne   Zagaris, Michael

Newspapers and Magazines:

San Francisco Chronicle, Jan. 1, 2, 4, 5, 6, 7, 8, 9, 10, 11, 12, 15, 17, 18, 23, 25, 26,
    1982; July 31, Aug. 9, 10, 2007.
San Francisco Examiner, Dec. 27, 1981.

Books:

Bayless, Skip, *God's Coach: The Hymns, Hype and Hypocrisy of Tom Landry's Cowboys.* New York: Fireside, 1990.
Dickey, *Glenn Dickey's 49ers.*
Harris, *The Genius.*
Montana, *Audibles.*
Myers, Gary, *The Catch: One Play, Two Dynasties, and the Game That Changed the NFL.* New York: Crown, 2009.
Walsh, *Building a Champion.*

36: THE CITY OF SAINT FRANCIS

Interviews:

Alioto, Angela	Jones, Cleve
Barbagelata, Paul	Maupin, Armistead
Britt, Harry	McLean, Lindsy
Calcagno, Vince	Reagan, Ron
Falzon, Frank	Selvin, Joel
Feinstein, Dianne	Volberding, Dr. Paul
Florez, Elisa	

Documentary Films:

Life Before the Lifeboat: San Francisco's Courageous Response to the AIDS Outbreak, produced and directed by Shipra Shukla, 2009.
We Were Here, directed by David Weissman and Bill Weber, Red Flag Releasing, 2011.

Newspapers and Magazines:

Los Angeles Times, Oct.22, 1985.
New York Times, May 22, Oct. 22, Dec. 14, 1985.
San Francisco Chronicle, Jan. 16, 1981; Sept. 18, 1998; July 26, 2003; June 8, 2004; Mar. 10, 2005; June 4, 2006.
San Francisco Examiner Image, June 15, 1986, "Safe Sex on the Silver Screen," David Talbot.
Mother Jones, Apr. 1985, "The AIDS Mecca of the World," Alexis Jetter; "At Risk," David Talbot and Larry Bush.
Noe Valley Voice, Feb. 2006, "Ruth Brinker: A Hero in Our Midst."
People, Nov. 4, 1985, "The Suicide of Dan White Brings a Notorious San Francisco Murder Case to a Bizarre End," David Van Biema.
Time, Oct. 24, 1983, "AIDS Dilemma."

Books:

Jones, Cleve, *Stitching a Revolution: The Making of an Activist.* San Francisco: Harper, 2000.
Shilts, Randy, *And the Band Played On: Politics, People and the AIDS Epidemic.* New York: St. Martin's Press, 1987.

INDEX

ABC, *Monday Night Football,* 372
abortion, legalization of, 251
Ace of Cups, The, 407
Acid Test happenings, 140
ACLU (American Civil Liberties
    Union), 283
ACT-UP, 395
Adair, Peter, 400
Agnos, Art, 204–6, 215–16, 223,
    251, 295
AIDS, 389–403
    and ACT-UP, 395
    AIDS Memorial Quilt, 401
    And the Band Played On, 400
    Behind the Green Door (safe-sex
        remake), 394–95
    and city funding, 395–96
    Coming Home Hospice, 394
    and Feinstein, 395–96
    HIV, 394, 399, 400, 401
    "I Will Survive," 400, 403
    Kaposi's sarcoma, 389–90, 394
    and medical marijuana, 393,
        402–3
    Project Inform, 394
    Project Open Hand, 393–94
    and Reagan administration, 395,
        396–98, 400
    San Francisco AIDS Foundation,
        394

    and San Francisco values, 395–96,
        398
    Shanti Project, 394
    and Sisters of Perpetual Indul-
        gence, 389, 394
    and volunteers, 392–95
    Ward 5B, San Francisco General,
        391–93, 396, 400
AIM (American Indian Movement),
    186
Albin, Peter, 113, 116
Ali, Muhammad, 214, 216
Alice B. Toklas Democratic Club,
    343–44
Alioto, Angela (Veronese), 146, 193,
    234, 395
Alioto, Domenica Lazio, 146
Alioto, Giuseppe, 146, 152
Alioto, Joseph L., 88, 103, 144–55,
    351
    death threats to, 169, 193, 286
    early years of, 144–47, 150, 169
    and gays, 234
    and Ginsberg, 233
    and Haight-Ashbury, 153–55,
        160–61, 163, 164
    Hallinan eulogy by, 405
    and Jim Jones, 276
    law-and-order image of, 151
    law practice of, 145, 152

Alioto, Joseph L. (*Continued*)
  and Mafia, 152–53
  as mayor, 143, 145–46, 151,
    153–55, 160, 218, 234, 247,
    251–52, 256, 354
  as natural politician, 148–49
  as poetry lover, 233
  political ambitions of, 152–53,
    256
  and protests, 149–51, 153–54
  and racial issues, 216, 217–19,
    221, 222
  reelection campaign of (1971),
    162–63
  reelection campaign of (1975),
    248, 249, 252
  and SLA, 192–93
  and unions, 147–49
Allen Temple Baptist Church, 277
Alta Coffee, 78
Altamont, 134–35, 136–42
"Amazing Grace," 334
American Civil Liberties Union
  (ACLU), 283
American Dream, xvii
American Indian Movement (AIM),
  186
American Legion, 145
American Public Health Association,
  396–97
Ammiano, Tom, 374
Amos, Sharon, 309
anarchists, 26–27, 144
Anchors Aweigh (movie), 236
Andrew, Sam, 94, 113–14, 117
Andriano, Sylvester, 145, 149
And the Band Played On (Shilts), 400
Angels of Light, 107
Animals (band), 55, 75
Apocalypse Now (movie), 156
Armstrong, Louis, 60, 81
Asher, Jane, 87
Asian Law Caucus, 228
Atkins, Susan, 130–33, 134

Atlanta Falcons, 367
Atwood, Angela, 176, 181, 191, 194,
  196
Avalon Ballroom, 115

Badlands (movie), 207
Baez, Joan, 334
Bailey, F. Lee, 201
Balin, Marty, 82, 138, 165
Bankhead, Tallulah, 102
Bank of America, 28, 183
Banks, Dennis, 186
Barbagelata, John:
  election challenged by, 254, 258,
    279, 284
  health problems of, 287, 289
  and Jim Jones, 269, 283, 284–86,
    287, 308
  and mayoral and other campaigns,
    252–53, 284, 351
  opposition to Moscone policies,
    260, 262–64, 288
  retirement from politics, 288, 289,
    322
  terror campaign against, 285–87
  and White, 322, 388
Barbagelata, Paul, 262, 285, 288
Barbary Coast district, xv–xvi
Barger, Sonny, 57–58, 138–40
Barnum, P. T., 70
Basie, Count, 60, 75
Bass, Charlotta, 14–15
Bates, Charles, 184, 188–89
Bayview–Hunters Point, racial ten-
  sions in, 33
Beatles, 87
beat underground, 27
Beau Brummels, The, 407
Beck, Glenn, 357
Beggs, Rev. Edward "Larry," 52
  and Human Be-In, 23, 42
  and runaways, 43, 44, 45, 47, 48,
    49
Beggs, Nina, 23–24, 42

Behan, Brendan, 291
Behind the Green Door (movie), 241–42
Behind the Green Door (safe-sex remake), 394–95
Belli, Melvin, 166
Bennett, Tony, 103
Bentley, Gladys, 102
Berg, Peter, 39, 40
Berry, Chuck, 75
Bertelli, Cheryl, 384
Biafra, Jello, 355–56
bicycle-friendly streets, xvii
Bierman, Sue, 248
Big Brother and the Holding Company, 94, 407
    beginnings of, 113–14
    benefit concert by, 58
    Cheap Thrills, 118
    at Fillmore, 58, 62
    and Human Be-In, 22
    and Janis, 114–18
    at Monterey, 91
Blackburn, Robert, 179
Black Cat, 85, 102
Black Cultural Association (BCA), 173, 174
Black Muslims, 206, 209–14, 217, 220–21, 222, 276–77
Black Panthers, 40, 372
    and Alioto, 151
    and SLA, 178, 179, 185
    and violence, 149–50, 151, 161, 172, 173
Black Self-Help Moving & Storage Company, 209, 210, 213, 221, 222
Blue Cheer, 93
Blum, Dick, 342, 347
Bogart, Humphrey, 72
Bortin, Michael, 198–200
Bowie, David, 166
Bradley, Don, 278
Brand, Stewart, 24, 90, 140

Brando, Marlon, 69
Brautigan, Richard, *Trout Fishing in America*, 38
Bridges, Harry, 11–12, 30, 32, 86, 88, 145, 147, 149
Briggs, John, 311, 312, 313, 318–19
Briggs, Marilyn, 241–42
Brinker, Ruth, 393–94
Britt, Harry, 344, 348, 352–53, 357, 374, 395
Brown, Rev. Amos, 208
Brown, Edmund "Pat," 47
Brown, James, 60, 65
Brown, Jerry, 256, 257, 281, 318
Brown, Paul, 362–63, 376, 384
Brown, Willie, 231
    and Feinstein, 343, 374
    and Huckleberry House, 49
    and Jim Jones, 269, 278, 280, 282, 283, 293, 307, 308
    as mayor, 224
    and Moscone, 250, 251, 254, 257, 261, 326
    street-wise, 224, 225–26
    and White, 326, 387
Brownie Mary (Rathbun), 393
Brubeck, Dave, 86
Bruce, Lenny, 28, 75, 86, 239
Bryant, Anita, 311–13, 394
Buchanan, Patrick, 393
Buford, Terri, 280
Bugliosi, Vincent, 194
Burdon, Eric, 55, 75
Burroughs, William S., 100, 128
Burton, John, 250, 258, 261, 264, 281, 343
Burton, Phil, 33, 231, 250–51, 253, 278, 343
Busch, Corey, 254, 256–57, 263, 283
Butterfield, Paul, 75
Byrds (band), 75, 93, 94

Caen, Bea, 85
Caen, Christopher, 88

Caen, Herb, 84–89
    and *Chronicle,* 82–83, 84, 85, 86,
        87, 89, 105, 239
    death of, 406
    early years of, 84–85
    and Feinstein, 356
    and 49ers, 374, 377–78, 384
    and "Frisco," 360
    and gays, 105, 190
    and Jim Jones, 291, 308
    love for the city, 84, 85
    and Moscone, 255, 261
    political edge of, 87, 89
    as "Sackamenna Kid," 85, 88
    and social issues, 88
    and violence, 214, 215, 216
Caen, Maria Theresa, 86, 87
Cahill, Thomas J., 16–17, 31, 34–35,
    150
Cakes, Patty, 119
Calcagno, Vince, 235–36, 238, 246,
    390
Califano, Joseph, 294–95
California:
    abortion legalized in, 251
    death penalty in, 223, 251
    Proposition 6, 318–19
    Proposition 13, 256
    school lunch program in, 251
    social needs vs. fiscal realities in,
        256, 257
    sodomy legalized in, 253
California penal system, 170–72, 173
California State Federation of Labor,
    32
Calvin, John, 397
Campbell, Bobbi (Nightmare),
    389–90, 400
Candlestick Park, 33, 360, 373, 374,
    379, 380, 383
Canepa, Ray, 320
Capaldini, Lisa, 392
Capote, Truman, 105
Carlin, George, 240
Carlos, John, 371

Carrigan, Father, 34
Carter, Bunchy, 172, 173
Carter, Jimmy, 202, 295, 318
Carter, Rosalynn, 281
Casablanca (movie), 72
Casady, Jack, 165
Caserta, Peggy, 28, 118
Casey, Tim, 200
Castro Street Fair, 399
Catholic Action, 145, 149
Catholic Church:
    and birth control funding, 33
    challenges to, 5
    and gays, 234
    and immigrants, 144–45
    influence of, xvi, 33, 35
    and Kandel's obscenity trial, 24
    and pedophilia, 388
    and runaways, 47, 49
    and unions, 145
Catholic Social Services, 164
Chamberlain, Wilt, 358
Charles, Ray, 60
Charles Lloyd Quartet, 75
Chessman, Caryl, 87
Chez Panisse, Berkeley, 236–37
Chief Joseph, 302
Child, Julia, 238
Chin, Gordon, 230–32
Chinatown, 26, 224–32
    and immigration reform law
        (1965), 225
    insular world of, 227
    Ping Yuen public housing, 228–29
    race-mixing prohibitions in, 231
    rent strike in, 228–29
    young activists in, 225–26, 227,
        229
Chinatown Community Develop-
    ment Center, 232
Chinese New Year Parade, 27
Christie, Julie, 87
CIA (Central Intelligence Agency):
    and double agents, 194
    and drugs, 127–29, 201

and Operation Chaos, 172
and Operation Phoenix, 173
Pacific Architects and Engineers,
   173
Cincinnati Bengals, 384
Cinque (DeFreeze), 173–76
   death of, 194–95
   and food program, 183
   and Foster murder, 178–79
   and Hearst kidnapping, 181–83,
      186, 190–95, 201
   media focus of, 181, 182, 191,
      195, 218
   move to LA, 193–95
   rap sheet of, 194
   and reward money, 193
   and Zebra murders, 218
City Lights Books, xvi, 26–27, 91
civil rights:
   activists from San Francisco State,
      27
   demonstrations, 16–17
   Hallinan family involvement in,
      14, 15
   and Operation Zebra, 218–20
   Shelley as supporter of, 32–33
   sit-ins, 47
Clark, Dwight, 365, 366–67, 379–83
Clausen, A. W. "Tom," 263–64
Cleary, Jack, 66–67, 129–30, 212,
   322, 328, 330
Club Sullivan, San Mateo, 60
Coblentz, William, 64, 186
Cockettes, 101–2, 103–7, 115, 135,
   245, 399
coffee, 77–78
Cointelpro, 172
Cold War, 12, 14, 15, 16, 32, 123
Collins, Itsie, 224
Columbia Records, 94, 135
Coming Home Hospice, 394
Communist Party, 11, 144, 145, 311
Compton's Cafeteria, 103
Conant, Marcus, 389–90, 402–3
Condor Club, 252

Conrich, Robert, 54
Constitution, U.S., 220
consumer regulations, xvii
Convent of the Sacred Heart High
   School, 226, 340
Cook, James, 221–22
Cooks, Jesse Lee, 209, 210–12, 221,
   222
Coppola, Francis Ford, 374
Cordova, John, 312
Coreris, Gus, 206, 216–17, 220–21,
   223
Cory, George, 103
Cotton Bowl (1979), 366
Country Joe and the Fish, 96
Cover, Michael, 397
Cow Palace arena, Halloween
   Hooker's Ball in, 240
Coyote (Call Off Your Old Tired Eth-
   ics), 239–40
Coyote, Peter:
   and Altamont, 137, 138
   and Diggers, 39–40, 41, 43
   and drugs, 136
   and Graham, 70
   and Human Be-In, 25
   and runaways, 43
Craig, Roger, 370, 372
Cream (band), 75
Creedence Clearwater Revival, 407
Cromwell, Oliver, 36
Crosby, David, 94
Crosby, Kathryn, 56
Cross, Douglass, 103
Cross, Randy, 361, 379, 381
Crumb, Robert, 25, 90–91, 242
Cutler, Sam, 136

Daley, Richard, 268
Dallas Cowboys, 359, 364, 366, 372,
   375, 376–84
Dalton, David, 117
Dash (gay bar), 102
Davies, Marion, xiii
Davis, Angela, 295, 305–6

Davis, Belva, 66
Davis, Bette, xiii, 102
Davis, Myles, 81, 86, 231
Day of the Locust, The (movie), 141
Dead Kennedys (band), 355, 407
Dean, Fred, 369, 379
Death Angels, 210, 212, 220, 221, 222
DeBartolo, Eddie Jr., 360–61, 363, 364, 365, 373, 378, 383, 384
DeBartolo, Edward Sr., 359–61, 363
DeBerg, Steve, 367
Deep Throat (movie), 241
DeFreeze, Donald "Cinque," 173–74
Delancey Street Foundation, 255
de la Renta, Oscar, 106
Demaris, Ovid, 152
Democratic Convention (1968), 151–52, 198–99
Democratic Party, working-class members of, xvi
Dernburg, Ernest, 124–26
Desmond, Mike, 6, 9–10
Deveron, 46–47
Devine, Dan, 366
Devo (band), 235
Diddley, Bo, 75
Diggers, 25, 36–41
    and Altamont, 136–37
    and community projects, 71
    contradictions of, 40–41
    and death of money, 37, 38
    end of, 131, 143
    feed-in at city hall, 36–37
    free ethos of, 36–37, 39, 41, 99, 158
    and health care, 51–52, 53
    and Hell's Angels, 40, 41, 57
    Invisible Circus of, 42
    and runaways, 35, 43–44
    "Stone Your Neighbor" night, 70
    street communiqués from, 37–38, 39
    and Summer of Love, 37, 40
    women doing grunt work for, 40

Dionysus, 141
Dirty Harry (movie), 215
Dobbs, Harold, 33, 148
Doda, Carol, 252
Donahue, Tom, 92–93
Donohue, F. Joseph "Jiggs," 12
Donovan, 35
Doors (band), 72–73, 75, 92
Douglas, Calvin, 309
Douglas, Michael, 215
drag queen shows, xvi, 102–7
DuBois, W. E. B., 14
Duncan, Isadora, 100
Dykes on Bikes, 240
Dylan, Bob, 23, 61, 170

Eagle Tavern, 237
Eastwood, Clint, 215
Edwards, Harry, 371–72
Egan, Frank, 1–9
Egan, Tommy, 13
Eisenhower, Dwight D., 15
Ellington, Duke, 60, 81, 230
Elliott, Lenvil, 381
El Matador, 85
Enrico's, 85
environmental regulations, xvii
Equal Rights Amendment, 356
Ernie's restaurant, 378
Ever Lovin' Trading Post, 157, 161

Fahnhorst, Keith, 367–68, 379
Falwell, Jerry, 396
Falzon, Frank:
    and Chief Gain, 320
    and White, 322, 325, 328–30, 346, 387–88
    and Zebra murders, 212
Family Dog collective, 81
Farm (commune), 142–43
FBI:
    Cointelpro, 172
    and Cold War politics, 14, 15
    and Hearst kidnapping, 182, 186, 187, 188–89, 193, 197, 200

police-state measures of, 177
and racial issues, 33, 172, 371
Febe's (club), 237
Feinstein, Bert, 226, 322, 340, 342
Feinstein, Dianne:
as acting mayor, 334–36, 339, 343
and AIDS, 395–96
ambition of, 340
on board of supervisors, 164,
226–27, 341–42
bodyguard of, 353
and cable cars, 350
death threats to, 286, 342, 350–51
early years of, 339–40
and 49ers, 374, 378, 384, 385
on gays and lesbians, 234, 240, 352
healing the city, 342–45, 353, 357
and Jim Jones, 269, 281
as landlord, 353, 356
and leadership, 335–36, 339, 340,
343, 344, 349, 353, 356–57,
395, 396
as mayor, 351–57, 395–96
mayoral campaign (1971), 162–63
mayoral campaign (1975), 252,
342, 355
mayoral campaign (1979), 350–51
and Moscone/Milk murders, 327,
330–31, 334–35, 347
political career of, 334–36,
340–43
and porn films, 242
and sexism, 355
and Sullivan case, 67
trekking in Nepal, 335, 342
and White, 322, 326–27, 388
and White trial, 345–47
Fellini, Federico, 245
Ferguson, "Sag" Darel, 159–60, 164
Ferlinghetti, Lawrence, 75
"An Elegy to Dispel Gloom," 333
and City Lights Books, xvi, 26–27
and 49ers, 374
and Ginsberg, 22, 27
Fertig, Jack (Sister Boom Boom), 355

Fillmore Auditorium, 60–63, 123
benefit concerts at, 58, 70
Black Muslim mosque in, 209,
217, 276–77
and Caen, 86
dance permit for, 62–64
Diggers night in, 70
and Graham, 58, 60–61, 62, 63,
67, 68–71, 74–75, 209
and Sullivan, 60–61
Fillmore district, 60–64
blacks pushed out of, 27, 61–62
demolition of, 26, 61–62, 154,
160, 208–9, 271, 277, 278
and Peoples Temple, 283, 305
and Sullivan, 60–61, 62–64
Third Baptist Church in, 208
Fillmore East, Manhattan, 70
Finley, Charles O., 178
Finocchio, Joe, 102
Fisher, Eddie, 69
Fisherman's Wharf, 238
Flamin' Groovies, The, 407
Fleet Week, 354
Florez, Elisa "Missy Manners," 395
Florida Health Department, 396
Flower Drum Song (musical), 231
Fog over Frisco (movie), xiii
Folgers Coffee, 78
folk and jazz clubs, 27
Folsom State Prison, 87, 170
Fong, Edsel Ford, 245
Fong, Heather, 352
food revolution, 236–38
Forbidden City nightclub, 230–31
Ford, Gerald R., 189–90
Fortson, Hue, 280, 301
49er Faithful, 358, 373, 379, 383–85
49ers, 358–75
and Clark, 365, 366–67, 379–83
January 10, 1982, game, 379–84
and Montana, 365–67, 370, 372,
380, 381–83
in 1981 season, 367–69, 372–75,
377–79

49ers (*Continued*)
    and race relations, 370–72
    and Super Bowl, 384–86
    The Catch, 382–83, 386
    and "us against the world," 372
    and Walsh, 363–73, 377–82,
        384–86, 399
    "West Coast offense" of, 362, 381
Foster, Jim, 354
Foster, Marcus A., 178–79, 180
Fotinos, John, 206, 216–17, 220,
    221
Fourth Amendment, 220
Fox, Jan, 244
Fox News, xvii
Francis of Assisi, Saint, 37, 398
Fratianno, Jimmy "the Weasel,"
    152–53
Frazier, Joe, 214
Freed, Alan, 92
Freed, Donald, 193
Freiberg, David, 73
Freitas, Joseph Jr., 259, 267–71, 282,
    284, 293–94, 308, 346
Fresno Bee, 291
Friedman, Myra, 116
"Frisco," 360
Fromme, Lynette "Squeaky," 190
Fuller, Bobby, 94Gain, Charles,
    258–60, 287, 319–21, 330,
    343, 347–48, 351

Gance, Abel, 374
Garcia, Jerry, 29, 30, 61, 73, 107,
    374, 406
Garland, Judy, 236, 319
Garry, Charles, 296, 306
Gaskin, Stephen, 142–43
Gavin, Steve, 290–92
Gay Freedom Day Parade, 236, 252,
    316, 321, 352
Gaynor, Gloria, 400
gays and lesbians, 233–47
    and AIDS, 389–403

    antigay actions, 311–13, 318–19,
        348
    bathhouses, 239, 320
    domestic partner legislation, 352
    drag queen shows, xvi, 102–7
    Dykes on Bikes, 240
    and Feinstein, 234, 240, 352
    and food revolution, 236–38
    gay carnival, 235–39
    gay liberation, xvi, 103–4, 265,
        332, 356
    gay marriage, xvii, 234
    and Halloween festival, 318–19,
        355
    and identity war, 232
    job seekers, 252
    and legislation, 251, 253, 265
    and Milk, 265, 312–19, 332, 333
    and Moscone, 253, 254–55, 313,
        316–19, 351
    in North Beach, 27, 102, 105
    Opel murder, 348–49
    in police department, 259, 352
    police raids on, xvi, 234
    and S&M safety, 352
    and "Tales of the City," 244–47
    teachers, 319, 374
    and White, 345
    and White verdict, 347–48
Geary Theater, xiii
Genet, Jean, 171
German, William, 78
Getlin, Josh, 263–64
Getz, Dave, 115, 116
Giannini, Amadeo Pietro, 28
Gilford, Rotea, 216, 217, 219
Ginsberg, Allen, 85, 92, 100, 127,
    233
    and Alioto, 233
    death of, 406
    "Howl," xvi, 27
    and Human Be-In, 22, 23
    and "seekers," xvii
Gitlin, Todd, 203

Gleason, Ralph J., 81–82
Glide Memorial Church, 42–43, 49,
    245, 277, 333, 341
Goddard, John, 62
Godfather (Bangkok tycoon), 229
"God Save the Queen," 102
Gold, Herbert, 86
Golden Gate Park, 74, 82
Goldman, Betty, 339–40
Goldman, Leon, 339–40
Goldman, Morris, 340
Goldwater, Barry, 176, 240
Good Earth commune, 157–68
Gooden, Theodore, 221–22
Goodlett, Carlton, 274
Good Times, 71, 141, 155
Gordon (AIDS patient), 392
Graham, Bill, 113
    and bands, 93
    birth and early years of, 69
    concerts staged by, 72–74
    and dance license, 61, 62, 63, 64
    death of, 406
    and Fillmore Auditorium, 58,
        60–61, 62, 63, 67, 68–71,
        74–75, 209
    and media, 71–72, 82, 93
    skimming the proceeds, 74
    and Smith, 58
Graham, Billy, 358
Graham, Bob, 269, 270, 271, 293–94
Graham, Bonnie, 63
Grand Central baths, 239
Grassroots, 62
Grateful Dead, 62, 77, 374, 407
    and Altamont, 136–37
    in concerts, 30, 87
    and Graham, 72, 73, 74
    in Haight-Ashbury, 28
    and Hell's Angels, 57
    house raided by drug squad, 25,
        29–30
    and Human Be-In, 22
    as local band, 23, 39

and runaways, 48
and Straight Theater, 48
Great Society, The (band), 407
Green, Larry, 209, 210–11, 213, 221,
    222
Green Bay Packers, 376
Gregory, Dick, 28
Grogan, Emmett, 39–40, 43, 44, 52,
    136, 143
Guevara, Che, 190
Gurley, Hongo Ishi, 114–15, 116,
    119–20, 121
Gurley, James, 112–14, 116–22
Gurley, Nancy, 111–22
Guyana:
    Jim Jones in, 273, 284, 293,
        294–97, 348
    Jonestown in, see Jonestown
    Peoples Temple in, 273, 284, 293,
        294–95, 298–304, 324

Haas, Walter Jr., 263
Hague, Quita, 210–11, 213
Hague, Richard, 210–11
Haight-Ashbury, 27–30
    comfort and help in, 126
    counterculture in, 24, 25, 27, 30
    drugs in, 128–29, 159, 161,
        166–67
    and Good Earth, 157–68
    and mayoral campaign (1975),
        248–49
    police harassment in, 31, 56, 161,
        163–64, 167
    redevelopment stopped in, 27,
        154–55, 160–61
    riots in, 143, 149, 150, 154
    and Summer of Love, 31, 35
    Victorian "painted ladies" in, 27,
        165, 225
    violence in, 124–26, 129, 142,
        153–55
Haight-Ashbury Free Clinic, 54–59,
    76, 124, 154

Haight-Ashbury Legal Organization
  (HALO), 30, 72
Halas, George, 376
Hale, Denise, 105
Hall, Camilla, 175, 176, 194
Hallinan, Patrick (father), 4, 12
Hallinan, Patrick (son), 11, 12, 14,
  15, 16
Hallinan, Terence "Terry":
  and Alioto, 154
  as district attorney, 118
  early years of, 12–13, 16
  and Hearst, 200, 201
  and his father's death, 405–6
  and Janis, 118
  and Milk, 264–65
  and social issues, 16, 27, 53, 154
Hallinan, Vincent, 2–17
  and Bridges, 11–12
  courtroom skills of, 3, 8, 9
  death of, 405
  and Egan, 4–9
  and fatherhood, 10–11, 12
  FBI pressure on, 15
  and Hearst case, 200
  imprisoned for political reasons,
    12, 13, 15
  IRS pressure on, 15
  law practice of, 4–5, 21, 405
  political activism of, 14–15, 16–17
  protégés of, 21, 25, 30, 120, 162,
    242, 264
  public opinion turned against,
    12–16
  and radical politics, 11, 13, 14, 16
  violence against family of, 12–13,
    154
  and Vivian, 2, 5–7, 9–10, 405–6
Hallinan, Vivian Moore:
  attempted rape of, 13–14
  death of, 406
  and Egan, 6, 7–8
  family of, 10–11, 12–13
  FBI pressure on, 15
  and grand jury, 7–8
  and radical politics, 11, 14, 15, 16
  and Vincent, 2, 5–7, 9–10, 405–6
Halloween Hooker's Ball, 240,
  259–60, 318–19
HALO (Haight-Ashbury Legal Orga-
  nization), 30, 72
Hamburger Mary's, 237
Hammett, Dashiell, xvii, 2
Hampton, Fred, 172
Hanna, Archbishop Edward, 145
Harris, Anthony, 210, 213, 214,
  220–21, 222
Harris, Bill, 176, 181, 195–96, 199,
  200, 201–2
Harris, Emily, 176, 193, 195–96,
  199–200, 202
Harris, George Edgerly III "Hibis-
  cus," 99–102, 103–7, 399
Harris, Marilyn, 27–29, 31
Harris, Mary Lou, 99
Hart, Lenny, 74
Hart, Mickey, 70, 73, 74, 135
Hartmann, Tory, 282
Hatch, Orrin, 395
Hauser, Fayette, 101–2, 103, 105–6,
  115, 117, 118–19
Hayden, Tom, 128
Headley, Lake, 193–94, 195
health care:
  and AIDS, see AIDS
  free, 53–59
  and Smith, 51–59
  universal, xvii
Hearst, Catherine, 180, 184–85,
  197–98, 201, 202
Hearst, Patty, 180–203, 374
  and bank robberies, 192–93, 199
  father's reaction to kidnapping,
    183–86, 189, 191, 193, 197–98
  kidnapping of, 181, 218
  media attention to, 181, 182, 184,
    186, 191, 196
  and public opinion, 202
  as SLA target, 180–81
  and Stockholm syndrome, 202

taken into custody, 200–201
as Tania, 190–92, 200–201
treatment by SLA, 181–82,
     190–92, 195–96, 199, 201–2
trial of, 201–2
Hearst, Randolph, 180
divorce of, 202–3
and food program, 183, 185–86
and Moore, 187–89
and Patty's defense, 200–201
and Patty's kidnapping, 183–86,
     189, 191, 192, 193, 197–98
Hearst, Veronica Beracasa, 202
Hearst, Will (nephew), 181, 183,
     184, 197
Hearst, William Randolph, xiii
Hearst Corporation, 77, 180–81
Hearst Foundation, 183
Hell's Angels, 29, 126
and Altamont, 136–41
and Diggers, 40, 41, 57
and free clinic, 51, 57
and Human Be-In, 23, 24
Helms, Chet, 90, 93, 113, 114, 115,
     116
Helms, Jesse, 243
Hendrix, Jimi, 62, 75, 91, 94, 117,
     119
Hennessy, Mike, 353
Herman, Jimmy, 147
Herman, Justin, 277
Hibiscus, 99–102, 103–7, 399
Hillsborough, Robert "Mr. Green-
     jeans," 312–13
Hills Brothers coffee, 78
Hinckle, Warren, 356
Hines, Earl "Fatha," 79
HIV (human immunodeficiency
     virus), 394, 399, 400, 401
Hoffman, Abbie, 38, 93
Holiday, Billie, 60
Hollywood, blacklisted filmmakers
     in, 14
homosexuals, see gays and lesbians
Hongisto, Richard, 164, 239–40, 258

Hooker's Ball, 240, 259–60
hookers' liberation group, 24,
     239–40, 259
Hoover, J. Edgar, 15, 172, 377
Hope, Bob, 102, 230, 360
Hot Potato, 323, 329
House Un-American Activities Com-
     mittee (HUAC), 16
Housman, Nathan S., 2, 9
Howlin' Wolf, 75
Hoyfield, Rick, 45
Hubbard, Alfred M., 127
Huckleberry House, 43–44, 45–46,
     48–50, 76
Hudson, Rock, 396, 397
Huggins, John, 172, 173
Hughes, Jessie, 1–2, 4, 9
Human Be-In, 22–23, 24–25, 31, 42,
     44, 124, 142
Humphrey, Hubert H., 151
hungry i, 28, 85
Hunter, Meredith, 139, 142
Hurok, Sol, 70
Huston, Will "Wild Bill," 159, 164,
     165, 166–67
Huxley, Aldous, 127

Ice Wagon Drivers' Union, 34
I Ching, 163
"I Enjoy Being a Girl," 245
"I Left My Heart in San Francisco,"
     103
immigration, xvii, 225
Internal Security Act (1950), 15
International Hotel, 229–30, 232
Invisible Circus, 42
Irish Catholics:
     in Castro and Noe Valley districts,
        26
     in city hall, xvi, 4, 17, 25
     immigrants, 144–45
     in police department, xvi, 25, 31,
        32, 34, 49, 208, 217, 242, 259,
        394
Irish Invincibles, 4

Irish Republican Brotherhood, 4
Irish Volunteers, collecting for, xvi
Isaacs, Cyril, 158
Italian Catholics:
    and anarchists, 26, 144
    in city hall, xvi
    immigrants, 144–45
    in North Beach, 26, 27, 146, 149
    in police department, xvi
Ivory Snow, 241–42
"I Will Survive," 400, 403

Jackson, George, 170–71, 174, 295
Jackson, Jonathan, 171, 295
Jackson, Wilbert "Popeye," 186–87,
    189
Jaffe, Dana, 165, 166, 167–68
Jagger, Mick, 136, 137, 139–40,
    141–42, 238, 350
Jefferson Airplane, 62, 94, 407
    and Altamont, 138
    and banquet, 86–87
    in concerts, 58, 74, 75, 86
    debut of, 81
    and Gleason, 82
    and Good Earth, 165
    and Human Be-In, 22–23
    and Summer of Love, 35
Jenkins, Dave, 147
Jennings, Duffy, 331
"Joe Hill," 405
John Birch Society, 276
Johnson, Bill, 363
Johnson, Lyndon B., 76, 151
Jones, Brian, 91
Jones, Cleve:
    and AIDS, 390, 394, 400–403
    and Milk, 314, 321, 331–32, 334,
        347
    and Peoples Temple, 282
    and White, 316
Jones, Diane, 392
Jones, Ed "Too Tall," 378, 380, 382
Jones, Rev. Jim, 267–74
    and black church leaders, 277

charismatic personality of, 277,
    289, 291, 300, 306
as civic leader, 269
early years of, 275–83
in Guyana, 273, 284, 293,
    294–97, 348
and media, 289, 290–92, 308
and Moscone election, 269, 271,
    279
peculiarities of, 283
and Peoples Temple, see Peoples
    Temple
and political connections, 269,
    274, 276, 278–83, 284, 285,
    287, 289, 292, 294–96
pulpit performances of, 277,
    299–300
sexual appetites of, 272
and Stoen, 270–74, 293
and suicides, 299–300, 302–4
violent fantasies of, 273
as weird and dangerous, 293,
    295, 296–97, 298, 299–305,
    307–8
Jones, Jim Jr., 272, 278, 279–81, 297,
    309–10
Jones, LeRoi, *Dutchman,* 75
Jones, Lynetta, 275
Jones, Marceline, 275, 278
Jones, Stephan, 275, 278, 309
Jones, Suzanne, 309
Jonestown, Guyana:
    aftermath of, 289, 306–8, 309–10,
        324, 333
    Congressman Ryan's visit to,
        298–99, 300
    escapes from, 306, 309
    as police state, 296–97
    suicides in, 299–300, 302–4, 305
    as symbol of mass lunacy, 274
    as unpredictable, 283
    White Night drills in, 297, 299,
        309
Joplin, Janis, 90, 94, 105, 132
    and Big Brother, 114–18

and concerts, 73, 86, 91, 117
and Diggers, 40
and drugs, 59, 115, 116–18, 122
and Hell's Angels, 57
and Human Be-In, 22
and Monterey, 91, 117

Kak (band), 407
Kaliflower commune, 99–101, 105
Kandel, Lenore, *The Love Book,* 24, 25
Kantner, Paul, 22, 23, 74, 138
Kaposi's sarcoma (KS), 389–90, 394
Karenga, Ron, 172, 173, 174
Katsaris, Maria, 273
Kaukonen, Jorma, 407
Keenan, Maurice, 348–49
Kefauver, Estes, 34
Keitel, Harvey, 59
Kelly, Gene, 230–31
Kennedy, Diana, 237
Kennedy, Edward "Ted," 180, 238
Kennedy, John F. "Jack," 32, 33, 127, 128, 176, 188, 254, 377
Kennedy, Joseph, 49
Kennedy, Michael, 242
Kennedy, Robert F. "Bobby," 77, 198–99, 254
Kentucky Jim, 158
Kerry, John, 243
Kesey, Ken, 24, 140, 239
Kever, Steve, 157, 158, 161, 163–66, 167, 168
Kezar Stadium, 358–59, 360
Kilduff, Marshall, 290, 292
King, Martin Luther Jr., 43, 150–51, 304
Kissinger, Henry, 281
KMPX San Francisco, 92–93
Kohn, Howard, 197
Koop, C. Everett, 397
Kopp, Quentin:
  and Chief Gain, 260
  and Feinstein, 341, 343, 351

and Milk, 265, 317–18
and Moscone, 260, 263, 265, 317–18, 324
and NWLF, 286
and Peoples Temple, 324
and White, 322, 346
Korean War, 14
Kozol, Harry, 201–2
KQED-TV, 151
Kramer, Larry, 395
Kramer, Ludlow, 183
Kraus, Bill, 400
Krupa, Gene, 85
KSAN-FM San Francisco, 93
Kwanzaa, 172, 174

Lacey, Father Tom, 316
Landry, Tom, 375, 376–77, 383
land-use war (1970s), 229–30
Lane, Mark, 306
Latino Mission district, 312
Laughing Policeman, The (movie), 215
Laundry Workers Union, 30
Lautzker, Larry "The Hat," 160
LaVey, Anton, 130–31
Leach, Rev. Norman E., 285, 305–6, 307–8
Leary, Timothy, 22, 38, 127
Lee, Ed, 227–29, 231–32
Lenny (movie), 239
Lesh, Phil, 28, 29
Lewis, Jerry, 69
Lewis, Peter, 73, 94, 95, 123, 133, 135
Lieberson, Goddard, 94–95
Little, Russell, 174, 179, 186
Little Richard, 60, 62
Loma Prieta earthquake, 223
Lomax, Louis, 371
Lombardi, Vince, 376
Longshoremen's Hall, 81, 405
longshoremen's strike (1934), 145
Longshoremen's Union, 147–49
Look magazine, 152–53

Los Angeles Police Department (LAPD), Criminal Conspiracy Section, 173
Lott, Ronnie, 370, 372, 386
Love (band), 62
Love Book, The (Kandel), 24, 25
Love Conspiracy Commune, 38
Love Generation, 31
LSD, 53, 91, 126, 127–28

MacDonald, Jeanette, 87
MacLaine, Shirley, 394
Mafia, 34, 146, 152–53, 377
Magnum Force (movie), 215
Maher, Bill, 341
Maher, John, 255
Malden, Karl, 215
Malick, Terrence, 207
Manilatown, 230
Manley, Ken, 65, 66
Manners, Missy (Florez), 395
Manney, Tom, 209, 210, 221, 222
Mansfield, Jayne, 103, 131
Manson, Charles, 132–33, 134–35, 136, 140, 176, 190
Mapplethorpe, Robert, 348
Marcello, Carlos, 377
Marigold (neighbor), 402
marijuana, medical, xvii, 385, 393, 402–3
marijuana laws, 30, 251, 261
Martin, Del, 234
Martin, Florence, 53
Martin, Peter, 26
Matek, Stanley, 396
Matrix (club), 81
Maud's lesbian bar, 373, 383–84
Maupin, Armistead, 243–47, 400
Mayor of Castro Street, The (Shilts), 389
Mays, Willie, 86, 198, 208, 358
McCabe, Charles, 82, 149, 244
McCarran Act (1950), 15
McCarthy, Leo, 204, 251

McCarthy, Robert "Mouseman," 156–59
McCarthyism, 14, 311
McCartney, Paul, 87
McElhenny, Hugh, 359
McElvane, Jim, 303
McGucken, Archbishop Joseph, 33, 262
McKernan, Ron "Pigpen," 29–30
McLean, Lindsy, 370, 399
McLuhan, Marshall, 87
McNeil Island, 12, 15, 132
McNight, Sharon, 393
Means, Russell, 186
Melcher, Terry, 133
Mel's Diner, 16
Mel's Sporting Goods, LA, 195, 201
Merry Pranksters, 140, 141, 374
Mertle, Elmer and Deanna, 268
Meyer, Cord, 127
Meyer, Mary, 127
Michaels, Lee, 407
Milk, Harvey, 253, 264–66, 288
    and Barbagelata, 253, 288
    bullhorn of, 332, 347, 401
    and death threats, 321
    finances of, 332
    and homosexuality, 265, 312–19, 332, 333
    and Jim Jones, 282, 283, 294–95, 324
    legacy of, 333, 334, 335, 343–44, 374, 402
    and political aspirations, 317, 389
    memorials to, 334–35, 401
    and Moscone, 265, 317–18, 324
    murder of, 327–28, 330–31, 347, 394
    popularity of, 264–65, 314, 331, 357
    and progressive revolution, 316–19, 324, 357
    and rent control, 323

and White, 314–16, 325, 326–27, 329
Miller, Christine, 300–303, 304
Miller, George, 249
Miller, Ira, 367
Miller, Jerry, 73, 94, 135
Mills, Al and Jeannie, 267, 268–70
Minority Coaches Fellowship Program, 371
Missabu, Rumi, 104, 106
Mission Emergency Hospital, 52
Mitchell, Jim and Artie, 240–43, 356, 394–95, 406
Mitty, Archbishop John, 145
MJB coffee, 78
Moby Grape, 73, 93–94, 123, 135, 408
Mojo Men, The (band), 408
Molinari, Jim, 257, 326, 328, 353–54
Mona's Club, 440, 102
Mondale, Walter, 281
Monroe, Marilyn, 98
Montana, Joe, 365–67, 370, 372, 380, 381–83
Monterey Pop Festival, 91, 117
Moonies, 278
Moore, Dan "Spud," 163, 164–65
Moore, Manuel, 209, 212, 214, 221, 222
Moore, Sara Jane, 187–90
Moore, Vivian, see Hallinan, Vivian Moore
Moose, Ed, 261, 373
Morabito, Tony, 358, 359
Moral Majority, 396
Morrison, Jack, 148
Morrison, Jim, 72–73, 87
Morrison, Van, 62
Moscone, Christopher, 255, 261–62, 317, 332, 347
Moscone, Eugenia Bondanza "Gina," 250, 261–62, 325, 332, 347, 351, 374–75

Moscone, George, 248–66
and city politics, 263–64
death threats, 321
early years of, 249–50
election of, 253–55, 269, 271, 279
and family, 261–62, 264, 323
finances of, 332–33
and gays, 253, 254–55, 313, 316–19, 351
and Jim Jones/Jonestown, 269, 271, 278–83, 293, 306–7, 324
legacy of, 333, 334, 335, 343, 351
as mayor, 247, 256–66, 318–19, 323, 357
mayoral campaign (1975), 248–49, 251–53, 255, 278–80
memorials to, 334–35, 401
and Milk, 265, 317–18, 324
murder of, 326, 327–28, 330–31, 394
personal life of, 260–62, 279–80
progressive values of, 251–52, 256, 259, 260, 265–66, 306–7, 316–19, 323, 324, 333, 351, 357
as street player, 256–57, 288, 317, 331
and White, 323–26, 329
Moscone, Jonathan, 261–62, 332
Moscone, Lee, 249–50
Moscone, Rebecca, 332
Most Holy Redeemer parish, 394
Mother Earth (band), 408
Mothers of Invention, 62
Motion Picture Association of America, 215
Mountain Girl, 29
Mouseman (McCarthy), 158–59, 160–61
Muhammad, Elijah, 209, 210
Murchison, Clint Jr., 376, 377
Murdoch, Rupert, 292
Murphy, Cornelius, 353
Murphy, George, 188

Murray, George, 149–50
Musburger, Brent, 371

NAACP (National Association for the Advancement of Colored People), 283
Napoleon (movie), 374
National Football League (NFL), 372–73, 376, 379
Nation of Islam, 209–10, 212, 217, 222
Nelder, Al, 164
Nelson, Tracy, 408
Nelson, Willie, 365
Newhall, Jon, 79, 80
Newhall, Ruth, 79, 80
Newhall, Scott, 76–82
    and the *Chronicle*, 76–78, 79, 80, 82, 162, 246, 356
    death of, 406
    family difficulties of, 78–80
    leg amputated, 79
New Left, 203
Newsom, Gavin, 231
Newton, Huey, 185, 231, 295–96
New Wave, 235
New West, 292–93, 294
New World Liberation Front (NWLF), 169–70, 187, 286–87, 342
New York City:
    raids on gays in, 234
    Stonewall riots, 103
Nichols, Nicky, 99
Nightmare, Sister Florence (Campbell), 389–90, 400
Nisker, Wes "Scoop," 91–93
Niven, David, 77, 348
Nixon, Richard M., 152, 180, 243, 254, 276, 377
Nixon, Tricia, 180
Nixon administration, 177
Nolan, Dick, 255
Nolan, Tom, 394
Norman, Tommy, 346

North Beach:
    bottomless dancing in, 252
    gay and lesbian clubs in, 27, 102, 105
    jazz clubs in, 27, 85
    Little Italy in, 26, 27, 146, 149
    topless bars in, 27, 33, 76, 87, 130
    tourists in, 27
Nureyev, Rudolf, 87
NWLF (New World Liberation Front), 169–70, 187, 286–87, 342

O'Connor, Mary, 48
O'Connor, Raymond J., 17, 47–49
O'Farrell Theater, 242
Olympic Club, 21
Olympic Games, Summer (1968), 371
Opel, Robert, 348–49
Operation Chaos, 172
Operation Phoenix, 173
Operation Zebra, 217–20
Opsahl, Myrna, 199, 200
Osceola (band), 164
Oswald, Lee Harvey, 128, 194

Pacific Architects and Engineers, 173
Pacific Gas and Electric Company, 286
Pacific Sun, 244
Paiva, George, 399
Pak, Rose, 224–27, 231, 353
Palace movie house, 101, 104–5, 107
Palmer, Paige, 235
Papa Al, 56–57
Park Emergency Hospital, 52
Pates, Gordon, 246
Paul Butterfield Blues Band, 75
PCP, 126
Pearson, Drew (Dallas Cowboy), 383
Pelosi, Nancy, 231
People in Need (PIN) food program, 185–86, 188

Peoples Temple, 267–74
  and aftermath of Jonestown,
    309–10, 345, 346
  children taken by, 284–85, 295
  defectors from, 267, 268–70,
    292–93, 299
  expansion of, 283
  in Guyana, 273, 284, 293,
    294–95, 298–304, 324
  "Inside Peoples Temple," 292
  investigations of, 269–71, 294,
    298, 306, 308
  and legal battles, 296
  loyalty tests and humiliations in,
    272
  and media, 290–92
  move to San Francisco, 258,
    276–77
  political connections of, 255,
    278–83, 284, 285, 293
  racial hierarchy in, 278
  in Redwood Valley, 276
  social outreach programs of, 277
  suicides in, 299–300, 302–4
  threats issued by, 285–86
  and voter fraud, 258, 271, 273, 279
  as weird and dangerous, 282–83,
    284–85, 289, 293, 307, 308
Peri, Don, 251
Perkins, Ray, 378
Perlman, David, 56
Peron, Dennis, 355, 385
Perrine, Valerie, 239
Perry, Joe, 359
Perry, Nancy Ling, 176, 179, 194
Peters, John, 141–42
Phipps, Diana, 44–45
Pike, James, 43
Pike, James Jr., 43
PIN (People in Need) food program,
  185–86, 188
Ping Yuen public housing, 228–29
Pittsburgh Steelers, 361, 376
Pizzaro, Allen, 139
Planned Parenthood, 33

Platypus Party, 162–63
Plunkett, Jim, 360
Policy, Carmen, 361, 363, 365
Poor People's Press, 286
porn movies, 240–43, 356
Price, Leontyne, 86
prisoner rights movement, 171, 172,
  174
prison reform, 170–71, 172
Progressive Party, 14
Prohibition, xvi, 146
Project Inform, 394
Project Open Hand, 393–94
Prokes, Michael, 290, 291
Proposition 6 (California), 318–19
Proposition 13 (California), 256
prostitute rights movement, 24,
  239–40, 259
Psychedelic Shop, 24
Pulp Fiction (movie), 58

Quicksilver Messenger Service, 62, 73
Quinn, John, 394
Quinn, William, 4, 5

racial tensions, 204–23
  Black Muslims, 206, 209, 212–14,
    217, 220–21, 222
  black power confrontations, 231
  in California prisons, 170–71
  Death Angels, 210, 212, 220, 221,
    222
  and FBI, 33, 172, 371
  and Fillmore demolition, 26,
    61–62, 154, 160, 208–9
  media stories on, 214–15, 218,
    220
  Nation of Islam, 209–10, 212,
    217, 222
  race riots, 33, 226
  racial profiling, 218–20, 260
  and SFPD, 208, 216, 217,
    218–20, 221, 222
  stopping the hate, 215–16
  Unknown Body #169, 213–14

racial tensions (*Continued*)
  white devil as grafted snake,
    209–10
  white vigilantes, 216, 221–22
  Zebra murders, 206–7, 209–23
  Zodiac killer, 207
Ramrod (roadie), 374
Randy (meth head), 124–26
Rathbun, Mary Jane "Brownie Mary,"
    393
Rauschenberg, Robert, 106
Reagan, Nancy, 95, 96, 397, 398
Reagan, Patti (Davis), 95–97, 397
Reagan, Ronald, 180, 379–80
  and AIDS crisis, 395, 396–98, 400
  and conservative politics, 95–96,
    352, 357, 371
  as governor, 47, 95, 150, 152
  and Hearst family, 183, 197
  and Jim Jones, 281
  and Moscone, 251
  and political campaign, 152
Reagan, Ron, 95, 96–97, 397
Reagan administration, and AIDS
    crisis, 395, 396–98, 400
real estate:
  anti–high rise campaigns, 88, 230
  and 1970s protesters, 229–30
  restrictions in, xvi
  speculators, 251
Reckless Claudia (movie), 242
Red Army Faction, 195
Reddick, Donald, 57
Redding, Otis, 75, 90, 117
Reed, Rex, 105
Reisman, Alex, 111–12, 114–15,
    117, 120–22
Reisman, Dorothy, 115
Reisman, Nancy Felice (Gurley),
    111–22
Remiro, Joe, 176, 179, 186
Reuben, David, 267–71, 273, 281,
    294, 298, 308
Reynolds, Jack "Hacksaw," 369, 370
Rice, Jerry, 372

Richards, Keith, 137, 139, 140
Rico (smack pusher), 159
Rifkin, Danny, 39
Riggs, Marlon, 400
Robeson, Paul, 14
Robinson, Smokey, 231
Rockett, Rita, 393
Rodgers, Judy, 237
Roff, Hadley, 147, 148, 354
Rogiers, Jacques (Jack Rogers),
    286–87
Rohan, Brian, 25, 30, 72, 133
Rolling Stone, 71, 82, 93, 189, 194,
    197
Rolling Stones, 93, 135
  and Altamont, 136–42
Romeo Void (band), 408
Romero, Cesar, 397
Ron "Leo," 159
Roosevelt, Franklin D., 11, 145
Rose, Frances, 211–12, 222
Rosenthal, Irving, 99, 100, 101, 105
Rossi, Angelo, 4
Roth, Philip, 238
Rozelle, Pete, 361
Rubin, Jerry, 22, 38
Ruby, Jack, 128
runaway children and teens, xvi, 23,
    35, 43–50, 56, 123, 130–31
Ryan, Joe, 262
Ryan, Leo, 298–99, 300, 306–7
Ryan, Margaret, 306
Ryan, Pat, 298

Sacred Heart High, 31, 145
Sahl, Mort, 28
St. Ignatius High School, 31, 209,
    262
St. James, Margo, 24, 239–40, 259,
    260, 320–21
Salon, xiv
Sam and Dave, 75
Sanders, Prentice Earl, 208, 211,
    213, 216, 217, 219–20, 222
San Franciscans Against Prop 6, 318

San Francisco:
  alternative reality in, 22
  antigun ordinance in, 356
  bands, playlist, 407–8
  built on a dare, xv
  cable cars, 350
  and chaos, 169
  city response to AIDS crisis, 395–96, 398, 401
  death threats to politicians in, 286, 321
  difference between Berkeley and, 22
  earthquake and fire (1906), xv, 146
  electing supervisors, 264
  environmentalism in, 356
  government corruption in, 288–89
  healing the city, 342–45, 353, 357, 386
  high-rise construction in, 351, 352–53
  labor unions in, 288, 356
  leadership in, 335–36
  as "Left Coast City," xvii
  libertine image of, xv–xvi
  longshoremen's strike, 11
  neighborhoods in, 26–27
  Proposition B, 263–64, 284, 287
  rent control in, 263, 352–53
  tourism business in, 259
  turning sour, 123–33, 169–70
  urban renewal in, 61, 277
  Victorian "painted ladies" in, 27, 165, 225
  and White verdict, 347–48
San Francisco AIDS Foundation, 394
"San Francisco" (show tune), 319
San Francisco Chronicle:
  Brown and Pak, 231
  and Caen, 82–83, 84, 85, 86, 87, 89, 105, 239
  and cultural revolution, 71–72, 76–83
  and Feinstein, 351–52, 356
  and Fillmore, 64
  and free clinic, 56, 58
  and Graham, 71–72
  and Jim Jones, 289, 290–92, 308
  and Moscone, 252, 255, 261
  and Newhall, 76–78, 79, 80, 82, 162, 246, 356
  and runaways, 44–45
  "Tales of the City," 244–47
  and Vietnam War, 80
  and Zodiac killer, 207
San Francisco Council of Churches, 285, 305
San Francisco Examiner, 77, 181, 186, 187, 192, 259, 260, 265, 307, 333
San Francisco General Hospital, 33, 126, 205, 211
  and AIDS, Ward 5B, 391–93, 396, 400
  Dr. Smith's detox center in, 51, 52
  patient-centered care in, 392
  volunteers in, 392–93
San Francisco Giants, 358
San Francisco Housing Authority, 228–29, 280–81, 292
San Francisco Labor Council, 32
San Francisco magazine, 245
San Francisco Mime Troupe, 39, 70
San Francisco Police Department (SFPD):
  and affirmative action, 344
  books confiscated by, 24, 25
  Catholics in, xvi, 25, 31, 32, 34, 49, 208, 217, 242, 259, 394
  and civil disturbances, 153–54
  civilian review board, 351
  civil rights lawsuit against, 217, 260, 319, 323, 344
  clinic harassed by, 56, 154
  corruption in, 9, 268
  distrusted by the public, 345, 348
  diversity in, 352
  and drug busts, 25, 29–30, 87, 161

San Francisco Police Department (*Continued*)
and Egan case, 3–4, 9
and Feinstein, 344–45, 351–52
and Fillmore Auditorium, 62
Gain as Chief of, 258–60, 287, 319–21, 343, 348
guarding the mayor, 193, 324, 326
guns confiscated by, 129
Haight-Ashbury harassment by, 31, 56, 161, 163–64, 167
and Halloween festival, 318–19
and Hearst arrest, 200
and Human Be-In, 25
and labor strikes, 145
and Moscone, 258–60, 319–21
and Moscone/Milk murders, 327–28
old-boy network in, 217, 258–59, 268, 351
public spotlight on, 8–9, 348
and racial tensions, 208, 216–20, 221, 222, 260
and runaways, 49, 56
and Sullivan murder, 65–67
and Summer of Love, 34, 35
vice squad, 240
and White, 320, 328–29, 330, 345, 346
and "White Night," 347–48
and whorehouse, 64
San Francisco Redevelopment Agency, 61
"San Francisco Sound," 82
San Francisco State College, 27, 142
black power confrontations in, 231
campus strike (1968–1969), 146
rioters at, 149–50, 154
San Francisco Suicide Prevention center, 333
San Francisco values, xvii, 257, 395–96, 398
San Francisco Warriors, 358

San Jose State College, 371
San Quentin prison, 170, 209, 210, 212
Santana, 408
Saroyan, William, 86
Sarria, José, 85, 102–3
Satanism, 130–31
Satcher, Earl, 187
Satyricon (movie), 245
Saxbe, William, 192
Sayre, Leonard, 120
Schmidt, Doug, 345–46
Scott, Donald, 218, 221
Scott, Jack, 196, 197
Scott, Micki, 196
Scrumbly (Cockette member), 106
Seale, Bobby, 218, 231
Sebastian (Palace impresario), 105
Seidemann, Bob, 114
Seifert, George, 373
Selvin, Joel, 71–72, 390
Serra, Richard, 161
Serra, Tony, 161–64, 170
sexual revolution, backlash of, 311
sex workers, 24, 239–40, 259
Shanti Project, 394
Shanty Malone's, 85, 86
Shaw, Bernard, 202
Shelley, Dennis, 32
Shelley, John Francis "Jack":
background of, 32, 47
and civil rights movement, 32–33
in Congress, 32–33
and death threats, 33–34
and Haight-Ashbury, 31, 56
as mayor, 17, 33–34, 36, 149
and Summer of Love, 31, 34, 36, 51
Shep (friend of Jones), 402–3
Shilts, Randy:
And the Band Played On, 400
The Mayor of Castro Street, 389
Shorenstein, Walter, 88–89, 229, 263
Silbert, Mimi, 255

Silver, Carol Ruth, 322, 347, 387
Simon, J. C., 209, 212–13, 214, 221, 222
Simpson, O. J., 204, 360, 367
Sinatra, Frank, 102
Sinclair, John, 128
Sing, Paul, 260
Sipple, Oliver, 190
Sister Boom Boom, 355
Sisters of Perpetual Indulgence, 355, 389, 394
1960s counterculture:
  assassinations, 124, 150, 172, 177, 188, 198
  churches grappling with, 42–43
  drugs, 59, 87, 116–18, 122, 124–29
  hippies, xvi, 80–82, 88, 95, 128, 129
  Human Be-In, 22–23, 24–25, 31, 42, 44, 124, 142
  New Left, 203
  political activism, 16, 95, 96
  radicalization process in, 176–77
  Summer of Love, see Summer of Love
  turning sour, 123–33
  Vietnam vets, 124–26
Sklar, Richard, 255, 283, 316, 351
Slick, Grace, 86, 115
Smith, David, 51–59, 125
  detox center of, 51, 52
  and free clinic, 54–59, 160
  and Good Earth, 160
Smith, Dorothy, 52
Smith, Elvin, 52
Smith, Rev. J. Alfred, 277
Smith, Julie, 292
Smith, Rev. Leon, 54
Smith, Tommie, 371
Snyder, Gary, 22, 23
Sodom, xv
sodomy, legalization of, 253
Soledad Brothers, 171

Soledad prison, 170, 175
Soliah, Kathy, 196–97, 198
Solomon, Freddie, 381, 382
Soltysik, Patricia "Mizmoon," 175, 179
"Someone to Watch Over Me," 104
Sopwith Camel, 62
Sox, Ellis, 51, 54, 56
Spanos, Alex, 360
Spence, Skip, 94, 135, 408
Spinelli, Marc "Count Marco," 82
Spoleto Arts Festival, 233
Springfield, Buffalo, 75, 94
"Stand By Your Man," 393
Stanford, Sally, 83, 85
Stanley, Owsley, 87
Stardust, Ziggy, 166
Starr, Kevin, 265, 292
Stars restaurant, 238
Stassen, Harold, 264
Steinbeck, John, 83
Steiner, Robyn, 174, 179, 180–81
Stepanian, Michael, 21, 25, 30, 72, 120, 264–65
Stevenson, Don, 135
Stills, Steve, 94
Stockholm syndrome, 202
Stoen, Grace, 271–72, 293, 295
Stoen, John, 272, 293, 295
Stoen, Tim, 270–74, 276, 284, 293, 294, 295
Stokes, Rick, 264–65
Stone, Robert, 133
Stonewall riots, New York City, 103
STP, 126
Straight Theater, 48
Streets of San Francisco, The (TV), 215
Stud (club), 237, 238
Student Nonviolent Coordinating Committee (SNCC), 53
Students for a Democratic Society (SDS), 199

Sullivan, Charles:
    dance license of, 61, 62–64
    death of, 65–67
    and Fillmore Auditorium, 60–61
Sullivan, Fanny, 65
Sullivan, Marion, 65–66, 67
Summerall, Pat, 381
Summer of Love:
    concerts in, 75
    and Diggers, 37, 40
    and drug experiments, 127–28
    and free clinic, 55
    and Human Be-In, 31, 42, 44,
        124, 142
    and mayor's office, 31, 34, 36, 51
    and runaways, 50, 123
    and SFPD, 34, 35
    turning sour, 123
    and Vietnam War, 123
Summer Olympics (1968), 371
Sunnydale housing project, 312
Sun Reporter, 274
Super Bowl (1982), 384–86
Sutro Baths, 239
Sweet Pam, 106
Sweet William, 24
Sylvester (disco queen), 104, 399
Symbionese Liberation Army (SLA),
        172–79
    background for, 172–75
    bank robberies by, 192–93, 199
    and food program, 183, 185–86
    and Foster murder, 178–79, 180
    as graveyard of 1960s New Left,
        203
    Hearst kidnapping, 180–203
    media focus of, 182, 184, 186,
        191, 193–94, 195
    move to LA, 193–95
    rewards for arrests of, 193
    safe houses of, 190, 196, 200
    violent actions of, 195

Talbot, Lyle, xiii
"Tales of the City," 244–47

Tate, Sharon, 134
Taylor, Elizabeth, 397
Teddybear, 56–57
Telegraph Hill Neighborhood Asso-
        ciation, 283
Temptations, 60, 65
Tennant, Woody, 352
Tent, Pam, 98–99, 100, 106
Them (band), 62
There's No Business Like Show Busi-
        ness (show), 98
Thieriot, Charles de Young, 76–77,
        244, 246
Thomas, Duane, 377
Thomas, Joe, 360–61, 364, 367
Thompson, Bill, 82
Thompson, Hunter S., 90, 238, 242
Thorazine, 52
Tittle, Y. A., 359
Tom of Finland, 348
Tork, Peter, 164
Tower, Jeremiah, 236–37, 238
Tracy, Phil, 292
Translator (band), 408
Travelers Aid, 44
Treasure Island Naval Base, 156, 158
Tresca, Carlo, 26
Tribal Thumb, 187
Trixie, and Hamburger Mary's, 237
Trout Fishing in America (Brautigan),
        38
Truth, Sojourner, 303
TUG (The Urban Guerrilla), 169–70
Turner, Ike and Tina, 60
Turner, Keena, 368, 379
Twinkies defense, 345

U2, 374
underground radio, 92–93
underground railroad, 44
United Farm Workers, 185, 283
United Prisoners' Union, 186, 187
United Slaves (US) organization, 172
US Conference of Mayors, 396
U.S. Steel, 88

Vacaville Prison, 173, 174, 201
Valenti, Jack, 215
Vejtables, The (band), 408
Velvet Underground, 62
Vernon, Paul, 102
Veronese, Angela Alioto, 146, 193, 234
Vidal, Gore, 106
Vietnam Veterans Against the War,
    243
Vietnam War:
    antiwar protests, 76, 80, 87, 89,
        123–26, 151, 177
    and drugs, 124–25
    and Summer of Love, 123
    supporters of, 151
    veterans of, 123–26, 156, 385
Volberding, Molly, 391
Volberding, Paul, 390, 391, 396, 398,
    400
Voye, Sally, 187
Voznesensky, Andrei, 75
Vreeland, Diana, 106

Wallace, Henry A., 14
Walsh, Bill, 361–73, 377–82,
    384–86, 398–99
Walsh, Steve, 398–99
Warhol, Andy, 106
Warner Bros., xiii
Washington Square Bar & Grill, 261,
    373
Watergate, 188
Waters, Alice, 236
Waters, John, 103, 105
Watson, Tex, 134
Watts, Alan, 93
Watts, Charlie, 137
Watts Clinic, Los Angeles, 53
Weather Underground, 161
Weed, Steven, 181, 184
Weinstein, Danny, 269
Weir, Bob, 29–30, 374
Weir, David, 197–98
Welch, Calvin, 160, 248–49, 250,
    351

Wenner, Jann, 71, 81, 82, 90, 93
"We Shall Overcome," 151, 229
West, Billy, 237–38, 390
West, Louis Jolyon "Jolly," 128, 201
Westbrook, Colton, 173, 174, 175,
    182, 183, 185, 194
Wheeler, Thero, 179
White, Charlie, 315, 325
White, Dan, 312, 319, 322–31
    confession of, 328–30, 346
    death of, 388–89
    financial pressures on, 323, 329,
        330
    and Milk, 314–16, 325, 326–27,
        329
    mock execution of, 348, 349
    and Moscone, 323–26, 329
    murders committed by, 325–28,
        331, 333, 334, 344, 361
    and police department, 320,
        328–29, 330, 345, 346
    released from prison, 387–88
    resignation of, 323–25
    statues of, 355–56
    as supervisor, 322, 323–24
    trial of, 345–48, 349
White, Danny (QB), 378, 380, 383
White, Mary Ann Burns, 315, 323,
    328, 388
"White Night," 347–48
Who, the (band), 75, 91, 117
WIBG Philadelphia, 92
Whole Earth Catalog, 24
Wickman, Chris, 167
Williams, Rev. Cecil, 218, 245, 277,
    333–34, 341
Williams, Dick, 178
Williams, Hannibal, 271, 277
Williams, Robin, 238, 243
Winchell, Walter, 84
Winterland, 86
Witches' Sabbath, 131
Wizard of Oz, The (movie), 236
Wofsy, Constance, 391
Wolfe, Tom, 87

Wolfe, William, 174
"Wonder Whore," 260
Wong, Julia, 228
Woodstock festival, 136
Worthington, Bert, 189
Wright, Eric, 383, 385, 386
Wright, Guy, 333
Wright, Jim, 306–7
Wright, Rosalie, 292

X-rated movies, 240–43

Yardbirds (band), 7
YMCA, 44
Yoshimura, Wendy, 199, 200, 201
Young, Charle, 380

Young, Loretta, 94
Young, Neil, 94
Youngbloods, The (band), 408
Younger, Evelle, 192
Youth Guidance Center (YGC), 46,
    47–49

Zagaris, Michael "Z-Man," 138–39,
    374, 378, 382, 385–86
Zappa, Frank, 62
Zebra murders, 206–7, 209–23
Zellerbach, Merla, 341
Zipkin, Jerry, 397
Zodiac serial killer, 207
Zumwalt, Elmo, 243
Zuni Café, 237–38, 390

ABOUT THE AUTHOR

DAVID TALBOT is the author of the *New York Times* bestseller *Brothers: The Hidden History of the Kennedy Years*. The founder of *Salon*, he has been hailed a "pioneer of online journalism" by the *New York Times*. Talbot has worked as a senior editor for *Mother Jones* magazine and has written for numerous publications. He lives with his family in San Francisco.

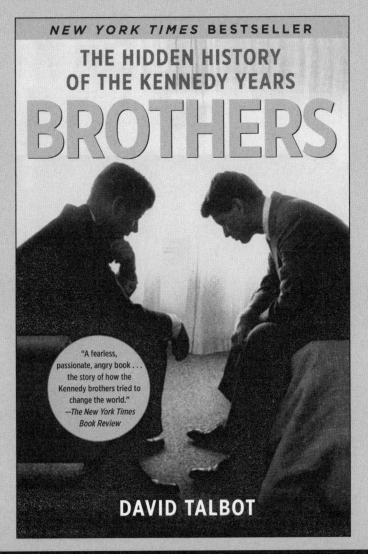

THE
AMERICAN
TABLE

More Than 400 Recipes That
Make Accessible for the First Time the Full
Richness of American Regional Cooking

by Ronald Johnson

Drawings by James McGarrell

Silver Spring Books

Cover designed by Hope Forstenzer
Original cover illustration by James McGarrell

Drawings by James McGarrell

Text designed and typeset by Syllables
Printed and bound by Sheridan Books, Ann Arbor, Michigan

Published by Silver Spring Books

Library of Congress Card Number: 00-104184

ISBN: 0-916562-50-6

Editorial Sales Rights and Permissions Inquiries should be addressed to:
Silver Spring Books, 8 Gray's Farm Road, Weston, CT 06883
www.silverspringbooks.com
email: editor@silverspringbooks.com

MANUFACTURED IN THE UNITED STATES OF AMERICA
1 3 5 7 9 10 8 6 4 2

Distributed by LPC Group
1-800/626-4330

to the meals
my mother served me

ACKNOWLEDGMENTS

A lot of the recipes in this book are worn smooth as river pebbles, and I can no longer say for certain where I first clipped them, who cooked them for me, even what part of the country they come from. The list of friends who have traded recipes over decades is too long to record, but they know who they are and how much thanked—most of their names have been embedded in the text.

In addition I would like to thank Anne Mendelson for her advice on textual matters, Molly Finn for cooking through the book, Herb Leibowitz and Judith Jones for their help in getting it published, but most of all Maria Guarnaschelli for her tenacious editing, and James McGarrell for his sprightly drawings.

Contents

ACKNOWLEDGMENTS   vii
FOREWORD
   The Culinary Ronald Johnson   xi
INTRODUCTION   xv

SOUPS
   Soups from Cold to Hot   3
   Meals in a Bowl   19

FISH & SHELLFISH
   Fish   41
   Shellfish   54

MEATS & FOWL
   Beef   77
   Veal   94
   Pork and Ham   102
   Lamb   122
   Variety Meats   132
   Chicken   143
   Domestic Game   159

SPECIAL DISHES
   Southern Beans and Rice   175
   Southwestern Foods   184
   Cupboard Meals   205

SIDE DISHES
Vegetables   219
Starchy Dishes   249
Salads and Slaws   268

SAUCES & CONDIMENTS
Sauces   289
Pickles and Relishes   299

BREADS
Quick Breads   315
Yeast Breads   330

DESSERTS
Summer and Winter Pies   347
Cakes, Torres, and a Cookie   362
Puddings, Ice Creams, and Fruits   376

METHODS & INGREDIENTS   395

INDEX   406

Foreword
The Culinary Ronald Johnson

*L*iving in Aspen, Colorado in 1967, a friend came to visit for several days, from New Mexico. After eating through most of the Southwest dishes I knew, he said "Write us a cookbook, The University of New Mexico Press needs a cookbook. You can cook, you can write, that's what we want." So I did and the next year they published it as *The Aficionado's Southwestern Cooking*, which has gone through seven printings and three covers as a paperback over the years. It has been one of UNM Press' best sellers ever.

Then in 1983, after opening a successful bistro style restaurant, *Brasserie 1600*, in San Francisco, and having the owner promptly sell it, I became a partner in a catering firm, and sat down to write *The American Table*. I wrote of my culinary past and about what we could salvage from our heritage to relish today. I avoided most of the expected dishes published everywhere (anyway if they were dull, like Indian Pudding) in order to find new classics.

Published in 1984 by William Morrow, the book won one of the Tastemaker Awards that year. Its many fans, some of whom have cooked through the entire book, kept it alive, through a paperback edition by Pocket Books in 1986 and a subsequent Fireside Books edition, in their Classic Cookbook Series.

(Editor's note: this essay was written some time ago; *The American Table* has been out of print altogether for almost ten years).

Through this book, I made the acquaintance of M.F.K. Fisher and Marion Cunningham, both of whom became mentors. M.F.K. I met at a party at North Point Press, our then mutual publisher, and then Marion telephoned me after combing the San Francisco telephone book for R. Johnsons, and said. "Are you the Ronald Johnson who writes cookbooks? I've been looking everywhere for you."

After the success of *The American Table*, on the way to a Cookbook Writers' Conference in Philadelphia, I negotiated with UNM to write an expanded version of my cookbook with them using updated tastes, techniques and particularly dishes I had found over some twenty years of living in Colorado, New Mexico and California, and visiting Arizona and Texas often. This was published as *Southwestern Cooking: New & Old* in 1985. Even old timers who like only the classic dishes seemed to love this cookbook. After it went out of print, it was reprinted in 1992 as a trade paperback by The Living Batch Press of Albuquerque, and was reprinted within the first six months of its publication.

Thereafter I acquired an agent and published two books with Simon & Schuster. One for the poor, and one for the rich who had little time, one a survival manual for living on the edge with a family to feed, and one on how to seem almost as if the cook has just left a little repast to warm up sort of thing. They were published in 1989 and 1991 as *Simple Fare* and *Company Fare*. Both were beautiful books, with little indication as to their intentions.

Since, I have nearly completed a book on American desserts. It is rich in calories, of course, for these days, but even so, dessert books have become steady sellers. And this, like *The American Table*, should become a classic text. Lately I've been working on a cookbook for singles with an amusing, often romantic, little essay for each short, easy recipe. Considering all those folks out there who hate cooking for themselves, this could be something a casual buyer picks up to give to a friend, on a whim, and that gets through to the well off single buyers, as well as bachelors and the divorced, widows and widowers who seldom buy cookbooks.

Looking back on this part of my career, I have been well published. Nothing can replace a publisher's confidence to stick to a book. *The American Table* is the most extreme case of this. It is a cookbook people fall in love with, and go out and buy four copies for friends, only to find the bookstore hasn't restocked. That this is one of the most delightfully written cookbooks of our time, with a fresh look at how the natives really eat, is indisputable. It will certainly outlive me and is cookable unlike comparable things like Alice Toklas.

I have an eye for recipes that put a twist on the classic tried and true, without trendy kiwi salsas and pesto made from grass. I'm what both Flo Baker and Marion Cunningham call "a home cook."

— Ronald Johnson

Editor's Note

I am one of those people Ron talks about — I fell in love with *The American Table* the minute I found it, and have loved it ever since. Plainly, the essay printed above was written some time ago. At the time, Ron was without an agent or a publisher, and was trying to promote himself — thus the absolutely accurate self portrayal of himself and particularly this cookbook. He wrote about himself without apology, but unlike many who celebrate their own achievements, in his case, the self praise was warranted.

This is a terrific book. Ron Johnson was undoubtedly, one of the great cookbook writers of our time. Silver Spring intends to reprint all of his out of print books, as well as his yet unpublished cookbooks (his American desserts for one) over the next few years, providing cooks and readers with enough recipes and writing to feed their own habits, and those of their friends and families.

Sadly, Ron died in 1998 of a brain tumor. He is sorely missed by many, those who knew him as one of the innovative poets of our time, and those who knew him as an extraordinary source of cooking ingenuity and common wisdom.

— David Wilk

Introduction

Thomas Jefferson was our first noted gourmet, to the point Patrick Henry complained the President "abjured his native victuals." In truth, Illinois pecans and Vermont maple syrup shared a shelf with Parmesan cheese, in his pantry, for he was intent on widening the common table with anything fine he could lay a hand on. He took pride in his macaroni maker, and a new gadget called a waffle iron. These had been brought back from Europe, along with a pocketful of rice he could have been executed for smuggling out of Italy. This packet started an industry which now exports back to Europe. He wrote back for new strains of vegetables for his garden at Monticello. Among the profusion grown there, he promoted both potatoes and tomatoes, then commonly believed poisonous. His back porch sported a bright spanking new machine to turn out ice cream, as did George Washington's, a few miles down the road.

"Native victuals" those days tended to be a sorry hodge-podge of salted pork, corn in all forms, beans, any stray game, with a daily molasses pudding to round it out. Not till a hundred years later, with the advent of the brothers Delmonico, did dining in the wide Jeffersonian style start to take on character and breed invention. The Delmonicos took a plot of ground outside New York City, where they grew endive, broccoli, and eggplant. They unveiled the avocado, and introduced salads made from native plants. There had always been pockets of fine food: some Yankee hostelries, many a Southern plantation, and in the quiet of the Shaker communities. With Delmonico's it became a fashion. Oscar of the Waldorf soon followed, and we were off and running.

Variety for everyman came about only with refrigerated shipping. By then, variety was no longer as individual as Jefferson had imagined, for large growers quickly standardized produce, and Prohibition had begun leveling vineyards (and as a by-product, excellent dining). The results were clear enough, though, even to a Kansas boyhood. My grandfather, who had settled in a covered wagon, was now able to order barrels of oysters still in the shell, packed in ice and sawdust, from "back East." Wheels of cheese came along the rails, along with canned goods of all kinds, and then, with swiftness—packaged mixes, puffed cereals, condensed milk, denatured breads.

As a consequence home canning from the garden fell off, and bread making became rare. There were few trustworthy cookbooks, magazines touted canned soups to substitute for sauces, and casseroles came to be born. Fruited gelatin salads rose in tribes. Abroad, Gertrude Stein and Alice Toklas were considering an American tour after decades away. They had been advised by a friend who had recently traveled there strange vegetable cocktails, and tinned fruit salads, might be pressed on one. "Surely" Alice wrote in her cookbook "you weren't required to eat them. You could have substituted other dishes. Not, said he, when you were a guest."

If Brillat-Savarin was correct in his remark that "The destiny of nations depends on how they nourish themselves," we were indeed in more trouble than Gertrude and Alice could have expected. Consider this dish, that very year the rage of Los Angeles:

CANDLE SALAD

4 slices canned pineapple	1 Brazil nut
2 bananas	¼ cup mayonnaise dressing
4 pieces of citron or green pepper	

*P*eel bananas. Cut them in two crosswise. Place a slice of pineapple on a salad plate; insert one half banana in center of each pineapple. Place a thin strip of Brazil nut in the top of the banana to represent a wick. The oil in the nut will burn if the nut is lighted. Let mayonnaise drip down the side of each candle. Make a handle to the candlestick of citron or of pepper. A piece of cherry may be used for a flame instead of the lighted nut.

As it turned out, they enjoyed their trip immensely. In hotels, Gertrude stuck to melon and oysters, while Alice investigated any unknown item, with the nose of a true cook. But home cooking really turned them round. They tasted turtle soup, home brewed orange wine they uncorked to find "ambrosia," abalone, sand dabs, soft shelled crab, passion fruit, and a confection called Tane Chambord which had since been lost to France. They ate wild rice for the first time, and sampled Oysters Rockefeller, both of which they served back in Paris.

They were lucky to be so fêted, and to travel when they did, for most of those Hotels have not survived, at least any to order oysters and melon in. Not only Hotels, the legendary truck stop, Pullman's ideas of fine railroad dining, the corner bakery, soda fountain—all vanished. Even when a good spot to eat does exist, there is no trusty way to find it, no one to point out one of the two cafes which still serve "mountain oysters in cream gravy" in Lexington, Kentucky, the best Basque table set in Eiko, Nevada, the most gracious Georgia fish camp, the little *brasserie-deli* a couple of nice boys down the way run, an annual "ramp" festival over the next hill, a Greek Church Supper around the block, or ultimate Burn to Palace right next door. They are all hidden as home cooking to any passing traveler.

The only answer to this I learned from fellow poet Jonathan Williams, whose migrations the birds might envy. His advice was to make far friends, and dine there (he also wrote about twenty letters a day). This encouraged me early on to learn the art of turning conversations to food and recipes—an art of some stealth, tact, and persistence, as this letter from Emily Dickinson to a neighbor shows:

> Sometime when our dear Mrs Hills has an unoccupied moment tho aware that her innumerable company of Angels leave her very few of what are called so, will she, please, tell Vinnie's sister how to make a little loaf of Cake like one she sent in April which is still a remembrance of nectar.
>
> It was what Austin calls Loaf Cake and the Almanac calls raised Cake— Then Vinnie spied a Loaf of Bread at our lost neighbors, which enthralled her—steamed Bran Brown Bread she thought it, from the same hand—and lovelier the same Heart—could I know the secret of that Though I desire crumbs for but a few Robins.

Timing is all, here, and one learns never to be discouraged by the overworked, as Alice discovered, seeking out a surprised and "inspired negress cook and the enormous kitchen over which she presided" who had no time for chit-chat.

I've gathered recipes for twenty years in this manner, here and about, looked through every tiny spiral-bound cookbook put out by local church ladies that came my way, and it's surprising how many fine recipes turn up from our amateur cooks. Sometimes a trick is turned, or an ingredient used, which would never occur to the tradition-bound chef who already knows what's right and what's not. This can be as simple as substituting a handy ingredient, as cooks have done with French recipes for years in New Orleans. Of course I stumble now and then on fine dishes from restaurants, but the large part of those collected here, to stand on my table, are simple "home cooking" at its everyday best.

Looking over this spread, as it is piled, is to make out distinct mountains through the jumble. The highest of these, perhaps, a toppling heap of recipes from the South.

I've lived in the four corners, and was brought up in the middle of this country, but my admiration is unbounded and continual for the pluck and inventiveness of cooks there. You can examine any local cookbook to find how far tradition, in the large old sense, is alive in many a kitchen still today. New England folk seem to share the British reservation about food talk of any kind, but in the South it is mannerly to comment the victuals, low and high, and sing the praises of the cook. Recipes are shared across the fence, church suppers look like groaning boards of lost plantations. If they had only New Orleans to show, they would have cause for pride.

And, leafing through, how often the sturdy hills of the Shakers crop up, fit for use after 200 years. But then they made almost every article they needed, and thought that form follows function from barn to chair, or a dish of "Alabaster" or "Yellow Velvet" for dinner. Sheer necessities of catering for a whole community, and duly recording it for daily revolving help, gave them an edge the single housewife seldom need sharpen. They left a trove of handsome recipes.

The Southwest seems to also carve a mesa, culinarily speaking, out from the rest. It was literally my first exotic food. My aunt, who had gone to live in New Mexico, brought tortillas and chiles back, on a visit, and it was like a trip to India for us all. Everybody crowded into the kitchen, and my mother there and then decided to import tortillas, and learn enough tricks to supply us with this strange delight forever. Though it rises alone, out of what the most of us eat, to me it's always worth climbing, at least once a month—I lust for it as some do for a Chinese dinner, dill pickles, popcorn, or ice cream late at night.

But from Vichyssoise through Ambrosia, I've gone on the notion that if Provence has more recipes than Oklahoma, it has had a long head start, and Oklahoma might have a few bright dishes yet for Provence. From what I've unearthed, I suspect our new chefs have a culinary El Dorado all around them, just waiting to be mined, from sea to shining sea.

San Francisco, 1983

SOUPS

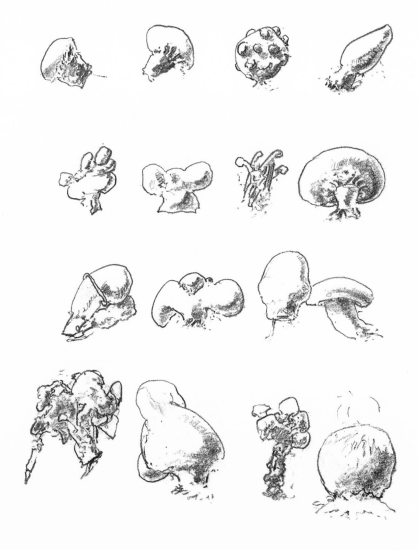

After a velvety oyster soup came shad and cucumbers, then a young broiled turkey with corn fritters, followed by a canvasback with currant jelly and a celery mayonnaise.

—Edith Wharton, The Age of Innocence

Soups from Cold to Hot

*E*xtremes of climate—scorching summers to snowdrifts piling the eaves—have left their mark on New World foods. Doughty settlers could skirt winters by the fireside, but it took more than a breezy verandah to keep the cream and butter cool and fresh when the temperature hovered in the hundreds. Most farms had an ice house where winter ice could be stored, laid down in sawdust, though it took advances in cutting and hauling to make the ice wagon a common sight in towns. In 1815, Brillat-Savarin noted a fellow exile from the French Revolution, a certain Captain Collet, who survived by introducing, to New York City, ices and sherbets: "It was especially difficult for them to understand how anything could stay so cold in the summer heat of ninety degrees." Louis Diat and others followed the admirable captain, to put the verandah breeze into the soup, to chill and lift the palate August nights.

LOUIS DIAT'S VICHYSSOISE

1½	cups chopped white part of leek	4	cups hot water
½	cup chopped onion	2	teaspoons salt
1	tablespoon butter	3	cups hot milk
3	cups peeled diced potatoes	2	cups heavy cream
			Minced chives

*I*n a kettle set over medium heat, sauté the leek and onion in the butter until they are soft. Add potatoes, water, and salt, then simmer, uncovered, over low heat 30 to 40 minutes, or until the potatoes are soft.

Either sieve the soup or purée it in a blender (a food processor will not smooth it enough, I find). Return purée to the kettle; add the milk and 1 cup of the cream. Bring to a boil. Set to cool in the refrigerator.

When cool, either sieve the soup again, or whirl in the blender. Finally, stir in the other cup of cream and taste for seasoning. Chill for several hours, and serve in soup cups sprinkled with chives.

Serves 8 to 10.

Louis Diat's creation for the old Ritz-Carlton is probably the most famed American soup, and justly so. Its origin is one of France's simplest staples, chilled, thoroughly puréed, enriched with extra cream, and with a sprinkle of chives for bounce.

"VICHYSSOISE" OF BEET GREENS

4	young beets with tops	1	cup milk
2	tablespoons butter	½	cup heavy cream
1	cup chopped onion	2	tablespoons lemon juice
2	cups peeled and diced potatoes		Salt
3	cups chicken stock		Lemon slices

*C*ut off the beet greens and wash thoroughly. Melt the butter in a kettle set over medium heat, and sauté the onion in it until limp. Add the potatoes and chicken stock and cook, uncovered, over medium heat 10 minutes.

Strip the greens from the beet stems and chop coarsely—there should be

1¾ to 2 cups of greens packed down. Add them to the soup, and cook 20 minutes more.

Place in a blender and—going from a slow speed to a fast one—purée thoroughly. Return to the pot, then add the milk, cream, lemon juice, and salt to taste (remember a cold soup will have less flavor than a hot one). Chill thoroughly.

The beets themselves can be cooked in salted water at any time during this process. They will take about 20 minutes, depending on size and age. When they are tender, drain them and run cold water over. Slip off their skins and chop into ¼-inch dice. To serve, place the chilled soup in chilled cups and garnish with slices of lemon and diced beets.

Serves 4 to 6.

This is adapted from a little 1962 book titled The Art of Creole Cookery, *by William I. Kaufman and Sister Mary Ursula Cooper, O.P., which promises on its cover "a delicious composite of familiar and not-so-familiar Creole recipes." A soup definitely and delightfully not-so-familiar, indeed it is a small triumph of regional invention. Beet greens are full flavored, suavest of all the leafy tops—but are unfortunately seldom used by anyone. Here they compose a subtle cold soup the color of celadon, which, sprinkled with dice of red beet root, and floating a yellow slice of lemon, makes a dish as easy on the eye as on the tongue. Serve it with a white wine, and The Duchess of Windsor's Cornpones (page 316).*

CHILLED PUMPKIN CREAM

1 can (1 pound) pumpkin (or 1½ cups fresh purée)	1 bay leaf
½ cup chopped onion	Salt and freshly ground pepper
2½ cups chicken stock	1 cup heavy cream
⅛ teaspoon ground mace	1 lime (or lemon), sliced
Pinch of curry powder	

Combine the pumpkin, onion, stock, spices, bay leaf, and salt and pepper to taste in a kettle. Bring to a rolling boil, then lower the heat and simmer 30 minutes with the pot uncovered.

Remove the bay leaf, place in a blender or food processor, and purée till almost—not quite—smooth. Chill in the refrigerator an hour or more.

When quite cold, stir in the cream and taste for seasoning. Chill several more hours, or overnight. (The soup acquires further taste with some sitting.) To serve, place in chilled soup plates, and garnish with thin slices of lime.
    Serves 6.

This is about the best use for a can of anything I've ever come across, but of course pumpkin seems to can with little loss of flavor. A surprising soup cold, there is no reason to limit this to summer—in fact it strikes rather a fine note to a Thanksgiving or Christmas dinner. At any time, serve it with white wine rather than red, and a basket of hot yeast rolls, Charleston Benne Wafers (page 327), or crisp Beaten Biscuits (page 327).

COLD CUCUMBER AND POTATO SOUP

1 cup chopped onion	2 cups chicken stock
¼ cup olive oil	Salt
4 cucumbers, peeled	1 cup buttermilk
1 pound potatoes (about 3 medium), peeled and sliced	Tabasco
	2 tablespoons minced chives

*S*auté the onion in olive oil, in a large kettle set over medium heat, until it is limp. Slice the cucumbers in quarters lengthwise and cut the seeds out with a small sharp knife. Chop the cucumbers in small dice and reserve ½ cup.
    Add all but the reserved cucumbers to the onion, stir, and cook a few more minutes. Add the potatoes and stock and bring to a boil, then turn down the heat and simmer 30 minutes with the pot uncovered.
    Salt the reserved cucumbers and let stand while the soup cooks, then wash them with cold water and drain.
    When the soup is cooked, purée in a blender, going from slow to fast speed, and pour into a bowl. Add salt to taste and cool in the refrigerator. When it has cooled, stir in reserved cucumber, the buttermilk, a few drops Tabasco, and taste again for salt.
    Lastly, stir in the chives and chill, covered, in the refrigerator 3 hours or more.
    Serves 4 to 6.

How fine this Iowa farm recipe is on a hot day. The buttermilk is its secret— tart and creamy, but still light. Though to be summoned from any larder (except for the chives—paprika will do) you will find it sits proud on any table set for company. Complement it with crusty bread and light dry wine.

AVOCADO CREAM

1 large ripe avocado	Pinch of curry powder
1 cup heavy cream	Salt
2 cups chicken stock	Tabasco
Juice of 1 lime	Minced chives
1 tablespoon light rum	

Whirl avocado, cream, stock, lime juice, and rum in a blender until smooth—going from a slow speed to a high one. Place in a bowl and add curry powder, salt to taste, and Tabasco (please, only a drop or two).

Cover and refrigerate several hours. To serve, put in cold cups or soup plates and sprinkle with chives.

Serves 4.

What could be simpler? It is also a kind of test dish for any would-be chef's palate—the final product suavely depending exactly on the balance of rum and curry, and both only faintly suggested, whispered rather than hollered. In Texas, it would be served with home-fried tortilla chips, and chilled light beer or white wine.

EPHRAIM DONER'S
POOR MAN'S CHILLED SALMON BISQUE

	Head, tail, and trimmings from 1 medium salmon	2	tablespoons rice
2	cups water	2	cups milk, scalded
½	cup chopped onion	1	tablespoon tomato paste
1	bay leaf	1	teaspoon anchovy paste
1	clove garlic, flattened and peeled	1	cup heavy cream
			Salt and freshly ground pepper
3	sprigs parsley	1	teaspoon lemon juice
	Pinch of ground cloves	2	tablespoons dry sherry
	Pinch of ground mace		Paprika

*P*lace salmon trimmings in a kettle with water, onion, bay leaf, garlic, parsley, spices, and rice. Bring to a boil, then lower the heat and simmer, covered, 20 minutes.

Lift out salmon and bay leaf, and boil the liquid, uncovered, till it is reduced by half and the rice is very soft—about 15 minutes. Meanwhile, pick all the pieces of meat off the salmon (don't forget the cheeks—they aren't as lovely a pink, but they are some of the best-tasting flesh on the fish).

Purée rice mixture, salmon, and scalded milk in a blender or food processor. Put in a large saucepan set over a low flame. Whisk in the tomato and anchovy pastes, then the cream. Heat gently, but don't let boil.

Taste for seasoning, then chill, covered, in the refrigerator for several hours. To serve, add the lemon juice and sherry, and again taste for seasoning. Place in chilled soup plates and dust paprika on top.

Serves 4.

Those lucky enough to find trimmings in their market will admire this silky soup. For very little, a cook may expect a singular lunch (with forethought always to good bread, green salad, chilled wine). Artist, and friend of artists, Ephraim Doner was the first person to teach me that even economy could be an art. May he still be waving his hands in joy over a box of castoff artichokes, promising a feast.

COLD CRAB GUMBO MARYLAND

1	tablespoon butter	¾	cup drained canned tomatoes
¼	cup chopped onion	¼	cup rice
¼	cup chopped celery	¾	cup crabmeat
2	tablespoons chopped green pepper		Salt and freshly ground pepper
¾	cup thinly sliced okra		Tabasco
4	cups chicken stock		Lemon juice

Melt butter in a soup pot over medium heat. Sauté onion, celery, and green pepper until they are soft. Add okra, stock, tomatoes, and rice. Bring to a boil, then lower the heat and simmer 1½ hours.

Remove from the heat and purée in batches in a food processor or blender. Put in a bowl, cover, and chill thoroughly. To serve, stir in the crab and season to taste with salt, pepper, Tabasco, and lemon juice.

Serves 6 to 8.

The only first-course gumbo, brought to an exquisite pitch, and unexpectedly cold. Treat it well with the finest Pinot Chardonnay your wine merchant points out, and either Zephyrs (page 317), The Duchess of Windsor's Cornpones (page 316), or homemade yeasty rolls.

GOLDEN GATE SOUP (HOT OR COLD)

6	carrots, scraped and sliced	1	bay leaf
1	medium onion, chopped		Pinch of ground mace
1	clove garlic, flattened and peeled	1	cup heavy cream (or half cream, half milk)
3	cups chicken stock	1	carrot, scraped and cut in very fine matchstick lengths
2	tablespoons rice		Curry powder (optional)
	Salt and freshly ground pepper		

Add all but the cream, matchstick carrots, and optional curry to a large kettle and cook over medium heat 30 minutes. Remove the bay leaf and purée the soup till quite smooth in a blender.

Return to the kettle, add the cream, and taste for seasoning. Add the matchstick carrots, and simmer 5 to 10 minutes more, or until the carrots are just tender.

Serve hot or cold. If cold, add a touch of curry during the cooking, and garnish the soup with a dollop of chutney.

Serves 4 to 6.

In catering I learned two things—first, that the rich like their elegance also inexpensive, and second, this soup, to prove the point. Draper Morrow, who taught me the business, trotted this out to social "dos" for years with nothing but praise, and little out of his pocket. Not only that, but he transformed its basic use of rice for thickening, and balance of mace and bay leaf, to any vegetable at hand—onions, turnips, cauliflower (with a little sherry), cucumbers, green beans, or peas. It is a gem, again and again.

SUMMER SQUASH BISQUE (HOT OR COLD)

1	cup chopped onion	Pinch of sugar
2	tablespoons butter	Salt
2	pounds summer squash	Freshly grated nutmeg
	(yellow, zucchini, or	2 cups heavy cream
	pattypan)	Minced parsley
2½	cups chicken stock	

*I*n a large kettle set over medium heat, sauté the onion in the butter until it is limp. Trim and slice the squash. Add, with the stock, and cook over medium heat 15 to 20 minutes, or until the squash is tender.

Place in a blender and purée, going from slow speed to fast. Return to the kettle. Season with sugar, salt, and nutmeg to taste. Stir in the cream and taste again for seasoning.

To serve hot, heat the soup without bringing to a boil. To serve cold, chill, covered, for 3 hours or more in the refrigerator. Place in soup plates and sprinkle with minced parsley.

Serves 4.

When you are able to obtain small farm-fresh squash this is a noble but inexpensive dish. Even with somewhat tired produce it holds up—with homemade bread of some kind and a friendly white wine. Chilled, it is worthy of the shiniest table.

GILDED LILY SOUP (HOT OR COLD)

2	cups chopped onion	4	cups chicken stock
2	bunches green onions, chopped with part of tops		Tabasco
			Salt
½	cup minced shallots	2	tablespoons flour
2	large cloves garlic, minced	1	cup heavy cream
5	tablespoons butter		Minced chives

*I*n a soup pot, sauté onions, shallots, and garlic in 3 tablespoons butter over medium heat. When they are limp, pour the chicken stock over and add a few drops of Tabasco, and salt to taste. Cover and cook gently 30 minutes.

Strain the stock into a bowl and place the onion mixture in a blender. Add some of the stock and purée to a smooth pale green.

Melt the remaining 2 tablespoons butter in a large saucepan, stir in the flour, and cook, while stirring, 4 to 5 minutes. Add the hot stock all at once, and cook, stirring, until it thickens. Add the onion purée and cook gently 15 more minutes.

To serve hot, taste for seasoning and ladle into soup plates with a sprinkle of chives. To serve cold, refrigerate in a covered bowl for 3 or more hours before garnishing.

Serves 4.

This is a "what if?" kind of soup, put together one evening I'd a gift of shallots, and chives blooming at the windowsill. What if there were a dish built around some harmony of all the culinary lilies: regular yellow onions, green onions, shallots, garlic, snipped chives?

WINTER TARRAGON TOMATO SOUP

1½	cups chopped onion	½	cup dry white wine (or vermouth)
½	cup butter		
1	quart canned tomatoes (or a large can of Italian plum tomatoes)	1	tablespoon sugar
		1	teaspoon dried tarragon
			Salt
			Sour Cream

*I*n a large saucepan or kettle set over medium heat, sauté the onion in butter till it starts to turn gold. This will take about 15 minutes, and the onions should be stirred so they take color evenly. Add the tomatoes, juice and all, and mash down with a potato masher.

Add wine, sugar, and tarragon and stir. Cover, turn the heat down, and simmer 45 minutes. Turn the heat off and let sit until you prepare the rest of the dinner.

When you are ready to get the meal started, purée the soup in a blender and push it through a sieve into a saucepan. Heat it, tasting for salt, and keep warm without boiling till serving time. Serve ladled into warm soup plates, and add a dollop of cold sour cream to each.

Serves 4.

Frankly, most tomato soups are boring, but not this one, which has been elaborated from one my mother used to prepare from home-canned tomatoes. Even with store-canned tomatoes it can be served to gourmets, and with garden fresh, if you raise your own, it's a downright wonder. Try it with The Duchess of Windsor's Cornpones (page 316), and a full-bodied white wine, for the best of all possible worlds.

GREEN CORN SOUP

4 to 5	ears corn		Pinch of sugar (optional)
3	cups milk	½	cup heavy cream
	Salt	2	tablespoons butter
	Tabasco		Minced parsley or chives
4	sprigs parsley		

*C*ut the corn kernels off the cob with the sharp blade of a knife, holding the ears over a bowl. Then use the backside of the knife to scrape the cobs and release all their "milk." Place the corn (you should have 2 cups) in a large saucepan with milk, salt to taste, and a drop or two of Tabasco.

Bring to a boil and add the parsley (and some sugar if the corn is not fresh from a field). Lower the heat and simmer gently 30 minutes. Remove the parsley sprigs and purée the soup in a blender. Rub through a sieve to make sure any hard parts of the kernels are removed.

Return the soup to the pan and cook gently till the consistency is slightly

thick. Add the cream and butter and let heat through without boiling. To serve, ladle into soup plates or bowls, and sprinkle with parsley or chives.
Serves 4.

"Green corn" in early recipes implies young corn rushed from the field, barely ripe. Nowadays we most must make do with market corn—so be on the look-out for a lively crop as fresh as possible. This is a perfect summer soup, sparing of flavors, to let the delicate kernels themselves permeate and thicken. Try Summer Cloud or Happy Valley Biscuits (page 322) with it.

SHAKER HERB SOUP

2	tablespoons butter	4	cups chicken stock
1	cup minced inner celery stalks with leaves		Salt and freshly ground pepper
2	tablespoons minced chives		Pinch of sugar
2	tablespoons minced fresh chervil		A few drops of lemon juice
2	tablespoons minced fresh sorrel	4	slices trimmed white bread, toasted
½	teaspoon minced fresh tarragon		Freshly grated nutmeg
		¾	cup grated aged cheddar

Melt the butter in a kettle, and when it has stopped sizzling add the celery and chives. Cook over a low flame 5 minutes, or until the celery is soft. Add herbs, stock, salt and pepper to taste, and a pinch of sugar.

Cover the pan and let simmer 20 minutes. Taste for seasoning and add a few drops of lemon juice—it should be faintly tart. To serve, place a slice of toast in the bottom of each soup plate, ladle the soup over, grate a wisp of nutmeg over, then sprinkle the cheese on top.
Serves 4.

The Shakers were purveyors of seeds and herbs, to the great benefit of their kitchens as well as their pocketbooks. You will probably need a garden too (or at least a windowbox of fresh herbs) for dried chervil has little flavor to it. A respectful substitute for sorrel would be ¼ cup minced watercress leaves— the full effect is worth a little subterfuge.

NEW ORLEANS SUMMER FAST DAY SOUP

1	head Boston or butter lettuce	3	cups water
1	onion		Pinch of sugar
½	cucumber, peeled and seeded		Salt and freshly ground
½	cup parsley leaves		pepper
2	tablespoons butter		Mint sprigs
2	cups shelled fresh green peas		

*C*hop lettuce, onion, cucumber, and parsley very fine (this is a perfect job for a food processor). Put in a saucepan with the butter, and stew gently with the pan covered for 15 minutes.

Cook the peas in another saucepan, with a handful of their pods for flavor, in the 3 cups water, along with some sugar and a little salt and pepper. When soft, remove the pods, and purée the peas with their cooking liquid in a food processor or blender.

Pour into the stewed vegetables, taste for seasoning, and simmer gently 15 to 20 minutes more, or until the flavors are melded. To serve, ladle into bowls or soup plates and garnish each serving with mint.

Serves 4 to 6.

Such a lively tasting soup could, I suppose, be well adapted to use frozen peas, though it is perfect for the somewhat overlarge peas shipped to market in spring and summer. The original recipe, culled from The Picayune Creole Cookbook *(a wonderful compendium of New Orleans cuisine, though often fuzzy as to process and desired effect), calls for a total of 2½ hours cooking; I suspect this would only tend to dissipate the flavor of its delicate vegetables. It should be partnered with a chilled fine dry white wine, and a French loaf or homemade rolls.*

PECAN SOUP

2	tablespoons butter		Tabasco
2	tablespoons flour	1	teaspoon Worcestershire
1	cup chicken stock, heated		sauce
3	cups milk, scalded	2	egg yolks
1	cup pecans	1	cup heavy cream
	Salt		Sour cream

*M*elt the butter in a large saucepan, stir in the flour, and cook over medium heat for several minutes as you stir. Add the hot stock and milk all at once, and stir the mixture until it thickens and is smooth.

Place half this mixture in a blender or food processor, add the pecans, and go at a clip until the pecans are finely granular (not a purée). Return to the pan, stir, and simmer 30 minutes, uncovered. Add salt, a drop or two of Tabasco, and the Worcestershire—the soup should not be hot from the Tabasco, only slightly perked up as to flavor.

Simmer 10 more minutes. Beat the egg yolks with the cream, and whisk them into the soup off the fire. This can sit, covered, for an hour or so to gather flavor, if you have time. To serve, heat without letting the soup come to a boil. Ladle into soup plates and garnish each with a dollop of sour cream.

Serves 4 to 6.

You'll want to attempt this exquisite, delicately flavored Southern soup when you are able to find new-crop pecans in bulk. The small packets of nuts available year round in the market are not only sometimes stale, but too expensive to bother with here. It's good to nose around every year and buy pound bags of shelled new-crop nuts, and keep them frozen. Rather than with wine, I like to serve this as I first had it from a candlelit Virginia table—with a small glass of the fine dry sherry known as Tio Pepe.

CHESTNUT SOUP

3	tablespoons butter	8	cups chicken stock
1	small onion, chopped	2	cups cooked chestnuts (see
1	carrot, scraped and sliced		Chestnut Purée, page 229)
1	stalk celery with its leaves,	¼	cup dry Madeira
	chopped	¼	cup heavy cream
3	sprigs parsley		Salt and freshly ground
2	whole cloves		pepper
1	bay leaf		

*M*elt the butter in a kettle set over medium heat. Add onion, carrot, and celery. Cover and steam over low heat 15 to 20 minutes.

Tie the parsley, cloves, and bay leaf in a cheesecloth bag and drop them in, along with the stock. Simmer another 30 minutes. Remove the cheesecloth bag and add the chestnuts and Madeira. Simmer only 3 minutes, then purée in a blender or food processor.

Return the purée to the kettle and add the cream and salt and pepper to taste. Heat to desired hotness, but do not let it ever boil. Serve in warm soup plates.

Serves 6.

Don't limit this gracious soup to holidays, though it does introduce a goose or turkey admirably. It is a dish in the fine old New England tradition, and it dates from before the chestnut blight, when native trees grew everywhere in abundance. Nowadays we get shipments from Italy—but always buy more than you need, for often many of them are moldy or withered inside. Offer it with a small glass of Madeira, and Parker House Rolls (page 331).

DELAWARE CLAM SOUP

½	cup shucked clams with their juice		Pinch of dried thyme
¾	cup minced green onions with tops		Salt and freshly ground pepper
3	tablespoons butter		Cayenne
2	tablespoons flour	1	egg
2	cups milk, scalded	2	tablespoons dry Madeira
1	cup heavy cream		Minced parsley

Drain and reserve the clam juice, and chop the clams coarsely. Sauté the onions in the butter in a kettle set over medium heat. When they are soft, add the flour and cook, stirring, several minutes.

Add the hot milk and cream all at once. Let boil up, then lower the heat. Add clam juice, thyme, salt and pepper to taste, and a bit of cayenne. Simmer 10 to 15 minutes.

Beat the egg together with the Madeira. Add some of the hot soup, bit by bit, while whisking, then beat it into the soup pot. Add the chopped clams and let the mixture heat through without boiling. (Actually, it is best to turn off the heat at this time and let the soup rest for some time—it brings out flavor.)

To serve, warm without boiling, and ladle into warm soup plates with a pinch of parsley.

Serves 4 to 6.

There are versions upon versions of clam soup, but this from Delaware is best of all, I think. I've even been tempted to try it with canned clams (whole clams, not the chopped, which are too full of tough bits). It is not as fine, but it holds up tolerably for those with no access to fresh sweet clams. Serve it with a white wine or the Madeira you have used in cooking, and perhaps Charleston Benne Wafers (page 327).

CHARLESTON SHE-CRAB SOUP

1	tablespoon butter	Pinch of ground mace
1	teaspoon flour	Salt and freshly ground
3	cups milk, scalded	pepper
1½	cups heavy cream	½ teaspoon Worcestershire
2	cups crabmeat, with their	sauce
	eggs	¼ cup dry sherry
¼	teaspoon onion juice	Paprika

Melt butter in the top of a double boiler over simmering water. Stir in the flour and cook 3 to 4 minutes, then add the milk slowly, whisking constantly. When smooth and thickened, add 1 cup of the cream, the crab, and all the seasonings except the sherry.

Turn the fire very low, cover the pot, and let it heat 20 minutes. Meanwhile, whip the remaining ½ cup cream until stiff. To serve, place a spoon of sherry in each soup plate and add the soup. Top with whipped cream and a dust of paprika.

Serves 4 to 6.

Legend is right. I have prepared this many times with fresh-caught crab, but it is not as good as eating it on a Carolina table made only from "she crabs." A subterfuge, I'm told, is to crumble a bit of hard-boiled egg yolk in the bottom of each soup plate. Whatever crab you can muster, however, this soup should be spooned as if you were serving caviar. It is adapted here from a Junior League sampler called Charleston Receipts (for further information on this splendid cookbook, see Maum Nancy's Scalloped Oysters on page 62). To be authentic, accompany it with Charleston Benne Wafers (page 327), and either a fine white wine or a respectable dry sherry.

Meals in a Bowl

What a rich heritage we have in hearty soups to warm the bones. Our stews, chowders, gumbos, and native *bouillabaisses* range from simple thrifty feasts, through lobster stew (our ancestors gave humble names to often elegant dishes) into the complex dark gumbos and court-bouillons of the Gulf States. Turtle soup, prepared with lacings of cream and Madeira, and a crumble of eggs, was considered one of the grandest dishes of all, but turtles were so easily caught they almost became extinct, and it is now rare to see this delicacy on any menu. A soup or stew could be made in one pot hung over the fire, and as such they were the first meals of the pilgrims, a staple of chuckwagon cooks, the constant companion of homesteaders.

SENATE BEAN SOUP

1	cup dried lima or navy beans	1	bay leaf
1½	cups chopped onion	¼	cup sliced carrot
1	clove garlic, minced	2	slices lemon
1	tablespoon butter	1	small ham hock
2	sprigs parsley		Salt and freshly ground
¼	teaspoon dried thyme		pepper
			Minced parsley

Wash the beans and cover them by several inches of water in a large kettle. Let sit overnight, then drain them and add 1 quart water. Place the kettle on a high fire, and while it comes to a boil sauté the onion and garlic in butter in a skillet, then add them to the kettle.

Tie parsley sprigs, thyme, bay leaf, carrot, and lemon in a cheesecloth bag. Add them with the ham hock to the bubbling beans. Lower the heat and cook 3 hours, or until the liquid is reduced and the beans are starting to fall apart.

Discard the cheesecloth bag, then remove the ham and let it cool. Scoop out 1 cup of the beans and purée them through a sieve, blender, or food processor, then return the purée back to the kettle.

Strip the meat from the hock and cut into small dice. Add to the kettle, with salt and pepper to taste, then reheat the soup slowly. Serve garnished with minced parsley.

Serves 4.

Anyone who dines in the restaurant in the United States Senate is well advised to try this specialty—really a meal in itself. There is some confusion as to exactly how this soup is made. One version even has mashed potatoes rather than puréed beans, but this seems closest in my memory to the soup as it is actually served. During the depression in Kansas, my mother used to make a similar dish she called "stewed butterbeans," which she would ladle over a slice of whole-wheat bread as a succulent budget stretcher. I still like it that way, so I usually double this recipe, and freeze batches of it to have as a simple dinner with a glass of beer and a salad.

KENTUCKY BLACK BEAN SOUP

½	pound dried black beans	¼	teaspoon sugar
1	onion, chopped	1	ham bone, 1 small ham
2	carrots, scraped and grated		hock, or ¼ cup diced salt
2	stalks celery, chopped		pork
2	cloves garlic, minced	3	cups chicken stock
2	tablespoons olive oil	¼	cup brandy
¾	cup peeled and chopped	⅛	teaspoon dried thyme
	(fresh or canned) tomatoes	2	strips orange peel
	Salt and freshly ground		
	pepper		

Soak the beans overnight in a large kettle of water. The next day drain them and rinse in cold water. Cook onion, carrots, celery, and garlic in olive oil in the bottom of a kettle until they are limp.

Add the beans, along with all the other ingredients. Bring to a boil, then reduce the heat and simmer, uncovered, 4 hours, or until the beans are tender. If necessary, cook down liquid the last half hour of cooking, to bring the beans to a creamy consistency.

Before serving, remove the hambone or hock and the orange peel. Chop any meat and return to the pot.

Serves 4.

One of our finest soups, often repeated in books on American cookery (none quite so fine, however, as this Kentucky version with a hint of orange peel). Black beans are not easily found these days, but they are usually available in Hispanic markets. The soup may be served as is, or puréed with slices of orange for garnish. For a hearty meal, serve fat squares of cornbread alongside, and a tossed salad.

ANCESTRAL TURKEY RICE SOUP

1	turkey carcass, broken up	¼	teaspoon dried thyme
6	cups water	4	sprigs parsley
3	stalks celery with leaves, sliced	4	peppercorns
			Salt
1	large onion, sliced	1	cup (more or less) turkey meat
2	carrots, scraped and sliced		
1	bay leaf	¼	cup uncooked rice ⊗

*P*lace the turkey bones in a kettle with the water, vegetables, herbs, pepper, and salt. Bring to a boil, then lower the heat and simmer, partially covered, for about 1½ hours. Strain, and if it is very greasy, chill the stock and remove the fat on top when it has hardened.

To complete the cooking, add the turkey meat and rice to the stock and simmer 20 to 30 minutes. Taste for seasoning and serve.

Serves 4 to 6.

Except for turkey sandwiches, this final rest of the holiday carcass has always been my favorite part of an overused and overbred bird. It was cooked by my mother and her mother before, and it is I'm sure one of the staples around the country in one form or another. It is conceived essentially as a supper, with perhaps the last of the cranberry relish and buttery toasted day-old rolls.

⊗ I added some leftover cooked wild rice

OXTAIL SOUP

3	pounds oxtails, cut in sections	6	peppercorns
	Flour	2	whole cloves
2	tablespoons vegetable oil	2	bay leaves
1	large onion, chopped	⅛	teaspoon dried thyme
2	carrots, scraped and sliced		Salt
2	stalks celery, sliced	2	tablespoons tomato paste
¼	cup parsley stems	1	cup diced carrot
4	cups beef stock (or as needed)	1	cup diced turnip
		2	tablespoons dry sherry

Shake the oxtail sections in flour. Brown them in oil either in a Dutch oven or, preferably, a pressure cooker, if you have one. They should get quite brown on all sides, so cook them at a high heat for 15 to 20 minutes, turning now and again to make sure they brown evenly.

Turn the heat down to medium, then add the onion and brown it as well, tossing with the tails. Add sliced carrots, celery, parsley stems, and stock to cover. Add spices, herbs, and salt to taste, then stir in the tomato paste.

Cover, turn the heat down low, and cook up to 6 hours, or until the meat falls off the bones. (I cook this 3 to 4 hours in a pressure cooker, for they can't really cook too much.)

When done, strain the broth (reserving the oxtails) and put it in the refrigerator to let the fat congeal on top. Remove the fat, put the soup in a kettle, and bring to a boil. Add the diced carrots and turnips and cook swiftly 15 minutes, or until the vegetables are done, and the soup has reduced slightly.

Carefully shred the meat from the oxtails, discarding the fat. Add to the soup, along with the sherry. Heat and serve in warm soup plates or bowls.

Serves 4 to 6.

Those curious people finicky about oxtails will find this old time New England rib-sticking soup the surest way to conversion. Strange that one of the sweetest, most savory parts of the whole beef should be its tail—but there it is. Though it used to be a grand first-course soup, I like its rich beefy essence as the center of a meal. You might begin with a first course vegetable or salad— an artichoke, say, or Celery Victor (page 278), then serve the soup with a red wine and homemade bread, and end with some substantial dessert.

BLACKEYED PEA SOUP

2 cups dried blackeyed peas	Freshly ground pepper
4 cups water	1 cup chopped canned or fresh
2 small ham hocks (or 1 large)	tomatoes
2 stalks celery with leaves, chopped	6 green onions with part of the tops, minced
1½ cups chopped onion	¼ cup minced parsley
1 clove garlic, minced	1 tablespoon olive oil
1 bay leaf	1 teaspoon wine vinegar
Pinch of ground cloves	Salt and freshly ground pepper

*W*ash and pick over the peas, then place them in a large kettle with 4 cups water. Bring to a boil, turn the heat off, cover, and let sit while the ham hocks cook.

Place the hocks in another kettle, cover them with water, and simmer 1½ hours, or until the meat is falling off the bones. Take the hocks out, let cool, then strip the meat from them and chop it coarsely.

Add the ham stock to the peas, along with the meat, celery, onion, garlic, bay leaf, cloves, and pepper to taste. Simmer, partially covered, for 1½ hours, or until the peas are soft. Add more hot water if it boils too low.

While the soup cooks, combine tomatoes, green onions, parsley, oil, vinegar, and salt and pepper to taste. Let this sit at room temperature.

During the final cooking of the peas, add salt to taste. Let the soup sit till you are ready to serve it, then heat it up, and ladle into a bowl or soup plates. Pass the tomato–green onion "relish" for diners to garnish their own soup.

Serves 6.

Black-eyed peas are about the most flavorful dried bean (and they are a bean, whatever their name) in the native cupboard, but though they are used constantly in the South, both fresh and dried, they get short shrift in other parts of the country. If they're not part of your repertoire, try this Tennessee soup— it makes a fine inexpensive family meal, which could become a favorite. Serve it with a frosty glass of beer, and Bacon Buttermilk Cornbread (page 318), then, later, pie and coffee.

POSOLE

1	pork loin or shoulder (3 pounds), trimmed of fat
3	cups chicken stock
1	onion, sliced
1	whole clove garlic, peeled
½	teaspoon dried oregano
	Salt
1	chicken (about 2½ pounds)
1	tablespoon bacon fat (or butter)
2	onions, chopped
2	cloves garlic, minced

1 to 2	tablespoons chili powder
2	large cans (1 pound 13 ounces each) white hominy, drained
1	cup chopped canned tomatoes
1	can mild green chiles (4 ounces), chopped
¼	cup chopped fresh coriander (or parsley)
	Garnishes as listed below

*E*arly in the day, or the day before, simmer the pork in a large kettle with the stock and enough water to cover the meat, sliced onion and whole garlic clove, and oregano and salt to taste. Cook 45 minutes, then add the chicken and cook 30 minutes more—always at a simmer. Strain the stock and refrigerate, along with the meats.

To cook the posole, lift fat off the cold stock and cut both the pork and meat of the chicken into ½-inch cubes. In the same large kettle, sauté the onion and garlic in the bacon fat until the onion is limp. Add the pork cubes and chili powder and cook several more minutes, stirring well. Add the stock— there should be about 8 cups of it. Then add hominy, tomatoes, green chilies, and coriander.

Simmer 20 minutes, then add the chicken cubes and cook another 15 minutes. Serve ladled into bowls, with small bowls of the following garnishes for guests to help themselves: Small strips of crisply fried tortillas, diced avocados, chopped green onions, tiny dice of cream cheese, lime wedges, sliced radishes, shredded lettuce tossed with a little salt and vinegar.

Serves 6 to 8.

Posole is an overlooked dish from the Southwest that makes a superb dish for entertaining. It is worthwhile making a large batch of it, even if you feed a small family, as it freezes admirably. Everyone likes the zesty taste of this combination soup and stew, and the table looks pretty spread with its array of garnishes. Serve it as well with a stack of fresh tortillas that have been sprinkled with a bit of water and put to steam in a warm oven, wrapped in foil. A plate of butter for these, and a pitcher of fine beer, then finally some such dessert as a flan with good coffee.

BEVERLY HILLS RANGOON RACQUET CLUB CHAMPIONSHIP CHILI

1	large can Italian plum tomatoes (or 3½ cups chopped fresh)	2½ cups chicken stock
		½ cup beer
2	cups chopped onion	2½ tablespoons chili powder
1	stalk celery, chopped	1½ teaspoons dried oregano
1	teaspoon sugar	1 teaspoon ground cumin
2	pounds pork loin	½ teaspoon dried thyme
2	pounds flank steak	1 tablespoon minced fresh coriander leaves

2	cloves garlic, minced		chopped
1	can (4 ounces) mild green	¼	cup oil
	chilies, chopped	½	pound natural Monterey Jack
2	pickled jalapeño peppers,		cheese, grated
	seeded and minced		Wedges of lime
1	small sweet green pepper,		Coriander sprigs (optional)

*T*his recipe takes nearly all day, but it can be speeded up considerably with a food processor and a pressure cooker.

To begin, mash the tomatoes in the bottom of a kettle. Add onion, celery, and sugar and cook an hour or more, gently. As they cook, cut the meat and prepare the other ingredients.

Trim the pork of fat, and cut into tiny cubes. Cut the flank steak in slightly larger cubes—not more than ¼ inch, however. When the tomatoes look (and taste) good, add all the ingredients listed from the chicken stock through all the peppers. Let this cook while you fry the meat.

Fry each meat separately in small batches over a hot fire, adding a little oil as you need it. As each batch is seared brown, lift it out into the chili pot. When all are done, pour a cup of hot water into the pan and whisk to scrape up all the brown pieces. Pour this into the pot, taste for salt and pepper, and simmer slowly until the meats start to disintegrate and it makes a composite mass. (This takes about 3 hours.)

Stir the chili now and again while it cooks, skim any fat off the top, and taste. (It tastes good all the way through the process of cooking—in fact, that is one of the rewards of spending the day making it.) When it is to your satisfaction, eat a bowl for yourself and refrigerate the rest.

The next day, heat it before serving, taste again, and stir in the Monterey Jack. If it is a good natural Monterey Jack it will dissolve in a creamy sauce as you stir. Serve immediately the cheese is dissolved and garnish with wedges of lime for guests to squeeze over the chili to taste. A sprig of coriander is nice, too.

Serves 6 to 8.

Chili is perhaps more American even than apple pie, but this particular dish (derived from C. V. Woods' champion winner) is brought to a certain pitch where it could favorably be compared to any fine curry. It takes at least 4 hours of cooking, though with a pressure cooker you can get by with less. (Try the tomatoes for 30 minutes, and the meat mixture should take an hour and a half or so.)

It is also very very rich—a good-sized bowl of it is almost more than any-

one could consume. So the rest of the meal should be made quite light. You could serve it with Avocado Slices Marinated in Rum (page 191) for a first course, then the chili with beer and home-fried tortilla chips, and finally some such dessert as Pink Grapefruit Ice (page 388). Since it takes all that work, I never make it in batches less than this. If you have only yourself to feed, however, it freezes well (except for the cheese, which should be added fresh) and assures you with a long string of superb suppers.

LONG ISLAND OYSTER STEW

4	tablespoons butter	Salt and freshly ground
2	cups milk	pepper
1	cup heavy cream	Paprika
3	cups fresh-shucked oysters with liquor	

*P*lace 4 soup bowls in a warm oven with a tablespoon of butter in each. Bring the milk and cream to a simmer in one saucepan, and in another pour the oysters with their liquor and poach them just till they plump and curl at the edges.

Immediately pour the hot milk and cream over the oysters. Add salt and pepper to taste, and ladle the stew into the warm buttered bowls. Sprinkle with a dust of paprika and serve immediately with any cracker you fancy, or good bread.

Serves 4.

Oyster stew is one of the best simple meals ever devised. Many recipes complicate the dish needlessly—even to the point of adding Worcestershire—but these are to be avoided. In the East the stew is always served with crackers, but some prefer a fresh loaf of crusty French Bread—I know I do.

LOBSTER STEW

1	lobster (2½ pounds), cooked		Cayenne
4	tablespoons butter		Salt
2	cups milk	2	tablespoons dry sherry (or
2	cups heavy cream		Madeira) (optional)

*P*ick out all meat from the lobster, reserving the coral. Discard the intestinal veins and the sacs near the base of the head. Crack the shell and bones from which the meat has been extracted, and put them in a large kettle.

Cut the larger pieces of lobster meat in small slices, and toss in the butter in a pan set over low heat, then turn off the heat.

Add the milk to the lobster shells (adding all juices that have escaped while shelling the lobster). Simmer 5 minutes, then strain into the pan with buttered lobster.

Mash the reserved coral with some of the cream, and add it to the pan with all the cream. Bring just to the boiling point, and season with a dash of cayenne and salt to taste. Swirl in sherry or Madeira just before serving in warm soup plates.

Serves 4 to 6.

Lobster Stew is flat out one of the glories of our cuisine. Unlike most of the "stews" it should be served as the first course to a banquet (preferably in the White House, to all visiting foreign dignitaries). In principle I don't like to fiddle much with any lobster, but this seems to concentrate flavor rather than to mask it as many elaborate lobster concoctions do.

SWEET SCALLOP STEW

1	pound scallops, cut in quarters if they are large	1	teaspoon flour
2	tablespoons butter	1	cup milk, scalded
½	cup minced green onions with part of tops	1	cup heavy cream
			Salt
			Butter

*I*n a large saucepan set over medium-low heat, sauté the scallops in butter for 3 to 4 minutes—or until they just stiffen slightly. Remove with a slotted spoon and reserve.

Add the green onions and sauté them till limp. Sprinkle the flour over and cook, stirring, another 3 to 4 minutes. Add the hot milk all at once, stirring until the soup thickens and is smooth.

Add about a quarter of the scallops, turn the heat down low, and cook gently a few more minutes. Place in a blender and whirl until smooth. Return to the pan and add the cream and salt to taste.

Add the remaining scallops and let the stew heat gently without boiling. Serve with a lump of butter on top.

Serves 4 to 6.

Another classic. There should never be anything to interfere with the sweet flavor and delicate texture of scallops, and this shows them at their simple, sensuous best.

NEW ENGLAND CLAM CHOWDER

¼	pound salt pork, cut in ¼-inch dice	¼	teaspoon dried thyme
1	onion, chopped	2	cups shucked clams
3	medium potatoes, peeled and cubed	2	cups milk, scalded
1½	cups water		Salt and freshly ground pepper

Sauté the salt pork in the bottom of a soup kettle set over medium heat. When it is crisp and golden, remove with a slotted spoon and reserve.

Sauté the onion in the pork fat released in the kettle, over low heat till pale gold. Add the potatoes, water, and thyme and cook gently for 10 minutes.

Drain the clams, strain the juices, and heat in another pan. Chop the clams coarsely as the juice heats. Add both the clams and hot clam juice to the onion, then the scalded milk. Add salt and pepper to taste and simmer, uncovered, 30 minutes.

To serve, ladle into soup plates and sprinkle the crisp salt pork over the top of the stew. Serve with crackers.

Serves 4.

This is a misunderstood soup, often gussied up in restaurants by thickening or by adding unnecessary ingredients to make up for the lack of fresh-dug clams. It is so pure, in fact, that there is probably no use cooking it without same—and washed beach, woodsmoke, salt breeze, good friends.

HYANNIS FISH CHOWDER

½ cup diced (¼ inch) salt pork
     (or bacon)
2 cups chopped onion
4 cups fish stock
3 cups peeled and cubed
     potatoes
   Pinch of dried thyme

   Salt and freshly ground
     pepper
3 pounds fish fillets, cut in
     pieces
2 cups milk, scalded
2 cups heavy cream
6 tablespoons butter
   Paprika

*I*n a soup kettle set over medium heat, sauté the salt pork until it releases its fat and is crisp and golden. Lift it out with a slotted spoon and reserve.

In the fat left at the bottom of the kettle, sauté the onion until limp. Add fish stock, potatoes, thyme, and salt and pepper to taste. Simmer, uncovered, 20 minutes, or until the potatoes are done.

Add the fish and simmer 5 minutes. Add the scalded milk, then the cream, and taste for seasoning. Turn off the heat and let the chowder stand for an hour to gather flavor.

To serve, gently heat the chowder without letting it come to a boil, add the butter, and ladle into warm bowls. Garnish with the crisp salt pork and a dusting of paprika.

Serves 6.

This was one of the favorites of Jack Kennedy, and was supplied to the press as such during his presidency. (All Presidents, for some reason, are required to have at least one recipe in their pocket.) In a chowder freshness is all—the daily catch of haddock or cod are treated to this bath of hot milk nightly throughout New England. Inland, it's perhaps not worthwhile using frozen fish, but there's no reason why a Southerner, say, couldn't take his local catfish to the uses of this Yankee dish.

IDEAL GUMBO

1 chicken (about 2½ pounds)	1 pound okra, tipped and
A meaty ham bone (or a	sliced (or 1 package
meaty ham hock)	frozen)
1 small onion, sliced	2 cups chopped tomatoes
2 stalks celery, chopped	(canned or fresh), with
2 sprigs parsley	their juices
1 whole clove garlic	3 bay leaves
1 bay leaf	1 teaspoon dried thyme
6 peppercorns	Tabasco
Salt	Freshly ground pepper
3 tablespoons fat (vegetable oil,	1½ pounds fresh shrimp,
bacon fat, or ham fat)	cooked and shelled
2 tablespoons flour	2 cups fresh crabmeat plus
2 cups chopped onion	cracked claws
3 cloves garlic, minced	2 dozen oysters, shucked
½ cup minced green pepper	Filé powder
	Hot steamed rice

*P*ut chicken to cook in a large soup kettle with the ham bone, onion, celery, parsley, whole clove garlic, bay leaf, peppercorns, salt to taste, and water to cover. Simmer, covered, an hour, or until the chicken is tender. Lift out both chicken and ham bone, and strain and reserve the stock.

(Much to-do is made over the New Orleans, or Creole dark roux, but it is really very simple, if a trifle time-consuming to prepare. A gumbo is worth anyone's time. French cooking recognizes only a simple mixture of butter and flour that is stirred until the particles of flour fully absorb the butter, the butter bubbling lightly all the while over low heat. That, and another roux with the butter let get golden for a "darker"-tasting sauce. Creole cooks went farther toward prizing this dark taste and developed an even browned roux made often with other fats that burn less easily than butter. It can take anywhere from 20 to 30 minutes of stirring to achieve flour granules so goldenly browned they no longer actually thicken the sauce to which they are the base.)

So make a dark roux with any tasty fat and the flour. Add onion, minced garlic, and green pepper. Stir them in the kettle till limp. Stir in the okra a few minutes, then add the tomatoes, herbs, and spices. Add the reserved stock and cook gently, uncovered, for 30 minutes, or until the okra has thickened the whole and it starts to look glutinous.

Add the cut-up meat from the chicken, the meat from the ham bone, the shrimp, and crab and crab claws. Simmer the gumbo gently for 2 or more hours, stirring now and again to make sure it doesn't stick to the bottom. (This long cooking of shrimp and crab will seem curious outside the South, but that's how it is usually done for the deepest flavor.)

Taste for seasoning near the end—it should be hot slightly with Tabasco, not too salty, and of a deep, rich flavor.

When you are ready to serve the gumbo, add enough filé powder (about a tablespoon) to thicken the gumbo to about the texture of a good stew. At the last add the oysters, and let the gumbo heat without boiling. (After adding filé powder the gumbo should never boil, or it will become stringy and much flavor is somehow lost.) To serve, ladle onto steamed rice on warm plates, and pass filé powder to sprinkle over.

Serves 6 to 8.

In practice no two gumbos are alike, and here are only approximations of what might go into yours. They may have many balances, and ham and chicken can be used alone—though a gumbo is usually conceived as a shellfish-based dish. The chicken is often, in the South, a game carcass—I have even found one recipe for home-smoked wild duck gumbo with fresh oysters. If you have fresh cheap seafood, there is no reason to use chicken at all.

Crab may be used alone, as in this recipe from Gourmet's Guide to New Orleans, *a splendid cookbook published in 1933, for Shadows of the Teche Gumbo, said to make the late painter Weeks Hall "desert his easel":*

Wash (1 doz.) crabs thoroughly, then boil them in just enough water to cover, and cook until done, saving water the crabs were boiled in. Remove the shells, picking out all the meat of the crab. Now put (2 lbs.) okra cut up in round slices and add it to the hot lard (1 kitchen spoon), to fry until dry. Add (4) cloves minced garlic. Fry all this together, then add the water in which the crabs were boiled. Add salt to taste, and set it all to boil about two hours.

The recipe goes on to add a tablespoon of flour to three ears of scraped corn, and this is added half an hour before serving, along with the crabmeat. Some vinegar is added to cut the okra toward the end. It can almost be sniffed through the Spanish moss of the Teche, almost tasted.

Probably the only way to cook a gumbo is to have eaten some and know where you're heading—plain sailing through fellow gourmet–traveled waters. You will find that either okra or filé powder can be used to thicken, though both are nice, and you will come to the darker the roux the better point and back, and above quite all you will find how a fine gumbo ages till (like a cassoulet) it is almost better at last dense taste.

Gumbos, though always listed as a soup, are definitely a main-dish stew served with dry fluffy rice. I serve them as one would a curry, on plates. Since they are so rich, I usually start the meal with a fine plain salad and The Duchess of Windsor's Cornpones (page 316), follow that with a gumbo and a fine white wine from California, then some such dessert as Roanoke Rum Cream (page 382).

TURKEY OYSTER GUMBO

	The remains of a turkey	¼	teaspoon dried thyme
½	pound ham	3	dozen small oysters, shucked
2	tablespoons butter		Salt and freshly ground
1	large chopped onion		pepper
2	quarts boiling water		Cayenne
1	bay leaf	2	tablespoons filé powder
3	tablespoons minced parsley		Hot cooked rice

*R*emove any meat from the turkey (there should be 1 to 2 cups), and cut it with the ham into ½-inch dice. Melt the butter in a soup kettle and sauté the meats and onion till the onion is limp.

Add boiling water, bay leaf, parsley, and thyme, and break up the turkey carcass and add it as well. Let this simmer, covered, over low heat for an hour or more, then remove the bones.

Add the oysters, salt and pepper to taste, and enough cayenne to make it slightly hot. Cook till the oysters begin to curl, then stir in the filé powder and cook without boiling until the gumbo thickens. Serve over fluffy hot cooked rice.

Serves 6.

What better and unusual way to serve the last of a turkey? An example of how the Creole cook constructs a gumbo from food at hand, in just proportions.

GUMBO Z'HERBES

4	pounds any combination of greens—turnip, mustard, beet, collards, spinach, watercress, lettuce, onion tops, radish tops, etc.	1	heaping tablespoon flour
		1½	cups chopped onion
		2	cloves garlic, minced
		1	green pepper, minced
			Salt and freshly ground pepper
2	cups water	¼	teaspoon dried thyme
1 to 2	meaty ham hocks (or 1 pound salt pork, or duck carcass or any game, or a veal knuckle, etc.)	1	bay leaf
		1	small pod of dried red pepper (or cayenne, or Tabasco)
			Filé powder
			Hot cooked rice
2	tablespoons bacon fat (or goose fat)		

Wash thoroughly whatever your garden, or market, can claim for fresh greens and place them in a large kettle. Add the water and bring the greens to a boil over a medium flame. If the kettle won't hold all of them, start with the first batch of greens and let it wilt, then add another batch, etc.

Place the meat over the greens, cover, and cook slowly an hour. Remove the meat, drain the greens, and save the "pot liquor." Place the bacon fat in another pot and thoroughly brown the flour in it over a low flame, stirring for 20 to 30 minutes.

Remove all meat from the bones and cut into ½-inch dice. Add the onion to the browned flour and cook till golden, then add garlic, green pepper, and the meat. Chop the greens and return them to the pot along with the "pot liquor," and let this boil up. Add salt and pepper to taste, then add thyme, bay leaf, and red pepper.

Simmer, uncovered, gently for 2 hours, and at the very end add enough filé powder to thicken it—about a tablespoon. (It should not boil after you add the filé.) Serve on hot cooked rice.

Serves 6.

This tonic apotheosis of southern "greens" is as wild as its name—from the French des herbes. Obviously no two versions are alike, even from the same cook, for it is possible to go from a full-scale production to a rather suave dish using the leftovers from a duck, cooked with lettuce and spinach. I like it. Of course it would never be served in a restaurant, but how pleasant to come upon it on a menu—a dish the like of which gourmets have scoured the homes of many a French peasant to find. If I were able to order it up, I would have oysters on the half shell, to begin, with good bread and white wine, then on to the gumbo with a robust red wine, with fruit and cheese or a light dessert to follow.

CREOLE COURT-BOUILLON

1	cup chopped onion		Salt and freshly ground
½	cup chopped celery		pepper
1	cup chopped green (or red)		Cayenne
	pepper	1	tablespoon paprika
½	cup chopped green onions	2	cups fish stock
	with part of tops	2	pounds redfish (or red
2	cloves garlic, minced		snapper or other fresh
¼	cup olive oil		firm fish)
	Flour		Vegetable oil
2	bay leaves	1½	tablespoons lemon juice
¼	teaspoon dried thyme	⅓	cup dry red wine
2	cups (fresh or canned	½	lemon, sliced
	preferably Italian Plum)		Hot cooked rice
	tomatoes		

*I*n a soup kettle set over medium-low heat, sauté the chopped vegetables in oil till they start to turn gold, then add 2 tablespoons flour and stir until the flour starts also to turn golden.

Add bay leaves, thyme, and then tomatoes—mashing them down with a slotted spoon or potato masher to break them up. Add seasonings, then stock, and simmer, uncovered, 30 minutes.

While this cooks, cut the fish into 1-inch strips, shake them in flour, and place on a plate. Heat some vegetable oil in a frying pan and sauté the fish for several minutes on each side over rather high heat, or until they start to brown.

Add the fish to the pot along with the lemon juice and wine, and simmer 10 to 12 minutes more. Add lemon slices, then taste for seasoning—it should be quite spicy and rather hot with cayenne—and serve in bowls over hot cooked rice.

Serves 4.

Though the Creole cook makes this dish from the tasty redfish from the Gulf, not available generally anywhere else, this rather primitive bouillabaisse, highly spiced and slightly dark from the roux of vegetables, is a fine way to treat any fresh firm-fleshed fish. It certainly has more gumption than any chowder. It might be preceeded by a salad or first-course vegetable, served with a fine red wine rather than a white, and followed by a rich dessert and coffee.

(The knowledgeable cook will wonder as to the title of this dish, for he knows a court-bouillon in French cookery is a simple bath of water, vinegar, vegetables, and herbs used to poach fish. The Creole cook throws all that to the winds, and puts everything in the pot.)

CIOPPINO

½	cup olive oil		Salt
1	cup chopped onion		Cayenne
2	cloves garlic, minced	3	pounds crabs, cleaned and cooked
3	tablespoons minced parsley		
1	cup dry white wine	1½	pounds sea bass (or other firm fish)
1	cup chopped fresh or canned (preferably Italian Plum) tomatoes	1	pound shrimp, shelled
		2	dozen clams in their shells
1	bay leaf	3	dozen mussels in their shells (optional)
2	whole cloves		
¼	teaspoon saffron threads		

Heat the oil in a heavy kettle and sauté the onion, garlic, and parsley until limp. Add the wine and let it cook for a few minutes, then add tomatoes, bay leaf, cloves, and saffron. Let simmer, covered, for an hour, or until the sauce has a well-balanced flavor. Season to taste with salt and cayenne.

Crack the crabs, remove the flesh from all but the large claws, and reserve. Cut the fish in bite-sized portions. Add the crabmeat, claws, and fish with the shrimp to the kettle and cook, uncovered, 15 minutes over low heat. Add the clams and mussels and steam them, covered, until they open.

Serve in warm soup plates or bowls, accompanied by either San Francisco sour dough bread, or any crusty French bread.

Serves 6 to 8.

Cioppino is a native California dish that has not yet been boosted as one of our great native bouillabaisses. At its best I have had it only at Italian festivals in San Francisco, but it is far from impossible in any seacoast kitchen.

FISH & SHELLFISH

There, having reduced some damp driftwood, which I had picked up on the shore, to shavings with my knife, I kindled a fire with a match and some paper, and cooked my clam on the embers for my dinner; for breakfast was commonly the only meal which I took in a house on this excursion. When the clam was done, one valve held the meat, and the other the liquor. Though it was very tough, I found it sweet and savory, and ate the whole with a relish.

—Henry David Thoreau, Cape Cod

Fish

*E*arly on, I always skipped the fish chapter of a foreign cookbook, with their eels and *loups* and faraway *fruits-de-mer*. Until I lived a long time in a seashore city, with equally unidentifiable Chinese finny things, I didn't figure out any catch should be cooked simply and lightly as possible. As a trout fisherman once advised me, on asking over the campfire: "It's how the critter takes to heat—he should skip just like he's still in the stream."

TARRAGON FILLETS
WITH CUCUMBER BUTTER

4 serving portions sole (or flounder or other tender fillet)	½ cucumber
	½ cup plus 2 tablespoons butter
	1 teaspoon lemon juice
White wine tarragon vinegar	Lemon slices
Salt	

Place the fish fillets on a plate and sprinkle them lightly with vinegar. (If you don't have a good tarragon vinegar, bring 2 tablespoons white wine vinegar to a boil, add some fresh or dried tarragon, let it cook briefly, and sprinkle over the fish.) Salt lightly and place the fish to marinate in your refrigerator.

Have the ½ cup butter at room temperature. Peel the cucumber, slice it lengthwise, and cut out the seeds. Mince finely in a blender or food processor. Drain the cucumber as well as possible—squeezing the juice out in your hands. Whip it bit by bit into the room-temperature butter until creamy. Add the lemon juice and incorporate it thoroughly. (All this can be done with a fork, or in any manner that incorporates the cucumber, but a food processor is best.)

Smooth the cucumber butter on a plate and place it in the refrigerator to harden. When it comes time to cook the fish, drain off any juice that has accumulated and pat dry with paper towels.

To prepare the dish, heat the 2 tablespoons butter in a frying pan large enough to hold the fish at once. When it begins to sizzle, add the fish to the pan and sauté over a medium flame 1 to 2 minutes a side. Place the fillets on a warm plate, salt again to taste, and top with pieces of cucumber butter. Garnish with lemon slices. If you have it, it's pretty to tuck in a sprig of fresh tarragon.

Serves 4.

A recipe assembled from two hints in Irma Rombauer's Joy of Cooking, *the one indispensable tool of any American cook. Everything can be found there, and can be depended on for style, economy, brevity—even wit. Her marinade of tarragon vinegar makes a surprise of supermarket fillets. The cucumber butter is subtler than it sounds, and should exactly balance the faint tarragon. The dish could either be a first course, with chilled white wine and hot rolls, or constitute a main course with some such starch as* Farmhouse Skillet Creamed Potatoes *(page 256), or* Thomas Jefferson's Pilau *(page 266).*

CRISP SOLE WITH ANCHOVY CREAM

4	serving portions sole (or flounder or other tender fillets)	½	teaspoon salt
		2	egg whites, beaten stiff
			Vegetable oil
½	cup flour	1	cup heavy cream
2	tablespoons olive oil	2	teaspoons (or to taste)
6	tablespoons water		anchovy paste

Wash and dry the fillets with paper towels. Mix flour, oil, water, and salt into a paste, then fold in the beaten egg whites just before ready to cook the fish.

To do so, heat about an inch of oil in a frying pan (this can be a small pan, and they can be done in batches). Dip the fillets in the batter, and fry them until gold on each side—this should take no more than 2 minutes a side. Remove to drain on paper towels, and keep warm while you prepare the anchovy cream.

Beat the cream stiff, adding the anchovy paste toward the end. Taste the sauce—it should not be too salt or fishy. To serve, slide the fillets onto warm plates and place a dollop of the cream on top of each.

Serves 4.

This is a recipe from Theodora Fitzgibbon's Country House Cooking *I picked up once, thinking it would be about American food, and promptly became enchanted by this British writer. So here I cheat, with only the flimsy excuse that I like the recipe, and that if so much of our food has stemmed from England at its dullest, there is no reason not to choose again from the best. Theodora Fitzgibbon, though not so well known as Elizabeth David, is surely one of the best writers on food we have. Perhaps only rivaled by France's Edouard de Pomiane for brevity and shine and sheer usefulness, the book above is a revelation of best family receipts and stout cooks long dead, obliged to hustle a sudden tea for Queen Victoria on a swoop, or edify a whole weekend of city guests such as Henry James. But any of her books, though difficult to find, are worth the price. As a first course, the recipe here needs nothing but the finest white wine. As a main dish, it could be accompanied by a simple green vegetable such as asparagus or green beans carefully turned out, and perhaps with a crisp pile of Saratoga Chips (page 254) cooked in the same fat.*

PAN-FRIED FILLETS
WITH FRENCH QUARTER SAUCE

4 serving portions sole (or flounder or other tender fillet) Milk Flour (or cornmeal)	Salt and freshly ground pepper 2 tablespoons butter 2 tablespoons vegetable oil French Quarter Sauce (page 293)

Dip the fillets in milk, then into flour or cornmeal seasoned with salt and pepper to taste. Lay on waxed paper until ready to cook. This is done in the butter and oil sputtering in a frying pan set over medium hot heat. Sauté until the fillets are gold on either side—a good guide is James Beard's 10 minutes per inch thickness for any preparation of fish.

Lift out the fish on paper toweling to drain. Serve warm, coated with French Quarter Sauce.

Serves 4.

It is the piquant New Orleans sauce that makes this dish stand out among simple preparations of fish—a little-known sauce with in fact many fine applications, and simplicity itself prepared with either blender or food processor. If you've never tried, do not hesitate to use cornmeal rather than flour, for it results in a fine crispiness flour cannot touch. Serve it with French bread and dry white wine.

CHILLED HYANNIS COD FILLETS

4 cod fillets (or other thick fish fillets or steaks) ¼ cup prepared horseradish, drained 2 cups sour cream ½ cup minced green onions with part of tops 1 teaspoon white wine vinegar	3 tablespoons minced fresh dill (or 2 tablespoons dried) Salt and freshly ground pepper 4 lettuce leaves 2 hard-boiled eggs, quartered 2 ripe tomatoes, peeled and quartered (or 8 radish roses)

Steam the fish, covered, in a little water for 8 to 10 minutes, or until it flakes easily. Lift out to a plate and let cool.

While the fish cooks, mix horseradish with sour cream, green onions, vinegar, dill, and salt and pepper to taste. Place half the mixture in a shallow dish large enough to hold all the fish in a single layer. Place the fillets on top of the sauce, spread the rest over, cover the dish, and refrigerate for at least an hour.

To serve, place a lettuce leaf on each plate, place a fillet in the middle, and garnish with eggs and tomato. Spoon any leftover sauce on top of the fish.

Serves 4.

Another recipe from the Kennedy Compound. Such an easy tangy horseradish sauce is the perfect foil for any strong-tasting, sturdy-fleshed fish such as cod, but it works with any cold fish. With a good crusty bread and chilled white wine, it makes an exceptional summer lunch or supper—and is easily assembled the day before.

FLORIDA ORANGE SNAPPER

4	red snapper fillets (or other fillets or steaks)	Salt
½	cup minced green onions with part of tops	Tabasco
		Freshly grated nutmeg
	Grated peel and juice of 1 orange	4 orange slices

*M*arinate the fillets with green onions, orange peel and juice, salt to taste, and a few drops Tabasco for at least 30 minutes.

Preheat oven to 400 °F.

Place fish with its marinade in a shallow casserole large enough to hold all the fillets in one layer. Sprinkle with a little grated nutmeg and bake basting once or twice, 10 minutes, or until the fish flakes easily with a fork.

Serve hot or cold, garnished with orange slices.

Serves 4.

Discovered in one of those ladies' church cookbooks, which promise so much and deliver so little, this is an excellent recipe from the Orange State. It is also a dieter's delight. As it's even better the next day cold—make too much and have enough for lunch. Either way, it should be served with a fragrant, not too dry white wine.

FRIED FISH WITH HUSH PUPPIES

4	serving portions any fish at all	1	recipe Hush Puppies (page
	Milk		320)
	Salt and freshly ground		Lemon wedges
	pepper		Parsley sprigs
	Cornmeal		Tartar Sauce (page 292)
	Fat for deep frying		

Dip fish, whole or in fillets, into milk, then roll in salted and peppered cornmeal. Lay on waxed paper and refrigerate 30 minutes or more, to set the cornmeal.

To cook, fry in deep fat (heated about 370°F, or sizzling up when a bit of cornmeal is dropped in) until they are golden on all sides. Drain on paper towels, and keep warm in an oven while you prepare the hush puppies in the same fat.

Serve each with a heap of hush puppies, lemon wedges, a sprig of parsley, and the tartar sauce.

Serves 4.

Seldom seen in cookbooks, this is the way Southerners cook fish—and they are to my mind right. The method is a joy on just-caught fish over a campfire, and it is an enhancement even to frozen fish fillets. It's easy, but the trick is to have the fat just the right temperature for it. If not hot enough, both the fish and the hush puppies will be greasy. Serve with cole slaw and cold beer.

MARYLAND BAKED FISH WITH CREAM

1	whole fish (4 to 5 pounds)	3	slices bacon
	(any catch of the day)		Cayenne
1	lemon, halved		Flour
	Salt	4	whole cloves
¼	teaspoon ground allspice	¾	cup heavy cream
2	tablespoons butter		Parsley sprigs
1	tablespoon Dijon mustard	1	pimento-stuffed olive slice

Preheat the oven to 375°F.

Take a fish that has been cleaned but left whole, and rub inside and out with some of the juice from the lemon. Sprinkle inside and out with salt and allspice. Mix the butter and mustard together with a fork, and place in the inner cavity.

Take a casserole large enough to hold the fish, and line it with aluminum foil so it comes up the sides of the casserole (this is for easy removal later to a platter. If you have a nice dish and wish to serve the fish at table, this will be unnecessary.) Grease the foil, and lay the bacon in the bottom. Rest the fish on the bacon. Dust with some cayenne and salt, and squeeze the rest of the lemon juice over. Dust the fish with a bit of flour—preferably through a sifter. Stick the cloves in the flesh, and pour cream around the edges.

Bake 35 to 40 minutes, or until the flesh flakes easily with a fork. Baste occasionally while it cooks, and when done remove to a serving platter and pour the cooking cream around and over it.

Serve garnished with a pride of parsley, and a sliced olive for eye.

Serves 4 to 6.

Ordinary baked fish, with a simple bread stuffing—perhaps with some grated cucumber tossed in—and strips of bacon cresting the top, is always welcome, but this antique Maryland recipe in a slightly spiced cream is superior in every way. I've tried it on all sorts of fish, and it worked in every case, though you'll want to stay away from very thin and thus very long fish, or you won't have a dish large enough to hold it. Since it is so simple it can be preceded with an interesting soup (with no cream of course) or a vegetable first course such as Celery Victor (page 278). To accompany it, try Zucchini-stuffed Baked Potatoes (page 258) or Portland Potatoes (page 259). That, and a toasting good white vintage.

POMPANO EN PAPILLOTE, ANTOINE

3	medium pompano (or trout)	2	tablespoons flour
3	cups water	4	green onions with part of
1	teaspoon salt		tops, chopped
1	stalk celery, sliced	1	cup cooked shrimp
1	small onion, sliced	1	cup cooked crabmeat
1	bay leaf	1	clove garlic, minced
	Pinch of dried thyme		Tabasco (optional)
2	cups dry white wine	2	egg yolks, beaten
6	tablespoons butter		Parchment baking paper

*H*ave the fish filleted and ask for the trimmings. Place the heads and bones in a kettle with water, salt, celery, onion, bay leaf, and thyme and simmer, uncovered, 30 minutes. Strain and reserve 1 cup of the stock. Pour the rest of the stock in a saucepan and add ½ cup of the white wine.

Poach the fillets in this 5 minutes. Remove from the heat, and let cool in the stock.

To make the sauce, melt 2 tablespoons of the butter in a saucepan. Stir in the flour and cook several minutes. Add the reserved cup of stock and let the sauce bubble up. Whisk smooth and turn the fire down very low.

In another pan, sauté the green onions in the remaining butter (4 tablespoons). When they are limp, add the shrimp, crab, garlic, and a drop or two of Tabasco if you like. Toss until the garlic starts to cook, then add the rest of the wine (1½ cups) and let cook, uncovered, 15 minutes over a low flame. Add the thickened sauce, and beat in the egg yolks. Stir until heated, but do not let it boil. This can sit until you are ready to assemble the dish.

Preheat the oven to 425°F. Make papillotes by cutting six 12 x 8-inch hearts from the parchment baking paper (which is usually found in food specialty shops). Brush each heart with oil, and dollop a little sauce on. Lay a fillet on the sauce, and top with the rest of the sauce. Fold the paper hearts over in half so they form an ice cream cone, or balloon, shape, and seal their edges by folding over and pinching together all around.

Lay the sealed hearts on an oiled baking sheet and bake for 15 minutes, or until the paper begins to brown. Serve at once, cutting open the paper at table.

Serves 6.

An elegant exuberance created in 1901 for the French balloonist Alberto Santos-Dumont. Antoine's honored him with a dish in the shape of his vehicle in what is by now famed as a culinary coup. Pompano is undeniably one of our best native fish, though it is not widely found outside the Gulf. Thus most of us must content ourselves with trout en papillote—itself a dish worthy the time and effort. But it takes not only time and effort, like most restaurant extravaganzas it also takes a lot of hard-earned cash, and culinary knowhow.

If you take this recipe in hand, look out for the new brands of parchment paper being offered in gourmet shops: they say clearly on the package that they are meant for lining cake pans (as if plain waxed paper weren't enough!). These brands are too light for papillotes—regular cooking parchment is about the weight of a good shopping bag, and that is exactly what to use if you haven't a source for parchment.

SALMON GEORGE WASHINGTON

1	piece (2½ to 3 pounds) fresh salmon	4	thin slices onion
	Salt and freshly ground pepper	1	clove garlic, peeled
	Pinch of dried thyme		Parsley sprigs
3	tablespoons butter	2	cucumbers
1½	cups heavy cream	2	teaspoons Dijon mustard
1	bay leaf		Lemon juice (optional)
			Lemon slices

*P*reheat the oven to 350°F.

Rub the salmon with salt, pepper, and a little thyme. Choose a baking dish large enough to hold the fish that also has a cover. Melt the butter in it, add the salmon, and turn to coat it thoroughly in the butter. Pour the cream around the fish and strew around bay leaf, onion slices, garlic, and 3 parsley sprigs.

Peel the cucumbers, slice lengthwise in quarters, remove the seeds, and cut each slice in half at the middle. Place them around the fish, cover, and bake about 40 minutes—or until the salmon flakes easily and the center bone can be pulled away.

Carefully remove the fish from the baking dish and lay on a baking sheet or some such surface. Slip off the skin, bone the fish, and reassemble on a hot serving platter. Place the cucumber around it and keep warm.

To make the sauce, strain the cream into a saucepan, turn the heat high, whisk the Dijon into it, and add a few drops of lemon juice if the sauce seems to need it. Boil down until slightly thickened, pour over the salmon, and serve with additional parsley sprigs and lemon slices.

Serves 4 to 6.

By far my favorite American fish dish, this is not complicated to prepare. It is also of incomparable subtlety and is a pleasure both to see and eat. If you don't find a good piece of salmon for it, salmon steaks do nicely—but as they take less time to cook, the cucumber must be simmered awhile in the cream on top of the stove, to complete the cooking. Since it has both sauce and vegetable the dish should probably not be served with anything else but a fragrant rounded white wine. I have been unable to trace the origin of this recipe. I've seen it written as "Martha Washington's Salmon," as well, but it doesn't appear in her family cookbook. At any rate, whoever named it, it is a proud dish for our first President.

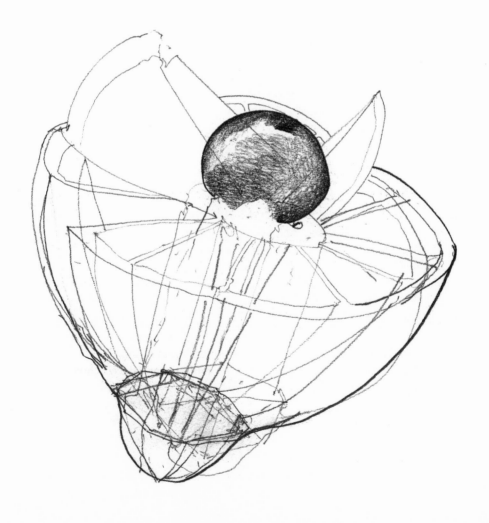

NORTHWESTERN SCALLOPED
POTATOES AND SMOKED SALMON

4	tablespoons butter, melted	1	cup heavy cream
4	medium potatoes, peeled and thinly sliced		Freshly ground pepper
			Ground allspice
1	onion, minced		Minced parsley
¾	pound smoked salmon, thinly sliced		

*P*reheat the oven to 325°F.

Grease a shallow casserole or gratin dish with some of the butter. Place a layer of potatoes on the bottom, sprinkle with half the onion, lay half the salmon on, then put another layer of potatoes over. Repeat the process, ending with a layer of potatoes.

Pour the cream over, sprinkle lightly with pepper and allspice, and dribble the rest of the butter on top. Bake for an hour, or until most of the cream is absorbed and the top is golden.

To serve, sprinkle parsley on top and bring to the table to be scooped directly out of the casserole.

Serves 4.

When you find relatively inexpensive scraps and trimmings from sliced smoked salmon, run to this dish! It's every bit as good as it sounds. Pair it with a simple fresh green vegetable, and you have a fine family dinner indeed.

SHAD ROE POACHED IN BUTTER

½	cup butter	¼	cup minced parsley
4	shad roe	2	tablespoons minced chives
	Salt and freshly ground pepper	8	slices bacon, cooked
	Lemon juice	2	lemons, quartered

*I*f you have a skillet large enough to hold all the roes, that's fine, but if not, either use two pans or fry the roes in stages—holding the first batch warm in the oven. Either way, melt butter over a low flame. Add the roes, sprinkle with salt and pepper to taste, and cook them about 6 minutes a side—making sure the heat is low enough never to discolor the butter. (Each roe should be golden on each side, but not crusty.)

Remove with a spatula to warm serving plates, squeeze a few drips of lemon juice into the skillet, and add the parsley and chives. Heat, stirring, and pour over the roes. Place crisp bacon beside them, along with lemon quarters, and serve immediately.

Serves 4.

Roe of shad, which used to be given along with the fish, are now so expensive I only allow myself this delicacy once a year, in season. They are our native caviar indeed.

TROUT WITH
LE RUTH'S SAUCE À LA NEIGE

4	trout		A few drops Tabasco (or
	Items at hand (see list below)		cayenne)
1	egg white	¾	cup bubbling hot butter
1	tablespoon lemon juice	2	pimiento-stuffed olives,
1	teaspoon white wine tarragon		sliced
	vinegar		

Steam the trout in a stock made up of some of the following: water, white wine, dry vermouth, a good white vinegar, lemon juice, vegetables such as onion, celery tops, parsley stems or a stray carrot, and any such herbs and spices as bay leaf, thyme, tarragon, cloves, or a strip of orange peel—perhaps, even, a couple of whole allspice.

The trout should steam with a lid on for 10 minutes. Lift them out onto a platter and let cool enough to slip their skins off, leaving neatly both head and tail intact. You can keep them warm, or chill them, covered.

In either case, to serve them, place egg white, lemon juice, and vinegar in a blender. Whirl at low speed and add the Tabasco. Dribble the hot butter in drop by drop as you whirl it. As it starts to thicken, you can increase the flow of the butter to a fine, very thin stream.

Frost the trout up to their heads and tails with the sauce, and place an olive slice for an eye on each.

Serves 4.

A dish constructed around a sauce invented, for a now forgotten Vice-President, by Warren Le Ruth—one of New Orleans' best restauranteurs. It is an inspired switch on a hollandaise by use of the then-new electric blender. In his restaurant, Mr. Le Ruth serves it on a fillet of trout encircling a lobster tail, but that is both elaborate and expensive for home cooking. It is a virtually unexplored sauce, simple to prepare and with a host of possibilities. It makes, for instance, a fine foil for artichokes or asparagus.

Shellfish

*U*ntil lately, native coasts have been blessed with an abundance of shellfish, so past largesse has left us a host of durable recipes—oysters being the best example. In Europe they are a delicacy presented hardly anywhere off the half-shell, whereas here we stew and stuff, and fry and roast with abandon. These recipes are a boon, particularly for those able to buy the rather coarse (and still inexpensive) Western oysters, or the fine Gulf oysters, packed fresh in bottles. Many of our shrimp dishes, too, can be prepared from the inexpensive little cooked shrimp available rather than elegant prawns. The rest is up to the tide, and purse.

CLAMS PHILLY

Salt

Cornmeal

4 dozen littleneck clams (or razor clams in the West)

6 green onions with part of tops, chopped

4 tablespoons butter

4 tablespoons dry sherry

4 tablespoons brandy

4 egg yolks

1 cup heavy cream

Cayenne

Toast points

*C*lams are sandy and need care in cleaning. They should be scrubbed with a brush and washed in several waters. Then soak them in salt water (⅓ cup salt to 1 gallon water), with cornmeal sprinkled over. Leave 3 or more hours—the meal helps rid them of sand, and makes them better tasting. After soaking, wash again under cold running water. Open clams over a bowl to catch their juices; use a sharp small knife, running it along the shell edge, to pry open. Cut the clams from the shell and reserve.

To cook the dish, strain the clam juices into a saucepan and bring to a boil. Lower the heat, and steam the clams, covered, in the juices 3 minutes. Drain the clams and reserve—the juices may be discarded or saved for fish stock.

Put the butter in a medium saucepan set over medium heat. Add the green onions and sauté until they are limp. Add both sherry and brandy, and boil down, uncovered, over high heat until reduced by half.

Beat the egg yolks with cream till light and frothy. Stir into the onion mixture. Cook stirring, over low heat, until the sauce is smooth and thickened—be careful not to let it boil. When the sauce is ready, add the clams and let them heat for 2 minutes.

Season to taste with salt and cayenne, and pour over toast points on warm plates.

Serves 4 (or 6 as a first course).

Years ago I had my first taste of raw clams when the late poet Walter Lowenfells took us out to a New Jersey fishermen's shack to buy just-caught clams from a bucket. He ordered two dozen for each of us, and though the first several were delightful, I found it increasingly difficult to get them down with no lemon, no bread, no wine, no nothing. Ever since I have shied away from this tonic delicacy, though I delight in most any cooked clam dish. After having tried many fancy stuffed clams of one kind and another, though, I find I settle on this classic clam dish to show fresh clams at their succulent best.

CLAM FRITTERS

less

1½	cups bread crumbs	Tabasco
1	cup minced clams *fresh*	Clam juice (or milk)
2	eggs, separated	Butter (or hot fat)
1	tablespoon minced parsley	Lemon wedges
	Salt *minced onions*	Tartar Sauce (page 292)

*P*ut the bread crumbs in a heavy frying pan over medium heat and toast them until golden, shaking now and again. Turn off the heat and set aside.

Drain the clams of their juice (reserving for later) and place them in a bowl with the egg yolks. Toss briskly, then stir in crumbs, parsley, salt to taste, and a few drops of Tabasco. Add enough clam juice or milk to make a heavy batter that will drop off a large spoon in a plop.

Beat the egg whites stiff and fold into the batter. I like these best cooked in butter—dropped from a spoon and then browned on either side over medium-high heat. They can also be cooked dropped from a spoon into hot fat (370°F) and fried till crisp and golden.

Serve on warm plates with lemon wedges and homemade tartar sauce.

Serves 4 as a first course.

Hands down, these win the classic fritter race. They are an old-time Eastern fritter, and it's the bread crumbs that seem to make the difference. The batter is so good, in fact, that you can use canned clams if need be (the whole ones, not the chopped), and they are delightful with bits of cooked fish, or mushrooms. The recipe is easily doubled or tripled for larger portions, and they do make a fine light supper with a glass of beer, a salad, and dessert.

If using canned it is more than one cup clams

DELTA CRAB PIE

4	cups ½-inch cubes from homemade-type bread	1	lemon, sliced paper thin and seeded
2	tablespoons dry sherry		Salt and freshly ground pepper
1	cup heavy cream		Milk
1	pound crabmeat		Watercress (optional)
½	cup butter, melted		

*T*oss the bread cubes with a good sprinkling of sherry, then soak in cream for at least 30 minutes—or until ready to assemble the dish.

Preheat the oven to 375°F.

Grease a soufflé dish, or a shallow gratin dish, with a little of the butter. Then layer the bread cubes, some crab, a douse of butter, a thin layer of lemon slices, salt and pepper to taste, then more butter. End with a layer of bread and the last of the butter.

Pour milk in to within ¼ inch of the top and pop into the oven. Bake 30 to 40 minutes, or until the top puffs up and is golden. Serve immediately, perhaps with a mound of watercress.

Serves 4 as a first course.

This is one of those marvelous, simple recipes handed down family to friend in the South. Its only exactions of the cook are fresh crab and thinnest lemon slices. If you are unsure of your knife, it may be prepared with grated lemon peel and squeezed juice.

GREEN CRACKER CRAB

½ cup celery	1½ cups crushed soda crackers
½ cup green onions, with part of tops	1 teaspoon Dijon mustard
½ cup green pepper	Tabasco
¼ cup parsley	¼ cup heavy cream
1 pound crabmeat	⅔ cup butter, melted

*P*reheat the oven to 350°F.

Carefully mince the vegetables fine with a knife (or place them in a food processor and chop with the steel blade. If using a processor, blot the vegetables with paper towels before proceeding). In a bowl, toss vegetables lightly with the crab and 1 cup of the crackers.

In another bowl, beat the mustard and Tabasco to taste into the cream. (This dish should be slightly hot, so use about ¼ teaspoon Tabasco, at least.) Toss this, with ½ cup of the melted butter, with the crab. Taste for seasoning at this point—the crackers may or may not have added enough salt.

To cook, grease a soufflé dish, or individual ramekins, with some of the rest of the butter. Place the crab mixture in the dish and sprinkle with the rest of the crackers, then dribble all the remaining butter over the top. Bake for 30 minutes, or until golden brown on top. Serve immediately.

Serves 4 as a first course.

This crisp dish is an example of how dishes freely travel. I found it in a wom-en's club cookbook, then later found it again looking through James Beard's superb memoir-cookbook Delights and Prejudices—*certainly where the lady or one of her friends had found it. It was remarkably unchanged, and she had resisted putting Worcestershire or whatnot in it. It is simple sounding as to ingredients, but it is better than any so-called deviled crab dishes you'll ever have a chance to eat. Serve it with an equally crisp dry white wine, and clov-erleaf rolls.*

GALATOIRE'S EGGPLANT
STUFFED WITH CRAB (OR SHRIMP)

2	medium eggplants	1	pound cooked crabmeat (or small shrimp, or half and half)
⅔	cup minced green onions with part of tops		
⅓	cup chopped onion	2	eggs
1	clove garlic, minced	¼	cup minced parsley
1	teaspoon dried thyme		Salt and freshly ground pepper
1	bay leaf		
2	tablespoons butter		Bread crumbs
1½	cups bread, soaked in water and squeezed dry		Paprika
			Melted butter

*P*reheat the oven to 350°F.

Trim the tops off the eggplants and split each in half lengthwise. Make crosswise slashes in the flesh of each, being careful not to pierce the skin. Par-boil in boiling salted water 5 minutes, or until the flesh can be scooped out with the skins left firm and intact. Scoop them so, squeezing out as much liquid as possible from the flesh, and chop or mash it fine.

In a frying pan, sauté green onion, onion, garlic, thyme, and bay leaf in 2 tablespoons butter gently for 5 minutes, or until the onion is limp.

Mash the soaked bread into the eggplant—the best way to do this is with your hands or through a ricer. It should all come to a light pulp. Add this to the onions. Beat in crab, eggs, parsley, and salt and pepper to taste—it should be a mite peppery. Cook gently 5 more minutes, then remove the bay leaf and stuff the mixture into the eggplant shells.

Place them in a greased baking dish, sprinkle each with bread crumbs, a dusting of paprika, and dribbles of melted butter. Bake 10 minutes, or until the tops are slightly crisp and the eggplant halves are warmed through.

Serves 4.

I was served this dish at Galatoire's on my first trip to New Orleans—my eye as usual scanning a menu for something I'd never heard of before. Useless years were spent thereafter attempting to reproduce its singular flavor and texture, both vying in subtleties. When research for this book turned it up, I was delighted to find no whit of remembrance was better than what I had before me. It needs little accompaniment but white wine and fine bread.

FAIRMONT HOTEL CRAB MUSTARD RING

1	envelope unflavored gelatin		Salt and freshly ground
¼	cup cold water		pepper
1	cup boiling water		Paprika
1	cup white wine vinegar	1	cup heavy cream, whipped
¼	cup sugar	1	pound cooked crabmeat
2½	tablespoons dry mustard		Cracked crab claws
1	teaspoon butter		Inner leafy celery stalks
4	eggs, whipped to a froth		

Sprinkle the gelatin over the cold water, stir in, and let sit till it softens. Add the boiling water and stir till dissolved.

In the top of a double boiler, mix the vinegar, sugar, mustard, butter, eggs, salt and pepper to taste, and a pinch of good paprika. Cook over simmering water, stirring with a whisk, until the mixture begins to coat the whisk. Remove from the heat, stir in the gelatin, and put in a bowl. Set in refrigerator until thick and syrupy (about an hour).

Whip the cream and fold it into the gelatin mixture, then ladle into a greased ring mold. Chill in the refrigerator till set.

To serve, unmold on a good platter, place the crabmeat inside the ring, and decorate the outer rim with crab claws and celery stalks.

Serves 6 to 8 as a first course.

The native habit of drowning delicate crab or shrimp in a "cocktail sauce" made of catsup, horseradish, Tabasco, and lemon makes me think we are not after all too far from barbarism at the table. The delicacy of fresh shellfish needs—if indeed anything at all beyond a squeeze of lemon—similarly delicate support. In the best tradition of San Francisco dining, this light sweet-sour gelatin with an aftertang of mustard makes the best of a very fine thing, in an admirable presentation for company. For a first course, it should be proudly

*brought to table and served on plates there, or, pretty as it is, it may form
the center of a party buffet.*

CAPITOL HILL
SOFT-SHELLED CRAB SANDWICH

1	soft-shelled crab, cleaned	2	slices good white bread
2	tablespoons butter		Tartar Sauce (page 292)
2	tablespoons vegetable oil		Lemon wedges
	Salt and freshly ground		
	pepper		

Wherever you buy soft shelled crabs will most likely also clean them for you, but if not, this is the way to do it. First you freeze the crab 5 minutes or so, to numb it, and proceed more or less as you clean cooked hard-shelled crab. You peel back the triangular "apron" on the underside, then scrape out the stomach and intestines that lie beneath it. Then you scrape out the spongy lungs under the points of the shell, snip off the head of the crab behind the eyes, and finally squeeze the body so the sand sac pops out of the head opening. Wash it well with water, and pat dry with a towel.

Sauté the crab in butter and oil over medium heat until it is golden on both sides—about 3 to 4 minutes. Salt and pepper it in the pan as it cooks, and lift out onto paper towels.

Serve between two slices of bread that have been spread with tartar sauce, with lemon wedges to squeeze on as you eat.

Serves 1 (may be adapted to any number).

There used to be a restaurant in Washington, D.C., that not only had the advantage of a deck looking out over the water but served these sandwiches— surely one of the best meals in the world, served with frosty ale and crisp slab fries. Soft-shelled crab is only available on our Eastern shores, and that seasonally (when the crab molts its shell). They should make it a national monument.

SOFT-SHELLED CRABS WITH ALMONDS

2 cloves garlic, flattened and
  peeled
½ cup butter
4 slices white bread, trimmed
  to rounds
4 medium cleaned soft-shelled
  crabs (or 8 small ones)

Salt and freshly ground
  pepper
½ cup slivered blanched
  almonds, toasted
Watercress

*I*n a large skillet, sauté the garlic in half the butter until it starts to get crisp and golden. Remove the garlic and sauté the bread rounds in the butter. The heat should be an even medium-high. When the bread rounds are crisp on both sides, place them on paper towels and keep warm.

Sprinkle the crabs with salt and pepper, add the rest of the butter to a skillet (if you use the same one, wipe it out first), and cook them 3 minutes a side, or till golden. Add the almonds during the last minutes and toss with the crabs.

Lift out onto the croutons placed on a warm plate, sprinkle the almonds over, and garnish with watercress sprigs.

Serves 4 as a first course.

Simple and superb. Everything is crunchy in a different way.

LOBSTER NEWBERG

3 tablespoons sweet butter
2 cups cooked lobster meat,
  cut in thick slices
2 tablespoons flour
1½ cups heavy cream
4 egg yolks

2 tablespoons dry sherry (or
  Madeira)
1 tablespoon Cognac
Salt
Cayenne (optional)
Toast points

*M*elt 2 tablespoons of the butter in a saucepan and toss the lobster in it, heating gently but thoroughly. Keep warm in a chafing dish or heated serving dish.

In the same saucepan, melt the remaining tablespoon of butter, stir in flour, and cook several minutes. Add the cream, beaten with the egg yolks, and cook until thickened and smooth, stirring the while. Do not let it boil.

Add the sherry or Madeira, the Cognac, cayenne if you wish, and taste for salt. Let it all heat several minutes, then pour over lobster with a sprinkle perhaps more sherry or Madeira. (In a chafing dish carefully regulate the heat or the mixture will curdle). Serve hot over toast points.

Serves 4.

So seldom do I get lobster I always want it red and plain with drawn sweet butter, but this justly famous dish (which originated at Delmonico's via one Ben Wenberg, a sea captain with fastidious tastes in food) is both suave and rich, in a sauce that seems, rather than mask the lobster, to extend and gently amplify. The story goes that the Delmonico brothers had a falling out with Wenberg, but liked his sauce so much they retained it as "Newberg."

MAUM NANCY'S SCALLOPED OYSTERS

1 cup fresh bread crumbs	Salt and freshly ground
6 tablespoons butter, melted	pepper
¼ teaspoon freshly grated	Pinch of cayenne
nutmeg	1 quart shucked oysters with
Pinch of ground mace	½ cup liquor
¼ teaspoon ground cloves	¼ cup Madeira

*P*reheat the oven to 350°F.

Take a small frying pan and sauté the crumbs with 2 tablespoons of the butter. Toss over medium heat until they are golden. Remove from the fire and mix in all the spices.

Grease the bottom and sides of a smallish casserole or soufflé dish with some of the butter, and sprinkle the bottom and sides with some of the sautéed crumbs.

Make 2 layers of oysters, some oyster juice, some buttered crumbs, some butter, and Madeira, ending with crumbs and a good dribble of butter on the top. Bake for 45 minutes, or until it is starting to bubble. Serve immediately.

Serves 4.

Every cookbook has its oyster scallop, but this is one apart. It has been adapted from Charleston Receipts, a Junior League cookbook (as so many of our best native ones are) to be obtained by inquiry to P.O. Box 177, Charleston, SC, 29402. It was first pointed out to me by a friend who had lived there, insisting it was quite simply one of the best cookbooks ever written or compiled on the culinary arts of the Southern black cook. At the same time it holds the pick of specialties from Charleston's considerably shiny and gracious tables, food that has been served to admiring guests unchanged since antebellum days.

OYSTER PAN ROAST WITH COLE SLAW

1	quart shucked oysters	¼	cup milk
	Flour	½	cup butter (or deep hot fat)
	Ground mace		Lemon wedges
	Fresh bread crumbs		Cole slaw
2	eggs		

Drain the oysters. Put flour mixed with mace and the bread crumbs on separate pieces of waxed paper, and beat the eggs with milk in a bowl. Dip each oyster in flour, then egg, then into the bread crumbs to coat. Put them on waxed paper.

Fry either in butter or deep hot fat, only a minute or two each side, or till golden. Drain on paper towels and serve with lemon wedges and a crisp mound of cole slaw.

Serves 4.

Superior to the familiar Grand Central Pan Roast nostalgic to New Yorkers, this simple, traditional dish makes one of the best meals ever devised—and that includes ones of great restaurant hoopla. Serve with thin brown bread to be authentic. And not with wine, but good beer. (The slaw should be Grison's Steak House Slaw, page 275.)

WILLIAMSBURG OYSTERS UNDER GLASS

1½	cups stone-ground cornmeal	12	thin slices Canadian bacon (or Virginia ham)
2	tablespoons flour		
½	teaspoon baking soda	2	tablespoons vegetable oil (or bacon fat)
1	teaspoon salt		
2	eggs	1	pint shucked oysters with liquor
1½	cups buttermilk		
½	cup plus 2 tablespoons butter, melted		Freshly ground pepper

Sift the dry ingredients together into a mixing bowl. Beat the eggs with buttermilk in another bowl, and add, with the 2 tablespoons melted butter, to the dry ingredients. Stir the batter until smooth.

Drop by spoonfuls onto a greased griddle to make twelve 3-inch pancakes. They should be cooked over medium heat, and turned when they begin to make bubbles on top. They need only a minute or so on each side to cook. Keep them warm on a plate in the oven while you prepare the ham and oysters.

Sauté Canadian bacon—or better yet good Virginia ham—in a little oil or bacon fat, until just lightly browned. Keep these warm with the pancakes.

Heat the oysters in a small saucepan with their own juices, until their edges just curl—don't try to overcook, they just need warming.

To assemble the dish, place the pancakes on a warm plate, lay a slice of Canadian bacon over each pancake, then arrange the oysters over the top. Sprinkle pepper over the top, and pour the ½ cup melted butter over. Serve immediately.

Serves 6 as a first course, 4 as a main dish.

A simple but indescribably sumptuous dish, deemed worthy of being served under a glass bell in Williamsburg. What doesn't show from the recipe is how delicate a foil these buttermilk cornmeal pancakes make to the thin cooked ham and plump oysters. No salt is needed, but I sometimes garnish the dish with lemon slices for those who might like a drop or so. Regular cornmeal is no substitute for stone-ground meal, here, but Canadian bacon is fine instead of the original expensive Virginia ham because a slice of it is exactly the size of the pancakes. Even without glass bells this dish makes an impressive beginning to an important meal—perhaps even for Christmas or Thanksgiving.

But I like it so well I don't wait for important dinners, for, with some crisp cole slaw, it makes a splendid quick supper or brunch for family.

OYSTER LOAF

1 loaf French bread (sweet or sourdough, preferably round)	Salt and freshly ground pepper
	Lemon juice
	Minced parsley
½ cup butter	Tabasco (optional)
2 dozen shucked oysters	

*P*reheat the oven to 375°F.

Slice the top third off your loaf and scoop out the center of both top and bottom, leaving a 1-inch crust all round. Slice the scooped-out portions thin, put on a baking sheet, and let dry out as the oven heats—enough to make bread crumbs.

Melt the butter and use half of it to coat the inside and top of the loaf generously. Put it in the oven and cook 10 minutes, or until the loaf is lightly toasted.

Meanwhile, make bread crumbs with a rolling pin, or in a blender or food processor. Drain the oysters and roll in the crumbs. Fry the oysters in the remaining butter (adding more if necessary) 4 to 5 minutes.

Layer the oysters in the toasted loaf, sprinkling with salt and pepper to taste, and with a few squeezes of lemon and sprinklings of parsley (and Tabasco if you like it). Put the top of the loaf back on, paint the outside of the loaf with a little more butter, put on a baking sheet, and cook 8 to 10 minutes. Bring to the table on a cutting board and slice in serving portions.

Serves 4 to 6.

In Consider the Oyster, *M.F.K. Fisher tells of a memory of a memory of an oyster loaf—her mother's tale of "midnight feasts" at her 1890s boarding school, where a loaf was smuggled into the dormitory by a chambermaid: "I can see it, and smell it, and I even know which parts to bite and which to let melt against the roof of my mouth, exquisitely hot and comforting, although my mother surely never told me," she writes. It was such a one as this recipe, surely, for oyster loaves used to be served extensively around San Francisco, but the dish is only common now in New Orleans, where it is called La Médiatrice (or "the mediator"), since it was usually purchased, in small French rolls, to soothe a waiting wife after a carousal through the late saloons of the French Quarter.*

It makes a good picnic dish still, if it is well wrapped so it keeps a modicum of warmth. And it really only wants a side dish of crisp cole slaw, with a flagon of beer or wine, to make a meal better almost than any memory of a memory. . . .

TONY'S HIGHWAY BARBECUE OYSTERS

Fresh oysters on the half shell   Lemon juice
Barbecue sauce   Minced parsley

This recipe takes a charcoal smoker. Lay the number of oysters you please over coals, drop a small spoon of sauce over each, and top with a squeeze of lemon and some minced parsley. Cover the smoker and let cook 6 to 8 minutes, or until the oyster's edges begin to curl in the shell. Serve on paper plates.

Can be adapted to any number.

A wonder captured by observation from Tony's in Marshall, California, Highway 1. The rest of Tony's food is good but pedestrian, but on weekends he throws open his barbecue and they come from all around, through the oysters being opened on the front porch, some with picnic baskets of slaw and sandwiches of black bread and sweet butter, some just to sit out on the dock and eat a plate of Tony's inspired invention.

OYSTERS ROCKEFELLER

No other American dish, it now comes to seem, has received so much praise and attention as this one invented in the 1850s by Jules Alciatore of Antoine's to replace snails Bourgignon. The original recipe (said to contain eighteen ingredients) has never left the restaurant, but has been so adapted and evolved in a host of ways that it has been called by Louis De Gouy a dish of "composite genius." M. De Gouy recounts that Alciatore exacted a promise on his deathbed that the exact proportions be kept forever a secret. He then goes on to relate as much as Alciatore told him: The sauce was compounded of green onions, celery, chervil, tarragon leaves and crumbs of stale bread pounded in a mortar with butter and Tabasco, with finally a dash of absinthe—no spinach (which is used in most versions), no proportions certainly, and definitely not eighteen ingredients.

One of the most elegant variations is reported by Alice B. Toklas, who served hers on silver sand rather than rock salt. She minced fourths of parsley and raw spinach with eighths of tarragon, chervil, basil, and chives. Topped with salt, pepper, bread crumbs and melted butter, this makes an extremely delicate version, though it omits the anise flavor usually associated with the dish. This is supplied by a Louisiana liquor called Herbsainte, or by Pernod, ground anise, or chopped fresh fennel.

Given so much leeway, I find it advisable to proceed as for snail butter and see what the garden and market provide. (Snail butter for about two dozen oysters is a mixture of ½ cup room-temperature butter, 2 tablespoons minced shallots or green onions, 2 to 3 minced cloves garlic, and 2 tablespoons minced parsley—and salt and pepper to taste.)

If fresh herbs are not available, then dried may do in combination with spinach, watercress leaves, parsley, green onion tops, and celery leaves. Tasting as you go, flavor with drops of lemon and Tabasco, then as much Pernod, etc., as it will take without tasting overtly of licorice. These can all be compounded easily in a blender or food processor, either with the bread crumbs, or with bread crumbs sprinkled later over the top. Serve 6 oysters per person laid on pans of rock salt, with sauce over their tops, and baked 4 to 5 minutes in a 450°F oven until hot and bubbly.

OYSTERS BIENVILLE

3	dozen oysters	1	cup minced mushrooms
2	cups minced green onions with part of tops	3	egg yolks
½	cup butter	½	cup heavy cream
2½	tablespoons flour	½	cup dry vermouth
2	cups chicken or fish stock, heated		Salt and freshly ground pepper
1½	pounds cooked shrimp, shelled, deveined, and minced		Tabasco
		¼	cup bread crumbs
		¼	cup grated Parmesan cheese
		⅛	teaspoon paprika

Shuck the oysters and reserve half the shells and all the liquor. Sauté green onions in butter until limp, then add flour and stir over a low flame until the mixture is golden brown. Add hot stock, shrimp, and mushrooms and simmer until the mixture begins to thicken. Set aside and allow to cool.

Beat the egg yolks with the cream and vermouth, then slowly pour the warm sauce into the egg mixture, stirring constantly to keep smooth. Add all the liquor from the oysters and season to taste with salt, pepper, and Tabasco.

Preheat the oven to 375°F.

Return the sauce to a low fire and let simmer 10 to 15 minutes, stirring to keep smooth. When it has thickened, remove from the fire.

To cook the oysters, place a good layer of rock salt (ice cream salt) over 6 pie plates. Place 6 oysters, each on the half shell, in each pan, and bake for 10 minutes, or just until they curl around the edges. Remove from the oven, turning the temperature to 400°F; spoon the sauce over the oysters and sprinkle with combined bread crumbs, cheese, and paprika. Bake 7 to 8 minutes, or until bubbly.

Serves 6.

This is another specialty at Antoine's, and one for which the recipe is blessedly available—and I think even better than Rockefeller. One of the best places to test them, in New Orleans, is at Brennan's, which features a plate of two oysters Rockefeller, two oysters Bienville, and two oysters Roffignac: such are the delights of that mild city! Like all restaurant food, it requires a lot of advance footwork, but is easily got to table, and there should be served with fine bread and even finer white wine.

DELMONICO SCALLOPS

2 pounds scallops (preferably small bay scallops)	¼ cup bread crumbs
3 tablespoons lemon juice	2 tablespoons Parmesan cheese
1 tablespoon olive oil	3 tablespoons finely minced ham
1 teaspoon minced parsley	1 tablespoon minced chives
Salt and freshly ground pepper	Vegetable oil for deep frying
Cayenne	Tartar Sauce (page 292)
1 egg, slightly beaten	Lemon wedges

Marinate the scallops in lemon juice, olive oil, parsley, salt and pepper to taste, and a hint of cayenne for 30 minutes or more.

To cook, beat the egg in one bowl and combine the bread crumbs, cheese, ham, and chives in another. Drain the scallops, and dip first in egg and then into the bread crumb mixture. Fry in deep hot oil (at 385°F) till golden, then drain on absorbent paper.

Sprinkle with salt, and serve with tartar sauce and lemon wedges.

Serves 4 (or 6 as a first course).

The Delmonico family established the first luxurious restaurant in the country, and they set a standard that was to make New York a culinary center on a par with Paris. They popularized unknown vegetables such as endive and eggplant, they helped a heavily meat-eating populace discover salads (many of them invented for New World plants) and ices. Many of their dishes were simple in execution, as these scallops prove, with all the fanciness in the presentation. This dish, for instance, was garnished with hard-boiled egg quarters and slices of sautéed green tomato topped with a mushroom cap browned in butter. It all sounds fresh and lively (and even likely) for a dish a hundred years old.

TIDEWATER SCALLOPED SHRIMP

4	tablespoons butter	1	tablespoon Worcestershire sauce
1	medium onion, finely chopped	2	pounds cooked shrimp, shelled and deveined
½	pound mushrooms, sliced		Salt and freshly ground pepper
2	tablespoons flour		
½	cup heavy cream	1	teaspoon sweet paprika
¼	cup dry sherry	½	cup bread crumbs
1	tablespoon lemon juice		

*P*reheat the oven to 350°F.

Sauté the onion in 2 tablespoons of butter till it is limp, then add the mushrooms and cook until they begin to release their juices.

Sprinkle the flour over and cook over medium heat, stirring, for several minutes. Pour the cream in and stir until the sauce thickens. Add sherry, lemon juice, and Worcestershire, then cover the pan and let cook gently 10 minutes.

Add the shrimp and seasonings, and taste (I find this dish might use a bit more sherry or lemon depending on the quality of the shrimp).

To serve, divide the mixture into 6 individual shells or ramekins, sprinkle with bread crumbs, and dot the other 2 tablespoons butter over the tops. Bake 20 minutes, or until browned and bubbly.

Serves 4 (or 6 as a first course).

Shrimp is so plentiful and cheap along the Southern coast still that it is served from breakfast through lunch and dinner. Needless to say this makes a visitor's mind (and tastebuds) boggle, and the restless recipe-hunter's pen get poised for action. My tactic is to invade the kitchen and help shell the daily catch, for there you uncover the best-kept secrets. Either as a first course, or main dish accompanied by a green vegetable and hot rolls, this recipe is in the finest tradition of home cookery. It's even tasty enough, for those stuck inland, to survive the frozenest shrimp.

SHRIMP AND CORN PIE

5 to 6	ears corn	1½	teaspoons Worcestershire
3	eggs, slightly beaten		sauce
¾	cup heavy cream (or milk)		Salt and freshly ground pepper
1½	cups cooked small shrimp, peeled and deveined		Pinch of ground mace
		6	tablespoons butter, melted

*P*reheat oven to 325°F.

Cut the corn from cobs with a sharp knife, then use the back of the knife blade to extract the "milk." You should have 3 cups kernels. Combine all the ingredients except 4 tablespoons of the butter.

Use part of the reserved butter to grease a gratin dish or casserole large enough to hold the shrimp-corn mixture in about a 1½-inch layer. Pour the mixture into it, then dribble the rest of the butter over.

Bake 30 to 40 minutes, or until the custard is set and the top has begun to take color.

Serves 4.

What a lovely, easy, delectable casserole this dish from the Carolinas is—it's a recipe that has been passed down from colonial times, and when fresh corn is available it remains one of my favorite seafood dishes for family dinners. Serve it forth with Cream Dilly Bean Salad (page 270) and either Summer Cloud or Happy Valley Biscuits (page 322).

FRANCES PARKINSON KEYES'
CUCUMBER ASPIC WITH SHRIMP

1	medium cucumber, peeled, seeded, and cut in ¼-inch dice	1	teaspoon white wine tarragon vinegar
	Salt	1	cup heavy cream
	Juice of ½ lemon	1	pound cooked shrimp, peeled and deveined
2	teaspoons unflavored gelatin	½	cup oil and vinegar dressing
2	tablespoons cold water		Minced parsley
¼	cup milk, heated		Parsley sprigs
¼	cup chopped pimiento		

*P*ut the cucumber in a bowl of salted ice water for 10 minutes. Drain and add the lemon juice. Soak the gelatin in cold water, and when soft dissolve in the hot milk. Add this to the cucumber, along with the pimiento and vinegar.

Whip the cream and fold it in. Place it in a lightly oiled 4-cup decorative mold, or a ring mold, and chill for 12 hours.

An hour before serving, toss the shrimp in the oil and vinegar dressing with plenty of minced parsley. To serve, unmold the aspic on a good platter, place the shrimp around it, pour shrimp marinade over the top, and garnish with parsley sprigs.

Serve with black bread and butter.

Serves 6 to 8.

My mother donates this favorite dish. It is an easily prepared, but sumptuous, first course for a summer dinner. The whipped cream gives it a particularly light texture for a gelatin preparation—so much so guests usually request the recipe. One warning—don't be tempted to save time by grating the cucumber, for that texture is not quite right for the dish. For less festive occasions, the shrimp may be omitted and the mixture put in individual molds and served on lettuce leaves as a simple salad.

PRAWNS MARIN

2	pounds good-sized shrimp	2 to 3	tablespoons cream sherry
4	tablespoons butter		A few drops Angostura
⅛	teaspoon curry powder		bitters (optional)
	Salt and freshly ground		
	pepper		

Cook the shrimp in water and whatever good things you have on hand (see Fish Stock in Methods & Ingredients Section). They will take 5 minutes. Drain, and peel and devein them when they are cool enough. Set aside till just before serving.

The dish may be prepared in a few minutes away from guests or in a chafing dish at table. Bring the butter to a sizzle over high flame and add the shrimp. Toss till they are coated with butter, then add the curry powder and salt and pepper to taste.

Add the sherry and let it bubble down to almost a syrup while still tossing—a matter of only a few minutes. Add a few drops of bitters if you like. Serve immediately on warm plates, with a full-bodied white wine and crusty fresh bread.

Serves 6 as a first course.

The unexpected sweetness of cream sherry is decisive for this invention of California chef Draper Morrow. It is a fine dish to serve as a first course when your main offering is a rich, complex one.

VIRGINIA SHRIMP PASTE

1½	pounds medium shrimp	1	teaspoon finely grated onion
½	cup butter at room	1	tablespoon dry sherry (or
	temperature		Madeira)
	Dash of ground mace		Salt and freshly ground
1	teaspoon Dijon mustard		pepper

Cook the shrimp in salted water 5 minutes. Let cool, then peel and devein them. Pound in a mortar, run through a grinder, or whirl in a food processor until a paste. Mix thoroughly with the other ingredients and place in a bowl covered with plastic wrap—or in a pot with melted butter poured over the top to seal it. Refrigerate overnight.

Serves 4.

In most cookbooks—even M. F. K. Fisher includes in her With Bold Knife and Fork *an example or so—this would be given as a spread served with cocktails. In parts of the South, however, it is served in a pot alongside a chafing dish of cooked grits, as part of a buffet hunt club breakfast, along with many another collation. As the shrimp paste melts in tiny granules through the only slightly larger granules of the soft grits, you will resolve slowly to go out next day and purchase a package so this dish will always be available. I serve it with scrambled eggs, and crisp bacon, for breakfast, or with an exemplary white vintage, for itself alone, at supper.*

SHRIMP AND CHICKEN ETOUFFÉE

6	tablespoons butter		Salt and freshly ground
¼	cup flour		pepper
1	cup minced onion	¼	teaspoon cayenne
½	cup minced celery	1	teaspoon lemon juice
½	cup minced green pepper	1	cup chicken stock
⅓	cup minced green onion tops	1	pound shrimp, shelled and
3	cloves garlic, minced		deveined
2	tablespoons minced parsley		Hot cooked rice
3	half breasts of chicken		

*I*n a large heavy saucepan, melt the butter over low heat, then add the flour and, stirring the mixture, cook over very low heat for 15 to 20 minutes, or until the roux is golden brown. Add all the vegetables (a food processor is a quick and efficient tool to mince all the vegetables finely and evenly) and cook another 20 minutes gently, stirring now and again to make sure they are all glazed and tender.

During this process, bone and skin the chicken breasts and cut each half in three or four pieces. When the vegetables look done, add the chicken and toss for several minutes. Season with salt and pepper to taste, then add the cayenne and lemon juice.

Stir in the stock and let the mixture cook, uncovered, until thickened and smooth, then cover the pan and cook gently 15 minutes. Add the shrimp and cook another 5 minutes. Taste for seasoning, and if necessary add water to make the sauce the consistency of a thick soup.

It is best to make the etouffée well ahead and let it sit at least an hour before serving, to gather flavor. To serve, reheat gently and spoon over hot cooked rice.

Serves 4.

The bliss of an etouffée in situ, made from Louisiana crawfish, is one of our finest culinary triumphs. Unfortunately the rest of us are unable to get crawfish, so I have poked around and found this fine example from a Biloxi, Mississippi kitchen. Etouffée means "stuffed" in French—here it refers to the blanket of vegetables cooked with the meats. It is very easily made (for an explanation of the Louisiana roux see under Ideal Gumbo, page 32), and is a splendid dish to double or treble for larger groups. Serve it with white wine and good French bread, with perhaps a salad course, then a handsome dessert.

MEATS &
FOWL

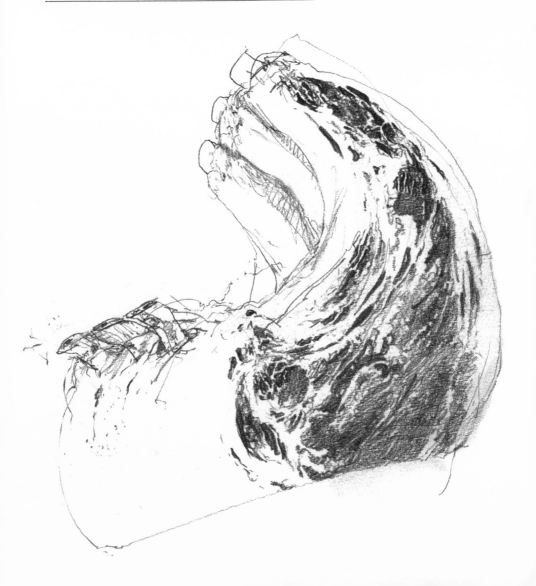

I lost the head of my first bull because I forgot to tell Mrs. Culbertson that I wished to save it, and the princess had its skull broken open to enjoy its brains. Handsome, and really courteous and refined in many ways, I cannot reconcile to myself the fact that she partakes of raw animal food with such evident relish.

—John James Audubon, Journals

Beef

When tender, hung grain-fed beef is available, it should be served simply as possible, without fuss of sauce or truffle. My family lived for a time in a small town in Missouri that had a plant known locally as "the a-bay-tor" (a Plains derivation from the French *abattoir,* a place to slaughter cattle). They had locally aged meats very few restaurants ever even get a whiff of, and restaurants get the cream of the finest Midwest crop. Most of the rest of us must make do with our friendly butcher for advice—if we have one at all—and even from him, more often lower grades and cuts that need long slow processes to gather flavor and ensure tenderness.

ROAST RIB OF BEEF WITH YORKSHIRE PUDDING AND HORSERADISH ICE CREAM

Early in the day prepare Horseradish Ice Cream:

¼	cup grated fresh horseradish		Salt
½	cup orange juice	1	cup heavy cream

Stir the orange juice and a pinch of salt into the grated horseradish in a bowl. Whip the cream stiff, and fold into the horseradish. Freeze in a refrigerator ice tray. Meanwhile, prepare the roast:

1	standing 4- to 5-rib beef roast	1	cup water (or beef stock)
	Freshly ground pepper		Salt
			Cold butter

Remove the roast from the refrigerator 1 to 2 hours before cooking. When it has reached room temperature, preheat the oven to 325°F.

Dry the meat with a paper towel and rub freshly ground pepper all over. Do not salt, as this has a tendency to toughen meat and draw out juices (anyway, good beef is tasty enough to need little salt).

Insert a meat thermometer in the thickest part of the roast—it should not touch the bone. Place the meat, fat side up, on a rack in a roasting pan. Cook without basting till the thermometer registers 130°F for rare, 140°F for medium-rare, 150°F for medium, or 160°F for well done. At this oven temperature you can caculate on timing your roast at about 20 minutes per pound. (Anyone who can afford rib roast these days can also afford a meat thermometer. It is the only way to ensure perfect meats, since oven temperatures vary more widely than one would think.)

Remove the meat from the oven, and immediately turn up the heat to 450°F. Let the meat stand while you cook your pudding—it will be a better texture for it. Pour off fat from the roasting pan, rescuing 3 tablespoons of it for Yorkshire Pudding:

2	eggs	½	teaspoon salt
1	cup milk	3	tablespoons beef drippings
1	cup flour		

Beat the eggs with the milk. Sift the flour with the salt, then combine with the egg-milk mixture. Beat until well blended. Add the beef drippings to a rather high-sided 8- or 9-inch baking pan, and put the pan in the oven to heat. When the temperature reaches 450°F, remove the pan and pour the pudding mixture in. Bake 10 minutes at 450°F, then reduce the heat to 350°F and bake another 15 to 20 minutes, or until the pudding is puffed way up and browned.

While the pudding cooks, add a cup of water—or stock—to the roasting pan, and over direct heat stir and scrape all its crustinesses together. Add salt to taste, and at the end add a nut of cold butter. Stir this in to smooth and slightly thicken the sauce.

To serve, slice the beef onto warm plates. Scoop the horseradish ice cream into individual small cups and place beside each serving of beef. From a side plate serve wedges of Yorkshire pudding. Put the sauce in a sauceboat to pass at table.

Servings: The cream and the pudding are for 4, and they may be easily doubled. For the roast, count on 1 rib per serving.

As beef grows more and more expensive, this kind of recipe is something most of us need only for special feasts—New Year's Day, or even Christmas when a turkey is too large for a small family. So when it is done at all, it should be with all the trimmings. Yorkshire pudding is traditional, and always welcome, and the horseradish ice cream makes an unusual condiment to perk up the whole affair. Needless to say, it should be accompanied with a splendid red wine.

LADYBIRD'S FILLET OF BEEF

1 whole fillet of beef	Fresh kumquats
Bacon (about ¾ pound)	Parsley sprigs
Broiled or sautéed mushroom	
caps	

*P*reheat the oven to 400°F.

Remove the fat from the fillet and wrap it entirely in bacon strips. Place in a roasting pan and cook for 20 minutes at 400°F, or until a meat thermometer reads 120°F (for rare meat) in the thickest part of the meat—that way some pieces will be rarer than others to the taste of the guests. Remove from the oven and place under a broiler until the bacon is crisp on both sides.

Cut carefully into 1-inch slices and reassemble as if whole. Garnish the platter with hot mushrooms and cold kumquats in equal proportions, then lay parsley sprigs down the center of the meat.

Serves 10 to 12.

The former first lady's recipe is a kind of paradigm of American cookery: no fancy sauces, no marinade of wine, no blazing of brandy, just best-quality ingredients combined in an attractive and contrasting manner. The kumquats are an unexpected relish to the meat, while mushrooms give it substance and added flavor. It is also graceful for company, for, as Mrs. Johnson assures us, it may be kept warm wrapped in a heavy towel, and put under a broiler to warm just before serving.

SIRLOIN CLEMENCEAU

4	medium potatoes, peeled and cut in ½" dice	8	mushrooms, sliced
	Vegetable oil	2	cloves garlic, minced
2	sirloin steaks, cut at least 1" thick	1	cup tiny peas, cooked
½	cup butter		Salt and freshly ground pepper
			Minced parsley

Cook potatoes in hot vegetable oil as in American Fries (page 253). Remove with a slotted spoon to paper toweling and keep warm.

Start the steak to grill in your favorite manner, while in a saucepan you sauté mushrooms with garlic in butter for 5 minutes. Add the peas and heat another minute.

To assemble the dish, cut each steak into two equal portions and place on warm plates. Toss the potatoes with mushrooms and peas, then with salt and pepper to taste; toss again with parsley. Bring to a quick heat and pour equally over the steaks.

Serves 4.

A hearty way to prepare an epicurean steak and potatoes, in not more than 20 minutes. Clemenceau is a staple New Orleans restaurant dish, equally adapted to serving over sautéed chicken rather than steak, and for that matter I see no reason not to treat hamburger with this unusual saucing. It is constructed around Brabant potatoes, with the addition of peas (in New Orleans they used canned petits pois, but certainly frozen or fresh peas may accomplish the thing as well). They also use an incredible amount of butter, which I have halved here.

Most restaurant dishes are assembled from ingredients prepared in advance, and this is no exception, for the potatoes may be prepared ahead and kept warm in an oven, then assembled while the steak is prepared. A fine dinner would be to prepare some such soup as Winter Tarragon Tomato (page 12), and then serve the sirloin accompanied only by a bottle of red wine, a green salad to follow, and finally a simple easily prepared dessert, like Roanoke Rum Cream (page 384) or Strawberries in Strawberry Sauce (page 392).

MARYLAND POT ROAST MADEIRA

3	tablespoons olive oil	2	whole cloves
3	pounds rump roast (or other boneless cut)	2	bay leaves
		1½	teaspoons good wine vinegar
1	large onion, chopped		Salt
2	cloves garlic, minced	1	tablespoon (¼ square) grated bitter chocolate
1	tablespoon flour		
½	cup white wine	1	tablespoon dry Madeira
2	cups water		Parsley sprigs
6	peppercorns		Orange slices

*H*eat the oil in a casserole the meat fits well into, and brown the roast thoroughly on all sides. Remove the meat, add the onion and garlic, and stir them until limp over low heat. Sprinkle the flour over the onion and cook, stirring, until the flour begins to stick to the bottom of the pan—a matter of about 5 minutes.

Add the wine and water, stir till the whole has begun to thicken, then place the meat back in the casserole. Tie the spices in a small bag and add with the vinegar. Cover tightly (with foil as well as a lid) and simmer very gently over lowest flame for 3 hours.

Halfway though cooking, remove the lid, turn the roast, and add salt to taste (remember, the sauce will be reduced later, so salt sparingly). When the meat is quite soft, wrap in foil and keep in a warm oven until ready to serve. It can be left in the oven, in this manner, for several hours if need be.

To make the sauce, skim off the fat from the top of the juices, remove the spice bag, and boil down over high heat until reduced by half. Place in a blender, and going from low to high speed, smooth out the sauce. The onions should thicken it slightly.

Return the sauce to the pan and stir in the chocolate over a low flame until it is dissolved. Add the Madeira and stir until silky. The chocolate will thicken the sauce—it should have the consistency of cream. Taste for seasoning and

let heat several minutes before serving over slices of the pot roast. It looks very nice indeed served with a sprig of parsley and a bright slice of orange.
Serves 6.

This old-time Maryland dish is one of our great regional specialties. It does only good to marinate the meat overnight in a slosh of wine if you have some on hand. The chocolate in its sauce yields a subtly dark savor usually associated with complex French reductions, and if you leave the meat in the oven as suggested, in foil, it assumes unheard-of tenderness. For the best of all possible worlds, serve it with Georgia Spoonbread (page 319) and a sound California red vintage.

SAVOY PLAZA POT ROAST

2	pounds boneless chuck, round, etc.	1	cup dry red wine
	Flour	½	cup beef stock
2	tablespoons vegetable oil	4	medium potatoes, peeled and quartered
2	medium onions, sliced		Juice of ½ lemon
1	clove garlic, minced		Minced parsley
	Salt and freshly ground pepper		

Cut the meat into 2-inch chunks and shake with enough flour to coat. Put a heavy casserole or Dutch oven over a high flame and put the oil in. When it is near smoking, sear the meat until all sides are brown and crusty—this should be done in batches, or the meat won't brown properly.

Turn the heat down to medium and add the onions and garlic. Stir them into the meat, and cook until the onion softens. Add wine, stock, and salt and pepper to taste. Cover, and simmer very gently for 2 hours. Add the potatoes, and cook another 15 to 20 minutes, till they are done.

Stir in the lemon juice just before serving, and taste for seasoning. Sprinkle well with minced parsley.
Serves 4.

Savoy Plaza's is one of the nicest variations on the theme of pot roast I know— although it really is more a sort of stew—its secret being perhaps the final squeeze of lemon. It would certainly make the reputation of any lesser restaurant, it is easily adjustable to any size family, and will be a family favorite to be cooked again and again. All in all, I would walk across town to eat it.

HOME BEEF BARBECUE

3	pounds rump roast (or other boneless cut)	1	clove garlic, minced
2	tablespoons vegetable oil	1	cup beer
1	onion, chopped	2	bay leaves
		1	cup Barbecue Sauce (page 294)

Dry the meat thoroughly. Place the oil in a Dutch oven and brown the meat well over a high flame. Turn the heat down, add the onion and garlic, and cook till they are limp. Then add the beer and bay leaves. Cover the Dutch oven with foil, as well as the lid, and place over very low heat. Cook gently for 3 hours, turning in the liquid several times as it cooks.

Preheat the oven to 375°F.

When done, remove the roast to another pan and glaze it with half the barbecue sauce in the oven for 15 to 20 minutes.

While it glazes, reduce the cooking liquid in the Dutch oven till it begins to thicken, then add the rest of the barbecue sauce. To serve, slice the meat and spoon some of the sauce over each portion.

Serves 6.

If not the authentic hickory-smoked barbecue, which takes all night over a glowing pit, this yet makes a very decent home substitute. It can be served with any of the traditional accompaniments, such as slaw and cornbread, but I like it best as my mother used to serve a similar dish: hot between slices of rye bread, with crisp sweet onion rings, and cold beer.

NEW ENGLAND
BOILED DINNER THREE WAYS

5	pounds corned beef (brisket)	8	carrots, trimmed and scraped
1	bay leaf	4	medium onions
6	peppercorns	4	parsnips, trimmed and scraped (optional)
1	clove garlic		
4	medium potatoes, peeled	1	small head cabbage, cut in quarters
4	turnips, peeled		

*P*lace the meat in a large kettle. Cover with water, then add the bay leaf and peppercorns. Bring to a boil and skim. When the liquid is clear, turn down the heat very low, cover the kettle, and barely simmer for 3 hours.

Add the vegetables, except for the cabbage, to the kettle; simmer 20 minutes. Remove the corned beef and keep warm. Add the cabbage to the kettle and cook about 10 minutes longer. Drain (saving the broth) and serve the sliced meat and vegetables decoratively on a warm platter. (Sometimes beets cooked separately are served as well for added color.) Accompany with horseradish and mustard pickle, along with a pitcher of the broth. Serve with a good dark beer.

Serves 4 (with enough left to make hash).

This is the American pot au feu. Although it is to be found in almost any cookbook—indeed it hardly needs a recipe—I have included it here because it may be used to concoct two more excellent thrifty meals for four people, and nothing wasted. One of these is Corned Beef Hash with Eggs, and the other a hearty soup (recipes for both follow). Although it is thought that the stock from corned beef is too salty for soup stock, and is always thus discarded after, here it comes into its own.

CORNED BEEF HASH WITH EGGS

2 to 3	medium potatoes	2	tablespoons melted butter
2	cups minced corned beef		Salt and freshly ground
½	cup minced green onions		pepper
	with part of tops		Paprika
1	tablespoon butter	4	eggs
2	tablespoons minced		Parsley or watercress sprigs
	parsley		Broth to cover
⅓	cup heavy cream		

*B*oil the potatoes (with skins on) in the corned beef broth until they are tender. Remove, let dry till you can handle them, then skin and crumble into the minced corned beef. (A richer hash may be made by adding any of the vegetables left over from a boiled dinner—about 1½ cups will be sufficient.)

Preheat the oven to 450°F.

Melt 1 tablespoon butter in a skillet and sauté the green onions and parsley until the onions are softened. Add potato-meat mixture, cream, salt and pepper to taste, and a dash of paprika. Toss all together.

Pour half the melted butter in a pie plate, pack in the corned beef mixture, and dribble the rest of the butter on top. Bake at 450°F for 15 minutes, then remove from the oven, turning the oven down to 350°F. Make 4 indentations in the top of the hash with a large spoon or custard cup, and break an egg into each. Salt and pepper, then bake 15 to 20 minutes, or until the eggs are set. Remove from the oven, slice in 4 wedges, and serve garnished with parsley or watercress.

Serves 4.

WINTER SOUP

4 cups stock from a New England Boiled Dinner (see preceding recipe)
2 cups peeled and cubed (¼ inch) potatoes
½ small cabbage, cored and chopped
½ cup minced green onions with part of tops

1 tablespoon butter
1 tablespoon flour
½ cup cream
Tabasco
Salt and freshly ground pepper
½ cup sour cream
Caraway seeds

*T*aste the stock—some corned beef is more salty than others, and if the stock seems excessively salty cut it with some water or chicken stock. Put it in a kettle and bring to a boil. Add the potatoes and cabbage, then lower the heat and let simmer.

Sauté the green onions in butter till limp, then add the flour and cook slowly for 5 minutes. Add some of the hot stock and cook, stirring, until the mixture thickens. Pour this into the soup, stir until smooth, and let simmer 30 minutes, or until the potatoes are beginning to crumble and the cabbage is very tender.

Add cream, a few drops of Tabasco, and taste for seasoning—you may need a very little salt, or wish some pepper. Place in soup plates and float a dollop of sour cream mixed with caraway seeds on each. Serve with rye bread, beer, and a good salad.

Serves 4.

THOMAS JEFFERSON'S RAGOÛT OF BEEF

2   pounds boneless beef round,
    cut in 1-inch cubes
Vegetable oil
½   pound ham, cut in ¼-inch
    dice
2   tablespoons butter
2   cups dry white wine
¼   teaspoon freshly grated
    nutmeg

8   peppercorns
3   whole cloves
4   stalks celery, cut slantwise in
    ½-inch pieces
1   teaspoon butter
1   teaspoon flour
Minced parsley

Dry the beef with paper towels. Film the bottom of a dutch oven with oil and put it over high heat. Brown the meat in batches, lifting the cubes out with a slotted spoon when brown on all sides. When all are done, tip out any fat in the pot and put in the ham and butter. Lower the heat to medium and toss several minutes, then add the beef, wine, and all the spices.

Cover the pot, lower the heat, and let simmer 1½ hours—or until the beef is tender. Add the celery and cook, uncovered, 10 to 12 minutes—the celery should still be a mite crunchy. Rub about a teaspoon of butter and a teaspoon of flour together until all the flour is absorbed. Thicken the sauce with little pieces of this—stirring after each addition. Use only enough to make a lightly thickened sauce.

Serve sprinkled with parsley, with buttered noodles, mashed potatoes, or even spoonbread.

Serves 4.

One of Thomas Jefferson's favorite dishes, this is a distinguished stew flavored with ham and spices rather than the usual garlic-onion-bay leaf, etc. It is a little heavy on the nutmeg, so I've cut it down, and you might want to even a little more. It has no salt because of the ham—Jefferson had the best Virginia hams at hand at Monticello—so you will want to taste it if you use ordinary market ham.

COLONIAL BEEF STEAK PUDDING

2 tablespoons vegetable oil	Salt and freshly ground
1 pound boneless beef, cut into	pepper
bite-sized pieces	⅔ cup sliced mushrooms
1 onion, chopped	2 tablespoons mixed butter and
1 cup plus 1 tablespoon flour	vegetable oil (or beef
1 cup beef stock, heated	drippings)
2 tablespoons tomato paste	2 eggs
½ teaspoon Worcestershire sauce	1 cup milk

*P*ut the oil in a medium saucepan set over high heat. Brown the steak in batches, then return all the pieces to the pan. Add the onion and cook over medium heat until limp. Add 1 tablespoon flour and cook a few minutes longer, stirring well. Add hot stock, tomato paste, Worcestershire, salt and pepper to taste, and the mushrooms. Cook gently, uncovered, 1½ hours, or until the steak is tender. When it is done, all of the liquid should be absorbed—if it tends to dry out either add some more stock or cover the pan.

To prepare the pudding, preheat the oven to 450°F. Put the butter and oil (or, better, beef drippings if you have any) in a 1½-quart casserole (with at least 2-inch sides so the pudding can puff up) and put the casserole in to heat.

In a bowl, whisk the eggs with milk, then sift the 1 cup flour and ½ teaspoon salt over, and beat the batter until smooth and bubbly. When the fat in the casserole starts sizzling, pour in the batter. Drop the steak mixture by spoonfuls on the top, and place immediately in the hot oven. Bake 15 to 20 minutes, or until the pudding is puffed and brown.

Serves 4.

Another variation on Yorkshire pudding invented by our ancestors. (The British to this day make a similar dish by dropping sausages in the batter and calling it Toad-in-the-Hole.) It seems a trusty dish to bring back for family suppers—it's easily prepared, fairly economical, and best of all, crusty and savory. It doesn't need much but a vegetable or salad to accompany it, and perhaps a sturdy red wine.

MASSACHUSETTS
BRAISED SHORT RIBS AND CELERY

2	pounds beef short ribs, cut in 3-inch lengths	2	carrots, trimmed and sliced
	Flour	¼	cup minced parsley
	Vegetable oil		Salt and freshly ground pepper
1	small bunch celery	1	cup red wine
1	cup chopped onion	¼	cup tomato paste
2	cloves garlic, minced		Beef stock

*S*hake the ribs with flour. Film the bottom of a stew pot with oil and brown the ribs thoroughly on all sides over medium-high heat. While they brown, prepare the vegetables.

Separate the celery stalks, remove tops and leaves, and pare away the tough ribbing on the outer stalks. Cut in 3-inch lengths, and mince enough celery leaves and tops to measure 1 cup—save the rest for soups or salads, etc. Prepare all the other vegetables.

When meat is well browned, remove from the pot and tip out most of the accumulated fat. Sauté celery tops, onion, garlic, carrots, and parsley till soft over low heat, then return the meat to the pot. Season with salt and pepper to taste, then add the wine. Let it boil up and cook 5 minutes or so, then add the tomato paste and enough stock to cover the meat.

Cover the pan and cook at a bare simmer on top of the stove for 3 hours— or until meat is nearly falling off the bones. Add the celery stalks and cook another 30 minutes. Skim off most of the fat, arrange the ribs and celery on warm plates and pour some of the strained braising liquid over them.

Serves 4.

A melting pot recipe, I suppose, as I got it from the kitchen of a great Greek lady in Lowell, Massachusetts, as I stood and watched. It didn't seem particularly Greek until she served it later with a huge dish of large macaroni moistened with the sauce and sprinkled with grated Parmesan. It could be made with any cut of beef, really, that is economical—the real secret I learned that day was how good all that celery was in a stew.

BRAISED OXTAILS WITH MUSHROOMS

3 pounds oxtails, cut up at joints	3 tablespoons finely chopped parsley
3 tablespoons vegetable oil	3 tablespoons tomato paste
1 cup finely chopped onion	1 cup red wine
2 cloves garlic, minced	2 cups beef or chicken stock
1 cup finely chopped carrots	Salt and freshly ground
1 cup finely chopped celery	pepper
16 mushrooms, caps separated from stems and stems finely chopped	2 tablespoons butter
	3 tablespoons Madeira

*I*n a Dutch oven or heavy casserole, sear the oxtails in 2 tablespoons of the oil till brown all over. Turn the heat down to medium, add the onion and garlic, and toss till the onion softens. Add the carrots, celery, mushroom stems, and parsley. Cook a few more minutes, tossing.

Stir in the tomato paste and the wine, and let the wine cook, uncovered, at a full boil down to half. Add stock and salt and pepper to taste, then cover the Dutch oven and let simmer 4 hours or more—the meat should be near to falling off the bones. (A pressure cooker is a great help in cooking oxtails, as it's almost impossible to overcook them. If you do so, it will take about 2½ hours.)

If possible, cook the meat early in the day, then refrigerate to harden the fat so it can all be lifted out. If not, soak up as much of the fat as possible and lift the oxtails out onto a plate.

Put the pan juices and vegetables in a blender or food processor and whirl until smooth. Put this, with the oxtails, back in the Dutch oven and bring to a rolling boil. Cook down till it is slightly thickened.

Meanwhile, sauté the mushroom caps in the butter and remaining 1 tablespoon oil in a roomy skillet. Cook these only 4 to 5 minutes, or until they start to exude juices, then add them to the oxtails. Add the Madeira and cook 10 minutes longer.

This dish seems to only gain on reheating, so it may be completely prepared ahead and simply reheated when dinner is to be got together.

Serves 4.

Mushrooms seem a particularly good partner for the rich glutinous meat of the oxtail. The recipe also makes lots of dark sauce, so you will need some-

thing to put it on. Try Georgia Spoonbread (page 319) or just plain fluffy mashed potatoes.

JOE'S SPECIAL

1 cup chopped onion	1 teaspoon dried basil
1 clove garlic, minced	Salt and freshly ground
3 tablespoons olive oil	pepper
1 pound fresh spinach (or 1	Freshly grated nutmeg
package frozen)	1 pound ground beef
1 zucchini, grated (optional)	4 eggs, beaten
2 tablespoons chopped parsley	Grated Parmesan cheese

*I*n a saucepan, sauté the onion and garlic in olive oil until the onion is transparent. Put the spinach to boil in a little water. Cook only a few minutes, then run cold water over it and drain well.

When the onion is done, add zucchini, parsley, and basil and cook a few minutes longer—the zucchini should still be slightly crisp. Remove this from the fire.

Squeeze all the water you can from spinach with your hands, then mince it fine. Add the spinach to the onion-zucchini mixture and season to taste with salt, pepper, and nutmeg.

In a large frying pan, cook the ground beef over medium heat until it begins to brown. If it is of high fat content, drain it on paper toweling, then return it to the frying pan, add the onion-zucchini mixture, and toss over medium heat until thoroughly mixed.

Add about three fourths of the beaten eggs, and turn and lift until the eggs are cooked. Add the rest of the eggs, and toss for a few minutes longer. Serve on warm plates with Parmesan cheese sprinkled over, and, if possible, with plenty of crusty sourdough bread.

Serves 4 to 6.

Joe's Special, with all its Italian overtones, has long been a favorite of San Franciscans, particularly as a late supper after theater, where one could sit at the counter of Original Joe's and watch it being made to order. Children particularly seem to like it (even with all that spinach), and it makes a quick, easy, satisfying family supper dish any time. It's best made with fresh spinach, but frozen does almost as well, and if San Francisco sourdough is not on hand you'll have to make do with whatever French bread you can get.

ALFRED LUNT'S MEAT LOAF

1	pound lean ground chuck	1	tablespoon butter
	Salt and freshly ground	1	cup coarsely grated zucchini
	pepper	⅔	cup sour cream
⅓	cup rice	¼	cup chicken stock
1	cup boiling salted water		Paprika
½	cup chopped onion		Minced parsley

Line bottom and sides of a pie plate with the meat, salt and pepper it, and leave aside while you prepare the filling.

Preheat the oven to 375°F.

To do this, heat 1 cup water to boiling, add salt, and cook the rice in it 20 minutes. Drain the rice and place in a bowl. Sauté the onion in the butter till limp and add to the rice. Stir in the zucchini and sour cream, and season lightly with salt and pepper.

Pour into the meat shell, pour the stock over the pie—loosening its sides to let the stock run down around the meat—and carefully place in the oven. Bake 40 to 45 minutes, or until the meat is done and the center is puffed and starting to turn straw colored.

To serve, sprinkle with paprika and parsley and cut into pie-shaped wedges. Serves 4.

This recipe is a tour de force of humble ingredients invented by the late actor Alfred Lunt, who seems to have been as creative in the kitchen as he was on stage. It is said that, when he and his wife Lynn Fontanne were on tour, they grew so tired of restaurant cooking Lunt would go shopping early in the day, then drop in on friends after the performance to use the kitchen.

SMOKED OYSTER BURGERS

1½	pounds best-quality ground		Freshly ground pepper
	beef	16	smoked cocktail oysters
1	tablespoon grated onion		Grated peel of 1 lemon
1	tablespoon heavy cream	4	slices bacon

Mix the beef with the onion, cream, and pepper to taste. Divide into 8 equal balls and flatten them to about 3-inch rounds. Place 4 oysters on 4 of the rounds, sprinkle grated lemon equally over them, then top with the remaining 4 rounds.

Pinch the edges together and ring each patty with a slice of bacon, securing with a toothpick. Broil over hot coals or under the oven broiler until they are to your taste. Remove the toothpicks and serve, with or without buns.

Serves 4.

The only true way to construct a hamburger is with the best possible local breads and condiments, but this little fantasia on the theme is good as it sounds, just as is. The first time I had one I couldn't quite believe my tongue. They are good served with My Mashed Potato Salad (page 281), or with New Potato Salad (page 280) and probably fine local beer rather than wine.

Veal

"Veal", Elizabeth David writes in her *French Provincial Cooking*, "is a meat which makes a good background for quite a variety of flavorings and sauces." That background, these days, both elusive and expensive, though we still have an unexpected foreground of recipes from former homestead slaughter. These range from sauces of Midwestern green tomatoes or Northeastern sand plums, to the Southern method of throwing in a handful of chestnuts and the Pennsylvania Dutch remembering Old World paprika and sour cream. The Shakers and the Creoles also chime in with their distinctive notes.

VEAL STEAKS
WITH GREEN TOMATO SAUCE

4	veal steaks, cut ¾ inch thick (or 8 veal chops)	6 to 8	green tomatoes
	Flour		Freshly grated nutmeg
	Salt and freshly ground pepper		Pinch of ground ginger
			Pinch of dried thyme
		½	cup beef or chicken stock
4	tablespoons butter	⅔	cup heavy cream
2	slices onion, punched in rings		

Shake the veal in lightly salted and peppered flour. Bring the butter to a sizzle in a frying pan large enough to hold all the meat in one layer, then put the meat in and sauté over medium heat for 5 minutes a side—or until golden. Remove the meat to a plate and add the onion to the pan. Sauté several minutes until the onion is limp, then place the meat over the onion.

Drop the tomatoes in a pot of boiling water for a couple of minutes, or until they can be peeled easily. Slip off the skins, and cut them in slices over the meat. Sprinkle with more salt and pepper, nutmeg, ginger, and thyme. Pour the stock over and let it come to a bubble, then cover the pan closely and simmer gently over lowest heat for 1 hour—or until meat is very tender.

At this point lift the meat out onto a warm platter, and keep warm in the oven. To make the sauce, mash down the tomatoes and onions with a large fork or potato masher. Stir in the cream, taste for seasoning, and bring the heat up to high. Stir till the mixture becomes a green tomato–studded gravy, partly silky smooth, part not. Pour this over the warm veal and serve.

Serves 4.

With green tomatoes often to be found among the underripe shipped to market these days, this gem of farmhouse cookery is one still to be emulated in apartments. The slight tartness of green tomatoes beautifully perks up bland veal, and there is plenty of sauce for mashed potatoes or Georgia Spoonbread (page 319). The wine should be white, and very dry.

GRILLADES AND GRITS

2	pounds veal, sliced ¼ inch thick (or beef Swiss steaks)	½	cup drained and chopped canned tomatoes	
	Salt		Minced parsley	
	Cayenne	½	teaspoon dried thyme	
2	cloves garlic, minced	1	bay leaf	
	Flour	1	tablespoon red wine vinegar	
¼	cup lard	2	teaspoons Worcestershire sauce	
1	cup chopped onion			
½	cup chopped green pepper	3	cups cooked hominy grits	
2	cups beef or chicken stock			

Cut the meat into 2-inch squares and flatten with a mallet or studded meat tenderizer. Rub salt, cayenne, and garlic well into the meat, then rub in flour. Melt the lard in a heavy skillet and fry the veal in batches over high heat until golden on each side. Reserve the meat on a plate.

Add onion and green pepper to the pan and stir till the onions are a straw color. Add 1 tablespoon flour and stir for several minutes, then add stock, tomatoes, ¼ cup minced parsley, thyme, and bay leaf. Cover and simmer 15 minutes.

Put the veal back in the pan, with the vinegar and Worcestershire and simmer, covered, for 1 hour, turning the meat now and again and checking to see it doesn't stick to the bottom of the pan. There should be plenty of rich brown sauce.

To serve the grillades, place on a warm plate inside a ring of cooked grits, and sprinkle additional parsley over.

Serves 4 to 6.

In New Orleans, home of this spicy concoction, beef is used often as veal. I find round steak perfect for this—one only has to cut the steak in 2-inch squares then carefully slice through the middle with a sharp knife to make thin pieces. With either beef or veal it rivals any so-called Swiss steak you've ever eaten. Before President Carter came into office you could probably count the Yankees on one hand who had even heard of grits, but now they are even available and used all over the country. Unfortunately, these are usually "instant grits" and not the kind the Southerners simmer for an hour or more. The best thing to do with these is to ignore the package directions, add more water, and cook them in a double boiler for 20 to 30 minutes—they have time that way to gather more flavor.

PENNSYLVANIA DUTCH PAPRIKA VEAL

4   slices bacon, cut in ¼-inch
        strips
1½   pounds veal steak, or any
        thin slices
¼   cup chopped onion
1   teaspoon paprika

Salt
1   cup sour cream
1   tablespoon tomato paste
½   cup water
Cooked egg noodles

*I*n a medium skillet, fry the bacon until it has rendered its fat but is not yet crisp. Remove it with a slotted spoon onto paper toweling. Cut the veal into serving portions and brown it quickly in the bacon fat, over a medium-high flame.

Toss in the onion and cook a few minutes more, until it is soft, then add the paprika and salt. Stir in the sour cream, tomato paste, the reserved bacon, and water.

Simmer, covered, for 20 to 30 minutes, or until the veal is tender. Check occasionally to see if it needs more water. Serve the veal with its sauce on cooked egg noodles.

Serves 4.

This is a definite addition to our repertoire of fine veal recipes. It does not differ substantially from many European paprika dishes, except perhaps in the delicacy of the paprika sauce itself, and of course all that bacon to savor the veal.

SHAKER VEAL FRICASSEE

4   pounds boneless veal shoulder
2   onions, quartered
2   stalks celery, cut in 2-inch
        pieces
1   teaspoon dried thyme
     Salt
6   whole cloves

6   peppercorns
4   tablespoons butter
⅓   cup finely chopped onion
¼   cup flour
     Heavy cream
4   egg yolks
     Juice of 1 lemon

½ teaspoon freshly grated
    nutmeg
1 cauliflower, cut in florets
    (optional)

12 mushrooms, quartered and
     sautéed in butter
     (optional)

*C*ut the veal into 2-inch pieces, making sure to discard any connective tissue. Put the quartered onions and the veal in a Dutch oven. Turn the heat to medium and add celery, thyme, salt to taste, cloves, and peppercorns. Add water to cover and simmer gently for 1 hour, with the cover on the pot.

When tender, remove the veal and keep warm. Strain the broth and reserve. Melt the butter in a medium saucepan and cook the onion and flour for 5 minutes or more, stirring. Measure the veal broth, and if there are not 2 cups, add enough cream to make up the balance.

Add this to the onions and bring to a boil, whisking till smooth and thickened. Remove from heat immediately. Beat the egg yolks with the lemon juice and the nutmeg. Beat some of the hot sauce into the yolks, then whisk the whole into the sauce.

Add the veal, and when ready to serve, allow to heat without boiling. To construct a more complex dish, add the cauliflower 30 minutes before the veal is done, and all the mushrooms when you add the veal to its sauce. Both should be slightly underdone.

Serves 8 to 10 (may be easily halved).

Visitors came from all over to eat the Shakers' veal and chicken fricassees at Hancock Village. The trolley ended a mile short of the village, in West Pittsfield, and they gladly walked all the way, braving summer dust and winter drifts. The veal fricassee—simply, slowly executed—especially combines great suavity with richness. It needs some absorbing foil, and for this I like to serve a side bowl of My Grandmother's Drop Noodles (page 263), stirred with some butter and minced parsley, but either creamy mashed potatoes or regular egg noodles will do.

CHARLESTON SMOTHERED VEAL WITH CHESTNUTS

1 slice (2 inches) of veal from the leg (about 3 pounds)	12 small white onions, peeled
Salt and freshly ground pepper	½ teaspoon dried thyme
	Minced parsley
1 pound chestnuts, peeled (see	1 cup diced (¼ inch) carrots
directions in Chestnut	1 cup diced (¼ inch) celery
Purée, page 229)	1 cup diced (¼ inch) turnips
3 cups chicken stock	1 tablespoon butter
6 slices bacon	1 tablespoon flour

*P*reheat the oven to 325°F.

Choose a casserole about 2 inches larger around than the veal slice. Lightly salt and pepper the meat. Boil the chestnuts for 5 minutes in the chicken stock, then drain them and reserve the stock.

To assemble the dish, lay 3 strips of bacon on the bottom of the casserole, lay the veal on, then lay the other slices of bacon over. Put the chestnuts over the top, and place onions in a ring around the meat. Sprinkle with the thyme and ¼ cup parsley. Scatter the diced vegetables evenly over the dish—to be fine these should be cut by hand.

Pour the reserved stock over, cover the casserole tightly—if necessary, with both foil and a lid—put in the oven and cook 2 hours. Baste with juices every 20 minutes, and when the meat is tender remove to a hot platter.

With a slotted spoon, arrange the vegetables and chestnuts over and around the meat, discarding the bacon strips. Rub the butter and flour together and whisk it bit by bit into the pan juices over high heat. This will make a slightly thickened sauce. Nap the meat with some of the sauce and serve the rest in a sauceboat. Sprinkle with additional minced parsley and serve.

Serves 6.

This is a superbly contrived company dish, needing only a basket of home-made rolls and a fine chilled white wine for accompaniment—that, and candlelight.

ROAST VEAL WITH WILD PLUMS

6   slices bacon
1   leg of veal (4 pounds), boned
       and tied (the butcher will
       do this)
    Butter
    Salt and freshly ground
       pepper
1   cup chopped celery tops

Juice of ½ lemon
1   bay leaf
6   whole allspice
¾   cup water (or stock)
1   cup preserved wild plums (or
       tart plum jam)
    Brown sugar (or dry mustard)

*P*reheat the oven to 300°F.

Cut the bacon in small strips. Take a small knife and cut into the roast, then insert the bacon strips with the tip of the knife—space these evenly over the whole roast. Rub the meat well with butter, and salt and pepper generously.

Lay the meat in a roasting pan, place the celery tops over, sprinkle with lemon juice, then add bay leaf, allspice, and water or stock. Insert a meat thermometer in the thickest part of the roast, put it in the oven, and roast until the thermometer registers 170°F—about two hours. Baste the meat frequently as it cooks, and half an hour before it's done add the plums.

When done, remove celery tops, bay leaf, and allspice and place the meat on a cutting board. Skim the fat from the surface of the pan juice, then stir the juices and plums till smooth over medium-high heat.

Taste for seasoning, and depending on the tartness of the plums you use, add brown sugar or dry mustard to taste (wild plums are quite sharp and tart and need a bit of sugar, while commercial plum jam requires the bit of dry mustard).

Serves 6.

If you live in an area that grows any of the varieties of wild plum—from beach plums to prairie sand plums—this will be a dish to savor often. If not, there are some plum jams that are tart enough to serve, and I've even used canned greengage plums for this that answered pretty well to the general effect. When growing up in Kansas, we used to make great expeditions for sand plums in season, and my mother would put them up both in jelly and jam. As a child I thought them rather too tart for comfort, but I long for them now.

Pork and Ham

My grandparents crossed Kentucky to Kansas in that "Prairie schooner," the covered wagon, no doubt hurrying along a school of pigs. The porker came along for the ride, as it were, from Old World to New, and made settlement a good gamble. They multiplied on the run, cost nothing to keep, and slaughtered they kept long months brined in a barrel. Salt pork kept most of the wilder margins of our country alive and kicking early on. Homesteads put every bit of the pig to use—from snout bristle into brush, down to dessert gelatin extracted out of trotter.

PORK ROAST WITH STUFFED ONIONS

1	rolled boneless pork roast (shoulder or butt) (4 pounds)	6	large flat onions (preferably Bermuda)
1	teaspoon dried thyme	2	tablespoons butter
	Salt and freshly ground pepper	¾	cup bread crumbs
½	cup beef stock	½	cup chopped walnuts
½	cup dry white wine	¼	teaspoon dried thyme
			Salt and freshly ground pepper
		1	cup heavy cream

*P*reheat the oven to 350°F.

Rub the meat with thyme and salt and pepper. Place in a roasting pan, pour the stock and wine around it, and roast 30 to 35 minutes per pound (or to an internal temperature of from 175°–185°F, depending on whether you like your pork just done or quite tender). Make sure the juices don't all cook away, and if they do so add a little water from time to time.

While the roast is cooking, begin to prepare the onions. Peel them, but leave the root ends on so they will remain whole. Slice the tops off each onion, and drop them in boiling salted water to cover. Cook until just tender—about 30 minutes. Drain and cool. Scoop out the centers to form cups with walls about ½ inch thick. Take the centers and chop fine.

Heat the butter in a pan and add chopped onion, bread crumbs, walnuts, thyme, and salt and pepper to taste. Mix well, then stuff the onions with the mixture.

30 minutes before the roast is done, place the stuffed onions around it, basting them several times with the pan juices.

To serve, remove the roast and onions from the roasting pan and keep warm. Skim the pan juices of most of the fat. Add the cream to the pan and cook over medium-high heat, stirring until the sauce is smooth and begins to thicken as it bubbles away. Slice the roast, place on warm plates with an onion, and pour some sauce over both.

Serves 6.

My mother used to serve pork roast in this manner, and I remain to this day fond of nut stuffed onions—though it has been years since I encountered them anywhere but my own kitchen. For some reason, many of our best things seem to have become rare as buffaloes. To my mind, one doesn't need much else on a plate here, but it could use a little color, such as a pile of slightly cooked and buttered green beans, or just a sprig of watercress. I like it, too, with white wine rather than red—but that may be an aberration on my part.

PLANTATION STUFFED
LOIN OF PORK WITH RUM PRUNES

1	pork loin (4 pounds, or 3 pounds boned)	½	teaspoon dried thyme
12	dried prunes	½	teaspoon dried sage leaves, crumbled (not powdered)
¾	cup dark rum	2	cloves garlic, minced
1½	cups croutons		Cayenne
	Chicken stock		Salt and freshly ground
1	tablespoon minced parsley		pepper
¼	cup minced green onions with part of tops		

*E*ither buy a boned pork loin, or bone it yourself—it takes only a long sharp knife or boning knife, no special knowledge, and about 5 minutes time to bone a pork loin. (It is also much cheaper than having a butcher do it. And don't worry about the neatness of the thing because it will be tied up later.)

Place the boned pork and prunes in a bowl and let them marinate in ½ cup of the rum for several hours.

Preheat the oven to 325°F.

Put the croutons in a bowl and moisten with some chicken stock. Add parsley, green onions, herbs and spices, and the rum marinade from the pork and prunes. Toss well.

Lay the pork flat out with the fat side down and lay a line of prunes the length of it. Pat the stuffing on top of the prunes. Wrap the meat back into its original shape, and tie it well with cotton string at 2-inch intervals. Bake for 2½ hours.

When done, remove the pork, pour off the fat from the pan, add the remaining ¼ cup rum and 2 cups chicken stock, and reduce, uncovered, over high heat to about half. Stir as it cooks, until a slightly thickened sauce is obtained.

Remove the string from the loin and slice it in ¼-inch slices. Pour some of the sauce over and serve on warm plates, accompanied by the remaining sauce.

Serves 6.

This Southern specialty from one of the great plantations makes an interesting company presentation—one both good to look at and to taste. Spoonbread is good (see Georgia Spoonbread on page 319) with it (I have two ovens, but if you don't, simply turn up the oven to the temperature for spoon bread when you take the pork out, and have the batter ready to pop in, for the pork will actually benefit by sitting, if kept warm). Otherwise, something like Cottage Roasted Jerusalem Artichokes (page 235) which can be basted with some of the pork juices, and a simple green vegetable will complement the roast nicely. It should be served either with a full-bodied white wine, or a sprightly red.

SHAKER APPLE CIDER PORK CHOPS

4	loin pork chops	1	tablespoon Dijon mustard
2	tablespoons butter	½	cup heavy cream
½	cup hard cider (or unsweetened apple juice)	2	tablespoons minced chives (or parsley)
	Salt and freshly ground pepper		

*C*hoose a medium frying pan just large enough for the chops. Put it over medium-high heat, add the butter, and when it stops sizzling add the chops, cover, and turn the heat down.

Turn the chops occasionally as they cook—in about 30 minutes they should begin to take on a good golden brown color on both sides. At that time add the cider, cover again, and let cook for 15 to 20 minutes more, turning once.

By this time the chops should be tender and most of the liquid evaporated. Pour off all the fat from the pan, then salt and pepper the chops and add mustard, cream and chives. Raise heat and whisk the sauce till smooth. It is probably easier to remove the chops and then put them back during this process.

Cook another few minutes, turning the chops in the sauce, until the cream is reduced and thickened slightly. To serve, place the chops on warm plates and pour the sauce over.

Serves 4.

Ah the wonderful Shakers! If you are able to find hard cider these days, this is an extraordinary way to prepare pork chops—if not, the best substitute would be unsweetened apple juice with a tablespoon or so of Calvados to give some boost. I know people don't drink much hard cider these days, but it would be nice to have more of it around to resurrect all the old dishes where it played such an important part. The best garnish for these chops is, of course, Fried Apple Rings (page 220).

PORK CHOPS BRAISED WITH QUINCES

	Salt	¾	cup peeled and grated quince
4	loin pork chops, cut ¾ inch thick	4	tablespoons honey
		½	cup water (or chicken stock)
1	tablespoon butter	2	teaspoons white wine vinegar
1	tablespoon vegetable oil		

*P*reheat the oven to 350°F.

Lightly salt the chops, then sauté in hot butter and oil until golden on both sides. Remove and put in a buttered casserole wide enough to hold the chops in one layer—and one that has a lid if possible. Sprinkle grated quince over each chop, dribble on the honey, and bring the sauté juices to a bubble. Add water or stock to the juices, along with the vinegar. Allow to bubble up and pour over the chops.

Cut a round of waxed paper to fit the casserole, butter it, and lay buttered side down over the chops. Cover with a lid as well, or foil if need be, and bake in the oven without peeking, for 1 hour. This can sit for some time before being served, with its juices poured over.

Serves 4.

On being handed a quince or two—not enough certainly for their legendary jelly or preserves—I dropped back on my files to uncover this recipe still waiting the advent of a quince crop. It is unearthly, and even more so if you use raspberry vinegar. Serve with halved baked yams slashed with curls of butter, and a white wine that is not too dry.

PORK CHOPS WITH
SCALLIONS AND SOUR CREAM

4	loin pork chops, cut about ¾ inch thick	Salt and freshly ground pepper
	Flour	Paprika

2 tablespoons vegetable oil
⅔ cup chopped green onions
   with part of tops
2 tablespoons minced parsley

½ cup beef or chicken stock
½ cup sour cream
   Parsley sprigs

Shake the chops with flour, salt, pepper, and some paprika. Put the oil in a skillet large enough to hold all the chops and sauté them over a medium-high flame until they are golden on both sides.

Pour out the fat from the pan, sprinkle the green onions and parsley over the meat, then pour in the stock. Cover and cook over low heat 45 minutes, or until the pork is tender but not dry. Check occasionally to see that the liquid hasn't boiled away—if so, add some extra water.

When done, lift the onion-covered chops out onto warm plates. Add the sour cream to the pan and cook, stirring, until the sauce is smooth and thickened. Pour over the chops, garnish with sprigs of parsley, and serve.

Serves 4.

This recipe is adapted from the Wisconsin novelist Edward Harris Heth's The Country Kitchen Cook Book. *It was first published in the late 1950s and has since been reissued, so is commonly available. I recommend it highly as one of the few cookbooks on native food that is jammed full with really usable and interesting recipes. Mr. Heth was a fine writer as well, and he arranges the book for seasonal cooking—from spring garden delights to the "blizzard cupboard"—with beautifully evoked scenes of country living, food gathering, and neighboring cooks.*

MISS DOROTHY'S STUFFED PORK CHOPS

4 loin pork chops, cut 1 inch
   thick
6 ounces cream cheese
¼ pound Smithfield or country
   ham, thinly sliced
1 cup dry white wine
¼ cup olive oil

¼ cup minced green onions
   with part of tops
2 tablespoons minced parsley
1 cup bread crumbs
2 tablespoons butter
   Salt
   Lemon juice
¼ cup heavy cream

Slice the chops with a small sharp knife held parallel to the surface, so that a pocket is formed through the flesh clear to the bone. Spread some of the cheese in each pocket, lay in slices of ham, and secure with toothpicks. Marinate in wine, oil, green onions, and parsley for a few hours—or even overnight.

When ready to cook, preheat the oven to 350°F.

Take a frying pan large enough to hold all the chops, put in the bread crumbs, and shake them over medium heat until they are evenly and lightly browned. Drain the chops (reserving the marinade for later) and turn them in the crumbs off the fire. When they are evenly coated, put them onto a plate and clean out any remaining crumbs in the pan.

Melt the butter in the pan and sauté the chops over medium heat until they are crisp and golden on each side. Add about ¼ cup of the marinade, then cover the pan and bake about 1 hour—or until quite tender.

When done, remove to warm plates, swirl a few drops of lemon juice and the cream into the pan juices, and when the sauce amalgamates as you stir it, pour over the chops and serve at once.

Serves 4.

A rich, sumptuous dish, and a specialty of Mrs. Dorothy Neal of Demorest, Georgia. Any good cured ham may be used if you can't locate the real Smithfield, or have no access to country hams. Westphalian Ham is to be found in many specialty shops, and is particularly fine here. Serve it with Miss Dorothy's Mashed Potatoes (page 250) and pickled crabapples.

NANTUCKET FIREMEN'S SUPPER

4	pork chops, about 1-inch thick	4	medium onions, sliced
	Salt and freshly ground pepper	4	medium potatoes, peeled and sliced
1	bay leaf	2	cups milk

*P*reheat the oven to 350°F.

Trim the chops of excess fat. Try the fat out in a frying pan set over medium heat. When the pieces are golden brown, remove them with a slotted spoon and fry the chops in the released fat 5 minutes a side.

Put chops then in a casserole of a size to hold them all in one layer. Add salt and pepper to taste and lay the bay leaf on top, then put a layer of onions then one of potatoes, over. Salt and pepper again.

Pour the milk over, cover the casserole closely with foil and a lid, and bake

2 hours. When the dish is done, all the liquid will be absorbed and the whole will be golden.

Serves 4.

The hearty simplicity of this one-dish meal makes it a family favorite any time. And like the firemen, the busy cook may put it in the oven and forget it for 2 hours—longer, if you turn the oven off and let it sit warm.

OLD-FASHIONED PORK CASSEROLE

1	pound boneless pork, cut in 1 inch cubes and trimmed of fat	1	onion, chopped
		1	large apple, peeled, cored, and sliced
½	teaspoon powdered sage	2	tablespoons minced parsley
3	medium potatoes, peeled and sliced		Juice of ½ lemon
			Salt and freshly ground pepper
2	teaspoons paprika	1	cup chicken stock

*P*reheat the oven to 350°F.

On a large strip of waxed paper, rub the sage into the pork cubes, coat the potatoes with a blush of paprika, make a pile of the onion, and sprinkle the apples with parsley and lemon juice.

You will need about a 1½-quart casserole for this. Make first a layer of half the potatoes in it, then a layer each of pork, apple, onion, etc., ending with potatoes on top. Salt and pepper as you go, to taste.

Finally add the chicken stock, cover the casserole tightly, and bake 2 hours, uncovering the last 30 minutes and pressing down gently into the juices.

Serves 4.

As casseroles go, this is a fine example, though you should be careful to trim as much fat off the meat as possible or it will be greasy. It needs little accompaniment except perhaps a pickled peach or crab apples—or even a nice homemade chutney.

GEORGIA BARBECUE SPARERIBS

1	cup chopped onion	1	teaspoon dry mustard
1	cup peach preserves	¼	teaspoon Tabasco
1	tablespoon catsup	4	pounds spareribs, left whole
¼	cup brown sugar, packed		Salt and freshly ground
1	teaspoon paprika		pepper
¼	cup white vinegar	2	lemons, thinly sliced
¼	cup Worcestershire sauce		

*P*reheat the oven to 400°F.

In a saucepan, combine the onion, preserves, catsup, sugar, and all the seasonings and simmer 10 to 15 minutes.

Rub salt and pepper into the ribs and place them in a shallow roasting pan, meaty side down. Brush them with some of the sauce and bake 30 minutes.

Turn the ribs, brush with some more sauce, and put the lemon slices on top. Bake another hour, brushing with sauce as the ribs cook several times more, removing the lemon slices before the last time.

To serve, slice into serving portions.

Serves 4.

Frankly, I will eat spareribs cooked almost any way, but this hot, tangy, sweet-sour sauce made with peach preserves is absolutely irresistible (Georgia grows the best peaches on earth!). Accompany them with any kind of good cornbread, or simple mashed potatoes, crisp cole slaw, and cold beer.

GOURMET SPARERIBS

4	pounds spareribs, cut in 2-rib sections	1	cup catsup
2½	teaspoons salt	¾	cup beer
½	teaspoon freshly ground pepper	½	cup minced onion
1	teaspoon granulated sugar	1	clove garlic, minced
¼	teaspoon paprika	½	cup minced green pepper
¼	teaspoon ground turmeric	⅓	cup vinegar
¼	teaspoon celery salt	¼	cup brown sugar, packed
		1	tablespoon Worcestershire sauce

1 teaspoon dry mustard	½ teaspoon dried basil
½ teaspoon Tabasco	

*P*reheat the oven to 325°F.

Cut up the ribs. Mix 2 teaspoons salt, ¼ teaspoon pepper, granulated sugar, paprika, turmeric, and celery salt and rub the mixture into the ribs. Mix all the rest of the ingredients, including the remaining salt and pepper, into a sauce—the best way to do this is either in a blender or food processor. Just put everything and whirl in pulses until there are no large lumps.

Place the ribs, meaty side down, in a baking pan large enough to hold them all in one layer and spoon some of the sauce over them. Bake 2 hours, basting with sauce every 30 minutes and turning the ribs once. After 2 hours, turn the heat off, and let the ribs sit in the oven another 30 minutes, or until ready to serve.

Serves 4.

I grew up, culinarily speaking, on Gourmet *magazine and the* Gourmet *cookbooks. Always one of the best ways to get the tone and temper of current American cooking is in the "Sugar and Spice" column, where readers send in their favorite recipes. Sometimes lovely old treasures turn up, and often an amateur cook turns a trick on a standard, making it new again. This recipe has been slightly adapted from that column to my own uses, but in essence it has remained the same—certainly one of the best ways to cook spareribs in the world. The ingredients are all the things one would ordinarily use in a barbecue sauce, but they are arranged differently. And what a difference! Wait till you smell them cooking—you'll hardly ever need another recipe.*

SPARERIBS AND SAUERKRAUT

12 to 16	ribs	1⅓	cups stock
4	cups sauerkraut		(beef, chicken, or either
1	cup chopped onion		with some white wine)
2	cups grated apple		Salt and freshly ground
			pepper
		4	bay leaves

*P*reheat the oven to 350°F.

Put the kraut in a large bowl of water and soak several minutes, changing the water, until some of the sharp flavor is left, but not too much. (This is all a matter of taste.) Drain in a colander and squeeze out all of the water by hand. Put the kraut in a casserole, toss with onion, apple, and stock, and cook, covered, in the oven 1 hour.

While the kraut is cooking, boil the ribs in a large pan of water for 15 minutes to remove some of their fat. Remove from the water and sprinkle all over with salt and pepper.

Place the sauerkraut mixture in the bottom of a shallow roasting pan big enough to hold the ribs in one piece. Put the bay leaves over, then the ribs. Put in the oven and cook 1½ hours, basting with the kraut juices every 15 to 20 minutes.

When done, the ribs should have browned on top and the kraut absorbed most of the juices. To aid this process, during the last half hour of cooking, lift the ribs, remove the bay leaves, and stir the kraut into the juices in the pan. Then place the ribs back over and baste.

To serve, place the kraut on warm plates, cut the ribs between bones, and spread 3 or 4 in a fan over the kraut for each serving. Garnish with parsley sprigs and flank with plain boiled potatoes. Dijon mustard makes a welcome side to the crisp ribs.

Serves 4.

Though it appears in some version in every one of our usual cookbooks, one seldom meets this fine native choucroute braisée *at table. It is not a dish for the faint hearted, nor (since the ribs are eaten by hand) the fastidious, but, served with a fine dry white wine or good cold dark beer, it is a feast for the rest.*

HOMEMADE COUNTRY SAUSAGE

2½	pounds boneless pork shoulder	½	teaspoon freshly ground pepper
½	pound pork fat	½	teaspoon dried thyme
2	teaspoons salt	½	teaspoon dried summer savory
½	teaspoon cayenne	¼	teaspoon powdered bay leaf
1	teaspoon powdered sage		Pinch of allspice

*C*ut the meat into dice and grind with all the other ingredients. Cook a bit to taste for seasoning—some prefer much more sage, and others like it hot with cayenne. Other ingredients are also sometimes added—coriander, nutmeg, cloves, etc. To cook, form into sausage patties and fry until crisp on both sides.

Store-bought sausage is usually rather crudely overflavored with sage or hot pepper, so those who want a better balanced product (with no preservatives) might wish to experiment at achieving their own variety. The easiest way to get the meat ground is to buy a pork shoulder and ask your butcher to grind it with some extra pork fat. The sausage will keep for a few days in the refrigerator, and it freezes well shaped into patties and placed between sheets of waxed paper. The patties make a fine breakfast dish topped with some sour cream and accompanied by scrambled eggs.

CHAURICE

5 pounds boneless lean pork	2 cups finely chopped onion
1 pound pork fat	1 clove garlic, minced
3 teaspoons salt	¼ teaspoon dried thyme
2 teaspoons freshly ground black pepper	½ cup minced parsley
½ teaspoon cayenne	1 teaspoon powdered bay leaf
½ teaspoon chili powder	½ teaspoon ground allspice
1 teaspoon paprika	Sausage casings (optional)

*E*ither have the butcher grind all the pork and fat together, or cut in dice and grind it twice through a food grinder. (A food processor has difficulty with pork.) Mix all the ingredients—except the sausage casings, of course—in a bowl with your hands until everything is well combined.

These can be used as sausage patties, or they can be made into sausage lengths. To do this, scald the casings, wash again thoroughly, and let dry. Fill with the sausage mixture, and tie in even lengths.

This highly seasoned Creole sausage is splendid to use in any way you like sausages. In the South it is most often served cooked in a sauce Creole (a good example of this can be found in Almond Chicken Creole, page 153). And it is then accompanied by mashed potatoes or grits for a supper or brunch dish.

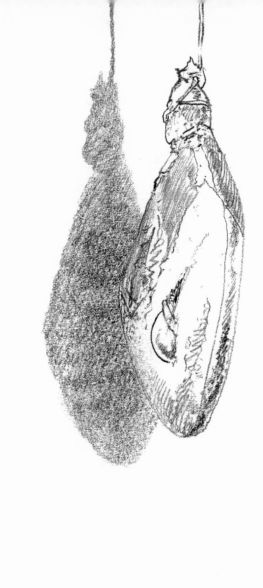

STUFFED BAKED HAM PONTALBA

1	(12 to 16 pounds) country-cured ham	½	cup Madeira
4	cups pecans, ground	4	bay leaves
1	tablespoon plus 2 teaspoons dried sage	1	onion, chopped
1	teaspoon dried thyme	1	apple, peeled, cored, and chopped
1	teaspoon ground cloves	1	cup light molasses
½	teaspoon cayenne		Freshly ground pepper
2	small cans truffles (optional), drained and truffles cut in quarters		Cornmeal
			Brown sugar

*E*ven if you buy the ham by mail, ask your butcher to bone it for you—he'll charge you, but it's an impossible task at home. Soak the ham in water to cover 12 to 24 hours, changing the water 2 or 3 times (the larger the ham, the longer soaking it needs). Remove the ham and scrub with a brush under cold running water.

Remove about ½ pound of the ham from around the boned cavity. Grind this through a food grinder, and combine with the pecans, 2 teaspoons sage, ½ teaspoon thyme, cloves, cayenne, truffles, Madeira, and 2 of the bay leaves, crumbled. Stuff the ham with this, and sew the opening tight. Sew a cloth securely around the ham.

Place in a large deep pan and cover with water. Add the onion, remaining 2 bay leaves, the 1 tablespoon sage, remaining ½ teaspoon thyme, the apple, and molasses. Bring to a simmer on top of the stove, then reduce the heat to low and let simmer partially covered for 6 hours—or until tender. Turn off the heat and let the ham get cold in its broth.

Preheat the oven to 400°F.

Finally, remove the ham and dust it with a mixture of pepper, cornmeal, and brown sugar. Bake 20 minutes, or until the glaze is richly browned. Serve at room temperature, cut into very thin slices. It will keep for several weeks.

Even in the South, of course, fine country-cured hams are a specialty item not found on just any grocery shelf. They are, however, available shipped from quite a few different firms as advertised in fine food magazines. They make an especially good holiday treat, as one ham will stretch over both Thanksgiving and Christmas—with all your visitors on and in between. The thinly sliced pieces make a focal point of a buffet, perhaps with some such dish as Maum Nancy's Scalloped Oysters (page 62) along with various vegetables, starches, hot rolls, pickles, and relishes, etc. You cook an unstuffed ham much as this one is cooked—with the necessary soaking, of course—but this fantasy preparation from New Orleans makes a fine thing even nicer. It makes a splendid hors d'oeuvre with Beaten Biscuits (page 327), and slices from the unstuffed portions make a special breakfast of Country Ham with Red-Eye Gravy (below). The extra bits and pieces not suitable for this kind of presentation may be used as an addition to biscuits, or in such dishes as Miss Dorothy's Stuffed Pork Chops (page 107) and Smithfield Chicken (page 148). Be sure to use every scrap!

COUNTRY HAM WITH RED-EYE GRAVY

4	slices cooked country-cured ham, cut ¼-inch thick	½	cup heavy cream
1	cup brewed coffee		Freshly ground pepper

*T*rim the extra fat from the ham slices. Try the fat out in a large skillet until the pieces are golden and have released their fat. Remove the pieces with a slotted spoon and fry the ham slices in the released fat over medium heat for several minutes on each side. Remove and keep warm.

Add the coffee to the skillet and turn the heat up to high. Scrape all the brown bits clinging to the pan with a spoon, and stir until the gravy turns reddish. Add the cream and pepper to taste, and cook slowly 10 minutes.

To serve, pour the gravy over the ham slices.

Serves 4.

One of the best of simple regional dishes for those lucky enough to obtain country ham. It may be prepared from ordinary smoked ham slices, but of course it won't be nearly so good. I had it at its best once while hiking the Appalachian Trail. A farmer found us in sleeping bags near dusk in his orchard, and after asking us if we'd seen any snakes (a formal conversational gambit in the Southern mountains), politely asked us for breakfast next morning. On a scrubbed, bleached kitchen table we were spread a feast of ham with plenty of red-eye gravy, fresh high biscuits, hot grits, new-laid eggs, good steaming coffee, and homemade wild strawberry preserves. After living for more than a month on dehydrated goods, it tasted like a banquet out of the Arabian Nights rather than fairly humble victuals.

TO GLAZE A HAM

There are about as many ways to glaze a ham as there are people who cook them. It can be as simple as a dusting of sugar over the fat, or it may involve much spicing and fruiting and dousings in liquids—from beer to champagne. First the ham is cooked, then the rind is removed, the fat trimmed to about ½ inch and slashed in a diamond pattern, each diamond stuck with a clove, and then you have a choice of the glaze itself. In principle this is usually brown sugar, some liquid such as vinegar or fruit juice, and a little dry mustard for nip. Then the ham is put back in a hot oven till the whole mess melts and glisters.

In the South the liquid of choice is bourbon, and then orange slices are pinned on with toothpicks, whereas in New England the choice for the sweet is maple syrup. In California this can all get rather out of hand, with one recipe calling for Dijon mustard, cloves, cinnamon, ginger, nutmeg, pepper, pomegranate jelly, both scotch *and* brandy, and brown sugar as well! There are also variations using bread crumbs—one interesting recipe from Williamsburg calling for crumbs, a little water from boiling the ham, butter, and homemade chowchow, and another, a favorite of President Hoover, which uses simply currant jelly and bread crumbs.

A favorite in my kitchen comes from a friend who uses a 16-ounce can of whole-berry cranberry sauce, with enough port wine to thin it. This is then put in a 400°F oven and watched closely, as it can quickly burn. But oh what a pretty berry-studded glow it makes! Perhaps the best of all, though, would be Mammy Pleasant's Bar-le-Duc Sauce for "a New Year's ham." She crushed 2 pounds of fresh currants with 1 pound raspberries, and added ¾ pound sugar for every pound of pulp. It was them simmered 40 minutes, or till the syrup thickened and jelled. It was then sealed in crocks for use as both a glaze and a sauce for the ham.

A freed slave, with one blue eye and one brown, Mary Ellen Pleasant is one of the most amazing characters in our culinary history. She cooked her way through Boston, Charleston, New Orleans (where she cooked for "The Voodoo Queen"), finally to bonanza San Francisco—starting at the age of nine. She amassed what could be called an up-and-down fortune. When rich she went from plantation to plantation, smuggled in dressed as a jockey, to arouse the slave revolt, and met John Brown to present him with a purse of gold collected from California Negroes. When poor she played hostess for rich playboy patrons who could throw money about on their palates.

In San Francisco she was the first to find new cheeses, Tahiti oranges, Ceylon cinnamon, Chinese tumeric, Puget Sound oysters, and citron from the Indies. She also quickly established a country place she turned into a truck farm for special vegetables, made raspberry vinegar, cheese with cowslip petals, strewed her butter with rose geranium leaves for cakes, adapted Chinese recipes for catering, served fried chicken with a shallot sauce, and came up with a greengage plum sorbet. "Mammy" Pleasant, as she termed herself in those Victorian times, may have been the first truly modern chef.

ALMOND HAM SLICES

1	center slice precooked ham, cut ½ to ¾ inch thick	1	egg, beaten
1	clove garlic, mashed	⅔	cup blanched almonds
	Flour	4	tablespoons butter

Rub the ham with the garlic, and discard any bits that cling. Dip the ham first in flour, then in beaten egg, and lay aside on waxed paper.

Grind ½ cup of the almonds in a food processor or chop them very fine by hand (a blender will make a paste of them). Dust the ham slice in the almonds, pressing them in on both sides, wrap in waxed paper, and refrigerate till needed.

To cook, sliver the remaining almonds and toast them golden in 1 tablespoon of the butter. In the remaining butter sauté the ham till the coating is golden brown on each side—over medium heat, this will take about 5 minutes a side. Cut the ham in serving pieces and sprinkle with the toasted slivered almonds.

Serves 4.

A superb way to serve a slice of good ham, or for that matter smoked pork chops. It needs tart currant jelly alongside, or perhaps chutney, and mounds of creamy mashed potatoes.

MY MOTHER'S HAM PLATTER WITH HOMINY AND PEACHES

4	serving slices precooked ham, cut ½ to ¾ inch thick (or 4 smoked pork chops)	3	tablespoons butter
		4	ripe peaches (or 8 drained halves canned freestones)

Bourbon (optional)
4   cups canned yellow hominy,
    drained

Salt and freshly ground
    pepper

Trim any fat off the ham. Try the fat out in a frying pan until the pieces brown and release their fat. Lift them out with a slotted spoon, add the butter to the pan, and fry the ham slices slowly on each side until slightly golden. This done, remove to a warming platter in the oven.

Place the peaches cut side down in the fat and brown them also on both sides. At this time you can blaze them with a good capful of bourbon, if you like.

In either case, lift the peaches out onto the ham platter and add the drained hominy to the pan. Add more butter if there is little fat, and toss the hominy until it too starts to become crusty and golden.

To serve the dish, rearrange the hominy, ham, and peaches attractively on the warm platter and bring it to table.

Serves 4.

A long-time favorite in our family. That it can be put together easily is not the least of its charms. I have used it for years as a rush meal got together with a slice of ham and two cans—accompanied by cole slaw or lettuce tossed with a simple creamy salad dressing. It deserves even a good white wine of its own—one rather more full bodied and mellow than dry and crisp.

HAM, YAMS, AND
CHESTNUTS, BAKED WITH PIPPINS

6   yams, baked, peeled, and
    sliced
1   pound cooked ham, sliced
1   pound chestnuts, peeled,
    cooked, and crumbled
4   green apples, peeled, cored,
    and sliced

Salt and freshly ground
    pepper
½   cup apple cider
¼   cup brown sugar, packed
⅛   teaspoon ground mace
¼   cup butter, melted

Preheat the oven to 350°F.

In a 2-quart casserole, alternate slices of yams, ham, chestnuts, and apples—beginning and ending with the yams. Sprinkle with salt and pepper over each layer of yams and chestnuts. (Not too much salt if the ham is salty.)

Pour the apple cider over. Mix the brown sugar with the mace and sprinkle over next, then dribble the melted butter on top. Bake, uncovered, for 45 minutes, or until bubbly. Serve warm.

Serves 6.

A superb New England way to offer up part of a baked ham—everything in it compliments everything else, and there is a host of flavors and textures all melded together. It makes a fine company dish if served with your best rolls and a glass of full-bodied white wine.

HAM LOAF WITH
RED CURRANT–HORSERADISH GLAZE

1	pound cooked ham, ground		Freshly ground pepper
½	pound pork, ground	½	cup bread crumbs (or crushed
1	onion, finely chopped		crackers)
1	apple, pared, cored, and	½	cup sour cream
	finely chopped	2	eggs
1	teaspoon dry mustard	3	tablespoons red currant jelly
¼	teaspoon ground allspice	2	tablespoons prepared
	Pinch of ground mace		horseradish
	Freshly grated nutmeg		

*P*reheat the oven to 350°F.

Mix all the ingredients (except the jelly and horseradish) thoroughly by hand. Place in a standard loaf pan and bake for 2 hours. The last half hour, baste with warmed currant jelly mixed with horseradish.

Serves 4 to 6.

This is a family standard, finely honed. It makes a good end to the last of a ham, served with a simple green vegetable, and perhaps Deep-fried Sweet Potatoes (page 260). If there is any left for the next day, it makes a splendid cold sandwich spread with plenty of Dijon mustard. All the chopping is a perfect job for a food processor—even the pork can be ground if cut in small pieces with most of the connective tissue cut out.

FARMHOUSE HAM HOCK BOILED DINNER

2 large meaty ham hocks (or 4 small ones)	8 medium potatoes, peeled and quartered
1½ pounds green beans, washed and trimmed	Salt and freshly ground pepper

*P*ut the hocks to boil in water to cover in a large kettle. Simmer gently 1½ hours, then add the beans, raise heat to medium, and cook for 10 minutes. Add the potatoes and cook another 20 minutes, or until the potatoes are tender.

To serve, remove the hocks, cut off the meat, and chop coarsely. Place the potatoes and beans on warm plates, ladle some broth over them, then sprinkle with ham and salt and pepper to taste. Serve with a cruet of vinegar and a small pitcher of the cooking broth.

Serves 4.

This is one of those humble dishes all cooks secretly like to cook for themselves when no one is looking. I know I do, and would even if I could afford lobster and truffles every day. To speed up the process, the hocks can be cooked in a pressure cooker 30 minutes or so.

Lamb

When America became beef country, after the far-feeding buffalo, no sheep could share its range, for they crop closer than cattle. I grew up in the heart of cattle lands without tasting any of this good woolly beast, and still my mother on travel treats it as an exotic to be approached on a menu with care. Even in these days of wide shipping, more veal is consumed in the country than lamb, which is hard to understand, since mutton was a British staple and *gigot* part of any Frenchman's larder. For one, I frankly dote on its distinctive taste, to the point of upstaging even pork and beef, so it was a pleasure to find some singular recipes from the native trove, delicious right down to the lowly shank and rib.

LEG OF LAMB
WITH PARMESAN POTATOES

1	leg of lamb (5 to 6 pounds)	8	large potatoes, peeled and sliced
3	cloves garlic, peeled and slivered	4	tablespoons butter
1	teaspoon dried rosemary	1	cup chicken stock
	Salt and freshly ground pepper		Freshly grated Parmesan cheese

*P*reheat the oven to 325°F.

Remove most of the fat from the lamb and lard it with garlic slivers all over. (The fell may be removed or left on, as you wish—some folks like the quality it takes on during roasting.) Rub the rosemary and salt and pepper into the roast.

Rub the bottom of a roasting pan the size of the leg of lamb with part of the butter, and layer the potatoes in it, salting and peppering and buttering each layer. Cover the potatoes with stock—it should come up almost to their tops—and place the lamb on top of them.

Roast about 15 minutes to the pound, or until a meat thermometer inserted in the thickest part of the flesh registers 140°F for rare, 160°F for medium, or 175°F for well done.

Remove the roast lamb to a carving board and look at the potatoes—the stock should almost all have cooked away and they should be gold and crusty. Sprinkle them with Parmesan cheese, and return to the oven for the cheese to melt while you carve the lamb.

Serves 8.

The potatoes in this sheepherder preparation sop up all the lamb drippings and become almost as tasty as the roast itself. If you are not afraid of a little oven cleaning, an even better way to roast it is to place the leg on an oven rack with the potatoes set fairly closely on the rack beneath. No other accompaniment is really needed except perhaps a simple green vegetable or watercress sprig, and a glass of good red wine.

BARBECUED BUTTERFLIED LEG OF LAMB

1	leg of lamb (5 to 6 pounds), boned and butterflied by the butcher	1	clove garlic, minced
¾	cup olive oil	1	teaspoon dried rosemary (or 1 tablespoon fresh)
¼	cup red wine vinegar	1	bay leaf, crumbled
½	cup chopped green onions with part of tops		Freshly ground pepper

Choose a pan large enough to hold the meat flattened out, and marinate it for 3 to 5 hours in the rest of the ingredients.

Start a charcoal fire, and when it has come to medium embers, grill the lamb set about 3 inches over the coals. Brush it from time to time with some of the marinade. It should be brown and crusty on the outside and still pink within in 35 to 45 minutes. To serve, let cool for 5 minutes, then slice on the diagonal.

If you don't have a grill, the lamb can also be cooked in an oven. Preheat it to 450°F and cook the lamb for 20 minutes—or until it has browned. Then reduce the heat to 325°F and cook 10 to 15 minutes per pound, according to whether you wish it rare or medium.

Serves 6 to 8.

This makes, I think, a much nicer party centerpiece than grilled steaks—which are often too thinly cut to cook properly outdoors. It is a quite common treat in California (where everything seems to be done outdoors), and the first time I had it the host brushed on the marinade with a sprig of fresh mint. New Potato Salad (page 280) makes a nice partner to the lamb, as does either fine beer or red wine.

CREOLE STUFFED SHOULDER OF LAMB

1	shoulder of lamb (3 to 4 pounds), boned	1	green pepper, seeded and chopped
	Salt and freshly ground pepper	4	tablespoons vegetable oil
1	cup chopped onion	1	cup drained and chopped tomatoes

3 tablespoons olive oil
1 clove garlic, minced
2 bay leaves

¼ cup minced parsley
¼ teaspoon dried thyme
8 to 12 small turnips, peeled
½ cup Madeira

*P*reheat the oven to 325°F.

Cut a large pocket through the center of the large muscle of the lamb, and salt and pepper it inside and out. Sauté the onion and green pepper in 1 tablespoon of the oil for several minutes, until the onion is limp. Combine this with the tomatoes, off the fire, and stuff the lamb with the mixture. Firmly skewer the pocket.

In a large Dutch oven, sauté the lamb in the remaining 3 tablespoons oil until browned on all sides. Turn off the heat and add the garlic, herbs, turnips, and Madeira. Bake, covered, 1 to 1½ hours, or until a meat thermometer inserted registers 150°F. Every 20 minutes or so, turn the meat and turnips. The turnips should be glazed brown all over by the time the roast is done.

To serve, remove the meat from the pan and let sit 15 minutes while you cook down the juices with the turnips, turning occasionally to glaze them more. Slice the meat and serve in a pool of the juices with the turnips alongside.

Serves 6.

All the definite flavors here, each strong in its own right, meld into one lovely succulence. It makes a relatively inexpensive company dish, not difficult to prepare if you find a butcher who will bone a shoulder for you. Serve it with a delicate Grits Soufflé (page 262) and a robust red wine.

ZUÑI LAMB STEW
WITH CORN AND GREEN CHILIES

1 pound boneless lamb shoulder, cut in 1-inch cubes
Flour
Salt and freshly ground pepper
2 tablespoons butter
2 tablespoons vegetable oil
1 clove garlic, minced
1 can (7 ounces) mild green chilies, chopped

1 cup chopped, peeled, and seeded fresh or canned tomatoes
3 cups corn kernels
6 juniper berries, crushed
1 teaspoon dried oregano
Salt
2 small dried red chili peppers

*P*at the lamb cubes dry with paper towels. Shake them in a bag of flour seasoned with salt and pepper, then sauté in batches in a large casserole in hot butter and oil. When the lamb is golden on all sides, lift out onto a warm plate.

Sauté the garlic in the same pot set over medium heat for a minute or two, then add the green chilies, tomatoes (with any juice if you use canned), corn, juniper berries, and oregano. Let this bubble up over high heat, then add the lamb, salt to taste, and the red chilies. Examine the chilies for any breaks in their skin—if they are not perfect, then remove the hot seeds before adding.

Stew slowly, covered, for 1½ hours, or until the lamb is quite tender. Check the pot now and again to make sure there is enough liquid—if not, add a little water, tomato juice, or stock.

When done, remove the red chilies, and serve in a heated dish.

Serves 4.

One place the sheep prospered was the scrublands of the West, where forage was too sparse for cattle. This native Indian dish uses everything the Zuñi have at hand—right down to local desert juniper berries. It's good served with a stack of warm tortillas, butter to slather over them, and a pitcher of cold beer.

RACK OF LAMB ALMONDINE

2	racks (6 to 8 chops each) of lamb	
	Salt and freshly ground pepper	

1	cup dry vermouth	
1½	cups toasted blanched slivered almonds	

*P*reheat the oven to 400°F.

Trim most of fat off the lamb, and rub with salt and pepper. Place the racks, bone side down, in a shallow roasting pan.

Roast for 25 minutes, or until the lamb is crisped and golden on the outside and pink and juicy inside. When done, remove from the pan and let sit while you prepare the sauce.

To do this, drain all the fat off, add the vermouth to the drippings, and stir over a medium flame till all the brown specks are dissolved and the liquid is reduced by half.

To serve, slice into serving portions, fan them on warm plates, sprinkle with almonds, then pour the vermouth sauce over.

Serves 4.

A rack of lamb is everybody's restaurant favorite, but there is no reason not to serve it at home. This fine recipe is a specialty of Le Ruth's in New Orleans.

It makes an unlikely pair, but I serve it with Shaker Alabaster (page 247) and the best red wine I can afford.

SALEM LAMB CHOPS WITH CAPER–BREAD CRUMB SAUCE

4	meaty shoulder lamb chops, cut ¾ inch thick	½	cup butter, melted
	Fresh bread crumbs	3	tablespoons minced capers
	Salt and freshly ground pepper	1	tablespoon caper juice
2	tablespoons butter	2	tablespoons white wine vinegar
1	tablespoon vegetable oil	¼	cup bread crumbs

*T*rim the chops of fat, and coat with bread crumbs, salt, and pepper. Melt the butter and oil in a frying pan large enough to hold all the chops, and brown them over medium heat 5 or more minutes a side, depending on the thickness of the chops—they should be golden brown on the outside and still pink on the inside.

While the chops are frying combine the melted butter with capers, caper juice, vinegar, and ¼ cup bread crumbs. Serve the chops on heated plates with some of the sauce at their sides, and the rest in a sauceboat.

Serves 4.

Serve these with Spokane Scalloped Onions (page 238), and you have a meal so delectable you won't notice the lack of fancy expensive loin chops.

NEW ORLEANS EPIGRAM OF LAMB

4	pounds breast of lamb		Melted butter
1	large onion, quartered		Salt and freshly ground pepper
2	carrots, trimmed and sliced		Bread crumbs
2	stalks celery, sliced		
¼	cup parsley stems	1	tablespoon butter
1	clove garlic	2	tablespoons flour
1	bay leaf	2	cups beef stock, heated
¼	teaspoon dried thyme	¼	cup Madeira
6	whole cloves	½	cup sliced mushrooms (optional)
6	peppercorns		

*T*rim the lamb of any fell and outside fat and put in a large kettle. Cover with salted water and bring to a boil with the onion, carrots, celery, parsley stems, garlic, bay leaf, thyme, cloves, and peppercorns. Simmer gently 1 hour, or until quite tender and the small bones will slip out easily.

Drain and let cool enough to be able to pull out all the bones. Press down with a heavy weight and chill till ready to serve dinner. (The stock can be used to make a barley soup.)

To prepare the dish, cut the breast into portions about 3 inches wide and cut these into three triangular pieces. Dip in melted butter, sprinkle with salt and pepper, then roll in bread crumbs.

Make a sauce by melting 1 tablespoon butter in a saucepan and stirring in the flour. Let cook several minutes over medium heat, then add all the hot stock at once. Turn heat low, and simmer 15 to 20 minutes, then add the Madeira and mushrooms and simmer another 5 minutes.

Preheat the broiler. Broil the pieces of lamb till golden on each side and serve with the Madeira sauce.

Serves 4 to 6.

For years I used to look at this unpromising cut of meat and wonder what could be made of it. After finding this recipe in that compendium of New Orleans cooking, The Picayune Original Creole Cookbook *(still in print from the Times-Picayune Publishing Corporation in New Orleans), I prepare lamb breast often. "Epigram" is an apt name for these concentrated nuggets of lambness, and their preparation is really simpler than it sounds.*

BARBECUED LAMB RIBLETS

2 racks lamb breast
   Salt and freshly ground
   pepper

1 cup barbecue sauce of your
   choice

*P*reheat the oven to 400°F.

Cut off any fell and fat from the top of the ribs—the surface should be mostly a thin layer of meat. Also remove as much fat from the bottom as you can. Rub the ribs all over with salt and pepper, then cut into 3- or 4-rib sections.

Lay the sections, meaty side down, in a large shallow roasting pan. Brush well with tangy barbecue sauce and bake for 1 hour, turning once, draining any fat off, and brushing the tops with more sauce.

Serves 4.

There is little meat to lamb ribs, but what there is is choice. This, plus the fact you eat them with your fingers, makes them a family rather than a company matter. I like them so much I often prepare them when I'm home alone—with corn on the cob (another finger food) and crisp slaw and beer.

"RAGOO" OF LAMB AND ASPARAGUS

1 pound boneless lamb, cut in 1 inch cubes from a rare-cooked leg (about 2 cups)	1 bay leaf Salt and freshly ground pepper
4 tablespoons butter Freshly grated nutmeg	¼ teaspoon dried rosemary
3 tablespoons flour	1 pound asparagus, cleaned and cut in 1-inch sections (reserving tips)
¾ pound mushrooms, cleaned and quartered	Juice of ½ lemon
2 cups beef stock, heated	

*I*n a frying pan, sauté the lamb cubes in butter for several minutes over a medium-high flame. The butter should not burn. Remove the cubes with a slotted spoon and scrape some nutmeg over them.

Add the flour and mushrooms to the pan and cook for several minutes, stirring. Add the hot stock and seasonings and simmer 10 minutes, stirring occasionally.

Add the asparagus (all but the tips) and cook 5 minutes. Finally add the tips and lamb and cook another 5 minutes, or until the asparagus is tender. Add the lemon juice and taste for seasoning. Serve immediately.

Serves 4.

This remarkably modern-looking dish is adapted from an old colonial receipt. It is an almost Chinese method for use of leftover lamb, though it may also be made from raw pieces if you cook the meat rather more than you would here. A fine way to serve it is with rice tossed with toasted pine nuts.

FOUR SEASONS GROUND LAMB

1 pound lean ground lamb	⅓ cup pine nuts
1 teaspoon curry powder	1 tablespoon butter
¼ teaspoon ground coriander	1 tablespoon vegetable oil
½ teaspoon paprika	⅓ cup ice water
Salt	Chutney

*P*ut the lamb in a bowl and combine with the spices and salt to taste. Sauté the pine nuts in the butter and oil over medium heat until they are golden, then drain them on paper towels. Mix them into the meat, then add the ice water, bit by bit, until the meat absorbs all of it. Shape into oval patties about an inch thick and refrigerate for 2 hours or more.

These are best cooked over a charcoal fire, but they can also be broiled or sautéed 5 to 7 minutes per side—they should be brown on the outside and still a little pink on the inside. Serve with dollops of chutney.

Serves 4.

Knowing my fondness for ground lamb, a friend sent me this recipe from New York's Four Seasons Restaurant. It is a delight served with something like saffron rice and a green vegetable—or perhaps Deep-fried Eggplant (page 233). Ground lamb is not easy to find, for some reason, for it seems to take a thrifty, smart butcher to realize that all the lamb scraps can be used up this way. And such a delicious way.

Variety Meats

*E*veryone has his terror among the innards, and mine seems to be tongue. For some it is as simple as an aversion to liver, this terror—but always it is irrational, having more to do with texture than actual flavor, or even a repugnance to handling in preparation. No matter, everyone has sweepingly silly dislikes, culinary or not, inexplicable to anyone else. This chapter is for that anyone else. Except for tongue (and brains, for which I could find no clearly home-grown recipe) there is a little of everything to go around, from liver to kidney to sweetbreads to heart.

MY LIVER AND ONIONS

2	tablespoons butter		Tabasco
2	cups sliced onions	4	slices bacon
	Freshly grated nutmeg	4	portions calves' liver
2	tablespoons heavy cream		Lemon juice
	Salt and freshly ground pepper		Minced parsley

*M*elt the butter in a saucepan, add the onions, and when they start to cook, toss and turn the heat as far down as possible. Cover the pan with a tight-fitting lid, and simmer until the onions become mushy—about 45 minutes. (Take care, they should not brown or burn. The onions themselves usually release liquid enough, if the heat is not too high, to stew beautifully.) When quite soft, whirl in a blender or food processor, with a pinch of nutmeg, the cream, salt and pepper to taste, and a drop or two of Tabasco. Return to the saucepan to keep warm.

Fry the bacon until it is crisp, drain it on paper toweling, and crumble. Dry the liver and sauté quickly in the bacon fat so that it is golden outside but still pink in the middle—the time will vary depending on the thickness of the liver.

Sprinkle with a bit of lemon juice and salt and pepper to taste. To serve, place the liver on warm plates, coat each slice with some onion purée, and sprinkle the bacon, then some minced parsley, on top.

Serves 4.

This dish exists as a result of twenty years or so refining the already excellent American dish of liver, onions, and bacon. Here, the three tastes and textures are simultaneous rather than side by side, and I am proud to call it mine. As liver is seldom submitted to guests, however, it remains a secret family triumph. There, I accompany it simply with creamy mashed potatoes and butter, and a bottle of mellow red wine.

LIVER MADAME BÉGUÉ
WITH FRENCH-FRIED SWEET POTATOES

1½ to 2	pounds calves' liver (or chicken livers)	¼	cup minced parsley
		½	cup dry white wine
	Salt and freshly ground pepper	1	tablespoon brandy (optional)
	Pinch of ground mace		Vegetable oil
1	cup chopped green onions with part of tops	1	recipe Deep-fried Sweet Potatoes (page 260)
			Lemon quarters
1	clove garlic, minced		Parsley sprigs

*H*ave your butcher cut the liver in 1-inch-thick slices, or buy a whole piece. Remove any outer skin and tough blood vessels, and cut the liver into 1-inch dice. (Or take chicken livers, cut in half through the separating strand, and prick several times with a fork to allow the marinade to permeate.)

Cover with salt, pepper, mace, green onions, garlic, parsley, wine, and brandy if you use it. Let marinate for an hour or more.

When ready to cook, drain, pat dry with paper towels, and fry in deep oil—it should have begun to smoke (375°F)—for about 1 minute, or until still just pink inside. Test a piece to see.

Drain on paper towels, and keep warm while you prepare the sweet potatoes in the same fat (skimmed). To serve, sprinkle with salt, place attractively on warm plates with lemon quarters, parsley sprigs, and a heap of crisp potatoes.

Serves 4.

A recipe with a curious history. I had passed over Madame Bégué's liver nonchalantly: "Secure a fine bit of calf liver, fresh and of good color. Skin well. Have a quantity of lard in frying pan, well heated. Slice liver in thick pieces. Place in lard and let cook slowly after seasoning with pepper and salt. Let lard cover liver. Simmer on slow fire and when cooked drain off grease and serve on hot plate." Then I found in a Prudence Penny cookbook from 1947 a recipe for Liver à la Madame Bégué that marinated the liver in onion and parsley for several hours before cooking in deep fat, with a garnish of lemon and parsley. Such is the secret life of recipes, that in the process of trying Prudence Penny's version I came on a marinade from the night before, and thought if it's to have onion and parsley—why not the whole shebang? The result is, if somewhat beyond La Bégué, ineffable. Do also try the French-fried sweet potatoes with it since you have the fat right there—they are every bit as good as the liver itself.

COUNTRY LIVER WITH HERBS

1½	pounds calves' or beef liver, sliced ½ inch thick	½	cup flour
	Milk (optional)	6	tablespoons butter
	Salt and freshly ground pepper	2	tablespoons white wine tarragon vinegar
1	teaspoon paprika	½	cup minced parsley
		2	tablespoons minced chives

*T*rim the liver of its tough outer skin and veins, then cover with milk and let sit an hour or so. The milk is not necessary if you use fine calves' liver, but it mellows beef liver considerably.

When ready to cook, drain the liver and pat dry with paper towels. Shake with salt, pepper, paprika, and flour. Melt the butter in a frying pan and sauté the slices over medium heat just until they are lightly browned—not more than 4 to 5 minutes a side. Remove to a hot plate.

Stir the vinegar into the pan juices, scrape up all the brown bits, and stir over a medium flame. Add the parsley and chives, and turn the liver in the sauce several times. Place immediately on warm plates and serve with buttered noodles.

Serves 4.

A farmhouse dish identical to the French aux fines herbes, except there white wine is used rather than vinegar. I find, though, that a delicate tarragon wine vinegar is actually more interesting in the finished product—a very fine dish indeed.

LIVER MARYLAND

2	tablespoons butter		Cayenne
3	slices bacon, cut in ¼-inch strips	1	cup sliced mushrooms
1	medium onion, chopped	½	cup Madeira
1	clove garlic, minced	1	tablespoon catsup
	Minced parsley	1	anchovy fillet, minced (or ½ teaspoon anchovy paste)
	Pinch of dried thyme		
	Pinch of dried summer savory	1½	pounds liver (either calf or beef)
	Pinch of ground cloves		
	Salt and freshly ground pepper		Flour
			Vegetable oil

Melt the butter in a saucepan over medium heat. Add the bacon, onion, and garlic and sauté until the onion is transparent. Add ¼ cup minced parsley, the remaining herbs, spices, and mushrooms, then turn the heat down low, cover the pan, and let simmer gently 1 hour. Check occasionally—the mushrooms should give off enough liquid, but if not add a little Madeira from time to time.

To finish the sauce, add ½ cup Madeira, catsup, and anchovy. Turn up the heat and let the sauce bubble, stirring until thick and rich.

To cook the liver, trim well and slice in bite-sized strips. Shake them in flour, then sauté in hot oil for several minutes—or until golden on the outside but still pink inside. Remove the pieces as they cook and put into the sauce. Heat several minutes and serve sprinkled with parsley.

Serves 4.

For liver fanciers this dish reaches new heights, and one suspects even those who are not might find something to savor in this complex balanced preparation. I don't know why Maryland seems to be such a font of fine cooking, but it was and is and will probably continue to be. The liver needs, of course, some such bland foil as potatoes, noodles, or toast points, and certainly a decent red wine.

CHICKEN LIVERS IN MADEIRA CREAM

1½	pounds chicken livers	1	teaspoon Worcestershire
4	tablespoons butter		sauce
1	tablespoon flour		Few drops of lemon juice
¼	cup dry Madeira	¼	cup minced parsley (or
1	cup heavy cream		chives)
	Salt and freshly ground		
	pepper		

*C*ut the livers in half where the small tendon holds them together, pat dry with paper towels, and sauté in the butter until they are lightly browned but still pink on the inside—about 8 to 10 minutes.

Remove about three fourths of the livers and keep warm. Sprinkle the flour over the livers remaining in the pan and cook a few minutes, stirring. Add the Madeira and cream, stir over low heat till the cream thickens, then purée in a blender or food processor.

Return the purée to the pan, and over low heat add salt, pepper, the Worcestershire, and a few drops of lemon to taste. If the sauce seems too thick, add a little more cream.

Add the reserved livers to the sauce and heat without boiling. To serve, place on warm plates and sprinkle with parsley—or better yet chives if you have them.

Serves 4.

What a suave concoction this is, with the livers making part of the sauce. They can be served with potatoes or noodles, but my favorite is to have them with toast points that have been sautéed in butter till crisp and brown. They are so rich you won't need much else but a vegetable and salad.

HUNTSVILLE DEVILED KIDNEYS

6	lamb kidneys (or 4 veal	1	tablespoon Worcestershire
	kidneys)		sauce
3	tablespoons butter		Cayenne
1	tablespoon Dijon mustard		Toast
2	tablespoons lemon juice		Minced parsley
1	tablespoon finely grated onion		

*I*f the kidneys have a thin filament still covering them, peel it off. Cut them in ¼-inch slices, and cut out any fat or white tissue. Mix the butter, mustard, lemon, onion, Worcestershire, and cayenne to taste in a frying pan set over high heat. When the mixture bubbles, put the kidneys in and toss until all traces of pink are gone—about 5 minutes. Serve immediately on toast, sprinkled with parsley.

Serves 2 (can be easily doubled).

One seldom finds many kidneys at once, but when you do it's easy to freeze them until you've collected enough for a meal. Look them over carefully, and choose only the freshest looking—if they seem even a little darkened or dry, they will have a strong odor and are beyond cooking. This recipe seems to be of British descent (they dote on deviled kidneys of any stripe) and comes from a pretty little ladies' club cookbook with unusually good recipes.

STUFFED LAMB KIDNEYS

6	lamb kidneys	1	egg, beaten
¼	cup finely mined onion		Milk
¼	cup finely minced celery		Salt
1	tablespoon butter		Paprika
1	cup bread crumbs	6	slices bacon
2	tablespoons minced parsley		

*P*reheat the oven to 400°F.

Wash the kidneys, peel off any filament, and slice them in half lengthwise. Cut out the knob of fat at the base of each and set aside.

In a small pan, sauté the onion and celery for several minutes or until limp, in the butter. Combine with the bread crumbs and parsley. Add the egg, and enough milk to make the dressing moist, then season to taste with salt and a pinch of paprika.

Cut the bacon slices in half and spread the dressing evenly over them. Lay each kidney half, uncut side down, on a bacon slice and wrap it up with the stuffing. Secure with a toothpick.

Place on a baking pan and bake 20 minutes. Serve immediately.

Serves 2 (can be easily doubled).

These may be served as a dinner dish, but I prefer them as part of a breakfast or brunch, with eggs and hot buttered toast.

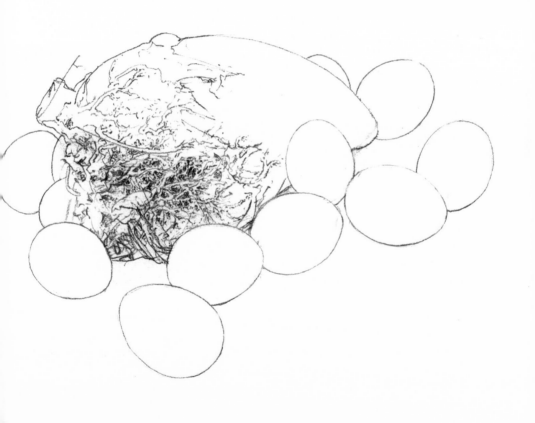

IOWA LEMON-BRAISED LAMB HEARTS

3	lamb hearts		Pinch of dried thyme
3	tablespoons butter		Salt and freshly ground
1	tablespoon flour		pepper
2	thin slices lemon		Pinch of ground mace
1	bay leaf	¼	cup minced parsley

Wash the hearts inside and out, then cut in slices across the grain—removing any of the larger veins, etc. Put the butter in a frying pan over medium heat, and when it sizzles brown the heart slices quickly.

Add the flour and let it become golden, then add the lemon slices, herbs, and spices. Cover with water, stir well, and let it come to a boil. Reduce the heat and simmer gently, covered, for 1½ hours.

When done, most of the liquid should have cooked away, the hearts should be tender and moist, and there should be a rich lemony sauce. To serve, discard the bay leaf and lemon slices, and place on warm plates sprinkled with parsley.

Serves 4.

For those who like the curious texture of heart (beef heart will also do in this recipe), this Midwestern dish will be a welcome one to try with either Purée of Cauliflower (page 228) or Shaker Alabaster (page 247), and of course a full-bodied red wine.

SWEETBREADS COUNTRY STYLE

2	pounds veal sweetbreads		Freshly ground pepper
	Juice of 1 lemon (or 2	¼	teaspoon dried thyme
	tablespoons vinegar)	4	slices bacon, cut in small
	Salt		strips
	Flour	3	tablespoons butter, melted

Soak the sweetbreads for several hours in ice water, changing the water twice. Drain, then soak again in ice water, with the juice of ½ lemon (or 1 tablespoon of the vinegar) and a little salt, for another hour.

Drain, and put in a saucepan with water to cover, the rest of the lemon juice or vinegar, and a little salt. Bring to a boil, lower the heat, and simmer 15 minutes. Drain, then put the sweetbreads in ice water for 15 minutes more. Take them out of the water and pat dry.

Separate the lobes of the sweetbreads, discarding any membrane and connective tissue. Refrigerate until ready to assemble the dish.

Preheat the oven to 450°F.

Shake the sweetbreads in a bag of flour, and put them in a casserole large enough to hold them in a single layer. Sprinkle with salt and pepper to taste, then the thyme. Scatter the bacon strips on top, then dribble with melted butter.

Bake 25 minutes, basting with the pan fat twice during the cooking. When they are done, the bacon and the sweetbreads both will have crisped.

Serves 4.

All that lengthy soaking and draining and soaking and draining, then the careful peeling away of membranes, makes most people steer away from preparing sweetbreads at home—though these same people may seek them out on restaurant menus. It's not really all that difficult, but it does take time and a bit of patience. With all this in mind, and the fact that restaurants want to make as much money out of this labor as possible, most preparations of sweetbreads are so sauced and mushroomed and sherried as to obscure their delicate flavor. But not this Midwestern farm recipe, which presents them at their simple sensuous best. They should be accompanied by similarly delicate flavors—perhaps Georgia Summer Squash Soufflé (page 243) and Colonial Green Beans with Mace (page 223).

VIRGINIA SWEETBREADS WITH HAM AND MUSHROOMS

1½	pounds veal sweetbreads		½	cup heavy cream
	Juice of 1 lemon		1	teaspoon lemon juice
	Salt			Cayenne
½	cup dry sherry		4	slices white bread, trimmed of crusts
4	tablespoons butter			
1	cup sliced mushrooms		4	thin slices ham

*S*oak the sweetbreads for several hours in ice water, changing the water twice. Drain, then soak again in ice water with the juice of a lemon and 1 teaspoon salt for another hour.

Drain, then cook with water to cover and ¼ cup of the sherry, at a simmer, for 15 minutes. Drain, place again in ice water for 15 minutes, then drain again and pat dry.

With your hands, separate the lobes of the sweetbreads, discarding outer membranes and connective tissue. Refrigerate until ready to assemble the dish.

Sauté the sweetbreads in 2 tablespoons of the butter a few minutes until they start to brown, then add the mushrooms and sauté a few minutes more, until the mushrooms are limp. Add the remaining ¼ cup sherry and the cream, and let the mixture boil over high heat until it thickens slightly. Add 1 teaspoon lemon juice and salt and cayenne to taste. Keep warm.

Preheat the oven to 375°F.

Sauté the bread in the remaining 2 tablespoons butter until lightly browned on both sides, and top each with a slice of ham. Place in four individual ramekins, and top with the sweetbreads and their sauce.

Bake 15 minutes, or until the sweetbreads begin to take color and bubble. Serve immediately.

Serves 4.

This fine old recipe is worth all the time and trouble of sweetbread preparation. In the opulent nineteenth-century tradition of dining, these would constitute one course out of many, but these days they will happily accommodate the main course of a meal, with soup, salad, and dessert. They deserve a fine mellow white wine.

Chicken

From the far-off days of my mother or grandmother chopping heads on the chicken-coop block is a long way to remember a flavor, particularly as there were then no comparisons. But I can yet as an adult recall the taste of a chicken ordered in an English village, brought up "on the ground" as we would say, but there one simply ordered "real." And a real bird it was—succulent from crisp skin to pulled wishbone. True, today's chickens cost little, as they leap off assembly lines into every pot, packaged and plucked of any true savor, but there we have them—and fortunately with a galore of past recipes to make even the most tasteless meat a daily shared delight.

NEW ENGLAND BAKED SPRING CHICKEN

1	chicken 3 to 4 pounds	6	sprigs parsley
	Salt and freshly ground	¾	cup dry sherry (or dry
	pepper		Madeira, or dry white
	Butter		wine)
1	large onion	2	slices bacon

*P*reheat the oven to 325°F.

Rub the chicken inside and out with salt, pepper, and butter. Chop the onion coarsely and stuff the cavity with it and the parsley. Put a lump of butter in, and skewer and truss.

Place in a baking pan and pour sherry over. Lay the slices of bacon criss-cross over the breast. Put in the oven and bake 2 hours, basting every 15 minutes or so.

Serves 4.

The slow cooking and basting here produce an extremely succulent, tasty meat. In fact, it is by far the best way to cook chicken for any dish calling for such, as the flesh is so beautifully textured (you can substitute chicken stock for the wine if you so wish, for this). Roast chicken can be served very simply with potatoes and carrots cooked round it, being doused also in the juices—or, if you feel extravagant, with whole cooked artichoke bottoms glazed in the juices toward the end, then filled with sautéed chicken livers.

CHICKEN STUFFED WITH CRAB APPLES

1	chicken (3 to 4 pounds)	1	onion slice
	Salt and freshly ground	2	slices bacon
	pepper	¼	cup dry sherry (or Madeira)
	Butter		Saffron rice
1	jar spiced crab apples (home		Toasted almonds
	style, not the bright red		
	ones)		

*P*reheat the oven to 325°F.

Rub the chicken inside and out with salt, pepper, and butter. Put a lump of butter inside the cavity, with the giblets, a slice of onion, and as many crab apples as will fit.

Skewer and truss the bird, and crisscross the bacon over its breast. Place in a roaster with ½ cup of the juice from the crab apples, and the sherry or Madeira.

Bake for 2 hours, basting every 15 minutes with the juices. During the last 15 minutes place the rest of the crab apples around the chicken to glaze and heat.

To serve, remove the bacon and place the chicken on a bed of saffron rice. Sprinkle with toasted almonds and garnish with the hot crab apples.

Serves 4.

Needless to say, this makes a spectacular company dish—and of course it may be carved in the kitchen, if you wish, before placing on the rice, to save any despair at carving before guests. The process can also be adapted for duckling, though the crab apple juice and sherry should be added to the pan after most of the fat has been rendered from the duck, and the bacon should be omitted.

PENNSYLVANIA CHICKEN
STUFFED WITH SAUERKRAUT AND APPLES

1	chicken (3 to 4 pounds)	½	cup chopped celery
	Salt and freshly ground	3	cups sauerkraut
	pepper	2	tart apples, peeled, cored,
4	tablespoons butter		and grated
1	medium onion, chopped	1	tablespoon caraway seeds

*P*reheat the oven to 350°F.

Rub the chicken inside and out with salt and pepper. Melt the butter in a large frying pan. Sauté the onion and celery in it till they are limp.

Place the kraut in a colander and run water over it in order to remove some of its sharpness. Drain thoroughly and add to the onion mixture. Add the apples and caraway seeds, salt and pepper to taste, and toss over medium heat for a few minutes.

Remove from the flame, and when cool enough to handle, stuff the chicken loosely, truss it, and rub with butter. Put the remaining dressing in a casserole or small roasting pan and nestle the chicken into it.

Tuck the giblets into the sauerkraut. Cover and bake for 1¼ hours, then uncover and bake another 45 minutes to brown.

Serves 4.

This hearty dish should be accompanied by a full-bodied, fragrant white wine, and either boiled potatoes sprinkled with parsley or My Grandmother's Drop Noodles (page 263).

MY BUTTERMILK FRIED CHICKEN

1	chicken, cut-up	1	bay leaf
	Buttermilk		Salt and freshly ground
¼	cup minced parsley		pepper
1	small onion		Flour
1	stalk celery, cut up		Vegetable oil
1	carrot, cut up		

*R*emove the wing tips from the chicken and put together with its neck and giblets. Marinate the chicken in buttermilk to cover, and minced parsley, for several hours.

Take the trimmings and giblets and place in a saucepan with water to cover, the vegetables, bay leaf, and salt and pepper to taste. Simmer for 2 hours, then drain and reserve the stock.

To cook the chicken, mix flour with salt and pepper. Without wiping the marinade off the chicken, shake the pieces in seasoned flour and lay aside on waxed paper.

Over medium-high heat, fry the chicken, in batches, in ½ inch hot oil till each piece is golden brown. As they are cooked, lift out into a baking dish that will hold all in one layer.

Preheat the oven to 300°F.

Pour enough buttermilk around the chicken to come up to less than half the depth of the chicken. Bake, uncovered, for 1½ hours, or until quite tender and crisp on top.

When done, remove the chicken and keep warm. To the pan of coddled drippings, add some of the chicken stock, stirring and scraping over high heat. Add this to a blender or food processor and whirl till smooth.

Place back in the pan and cook over medium heat, adding stock and stirring, until the sauce is the consistency of thick cream.

Serve the chicken, in a pool of the sauce, on warm plates. Pass the rest of the sauce in a sauceboat at table, with hot biscuits.

Serves 4.

My fried chicken is the horror of some purists, who insist that it is neither fried nor has the "right" kind of gravy. That there are as many ways of frying chicken as there are cooks is no argument to such people, and I can only say that this is the way I fry chicken. It is particularly savory, with much delicate crust on top and a creamy underside. It also makes a good sauce I think much better than floury milk gravy. If you wish, it may be served with the coddled drippings as they come from the pan, rather than the sauce—it may be less pretty, but this residue is wonderful spread on biscuits.

ALABAMA FRIED CHICKEN WITH MILK GRAVY AND FRIED BISCUITS

1	chicken, cut up		Flour
1	egg		Fat for deep frying
½	cup milk	½	cup chicken stock, heated
	Salt and freshly ground	1½	cups milk
	pepper	1	recipe biscuit dough

Wash and dry the chicken. Beat the egg with the milk and some salt and pepper. Dip the chicken in this, then shake in flour. Put in refrigerator to "set" for 30 minutes or more.

Preheat the oven to 350°F.

In a frying pan or deep fat cooker, bring 1 inch fat to 350°F. Fry the chicken, first on one side, then the other, till golden brown on both.

Place in the oven for 20 minutes while you make the gravy and fried biscuits.

To prepare the gravy, drain off the fat from the pan, putting 2 tablespoons of it and any fried bits in a saucepan. Add 2 tablespoons flour and cook, stirring, until golden over medium heat. Add the stock, milk, and salt and pepper to taste. Cook, stirring, until the gravy thickens, then turn the fire low and let bubble 10 minutes, or until ready to serve. If it gets too thick, add some more milk.

To prepare the biscuits, heat the deep fat to 375°F. Roll out the biscuit dough ¼ inch thick and cut into strips 1 x ½ inch. Drop these strips, in batches, into the hot fat and fry until golden brown on the bottom. Turn and fry until the other side is brown. Lift out with a slotted spoon onto paper towels, and salt lightly.

To serve, place the pieces of chicken on warm plates with a heap of fried biscuits. Pass the milk gravy separately.

Serves 4.

This one is for purists, not to mention those who fancy fried biscuits.

SMITHFIELD CHICKEN

1 chicken, cut up	2 cups heavy cream, heated
1 medium onion, chopped	Freshly grated nutmeg
1 carrot, sliced	2 cups bread crumbs
1 stalk celery, sliced	½ cup minced green onions
2 sprigs parsley	with part of tops
2 whole cloves	2 tablespoons minced parsley
4 peppercorns	1 teaspoon dried summer
Salt	savory
2 tablespoons butter	Freshly ground pepper
2 tablespoons flour	8 thin slices Smithfield ham

*S*tew the chicken in water to cover with the onion, carrot, celery, parsley, cloves, peppercorns, and salt to taste for 1 hour, or until the chicken is tender.

Remove from the broth, and when cool remove all the flesh and discard the bones and skin; strain the broth and reserve. Cut the meat into bite-sized pieces and place in a baking dish that can be brought to table.

Melt the butter in a saucepan, stir in the flour, and cook over low heat for several minutes, stirring. Add the hot cream all at once, then cook, stirring, until the sauce thickens and is smooth. Add salt to taste, some nutmeg, and let simmer 15 to 20 minutes over very low heat.

Preheat the oven to 300°F.

Pour the sauce over the chicken and let stand while you make the stuffing. Mix the bread crumbs with the green onions, parsley, savory, and salt and pepper. Add just enough of the reserved broth to make the stuffing hold together. Reserve ¼ cup of the stuffing, and divide the rest into 8 heaps.

Place the stuffing in the center of each slice of ham and roll the slices around in the shape of peaked croquettes. Nestle these down into the chicken in an attractive arrangement.

Sprinkle the reserved stuffing on top and bake at 30 minutes, or until the sauce begins to bubble and brown lightly. Serve immediately.

Serves 4.

When Smithfield Ham is available in your specialty store, seize on it, for this is certainly one of our most distinguished chicken dishes. It is particularly gracious to modern tasteless birds, which are too bland for most roasting and stuffing treatment. The ham gives a savor to the whole that is well worth its expense. Other cured hams can be used, certainly—Westphalian Ham particularly makes a splendid, if not authentic, substitution.

COLONIAL CHICKEN PUDDING

1	chicken, cut up	¼	teaspoon dried thyme
1	medium onion, chopped	1	bay leaf
1	carrot, sliced		Flour
1	stalk celery, sliced	4	tablespoons butter
2	sprigs parsley	3	eggs
	Salt and freshly ground	1	cup milk
	pepper	2	tablespoons butter, melted

*T*ake the back, neck, wing tips, and giblets (except the liver) of the chicken, and cover with water in a kettle to cover. Add the onion, carrot, celery, parsley, and seasonings, then simmer about 1 hour. Strain and reserve the stock.

Shake the pieces of chicken with flour seasoned with salt and pepper. Heat the butter in a frying pan, and sauté the chicken until brown-gold all over. Add enough stock to come up halfway on the chicken, cover the pan tightly, and cook gently 45 minutes, or until the chicken is tender.

Preheat the oven to 450°F.

Transfer the chicken pieces with a slotted spoon to a greased baking dish, 1½ inches deep or more, and large enough to hold all the chicken in a single layer. Reserve the juices in the pan.

Make a batter by sifting 1¼ cups flour with ½ teaspoon salt into a bowl. Beat the eggs until frothy, pour the milk and melted butter into them, and mix well into the flour till the batter is smooth. Pour this over the chicken, making sure all the pieces are covered as evenly as possible.

Pop immediately into the hot oven. Bake 15 minutes at 450°F, then lower the heat to 350°F and continue baking for another 20 to 25 minutes, or until the topping puffs up and is browned—like a Yorkshire pudding.

While the pudding bakes, scrape the juices from the chicken pan into a blender or food processor, whirl, and return to the pan. Cook down gently, and if it is necessary, thicken with a bit of soft butter worked with flour.

Serve the sauce separately in a sauceboat, as you bring the pudding to table.

Serves 4.

Considering this pudding seems a common one in colonial days, and is so particularly delicious, it is curious that it is seldom served these days. It is much more interesting than any of the various pot pies, etc., and is quite a simple dish to master. It makes even a quite ample company meal with good white wine, a fresh light soup before, an interesting salad or vegetable after, and any outstanding dessert.

SHAKER CHICKEN IN CIDER CREAM

1	chicken, cut up		Salt and freshly ground
4	tablespoons butter		pepper
½ to ¾	cup hard cider	1	cup heavy cream
	Grated rind of 1 lemon		

*I*n a large frying pan, sauté the chicken in the butter over a medium flame until it is golden on both sides. Add ½ cup cider, then cover the pan and cook over low heat for 30 to 40 minutes, or until tender.

Check while cooking, and if the chicken tends to get dry, add more cider. When done, lift the pieces out with a slotted spoon onto a warm platter and keep warm in the oven. Add enough cider so there is about ¼ cup liquid in the pan, along with the lemon rind and salt and pepper to taste.

Add the cream, turn the heat up high, and cook, stirring with a whisk, until the sauce thickens slightly. Pour over the chicken and serve.

Serves 4.

A delicious dish reminiscent of Normandy in its use of cider. If hard cider is not available, unsweetened apple juice is acceptable—with a squeeze or so of extra lemon juice, or a dash of Calvados, added along with the grated rind. It should be served with Fried Apple Rings (page 220) and a fragrant chilled white wine.

CHICKEN CHARLESTON

1	chicken, cut up	2½	teaspoons curry powder
4	tablespoons butter	1	cup heavy cream
4	cups chopped onion	⅓	cup dark rum (or brandy)
1	clove garlic, minced		Hot cooked rice
	Salt and freshly ground		
	pepper		

Wash and dry the chicken pieces. Melt the butter in a frying pan and sauté the chicken lightly. Lift the pieces onto a plate. Add the onion and garlic to the pan and cook over medium heat until straw colored. Sprinkle with salt and pepper. Place the chicken pieces, skin side down, into the onion, cover, and cook slowly on top of the stove for 15 minutes.

Remove the cover, turn the chicken, and cook slowly, uncovered, 20 minutes more. Add water if it gets too dry. Remove the chicken from the pan when its juices run golden when stuck with a fork, and keep warm.

Sprinkle curry powder over the onion and cook a few minutes, stirring, then add the cream and rum. Boil down, stirring, until the sauce is slightly thickened. Taste for seasoning, pour over the chicken, and serve with fluffy rice.

Serves 4.

This Charleston extravaganza is one of my all time favorites to serve company. It is rich and delicately flavored (neither the curry nor rum should be so evident as to overwhelm either the chicken or onion flavors) as well as both easy and elegant. The original recipe had twice as much butter and cream, but that was perhaps gilding the lily too much! It is at its best served with Thomas Jefferson's Pilau (page 266) rather than plain boiled rice.

CHICKEN IN GREEN CORN

1	chicken, cut up		Salt and freshly ground
2	tablespoons butter		pepper
6 to 8	ears of corn	½	cup heavy cream
		6	slices bacon, cut in half

Preheat the oven to 325°F.

Wash and dry the chicken pieces, then sauté until golden in the butter. Place the pieces in a casserole of a size to hold them all nicely in a single layer, then add salt and pepper.

Scrape the corn kernels into a bowl with the sharp side of a knife, then scrape the "milk" out with the dull side; you should have 4 cups. Salt and pepper this to taste, and pour over the chicken..

Add the cream and place the bacon in a pattern over the top. Put in the oven, covered with foil or a lid, for 30 minutes. Then uncover and cook 30 more, or until the bacon crisps and curls.

Serves 4.

Green corn means always fresh young corn rushed from the field, but any fresh market corn is fine here. It is a dish to come to over and over for family, served with cole slaw and hot biscuits. (But one has an idea that secretly company would sometimes prefer such homely fare to more elegant dishes.)

ALMOND CHICKEN CREOLE

1 chicken, cut up	2 cups drained and chopped
Flour	canned tomatoes
Salt and freshly ground	½ cup beer
pepper	¼ cup dried currants (or raisins)
Olive oil	½ cup toasted blanched,
2 cups chopped onion	slivered almonds
1 clove garlic, minced	Saffron rice
½ cup chopped green pepper	

Rinse and dry the chicken pieces. Shake in flour seasoned with salt and pepper. Heat enough olive oil to cover the bottom of your frying pan and brown the pieces over medium heat until golden on all sides. Remove with a slotted spoon and keep warm.

Add the onion and garlic to the oil, then the green pepper, and cook till soft. Add the tomatoes and bring to a boil. Replace the chicken in the bubbling vegetables, and add beer and salt to taste.

Spoon the sauce over and around the chicken, cover, and simmer 45 minutes, turning the chicken several times. Add currants or raisins the last 10 minutes of cooking. If necessary, this may be kept warm some time before serving.

To serve, place the chicken in a ring of saffron rice and sprinkle with toasted almonds.

Serves 4.

If it had a pinch of curry, this would be called "Country Captain"—I find it simply delicious as is. Frankly this sauce Creole (for that is what it is) seems the best of all tomato sauces, perhaps because of the beer. With the presentation on a bed of yellow rice, and sprinkled with almonds, it makes a fine, inexpensive company dish. For that it is pleasant to begin with some such first course as Watercress Salad à la Germaine (page 285), with perhaps hot rolls or homemade individual loaves of bread, then the chicken itself served with a fine California Chardonnay, and lastly a dessert such as Roanoke Rum Cream (page 382).

CHICKEN FRICASSEE

1	chicken, cut up	⅓	cup minced parsley
	Salt and freshly ground	1	medium onion, chopped
	pepper	2	cloves garlic
1	bay leaf	4	tablespoons butter
6	peppercorns	¼	cup flour
2	whole cloves	2	egg yolks
1	teaspoon dried summer savory	1	cup heavy cream, heated
1	teaspoon dried tarragon		

*R*emove any fat from the chicken and render it by placing it in a small saucepan with some water and letting it cook down gently 15 minutes, or until the water is cooked away and only liquid fat and golden nuggets are left. Take out the nuggets and measure 3 tablespoons of the fat into a frying pan.

Wash and dry the chicken, sprinkle with salt and pepper, then brown thoroughly in the fat over medium heat. Put in a stew pot, add boiling water to cover, the spices, herbs, and onion.

While the water comes to a boil, put the cloves of garlic in hot water to cover and simmer gently for a few minutes. Drain, slip off their skins, and add them to the pot. Cook gently an hour, adding salt to taste the last 10 minutes.

Remove the chicken pieces with a slotted spoon and keep warm. Strain the stock and measure—there should be 3 cups. If not, add more chicken stock to make it up.

In a saucepan, melt the butter, stir in the flour, and cook several minutes, stirring. Pour 1 cup of the stock in. Simmer a bit, stirring till smooth, then add the rest of the stock, stirring again till free from lumps. Cook, uncovered, over low heat 10 minutes.

Beat the egg yolks in a bowl, then add the hot cream gradually, stirring constantly. Add this to the thickened stock, along with the chicken pieces, and heat slowly without allowing the mixture to boil. Serve with homemade dumplings, or noodles.

Serves 4.

What a lost world the word fricassee calls up! It is still the Sundayest of Sunday dishes, suave, rich, and satisfying to the soul as well as body.

CHICKEN CHILE VERDE TAMALE PIE

1	chicken (2½ to 3 pounds)	1	can (4 ounces) mild green chilies, drained and chopped
1	onion, sliced		
1	clove garlic, flattened		
	Salt	2	jalapeño peppers (bottled en escabeche), seeded and minced
6	peppercorns		
1	bay leaf		
½	teaspoon dried oregano	¼	cup flour
1	cup chopped green onions, with part of tops	1¼	teaspoons sugar
			Juice of ½ lemon
1	clove garlic, minced	3	cups milk, scalded
5	tablespoons minced parsley	1	cup cornmeal (preferably stone-ground)
2	tablespoons minced fresh coriander (optional)		
		1	tablespoon butter
1	medium green pepper, seeded and grated (discarding the skin)	3	eggs, separated
		¼	cup pumpkin seeds (or toasted pine nuts)

*E*arly in the day, or the day before, boil the chicken in water to cover with the sliced onion, garlic, salt to taste, peppercorns, bay leaf, and oregano for 45 minutes. Let chill in the stock. When the fat has hardened, remove and save it. Remove the flesh from the chicken, melt the stock down, and strain it into a large pan. Boil the stock down, uncovered, till you have about 4 cups.

In another suacepan, sauté the green onions and minced garlic in 2 table-spoons of the chicken fat for several minutes, then add, one by one, 2 table-spoons of the parsley, coriander, green pepper, green chilies, and jalapeños. Cook 5 minutes, stirring now and again. Stir in the flour and let cook another 5 minutes, then add the stock all at once and stir until smooth over high heat. Add ¼ teaspoon of the sugar and the lemon juice, then taste for season-ing. Let simmer, uncovered, 20 minutes, then remove from the fire, add the chicken meat, and pour into a 12 x 9-inch casserole.

Preheat the oven to 350°F.

Sprinkle the cornmeal over the hot milk in a saucepan and stir 5 minutes over medium heat, or until the mixture is smooth and thick. Stir in 1 tea-spoon salt, remaining 1 teaspoon sugar, and butter, then the remaining 3 ta-blespoons parsley. Stir in the egg yolks, one by one, then whip the whites stiff (but not dry) and fold carefully in.

Spoon the tamale mixture in dollops over the chicken mixture and spread out as far as you can to the edges. Sprinkle pumpkin seeds or pine nuts over the pie and bake 40 to 45 minutes, or until golden, puffed, and bubbly.

Serves 6.

There are as many tamale pies as cooks in the Southwest, most simply a meat-chili mixture, perhaps with beans and some cheese, nestled in a cornmeal mush. As you can see, this both breaks and keeps the rules. It sounds like a lot of work, but it is the most interesting way I've ever found to stretch one chicken over six people. It should be accompanied by a fine beer rather than wine, and a sound green salad.

BREAST OF CHICKEN MAITLAND

2	whole chicken breasts, halved	2	teaspoons flour
1	cup chicken stock	1	teaspoon Worcestershire
	Salt and freshly ground		sauce
	pepper	1	tablespoon dry sherry
¼	cup sausage meat	½	cup pecan halves
4	green onions with part of		
	tops, chopped		

Take the skin off the chicken breasts and lay them, flesh side down, in a saucepan large enough to hold them in one layer. Pour the stock over, and sprinkle with salt and pepper to taste. Bring to a boil, cover, then lower the heat and cook gently 25 to 30 minutes.

Remove the breasts and keep warm; reserve the stock. In a small pan, fry the sausage until it releases its fat. Add the green onions and cook together until the onions start to brown. Add the flour and cook another few minutes, stirring. Scrape into a blender.

Add the stock to the blender and whirl over high speed, then place back in the pan and cook over medium heat until it thickens. Add the Worcestershire and sherry, then taste for seasoning. Just before serving, add the pecan halves to the sauce and pour over the breasts.

Serves 4.

An unusual dish, and an adaptation of a specialty from Dunbar's in New Orleans. It is relatively simple to prepare and has an especially rich flavor from the unexpected (and here almost unidentifiable) bits of sausage. It can be accompanied by a starch if you like, or as a course on its own, garnished with watercress and accompanied by a fine white wine.

NEBRASKA CHICKEN CUTLETS

2	whole chicken breasts, halved, boned, and skinned	Fine dry bread crumbs
	Juice of 1½ lemons	Vegetable oil
6	tablespoons flour	4 tablespoons butter, melted
	Salt and freshly ground pepper	1 teaspoon paprika
1	egg, beaten	Parsley
		Lemon wedges

*P*ound each boned breast thin between waxed paper with a rolling pin. Put on a plate, pour the juice of 1 lemon over, and let marinate an hour, covered, in the refrigerator.

To assemble for cooking, dredge each breast in flour mixed with salt and pepper, dip that in beaten egg, then in bread crumbs. (These can also sit awhile in the refrigerator to "set" the coating if you have time.)

Heat oil in a frying pan to the depth of about ⅛ inch and fry the cutlets 2 to 3 minutes on a side, or until golden. Remove to warm plates and pour over them the 4 tablespoons melted butter mixed with the juice of ½ lemon and paprika. Garnish with parsley and more lemon wedges.

Serves 4.

Now that both price and quality of veal are in question, this is a good compromise for those who like their schnitzel. The cutlets may be sauced, in fact, in any of your favorite ways for veal scallops or schnitzel—anchovies or capers are particularly good additions to the above butter lemon sauce.

BREAST OF CHICKEN, DELTA STYLE

2   whole chicken breasts,
    halved, boned, and
    skinned
½   cup dark rum
½   cup fresh bread crumbs

Salt and freshly ground
    pepper
⅓   cup clarified butter
½   cup chutney
Parsley
Lemon wedges

*P*ound each boned breast thin between waxed paper with a rolling pin. Place in a shallow dish and marinate in the rum for an hour or more in the refrigerator.

To cook, drain the breasts, reserving the rum, and roll in bread crumbs seasoned with salt and pepper. Fry 2 to 3 minutes per side in clarified butter. Mix the chutney with 4 tablespoons of the rum marinade and top the breasts with it. Garnish with parsley and lemon wedges.

Serves 4.

These are well accompanied by Thomas Jefferson's Pilau (page 266), or simply buttered rice tossed with toasted pine nuts as I first had the dish. Any chutney will do, but homemade peach chutney is used in the South. And certainly it deserves a chilled, full-bodied white wine.

Domestic Game

A couple of centuries of wilderness behind us, there are many secrets of our savage larder that could have turned up here: venison hamburger, ragoûts of tiny quail and pies of prairie chicken, pheasant slumgullion, roast porcupine, possum grilled with sassafras twigs. Squirrel and turtle, canvasback and antelope—anything that moved (and could be shot or netted) was eaten. It is in this field our amateur cook really shines in inventiveness and native presumption. But I've had to content myself, like the most of us who do not hunt, with what we can catch in the market in the way of domesticated game: duck, goose, rabbit, a holiday turkey breast for a small family, and a few uses for the rest of that national favorite. Besides those listed here, other fine dishes that use leftover turkey are Ancestral Turkey Rice Soup (page 22), Turkey Oyster Gumbo (page 34), and Turkey Pilau with Walnuts (page 177).

ROAST LONG ISLAND DUCKLING

2   ducklings (4 to 5 pounds
    each)
2   carrots, scraped and sliced
2   onions, sliced
1   stalk celery, trimmed and
    sliced
1   sprig parsley
1   bay leaf

Pinch of dried thyme
Salt and freshly ground
    pepper
1   lemon, halved
    Celery leaves
1   tablespoon cold butter
1   recipe Chestnut Purée (page
    229)

*P*reheat the oven to 450°F.

Remove the wing tips and cut the necks from the ducks. Add them to a kettle of water, along with the giblets (except the livers—use these for an appetizer). Add half the carrots and onions, the celery stalk, parsley, bay leaf, thyme, and salt and pepper to taste. Bring to a boil, skim, and simmer while the duck is cooking.

Rub the ducks inside and out with the lemon, salt them lightly, and place a few slices of onion and some celery leaves in the cavities. Prick the skin all around the thighs, backs, and lower breasts with a sharp fork. Put the ducks, breasts up, in a roasting pan, scatter the remaining onions and carrots around, and place in the oven.

Immediately turn the heat down to 350°F, and after 15 minutes turn the ducks on their sides. Half an hour later, turn on the other side. Fifteen minutes before done, put breast up and salt the ducks—they should roast about an hour and a half, or until the juice runs from a faint rose to pale yellow when you prick a thigh. Remove the fat from the pan as it accumulates with a bulb baster.

When done, remove the ducks and place on a serving platter; keep warm. Remove all the fat from the roasting pan and add 1½ cups strained duck stock. Boil this down, mashing the vegetables, until it has reduced by half. Remove from the heat and whisk in 1 tablespoon cold butter to finish the sauce.

To serve, carve the ducks and place on warm plates with a pile of Chestnut Purée (page 229) and perhaps fresh Cranberry-Orange Relish (page 311) in an orange cup.

Serves 4.

Domesticated ducks are an entirely different bird from the wild duck—they have been bred so they have an incredible amount of fat that must be drained off as they cook. However, they are more tender, so the legs can be eaten as well as the breasts, and when cooked properly so most of the fat is rendered from the skin, the skin itself is crisply succulent. Serving them with two contrasting purées makes a handsome preparation, and you will want to serve a vintage red wine.

NEW ORLEANS
ROAST DUCK WITH SAUCE PARADIS

1	duckling (4 to 5 pounds)		Cayenne
1	carrot, sliced	5	tablespoons butter
1	small onion, sliced	¼	cup flour
1	sprig parsley	½	cup dry Madeira
1	bay leaf	3	tablespoons red currant jelly
	Dried thyme	1	cup green seedless grapes
	Salt and freshly ground pepper		

*R*emove the wing tips and cut the neck from the duck. Place them, and all the giblets but the liver (reserve this for later), in a kettle with the carrot, onion, parsley, bay leaf, pinch of thyme, salt and pepper to taste, and water to cover. Simmer an hour or so, then strain. You will need 2 cups stock, so if necessary boil it down so the stock will be rich as possible.

Preheat the oven to 475°F.

Rub the duck inside and out with salt, pepper, cayenne, and dried thyme. Prick skin all around the thighs, back, and lower breast with a fork. Place, breast up, in a roasting pan and roast 20 minutes, then remove and sprinkle with more pepper, cayenne, and thyme. Lower the heat to 350°F and roast the duck 1½ hours, basting frequently with its own fat (use only a little for this, discarding fat as it accumulates.) During the last 20 minutes, turn the heat back up to 475°F. Dust the duck again with pepper and cayenne, baste, and return to the oven to crisp.

To make the sauce, melt 4 tablespoons of the butter in a saucepan, and when it bubbles add the flour. Cook, stirring, over medium heat, then lower the heat and cook until the flour becomes straw gold. Add 2 cups stock and stir until the mixture thickens and becomes silky. Add the Madeira, jelly, and cayenne to taste, then stir until the jelly melts.

Chop the reserved liver in tiny dice, and toss quickly over high heat in the remaining 1 tablespoon butter. Cook only about a minute or so—the flesh should still be slightly pink on the inside. Add to the sauce along with the grapes, turn off the heat, and let sit, covered, until needed.

To serve, cut the duck in half and ladle the sauce over.

Serves 2.

It has become fashionable to serve duckling pretty rare these days, and this recipe will seem terribly overcooked to such folk. However, this method results in extremely tender meat, and an exceptionally crisp skin. The sauce is also a fine one—the original calls for truffles, which is very elegant, but I think the duck liver does just as well, since canned truffles don't really have much flavor. You'll want an excellent red wine, and perhaps yeast rolls, to accompany the feast.

THOMAS JEFFERSON'S SALMI OF DUCK

1	duckling (4 to 5 pounds)		Salt and freshly ground
1	duck liver		pepper
3	tablespoons butter	½	pound mushrooms, sliced
½	cup Madeira		Lemon juice
			Minced parsley

*R*oast the duck as described in Roast Long Island Duckling (page 160), reserving all the giblets. When done, cool and strip off all meat from the carcass and reserve. If you wish, add the carcass (not the skin) to the kettle to cook along with the giblets (except the liver) at this time.

When the stock (make the stock using the same vegetables as in Roast Long Island Duckling) is flavorful, strain it and make the duck sauce ahead of time so the salmi can be put together at the last minute (in fact this is a splendid dish to be made in a chafing dish at table).

To put the dish together, sauté the duck liver in 2 tablespoons of the butter. When it is golden but still pink inside, mash it to a paste in the pan. Add the Madeira and salt and pepper to taste. In another pan, toss the mushrooms in the remaining 1 tablespoon butter till they start to give out juices, and add them as well. Add the duck stock, the duck meat, and a few drops of lemon juice and some minced parsley. Heat through and serve.

Serves 3 to 4.

A salmi was often prepared in the days when there was plenty of leftover game— wild duck, pheasant, quail, etc. Though few of us now have game at all, not to mention any left, it is still a carefree way to serve duck, since all the preparation is accomplished well before company arrives and no carving is involved. I like to serve it with tiny fresh peas or green beans, and Saratoga Chips (page 254).

STUFFED ROAST GOOSE WITH CRANBERRY ICE IN ORANGE SHELLS

1 goose (8 to 9 pounds)	1 apple, peeled, cored, and grated
1 small onion, sliced	¾ cup chopped cooked prunes
1 carrot, sliced	½ cup peeled and chopped cooked chestnuts
1 stalk celery, sliced	
1 sprig parsley	¼ cup chopped celery leaves
1 bay leaf	¼ cup minced parsley
Pinch of dried thyme	1 fresh sage leaf, minced
Salt and freshly ground pepper	Salt and freshly ground pepper
½ lemon	1 recipe Cranberry Ice in Orange Shells (page 389)
2 onions, chopped	
3 cups diced crustless bread	

*P*reheat the oven to 425°F.

Trim wing tips from goose, and put with the giblets (not the liver—sauté that in butter and chop for the stuffing), sliced onion, carrot, celery, parsley sprig, bay leaf, thyme, and salt and pepper to taste in a large kettle. Add water to cover, bring to a boil, skim, and simmer while you cook the goose.

Remove any loose fat from the cavity of the goose. Prick it around the thighs, back, and lower breast with a sharp fork. Rub the cavity with lemon. Put any extra goose fat you can pull off in a small saucepan, and cook it over low heat until you have rendered at least 2 tablespoons of fat. Use this to sauté the chopped onions until they are transparent.

Put the onions and bread cubes in a bowl, and add the rest of the ingredients up to the Cranberry Ice. Add enough stock to moisten the dressing lightly.

Stuff the goose and truss it. Cook exactly as you do duck (see Roast Long Island Duckling, page 160), but baste it every 15 minutes with some boiling water to help remove excess fat. Roast the goost at 425°F 20 minutes, then lower the heat to 375°F and cook 20 to 25 minutes per pound. It is done when the drumsticks move slightly and the juices run pale yellow when you prick the thigh with a sharp fork.

When done, remove the goose to a serving platter and keep warm while you prepare the sauce. Drain all fat from the roasting pan (being careful to save it—goose fat is excellent for cooking potatoes, and will keep for months in the refrigerator).

Strain the stock, add it to the roasting pan, and boil down, uncovered, to half. You may wish to cut up the giblets and add them, or to whisk in some cold butter off the heat to give the sauce extra body.

To serve, carve the goose and arrange on warm plates with some of the sauce over, a heap of dressing, and cranberry ice in orange shells beside each portion.

Serves 6.

As it becomes increasingly difficult to find a turkey that tastes at all real, and has never been frozen, I turn more and more to goose for holidays. The cranberry ice makes an attractive and refreshing contrast, rather than the usual cranberry relish. You need only hot rolls and a fine bottle of red wine to complete your feast.

RABBIT TARRAGON

1	rabbit (2 to 3 pounds), cut up	1	teaspoon Dijon mustard
	Salt	½	cup heavy cream
	Flour	¼	cup canned beef bouillon (or
½	cup butter		concentrated stock)
⅔	cup dry white wine		Sprig of fresh tarragon or
4	juniper berries (optional)		parsley
1	teaspoon dried tarragon (or 2 tablespoons chopped fresh)		

*R*eserving the liver, shake the rabbit in lightly salted flour. Sauté in the butter in a large frying pan, over medium heat. Be careful not to let the butter burn. Turn each piece till golden, then add the wine and juniper berries, and let it bubble up. Cover tightly, turn the heat to low, and simmer gently 40 minutes.

While the rabbit cooks, mix the tarragon into the mustard, then slowly incorporate the cream. Let this sit to gather flavor. Take the liver, chop it into tiny dice, and sauté in a bit more butter for only a minute or two over high heat. This may sit, also, till needed.

To assemble the dish, add the tarragon cream to the rabbit, mix all around to flavor the meat, and let simmer, uncovered, 5 more minutes. Remove the rabbit pieces to a warm plate. Turn heat up high, add the beef bouillon, and boil the pan juices down, uncovered, till the sauce is silky. Strain it in a fine sieve to remove the tarragon and juniper.

Finally, scrape the liver pieces into the pan, add the strained sauce, and heat for several minutes. To serve, glaze the rabbit with the sauce and decorate with a sprig of fresh tarragon or parsley.

Serves 4.

Inspired by a simple rabbit dish with tarragon I dined on in France years ago, this dish has taken on new characteristics through many subsequent cookings. It is best, of course, with fresh tarragon, but quite tasty enough without. I like to serve it with the same white wine it has been cooked in rather than a red, but that is up to you. Either Zucchini-stuffed Baked Potatoes (page 258), or Portland Potatoes (page 259) make a fine partner.

CAJUN RABBIT WITH ORANGE RICE

1	rabbit (2 to 3 pounds), cut up	2	tablespoons butter
	Red wine	1	tablespoon vegetable oil
2	cloves garlic, flattened	1	tablespoon flour
	Pinch of dried thyme		Salt and freshly ground
1	bay leaf		pepper
	Sprinkle of ground allspice		Orange Rice (page 265)
1	slice orange peel		

*P*ut the rabbit to marinate in red wine to cover, the garlic, thyme, bay leaf, allspice, and orange peel. Leave it for 24 hours, turning once or twice during the time.

When ready to cook, remove the rabbit from the marinade (save 1 cup of it), and pat dry with absorbent paper towels. Let the butter and oil sputter in a frying pan, then add the rabbit pieces, and sauté till golden on each side over medium heat.

Remove the rabbit with a slotted spoon and add the flour to the pan. Whisk it into the fat till golden, then add the reserved 1 cup marinade. Stir until thickened and smooth, then put the rabbit back in the pan. Cover and simmer over low heat 45 minutes, or until tender. Turn once or twice during the cooking, and when a fork pierces the meat easily, remove and keep warm in the oven.

Rapidly boil the sauce down over high heat till it coats a spoon, and glaze the rabbit with it. Serve in a ring of orange rice.

Serves 4.

This recipe I would enter in The Great American Regional Cookery Sweepstakes, if we had one. Both rabbit and rice are adapted from Mary Land's epic Louisiana Cookery, *published in 1954. It runs bristling clear through the higher flights of Brennans and other New Orleans watering holes, through humbler fare of Creole and Acadian at home, right down to campfire edibles from the backwater hunter: "banquette, byroad, and bayou" indeed. You will learn how best to handle a catch of possum or muskrat, how snipe (steeped in local orange wine) or octopus (she offers a tempting fricassee of its tentacles), how the lowliest gleanings from the field (my favorite being a pretty-sounding stew of marsh marigolds and early blue violets, with salt pork). Unfortunately, few attempts are made at measure, process, or progression, and not some few receipts are puzzling to the point of incomprehensibility. However, to the cook and cookbook reader alike she offers still more than most, in the way of pleasure and simple culinary profit—her recipe for Fowl à la Westerfield is almost worth the price of the book itself, if you can find it. She begins "Take one quail, dressed; one duck dressed; one goose, dressed; one turkey, dressed." Each are then sautéed in butter, the quail is stuffed with pecans and stuffed in the duck, apples are stuffed around that, then the duck is stuffed in the goose with orange segments, and lastly the goose is stuffed into the turkey with cornmeal dressing around it! No advice given as to carving all this, but as we will never cook it, that seems purest quibble.*

LOUISIANA
BREAST OF TURKEY EN DAUBE

1	half breast of turkey	4	carrots, sliced
4	stalks celery with some leaves, chopped	½	cup minced parsley
		2	cloves garlic, minced
2	onions, chopped	¼	teaspoon dried thyme

2 bay leaves	1 cup fine dry white wine
⅓ cup diced (¼ inch) salt pork	2 tablespoons brandy
6 whole cloves	3 tablespoons butter
Salt and freshly ground pepper	3 tablespoons flour

*B*one the breast of turkey as you would a chicken breast. Simply cut along the breastbone separating the meat, then detach the flesh from the rest of the bones—they are large and this is easily done. Do not remove the skin from the breast, but locate the large white tendon on the underside and carefully pull it out with the assistance of a small sharp knife.

Put the bone with any meat clinging to it in a kettle, cover with water, and add half the celery, onions, carrots, parsley, garlic, thyme, and bay leaves, and some salt and pepper to taste. Simmer an hour or more, or until the stock is flavorful.

To cook the turkey make a bed of the salt pork, the rest of the vegetables, cloves, and salt and pepper in a Dutch oven or casserole. Place the turkey on top, pour the wine, brandy, and 2 cups of the stock over, and bring to a boil. Lower the heat and simmer gently, with the pot covered, for 1 hour, basting occasionally as it cooks.

After an hour, drain the liquid off into the stock kettle. Cover the pan and keep turkey warm while you prepare the sauce.

Stir the butter and flour together in a saucepan over low heat until it turns a delicate straw color—about 10 minutes. Strain 4 cups stock into the pan and simmer until it thickens, stirring as it cooks. Taste for seasoning and add more salt, pepper, or brandy as needed.

To serve, slice the meat and mask with the sauce. Garnish with either parsley or watercress.

Serves 6 to 8.

Turkeys around holidays tend to be so processed and packaged, and pumped with such adulterated oils, I can't recommend this most indigenous of fowls (Benjamin Franklin nominated it for Native Bird). The only thing is to look about in markets for signs advertising turkeys never frozen, and that still is a long shot. For even a small family a small turkey can be burdensome, after a few meals of leftovers. So this unusual Louisiana daube, adapted to the use of turkey "pieces" now so often found, is my choice for a Christmas or Thanksgiving that does not include all the aunts and uncles.

Good accompaniments would be, preceding the daube, Chilled Pumpkin Cream soup (page 5), with Parker House Rolls (page 331), then the daube with Rum and Orange Yams (page 261) and Colonial Green Beans with Mace (page 223) and perhaps a dab of Blueberry Rhubarb Relish (page 311). Then a course of Jerusalem Artichoke Salad (page 270), on to My Persimmon Pudding (page 380), and a dry native champagne throughout.

WYOMING TURKEY PUDDING

5 cups diced (½ inch) cooked turkey	1 onion, chopped
5 cups bread cubes	½ cup plus ⅓ cup butter
Salt and freshly ground pepper	¼ cup flour
½ teaspoon celery seed	4 cups turkey or chicken stock, heated
½ teaspoon poultry seasoning	4 eggs

*P*reheat the oven to 350°F.

Put the bread in the oven—as it warms—to toast. When the bread cubes are golden, remove and mix with the seasonings.

Sauté the onion in the ½ cup butter till it is transparent, then toss with the bread till the cubes are coated with butter. Reserve 1 cup of the bread cubes for later.

Line a large shallow greased casserole with the bread dressing and arrange the turkey in the middle. Melt ⅓ cup butter in a saucepan, add the flour, and cook, stirring, for 10 minutes over low heat. Add the hot stock all at once and cook, stirring till it is smooth and thickened, for 10 minutes more.

Beat the eggs and pour the thickened stock bit by bit into them, beating constantly. Pour over the turkey and sprinkle with the reserved bread cubes. Bake 45 minutes, or until the custard is set.

Serves 6 to 8.

A church-supper delight to stretch leftover turkey.

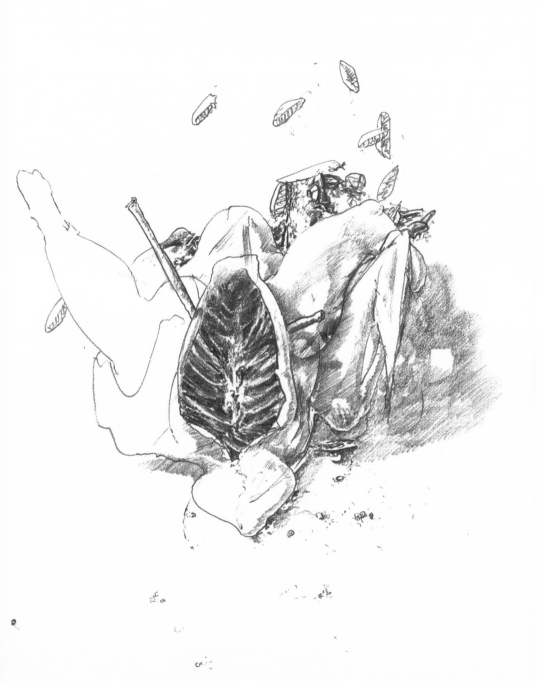

DOWNEAST TURKEY OYSTER SHORTCAKE

3 tablespoons butter
¼ cup flour
2 cups milk, scalded
   Salt and freshly ground
      pepper
1 teaspoon sweet paprika

1 cup diced (½ inch) cooked
      turkey, preferably white
      meat
1 cup shucked oysters
   Helene's Drop Shortcakes
      (page 324) (or cornbread)
   Pimiento strips

*I*n the top of a double boiler, melt 2 tablespoons of the butter and stir in the flour. Let cook over simmering water for 15 minutes. Add the hot milk all at once and cook, stirring, until the mixture is smooth. Add salt, pepper, and the paprika and cook gently 10 minutes.

Add the turkey to the cream sauce. Cut the oysters in half (unless they are quite small) and sauté in the other 1 tablespoon butter until their edges curl— only a couple of minutes or so. Add to the creamed turkey and heat for a few minutes.

Serve between and over any biscuit-type shortcakes, or split and buttered cornbread. Garnish with strips of pimiento.

Serves 4.

An old-fashioned dish that makes an unusually good lunch or supper. It is about my favorite among turkey leftover dishes. It may, certainly, be prepared with chicken, and though in the East it is always made with shortcake, in the South you will find it between cornbread flavored with a bit of poultry seasoning. Out West it comes to table on toast. Mushrooms may be substituted for the oysterless.

TURKEY IN MOLE SAUCE

6 tablespoons sesame seeds
2 green peppers, seeded and
      cut up
1 teaspoon anise seeds

5 cloves garlic, coarsely
      chopped
¾ cup blanched almonds,
      coarsely chopped

2   cups canned tomatoes,
        drained
3   tortillas, chopped
1   teaspoon salt
½   teaspoon ground cinnamon
½   teaspoon ground coriander
2   ounces unsweetened
        chocolate, grated
2   tablespoons chili powder

½   cup vegetable oil
2½ cups turkey or chicken
        stock, or as needed
6   cups diced (½ inch) cooked
        turkey (or chicken)
    Hot cooked rice
    Fresh coriander
    Sliced limes

*T*oast 4 tablespoons of the sesame seeds and set aside.

In a blender or food processor, purée the peppers, anise seeds, 2 tablespoons untoasted sesame seeds, tortillas, garlic, almonds, and tomatoes. It should be a very fine purée. Add all the spices and chocolate and whirl until it makes a paste.

Heat the oil in a large saucepan and add the paste. Cook 5 minutes over medium heat, then add 2 cups stock. Cook over low heat 10 to 15 minutes, or until quite thick. Thin with extra stock until the consistency of heavy cream.

Add the turkey and let heat through. Serve on rice, sprinkled with the toasted sesame seeds and garnished with sprigs of coriander and slices of lime.

Serves 8.

The most surprising way to put a leftover turkey to account. It should be served either with a good full-bodied white wine or a fine beer, and perhaps Guacamole (page 190) on lettuce leaves. In the Southwest I have had it also superbly at an outdoor fiesta where guests spooned it into warm soft tortillas, topped it with guacamole, and rolled it up themselves to eat. Wonderful!

SPECIAL DISHES

In other words, the usual should be made unusual; extraordinariness should cloak the ordinary. So long after my decision to serve enchiladas on a Paris roof to Colette and the Prince, I still believe firmly in the attributes of the unexpected!

—*M.F.K. Fisher,* An Alphabet for Gourmets

Southern Beans and Rice

The great rice and bean dishes tucked away in the South are to be found in homes, not restaurants. The restless recipe pioneer learns to sniff them out, if necessary by raising a pot lid on the back of a stove, to see what the cook eats. These days that cook is likely to be the hostess herself, who, like almost anyone in the South, will copy a recipe for the simple admiration of a dish. What secrets you uncover this way! You find how flexible the Jambalaya—all different as can be—and how full of sass and spice the pilaf (often termed "pilau" or even "perloo" along the byways). There are also even more secret dishes like red beans and rice, or Hopping John, only piping for family and friends, and not likely for any snooping Yankee. These are some of the best.

MISS EMILY'S PERLOO

1	cup rice	1	green apple, peeled and cored
2	tablespoons butter	½	cup raisins
½	teaspoon salt	1	cup diced (½ inch) cooked chicken
⅛	teaspoon freshly ground pepper	1	cup diced (½ inch) cooked ham
⅛	teaspoon crushed saffron threads	1	cup cooked shrimp, shelled and deveined
¾	cup chopped green pepper		Slivered blanched almonds, toasted
½	cup minced green onions with part of tops		Peach chutney
3	cups chicken stock		

*I*n a heavy casserole, sauté the rice in the butter over a medium flame, stirring, for 6 to 7 minutes, or until the rice is opaque. Lower the heat and stir in the salt, pepper, saffron, green pepper, and green onions.

Add the chicken stock and bring to a boil. Lower the fire, cover, and simmer gently 15 to 20 minutes, or until the rice has absorbed most of the liquid and is nearly done.

Grate the apple over the rice, add the raisins and meats, stir up the rice, and cover again. Cook 15 more minutes, tossing occasionally.

To serve, place servings of the perloo on warm plates, sprinkle toasted almonds over, and place a dollop of chutney on top.

Serves 6.

Miss Emily—whoever you were—yours remains one of my favorite company dishes. I have even put up peach chutney for it, though of course any chutney will do. To prepare it for company, if need be, after you stir in the meats, etc., simply place the casserole in a 300°F oven for 30 minutes, then turn the heat off and let the pilaf sit till needed. It should be served with some such very fine chilled white wine, as a Chardonnay.

HAM AND EGGPLANT
PILAU MADAME BÉGUÉ

1	small eggplant	2	cups water
	Salt		Freshly ground pepper
	Ham fat (or butter)	2	bay leaves
1	cup chopped onion	¼	teaspoon dried thyme
1	cup ham, diced (½ inch)		Diced pimiento
	cooked		Minced parsley
1	cup rice		

*P*eel the eggplant and cut into 1-inch cubes. Salt lightly and let sit 30 minutes or more to sweat. Press as much juice as possible from the cubes, then refresh with water. Squeeze again.

Render some pieces of ham fat until there is about a tablespoon (or use butter). Sauté the onion and green pepper in the fat, then add the ham and eggplant. Toss all over a medium flame.

Add the rice and 2 cups water. Add pepper, bay leaves, and thyme—it will need no salt because of the salted eggplant and ham. Cover and cook 30 minutes, stirring occasionally. Serve sprinkled with diced pimiento and parsley.

Serves 4.

Sound, simple, and inexpensive to boot, this is New Orleans cooking at its homely best. Madame Bégué would have, in her restaurant, used this as a side dish, I suspect, but it makes a lovely main family dinner using up the rest of a baked ham. It even remains a sound one if you have no ham, and substitute a quarter pound of cut-up bacon (partly fried and all but a tablespoon of fat discarded).

TURKEY PILAU WITH WALNUTS

4	large onions, chopped	12	whole cloves
½	cup butter	1	stick cinnamon
2	cups rice	½	cup dried currants or raisins
2	cups diced (½ inch) cooked turkey		Salt and freshly ground pepper
3½	cups turkey or chicken stock	⅔	cup chopped walnuts

Sauté the onions in the butter in a heavy casserole. When they are soft, add the rice and sauté, stirring, over low heat until it turns golden.

Add the turkey and stock, then all the ingredients except the walnuts. Cover the pan and simmer 20 to 30 minutes, or until all the liquid is absorbed.

Remove the cinnamon stick (the cloves are really not worth retrieving), and fold in the walnuts. Serve warm with chutney, or cranberry relish.

Serves 6.

Perhaps this is the most creative way of all to turn a leftover turkey to account. Like any of the pilafs, it may sit awhile if need be, for company.

CREOLE JAMBALAYA

4 medium onions, chopped	½ pound Chaurice (page 113)
2 tablespoons lard (or butter)	(or hot Louisiana sausage,
1 green pepper, seeded	smoked Polish or French
chopped	sausages), sliced ¼″ thick
6 green onions, chopped with	2 cups rice
part of tops	3 cups beef stock (or ham
Minced parsley	cooking liquid)
1 pound lean pork, cut into	Salt and freshly ground
small cubes	pepper
1 cup chopped cooked ham (or	Pinch of cayenne
ham hocks cooked in	½ teaspoon chili powder
water)	2 bay leaves
	¼ teaspoon dried thyme
	Pinch of ground cloves

In a heavy casserole, sauté the onions in lard till they are quite golden-brown. (Or, if using butter till they are transparent and limp.) Add the vegetables, 1 tablespoon parsley, and the pork and cook 15 minutes over medium heat, stirring occasionally.

Add the ham and sausage, then the rice, stirring until each rice grain is coated in oil. Add the stock and seasonings. Cover, then turn the heat down low and cook 30 minutes, uncovering now and again to stir.

Finally, remove the cover and cook 15 minutes more to allow any extra liquid to be absorbed. Sprinkle with chopped parsley and serve.

Serves 6.

Jambalayas are a native pilaf flexible as to ingredients, but always dark and spicy. Like gumbos, they come in many versions, but this recipe is probably best for inlanders for whom shellfish are rare and dear. To vary the recipe above, you can omit or reduce some of the meat ingredients and include shrimp or oysters. Or you could try a chicken, cut up and browned in oil—with water or chicken stock added rather than the beef. Anyway you prepare it, jamba-laya makes a rich, satisfying meal easily put together. Some people even find it faintly addictive.

NATCHEZ SHRIMP JAMBALAYA

6	slices bacon, chopped	½	teaspoon Worcestershire sauce
1	cup chopped onion		
1	clove garlic, minced	3	tablespoons tomato paste
1	green pepper, seeded and chopped	3	cups fish stock (or 1 cup bottled clam juice and 2 cups water)
¼	teaspoon dried thyme		
2	bay leaves	1½	cups rice
	Pinch of ground cloves	¼	cup minced parsley
	Pinch of ground allspice	1	pound small cooked shrimp, shelled and deveined
	Tabasco		

*R*ender the fat from the chopped bacon in a heavy casserole set over medium heat. When the bacon has begun to brown, add the onion, garlic, and green pepper. Sauté until the onion turns golden.

Stir in the seasonings, tomato paste, and stock. Stir until the mixture is smooth and begins to bubble, then add the rice and cover the pot. Turn the heat down low and cook 20 to 30 minutes, or until the liquid is absorbed.

Finally, stir in the parsley and shrimp and let heat through.

Serves 4 to 6.

An admirable and relatively inexpensive company dish—or at least it makes a pound of shrimp go a very long, tasty way. It can be held warm for some time, as can all the jambalayas, and served with a simple green salad, fresh bread or rolls, and an elegant dessert, it makes a complete repast.

RABBIT JAMBALAYA

1	rabbit (2 to 3 pounds)	4	cups vegetable oil
1	onion	4	tablespoons butter
1	carrot	2	cups chopped onion
1	stalk celery	1	green pepper, seeded and
1	bay leaf		chopped
¼	teaspoon dried thyme	2	tablespoons tomato paste
2	sprigs parsley	1	bay leaf
6	peppercorns		Pinch of ground cloves
	Cayenne		Pinch of ground ginger
	Salt	1	teaspoon Worcestershire
	Dried thyme		sauce
	Flour	1½	cups rice

*C*ut the rabbit meat off the bones. (Don't worry about some of the thinner pieces, but be careful to save the kidneys along with the meat.) Put the bones in a large kettle with the whole onion, carrot, celery, bay leaf, thyme, parsley, peppercorns, and salt to taste. Cover with water, bring to a boil, skim the pot, and cook about 2 hours. (This can be speeded up to an hour, in a pressure cooker).

Cut the meat into bite-sized pieces. Sprinkle with a generous dash of cayenne, and a little salt and thyme, then shake the pieces in a bag of flour. Heat the vegetable oil in a medium frying pan over medium-high heat. Sauté the rabbit pieces in batches till they are golden all over, and scoop out into a casserole. Discard the oil from the frying pan.

Add the butter to the pan and cook the chopped onion and green pepper over medium heat until the onion is limp. Add 4 tablespoons flour and stir until it starts to turn gold—about 10 minutes. Strain the rabbit stock and add 3 cups of it to the onions, stirring until a smooth sauce is achieved. Stir in the tomato paste, bay leaf, spices, and Worcestershire. Pour this over the rabbit.

Cover the casserole and simmer 20 minutes. Add the rice, cover again, and cook gently over low heat 30 more minutes, or until the rice is cooked and has absorbed all the liquid.

Serves 4 to 6.

Southerners treat all kinds of game to this kind of preparation. I even once had home-smoked wild duck made into a jambalaya, certainly a memorable experience. It's nice to serve this with a topping of homemade chutney, and either a red or white wine.

RED BEANS AND RICE

1	pound dried red beans		Pinch of dried thyme
1	cup chopped onion		Pinch of ground cloves
2	cloves garlic, minced		Cayenne (or Tabasco)
½	cup chopped celery tops		Salt
¼	cup chopped parsley	1	can beef bouillon (or ham
⅓	cup diced (¼ inch) salt pork		braising liquid)
2	ham hocks (or ham bone	1	pound hot sausage meat
	with meat on it)		Hot cooked rice
2	bay leaves		

Wash the beans and discard any discolored ones. (Most beans these days are more carefully packaged than they used to be and you seldom find small stones among them, but it does no harm to check.) Cover with water in a large saucepan and bring to a boil. Turn the heat off, cover, and leave for an hour or more to soak and plump.

Bring the water again to a boil and add onion, garlic, celery, parsley, salt pork, ham hocks, bay leaves, thyme, cloves, and a dash of cayenne or Tabasco. (This dish can be hot as you like, but some of its subtlety is lost if the pepper takes over. I personally like to make the sausage a bit hot as a contrast, and then serve the dish with a bottle of Tabasco at table so guests may pick their own degrees.)

Lower the heat so the beans are just bubbling, and let cook until the beans are softened—about 1½ hours. Check now and again to make sure the beans have enough water. When the beans are soft, add salt to taste, and the bouillon—salt added to beans at the beginning of cooking tends to make them hard.

Preheat the oven to 350°F.

Remove the ham hocks or bone and separate the meat from them, then chop. Roll the sausage in nut-sized balls and add them, along with the ham. Cook slowly, uncovered, in the oven until a slight crust forms on the top (about 30 minutes). Stir and let crust form again. Do this several times—the beans at serving should have begun to break down so the dish is slightly mushy. (Like the French *cassoulet* this is best on second or third reheating, and it also freezes well.)

Serve the beans in a ring of fluffy rice.

Serves 6.

This is a quite overlooked dish outside the South, and even there it is considered "country" and thus never to be served guests. Actually it is probably the most inexpensive dish imaginable as company fare, and all but the most finicky will find it a splendid example of American regional cooking. I serve it with beer rather than wine (another economy) since it is a little hot and spicy for wine, and a salad and dessert.

PODRILLA À LA CRÉOLE

2	cups dried red kidney beans		Few drops of Tabasco
¼	pound salt pork, cut into ¼-inch dice		Freshly ground pepper
		4	cups hot cooked rice
1	bay leaf	3	slices bacon, cooked and
¼	teaspoon dried thyme		crumbled
¼	cup minced parsley		

Soak the beans overnight in water. Next day, bring the beans in the water to a boil and simmer gently 30 minutes. Fry the salt pork until golden, then add it with 3 tablespoons of the rendered fat to the beans. Add bay leaf, thyme, parsley, and Tabasco and pepper to taste to the bean pot and simmer 1 hour, or until the beans are tender.

Taste for seasoning—the beans should be slightly peppery, and there should be enough salt from the salt pork. To serve, fill a buttered ring mold with the cooked rice and press it gently. Turn it out onto a heated platter. Remove the bay leaf from the beans and fill the center of the rice ring. Sprinkle with crumbled bacon.

Serves 4 to 6.

A favorite side dish with Thomas Jefferson. To prepare it as a succulent main dish, another version adds a clove of garlic and a chopped onion along with the salt pork, then a chopped green pepper and a cup of chopped tomatoes near the end.

HOPPING JOHN

1 pound dried black-eyed peas	1 cup finely chopped red onion
1 onion, chopped	(or green onion chopped
1 meaty ham hock (or a ham	with part of tops)
bone)	¼ cup minced parsley
Freshly ground pepper	1 tablespoon vinegar
Salt	1 tablespoon olive oil
1 cup peeled, seeded, and diced	Freshly ground pepper
fresh ripe tomato	Hot cooked rice

Soak the peas overnight in water to cover. The next day bring to a boil in the water and add the onion, ham, and pepper. Lower the heat and simmer an hour, or until the peas are nearly soft.

Add salt to taste and continue cooking slowly until the peas are done. Water should be added at any time they tend to get dry—but the water should be boiling when you add it.

Combine the tomato (canned may be used if summer tomatoes are not available) with red onion, parsley, vinegar, olive oil, and salt and pepper to taste. Let sit for an hour or so in the refrigerator to mellow and gather flavor.

To serve, remove any meat from the ham and chop it fine. Place the peas on a bed of rice, sprinkle with ham, and top with the tomato-onion relish.

Serves 4 to 6.

In many Southern homes, Hopping John is served each New Year's Day with the toast that the more black-eyed peas one eats the more prosperous will be the coming year. I like to perpetuate this custom wherever in the world I find myself, and invite friends for Hopping John, hot cornbread, and pecan pie— welcome and simple after rich indulgences from the holidays. But I don't stop there—it's one of my favorite dishes anytime.

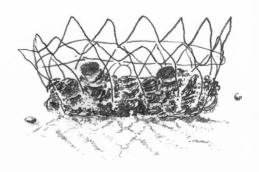

Southwestern Foods

*B*ased on harmonious combinations of corn, beans, and chilies, the fourth leg to the American table is a happily self-contained cuisine. Not only is it different from any of our other food, it is also served differently. It is possible (I know I do it sometimes) to serve Southwestern dishes in courses, but generally, after some appetizer, one is served a plate heaped and crammed full of different things: one enchilada, one taco, one quesadilla—all with differing fillings—and these nestled among refried beans and lettuce garnish and sliced radishes, etc., etc., etc. All this, of course, is highly influenced by foods south of the border, but Southwesterners have evolved a cuisine different from anything you will find in Mexico. It has acquired the rather derogatory name of "Tex-Mex" food, probably from the fact that there are (even in the Southwest itself) so few really fine restaurants that serve it, but as it is cooked in the home it is one of our glories—and best-kept secrets.

RED CHILI SAUCE

½	pound dried red chilies (New Mexican, ancho, or pasilla)	2	cloves garlic, peeled
3	cups chicken stock	2	teaspoons dried oregano
		½	teaspoon salt

*R*emove the stems and seeds from the chilies. (These are very hot, so some people use rubber gloves for the process—I don't, but I take care not to rub my eyes, etc.) You can also remove any vein ribs inside the chilies: these are where the seeds gather and are hotter than the flesh of the chilies.

Place the seeded chilies in a saucepan with the stock. Simmer, covered, 15 minutes. Place in a blender or a food processor with the garlic cloves, oregano, and salt. Blend until smooth. Place this mixture back in the saucepan and simmer for 15 minutes more.

This makes 3 cups chili paste, which can be thinned with water or stock if you need a sauce of lighter consistency. It freezes well.

In the Southwest, fresh red chilies are available in season, and later they are dried and hung in great fragrant strings, called Ristras, *to be picked during the long winters. In other parts of the country Hispanic markets carry not only these, but also the darker-flavored ancho and pasilla chilies. By all means, search out chilies if possible, for this basic sauce, so full of zip and freshness, is a far cry from the canned sauce found in every market.*

GREEN CHILI TOMATILLO SAUCE

1	cup chopped mild green chilies (either fresh or canned)	1	tablespoon minced parsley
		1	tablespoon minced fresh coriander
¾	cup peeled and chopped tomatillos (either fresh or canned)	1	tablespoon flour
		½	cup chicken stock
1	tablespoon butter		Salt
1	clove garlic, minced		Pinch of sugar

*I*f you use fresh chilies, you will need 10 to 12 Anaheim chilies. Roast them in a 400°F oven on a cookie sheet for 10 minutes or so—or until the skins blister all over. Remove, sprinkle with cold water, cover with a moist towel, and let sweat for 10 minutes. Slip the skins off, remove the tops, and scrape out all the seeds. Tomatillos have a thin dry papery skin that must be peeled off before using.

Heat butter in a saucepan set over medium heat. Add the garlic and sauté a minute or two, then add the chilies and tomatillos. Sauté over medium heat for 5 minutes, then add parsley, coriander, and flour. Cook 3 to 4 minutes, then add the stock. Stir as it thickens, and add salt to taste and a pinch of sugar. Let cook, uncovered, 15 to 20 minutes. Don't overcook—if you use fresh tomatillos they should still be a mite crisp.

Makes 2 cups.

Prepared with fresh ingredients, this sauce from New Mexico chef Richard Freeby is one of the best Southwestern sauces of all, and even with canned ingredients it is better than any restaurant green chili sauce I've ever tasted. In New Mexico a sauce like this, or the preceding red sauce, is used in nearly every dish. When you order in a restaurant, the waiter will immediately say, "Red or green?" It is so instinctive that I sometimes expect this response when ordering a cup of coffee. My favorite use for this sauce is as a topping for cooked pinto beans, with a dollop of sour cream. Canned green chilies are to be found practically everywhere, but you will probably have to seek a Hispanic market for either fresh or canned tomatillos—they look, when peeled, somewhat like tiny green tomatoes, but they come from another family altogether, and have a much more acidic taste than green tomatoes.

ALDA'S CHILI MEAT SAUCE

1½	pounds ground beef	1	can (4 ounces) mild green
2	tablespoons bacon fat (or		chilies, chopped
	vegetable oil)	¼	cup minced fresh coriander
2	large onions, chopped	¼	cup chili powder
2	cloves garlic, minced	1	teaspoon sugar
1½	cups canned tomatoes (or ½		Salt
	cup tomato sauce, or 4		Pinch of ground cloves
	tablespoons tomato paste)	½	teaspoon dried oregano
1	cup beef or chicken stock		
	(or beer)		

*S*auté the ground beef in a casserole or Dutch oven until it starts to brown. Remove with a slotted spoon to absorbent paper in order to drain off the fat, and pour off any fat in the pan. Add the bacon fat, then sauté the onions and garlic over medium heat until the onion is limp. Add the beef and all the other ingredients.

Turn the heat low and simmer for 3 to 4 hours, or until the sauce is dark, dense, and tasty—adding stock or beer from time to time if it gets too dry. (If you have a pressure cooker, cook it for 1½ to 2 hours.)

Makes 5 cups.

This is a recipe from my Aunt in Gallup, New Mexico—though it has picked up many of my own (and my mother's) touches from having cooked it for so many years. Aside from its first use—on cheese and green onion enchiladas—it may garnish huevos rancheros, make a further foundation for a taco or tostada, and combined with beans it can become chile con carne or the filling for a tamale pie.

GREEN CHILI SALSA

½ cup chopped fresh or canned tomatoes	2 jalapeño peppers (bottled en escabeche), seeded and minced
½ cup chopped green onions with part of tops	Salt and freshly ground pepper
1 4 ounce can mild green chilies, chopped	Pinch of sugar
1 clove garlic, minced	1 tablespoon lime or lemon juice
3 tablespoons minced parsley	
3 tablespoons minced fresh coriander	

*C*ombine everything and let sit in the refrigerator for at least an hour before serving.

Makes 1½ cups.

Bottled, salsas are pure fire and no taste, and most all recipes and restaurants use such commercial products. Homemade salsa is a must. This, the lesser of two hots, can be interchangeable with Frances Sommer's Jalapeño Salsa (recipe follows) in any dish. Salsa can go on anything but the dessert in Southwestern cooking. Its first use can be with homemade Tortilla Chips (below) as a dip for appetizers, then it can go on the beans, or any of the tortilla combinations.

FRANCES SOMMER'S JALAPEÑO SALSA

6	jalapeño peppers (bottled en escabeche)	1	tablespoon lime or lemon juice
½	cup chopped green onions with part of tops	½	teaspoon Worcestershire sauce
2	tablespoons minced parsley		Pinch of sugar
¼	cup minced fresh coriander Salt	½	cup fresh or canned tomatoes, chopped
1	tablespoon olive oil		(optional)

Slice the jalapeños lengthwise first, and remove all the seeds under running water—otherwise this sauce will be too hot for ordinary human consumption. Combine all the ingredients (Mrs. Sommer sometimes adds a slosh of white wine, as well) and let chill for an hour or so before serving.

Makes 1 cup.

Frances Sommer is the wife of photographer Frederick Sommer, and I owe to her some of the best meals I've ever had in Arizona—or elsewhere. I had to watch her to get the recipe, and like her I cook it without measuring these days. It is, I suppose, my favorite all-around American sauce for hot or cold meats, fish and shellfish, as well as for every Southwestern feast.

TORTILLA CHIPS

Corn tortillas	Salt
Vegetable oil	

Cut tortillas in eighths, like a pie. Put about ½ inch of oil in a heavy cast-iron frying pan and set it over high heat. When the fat starts to shimmer (but not smoke), test one chip: when the oil stops bubbling around it, it should be golden and crisp. If it is still chewy the fat is not yet hot enough, and if it gets more brown than gold the fat is too hot.

Cook the rest in batches of one layer in the frying pan. Lift out with a slotted spoon, and drain on absorbent paper. Salt while they are warm.

No meal in the Southwest is complete without these. They can now, of course, be bought packaged like potato chips everywhere, but they are nothing like homemade (which usually disappear before your eyes as you cook them). They are used at the beginning of a meal as an appetizer to scoop up salsa or guacamole, and they look very pretty stuck in a pile of refried beans (where they are also used as a kind of spoon to eat the beans). A basket ought to be put on the table, in fact, to use for anything.

REFRIED BEANS

1	pound dried pinto beans (or half pinto and half black beans)	Salt
		Lard or bacon fat
		Sour cream
1	onion	Frances Sommer's Jalapeño Salsa
1	clove garlic	(page 188)
3	slices bacon	Tortilla Chips (see preceding
2	teaspoons chili powder	recipe)

Soak the beans in water overnight, or cover with water, bring to a boil, and let sit an hour covered. When ready to cook, bring to a boil, then lower the heat to a simmer and add the onion, garlic, bacon, and chili powder. Simmer several hours, adding hot water if the beans get too dry.

When the beans are tender, add salt to taste, and cook them till they start to almost fall apart. They should have about an inch of cooking liquid over them by the end, for you will need the bean liquid later. If they are too dry, simply add hot water and stir the pot.

Heat lard or bacon fat in a skillet, and add about 1 cup beans per serving to about 1 tablespoon fat. Toss the beans in the fat, then mash them with a potato masher and let fry over low heat until a crust forms on the bottom. If they get too dry, add some bean liquid, and let crust again.

Serve the beans, crust up, with sour cream on top, a little jalapeño salsa, and tortilla chips stuck point down in them.

Delicately crusted with creamy dark insides, I think none of our starches quite outdoes refried beans, for glorious sustenance. Though in the Southwest most all refried beans are made from pinto beans, I like to use half black beans with them for superior flavor—if you can get them, try it. Topped with sour cream, jalapeño salsa, and with three or four tortilla chips stuck in (with a handy basket of more to eat the beans with), they are as good as any dish in the whole cuisine.

LETTUCE GARNISH

*T*his is the only time I ever use iceberg lettuce. In salads it is the most boring of all the lettuces, but it is the only lettuce that can stand up to being sliced like cole slaw, as is done in the Southwest. It is an indispensable garnish to any platter. The best way to slice the lettuce is to detach the leaves, pile them up, and cut with a long sharp knife in shreds. They should then be put in a bowl of water to crisp, and drained and dried before using. Usually the lettuce is completely unadorned, but it is nice sprinkled with just a hint of white wine tarragon vinegar and a little salt. Or I often shred radishes and let them soak with some salt and vinegar, then sprinkle them over the lettuce.

GUACAMOLE

2	large avocados, peeled and seeded	1	clove garlic, minced to a paste
	Juice of lemon (or lime)		Tabasco
4	green onions, chopped with part of tops	½	teaspoon chili powder
1	tomato, peeled, seeded, and chopped (optional)		Pinch of sugar
			Salt

*E*ither mash the avocados fine or chop them up. (There are people who prefer their guacamole to be almost a purée and those who like it chunky—I like either). Sprinkle immediately with lemon or lime juice, then add all the rest of the ingredients. Taste for seasoning, place the avocado pit in the bowl, cover with plastic wrap, and refrigerate for at least 30 minutes to mellow. If kept too much longer the avocados will start to darken.

Serves 4.

Arguably our finest native salad, all by itself on a leaf of tender lettuce, with a basket of warm Tortilla Chips (page 188) to scoop it up. In the cuisine of the Southwest it is used also as a cocktail dip, or one of the toppings and/or fillings of enchiladas, tacos, tostadas, burritos—you name it. It is also lovely as a cold sauce for grilled meats or for cold or hot fish.

AVOCADO SLICES MARINATED IN RUM

2	large avocados, peeled, seeded, and sliced	2	tablespoons light rum
3	tablespoons lime juice	1	clove garlic, minced
½	cup olive oil		Salt and freshly ground pepper

Toss the avocado slices in the remaining ingredients, cover with plastic wrap, and refrigerate for an hour or so before serving. (The lime, rum, and oil combination keep the avocados from darkening.)

Serves 4.

A kind of superior guacamole. The avocado slices make, arranged in a fan on Boston lettuce leaves, a fine first course to any meal, or they can replace the lettuce garnish on a Southwestern platter.

PICKLED JALAPEÑOS
STUFFED WITH WALNUT CHEESE

5 to 6	jalapeños (bottled en escabeche)	¼	cup finely minced walnuts
1	package (3 ounces) cream cheese		Salt

Remove the stems from the jalapeños with a sharp knife, and take out their seeds with a small knife under the faucet. Drain. Mash the cream cheese with walnuts and salt to taste, and stuff the peppers with the mixture. Chill for an hour or more in the refrigerator. To serve, slice into rings.

Serves 4 to 6.

Stuffed, then chilled and sliced, these make for more than garnish to shredded lettuce, taco or tostada. In fact, they lift any Southwestern meal to notice down to the finest detail. They may also be used to top Tortilla Chips (page 188), for an appetizer.

CHORIZO

1 pound ground lean pork	1 bay leaf
1 teaspoon salt	4 cloves garlic, minced to a
2 tablespoons chili powder	paste
A pinch each of ground	2 tablespoons vinegar
cinnamon, ground cloves,	
dried oregano, dried	
thyme, ground cumin,	
freshly ground pepper,	
ground ginger, nutmeg,	
coriander seeds	

*P*lace the pork in a bowl. Put all spices from the salt to the bay leaf in a blender, and whirl till the coriander seeds and bay leaf are powdered. Add to the pork along with the garlic and vinegar, mix well, and refrigerate for a day or more. (This can be made, divided in ¼–½ cup batches, and frozen for future uses.)

Chorizo is available in the stores, but none of it is as good as your own home-made variety. Its uses are legion in Southwestern cooking, from simple frying, crumbled as filling for a taco, etc., to adding spice and spark to many casseroles, meat loaves, and egg dishes.

CARNITAS

1 pork shoulder (4 to 5	½ teaspoon dried oregano
pounds)	2 onions, chopped
Salt	1 clove garlic, flattened with a
½ teaspoon ground cumin	knife
½ teaspoon coriander seeds	2 carrots, scraped and chopped

*P*lace the pork in a large kettle with water to cover. Add salt to taste, and the remaining ingredients and bring to a boil. Lower the heat and simmer 2½ hours.

Preheat the oven to 350°F. Take the pork out of the kettle and place in a shallow baking pan. Bake 45 minutes to 1 hour, or until the meat is well browned all over.

Remove the meat from the oven, discard as much fat as possible, and shred the meat with knife and fork.

All this boiling and baking produces an incredibly soft-textured meat, yet with crispy edges. Simply with cooked pinto beans and salsa it makes one of the best fillings for tortillas in the whole cuisine.

TINGA

2 cups Carnitas (see preceding recipe) (or leftover baked pork, shredded)	1 cup chopped tomatoes
1 tablespoon bacon fat (or vegetable oil)	1 jalapeño pepper (bottled en escabeche), seeded and minced
½ cup chopped onion	½ cup stock (preferably from Carnitas)
1 clove garlic, minced	1 cup water
½ cup Chorizo (page 192)	Salt

*P*repare the meat and measure it. Sauté the onion and garlic in the fat till soft, then add the chorizo to the pan and mash to crumble it. Cook slowly, uncovered, 10 minutes, stirring now and again to cook the sausage.

Add all the rest of the ingredients and cook, uncovered, over medium-high heat until the liquid has cooked away and the Tinga begins to brown. Remove from the heat.

Tinga may be served by itself, topped with onion rings that have been soaked in salted water, then sprinkled with vinegar, and avocado slices. Accompanied by warm fresh tortillas, it makes an excellent meal. It also makes a splendid filling for tacos, or tostadas, etc. (also topped with chopped onion and avocado).

PICADILLO

1 pound ground beef	¼ teaspoon ground cumin
1 cup Chorizo (page 192)	Salt
1 onion, chopped	1 bay leaf
1 clove garlic, minced	½ cup raisins
1 cup chopped canned tomatoes	½ cup slivered blanched
1 tablespoon vinegar	almonds (optional)
Pinch of sugar	½ cup chopped pitted black
1 teaspoon ground cinnamon	olives (optional)
Pinch of ground cloves	

*P*ut the beef and chorizo in a frying pan and cook, mashing down to crumble the meats, until the beef starts to brown. If too much fat is released, drain on absorbent paper and put back in the pan.

Add the onion and garlic and cook a few minutes, then add all the other ingredients except the raisins, almonds, and black olives. Let simmer, covered, 30 minutes, then add the raisins, etc., and cook, uncovered, 10 to 15 minutes.

This dish is sometimes served as is, with bowls of garnish such as grated cheese, shredded lettuce, guacamole, chopped tomatoes, little chunks of cream cheese, etc. But it is perhaps best as a filling for tortillas in the form of enchiladas, tacos, tostadas, etc. One seldom comes upon it, but one of the most spectacular ways to eat it is as a stuffing for green chilies, which are then fried in a light batter and served with a fresh tomato sauce.

CHEESE AND GREEN ONION ENCHILADAS

Corn tortillas	Sharp cheddar, grated (or
Vegetable oil	Monterey Jack)
Alda's Chili Meat Sauce (page	Green onions, chopped with part
186)	of tops

*H*eat ¼ inch oil in a small frying pan and fry tortillas in it only a second or so on each side—just until they soften. They should not get crisp. Do this with a pair of tongs, and as they bubble up and soften, dip each one in a pot of hot chili meat sauce, then lay on a plate.

Sprinkle each tortilla with cheese and green onion (about 3 heaping tablespoons cheese to 1 heaping tablespoon onion) and roll up. Place side by side in a baking dish and sprinkle with any leftover cheese and onion. Cover with foil and let sit until ready to serve.

To serve, heat the chili meat sauce, and warm the enchiladas in a 350°F oven 5 to 10 minutes—or just until the cheese begins to melt. Serve with a good spoonful of chili meat sauce on top.

Serves 1 to 2 per person, depending on other dishes.

My favorite simple enchilada is definitely this one. In fact, I seldom serve a Southwestern meal without it. Two of them, with Refried Beans (page 189) and Lettuce Garnish (page 190), make a splendid meal anytime—but they are also nice as one of a selection of tortilla dishes. They can also be made with plain Red Chili Sauce (page 185) for a tasty meatless main dish.

GREEN CHILI ENCHILADAS

	Vegetable oil	2	tablespoons minced fresh coriander
6 to 8	corn tortillas		Salt
½	cup chopped green onions with part of tops		Pinch of sugar
1	clove garlic, minced	1	tablespoon cornstarch
2	tablespoons minced parsley	1	cup milk
1	green pepper, seeded and grated (discarding the skin)	1	tablespoon lemon juice
		1¾	cups grated natural Monterey Jack cheese
1	tablespoon olive oil	¼	cup toasted pinon nuts, or pumpkin seeds
1	can (4 ounces) mild green chilies, chopped		

*H*eat oil—about ¼ inch—in a small frying pan, and with a pair of tongs dip the tortillas in just until they bubble and soften. Place on a plate.

Sauté green onions, garlic, parsley, and green pepper in olive oil in a medium saucepan over medium heat. After 5 minutes, add the chilies, coriander, salt to taste, and a bit of sugar. Cook 5 minutes.

Dissolve the cornstarch in the milk; then add it, with the lemon juice, to the saucepan and simmer 10 minutes. Stir now and again, as the sauce thickens to make sure it is smooth. Taste for seasoning, and reserve.

Preheat the oven to 350°F.

To assemble the dish, warm the sauce up and add 1 cup of the cheese. Place a tortilla in the bottom of a round casserole the size of a tortilla, like a soufflé dish. Top with some of the sauce, then continue layering tortillas and sauce. Finally, top with the rest of the sauce, a sprinkling of pinon or pumpkin seeds, and the rest of the cheese.

Place foil over the dish, and when ready to serve, heat in the oven 10 to 15 minutes, or until starting to bubble. Slice in pie-shaped wedges, and lift out onto plates.

Serves 4 to 6, depending on other dishes.

Enchiladas come in two forms—the rolled up and the pie stack. This is perhaps the best of the stacked, with a splendid sauce, only faintly hot, that contrasts well with more fiery dishes.

AZTEC PIE

5 corn tortillas	⅔ cup heavy cream (or milk)
6 ounces cream cheese	1 teaspoon salt
1 can (4 ounces) mild green chilies	

*P*reheat the oven to 350°F.

Divide the cheese in fourths, and spread it on 4 of the tortillas. Put the green chilies in a blender or food processor, and whirl till smooth. Spread a little of this on each cheese-coated tortilla.

Stack all the tortillas except for the plain one in a round casserole the size of a tortilla—a soufflé dish is perfect. Mix the cream and salt together and pour over the tortillas. Top with the last tortilla, and cover tightly with foil. Bake 20 to 30 minutes—or until all the liquid is absorbed. Serve cut into pie-shaped wedges.

Serves 4 to 6, depending on other dishes.

A splendid bland dish I serve often to balance all the hot spicy ones.

SIMPLE TACOS

Vegetable oil	Cooked pinto beans
Corn tortillas	Grated cheese
Alda's Chili Meat Sauce (page	Shredded lettuce
186) (or Carnitas [page 192] or	Sliced radishes
fried Chorizo [page 192])	Chopped green onions

*H*eat oil in a small frying pan—there should be at least ½ inch in the pan. When quite hot, take each tortilla with tongs and start to fry in the oil. As they cook, while they are still pliable form into a U shape by folding over with the tongs and frying first one side and then the other. Make sure, as they crisp, that you maintain at least a 2-inch opening at the top of the U. When they are crisp and golden all over, drain on absorbent paper.

These can be made well ahead during the day, and reheated in a warm oven. To serve, warm them, fill with a good spoonful of hot meat sauce, then some warm beans, cheese, lettuce, radishes, green onions, etc.

Tacos are one of the best simple balanced meals, all in one package, ever devised. To my taste, they beat almost any sandwich or hamburger anytime. In practice they can be filled with almost any spicy hot meat (or chicken) mixture, with perhaps beans as well, then garnished with any selection of cheese, lettuce, guacamole maybe, and hot salsa, chopped fresh tomato, what have you.

CHICKEN TACOS WITH
GREEN CHILIES AND SOUR CREAM

8 to 10	corn tortillas	¼	cup minced fresh coriander
	Vegetable oil	1	cup sour cream
2	cups chopped onion		Salt
1	can (4 ounces) mild green		Grated Monterey Jack cheese
	chilies, chopped		Sliced avocados
2	tablespoons butter		White wine vinegar
2	cups cooked chicken,		
	diced (½ inch)		

*F*ry tortillas in the oil as in Simple Tacos (see preceding recipe). Sauté onion and chilies in the butter for 5 minutes, or until the onion is tender. Add the chicken and coriander and heat through. Add the sour cream and salt to taste, and warm through—do not let it boil.

Fill the tacos with a good bit of the chicken mixture, and top with cheese, avocados, and a sprinkle of vinegar and salt.

8 to 10 tacos.

A sensuous, mild combination, useful when other dishes are hot and spicy. It is also one of the best ways ever devised to use leftover chicken.

SIMPLE TOSTADAS

Corn tortillas

Vegetable oil

Alda's Chili Meat Sauce (page 186) (or Carnitas [page 192], or fried Chorizo [page 192])

Cooked pinto beans

Grated cheese

Shredded Lettuce Garnish (page 190)

Sliced radishes

Chopped green onions

Green Chili Salsa (page 187) or Frances Sommer's Jalapeño Salsa (page 188)

*F*ry tortillas in about ½ inch hot oil. As they cook, press down with tongs in the middle so they form a crisp cup as they fry. Drain on absorbent paper. (Like taco shells, they can be cooked well ahead during the day and reheated in a warm oven—they only get nicely crisper.)

Serve a basket of the tostadas with warm bowls of meat sauce (or other meats) and pinto beans, and an assortment of garnish for guests or family to pile up as they wish. (And plenty of napkins).

When I cook Southwestern food, and have scraps of this and that left, I always feast on tostadas for a meal of their own at the very end. With glasses of fine frosty beer, they make a wonderful simple party dish for guests, set on a buffet with the warm things in chafing dishes, and bowls and bowls of garnish— aside from those listed you can have two different cheeses, pumpkin seeds, Guacamole (page 190), two different kinds of salsa, chopped fresh tomatoes. On, and on. And scaled down a bit, they make a favorite family dinner— always pleasing.

BLACK BEAN TOSTADAS WITH SOUR CREAM

12	corn tortillas	2	cups sour cream
	Vegetable oil	1	can (4 ounces) mild green
2	cups Refried Beans (page		chilies, chopped
	189) made with half pinto		Parmesan cheese (or dry
	and half black beans (or		Monterey Jack), grated
	with ½ can of undiluted		
	black bean soup added to		
	plain refried beans)		

*F*ry the tortillas in the oil as in Simple Tostadas (see preceding recipe). Drain on absorbent paper and keep warm. Heat the beans and make sure they have enough liquid in them to spread well (but not be soupy). Mix the sour cream with the green chilies.

To assemble, spread the crisp tortillas with warm beans, then top with the chili sour cream and sprinkle with Parmesan, or aged dry Monterey Jack freshly grated.

Serves 6 to 12, depending on other dishes.

There is something about this combination which I find nigh irresistible. You would not want to serve them with a platter that includes refried beans, but they make themselves a fine meatless meal with a substantial lettuce garnish—including tomatoes, radishes, sliced avocados (or Guacamole—see page 190), etc. And of course cold, full-bodied beer.

PICADILLO TOSTADAS

12	corn tortillas	Salt
	Vegetable oil	Avocado slices
1	recipe Picadillo (page 195)	Lemon juice
	Sweet onion rings	

*F*ry the tortillas in the oil as in Simple Tostadas (page 199). Drain and keep warm. Heat the picadillo, prepare onion rings and place them in a bowl of cold salted water, and dribble lemon juice and salt over the avocado slices.

To assemble, spread warm picadillo over the shells and top with onion rings and avocado slices.

Serves 6 to 12, depending on other dishes.

A very spicy tostada, but since it has no chilies it is not a hot one. The avocado and onion rings top it prettily and succulently, but if you serve these by themselves rather than as a platter of specialties, you might wish to have bowls of various garnish as in Simple Tostadas (page 199), for guests or family to top their own.

SIMPLE QUESADILLAS

Corn tortillas	Chili powder
Monterey Jack or sharp cheddar, grated	Vegetable oil

*P*lace about 3 tablespoons cheese on one half of each tortilla, then dust the whole with a bit of chili powder. Fold over in half moons, and fasten with toothpicks.

Fry a minute or so in about ½ inch hot oil, drain on absorbent paper, remove the toothpicks, and serve warm.

The Southwestern grilled cheese sandwich. If done with inferior cheese, they are rather tasteless and stringy—but with either natural Jack or the best aged cheddar they are beautiful crispy snacks. To make them even better, try coating each with Guacamole (page 190).

GORDON BALDWIN'S QUESADILLAS

4	wheat flour tortillas	1	sweet onion, sliced and punched into rings
½	cup grated Monterey Jack cheese	1	can (4 ounces) green chilies, chopped
½	cup grated cheddar cheese		Melted butter
	Grated Parmesan cheese		

*L*ay out the tortillas and distribute the ingredients as listed (except for the melted butter) over half of each tortilla. Fold over so they make half moons and brush each side with melted butter.

Place under a broiler and broil each side about 2 minutes. Serve immediately.

Serves 4.

Quesadillas are usually prepared with corn tortillas, but these made with flour tortillas, simply broiled and not fried in deep fat, seem to outdo them all. They can, if you wish, be topped with a cold salsa at table.

SIMPLE BURRITOS

Large flour tortillas
Carnitas (page 192)
Cooked pinto beans

Green Chili Salsa (page 187) or
    Frances Sommer's Jalapeño
    Salsa (page 188)
Grated Monterey Jack cheese
    (optional)

Sprinkle large flour tortillas with a bit of water, wrap them in foil, and heat about 10 minutes in a 350°F oven to steam and soften.

Make sure the carnitas and beans are warm, then assemble the burritos by placing about ¼ cup each carnitas and beans on one edge of the tortilla, then top it with salsa (and cheese if you wish). Roll the tortilla once towards the middle, fold over the side edges to make an envelope, then finish rolling up. Serve at once.

These are a specialty of a taqueria several blocks from where I live, and though I live in San Francisco with all its restaurants, I think this is my favorite lunch out—and all rolled before your eyes in minutes. Fast food can be good indeed. You can fuss with their filling, and slather them with guacamole, etc., but their simplicity is hard to improve on.

CHIMICHANGAS

Wheat flour tortillas
Alda's Chili Meat Sauce (page
   186)
Cooked pinto beans

Vegetable oil
Guacamole (page 190)

*R*oll up flour tortillas with meat sauce and pinto beans as in simple Burritos (see preceding recipe). You will not need to steam the tortillas, simply use them as they come from the package. Fasten each with a toothpick.

Heat at least 1 inch of oil in a heavy frying pan, and when it starts to shimmer fry the rolls until golden on all sides—this will take only 2 to 3 minutes. Drain them on absorbent paper and keep warm. To serve, slather generously with guacamole. (Or serve sprinkled with shredded lettuce, grated cheese, slices of radish, cubes of tomato, etc.)

Chimichangas are simply burritos deep fried, but like all changes of this sort— what a difference! Like any of the Southwestern tortilla dishes you can, of course, fill it with practically anything, but this version is so good I stick with it as a rule.

HUEVOS RANCHEROS

Alda's Chili Meat Sauce (page 186) (or Red Chili Sauce [page 185])
Corn tortillas
Vegetable oil

Eggs
Grated cheddar cheese
Green onions, chopped with part of tops (optional)

*H*eat the sauce in a saucepan. Meanwhile, fry tortillas in hot oil only a minute or so to soften, then dip each in the sauce and lay on a plate. Keep them warm in the oven. Fry 2 tortillas for each person.

Either fry or poach 2 eggs per person, and lay them, when done, on the tortillas. Pour the hot sauce around and over them (not covering the yolks). Sprinkle with cheese and let warm in a medium oven till the cheese just begins to melt. Sprinkle with green onions—if you use them—and serve at once.

May be adapted to any number.

I am frankly not as fond of eggs as many people seem to be, but these I can eat anytime. They are usually, of course, served for breakfast, but they also make a fine light supper.

NATILLAS

2 cups milk	⅛ teaspoon salt
3 eggs	1 teaspoon vanilla
½ cup sugar	2 sticks cinnamon
2 tablespoons cornstarch	

*P*ut the milk in a saucepan and bring it just to the boiling point. While it heats, separate the eggs in this manner: place three yolks and one white in one bowl, and reserve the other two whites in another bowl for later.

Beat the yolks and white until light and frothy. Combine sugar, cornstarch, and salt and beat into the egg mixture.

Pour a bit of the hot milk into the eggs, then a little more, beating with each addition Beat the whole thing into the milk. Cook in a double boiler set over simmering water until the mixture thickens—about 10 minutes. It should be stirred almost constantly.

When thick, remove from the fire and let cool to room temperature. Stir in now and again so a skin doesn't form on top. When cooled, stir in the vanilla.

Whip the reserved egg whites until they hold a soft peak. Fold them gently into the custard—this should be done carefully so that there are pockets of egg whites in the pudding here and there, and the whole thing is not completely smoothed out.

Divide the pudding into 4 serving cups and chill in the refrigerator. To serve, break the cinnamon sticks in half and stick one in each pudding.

Serves 4.

For sweets after a hearty Southwestern meal, even the best restaurants in the Southwest seldom go beyond the bounds of a plain flan or undigestible deep-fried sopapillas dribbled with honey. But after all the complexities of this hot and spicy cookery, one wants only the lighest clearest taste to end the meal: fresh sliced pineapple, melon balls with lime, a fresh fruit ice. My choice for a simpler family meal, however, would be this wonderful bland pudding.

Cupboard Meals

*E*veryone is caught sometime with a sturdy meal to put together from what at first looks like thin air. Rather than scramble a couple of eggs, there are main dishes you can serve with a flair, quickly produced from any cupboard or refrigerator. In a pinch, from the corner or country store. They are the secretest of meals, we eat on our own, or whip together for the kids, who hunger for such private festivities, humble abracadabra. The best of these would be a simple soufflé—the dish that really *is* thin air—but that would be to crop in ever Frencher fields.

JAMBALAYA AU VALOIS

V. good
5-15-08

4 smoked sausage links, sliced (about 1 cup)	2 tablespoons tomato paste
2 tablespoons butter, bacon fat, or olive oil	~~Salt~~ and freshly ground pepper
2 cups chopped onion	~~2~~ cups hot water *or ch broth*
1½ cups rice	½ cup minced parsley
	2 cloves garlic, minced

*U*se a roomy pan with a cover for this dish. Put it over medium heat, and sauté the sausage slices in the fat. Add the onion and stir till it turns limp.

Add the rice, and stir 5 to 8 minutes over low heat. The rice will turn opaque and be filmed with oil. Stir in the tomato paste and salt and pepper to taste (it should be fairly peppery), and add the hot water.

Turn the heat up, let it come to a boil, and cover closely, then turn the heat low. Let steam gently 20 minutes. To serve, stir in the minced parsley and garlic and place on warm plates.

Serves ~~3~~

I used Hillshire farms (2/3) smoked Turkey Sausage (9 pkg)

This, as well as the next recipe, comes from a rare Gourmet's Guide to New Orleans, *put out in 1933. It seems to have been put together like any ordinary ladies' club cookbook, but most of the contributors are so fine, and knowledgeable about odd little recipes, that the book is a delight from cover to cover. I use ordinary smoked breakfast sausage for this dish—the smokiness is what gives it zip.*

BOULETTE DE SAUCISSON

¾ pound sausage meat	2 tablespoons vegetable oil
2 cloves garlic, minced	1 cup chopped onion
Pinch of cayenne	2 cans (14½ ounces each) hominy, drained
Pinch of dried sage	Minced parsley
Pinch of ground allspice	
Flour	

*U*se ordinary mild sausage, and mix in the garlic and spices. Let sit at least an hour to assimilate the flavors.

Roll the sausage into marble-sized balls, and shake them in flour. Sauté in the oil in a frying pan over medium heat until they begin to brown slightly. Add the onion, and cook it till limp. Add the drained hominy and cook several minutes more, always stirring and tossing.

Sprinkle the parsley over and toss thoroughly. Serve on warm plates.

Serves 4.

A lively dish that, in New Orleans, would likely be a breakfast dish, served with hot biscuits and coffee. But it also makes a fine quick supper, with beer, bread, and a salad.

BACON AND PARSLEY PUDDING

2	eggs	½	pound bacon, cut in ½-inch
½	teaspoon salt		slices
1	cup milk	2	tablespoons minced parsley
1	cup sifted flour		Grated Parmesan cheese

*P*reheat the oven to 450°F.

Break the eggs into a bowl and beat till frothy. Add the salt and half the milk, stirring. Sift in half the flour and stir till smooth, then add the rest of the milk and flour. Beat the batter till smooth.

Sauté the bacon in a frying pan until it is lightly brown, and remove to paper toweling. Pour ¼ cup of the bacon fat into a 10-inch oval gratin dish (or an 8 x 8-inch baking pan) and place it in the oven till it is very hot.

Stir the parsley into batter and pour into the hot gratin dish. Crumble the bacon and sprinkle it over the batter, along with some Parmesan cheese. Bake 15 minutes at 450°F, then reduce the heat to 375°F and cook 10 minutes more, or until the pudding is puffed high and golden. Serve at once.

Serves 3 to 4.

A descendant of Yorkshire pudding that makes a good quick, light supper with a green salad and a glass of wine or beer. It is an equally good breakfast or brunch dish with fresh fruit and coffee. If you like, it can be prepared with ½ pound of sausage cooked in tiny balls rather than the bacon.

NEW ENGLAND CLAM HASH

4	slices bacon, cut in slivers		Salt and freshly ground
⅔	cup chopped onion		pepper
4	medium potatoes, cooked,	⅓	cup heavy cream
	peeled, and diced	1⅓	cups fresh or canned whole
3	tablespoons butter		clams, drained
⅓	cup minced parsley		Paprika

*F*ry the bacon gently in a medium frying pan. When cooked but not yet crisp, add the onion to the pan and cook over medium heat until limp.

Add the potatoes and butter, tossing, then the parsley and salt and pepper to taste, then the cream. Toss the mixture over medium heat, then mash down and let cook until a brown crust starts to form on the bottom when you lift it over—about 10 minutes.

At this point add clams to the mixture, and mix well in. Cook another 5 to 8 minutes, lifting now and again to distribute the golden crust from the bottom. Serve on warm plates with a dusting of paprika.

Serves 3 to 4.

Of course this ought to be prepared from fresh clams, but I find it makes a quite good scratch meal with a tin from the shelf, for either breakfast or supper.

B. & O. RAILROAD CLAM POT PIE

4	cups peeled and thinly sliced		Heavy cream
	potatoes	4	eggs
1	cup chopped onion		Salt and freshly ground
2	tablespoons butter		pepper
1	cup whole clams, with their	1	recipe biscuit dough
	juice (fresh or canned)		

*P*reheat the oven to 375°F.

Parboil the potatoes in boiling salted water for 5 minutes. Drain in a colander and run cold water over. Sauté the onion in butter until it is limp.

Drain the clams, and measure the juices in a cup measure. Add enough cream to make 2 cups. Beat the eggs into the cream.

In 4 individual pot pie dishes, or in one soufflé dish, layer the potatoes, then add a sprinkle of onion and clams, some salt and pepper, then another layer of potatoes, etc. Pour the cream-egg mixture over.

Roll out the biscuit dough in 4 small rounds, or in one large one to fit your dish. Place over the filling mixture, tucking any extra under the edges. Place in the oven and bake 30 minutes, or until the crust is puffed and golden and the filling bubbly. Serve immediately.

Serves 4.

Such an easy and inexpensive dish makes one long for the lost days of railroad dining cars. For a hasty simple lunch or supper, I quite frankly prepare it from canned clams and packaged biscuit mix.

FARMHOUSE ONION PIE

2 large onions, thinly sliced	Freshly grated nutmeg
2 tablespoons butter	¼ to ½ cup grated sharp
2 eggs, lightly beaten	cheddar
¾ cup milk	1 cup fine cracker crumbs
Salt and freshly ground	4 tablespoons butter,
pepper	melted

*P*reheat the oven to 350°F.

Sauté the onions in 2 tablespoons butter until they are limp but not browned. Spoon into a pie plate. Mix the eggs with milk, spices and cheese, and pour over the onions. Mix the cracker crumbs with the melted butter and spread on top of the pie. Bake 30 minutes, or until the custard has set.

Serves 4.

A kind of country cousin to the quiche, and like the quiche it has possibilities of many variations. Any kind of cheese—good cheese—is pleasant, and a cup of shrimp in place of one of the onions is very good indeed. In fact it is one of those recipes which is useful on many occasions—a first course, a brunch, or supper—and best of all it is made from inexpensive ingredients usually found in any cupboard.

HUNT CLUB CREAMED CHIPPED BEEF

5	ounces chipped beef	1	tablespoon finely grated onion
2	cups heavy cream		Toast or waffles

Shred the chipped beef fine. Place in a bowl and pour boiling water over it, then drain immediately in a sieve (this will eliminate some of the saltiness of the beef).

Put the beef in a saucepan with cream and grated onion, and let boil over medium heat until the cream starts to thicken. This will take 15 to 20 minutes. Serve immediately over hot toast or waffles.

Serves 4.

Years ago I was invited to a private club by a gentleman who claimed it was Friday, and every Friday he made it a ritual to eat the creamed chipped beef at his country club. Now who honestly could refuse such a mystery, for who would drive twenty miles once a week for chipped beef on toast? At last it came, on good china, with mellow red wine, sprightly with parsley tufts, and it was inimitable. The only secret I could budge from the place was that it was cooked down in cream alone—there was no flour. This faintly approximates that far-off, unexpected feast.

McSORLEY'S TAVERN LUNCH

One of the tastiest native meals I've lucked upon comes from this famous New York watering hole. For many years women were not allowed inside, and among the regulars—from heavy laborers to smart businessmen—there have always been a smattering of artists and poets. All were there for good conversation and the best ale in the city.

When I first visited in the late 1950s, I saw a plate being delivered to a customer that consisted of a wrapped pack of fresh saltine crackers, a whole soft unwrapped Liederkranz cheese, and a Bermuda onion sliced thin as anyone could wish. We quickly caught on to this simple feast for the utterly fearless, and I continue eating it even though I don't have McSorley's around the corner.

Their famous ale cannot be reproduced, but you can come near with any fine local brew, or some dark and tasty imported beer. Liederkranz is our first native cheese and is available anywhere, as are the saltines. And though sweet onions have unaccountably disappeared from markets, by and large, any good-sized flat onion may be sliced thin and mellowed in salted ice water an hour or more, changing the water twice.

THING

Per person:

2 medium potatoes	⅔ cup cottage cheese
Vegetable oil	⅓ cup chopped green onions
Salt and freshly ground	with parts of tops
pepper	

*P*eel the potatoes and cut into ½-inch dice. Put in cold water to cover, then drain and pat dry with toweling. Fry in hot oil over high heat until they are crisp and brown.

Lift out onto paper towels to drain, and sprinkle with salt and pepper. Serve on plates, topped with a mound of cottage cheese and sprinkled with green onions.

This dish was given me in conversation (as most good recipes usually are) nearly twenty years ago, and as it was never named by the lady who passed it on, it acquired the name "Thing" from poet Jonathan Williams, who insisted it was his favorite breakfast dish. I have never grown tired of its pleasant contrasts, and served with hot coffee, or cold beer, its usefulness as a brunch or late supper dish is undeniable. It is perhaps the meal I most often sit down to when alone.

POTATO OMELET JOHN SHARPLESS

Per person:

2 medium potatoes	Parsley, minced
2 tablespoons butter	1 egg
Salt and freshly ground	1 tablespoon heavy cream
pepper	Grated cheese
Freshly grated nutmeg	

*P*eel and coarsely grate the potatoes. Put in cold water, and when you are ready to cook them, drain and press dry between paper toweling. Melt half the butter in an omelet pan (or larger frying pan if you are serving several). Add salt and pepper and nutmeg to the potatoes, and press them into the pan—shaking to make sure they don't stick.

Melt the rest of butter over the top, turn the heat down to medium, and cook till the potatoes start to turn golden on the underside. Cover the pan, turn the heat down to low, and cook slowly for 20 minutes or so, or until there is a good crust underneath and the potatoes on top taste done (but still al dente a bit).

Beat the egg and cream together with a little parsley and pour over the potatoes, stirring into the cake but not disturbing the bottom crust. Place under the broiler until the eggs are just set. Sprinkle lightly with any grated cheese, shake the pan, and flip crust up onto a hot plate, then sprinkle a little more cheese on top. Cut into wedges and serve.

With its combination of crustiness and soft creamy insides, this dish makes a satisfying meal anytime. It also lends itself to variations of all kinds—you could add onion, chives, herbs, black olives, salt pork or bacon, pimiento, green pepper, etc., etc., etc. Writer-chef Sharpless says this was the dish that gave him the special reputation of being able to prepare a gourmet meal from nothing.

PENNSYLVANIA DUTCH NOODLES WITH EGGS

Per person:

1 cup loosely packed fine-cut egg noodles	Salt and freshly ground pepper
2 tablespoons butter	Minced parsley or chives, or
1 egg	paprika

*C*ook the noodles in boiling salted water 4 to 5 minutes, or till just tender. Drain, and pour cold water over them.

In a frying pan over medium heat, cook the butter until it turns golden brown, then add noodles and cook another 4 to 5 minutes, or until they begin to crisp slightly and turn golden.

Add the egg beaten with salt and pepper, and stir a minute or so until set. To serve, place on a warm plate and sprinkle with parsley, chives, or paprika.

A fine dish reminiscent of spaghetti carbonara, though the browned butter gives it a nuttier taste. I like it very much indeed served with sausages and applesauce, or Fried Apple Rings (page 220).

DENVER OMELET

½	cup chopped onion	1	pimiento, chopped
¼	cup chopped green pepper		Salt and freshly ground
3	tablespoons butter		pepper
⅓	cup diced (¼ inch) ham	6	eggs

*I*n a small saucepan over low heat, sauté the onion and green pepper in 1 tablespoon of the butter until tender. Add the ham and cook a few minutes longer, then add the pimiento and remove from the heat.

Beat the eggs lightly with salt and pepper to taste and add the ham mixture. Put an omelet pan over medium heat, and when it is hot enough to make a bit of water sizzle, add 1 tablespoon of the butter. When it stops bubbling, immediately pour half the egg mixture in.

Stir slightly and hold the edges of the egg up to let uncooked egg pour under, shaking the pan now and again to see it doesn't stick. When set, but still a bit undercooked on top, shake the pan a final time and slide it out onto a warm plate, flipping the pan over to fold the omelet onto itself. Repeat the process for a second omelet.

If you like, you can glaze the top with a bit more butter. Serve immediately.

Serves 2 (easily doubled).

This is one of the best, and best known, American omelets. If it is scrambled and placed between slices of toast it becomes a Denver sandwich, and that is equally good.

NEW YORK EGG AND ONION SANDWICH

1	medium onion, sliced into thin rings		A few drops Tabasco
2	tablespoons butter	4	slices rye bread
	Salt		Mayonnaise
3	eggs, beaten lightly		

*S*auté the onion slices in the butter over low heat in a saucepan till they start to turn limp. Cover the pan and let them stew gently for 10 minutes, or until they are quite soft and have released some juices. (Peek and stir occasionally to see they are not burning on the bottom—if so, the heat is too high.)

After 10 minutes, take the cover off and turn the heat up to medium in order to boil any liquid down. This should only take a few minutes. Add the eggs and a few drops Tabasco, and stir until the eggs are set. Place on rye bread spread with mayonnaise, and slice the sandwiches in half.

Serves 2 (easily doubled).

This almost-omelet, served with perhaps a dill pickle and whatever else you fancy, makes a very satisfying quick meal. Beer is almost obligatory—though the most famous egg and onion sandwich, that from Mary Chase's play Harvey, was eaten simply on the run.

EGGS GOLDENROD

4	eggs, hard boiled	1½	cups milk, scalded
3	tablespoons butter		Salt
3	tablespoons flour		Toast

*S*hell the eggs and take out the yolks. Chop whites either coarsely or fine, as you wish. Melt the butter in a saucepan set over low heat, stir flour in, and cook 3 to 4 minutes, stirring. Add the milk all at once and stir till the sauce is thick and smooth. Cook the sauce slowly about 5 minutes.

Add the chopped whites to the sauce and cook another few minutes to heat them through. Season to taste with salt. Pour the sauce over toast, and over each serving rub egg yolk through a sieve.

Serves 2 to 4.

For no good reason I can see this dish is almost never cooked these days— perhaps because it was considered a dish from the nursery? At home we never thought it such—it was something like Welsh rabbit to warm the soul and tummy on winter evenings, and how suave the cream sauce, how pretty the dusting of bright yellow on top the color of meadow goldenrod. It is good with broiled tomato halves, for color contrast, and ham or bacon on the side, if you wish. Some like it spiked with Tabasco, or with curry in the sauce, or with a pinch of paprika to blush the top, but these I think only confuse its beautiful simplicity.

EGGS NEW ORLEANS

8	eggs		Tabasco
¼	cup tomato sauce	3	tablespoons butter
1½	tablespoons dry sherry	⅓	cup toasted slivered almonds
	Grated rind of 1 large		Buttered toast
	orange		Orange slices
	Salt		Watercress

*B*eat the eggs lightly with tomato sauce, sherry, orange rind, salt, and Tabasco to taste. In a frying pan, set over medium heat, melt the butter, and when it starts to foam add the eggs.

Scramble gently with a fork, and when the eggs are done (but still moist), place on buttered toast. Sprinkle almonds over the top and garnish with orange slices and sprigs of watercress.

Serves 4.

A dish of great subtlety in which no flavor is more pronounced than another. Cooked, the eggs assume an almost apricot color, which is as unusual as their taste. Use a very good, very dry sherry here.

SHAKER MAPLE TOAST

Bread
Maple syrup (or any syrup)
Butter

*T*ake as many slices of bread as you have persons, and spread maple syrup on both sides. Stack them up and let the syrup completely soak in. Let stand about 5 minutes, then check to see the bread is soaked through.

To cook, melt butter in a frying pan, and fry the bread slices over medium heat until crisp and golden brown on both sides—adding more butter as needed. Serve with sausage or bacon.

We Americans seem always fond of such sweet things as waffles, pancakes, French toast, etc. This, I think, outshines them all—crisp and sweet and sticky all at once, and beloved by children of all ages.

SIDE
DISHES

Or that noble dish of green lima beans now already beautifully congealed in their pervading film of melted butter; or that dish of tender stewed young cucumbers; or those tomato slices, red and thick and ripe, and heavy as a chop; or that dish of cold asparagus, say; or that dish of corn . . .

—Thomas Wolfe, Of Time and the River

Vegetables

Their trick is simplicity. At the same time, any vegetable is expected to provide the unexpected, to assume the role of texture or taste contrast, and generally shine beyond the dutiful squirt of lemon, toss of shiny butter. This kind of recipe is hard to come by, and any cook can use more of them. The questing recipe hunter has all the more to prod and pry—for if he admires an obscure turnip concoction, or a new way of turning out the humble carrot, he at the same time runs the risk of offending the host or hostess's pride in their centerpiece *coq au vin* or angel cake. My solution is to admire whatever looks like much time expense and trouble was spent on, and then remark how fine the carrots were. It usually works.

FRIED APPLE RINGS

4	cooking apples (Greenings, Granny Smiths, Pippins, Gravensteins)	Salt
		Lemon juice
		Minced parsley
4	tablespoons butter	

*T*ake good, sharp-flavored cooking apples (if not available, Golden Delicious will do) and core and slice them in rings—leaving the skin on. Melt the butter in a frying pan, toss the apples till coated with butter, then fry gently over medium heat, turning every few minutes.

Cook 15–20 minutes, or until the rings start to brown slightly and have become almost translucent. Sprinkle with salt, a few drops of lemon juice, and minced parsley.

Serves 4.

Usually apples are fried with brown sugar, with perhaps a bit of rum or bourbon added toward the end. That is, of course, very nice, but with fine apples the method here is even nicer, with the only sweetness coming from the apples themselves. They are most often served with ham, pork, or sausages, but they are also excellent with many chicken dishes—and most certainly with Shaker Chicken in Cider Cream (page 150).

GRATIN OF APPLES, SWEET POTATOES, AND RUTABAGAS

2	pounds sweet potatoes, peeled and cut in ½-inch dice	Salt
1	pound rutabagas, peeled and cut in ½-inch dice	½ cup butter, melted
		Bread crumbs
1	pound cooking apples, peeled, cored, and cut in ½-inch dice	

*P*reheat the oven to 325°F.

Parboil the sweet potato dice 10 minutes, then drain and toss with the other vegetables, salt to taste, and melted butter.

Put in a baking dish with a good tight lid and bake at 325°F for an hour, tossing twice during the time. The different vegetable cubes should be tender but still hold their shapes.

Place them in a gratin dish, spreading so they are between 1½ to 2 inches deep. Sprinkle lightly with bread crumbs. Turn the oven up to 425°F, and when you are ready to serve them, place in the hot oven for several minutes, or until the vegetables are golden on top.

Serves 6.

A beautiful, festive dish to partner pork, ham, or best of all goose. They are good with some meat sauce poured over them, though you won't want to mask this colorful mélange completely with a heavy gravy.

STUFFED ARTICHOKES BIG SUR

4 artichokes	Salt and freshly ground
1 lemon	pepper
2 cups parsley leaves	2 tablespoons olive oil
1 clove garlic	3 tablespoons butter, melted

*R*emove the tough outer leaves on the artichokes. Slice off the stem and the top third of the leaves. Trim their bottoms with a vegetable peeler and drop them in a bowl of cold water with the juice of half the lemon. Remove them one at a time, spread the leaves, and scoop out the choke with a spoon.

To cook, mince the parsley with garlic and add salt and pepper to taste. Remove the artichokes to a saucepan in which they will all be able to stand upright. Stuff the center cavity with the parsley-garlic mixture and add an inch of water to the pan. Dribble olive oil over. Cut the remaining half lemon in eighths and place two of these, skin side up, over each artichoke.

Bring to a boil, turn down the heat to medium, cover the pan, and cook 30 to 40 minutes—or until a fork goes into the heart easily. When done, the artichokes may sit for up to 30 minutes kept warm. To serve, pour melted butter over the tops.

Serves 4.

A fine California (Italian-influenced) recipe for anyone's files. Most stuffed artichokes seem not to add anything to that subtle vegetable, but these have a wonderful savor that really doesn't seem to call for any extra dipping butter as you eat them. They should be served as a first course, with crusty fresh bread. A faint metallic taste is the consequence of drinking wine with artichokes, so it is best to hold wine for the following course.

ARTICHOKES À LA NEIGE

4	artichokes	1	recipe Sauce à la Neige (page
½	lemon		52)

*P*repare the artichokes as in the preceeding recipe, but also snip off the ends of the outside leaves with scissors all around so they appear in graduated scales to the top.

Boil over medium heat 20 minutes, or until a fork will pierce their bottoms easily. Remove and let drain upside down. Serve still warm, at room temperature, or chilled, with sauce à la neige dolloped over their tops.

Serves 4.

Sauce à la Neige, usually reserved for fish in its New Orleans habitat, is a perfect complement to artichokes I find. It is a very easy sauce, fortunately, to master, and it has the virtue of appearing here like snow capping an Oriental jade mountain.

ASPARAGUS SAN FRANCISCO

2	pounds asparagus		Salt
¼	cup ground pecans	1	tablespoon lemon juice
⅓	cup bread crumbs		Lemon quarters
4	tablespoons butter		

*R*emove the tough ends of the asparagus, tie in bundles of 12, and cook standing up in 2 inches of water so the stems boil and the tips steam. (If you don't have an asparagus steamer, use the bottom of a double boiler with the top inverted over as a lid.) Cook for about 12 minutes—or until just tender.

While the asparagus cooks, sauté the nuts and bread crumbs in 3 tablespoons of the butter until lightly browned. Salt the mixture to taste. Heat the lemon juice and remaining 1 tablespoon butter together.

When the asparagus is done, drain and untie it. Place on warm plates, pour the lemon butter over, then sprinkle with the nut-crumb mixture. Garnish with lemon quarters.

Serves 4.

A sumptuous variation on asparagus Polonaise that should be served as a course by itself, perhaps with a glass of wine, and certainly a crust of good bread. This preparation can be adapted for green beans, broccoli, or Brussels sprouts.

COLONIAL GREEN BEANS WITH MACE

1	pound green beans, trimmed and French sliced	Salt and freshly ground pepper
2	tablespoons butter	Pinch of ground mace
		A few drops lemon juice

Drop the beans in rapidly boiling salted water, a handful at a time, making sure the water never stops bubbling. Cook 6 to 8 minutes, or until just tender, then drain and run cold water over to make sure they stop cooking.

Melt the butter in a pan over medium heat, toss the beans in it, and season to taste with salt, pepper, mace, and lemon juice. Serve immediately.

Serves 4.

Mace is a spice not now so widely used as in colonial time, but it makes a particularly happy marriage with green beans.

COUNTRY GREEN BEANS

1	pound green beans, trimmed	Chicken stock (or stock made with a ham bone, onion, and peppercorns, etc.)

Simmer the whole beans in stock to cover for 30 minutes. Drain and serve (the stock may be saved for soups).

Serves 3 to 4.

These go against all we have been taught about green beans—that they should be bright green, slightly crisp still, and served with perhaps only a sprinkle of almonds browned in butter over them. But if you simply consider this another vegetable altogether, and attempt it, you might end by liking this method—I know I do. The stock gives the beans enough savor that butter seems redundant, here, for those who worry about calories, and they go well with all kinds of simple country dishes like meat loaf, spareribs, etc.

YALE BEETS

1	orange	2	teaspoons cornstarch
1	lemon	⅓	cup sugar
10 to 12	medium fresh beets, cooked and sliced (or canned beets)		Salt
		2	tablespoons butter

*P*eel the orange and lemon with a vegetable peeler, then cut the peels into tiny julienne slices. Save the fruit. Put in a small pan of boiling water and let cook over medium heat 5 minutes. Drain and reserve.

Reserve ¼ cup of the beet cooking water (or the juice from the can) and mix it with the cornstarch, juice from both the orange and the lemon, sugar, and salt to taste. Cook over a gentle heat until the mixture clears and thickens.

To serve, bring the sauce to a simmer and slip the beet slices in. Cook several minutes to warm through, then swirl in the butter. Place the beets in a serving bowl and sprinkle the orange and lemon peel over.

Serves 4 to 6.

It is said that Yale beets set out to rival that rather horrid preparation known as Harvard beets. If so they must be accounted a success. They are both attractive and pleasantly sweet-sour, and they make a tasty and colorful side dish (or even first course) for many simple meats.

BEETS WITH
THEIR GREENS IN SOUR CREAM

10	young beets with their leaves	Salt and freshly ground pepper
2	tablespoons butter	Sour cream
1	tablespoon finely grated onion	Lemon wedges

*T*op the beets and put their greens in a large pan of water. Put beets in boiling salted water to cover, and simmer about 15 minutes, or until a fork pierces them easily. Place in cold water and slip off their skins. Cut into ½-inch dice.

Change the water on the greens, and make sure they are thoroughly clean. Strip the leaves off the stems and put in a large pot. Add the butter and grated onion, cover, and let cook down slowly, as you would spinach, in their own water. This will take no more than 5 minutes. Remove them with a slotted spoon, pressing down to remove as much liquid as possible.

Chop the greens coarsely, and boil down any of the liquid they released so you have only a couple of tablespoons of liquid. Put the greens back in the pot, add the diced beets, and toss with 2 tablespoons sour cream. Salt and pepper to taste.

To serve, place on warm plates, garnish with a dollop of sour cream and lemon wedges, and bring them quickly to table. If they must wait, toss with the 2 tablespoons sour cream just before serving.

Serves 4.

As a course by itself, with yeasty homemade rolls or The Duchess of Windsor's Cornpones (page 316), and a glass of either fine white or red wine, this dish can hold its own with a plate of spring asparagus or the lofty artichoke. One would not ordinarily think of serving beets to impress company, but that's exactly what I do with this dish.

COLONIAL FRICASSEE OF CABBAGE

4 tablespoons butter	1 tablespoon lemon juice
1 pound cabbage, cored and coarsely grated	Salt and freshly ground pepper
	Pinch of mace

*M*elt the butter in a saucepan over medium high heat. Toss the cabbage till it is coated with butter, and when it is heated through, add the lemon juice and seasonings.

Turn the heat low, cover the pan, and cook 8 to 10 minutes, tossing once during the cooking. The cabbage should still be slightly crisp. Taste for seasoning and serve immediately.

Serves 4.

A simple and good way to cook cabbage, and its simplicity is not harmed by the addition of a pinch of fresh herbs (say, summer savory, or a bit of thyme) if you have them. Cabbage has a bad name since it is so often overcooked to almost a mush, but treated with as much care for timing as you would any green bean, it is a delight—and inexpensive, too.

SHAKER CABBAGE IN CARAWAY CREAM

1	pound cabbage	1	teaspoon sugar
½	cup water	1	teaspoon curry powder
2	tablespoons butter	2	teaspoons caraway seeds
2	tablespoons flour	1½	tablespoons white wine
1	cup milk, scalded		vinegar
	Salt	½	cup sour cream

Core the cabbage and shred fine with a sharp knife. Put it with the water into a large saucepan, cover, and steam over medium heat 6 to 8 minutes, or until the cabbage has wilted. Remove from the heat and let sit.

In a saucepan, melt the butter, then stir in the flour and cook over medium heat for several minutes, stirring the while. Add the milk all at once and stir until a thick and smooth sauce is achieved. Add salt to taste, along with the sugar, curry powder, and caraway seeds. Stir this into the wilted cabbage.

Cover and let cook over very low heat 20 minutes, stirring now and again to make sure the cabbage doesn't stick to the pan. To serve, stir in the vinegar and sour cream and turn into a serving bowl.

Serves 4.

What an incredibly good vegetable the Shakers have come up with. In the final dish the flavors are balanced in a way that quite makes cabbage seem a luxury vegetable. Beauty and proportion to the Shakers were innocent delights, and they sought it all around them—from a table or chair, to a cabbage cooked for their fellows.

CARROTS DRAPER MORROW

1	pound carrots		Dash of mace
4	tablespoons butter	½	cup heavy cream
	Salt		

Scrape the carrots and either grate them very fine by hand, whirl in a food processor, or cut in 1-inch chunks and put in a blender with cold water to the top—blending until they are quite fine, then draining well. All these methods are equally good.

Heat the butter in a saucepan over medium flame, then add carrots, salt to taste, and mace. Cover, turn the heat down, and cook 10 to 15 minutes. Stir the carrots now and again to make sure they cook without sticking or burning—they should just slowly steam in the butter.

Finally, add the cream and cook 10 minutes more, uncovered, stirring now and again until the whole is a suave, creamy mass.

Serves 3 to 4.

Perhaps the finest way to show a humble vegetable to effect, these carrots will hold their own with almost any meat that does not have a cream sauce. Freshly grated nutmeg may be substituted for the mace, and if carrots are long from the field and need a bit of extra flavor, it makes the dish even richer to add a slog of good brandy, or sharper with a few drops of Tabasco or lemon juice.

ROOT PUDDING

1	cup coarsely grated carrot,	2	cups coarsely grated potato
1	medium onion, coarsely grated		Salt and freshly ground pepper
1	medium turnip, peeled and coarsely grated	6	tablespoons butter, melted
		3	tablespoons heavy cream

*P*reheat oven to 350°F.

This is, of course, a very simple dish to prepare with a food processor, but it doesn't take much effort to grate the vegetables by hand. Put them into a bowl, sprinkle with salt and pepper to taste, and toss with some of the butter.

Grease a pie plate or gratin dish with more of the butter, and lightly press the mixture in. Dribble cream over, then the rest of the butter. Bake uncovered for an hour, or until golden but still moist and rich.

Serves 4.

A fine old-fashioned way to treat winter vegetables. It is also a dish that can accompany most any meat or chicken, or even game. I like to sneak in a little grated nutmeg as well.

MY MOTHER'S
SOUR CREAM PEAKED CAULIFLOWER

1	head cauliflower, trimmed		Salt
1	tablespoon white wine	1	cup sour cream
	tarragon vinegar	⅓	cup fresh bread crumbs
5	tablespoons butter		

*P*reheat the oven to 350°F.

Steam the cauliflower in ½ inch water and the vinegar 10 to 15 minutes. When a sharp knife will just penetrate the heart of it, remove and place upside down in a bowl. Cut about 2 tablespoons of the butter into bits. Let the bits melt a good sprinkling of salt down the branches of the cauliflower as it sits.

Place the cauliflower right side up in a baking dish that is about its size—a soufflé dish is excellent. Sprinkle with more salt, and about 1 tablespoon more of the butter, in dots. In a frying pan, melt the remaining 2 tablespoons butter, add the crumbs, and stir over medium heat until golden.

To cook the dish, spread sour cream thickly over the cauliflower, sprinkle buttered crumbs over, and bake 30 minutes at 350°F. To serve, slice in pie-shaped wedges.

Serves 4.

All childhood longings aside, this is my favorite alternative to the usual cauliflower in a cheese sauce.

PURÉE OF CAULIFLOWER

1	head cauliflower	1	tablespoon butter
	Salt		Dash of Tabasco
1	tablespoon dry sherry		Freshly grated nutmeg
1	tablespoon heavy cream		

*R*emove the green leaves from cauliflower, cut out the core, and break into individual florets. Put in a saucepan with about a cup of water, some salt, and the sherry.

Cook over low heat 20 minutes, or until a knife point just pierces the stems.

Drain the liquid into a bowl and place the cauliflower in a blender or food processor.

Add the cream, butter, and 3 tablespoons of the cooking liquid and whirl till smooth. Add seasonings to taste.

Serves 4.

This should not be kept too long before serving. It is a wonderfully delicate dish—actually a kind of essence of cauliflower. For a company dinner it makes a fine show of flavor and texture with equal portions of glazed carrots and fresh green beans.

CHESTNUT PURÉE

1	pound (plus) chestnuts	½	cup milk
1	stalk celery	2	tablespoons butter
1	sprig parsley		Heavy cream
½	bay leaf		Salt and freshly ground
	Pinch of dried thyme		pepper
2	cups beef or chicken stock		

With a sharp small knife cut a small strip off each chestnut. Discard any "off" ones—(depending on how good the crop is, you may need more than a pound).

Put the chestnuts in a pan with cold water to cover, bring to a boil, and cook 1 minute. Remove from the heat and peel. They will need to keep hot for peeling, so if they start to be difficult, return the pan to the fire again and bring to a boil. Use a cloth or paper towel to hold them while peeling.

Put the chestnuts in a pan with the celery and the herbs (tied in a cheesecloth bag). Cover with stock. Simmer 45 minutes to an hour. When the chestnuts are tender, discard the celery and herbs and drain the chestnuts.

Sieve or rice them, adding the hot milk, butter, and enough cream to bring them to a desirable consistency. Taste for salt and pepper. (This may be kept hot for an hour in a double boiler.)

Serves 4.

If I didn't have to peel the chestnuts, I'd have this on the table nearly all the time. As it is, I anticipate it two or three times over the holidays, and plan whole meals around it. An instance of this is Roast Long Island Duckling page 160) with Chestnut Purée. It is also splendid alongside the stuffing, in equal portions, from a turkey or goose.

CORN ON THE COB

*T*he best way to prepare this most American of dishes is to put the kettle on to boil before picking the corn, then to run back to the kitchen. However fewer and fewer of us have gardens to run from, and must settle for the less than fresh corn in markets. It is never as sweet and flavorful, but even some of the frozen varieties are acceptable, and any ear of corn in the market still has the makings of a feast about it. To prepare corn, shuck the ears and rub to remove the silk. Trim the ends, put in a kettle, cover with cold water, add some salt and sugar, and turn on the heat to high. When the pot comes to a boil the corn is ready to serve, and should be, of course, eaten with the hands with slathers of butter, and a little salt and pepper.

COLONIAL CORN PUDDING

4 to 5	ears fresh corn	¼	cup buttermilk
3	eggs		Salt and freshly ground
1	cup heavy cream		pepper
¾	cup milk	2	tablespoons butter, melted

*P*reheat the oven to 350°F.

Scrape the corn from the cob first with the sharp edge of a knife to remove kernels, then with the back of the knife to make sure all the milky juice is extracted. You should have 2 cups.

Beat the eggs well, then beat in the cream, milk, and buttermilk. Add the corn and salt and pepper to taste. Grease a 1½-quart gratin dish, or an 8 × 8-inch baking pan, with part of the butter. Add the corn and dribble the rest of the butter on top.

Place in a larger pan with about 1 inch hot water in it and bake for an hour—or until the top of the pudding is golden, and a knife inserted comes out clean.

Serves 4 to 6.

Just writing about this dish makes me long for it again. Surely it is one of our best native dishes. In earlier times it was an ordinary breakfast dish— rather more sweetened than need be—and it is indeed pleasant to have some left over the next day, served at room temperature with crisp bacon. I like the extra flavor buttermilk yields here, but it can be prepared with any combination of cream and milk, or with milk alone.

SUCCOTASH

¼ cup diced (¼ inch) salt pork (or bacon)	1 pound fresh (or frozen) lima beans
5 to 6 ears of corn, scraped from the cob	Salt and freshly ground pepper
⅔ cup heavy cream	3 tablespoons butter

*T*ry out the salt pork in a heavy saucepan over low heat. When it has given out some of its fat and begins to brown, add the corn, tossing the mixture with a spoon. Add the cream, cover, and let simmer 20 minutes—occasionally peeking and stirring.

Meanwhile, cook the lima beans separately in salted water, and drain. Add to the corn, with salt and pepper to taste, and the butter. Cover and let simmer another 10 minutes—or until there is a good balance between the vegetable flavors.

Serves 4.

Succotash (a variation of the Narrangansett msickquatash) *was the first dish the Pilgrims learned from the Indians. It seems to have originally been a dish made from corn and dried beans, and it still is prepared in parts of New England with cranberry beans. Nowadays, however, fresh limas are usually preferred. It is a stodgy kind of vegetable, to me, but many dote on the combination.*

CORN, OKRA, AND TOMATOES

4 slices bacon	1 small green pepper, seeded and minced
1 onion, chopped	
2 cups okra, cut into ¼ inch rings	½ teaspoon sugar (optional)
	Salt and freshly ground pepper
4 ears corn, scraped from the cob (2 cups)	
1 cup peeled and chopped tomatoes (or canned tomatoes)	

*F*ry the bacon till it crisps, drain it on paper towels, and crumble. Sauté the onion and okra in the bacon fat until the onion softens.

Add the corn kernels and cook slowly 10 minutes, stirring to prevent sticking. Add tomatoes, green pepper, and seasonings, cover, and cook slowly 20 to 30 minutes, stirring now and again.

To serve, put into a serving dish and sprinkle with bacon.

Serves 6.

This is the Southern succotash, and it is my personal favorite among that far-flung family. But then I like okra. If one has only store produce, canned tomatoes do well, and frozen corn and okra still make a fine dish. Try it with fried chicken or pork chops.

SHAKER YELLOW VELVET

4 to 5	ears corn (2 cups)	1	pound yellow summer squash, trimmed
⅓	cup heavy cream		Few drops Tabasco (optional)
	Salt and freshly ground pepper	4	tablespoons butter
½	teaspoon sugar (optional)		

*S*crape the corn of its kernels with the sharp side of a knife, then scrape the "milk" out with the back side. Put in a saucepan with the cream, salt and pepper to taste, and a little sugar if the corn isn't fresh from the garden. Simmer 15 to 20 minutes, or until the corn is almost done.

Meanwhile, cook the squash in salted water to cover 15 to 20 minutes—or until it can be pierced easily with a fork. Drain and mash it (a food processor is easiest for this, but it can either be put through a ricer or puréed with a potato masher).

Add to the corn, with the Tabasco, butter, and salt to taste. Simmer another 15 minutes, or until the mélange has acquired some character.

Serves 6.

Yellow velvet indeed!

CHARLESTON CUCUMBERS

3   medium cucumbers
4   tablespoons butter
1   medium onion, finely chopped
¼   cup white wine tarragon
     vinegar

Salt and freshly ground
    pepper
Minced parsley

*P*eel the cucumbers and slice in quarters lengthwise. Cut down the center of each slice with a knife to remove the seeds, then cut the slices in 1-inch lengths. Put in salted water to cover, and simmer 12 to 15 minutes, or until done but still slightly crisp. Drain and reserve.

Heat the butter in a saucepan, add the onion, and sauté over low heat until limp. Add cucumbers, vinegar, and salt and pepper to taste. Cook, uncovered, 5 minutes over medium-high heat, stirring occasionally and letting the vinegar cook mostly away. Toss with parsley and serve.

Serves 4.

Every time I prepare this dish I am delighted anew at both its flavor and the lovely pale jade color. It is certainly one of the best accompaniments to fish ever devised, but it is also splendid with chicken as a kind of combination relish and vegetable.

DEEP-FRIED EGGPLANT

1   eggplant
    Salt
    Milk

Flour
Freshly grated nutmeg
Vegetable oil

*P*eel the eggplant and slice as for French fries. Salt, then let drain 15 minutes or more on absorbent paper. Put in a bowl and cover with milk and let sit until you are ready to cook.

At that time, drain off the milk and shake the slices in a bag with flour and nutmeg. Fry in deep hot oil at about 375°F (or until a test slice enters the fat sputtering and becomes straw brown—not dark brown—by the time the sputters subside). Remove with a slotted spoon and drain on absorbent paper. Salt and serve quickly.

Serves 4 to 6, depending on the size of the eggplant.

Even people who say they do not like eggplant often admire these delicate puffy strips. They are crisp on the outside and almost creamy at the center, though they should be served as soon as possible after cooking or their light-ness subsides. They make an excellent companion for lamb.

LOUISIANA RATATOUILLE

1 medium eggplant, peeled and cut into 1-inch cubes	Freshly ground pepper
Salt	Pinch of ground cloves
1 cup chopped onion	Pinch of dried thyme
4 tablespoons olive oil (or bacon fat)	4 garden-fresh beefsteak tomatoes (or 1 can [1 pound] Italian plum tomatoes)
1 pound okra, trimmed and sliced	2 tablespoons red wine vinegar

*P*ut the eggplant in boiling salted water and cook 10 minutes. Drain. Cook the onion in a frying pan with 2 tablespoons of the oil, for several minutes, or until limp. Add the okra and toss with salt, pepper, cloves, and thyme. Cover, and cook slowly 10 minutes.

Meanwhile, preheat the oven to 325°F.

Drop the tomatoes in boiling water for a minute, remove with a slotted spoon, and peel and slice. (Or, if you are using canned tomatoes, drain and chop coarsely.)

To assemble the dish, oil a shallow baking dish. Make a layer of the eggplant in the dish, cover with the onion-okra mixture, and finally arrange the sliced tomatoes on top. Sprinkle with the rest of the oil, cover with a lid or foil, and bake 1½ hours.

Remove from the oven, sprinkle with the vinegar, and return to the oven for another 10 to 15 minutes. Remove and let cool.

Serves 6 to 8.

A dish that should be served at room temperature, or cold the next day. I like it better than most ratatouilles I've tasted, and I also secretly like it better with bacon fat than with olive oil.

GREENS

2 bunches turnip, mustard, or
    collard greens
2 cups water
¼ pound salt pork (or bacon),
    finely diced
    Salt and freshly ground
    pepper

¼ cup chopped onion
    (optional)
2 to 3 turnips, peeled and cut
    into ½-inch dice
    (optional)

Clean any mixture of greens in a large pan of water. Strip the leaves off the stems and place them in a large kettle with 2 cups water. Sprinkle salt pork over the top and add salt and pepper to taste (remember the salt pork will add almost enough salt to the completed dish).

Add the onion if you wish the extra savor, and if you've used turnip greens, add the turnips as well. Bring to a boil, then cover the pot, turn fire down low, and let simmer several hours. (In some places in the South they are cooked nearly all day—I find a pressure cooker ideal for greens, and they are just right in about an hour.)

Serve 4 to 6.

Most people not brought up in the South find the mention of this dish rather appalling. It goes against all rules for cooking delicate greens, certainly, but for rough, bitterish greens it is simply wonderful. And don't worry about loss of vitamins, for the juice left is not called "pot liquor" for nothing. It is a broth of minerals and vitamins that may be used to cook cornmeal dumplings (though I can never get them to hold together), or to sauce cornbread, etc. Greens should be served with equally forthright meat such as barbecued pork or fried chicken.

COTTAGE ROASTED JERUSALEM ARTICHOKES

1½ to 2 pounds Jerusalem
    artichokes

1 roast beef in progress (or leg
    of lamb, baked chicken)

Most people peel Jerusalem artichokes, but it is not really necessary—so peel or not, as you wish. Slice them about ½ inch thick. An hour before your roast is done (assuming it is cooking at 325° to 350°F), place the slices around the roast in its pan drippings. Baste and turn them occasionally, and remove them when they are golden brown. Serve around the meat.

Serves 4 to 6.

No relation to the "globe" artichoke, these are tubers from sunflower roots (and sometimes marketed as "sunchokes"). They have a lovely crispness rather like a water chestnut, and are delightful cooked around a roast rather than the usual potatoes. They are also good for those on diets, as the tubers have virtually no starch.

FRIED OKRA, KENTUCKY STYLE

1	pound okra	3	tablespoons bacon fat (or 2
	Salt and freshly ground		tablespoons butter and 1
	pepper		tablespoon vegetable oil)
½	cup white stone-ground		Lemon wedges
	cornmeal		Tabasco

*T*rim the okra by cutting off the tops of the pod and the tip end. Place in a kettle of boiling water and cook till almost tender—about 5 minutes, depending on the size of the pods.

Drain, sprinkle with salt and pepper, and shake in a bag of cornmeal. Heat the bacon fat in a skillet large enough to hold all the okra and sauté them till they are golden, turning once during the cooking. Serve with wedges of lemon and Tabasco.

Serves 4.

For those who like okra, this is one of the very best ways to prepare it. (For those who do not like okra, there is no hope.) There are two other basic ways to cook it, as well. If you have small tender okra, simply boil it (whole and just trimmed on top) in salted water as little as possible until it is done to taste, then dress and toss with butter, lemon juice or white wine vinegar, salt, and pepper. Larger okra are prime for the final method in which you top the pods and slice them about ¼ inch thick. Drop them as you slice into a bowl of cornmeal. Salt and pepper, and toss to coat the slices. Fry these in hot fat until golden, then drain on paper toweling.

FRENCH-FRIED ONION RINGS

2 large mild onions, peeled and   Flour
     cut in ¼-inch slices   Salt and freshly ground pepper
1 cup water   Vegetable oil
1 cup milk

Put the onions in a bowl and cover with water and milk. Let them sit for 30 minutes or more. To cook, drain the onions, then separate into rings and shake them in flour generously seasoned with salt and pepper. Fry in hot oil (350° to 370°F) until they are golden brown, remove to paper toweling, sprinkle with salt, and serve quickly.

Serves 3 to 4.

Twenty years ago these were served everywhere to great delight. Now they come frozen, constructed of reconstituted onion pulp and, oddly enough, breaded. They are so awful that I wonder who remembers the real right thing, so much better than any French fry with a steak or hamburger.

BRAISED ONIONS, FRENCH QUARTER STYLE

6 Spanish or Bermuda onions   Salt
     (or any large flat white   ½ teaspoon dried thyme
     onion)   ½ cup Madeira
12 whole cloves   ¼ cup capers
1 cup water   1 teaspoon caper juice
½ cup beef stock

Trim the onions, but don't cut through the root end completely so they will hold together during cooking. Stick 2 cloves in each onion and place them in a saucepan or casserole large enough to hold all of them. Add water, stock, and thyme, and just a pinch of salt.

Bring to a boil, cover, and cook over low heat 30 minutes, or until the onions are tender. Remove the onions with a slotted spoon and keep warm.

Turn the heat on high and boil the liquid down, uncovered, to about ½ cup. Add the Madeira, capers, and caper juice, and taste for seasoning. To serve, pour the sauce over the onions.

Serves 6.

What an ideal way to begin a meal, in the French manner, with crusty bread and a glass of wine. The meal itself could only be a simple romantic one such as a tossed herb omelet, and fine fruit and cheese, then steaming thimbles of coffee.

SPOKANE SCALLOPED ONIONS

6	onions, sliced	Salt and freshly ground
3	tablespoons butter, melted	pepper
½	cup heavy cream	Freshly grated nutmeg (or
1	egg, beaten	mace)
2	tablespoons dry sherry (or Madeira)	

*P*reheat oven to 350°F.

Place the onions in a large kettle of boiling salted water and parboil 10 minutes. Drain thoroughly and put in a 1½-quart casserole greased with a bit of the melted butter.

Mix the cream with egg and pour over the onions, then add the sherry and seasonings. Toss lightly to make sure the flavorings are spread evenly. Dribble melted butter over the top and bake 45 minutes, or until the top is crusty gold.

Serves 6.

All savory simplicity, and right with many a meat. It may easily sit in a warm oven for a spell, and it makes an inexpensive side dish for company. You could halve it for family by using only an egg yolk, etc.

CAROLINA PARSNIP SOUFFLÉ

1	pound parsnips	1 cup milk, scalded
	Salt	3 eggs, separated
3	tablespoons butter	Freshly ground pepper
3	tablespoons flour	Freshly grated nutmeg

*P*reheat oven to 350°F.

Peel the parsnips, and if they are large, quarter them and cut out the inner tough core. Chop and place in a pot of boiling salted water. Boil 30 minutes, or until tender. Drain and put them through a ricer or sieve.

In a saucepan, melt the butter over medium heat. Add the flour and cook, stirring, several minutes. Add the milk all at once and stir until the sauce is thick and smooth. Take off the fire and beat in the egg yolks one by one, then add salt, pepper, and nutmeg to taste.

Whip egg whites stiff (but not dry) and fold them into the parsnip mixture. Put in a greased soufflé dish and bake at 350°F 40 minutes, or until puffed and set.

Serves 4.

The best parsnip dish I know of, from anywhere. It makes an unusual accompaniment to sturdy braised or sautéed meats of all kinds. It is especially good with pork, and I once served it with rabbit to great acclaim.

BRAISED PEAS WITH CUCUMBERS

1 cucumber	Pinch of sugar
2 tablespoons butter	¼ cup chicken stock
Salt and freshly ground pepper	1 package frozen tiny peas (or one pound fresh, shelled)
1 teaspoon minced chives (or some parsley)	

*P*eel the cucumber, cut it lengthwise in quarters, then scoop out the seeds. Cut the strips into ¼-inch dice and put in a saucepan with the butter. Cover the pan and cook the cucumber over medium heat for 4 to 5 minutes. Add salt and pepper to taste, the chives, and the sugar.

Add the stock and bring to a boil, then add the peas, and when they come again to a boil, cook another 2 minutes, covered.

Serves 4.

If I remember rightly, this comes from a handbound "book" mimeographed by homesick Korean army wives. Nothing of much interest turned up in it, but this recipe I use constantly. Though infinitely better with fresh garden peas, or course, the cucumbers here bring out frozen peas to distinction.

CREAMED SPRING PEAS AND NEW POTATOES

*E*ach season's creamed peas and potatoes was the very best vegetable I can remember eating through my childhood, and I have tried in vain to reconstruct the dish from current store produce. No peas seem fresh enough, though new potatoes are found now and again with much flavor. The closest you may come, if you yourself don't grow peas, is to use fresh Chinese snow peas (or even frozen in a pinch).

To do this, boil the potatoes in their skins in salted water, then drain and keep warm. Prepare a simple white sauce using the proportions of 1 tablespoon butter and 1 tablespoon flour to 1 cup hot rich milk or light cream. Trim the snow peas, put in water to cover, and cook only till they come to a boil. Drain, then stir into the sauce with potatoes and season to taste with salt and freshly ground pepper.

POMPION

4	cups pumpkin (or any winter squash), cut in ¼-inch dice		Salt and freshly ground pepper
1	shallot, minced	1	cup heavy cream
¼	cup minced parsley		Grated Parmesan cheese
¼	cup flour	3	tablespoons butter, melted

*P*reheat the oven to 350°F.

Cut off the hard peel of a pumpkin or any red-fleshed winter squash such as Hubbard or butternut. Dice and place in a bowl.

Toss the pumpkin with shallot (a scrap of garlic minced with some green onion may substitute for the shallot, if you wish), parsley, flour, and salt and pepper to taste.

Use some of the butter to grease a 12 x 8-inch gratin dish. Add the pumpkin, pour the cream over, sprinkle with Parmesan, and dribble the rest of the butter over. Bake at 350°F for 1 hour, or until the pumpkin is quite dark gold and the cream has been absorbed.

Serves 4 to 6.

This dish, named for the early explorer's word for pumpkin, will be a revelation for those who have only tasted squash and pumpkin sticky sweet and spiced. *This preparation is rich and handsomely flavored, and is at home with turkey, game, or pork.*

PENNSYLVANIA GRATED RUTABAGAS

6 tablespoons butter	6 slices bacon, fried and
2 pounds rutabagas, peeled and	crumbled (optional)
coarsely grated	Minced parsley
Salt and freshly ground	
pepper	

*M*elt the butter in a large frying pan, and when it begins to sizzle add the rutabagas and salt and pepper to taste. Cover the pan and cook gently 15 minutes, tossing now and again as they cook.

Uncover and cook 15 minutes more, or until the rutabagas are soft and start to brown slightly. Serve sprinkled with bacon and parsley.

Serves 4 to 6.

Cooked so, these make a light unusual dish to partner pork, game, or even lamb. A hint of nutmeg or mace will not be out of place, and minced chives tossed in the end of cooking (rather than the bacon and parsley) make it more delicate. Rutabagas have a coarse, unlovely reputation, and it is true that cooked to a mush as usual they are almost as unsavory as a soggy Brussels sprout, but this is a dish apart.

SPINACH WITH
CREAM CHEESE AND CHIVES

2 pounds fresh spinach, washed	Milk
and stripped of stems	1 tablespoon minced chives
1 package (3 ounces) cream	Salt and freshly ground
cheese	pepper

*P*lace the spinach leaves in a large kettle with just the water that clings to the leaves. Cover the kettle, put over medium heat, and let the leaves wilt—this will take only about 5 minutes. Immediately dump them into a colander and run cold water over.

Squeeze out all the water with your hands and chop the spinach fine. Put the chopped spinach in a small saucepan with the cream cheese and stir over low heat until it forms a paste.

Add enough milk to make the mixture soft and creamy, then add the chives and salt and papper to taste. Cover, and let cook gently for 10 minutes.

Serves 4.

A beautiful and easy way to serve spinach. It has a slightly different quality than the usual French method of marrying cream, butter, and spinach—and chives make a welcome change from the traditional nutmeg. I suppose it would be possible to concoct this dish from frozen spinach and chive cream cheese, but with a good deal of loss in flavor.

GEORGIA SUMMER SQUASH SOUFFLÉ

2	pounds yellow summer squash (or patty pan or zucchini)	¼	cup minced parsley (optional)
		¼	cup bread crumbs
	Salt	1	egg
4	tablespoons butter, melted		Milk
1	cup chopped onion		Freshly ground pepper

*P*reheat the oven to 350°F.

Boil the squash in salted water till just tender. Drain, then mash coarsely with a potato masher.

Sauté the onion and parsley (if using) in 2 tablespoons of the butter until the onion is limp. Add this to the mashed squash along with the bread crumbs. Break the egg into a cup measure and add enough milk to make a full cup, then mix gently into the squash.

Add salt and pepper to taste (if the squash is not quite small and fresh, sometimes I also add a pinch of sugar or a drop of Tabasco).

Grease the bottom and sides of a gratin dish with some of the butter, then add the squash and dribble the butter that is left on top. Bake 45 minutes, or until puffy and golden on top.

Serves 4 to 6.

Of course not a soufflé in the French sense of the word, this is more a pudding. Nevertheless, homely as it sounds it is one of the very best ways to cook tender little squash there is, and I never tire of it.

ACORN SOUFFLÉS

2	matched acorn squash		Salt and freshly ground
2	tablespoons minced shallot		pepper
2	tablespoons butter	⅓	cup heavy cream
	Pinch of ground mace	2	eggs, separated, plus 2 egg
	Lemon juice		whites
			Parmesan cheese (optional)

*P*reheat the oven to 350°F.

Bake the squash whole for 1 hour, or until a toothpick enters the skins easily. Remove from the oven, then slice in half lengthwise so they form four equal cups. Spoon out the seeds and discard.

Sauté the shallot (or chopped green onions with a scrap of garlic) in the butter till soft, and place in a bowl. Scoop out the flesh of the baked squash and mash it into the shallot, or rice through a ricer into the bowl.

Add mace, a few drops of lemon juice, salt and pepper to taste, cream, and the 2 egg yolks. Taste for seasoning. Beat the 4 egg whites till they hold peaks but are not dry, then fold into the squash mixture carefully.

Place the squash shells in a buttered baking dish, heap the soufflé mixture in each shell, and sprinkle with parmesan cheese. Bake 20 to 30 minutes at 350°F, or until puffed up and golden. Serve immediately.

Serves 4.

These beautiful soufflés can make either a first course or a side dish to meats. They lend a simple roast pork distinction, or a grilled lamb chop substance. They are, I think, splendid enough for holiday goose or turkey, and at the same time they are comfortable as a small supper with some sausage and applesauce.

HERBED CHERRY TOMATOES

2	tablespoons butter	2	teaspoons minced fresh basil
1	shallot, minced		(or 1 teaspoon dried)
2	green onions, minced with	1½	cups cherry tomatoes,
	part of tops		washed and stemmed
1	tablespoon minced parsley		Salt and freshly ground
			pepper

Melt the butter in a frying pan. Add the shallot, green onion, parsley, and basil and cook over low heat a few minutes, or until the shallot and onion are wilted.

Add the tomatoes, sprinkle with salt and pepper, and stir very gently as they cook over low heat. Cook 5 minutes or until they are heated through (too much cooking will cause their skins to burst).

Serves 4.

Even cherry tomatoes are in a decline these days, and come to market still greenish. But if you can find ripe tasty ones, this makes an attractive vegetable garnish to almost any plate.

CARAMELIZED GREEN TOMATOES

2	pounds small green tomatoes	4	tablespoons butter
	Flour	½	cup light brown sugar

Remove the stem ends of the tomatoes and cut them in half crosswise. Dip the cut ends into flour, and fry in hot butter in a large frying pan over medium heat until they are golden on the cut side. This will take 6 to 8 minutes.

Turn them over and sprinkle sugar on and around them. Cook gently for 5 minutes, then turn them cut side down again and cook until caramelized—about another 5 minutes. Serve cut side up to garnish meats, etc.

Serves 4 to 6.

Edible tomatoes have nearly disappeared in American markets, even in season. Among them, however, the diligent will often find nice tart green tomatoes that are quite good. This recipe may also be adapted to large green tomatoes cut in slices, but they take less time to cook. They are good with ham, or pork in almost any form, but they can be used anywhere a delicate sweet-sour flavor seems fit.

GRATIN OF CURRIED GREEN TOMATOES

6	medium green tomatoes, sliced		Salt and freshly ground pepper
2	medium onions, sliced	1	cup sour cream
2	tablespoons butter	½	cup buttered bread crumbs
1	teaspoon curry powder		

Preheat the oven to 350°F.

Sauté the tomatoes and onions in hot butter till the onions are limp and the tomatoes are cooked but not mushy.

Add the curry powder, salt and pepper to taste, and stir gently. Let cook a few more minutes, then stir in the sour cream. Pour into a buttered 10 × 6-inch gratin dish and top with buttered crumbs. Bake for 30 minutes, or until golden and bubbly.

Serves 4 to 6.

Another favorite vegetable. Somehow green tomatoes have an affinity for curry powder (and ginger as well) and this dish shows them at their finest. I like it particularly with roast lamb, or pork, but it is useful for many meals more.

JAMES BEARD'S
TURNIPS WITH MUSHROOMS

	Salt		Freshly ground pepper
6	turnips, peeled and sliced ¼ inch thick	½	pound mushrooms, cleaned and sliced ¼ inch thick
6	tablespoons butter		Minced parsley (or chives)

Cover the sliced turnips with boiling salted water and cook over medium heat 8 to 10 minutes, or until tender but still crisp. Drain and toss with 2 tablespoons of the butter and some pepper.

While they are cooking, sauté the mushrooms in the remaining 4 tablespoons butter, seasoning with salt and pepper to taste. This will take only 3 to 4 minutes.

Scrape the mushrooms and their juices into the turnips and cook gently for 2 minutes more. Serve sprinkled with parsley or chives.

Serves 4 to 6.

A recipe picked up on the trail of the indefatigable James Beard, our most venerable and intelligent champion of native food—though I'm not sure how much it has changed during the years I've cooked it with pleasure. Typical of Mr. Beard's forthright gustatory sensibilities, here two earthy flavors play off and complement each other toward a new succulence. As partner to a lamb chop—or for that matter game—they are not to be beaten.

SHAKER ALABASTER

4	medium turnips, peeled and halved	Salt
4	medium potatoes, peeled and halved	Heavy cream
		Tabasco (or white pepper)

*P*lace the turnips and potatoes in a saucepan of boiling salted water to cover and boil 20 to 30 minutes—or till a knife pierces each easily. Drain, then put turnips in a blender or food processor. Return the potatoes to the saucepan.

Put paper toweling over the potatoes, and cover with a lid to sit till dry— about 5 minutes. Add ¼ cup cream to the turnips and whirl to a fine purée. Mash or rice the potatoes, add the turnips, and beat smooth.

Add as much more cream to the mixture as will make it slightly more liquid than regular mashed potatoes. Season to taste with salt and Tabasco. Put in the top of a double boiler over simmering water (or in a 300°F oven) till puffed slightly—about 20 to 30 minutes. They may stand for as long as an hour.

Serves 4.

A beautiful conceit of the Shakers, with nothing to yellow the whiteness, and a surprisingly good accompaniment to any duck dish, to braised meats with lots of sauce, or to a lamb chop for all that. Surprise is the word—they are always surprising.

ZUCCHINI FRITTERS

2 cups coarsely grated zucchini	½ teaspoon salt
1 teaspoon lemon juice	Freshly ground nutmeg
1 tablespoon grated onion	¼ cup flat beer
¼ cup minced parsley	Vegetable oil
½ cup flour	Grated Parmesan cheese
1 teaspoon baking powder	(optional)

*P*ut the zucchini in a bowl, sprinkle with lemon juice, and mix with the onion and parlsey. Sift the flour, baking powder, and salt over, grate some nutmeg in, and mix together lightly. Pour the beer in and mix again thoroughly.

Heat at least 1 inch oil in a pan, and fry walnut-sized spoonfuls of the zucchini mixture till crisp and golden. Drain on paper toweling, and sprinkle with Parmesan cheese if you wish before serving.

Serves 4.

Zucchini fritters make very good combination starch and vegetable to serve with all kinds of meats. In my house they tend to disappear before they can even get to table.

Starchy Dishes

*H*enry James (no noted gourmet) once asked his British cook if she could not do other than boil or mash a potato to accompany his chop, and suggested she might fry them. She, in turn, suggested that method might be French, and no, she didn't know of any other ways. Henry knew otherwise. His French visits bristled with ways of surprising a chop, and he suspected even his brash countrymen knew a trick or two, for he had tasted the newly invented "Saratoga chips"—that paper-thin crisp heaped beside the duck, prepared in a way that certainly couldn't be called French. In fact, the potato is a magical vegetable, quick to take on new character with every marginal change in shape, or twist in cooking. We have a host of ways (and nearly as many with the noodle and grain of rice) treasured up, out of the past, for one and all.

MISS DOROTHY'S MASHED POTATOES

Per person:

1	medium potato	1 to 2	tablespoons butter
	Salt		Freshly ground pepper
	About ¼ cup milk, scalded		

Boil the potatoes in salted water till they are tender, or a fork will pierce them easily. Drain well, return to the pot, and cover first with a double layer of paper toweling, then with the pot lid. Let sit 5 minutes, or until the potatoes are dry and mealy.

Peel, rice them into a bowl, and with a potato masher (or better yet with an electric mixer) work in milk, bit by bit, until you think there is too much, and then add a little more. It is better to add too much than too little.

Beat in the butter, and salt and pepper to taste. Put the potatoes in the top of a double boiler set over hot water (or covered in a 300°F oven) and let them sit over low heat for 20 to 30 minutes. They will puff up and have a very light consistency without being filmed with butter or cream as most recipes tell you. (They can be held up to an hour in this manner, and really only get better.) Serve with a little more butter in a pool on top if there is no sauce to the meat.

This, along with my mother's pie crust, are just about the only two things I have learned firsthand from great cooks. Anyone can make complex things, but to make the simplest ones fine is the mark of the truly expert.

MY MASHED POTATOES

Preheat the oven to 425°F.

For these you proceed exactly as for Miss Dorothy's Mashed Potatoes (see preceding recipe), except you take good strips of peel with a vegetable peeler from the potatoes before boiling.

When you have the mashed potatoes in a double boiler or warm oven, pile the strips of peel up in stacks and cut them in julienne strips (about ⅛ inch wide) with a sharp knife. Toss with a bit of melted butter—only about a tablespoon per cup of peel is necessary.

Place in a shallow pan and bake 15 minutes, or until the strips of peel are crisp as potato chips and golden brown. They should not get dark brown. They may be kept warm until you are ready to serve the potatoes, then sprinkle a pile of crisp strips over every serving. These are quite tasty enough without any salt.

Vitamins aside, this makes quite the most possible of an already good thing. It probably is a sin to waste anything as good as these peelings. In fact, even when you prepare other potato dishes remember they can be cooked as they come from the peeler in large strips to make an excellent appetizer. They can also be prepared from baked peel (about 5 minutes), or boiled peel (about 20 minutes). Warning: If you see a hint of green under the peel of any potato, don't use it. This means the potato has been stored improperly, and the green part is slightly poisonous.

OHIO BUTTERMILK
MASHED POTATO SOUFFLÉ

4	medium potatoes	2	teaspoons sugar
	Salt	2	tablespoons butter
¼	teaspoon baking soda	½	cup (or more) milk
½	cup buttermilk	2	tablespoons butter, melted

*B*oil the potatoes in salted water till a fork goes through. (It is preferable to do this with the skins on, for flavor, but not necessary.) When done, drain and return to the pan. Place a double paper towel over the pan, then cover with the lid. Let set to dry 5 minutes or so.

Preheat the oven to 325°F.

While the potatoes sit, stir the soda into the buttermilk. Place 1 teaspoon salt, the sugar, and butter into a bowl. Peel the potatoes and place in a ricer. Rice them into the salt, sugar, and butter. Mash with the soda-buttermilk until smooth. Add enough milk to make the mixture thickly soupy rather than stiff. (2 cups liquid in all are just right for 1½ pounds potatoes, but in practice no two batches are quite alike. Don't worry, but don't make them too dry either.)

Use a bit of the melted butter to grease a soufflé dish. Put the potatoes in, smooth over with a spatula, and dribble the rest of the butter on top. These can sit awhile if you wish, for 30 minutes or so, and then be cooked at 325°F for 30 minutes. They can cook in a slightly higher oven, even, but they should not brown. The final dish should just puff up slightly, and still be creamy.

Serves 4.

More "mashed" than soufflé, these farmhouse potatoes are still about the best tasting in the world.

MY NESTED POTATOES

4	medium potatoes	4	tablespoons butter, melted
	Salt	½	cup sour cream (optional)

*P*reheat the oven to 350°F.

Boil the potatoes till tender in salted water, then drain and return to the pan. Place paper toweling over the pan then cover with the lid. Let sit to dry 5 minutes or more.

While the potatoes sit, use some of the melted butter to grease the bottom and sides of a soufflé dish. Peel the potatoes and place in a ricer, then rice them carefully into the dish. (The reason for a soufflé dish is that the sides of it are high enough so the riced potatoes are not mashed down in any way.)

Put directly in the oven and cook 30 minutes, or until the potatoes begin to get golden and a slight crust begins to form on top. Gently pour the remaining melted butter over the potatoes, and cook another 30 minutes.

Properly made, the potatoes will be crisp and golden all over, and not stick to the sides or bottom. You will be able to tip them out and place on a warm plate without changing their shape. Shake the dish to see if they are loose, and if not cook some more.

When done, unmold on a serving plate and fill the center of the nest with sour cream if desired. Bring to table and slice in pie-shaped wedges.

Serves 4.

A ricer necessarily produces a ring mound with a center depression, and these potatoes are formed around this. I have given the smallest amount of butter here, but there is no use being stingy about it, and I use sometimes nearer ½ cup. After the potatoes are crisp extra butter on top will not harm the light puff inside. I don't think they need any salt or pepper, but you might.

AMERICAN FRIES

4   medium potatoes   Salt and freshly ground pepper
    Vegetable oil

*P*eel the potatoes and cut into ½-inch dice. Drop into a bowl of cold water to wash the starch off. Drain and dry on paper toweling.

Heat oil to the depth of about 1 inch in a large frying pan set over high heat. When the oil begins to shimmer, test a potato cube—and it should sizzle up immediately and cook in earnest.

Add all the potatoes and fry until golden brown (they should be turned now and again to ensure that they cook evenly). When done, lift out with a slotted spoon onto paper toweling, and sprinkle with salt and pepper.

Serves 4.

Essentially French fries in another form, these also form the basis of Brabant Potatoes (see following recipe) and all its variations—see Sirloin Clemenceau (page 80).

BRABANT POTATOES

4   medium potatoes   ¼   cup minced parsley
    Vegetable oil   Salt and freshly ground
¼   cup butter   pepper
2   cloves garlic, minced   Good wine vinegar (optional)

*C*ook the potatoes as in the preceeding American Fries.

Preheat the oven to 175°F.

When the potatoes are done, and drained, put the butter in a small saucepan and cook the garlic in it till the garlic starts to turn golden—be careful not to burn it. Remove from the heat.

Put potatoes in a baking dish, pour the garlic butter through a sieve over them, and discard the garlic. Sprinkle the parsley and salt and pepper to taste over the potatoes, and toss thoroughly.

Place in the oven and cook 15 to 20 minutes. If you wish, sprinkle a very little vinegar over them before serving.

Serves 4.

It is a mystery to me why this dish—widely cooked in both homes as well as restaurants in New Orleans—never seems to travel. These fries are certainly livelier than any French fry, and are easier to prepare, since they have to sit in the oven for a time rather than being rushed to the table.

BALTIMORE FRIES

1½ pounds red potatoes, each 2	Salt
inches in diameter	Vegetable oil

Scrub the potatoes and cut them in quarters. Drop in boiling salted water and cook 15 minutes—they should be almost done but not soft. Drain and dry on taper toweling.

Heat at least 1 inch of oil in a large frying pan, and when it starts to shimmer (but not smoke) add one potato quarter to test. In 4 minutes it should be golden brown all over. Cook the rest of the potatoes, drain on paper toweling, and lightly salt them. Serve immediately.

Serves 4.

An example of how potatoes, by being a slightly different form, and by being cooked slightly differently, can take on magic newness and goodness. These are not widely known, and I like to surprise guests with them alongside steaks or chops or many another dish.

SARATOGA CHIPS

4 baking potatoes	Salt
Vegetable oil	

Peel the potatoes (or not, if you like chips with skins on) and slice as thin as possible—a vegetable grater usually has a slicer on it that makes these well, but they are best carefully done with a regular vegetable peeler, one by one. Soak the slices 1 to 2 hours in cold water, changing the water once.

Drain and dry thoroughly before cooking. To do this, bring oil to heat in a deep-fat fryer. The fat should be 375°F, or at the point a test slice enters the fat sputtering and becomes straw-brown by the time its sputters subside.

Fry the chips in batches, making sure they don't stick together. Drain on paper toweling, and sprinkle with salt while still hot.

Serves 4.

These homemade potato chips are the traditional partner to game, in this country, but they are perfect with steaks or grilled chops, even hamburgers. But be prepared—your family or guests will most likely eat all you can turn out. These were the invention of one George Crum, chef of Moon's Lake House at the fashionable nineteenth century spa, Saratoga Springs. It is said a finicky patron returned his French fries saying they were not thin enough, and Crum sliced some potatoes paper thin. A new dish was born—and as Brillat-Savarin says, "The discovery of a new dish does more for human happiness than the discovery of a star."

RUSSIAN HILL POTATOES

1½ cups coarsely grated potatoes	4 tablespoons butter, melted Salt and freshly ground pepper

*P*ut the grated potato in a bowl of water, then drain and rinse under the faucet in a sieve or colander. Squeeze the water out by hand and put the potatoes in a bowl. Use a bit of the butter to grease a 10-inch cast iron frying pan (or a nonstick pan) and toss the rest with the potatoes. Add salt and pepper to taste.

Put the frying pan over high heat and spread the potatoes in with a spatula. When they start to take a bit of color on the underside, lower the heat and cook 20 minutes, shaking now and again to make sure a crust forms evenly without burning. (It is better to cook it too slow, after it first forms a crust, than too fast.)

When the bottom is a gold-brown crust, flip the cake onto a plate, crust side up, then slide it back into the pan on the uncooked side. Cook another 15 to 20 minutes, adding more butter if needed, until the whole is a lacy golden brown throughout, and can be lifted with a spatula (or hand) onto a plate.

Cut in 4 pie-shape wedges and serve. (The potatoes can also be held in a warm oven, if need be, for 30 minutes or so.)

Serves 2 to 4.

My only complaint about this dish is that it's almost impossible to make enough unless you have a battery of skillets going. Once you get the hang of them, they are really quite easy, though, and they go well with everything but fried meats. They put hashed browns in the shade, at breakfast, as well.They are the invention of chef John Sharpless, who cooks them in a hot oven as restaurant cooks do everything, but I get better results on top of the stove.

FARMHOUSE
SKILLET CREAMED POTATOES

¾ cup heavy cream	Salt and freshly ground pepper
¾ cup milk	Freshly grated nutmeg
2 tablespoons butter	
4 to 5 medium potatoes, peeled and cut into ¼-inch slices	

*P*lace the cream, milk, and butter in a frying pan. Slice the potatoes into the pan and add salt, pepper, and nutmeg to taste. Turn up the heat and bring to a simmer.

Cover the pan, turn the heat way down, and cook gently 30 minutes. Uncover and turn the potatoes with a pancake turner. Check the seasonings and simmer another 30 minutes, uncovered, or until the potatoes are tender and their sauce is thick and creamy.

Serves 4.

These are purely wonderful. The sauce achieved is incomparably better than potatoes in a white sauce. They can accompany practically any meat that is not sauced itself.

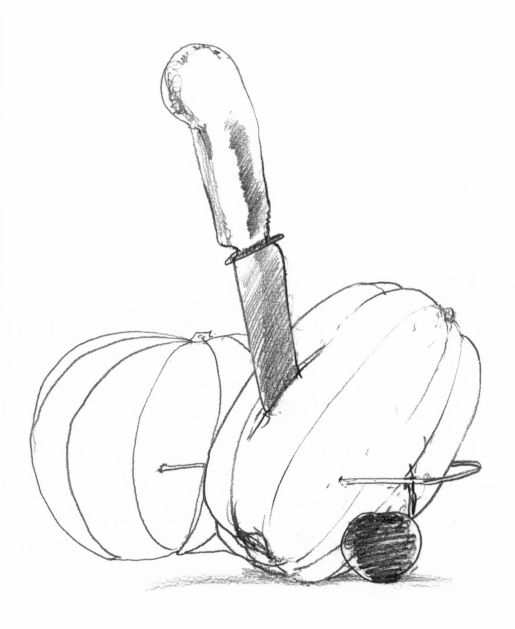

THRICE-BAKED POTATOES

2 large baking potatoes, scrubbed and oiled	Salt and freshly ground pepper
4 tablespoons butter, melted	Milk
	⅓ cup grated Parmesan cheese

*B*ake the potatoes at any temperature till they are soft. Remove from the oven and let cool until you can handle them. Cut them lengthwise and scoop out the flesh from the shells. Turn the oven to 425°F.

Brush the shells well with 1 tablespoon of the melted butter, put them in the oven on a baking sheet, and cook 10 to 15 minutes, or until they are crisp and golden.

While the shells cook, prepare the flesh as you would for Miss Dorothy's Mashed Potatoes (page 250), adding plenty of milk and 2 tablespoons of the butter and most of the Parmesan. They should be very creamy.

Finally remove the crisp shells from the oven, fill them with whipped potatoes, and sprinkle with the last of the butter and Parmesan. Bake 10 more minutes, or until the potatoes begin to take color on top.

Serves 4.

A recipe for devotées of potato skins, and those interested in the possible evolution of the baking potato. They are crunchy and creamy all at once, and you have used very little fat—or at least much less than you would for a regular baked potato.

ZUCCHINI-STUFFED BAKED POTATOES

2 large baking potatoes	Salt and freshly ground pepper
2 tablespoons butter	Parmesan cheese
2 medium zucchini, coarsely grated	

*B*ake the potatoes—this can be done at practically any oven temperature, if you have other things going. When they are soft, remove from the oven, slice lengthwise, and scoop out the flesh into a bowl. Reserve the potato shells.

Either mash the potato or put it through a ricer. Melt the butter in a small pan, and when it sizzles, toss the grated zucchini in it over medium heat 3 to 4 minutes—or till cooked but still firm to the bite. Add salt and pepper to taste as it cooks.

Fold the zucchini lightly into the potatoes, then spoon back into the potato shells. Sprinkle with cheese. (These can be held, covered, for an hour or more before baking.)

About 20 minutes before your meal is to be ready, preheat the oven to 425°F.

Bake the potatoes 5 to 10 minutes—or until heated through, with the tops beginning to brown.

Serves 4.

These wonderful things seem to be the invention of Colorado chef Barbara Conwell, and they come from a splendid Junior League of Denver cookbook called Colorado Cache *that offers "a goldmine of recipes"—as indeed it does. Copies may be obtained from The Junior League of Denver, Writer's Center II, Suite 400, 1805 South Bellaire Street, Denver, CO 80222. They are a kind of spinoff of Julia Child's famous grated zucchini recipes, and everyone I've ever served them to goes into ecstasies and copies the recipe down. They can be prepared ahead, and in any amount, and couldn't be better, as a combination starch and vegetable, with any casual or stately meal. They are also much less calorific than a baked potato with all the trimmings.*

PORTLAND POTATOES

4	baking potatoes	8	slices thin bacon
	Salt		Paprika

Scrub the potatoes and drop them unpeeled in boiling salted water. Boil until just tender, then drain and put them back in the pan. Cover with paper toweling and the lid, and let sit 5 minutes.

Heat the oven to 350°F.

Peel the potatoes and place in a baking dish. Cut the bacon slices in half and wrap 4 slices around each potato, securing with toothpicks. Sprinkle with a dust of paprika.

Bake 20 to 30 minutes, or until the bacon crisps golden. Remove the toothpicks before serving. (These may be kept warm some time in the oven, if necessary.)

Serves 4.

Easy to prepare and delicious, these certainly look better on a plate than a boiled potato, and basted naturally they need neither sauce nor condiment.

DEEP-FRIED SWEET POTATOES

4	medium sweet potatoes	Salt
	Vegetable oil	Freshly grated nutmeg

*P*eel the sweet potatoes, square off the ends and sides, and cut, like French fries, in ¼-inch strips. Heat oil in a deep-fat fryer until it is 375°F (or until a sample sputters when dropped in, and gets brown when the bubbles subside).

Drop the potatoes, in batches, into the hot fat. Remove with a slotted spoon, drain on absorbent paper, and sprinkle with salt and freshly grated nutmeg.

Serves 4.

If you appreciate French fries, you will find the nutty flavor of a mound of these a welcome surprise with many dishes—from plain lamb chops to Madame Bégué's Liver (page 134). Some recipes call for them to be cut thicker and parboiled before frying, but I think these are superior.

BAKED YAMS

*G*et yams all of a size so they bake evenly. They can bake at any temperature, and as there is little danger of cooking them too much, add along with meat in the oven as it cooks, or before.

At 350°F, medium-sized yams take a minimum of an hour to get done. Squeeze them to test, and when they are quite soft they are ready. They can be kept warm for an hour or more if need be. To serve, slice in half lengthwise, then cut slashes through the flesh and melt butter into them, as much as they will hold, and sprinkle with a bit of salt.

The yam is much better than the regular sweet potato. They can be distinguished in the market for their quite dark color, and on the tastebuds by a texture just this side of an avocado. They not only have more flavor than a sweet potato, they are also sweeter and so need no sugar. Baked, they outshine plain potatoes by far. Though they are usually served with pork or ham, I like to serve them, to the surprise of company, with any dish (and it doesn't have to be American, either) not overly delicate, or with which the sweetness of the yams would not be out of place.

RUM AND ORANGE YAMS

2   pounds yams, baked (page   1   tablespoon rum (or brandy)
        260)   Salt
     Juice and finely grated peel of   ½   cup finely chopped black
        1 orange   walnuts (optional)
2   tablespoons butter

*H*alve the cooked yams and scoop the flesh into a ricer. Rice the yams into a bowl, then add the juice and grated peel of the orange and the rest of the ingredients except the nuts.

Mash and beat the ingredients into a light purée, then fold in the nuts. The yams can be kept in a double boiler for 30 minutes to an hour, and they will puff slightly. (Or you can cook them in a 300°F oven for the same time, perhaps with a dribble of butter over the top.)

Serves 4.

If anything, this is my version of dread candied sweet potatoes with marshmallow topping. These have only the fine natural sweetnesses of the yams and orange, and I think a better texture and depth of flavor. The black walnuts are my mother's addition, and they make the dish into a masterpiece. I have tried regular walnuts, but they do not so equally balance the orange and rum flavors, and seem there only as a pretext for texture.

GRITS PONTCHARTRAIN

1   cup grits   6   egg yolks (or 3 eggs)
     Salt   1   cup diced (¼ inch) sharp
4   cups water   cheddar cheese
1   cup heavy cream   2   tablespoons butter, melted

*P*reheat the oven to 350°F.

Cook the grits in salted water according to package directions. When done, remove from the fire and let cool a bit.

Beat the cream with the egg yolks until frothy, then mix into the grits. Add the cheese and mix in as well. Butter an 8-inch casserole with a bit of the melted butter. Add the grits, then dribble the rest of the butter over the top.

Cover with a lid, or foil, and bake 30 minutes. To serve, cut in squares (or pie-shaped wedges if the pan is round) and place on warm plates to accompany sausage, bacon, or kidneys, etc.

Serves 4 to 6.

Good solid American fare, made so well as to please those who have never heard (and have never wanted to) of Southern grits. They are slightly more delicate when all egg yolks are used, but if you are not planning meringues the next day the difference becomes a matter of small note. The very best aged sharp cheddar should be used, however, for there is no substitute for good cheese.

GRITS SOUFFLÉ

1 cup grits	Tabasco
Salt	4 tablespoons butter, melted
4 cups water	Grated Parmesan cheese
1 cup heavy cream	
3 eggs, separated, plus 1 egg white	

*P*reheat the oven to 350°F.

Cook the grits in salted water according to package directions. When done, remove from the fire and let cool a bit.

Beat the cream with the 3 egg yolks and mix well into the grits. Add a few drops of Tabasco and salt to taste. Mix in 2 tablespoons of the melted butter.

Beat the 4 egg whites till stiff but not dry, then fold them carefully into the grits. Butter a soufflé dish with some of the remaining butter and gently spoon the mixture into it. Sprinkle with some Parmesan and dribble the last of the butter on top.

Bake 30 minutes, or until the soufflé is puffed and golden on top.

Serves 4 to 6.

In effect another kind of spoonbread, this may be used as a starch dish to accompany nearly any meat, with butter if there is no sauce. In the south it would most often be served for breakfast, and it does make a special treat with eggs and sausage, etc.

PENNSYLVANIA NOODLE PANCAKE

1	pound wide egg noodles		Freshly ground pepper
	Salt		Paprika
4	tablespoons butter	¼	cup minced parsley

Cook the noodles in boiling salted water until just tender. Drain well and toss with half the butter. Season to taste with salt and pepper, then toss with paprika and the parsley.

Melt the rest of the butter in a large skillet. Add the noodles, press down, and cook slowly until a golden brown crust has formed on the underside.

Shake the pan occasionally as the noodles cook to make sure they do not stick. When the crust has formed, flip them out like a pancake onto a plate, with the crust on top. Sprinkle with extra paprika, and serve cut into pie-shaped wedges.

Serves 6.

An excellent change from plain buttered noodles, and also a good way to use leftover noodles—adjusting the recipe, of course, if there is a smaller amount of noodles. They may be topped with a dollop of sour cream, if you like.

MY GRANDMOTHER'S DROP NOODLES

3	eggs	1	cup (plus) flour
3	tablespoons water		Beef or chicken stock
½	teaspoon salt		

Beat the eggs, water, and salt to a froth. Add the flour slowly, beating with a fork till smooth after each addition. Add flour until the dough becomes a little stiff and begins to leave the side of the bowl as you mix it. (Three large eggs will take 1½ cups flour).

Have the stock simmering in a kettle. Drop the dough in by the ¼-tea-spoon, dipping the spoon into the hot stock each time so the dough doesn't stick to the spoon. Cook about 6 minutes—or until they are no longer doughy at the center.

Remove with a slotted spoon and serve either lightly buttered or with sauce from a meat or chicken dish.

Serves 4.

This pioneer-style recipe makes a kind of spaetzle. *If cooked too long they become tough, but captured right they are light but chewy—a texture truly not to be found in any other noodle, and what could be simpler. My grand-mother used these to stretch a budget over seven people at family table by boiling a meaty soup bone up—the meat and noodles were served in some broth in a soup plate. I still like them with things like fricassee.*

SOUTHERN DRY RICE

1	cup long-grain rice	Salt (optional)
1¼	cups water	Toasted sesame seeds (optional)

*P*ut the rice in a sieve and wash it in several waters as follows: dip the sieve in a bowl of water, then under running water, then back in a bowl of clean water, etc. This will wash off all the starch on the rice.

Bring 1¼ cups water to a boil. Add the rice and bring back to a simmer, then cover the pan and cook over as low a fire as possible for 15 minutes. Do not lift the lid until 15 minutes are up.

Test the rice—every grain should stand apart and they should be still a bit firm to the tooth. If you wish it less al dente, cook very slowly another 5 minutes. Sprinkle with sesame seeds, if you like, before serving.

Serves 4.

Dry rice is a radical departure from the way you usually cook rice, but it is well worth trying. Once you get the knack of it you might not want rice any other way. It somehow doesn't need salt if it's to be served with a sauce or gravy, but add it if you wish. I like it simply buttered and sprinkled with sesame seeds that have been toasted in a dry skillet, as they do in Charleston.

ORANGE RICE

1	cup long-grain rice	½	cup finely chopped pecans
1½	cups orange juice	2	tablespoons butter
1	tablespoon lemon juice	1	teaspoon grated grapefruit rind

W ash the rice through several waters, as in Southern Dry Rice (see preceding recipe), and drain. In a medium saucepan, bring the orange and lemon juice to a boil, add the rice, cover, and cook over as low a fire as possible for 15 to 20 minutes, or until the rice is slightly nutty still but the liquid is absorbed.

Sauté the pecans in the butter till they are toasted through, and toss them, with the grated grapefruit rind, into the cooked rice. Serve immediately.

Serves 4.

Adapted from Mary Land's Louisiana Cooking, *this is wonderfully paired with her recipe for Cajun Rabbit on page 165. It is also particularly good with simple fish, or barbecue, on a warm day as well. It tastes every bit as good as it sounds.*

KENTUCKY RED RICE

⅓	cup diced (¼ inch) salt pork (or bacon)	2	tablespoons tomato paste
1	tablespoon butter	2	cups water (or chicken stock)
½	cup minced green onions with part of tops		Salt and freshly ground pepper
1	heaping teaspoon sweet paprika	1	cup long-grain rice

S auté the salt pork in the butter over medium-low heat until it is slightly golden. Add the green onions and cook them till limp, then add the paprika and stir the pot for a few minutes off the fire.

Stir in the tomato paste, add the water or stock, bring to a boil over high heat, add salt and pepper to taste, and finally add the rice.

When the pot returns to a boil, lower the heat, cover the pan tightly, and simmer 20 minutes, or until the rice is done but not too soft. Serve immediately.

Serves 4.

A sort of home grown risotto, and a very good one, too. The tiny cubes of salt pork give another savor altogether than is to be got from olive oil or butter. I first had it as a side dish to cold sliced meats, with homemade rolls and an assortment of chutneys, pickles, and relishes, but it makes a fine accompaniment to many a meat.

THOMAS JEFFERSON'S PILAU

1 cup rice	⅓ cup pistachios
2 cups water (or chicken stock)	⅓ cup pine nuts
4 tablespoons butter	Ground mace
½ teaspoon salt (if using water)	

Wash the rice thoroughly. In a large saucepan, bring water or stock to a boil, along with 1 tablespoon of the butter and the salt (if used). Add the rice, stir, and when the water comes to a boil, lower the heat well, and cover the pan. Let simmer gently 20 minutes.

Cover the pistachios with boiling water and let sit a minute. Drain and rub off their skins. Sauté the pine nuts and pistachios in the remaining 3 tablespoons butter over low heat, tossing until they are golden. Remove from the heat (the butter shouldn't burn, but if it has, drain the nuts and toss with new butter).

When the rice is done, toss it gently with the nuts, pile on a platter, and sprinkle with mace.

Serves 4.

A fantasy dish like something out of dear Alice Toklas. If pistachios and pine nuts seem too expensive, it is equally interesting with toasted almonds and pumpkin seeds, say, or what your cupboard affords. It works as well, with fish, if cooked with half clam juice and half water.

FEATHERED RICE

1 cup long-grain rice	3 tablespoons butter (optional),
2½ cups boiling water	cut into bits
1 teaspoon salt	

*P*reheat the oven to 400°F.

Spread the rice on a cookie sheet and bake, stirring occasionally, for 10 to 15 minutes, or until golden brown.

Turn the oven down to 350°F, and remove the rice to a casserole with a cover. Add the boiling water, and salt, cover the pot closely and bake for 30 minutes, or until the rice has absorbed all water and is light and puffy.

If you wish butter, fold the bits in lightly before serving (I don't think it needs any at all if the meat has sauce).

Serves 4.

This process completely changes ordinary rice into another consistency and flavor—the one light and feathery, the other rich and nutlike. I don't know why it is not served more often, for it makes an easy alternative to the usual starches. It is particularly happy with game dishes where you might wish to serve expensive wild rice—no one will miss that rather overpraised delicacy.

Salads and Slaws

*T*he state of the American salad reminds me of this recipe, from an old-timer, for sheepherder's salad: "Well, you take some cold beans and some cold potatoes and cut the potatoes up and throw them in with the beans, and some cold meat if you got it, and cut up an onion or anything else that's around, and put the oil off some sardines on it and some vinegar and salt and pepper, and if you got some cold pancakes left, why, just cut them up, too, and shake the whole works together and you got something."

The first rule for a salad should be that you don't have to throw everything in the refrigerator in, but to find two that look likely as partners. See if there isn't some herb that will compliment both, then toss with the best vinegar and oils you can afford. The second rule should be (with the exception of Southwestern Lettuce Garnish and the Shaker bean salad listed here) never even buy iceberg lettuce, let alone use it in a salad. Look for tender Boston lettuce, for chicory and escarole, remember the spinach and watercress—and if necessary go out and pick dandelion leaves off the front lawn. *Then* you got something!

DRESSING A GREEN SALAD

Nothing could or should be simpler. Choose among the freshest greens of garden or market, then wash them carefully, shake out any excess water from the leaves, and dry thoroughly—one of the new spin dryers is best, or you can roll the salad up in paper towels and place in the refrigerator till ready to serve.

The chilled dry greens want only a toss, first lightly with oil (to coat the leaves), then with good vinegar, in the proportion Escoffier proposed: "Be a miser with vinegar and a spendthrift with oil." The salad needs then to be adequately salted and peppered, given a tang from some good mustard, and flavored as you wish with minced onion or garlic.

Years ago I learned a trick for all this from a fine French cook. She mixed the vinegar with a little grated onion or minced garlic, salt and pepper, Dijon mustard, minced parsley and fresh herbs, etc. in a salad bowl. This was let to steep for 30 minutes or so, then at serving time she placed the lettuce leaves in the bowl, poured olive oil over, first tossed the leaves to coat with oil lightly, and finally she tossed deeply and deftly from the bottom of the bowl to bring up the flavored vinegar.

A good cook has his habits, and knows the value of a drop of bitters, what dried herb or fresh will complement his whole meal, and how to secure the best available oils, vintage vinegars.

There are no other secrets.

SAN FRANCISCO GREEN SALAD WITH WALNUTS AND ORANGE PEEL

1 head Boston lettuce	⅔ cup coarsely chopped walnuts
Grated rind of 1 orange	½ cup oil and vinegar dressing

Wash the lettuce leaves, gently shake the water off them, and pat dry. Chill. At serving time, toss everything together till all the leaves are coated.
Serves 4 to 6.

Working with caterer Draper Morrow, in San Francisco, we always called this "Boring Salad," after a Nob Hill client who declared it so over the telephone, when described to her as a possible tossup. Of course it is anything but bor-

ing, and equal to any occasion great or small. Mr. Morrow's only secret was the quality of his oil and vinegar.

JERUSALEM ARTICHOKE SALAD

½ pound Jerusalem artichokes
⅓ cup oil and vinegar dressing

1 head Boston lettuce, washed, dried, and chilled

*T*he artichokes can be peeled or not, as you wish. If not scrub them first, then slice thin. Combine them with the dressing and let them marinate several hours.

To serve, toss with the lettuce leaves and place on chilled salad plates. Serves 4 to 6.

When these little sunflower tubers are available, they make a splendid salad in this manner. By all means try them if you've not before—they are crisp as water chestnuts and have as subtle a flavor as artichokes themselves.

CREAM DILLY BEAN SALAD

1 pound green beans
   Salt
¼ cup white wine vinegar
1 clove garlic, flattened and
   peeled

1 tablespoon chopped fresh dill
   (or 2 teaspoons dried)
   Freshly ground pepper
¼ cup olive oil
¼ cup heavy cream

*T*rim the beans and leave them whole if not too large—in that case, cut them lengthwise as for French-cut green beans. Drop into boiling salted water and cook 6 to 8 minutes—or until they are cooked but still a bit crisp.

Drain, run cold water over, and pat dry with paper toweling. Place in a bowl to marinate with the vinegar, garlic, dill, and salt and pepper to taste. Put in the refrigerator for several hours, tossing now and again to distribute flavors.

To serve, shake the oil and cream together until smooth. (Sometimes this will take some doing, so they won't separate. I use a small jar with a tight fitting lid and shake them until they hold in suspension.)

Drain the excess vinegar off the beans, pick out the garlic clove, and toss well with the oil and cream.

Serves 4.

This Midwestern salad is one of my favorites for all kinds of meals. It is even good enough to make a first course with fine bread to accompany it, and on hot days it can replace the vegetable that usually partners the meat.

SHAKER STRING BEAN SALAD

2 cups cooked green beans
2 cups finely shredded iceberg lettuce
2 cups minced green onions with parts of tops
2 teaspoons chopped fresh summer savory (or 1 teaspoon dried)

6 nasturtium leaves
12 nasturtium flowers
1 tablespoon capers
½ cup oil and vinegar dressing

*T*oss all together and be sure the nasturtium leaves and flowers show themselves off.

Serves 6.

I suspect this recipe may be good even with canned green beans, though I usually prepare too many Country Green Beans (page 223) for use the next day in this. It could be gussied up with romaine, but though I thought I'd never say I liked iceberg lettuce, it makes a fine lacy texture here if sliced thin as slaw. The green onions are a whiz in a food processor, and all in all it is an excellent dish to add to your files even if you haven't nasturtiums to harvest. The original recipe calls for pods of nasturtiums as well, whatever they are. But as nasturtium seeds were often put up in the past to substitute for capers, I throw some of those in to boot.

COACH INN FOUR BEAN SALAD

2	cups cut-up stringless green beans (1-inch lengths)	2	teaspoons chopped fresh summer savory (or 1 teaspoon dried)
2	cups baby lima beans		
2	cups cooked kidney beans (or canned)	¼	cup minced parsley
		6	green onions, minced with part of tops
2	cups cooked chick-peas (or canned)	2	stalks celery, minced
¼	cup good vinegar	1	clove garlic, minced
¾	cup olive oil		Lettuce leaves, washed, dried, chilled (optional)
1	tablespoon Dijon mustard		
	Salt and freshly ground pepper		Pimiento strips (optional)

Cook each of the beans separately, until tender but still a bit crispy. Drain all, and mix while warm with the other ingredients.

Let sit in the refrigerator, tossing now and again, for an hour or overnight. Serve as is, or on lettuce leaves, garnished with pimiento strips.

Serves 8 to 10.

This colorful and tasty American salad is as pleasant as many French "composed" salads. Served with a crusty bread, there is no reason it mayn't be served as a first course, take the place of a hot vegetable entirely for a light summer supper, or be one of the mainstays of a picnic.

GREAT NORTHERN BEAN SALAD

1	cup dried Great Northern beans (or other white beans)	½	cup chopped celery
		½	cup chopped onion
		½	cup chopped sweet pickles
3	cups water	½	cup sour cream
¼	cup oil and vinegar dressing	½	cup mayonnaise
1	clove garlic, minced		

Put the beans in a 2-quart pan with 3 cups water and bring to a boil. Cover the pan, turn the heat off, and let sit for an hour or so.

Then simmer gently for an hour or two, or until the beans are tender—but not falling apart. Drain the beans and toss in a bowl with the salad dressing and garlic while they are still warm.

Put the bowl in the refrigerator and let marinate for several hours. To serve, toss with the remaining ingredients.

Serves 4 to 6.

A Northwestern speciality that can stand with any potato salad, and it is simpler than most of those. I had it once in Seattle as the sole accompaniment to a barbecued butterflied leg of lamb, and thought it could not be improved upon.

COLE SLAW

*T*he whole country seems to have collective amnesia on the subject of cole slaw. First came the rage for sweetness (even unto the adding of such things as pineapple and marshmallow bits), then everyone started grating the cabbage rather than cutting it in slivers, and finally came the strange notion that it ought to sit in its dressing a long time so all fine crispness is lost. No wonder it has fallen in disrepute as an accompaniment to good meals. The dressing for any slaw should no more be sweet than any tossed green salad, surely, and the cabbage should be treated with as much respect as lettuce— tossing at the last moment before serving.

Cutting cabbage is really no great chore either. It *is* difficult, even with a sharp knife, to make delicate shreds if you quarter the cabbage and then cut. But if you detach the cabbage leaf by leaf, then place the leaves in stacks, it goes like a breeze. This done, it ought to be kept in cold water to crisp further, then redrained and dried either with paper toweling or by whirling in a salad spinner. Now you have a salad that can go hand in hand with fried brook trout, plump oysters fresh from their shells, barbecued ribs, steaming bowls of chili, the feasts of autumn.

GRISON'S STEAK HOUSE SLAW

1	pound cabbage, cored and thinly sliced	1	teaspoon finely grated onion
1	cup sour cream		Pinch of sugar
½	cup mayonnaise		Salt and freshly ground
1	tablespoon prepared horseradish		pepper

*P*lace the cabbage in a bowl of ice water in the refrigerator to crisp. Mix the sour cream, mayonnaise, horseradish, onion, sugar, and salt and pepper in a small bowl. This should sit at least 30 minutes to gather flavor.

To serve the slaw, drain the cabbage, pat dry with paper toweling, and toss with the dressing.

Serves 4 to 6.

The classic slaw is made with a boiled dressing—most usually sweet beyond belief. I've tested a boiled dressing decreasing the sugar in favor of tarragon, and it is good, but this dressing from an old San Francisco restaurant remains my favorite easily prepared slaw.

OLD-FASHIONED COLE SLAW

1	pound cabbage cored and thinly sliced		Tabasco
¼	cup olive oil	1	tablespoon sugar
1	tablespoon flour	¼	cup wine vinegar
½	teaspoon salt	½	cup heavy cream
2	teaspoons dry mustard	1	egg yolk
			Tarragon (optional)

*P*ut the cabbage in a bowl, cover it with cold water, and keep in the refrigerator until needed.

Put the oil in a saucepan over low heat, whisk in the flour until smooth, and cook several minutes. Add salt, mustard, a drop or so of Tabasco, and the sugar. Stir to blend, then add the vinegar.

Beat the cream with the egg yolk, then stir this into the sauce over low heat. Add some chopped fresh (or dried) tarragon, if you wish, and stir the sauce till it is thick and smooth.

Remove from the fire and taste for seasoning. You may wish to make it sweeter, or more tart, etc. (Also, if it is too thick, you may thin it with more cream.)

Let the dressing chill for a couple of hours before tossing with the cabbage. To serve, drain the cabbage and pat dry with paper toweling—it should be very crisp from sitting in the cold water. Toss with the dressing and serve.

Serves 4 to 6.

The classic slaw with boiled dressing. Most usually, these days, this dressing is made sweet beyond reason, but it really only needs, to my taste, a hint of sugar to balance the vinegar. It is a slaw that might be served with simple fried fish, hamburgers or any barbecue, or fried chicken.

MY SLAW

1	pound cabbage, cored and thinly sliced	½	teaspoon (or to taste) prepared horseradish
⅔	cup mayonnaise	1	tablespoon lemon juice
	Grated peel of 1 orange		Salt
			Capers

Place the cabbage in a bowl of cold water, and keep in the refrigerator.

Mix the mayonnaise, orange peel, horseradish to taste (some is bland and some blazing—the dressing should not be overly hot), lemon juice, and salt to taste. Chill for an hour or so, to mellow.

To serve the salad, drain cabbage, pat dry with paper toweling or spin in a salad dryer, and toss lightly with the dressing. Garnish with capers.

Serves 4 to 6.

The orange and horseradish give a zing to an otherwise bland dressing.

WILTED SOUR CREAM SLAW

1	pound cabbage, cored and coarsely grated	¼	cup wine vinegar
2	tablespoons minced onion		Salt and freshly ground pepper

3 tablespoons minced parsley	1 teaspoon caraway seeds
3 tablespoons olive oil	1 teaspoon Dijon mustard
Pinch of sugar	1 cup sour cream

*P*our boiling water over the grated cabbage and let sit 5 minutes. While it is sitting, mix all but the sour cream together. Test the cabbage—it should have cooked slightly, and still be a bit crisp. (If you think you'd like it more wilted, pour some more hot water over it and let it sit a bit more.)

Finally, drain the cabbage and mix with the dressing while still warm. Toss gently with sour cream and serve on salad plates.

Serves 4 to 6.

A fine addition to our slaws, and one particularly good with pork, or fat, garlicky steamed sausages.

CARROT SLAW

1 pound small carrots	Pinch of sugar (optional)
2 tablespoons olive oil	1 tablespoon minced fresh mint
Lemon juice	(or minced chives)
Salt and freshly ground	
pepper	

*S*crape the carrots and cut them in quarters lengthwise. Cut out the yellow cores unless they are very young and tiny. Grate the orange part very fine (they can be whirled in a food processor almost to a coarse paste, or put in a blender with a lot of water and whirled until fine then drained thoroughly, but the very best texture is achieved in the most tedious way—with a hand grater that has a side with holes for shredding very finely).

Mix the carrots with the oil and lemon juice, salt, and pepper to taste. Add a pinch of sugar if they don't seem tasty enough, or young enough, then mix in the mint or chives. Let sit in the refrigerator for 30 minutes to gather flavor.

Serves 4.

I suppose children are still being fed that particularly ugly combination of grated carrots, raisins, and mayonnaise—and all in the name of "health," too. I do not see anything healthy about them especially, and raisins can be eaten in many another way, but these delicate grated carrots are enough to wipe the far-off taste of those from our young mouths.

CELERY VICTOR

1 bunch celery	Pimiento strips
2 cups chicken or beef stock	2 eggs, hard boiled and
1 cup oil and vinegar dressing	chopped (optional)
(made with Dijon mustard)	Fresh-cracked crab claws
Anchovy fillets, washed in	(optional)
water	

*R*emove the outer stalks from the celery and cut off the top part with its leaves. Split the whole bunch lengthwise, first in half, then quarters. Save the tender inside leaves for garnish and the rest for other uses.

Simmer the celery quarters in stock 20 to 30 minutes, or until tender. Let cool in their broth. Drain, then marinate in dressing for several hours in the refrigerator, turning now and again.

To serve, drain the celery, place on salad plates, and garnish with crossed fillets of anchovy, strips of pimiento, some of the reserved celery leaves, and eggs if you wish. (The finest celery Victor I've had also included 2 cracked crab claws.)

Serves 4.

A justly famed California first course, with Italian antecedents. There it is served with crusty sourdough bread, but dinner rolls or other hot breads may accompany it as well. If the vinaigrette is light, I like also to drink with it whatever wine is to be served for the main dish.

JADE CUCUMBER STICKS

2 large cucumbers	2 tablespoons white wine (or dry
Salt	vermouth)
¼ cup tarragon white wine	Pinch of sugar
vinegar	Fresh tarragon sprigs (optional)

*P*are the cucumbers and cut in eighths lengthwise. Cut out the seeds of each slice, then cut the slices in half. Drop in boiling salted water, let the pot return to a boil, and cook exactly 1 minute.

Immediately drain and run cold water over the cucumbers until they are tepid. Pour the vinegar, wine, and sugar over them and toss. Chill, turning now and again, for 30 minutes to an hour. Serve with tarragon sprigs if you have them.

Serves 4.

These are a jewel. They are lovely as a garnish for fish, on a warm day, or they can make up a plate with stuffed eggs, green onion curls, and radish roses—particularly nice for a picnic.

CAROLINA OKRA SALAD

1	pound small okra		Tabasco
	Salt	¼	teaspoon grated lemon rind
1	tablespoon white wine tarragon vinegar	4	green onions, minced with part of tops
3	tablespoons olive oil Freshly ground pepper		Nasturtium flowers (optional)

*T*rim and wash the okra—if small and fresh enough, do not cut off the tops, as this causes some of the insides to escape. Drop in boiling salted water and cook barely 5 minutes. Drain, and while hot toss with the vinegar.

Add oil, salt and pepper to taste, a few drops of Tabasco, and the lemon rind. Let marinate in the refrigerator an hour or more, tossing now and again.

Shortly before serving, toss again with the green onions. Serve garnished with nasturtium flowers.

Serves 4.

It is possible to substitute whole frozen okra for this, but it will never be as crisp and flavorful. The best bread to serve with the dish would be Zephyrs (page 317), because of the contrast between the two different crispnesses.

LYLE'S BLACK-EYED PEA SALAD

3	cups cooked black-eyed peas	⅓	cup chopped green onions with part of tops
2	tablespoons lemon juice		
¼	cup olive oil Salt and freshly ground pepper	⅔	cup fresh or canned chopped tomatoes
			Sweet onion rings

*F*rozen black-eyed peas are perfect for this salad. They have a fresher taste than dried, and they cook to tender (with just a bit of snap) in 18 minutes. They should then be drained and tossed, while still hot, with the lemon juice, oil, and salt and pepper to taste.

Let sit 30 minutes, then toss in the green onions and tomatoes. Chill for at least 1 hour to bring out flavors. Cut rings from Bermuda, Spanish, or sweet red onions and chill in icy salted water for an hour, changing the water twice.

To serve, place the peas on salad plates and garnish with onion rings.
Serves 4.

A recipe from Lyle Bongé, one of the country's best photographers (and cooks). In Texas such a dish is called "poor man's caviar" and is served as an appetizer, but I like it as part of the meal along with hot cornmeal Zephyrs (page 317) or The Duchess of Windsor's Cornpones (page 316).

NEW POTATO SALAD

2 pounds tiny new potatoes	½ cup olive oil
Grated rind of 1 lemon	Salt and cracked pepper

*B*oil the new potatoes in salted water until tender—they take a surprisingly long time to cook considering their size. When done, drain, then place them in a bowl.

While warm, toss with lemon rind, olive oil, salt to taste, and rather a lot of coarsely milled pepper. Poke holes with a fork several times in each potato, toss again, and chill.

Toss several times more as you open the refrigerator. They should sit several hours before serving.
Serves 4 to 6.

The simplest and best of potato salads. It is superb tasting by itself, with all the sweet flavor of the new potatoes in evidence, and it makes a fine appetizer. Or, it makes a lovely salad plate nestled in shredded lettuce and garnished with deviled eggs and radish roses.

MY MASHED POTATO SALAD

4   large potatoes (2 pounds)
Salt
4   green onions, with half their
     tops
¼   cup parsley leaves
½   cup celery leaves and/or heart
     stalks
2   tablespoons chopped green
     pepper
1   teaspoon dried summer
     savory (or 2 teaspoons
     fresh chopped)
1   clove garlic

¼   cup tarragon white wine
     vinegar
1   tablespoon Dijon mustard
Freshly ground pepper
½   cup olive oil
About ⅔ cup milk, scalded
½   cup mayonnaise
Lettuce leaves, washed,
     dried, and chilled
Paprika
Radish slices (optional)
Sliced hard-boiled eggs
     (optional)

*B*oil the potatoes till tender in salted water, then drain and return to the pan. Place paper toweling over the pan, then the lid, and let the potatoes sit 5 minutes to get dry and flaky.

While the potatoes are cooking, mince very fine all the herbs and vegetables—a food processor is a boon for this. When chopped, place in a bowl with the vinegar, mustard, salt and pepper to taste, and the olive oil.

Put the cooked potatoes in a ricer, then rice directly onto the vegetable-oil mixture. Mash thoroughly with a potato masher, and add enough scalded milk to make them light and fluffy.

Fold in the mayonnaise and place, covered, in the refrigerator for an hour or more to mellow flavors. Serve on lettuce leaves, dusted with paprika, and garnished (if you wish) with radish slices and sliced hard boiled egg.

Serves 4 to 6.

Some years ago I heard rumors of a mashed potato salad consumed in Atlanta, Georgia, and set out to construct one if I could. The secret, if there is any, is not to use leftover mashed potatoes certainly, but to rice them hot onto the herbs and oil. The recipe here is for the most elaborate of versions, and I seldom prepare it the same way twice. At simplest best it folds in only mayonnaise, a little crumbled hard-boiled egg, and a speck of pickle or capers.

FRESH SPINACH AND MUSHROOM SALAD

1	pound young spinach	½	cup oil and vinegar dressing
¼	pound mushrooms		

Wash the spinach and tear the leaves from the stems. Drain and pat dry with paper toweling, then chill in the refrigerator.

Clean mushrooms, slice thin, and marinate in the dressing for 1 hour, or until you are ready to serve the salad. At that time, toss the two gently together in a salad bowl and serve on salad plates.

Serves 4.

When you find tender spinach in the market, it is one of the best salad greens of all. Mushrooms set it off perfectly without the need for a mess of other vegetables thrown in, or dressings overelaborated with blue cheese.

WILTED SPINACH AND WATERCRESS SALAD

1	pound tender spinach		Salt and freshly ground
1	bunch watercress		pepper
4	slices bacon	¼	teaspoon dry mustard
1	egg	¼	teaspoon dried tarragon
1	cup light cream	6	green onions, chopped with
¼	cup wine vinegar		part of tops
1	tablespoon sugar	8	radishes, sliced

Wash the spinach and watercress and remove tough stems. Tear into bite-sized pieces, then drain and dry thoroughly but gently.

Cut the bacon into small strips and fry slowly in a saucepan. When it is crisp, remove with a slotted spoon and drain on paper toweling. Pour out the hot bacon drippings and measure 2 tablespoons back into the pan.

Beat the egg in a bowl with the cream until it is frothy. Add the vinegar, sugar, salt and pepper to taste, the mustard, and tarragon. Add this to the bacon fat in the pan and stir over a low flame until the mixture thickens. Do not let it come to a boil.

When it has thickened, pour hot over the greens in a salad bowl. Toss thoroughly, and serve immediately garnished with bacon bits, green onions, and radishes.

Serves 4 to 6.

Maybe nothing in our gastronomic pantheon is purer than a summer wilted lettuce salad, its limestone lettuce cut hot from the garden to be tossed quickly in hot bacon fat, sprinkled with sugar and vinegar, thence to be put on plates topped with crumbled bacon, radish slices, and green onion. There is no way to repeat it, but this comes near as possible with grocery produce and subterfuge. It should always be served as a course alone, with a basket of rolls or bread to break.

COUNTRY TOMATO SALAD

Garden-ripe tomatoes	Wine vinegar
Fresh basil	Olive oil
Salt and freshly ground pepper	Parsley sprigs
Pinch of sugar	Onion rings (optional)

*P*ut tomatoes in boiling water for about 5 seconds, then remove with a slotted spoon and run cold water over them. Peel—the skins should almost slide off—and slice them carefully about ¼-inch thick into a shallow wide bowl.

Tear basil leaves and scatter over them, sprinkle with salt and pepper to taste, a bit of sugar, some good vinegar (not too much), and some olive oil. (They do not need even a great deal of oil, just enough to give the juices some body.)

Let marinate, either in or out of the refrigerator, for at least 30 minutes. Serve in an overlapping fan with some of the juices poured over, and a sprig of parsley for garnish. If you like, they may be combined with the mildest onions you can find, sliced and punched into rings, and sweetened in a bowl of iced salted water for 30 minutes or more.

When I come upon any real vine-ripened tomatoes—an all-too-rare occurrence without my own garden—this is the first dish I rush to the kitchen to prepare. It is one of the glories of American saladry, but it can do little for our store plastic "tomato."

CREAM TOMATO SALAD

4 ripe beefsteak tomatoes (or 1
     large can Italian plum
     tomatoes)
1 Bermuda, Spanish, or mild
     red onion, chopped
¼ cup minced parsley

Salt and freshly ground
   pepper
2 tablespoons wine vinegar
¼ cup olive oil
¼ cup heavy cream

*P*eel the tomatoes as in Country Tomato Salad (see preceding recipe), but rather than slicing them, cut into cubes. (If you are using canned tomatoes, drain, then cube.)

Add onion, parsley, salt and pepper to taste, and vinegar. Shake the oil and cream together in a small jar with a lid until they no longer separate, and toss the tomatoes gently with it.

Let sit 30 minutes at room temperature before serving.

Serves 4.

Though fresh tomatoes are best here, it is the one tomato salad I have found in which canned tomatoes (if they are good ones) can hold their own. The addition of cream gives the salad a particular suaveness that is very refreshing. It should be served with good homemade bread, or a crusty French bread to sop up the juices.

TURNIP SLAW WITH CAPERS

3 cups (loosely packed) coarsely
     grated turnips
2 teaspoons lemon juice

¼ cup olive oil
   Salt and freshly ground
     pepper
1 tablespoon capers

*T*oss the turnips with lemon juice, olive oil, and salt and pepper to taste. (They might need a little more lemon juice to your taste, but they should not be tart enough to obscure the fresh light turnip flavor.)

Let sit in the refrigerator 30 minutes, tossing now and again. Serve on salad plates with a scattering of capers.

Serves 4.

A preparation from the late great Edouard de Pomiane who was practicing nouvelle cuisine long before it had a name. Even though it has been a mainstay of my kitchen for years, and I call it slaw rather than navets râpées, it is only hopeful thinking on my part to claim it as American. My excuse is that much of this book was inspired by Pomiane's example, and I think more people ought to know of him. Two of his books are still in print in the country: French Cooking in Ten Minutes, from McGraw-Hill, and Cooking with Pomiane, from The Cookery Book Club. His recipes are all witty and simple and sizzle and bounce.

WATERCRESS SALAD À LA GERMAINE

1   bunch watercress
4   ounces cream cheese
1   tablespoon olive oil

1   tablespoon white wine
    tarragon vinegar
Salt and freshly ground
    pepper

Wash the watercress, cutting off the larger stems as you go. Drain it in a colander and pat gently with paper toweling; reserve chilled.

Divide the cream cheese in half—put one in your refrigerator and the other in a warm bowl. When the cheese in the bowl has softened, mash it with olive oil, vinegar, salt to taste, and rather a lot of freshly ground pepper.

To serve the salad, put the chilled watercress into the bowl on top of the cream cheese dressing, and cut the chilled cream cheese into small pieces on top of the cress. Toss gently with a fork and spoon and lift onto chilled salad plates.

Serves 3 to 4.

A salad named after the daughter of Count Arnaud Cazenave who established Arnaud's Restaurant in New Orleans. She was renowned in that city for her elaborate hats, but she should be famed everywhere as one of our finest restaurateurs. The salad is perfectly balanced and may follow any superb main course.

ZUCCHINI SLAW

2	tablespoons Dijon mustard	½	teaspoon sugar
¼	cup olive oil	4	medium zucchini, trimmed
2	teaspoons red wine vinegar		

*S*hake the mustard, oil, vinegar, and sugar in a jar till smooth. Coarsely grate the zucchini into a bowl, and toss with the dressing. Cover and let sit in the refrigerator for 15 to 20 minutes. Taste for seasoning—I don't think it needs any salt, but you might.

Serves 4.

A zesty, easy invention. Scooped onto a tender lettuce leaf, garnished with sieved hard-boiled egg yolk over the top, surrounded by a small ring of chopped boiled egg white, with maybe a sprinkle of capers, it can easily stand with any salad.

SAUCES &
CONDIMENTS

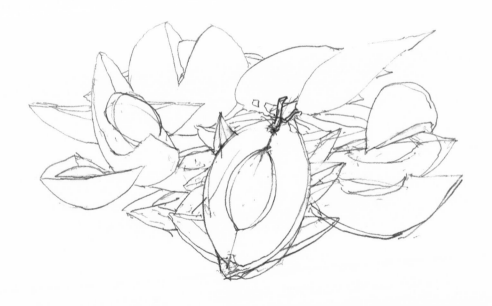

On a hot day in Virginia, I know of nothing more comforting than a fine spiced pickle, brought up troutlike from the sparkling depths of the aromatic jar below stairs in Aunt Sally's cellar.

—Thomas Jefferson, Letters

Sauces

*E*xcept in Southwestern cooking, where they take on great importance, and a deal of hot spiciness, the book of native sauces remains embarrassingly slim no matter who finds what to write about it. For some reason, home cooks even are impatient preparing an ordinary white sauce—so much so that when canned concentrated soups became commonplace, recipes using them instead of sauces cropped up like toadstools in every little cookbook and magazine. No matter that these were all too salty for that use, cooks went right ahead inventing new uses for all cream soups on the market. The one that swept the country, when I was a child, was a tunafish casserole that used canned mushroom soup plus salty tuna plus crumbled salty potato chips! It must have given a whole generation high blood pressure. Others creamed perfectly fine vegetables, like green beans, in celery soup sauce, and then sprinkled cheese and nuts on top. Fortunately this craze seems to have largely passed—though we still have few sauces. Consequently this will seem a very strange chapter indeed for cooks used to thumbing their Escoffier.

GOURMET CATSUP

1	can (28 ounces) tomato purée	1½	teaspoons dried thyme
1	medium onion, chopped	1½	teaspoons dried marjoram
1	clove garlic, chopped	2	tablespoons (or to taste)
¾	cup dry red wine		brown sugar
¾	cup red wine vinegar		Salt and freshly ground
2	tablespoons minced parsley		pepper
1	bay leaf		

*P*reheat the oven to 325°F.

Combine half the tomato purée with the onion and garlic and blend till smooth in a blender or food processor. Put in a casserole and bake in the oven for an hour or more, or until slightly thickened. Stir the sides down occasionally as it cooks.

While the purée is catsuping, put the wine, vinegar, and herbs in a saucepan and boil them down, uncovered, till you have barely ¼ cup liquid. When the catsup stirs thickly, take out of the oven, and strain the herb vinegar into it.

Add brown sugar and salt and pepper to taste. Store, covered, in the refrigerator.

This is the favored sauce of the land. Both commercial or homemade catsups, however, are more ordinarily prepared with spices such as cloves, mace, allspice, and even cinnamon. This easily got together recipe has a much fresher and more delicate aftertaste, I think—even more so if you are able to use fresh herbs (about a tablespoon each). The catsup will keep for months in your refrigerator.

CURRIED APRICOT CATSUP

1	cup dried apricots	1½	teaspoons curry powder
3	tablespoons honey	¾	teaspoon ground ginger
2	tablespoons dry mustard	2	tablespoons dry sherry

*S*immer the dried apricots in water to cover for 20 minutes, or until quite soft. Drain, saving the juice in a bowl, and put the apricots through a ricer or sieve.

Beat in the rest of the ingredients, and as much of the apricot cooking juice as will make a fine paste. Store in a covered jar in the refrigerator.

Makes 1½ cups.

Old recipes offer many kinds of reductions made from cucumbers to goose-berries, rather than just tomatoes. I have tasted a few fine aged mushroom, and even one dark black walnut ketchup, but this strange ruse of a friend has become a distinguished inhabitant of my refrigerator. I always serve it as part of a range of picklings and chutney with any of our pilaf dishes (such as Miss Emily's Perloo, page 176), and many of our meats. It may also add the final touch to a barbecue sauce, or marry a bit of boiled-down cream in the sauté pan from pork chops, or chicken, with a couple of cooked dried apricots for garnish.

HOMEMADE FRENCH-STYLE MUSTARD

¼	cup dry mustard	½	teaspoon salt
¼	cup white wine tarragon vinegar	3	egg yolks
⅓	cup dry white wine	1	teaspoon dried tarragon (optional)
1	teaspoon sugar		

*I*n a bowl, whisk together the mustard, vinegar, wine, sugar, and salt, then let sit several hours.

To cook, beat the egg yolks and tarragon into the mustard, then stir in a double boiler set over hot water 5 to 6 minutes, or until it has definitely thickened.

Remove from the heat and spoon into a jar. Store, covered, in your refrigerator.

An easy creamy mustard, flavorful enough to enhance salad dressings, and to be used in all recipes that designate Dijon-style mustard in this book. If your children insist it must be bright yellow, add some turmeric in the first stirring. It is also a good base on which to experiment with other herbs, green peppercorns, grated rind of lime, cloves, horseradish, tomato paste, to put by your own specially spiced and pretty product.

BLENDER MAYONNAISE

1	egg	1	tablespoon lemon juice (or white wine vinegar)
½	teaspoon salt		
¼	teaspoon dry mustard	1	cup olive oil (or vegetable oil, or half of each)

*P*ut the egg into the blender jar (or into the food processor, which works equally well). Add the salt and mustard and whirl until the egg is foamy. Add the lemon juice and blend a bit more.

Pour the oil in droplets through the top hole, as you blend at top speed. As more and more oil is absorbed into the egg, it is possible to add it in a very thin stream, but don't push this too much or the sauce will separate. (If it does, mix 2 tablespoons of the turned sauce into a teaspoon of Dijon-style mustard, and start the whole process over, pouring the turned sauce drop by drop into the mixture.)

When all the oil is absorbed, taste for seasoning. If you wish a thinner sauce, add a little more lemon juice.

Makes 1¼ cups.

Hand-whipped mayonnaise is better, but not that much, and I like blender mayonnaise because it is the only way to make fresh green mayonnaise, when herbs are fresh in summer. A tarragon one is nice for fish, or one with basil on top of a tomato slice, or a judicious mixture (about ¼ cup) makes a delicious spread for sandwiches—or wherever one would use mayonnaise.

TARTAR SAUCE

1	cup homemade mayonnaise (see preceding recipe)	1	tablespoon finely chopped green olives
1	teaspoon Dijon mustard	1	tablespoon chopped capers (optional)
1	tablespoon minced parsley		
1	teaspoon minced green onions with part of tops	1	egg, hard-boiled and chopped (optional)
1	tablespoon finely chopped sweet pickles		Salt and freshly ground pepper

Mix all thoroughly and let chill in a covered jar or bowl for at least 30 minutes before serving.

Any cook worth his salt ought to be able to put together this sprightly accompaniment to fish, sandwich spread of note, and friend to all cold meats. It lasts a week at least in the refrigerator—where it gets even better, becoming a temptation to pan-roast oysters next day.

FRENCH QUARTER SAUCE

2	tablespoons good vinegar	1	tablespoon parsley leaves
6	tablespoons olive oil	1	tablespoon coarsely chopped green onion tops
3	tablespoons Dijon mustard		
1	clove garlic, minced	1	hard-boiled egg yolk
6	anchovy fillets		

Combine the ingredients one by one in a blender or food processor. Cap in a jar and store in the refrigerator.

I would admire always, as Southerners say, to be served this sauce with cold shrimp and crab, rather than the usual doleful hot tomato-ness known as "cocktail sauce." It is also excellent mixed with cream to the consistency of salad dressing, for tender lettuce leaves.

PIÑON AND PARSLEY SAUCE

½	cup minced parsley	¼	cup olive oil
½	cup chopped pine nuts		Salt
2	tablespoons lemon or lime juice		Pinch of sugar
1	jalapeño pepper (pickled en escabeche), seeded and minced		

Combine all the ingredients and let sit, covered, in the refrigerator for at least 30 minutes before serving.

A pleasant—and not too fiery—Southwestern sauce with many uses. It is very good with cold shrimp, or over plainly sautéed fish fillets, or with cold roast beef. I even had it once tossed with hot steamed cauliflorets—a delicious experience.

GREEN GODDESS DRESSING

1   cup mayonnaise
4   anchovies, chopped
1   tablespoon minced parsley
1   tablespoon minced chives
2   teaspoons minced fresh
    tarragon (or 1 teaspoon
    dried)

1½   tablespoons white wine
    tarragon vinegar
Salt and freshly ground
    pepper

*C*ombine all the ingredients and store covered, at least 30 minutes in the refrigerator to bring out flavor.

Green Goddess dressing was originated at the famed Palace Court, of the Palace Hotel in San Francisco, as a salad dressing. Since then it has gone into the native repertoire with additions of any number of greeneries, sour cream, etc. Prepared as above, however, I think the original makes a fine substitution for tartar sauce with fish, etc.

BARBECUE SAUCES

*P*robably to outsiders a native barbecue, of whatever stripe, would appear peculiarly typical of our New World ways. Things haven't changed much since the press brouhaha over Eleanor Roosevelt serving hot dogs to George VI on the lawn. Spanish explorers gave the name *barbacoa* to the Indians' practice of cooking meat on a stick over a fire—a method that was to prove necessary to many a settler as well. In the West and South, barbecue comes nowadays to mean more than chops grilled outdoors. Pits are dug and lined and brought to coals by professionals, and whole haunches are slowly fired all night for the neighborhood to flock to, dance and drink to.

Most of us make do with stoves in the winter, and an occasional hickory grill set up in our summer backyard. But whenever and whoever we are, no two barbecues are alike, and everyone has a secret ingredient. (Or a secret,

period.) This can be the use of a thyme sprig as the basting tool for a delicate orange-soy marinade, or a downright full-scale production. My favorite of the latter is a sauce I sometimes put up for gifts. It seems to be the result of an admirer's request to a Florida chef:

PENDENNIS CLUB BARBECUE SAUCE

1	bottle chili sauce	1	bottle Worcestershire sauce
1	bottle catsup	1	bottle Major Grey's chutney
1	bottle A-1 sauce	1	cup fine bourbon

*T*his should be whirled a little in a blender or food processor to break up the large pieces in the chutney. It keeps forever in the refrigerator, only becoming better. The recipe comes from Jean Hewitt's *The New York Times Heritage Cook Book,* which is probably the best available compendium of amateur cook's recipes from all over the country.

Other than that I have no secrets, except I never ever measure—so every sauce may be different. I work from a dollop of this to a drop of that. In between, I stick a finger in the sauce to taste, until it seems just right. The things to hold in mind here are that you are making a spicy, slightly sweet-sour sauce. The sweet can come from anything (like the peach preserves in Georgia Barbecue Spareribs on page 110), and a sour can range from lime juice to the best vinegars. The rule of thumb is if you use delicate flavors or fresh herbs, don't overpower needlessly. As suits the republic, this is a sauce fiercely individual, so go for your own spot of sherry or grate of fresh ginger, splash of soy.

The recipe following is only a skeleton from which to work, and also, as it only makes a cup and a half, you might want to prepare it in larger batches in order to have some on hand.

COMPOSITE BARBECUE SAUCE

1	onion, chopped	2	tablespoons wine vinegar
1	clove garlic, minced	2	tablespoons Worcestershire
4	tablespoons butter (or bacon fat)		sauce
			Juice of ½ lemon
1	cup beer	2	tablespoons brown sugar

1   can (6 ounces) tomato paste
1   teaspoon salt
1   teaspoon paprika
½   teaspoon dry mustard
1   teaspoon freshly ground
      pepper
    Tabasco (or cayenne)

½   teaspoon dried rosemary
1   tablespoon soy sauce
      (optional)
1   teaspoon chili powder
      (optional)
3   drops liquid smoke (optional)

*P*ut a saucepan over medium heat and sauté the onion and garlic in the fat till the onion is limp. Add the rest of the ingredients, stirring as you go. Cook over low heat 20 to 30 minutes, or until the sauce is balanced to taste. If it gets too thick, add some more beer.

Strain through a sieve, pressing down on the onion to release its essence, and keep in a covered jar in the refrigerator.

BOTTLED SAUCES

*C*ondiments, really—we have inherited from the British a taste for spiced dusky sauces. Of these descendants from home-bottled mushroom or walnut catsups, the most widely known and used being Worcestershire. Practically everyone uses it to some degree, and though it is possible to overdo a good thing, it builds a rich dark base in barbecue, or gives a proud shove to stews, meat loaves, hamburgers—what have you. "Wooster," as it is pronounced, needs no introduction.

With its bright and handsomely designed label, Tabasco was made first by the Avery family, who found in the wake of the Civil War some business was needed to bring in hard cash. An invention of a plantation cook (presumably black) was turned into a best seller, out of local vinegar and some tiny red peppers brought home by a soldier in the Mexican War. Their Louisiana product is quite quite hot, but used sparingly it has a hundred uses. As a rule of thumb I use it where the French suggest white pepper, though Tabasco is much livelier. It is a long true friend to any kitchen. When sauce or stew seems not up to par, drop in two shakes of the bottle, and taste a singing difference. Don't put in any more—the secret of Tabasco is to have the lightest of hands.

Angostura Bitters is in everybody's cupboard, disguised as a cocktail ingredient. But it is tonic brace to many foods: salads, soups, fruits, mincemeat, and as you use it now and again, you'll get the hang of its unidentifiable yet distinctive tone unlike quite anything else. (But all this information can be studied on its old-fashioned be-medaled label.)

Recently imported from Bermuda, and found only in fancy food sections, is a sauce that has some of the qualities both of bitters and Tabasco: Outerbridge's Original. If you find some, snap it up. Made from peppers and more than a dozen different unstated spices, it is steeped in casks of sherry for months before bottling—with a few of the pretty little peppers inside. Like Tabasco, hot, it gives more subtlety, complexity, aroma. A few drops will give you a reputation for champion salad dressings. It is the secretest of secrets, as yet.

Older, but hardly known outside the South, is Jamaica's Pickapeppa Sauce. It is closest to A-1 sauce, but very much more condensed and fragrant. It has a label of a red and green parrot contemplating a bough with a single red pepper, and is made from tomatoes, onions, sugar, vinegar, mangoes, raisins, tamarinds, salt, pepper, and unnamed spices. Dollop it in barbecue sauces, cheese dishes, meat loaf, bland gravies—a dab of it is even fine brushed on plain broiled fish. Some folks (in Texas) won't eat eggs without it.

Pickles and Relishes

*I*f we can't boast much about sauces, we certainly can about our chowchows and piccalillis. The Pennsylvania Dutch think no meal should be put on the table without seven sweet and seven sour condiments, and in the South even a simple repast may have a petaled plate with clove-stuck brandied peaches, translucent blades of pickled watermelon rind, dilled okra, and summery hot corn relish nestled in its sections. In parts of the country a cook is not to be considered unless she puts up her own chutney every fall. With the advent of the freezer, many gardeners started automatically freezing any surplus, but those who stuck to their kettles know the satisfaction of row on row of colorful jars waiting in the pantry, the year through.

PUTNEY CHUTNEY

6	green tomatoes, peeled and chopped	1	cup sugar
6	green apples, peeled, cored, and chopped	1	cup (packed) brown sugar
8	green peppers, seeded and chopped	2	cups vinegar
		1	cup raisins
3	large onions, chopped	1	cup chopped crystallized ginger
1	clove garlic, minced	1	tablespoon salt
4	lemons	1	tablespoon ground ginger

Preheat the oven to 325°F.

Put the tomatoes, apples, green peppers, onions, and garlic in a large kettle. Add the juice of two of the lemons, and chop the other two, being careful to remove the seeds. (A food processor is a good tool for all this, but be careful not to get everything too fine.)

Add all the other ingredients and bring to a boil over medium heat, stirring now and again. As soon as the mixture is heated through, put the kettle in the oven and cook, uncovered, for 1½ hours, stirring every 15 to 20 minutes.

The chutney will be done when the mixture becomes a bit thickened and starts to take on a darker color. Bottle immediately in sterilized jars.

Makes 9 to 10 half pints.

This chutney makes a particularly fine balance of flavors, and though it can be cooked on top of the stove, I like this method as there is little fear of burning, and only minimal stirring is required.

When you make chutney, remember any recipe can be played with, and there are no hard and fast rules. For instance, here are three other apple-green tomato chutneys I picked up from the files of a friend: (1) 4 cups apples, 4 cups green tomatoes, 2 onions, 1 cup brown sugar, 1 cup raisins, ½ cup shredded almonds, 1 small ginger root; (2) 8 green apples, 4 green tomatoes, 3 green peppers, 3 onions, 3 tablespoons salt, 1 tablespoon celery seed, 1½ cups sugar, 1½ cups vinegar; (3) 12 apples, 6 green tomatoes, 1 cup raisins, 2 tablespoons mustard seed, 4 green peppers, 2 cups sugar, 4 small onions, 1 quart vinegar, 2 tablespoons salt.

This, as you see, gives quite a lot of leeway—and also bear in mind that chutneys may be constructed around most any fruit—the most popular being apples, peaches, and pears, though the more exotic run to gooseberries, plums, or rhubarb.

MOCK MANGO CHUTNEY

9	cups unripe peaches, peeled and cut in dice (½ inch)	2	cups white wine vinegar
2	tablespoons plus 1 teaspoon salt	4	cloves garlic, minced
		¾	cup Worcestershire sauce
¾	cup peeled and minced fresh ginger	1	cup minced onion
		¼	teaspoon cayenne
2½	cups sugar	1½	cups lime juice

*P*ut the fruit in a crock with water to cover and 2 tablespoons salt. Let sit for a day or two in a cool place.

When ready to cook the chutney, put the ginger in a large saucepan with a good bit of water, bring to a boil, and simmer over a medium-low heat 45 minutes to an hour, or until the ginger is tender. Drain it and save the water.

Pour 1¼ cups of the ginger water back in the saucepan, mixing with sugar, vinegar, garlic and Worcestershire. Boil over medium heat until the sugar dissolves, stirring occasionally. Drain the peaches and add them to the syrup. Cook gently until the fruit is clear—15 to 20 minutes.

Remove the peaches with a slotted spoon to a bowl, and add the 1 teaspoon salt, onion, cayenne, and lime juice to the saucepan. Cook over low heat (or in a 325°F oven) until it is thick, making sure not to burn it. (If you cook on top of the stove, it will mean nearly constant stirring.)

When the mixture is thick, return the peaches and bring to a boil. Taste for seasoning and pour into sterilized jars.

Makes 6 half pints.

A fine chutney that produces at home something like the imported bottled chutneys at fancy prices in the store.

PICCALILLI

4	cups finely chopped cabbage	2	cups water
12	green tomatoes, cored and chopped	12	cups vinegar
		3	cups sugar
12	cucumbers, chopped	½	cup mustard seed
6	onions, chopped	1	tablespoon dry mustard
4	cups chopped celery	1½	teaspoons freshly ground pepper
3	green peppers, seeded and chopped		
		1½	teaspoons ground cloves
2	red peppers, seeded and chopped	3	teaspoons ground cinnamon
½	cup salt	½	teaspoon cayenne

Put all the vegetables in a large bowl or crock with ½ cup salt. Mix thoroughly and let stand 2 hours. Drain thoroughly.

Combine 2 cups water with 4 cups of the vinegar in a large kettle and bring to a boil. Add the drained vegetables, bring to a boil, and simmer 10 minutes. Drain again thoroughly, discarding the liquid. Pack the vegetables in sterilized jars. Combine 3 cups sugar with the remaining 8 cups vinegar in the kettle and cook until the sugar is dissolved. Add the spices and bring again to a boil.

Pour the syrup over the vegetables and seal the jars.

Makes 12 pints.

Piccalilli is a fine crisp, slightly hot relish for any cold meat, or hamburgers and hot dogs. No one remembers where it got its name—but the Shakers, with their penchant for a lively name, used to put up huge crocks full of summer vegetables all spiced and chopped and vinegared that they called "pickled lilly."

CHOWCHOW

4	cups chopped green tomatoes	1	tablespoon mustard seed
4	cups chopped cabbage	1	tablespoon celery seed
4	cups chopped cucumbers		1-inch stick cinnamon
1	cup chopped onions	12	whole allspice
1	cup chopped green peppers	12	whole cloves
	Salt	6	cups vinegar

⅓ cup sugar   ½ teaspoon turmeric
2 tablespoons dry mustard

Cover the vegetables with a brine made of ½ cup salt to 2 quarts water. Let stand in a crock overnight, then drain thoroughly. Taste for salt, and if too salty, rinse and drain again.

Put the whole spices in a muslin bag and tie securely. Add to the vinegar in a large kettle and simmer 15 minutes. Add sugar, dry mustard, turmeric, and drained vegetables and bring to a boil.

Simmer gently for 1 hour, then remove the spice bag and bottle in sterilized jars. Seal.

Makes 6 pints.

Chowchow seems to be originally a Chinese name for any mixture, but the British inherited it from India, where it designated any mustardy pickle. It comes in all varieties—some with little pieces of green bean, cauliflowerets, lima beans, scraped corn, red peppers—but this one is good because it is a quite sour chowchow, particularly good if served also with some sweet pickle such as watermelon rind.

STATE FAIR CORN RELISH

2 cups vinegar   3 cups peeled and chopped
1 cup sugar   fresh or canned tomatoes
1 tablespoon salt   1½ cups chopped green peppers
1 teaspoon celery seed   ¾ cup chopped red peppers
1 teaspoon mustard seed   1 cup chopped unpeeled (if
4 cups corn cut from the cob   unwaxed) cucumbers
                                                    1 cup chopped onion

Bring the vinegar, sugar, salt, celery seed, and mustard seed, to a boil in a large kettle.

Add all the vegetables, bring again to a boil, lower the heat, and simmer gently 1 hour. (Or put in a 325°F oven an hour or more, or until the whole is thick and melded in flavor.)

Seal immediately in hot sterile jars.

Makes 11 to 12 half pints.

The very best blue-ribbon relish, with all one taste of summer sealed in.

PHILADELPHIA PEPPER RELISH

3	cups finely chopped cabbage	⅓	cup cider vinegar
1	cup finely chopped green pepper	¼	cup (packed) light brown sugar
½	cup finely chopped red pepper	2	teaspoons mustard seed
1½	teaspoons salt	1	teaspoon celery seed

Salt the finely chopped vegetables and chill overnight in the refrigerator.

Next day, drain the mixture and squeeze out any excess moisture with your hands. Spoon into a quart jar.

Cook the remaining ingredients over moderate heat until the sugar is dissolved, then pour over the vegetables, shake to combine, and chill, covered, in the refrigerator for at least 3 days before serving.

Makes 1 quart.

Another "fresh" relish, and a very simple one too, to have on hand for hamburgers, hot dogs, and many other meats and sandwiches. It keeps well for several months, though mine is generally gone long before then. The fine chopping is most easily done in a food processor.

BEST BREAD AND BUTTER PICKLES

7	unwaxed cucumbers, sliced ¼ inch thick (with skins on)	¼	cup salt
5	medium onions, thinly sliced	2½	cups vinegar
1	green pepper, seeded and chopped	2½	cups sugar
1	red pepper, seeded and chopped	1	tablespoon mustard seed
		1	teaspoon celery seed
		12	whole cloves
		¾	teaspoon ground turmeric

Place the vegetables in a bowl or crock with the salt and ice cubes to cover. Let stand in a cool place (or the refrigerator) 3 to 4 hours, then drain thoroughly.

Put the rest of the ingredients in a large kettle, add the iced vegetables, and heat just to the boiling point, stirring now and again. Do not let the pickles boil.

Immediately pack them in pint jars and pour the pickling liquid over. Seal and store.

Makes 6 pints.

A very pretty pickle indeed. Bread and butter pickles are, I suppose, America's most typical home-canned product, and they are my favorite all-around cucumber pickle for simple munching.

ICICLE PICKLES

1 quart cucumbers (preferably small unwaxed ones 3 to 4 inches long), cut lengthwise in eighths	1 teaspoon celery seed
	1 cup vinegar
	¾ cup sugar
	1 tablespoon salt
1 small onion, sliced	½ teaspoon curry powder
1 tablespoon mustard seed	

Soak the cucumber spears in ice water 2 to 3 hours. Drain them, then pack in a hot sterilized jar (or jars) with the sliced onion, mustard seed, and celery seed.

Bring the vinegar, sugar, salt, and curry powder to a rolling boil, then pour over the cucumbers. Seal immediately.

Makes 1 quart.

A very easy pickle, and one that can easily be doubled and redoubled, etc. The unexpected curry powder gives them an unusual punch.

TRIPLE PICKLES

4 cups peeled and sliced thinly cucumbers	2 cups vinegar
	1 cup sugar
4 cups sliced (¼ inch) green tomatoes	1 tablespoon mustard seed
	½ teaspoon celery seed
2 cups sliced thinly onions	12 peppercorns
¼ cup salt	½ teaspoon turmeric

*L*ayer the vegetables in a bowl or crock, with a sprinkling of salt over each layer. Cover and let stand in a cool place overnight.

In a large kettle, bring the rest of the ingredients to a boil. Drain the vegetables thoroughly. Add them to the kettle and boil 5 to 10 minutes, or until the cucumber and tomatoes become clear. Do not overcook, however.

Pack the pickles into sterile jars and seal.

Makes 7 half pints.

As I am quite frankly fond of green tomatoes, this pickle (not so sweet as bread and butter pickles) makes a handsome relish with meats, or particularly on hot dogs and hamburgers, but it takes about a double recipe to last me a whole year.

SPICED CRAB APPLES

4	pounds crab apples	2	sticks cinnamon
4½	cups sugar	1	tablespoon whole cloves
4	cups white vinegar	1	blade mace (optional)

*P*ick over the apples to make sure they have no spots, and are firm and ripe. Leave the stems on, but prick each with a fork.

Combine the sugar, vinegar, and spices in a large kettle and cook slowly 5 minutes. Add the fruit and bring to a boil, then turn down the heat and cook slowly until the apples are tender but not broken.

Pack into hot sterile jars, filling to within ¼ inch of the tops. Pour the syrup over and make sure that it covers the fruit. Seal immediately and store.

Makes 6 pints.

When crab apples are available, this is one of the most typical and pleasant of American garnishes for either hot or cold meats. Unfortunately, it is necessary to put up your own, as all commercial varieties are packed with a rather garish red coloring.

DILLED GREEN BEANS

4 pounds green beans (young and stringless)	Garlic cloves
	Fresh dill (or dill seeds)

Hot peppers (optional)	5	cups vinegar
Mustard seed (optional)	5	cups water
Bay leaves (optional)	½	cup salt

Wash the beans and pack vertically in hot sterilized jars. Into each jar put a split garlic clove, an umbel of dill, and any of the optional ingredients you might wish.

Heat the vinegar, water, and salt to a boiling point and pour over the beans. Seal.

Makes 7 pints.

These wonderful tidbits are ready to eat in a week or so. They will keep for a month or more, but for longer shelf life the sealed jars should be processed in a pot of boiling water for 5 minutes. Although they are oftenest served with meats as a relish, they also make excellent appetizers.

PICKLED OKRA

2	pounds young okra (about 3 inches long)		Onion slices
	Celery leaves (or seed)		Mustard seed
	Dill weed (or seed)	2	cups vinegar
	Garlic cloves	1	cup water
	Hot peppers	1	tablespoons sugar
		2	tablespoons salt

Wash the okra and trim the stems a bit (don't cut off too much though). Pack them in sterile jars, stem end down for one row, and stem end up for another.

Add whatever seasonings above you wish to each jar—for instance a split clove of garlic, an umbel of dill, and a small hot pepper.

Mix the vinegar, water, sugar, and salt together and boil for several minutes. Pour over the okra and seal. These should stand at least a month before serving.

Makes 4 pints.

My favorite pickle of all—wonderful as an appetizer, with a slice of French pâté (rather than a cornichon), beside a sandwich, or as part of any assortment of relishes for a grand meal.

WATERMELON RIND PICKLES

1	rind of watermelon	1	tablespoon whole allspice
3	tablespoons salt	1	tablespoon broken-up
5	cups sugar		cinnamon stick
2	cups vinegar	1	lemon, sliced
1	tablespoon whole cloves		

*P*repare the rind by removing all green and pink, and cut into 1-inch cubes. Depending on the size of the melon this will make 8 to 12 cups. Place the cubes in a crock, cover with water, and add the salt. Let stand overnight.

Drain the cubes, cover with fresh water, and cook in a large kettle until the cubes are tender—45 minutes to an hour. Drain the cubes.

Mix the sugar and vinegar in the kettle and boil for 10 minutes. Tie the spices and lemon slices in a spice bag and drop into the pot, add the rind, and cook till it is transparent—another hour or so.

Remove the spice bag, pack the rind into sterile jars, and fill with syrup. Seal.

Makes 5 to 6 pints.

Our sweetest pickle by far, with a lovely look and crisp texture, one needs only a cube or two to be satisfied. They are particularly fine with thin slices of salty country-cured ham.

DIXIE PICKLED PEACHES

3	pounds peaches (about 12)	4½	cups sugar
12	whole cloves		4-inch piece of stick
3	cups vinegar		cinnamon, broken up

*D*rop the peaches in boiling water, remove with a slotted spoon, and slip the peels off. Stick a clove in each peach and place them in hot sterile jars.

Bring the vinegar, sugar, and cinnamon pieces to a boil and cook until the sugar dissolves. Ladle the syrup over the peaches, and add a few pieces of cinnamon to each jar.

Seal at once and refrigerate.

Makes 2 quarts.

The traditional accompaniment to baked ham in the South, where they are to be seen glimmering from a silver bowl beside the platter of hot steaming biscuits.

SHAKER APPLESAUCE

2 pounds green cooking apples (or any cooking apple such as Gravensteins)	Sugar (optional)
	Lemon juice (optional)
	Cinnamon (optional)
2 cups hard apple cider	

Cut the apples into quarters and core. Place them in a kettle with the cider, cover, and cook over medium heat about 10 to 15 minutes, or until they are soft.

Remove the apples with a slotted spoon and purée them through a ricer. Turn the heat to high under the cider and let it boil down till it becomes almost syrupy, then add to the apples and let cool.

If your apples are tasty, this is about all that is necessary for an excellent tart applesauce. But you may add sugar to taste, lemon juice to heighten flavor, or cinnamon for memory's sake.

If you are able to obtain good hard cider this makes an applesauce beyond belief, appley beyond appley, to accompany pork, ham, or even duckling.

FRESH TURNIP RELISH

1 cup grated turnip	2 tablespoons sugar
1 cup grated white onion	2 tablespoons prepared horseradish
⅓ cup white wine vinegar	

Combine all the ingredients and chill thoroughly in the refrigerator. This can be eaten as soon as it is chilled, but it is better after at least 24 hours, and it will keep a week or more.

An unusual "fresh" relish that makes a quite lively contrast to almost any cold or hot meat.

CRANBERRY ORANGE RELISH

1   pound cranberries
1   large seedless orange

1 to 2   cups sugar (depending on
            your taste)
2   tablespoons brandy
      (optional)

Wash the berries and pick out any bad ones. Either put the berries and orange through a grinder or chop them fine in a food processor.

Add the sugar and brandy, mix thoroughly, and store, covered, in the refrigerator for at least 2 days before serving.

Makes 3 cups.

Our best known and most widely served chutney is this "fresh" one meant to be kept in the refrigerator to age rather than be canned. As the flavor only gets better with age, you should make the relish several months before you first use it, though. My friend Dorothy Neal says she has tasted it a year later and found it still more delicious. I make it when cranberries first come on the market in the fall, and make enough to last through the holidays and on into the next year, for it is a graceful, bracing, colorful condiment to any meat you see fit—not just turkey.

BLUEBERRY RHUBARB RELISH

2   cups blueberries (fresh or
       frozen)

4   cups rhubarb
½   cup sugar (or to taste)

In the past the blueberries for this recipe were ground in a meat grinder, and the rhubarb was finely diced. If you have a food processor, everything is much easier. Place the blueberries in the processor (thawed, if frozen) and run with the metal blade until they are ground fine. Slice the rhubarb fairly thin, put it in with the blueberries, and add the sugar. Process with an "on and off" motion until the rhubarb is cut in tiny pieces. Taste for sugar, and also check to see there are no large pieces of rhubarb—if so, process several twitches more.

This is a little-known relish from the Northwest, where blueberries abound. It is similar to the familiar cranberry-orange relish, and is used in the same manner, but the combination has an exotic—almost unearthly—flavor that no one is quite able to identify. Unlike cranberry-orange relish, it doesn't seem to keep more than several weeks in the refrigerator, but it needs at least a day to age before serving, and it freezes well if you make it in large batches. It compliments turkey, game, chicken, pork, and ham.

BREADS

God bless you for the Bread!
Now—can you spare it? Shall I
send it back? Will you have a
Loaf of mine—which is spread?

    —Emily Dickinson, Letters

Quick Breads

I know of no other cuisine that puts forth such a large range of breads. The tiniest village in Europe often has one proud loaf unlike their neighbors, but here a great variety may be turned out even from one home—biscuits of all kinds, cornbread in several different forms, flapjacks, waffles, loaves both wheat and white, plump rolls for holidays. A definitive cookbook such as *The Joy of Cooking* often lists over a hundred such breads. It is our tradition of quick breads, using baking powder rather than yeast, that accounts for much of this wide range. In most of the South they are made up for every meal, still. I don't go that far, but the breads put down here I cook, and cook often. Many of the best of these breads, though, need good cornmeal with the germ still in it—I have friends send it, stone ground, from the South, but most parts of the country never get a sniff of it. For those, look under cornmeal in the Methods and Ingredients section on page 399 for suggestions on how to handle tasteless market meal.

THE DUCHESS OF
WINDSOR'S CORNPONES

2   cups stone-ground white
    cornmeal (or 1½ cups
    ordinary meal and ½ cup
    masa harina—see page 401)
1   teaspoon baking powder
1   teaspoon salt

½   cup milk
1   cup boiling water
    (approximately)
3   tablespoons melted bacon fat
    (or butter)

*P*reheat the oven to 425°F.

Measure the cornmeal, baking powder, and salt into a bowl and mix well with a fork. Stir in the milk, then add ¾ cup of the boiling water. (There is no telling how much water to use with a particular meal, though it is safe to say it's better to use too little rather than too much. Let it sit 10 minutes, and see—its consistency should be that of wet sand, so that it holds a shape in the hand. If it looks too thick, add the other ¼ cup of water—or more. One cup is exactly right for good Southern meal.)

To cook the pones, put the fat in a heavy 12-inch frying pan and put it in the oven as it heats. (If you use butter, this will take only heating up so it bubbles, but with the preferable bacon fat it ought to heat almost to smoking.)

Pour the melted fat into the cornmeal mixture and stir it in. Form pones by scooping up a small handful of meal and shaping it with the other hand the length of your fingers—in the manner of prayer.

Drop these shapes in a radial pattern around the bottom of the sizzling hot skillet as you form them. If you don't have a large heavy pan, the alternative is to use cast-iron cornstick pans treated with fat in the same manner (In fact they make the best possible cornsticks, and as they are prettier I most often make them rather than pones for company—one recipe will fill 2 regular cornstick pans.)

Put the skillet or cornstick pan back into the hot oven and bake 20 minutes, or until the pones are golden on top with browned crisp bottoms and steamy insides. Serve immediately to be split and buttered.

Makes 12.

Published in 1943, all crisply upper Baltimore in the old sense, Some Favorite Southern Recipes *by the Duchess of Windsor is the very example of inherited local bride's cookery, each dish put down deft enough to program a new cook (for one doubts The Duchess bothered herself much in the kitchen). As good as these recipes all are, one hopes the Simpson cornpones survived the Riviera and itinerary, for the Duchess goes on to "some foreign recipes" learned on her travels—some handy haddock rules, a reckless Bahamian turtle pie, a sound chicken curry, and a simply lovely dish of boned loin of lamb cut open, broiled with mustard, then laid on sautéed eggplant slices with a garnish of water-cress and pan juices, thence to a risotto of leftovers, and a glacé aux mangoes. I would forego any of them for the cornpones of the Duchess anytime—indeed, they are one of my favorite breads.*

ZEPHYRS

2 cups boiling water	1 tablespoon lard, bacon fat, or butter
½ cup stone-ground cornmeal (or ⅓ cup regular cornmeal plus masa harina to measure ½ cup—see page 401)	½ teaspoon salt
	2 egg whites

*P*our the boiling water over the cornmeal, fat, and salt in the top of a double boiler. Cook over simmering water for 20 minutes, stirring now and again to make sure it stays smooth.

Remove from the heat, film the top with butter, and let cool. (This can sit covered a good while before you make the zephyrs, but it must be whisked smooth before cooking.)

Preheat the oven to 375°F.

Whip the egg whites stiff but not dry and gently fold them into the cooled mush. Drop by tablespoonfuls on a greased cookie sheet (one should hold them all) and bake 30 minutes, or until still soft and mushy inside but crisp without. Makes 24.

These light crisp mouthfuls are one of the pleasantest treasures of all our hot breads. Exactly what they sound, they are a cornmeal mush cooked crisp with only egg white for leaven. Topped or not with a dab of soft butter, the amount above is perfect for 6 at soup—though if served with a main course, as a starch, the amount serves barely 2 they are so briefly delicious.

BACON BUTTERMILK CORNBREAD

4	slices bacon (optional)	1	tablespoon sugar
¾	cup stone-ground cornmeal (or regular cornmeal)	1	teaspoon salt
		4	tablespoons cold butter
1	cup flour (or if using regular meal, ½ cup masa harina and ½ cup flour)	1	cup buttermilk
		2	eggs, separated
		¼	teaspoon baking soda
2	teaspoons baking powder	1	tablespoon water

*P*reheat the oven to 400°F.

This makes a superior cornbread without the bacon, but if you are using it, slice the strips into ⅛-inch slivers. Put them in an 8-inch square baking pan and put it into the oven as it heats.

Combine the dry ingredients and cut in the cold butter till it is reduced to the size of peas (this can be done with a couple of crisscross knives or with a twitch or two in a food processor).

Beat the buttermilk with the egg yolks. Dissolve the baking soda in the water. Stir these both into the dry ingredients till just moistened.

Beat the egg whites stiff but not dry. Remove the bacon from the hot pan— the strips should have begun to cook and release fat. Sprinkle the bacon over the cornmeal mixture and fold in along with the egg whites.

Spoon the batter into the hot greased pan and bake 20 to 25 minutes, or until gold and springy.

Serves 6 to 8.

Though bacon is optional in this recipe, I like the way the pieces render a bit of fat while cooking so there are spots and pockets of goodness throughout. If you wish to omit the bacon, grease your baking pan with butter and heat just before adding the cornmeal mixture—this assures a good crust. Be sure not to bake this bread too much, for it will dry out if left too long in the oven. Any leftover pieces are definitely to be split and spread with butter to broil the next morning (or for lunch or dinner).

TEXAS JALAPEÑO CHEESE CORNBREAD

*M*ake this exactly like Bacon Buttermilk Cornbread (see preceding recipe), except leave out the bacon and in its place fold in 1 cup grated sharp cheddar cheese, and ¼ cup jalapeño peppers (bottled en escabeche), seeded and minced.

This is a fine half-bread sired between Southern and Southwestern cuisines. Texans serve it with their large steaks and generous barbecues usually, though I had it once with simply a platter of well-seasoned beans, and a glass of beer, and felt well fed. It is also good the next day, split and toasted with butter— and when cut in small pieces it makes a very good appetizer.

SHAKER CORNBREAD (OR MUFFINS)

<table>
<tr><td>¾</td><td>cup stone-ground cornmeal (or regular cornmeal)</td><td>½</td><td>cup flour (or masa harina if you use regular meal— see page 401)</td></tr>
<tr><td>3</td><td>teaspoons baking powder</td><td></td><td></td></tr>
<tr><td>1</td><td>teaspoon sugar</td><td>2</td><td>eggs</td></tr>
<tr><td>1</td><td>teaspoon salt</td><td>1¼</td><td>cups milk</td></tr>
<tr><td></td><td></td><td>3</td><td>ears corn, scraped (1 cup)</td></tr>
<tr><td></td><td></td><td>3</td><td>tablespoons butter, melted</td></tr>
</table>

*P*reheat the oven to 350°F.

Sift the dry ingredients together in a bowl. In another bowl, beat the eggs with the milk, then mix them into the dry ingredients.

Fold in the corn kernels and melted butter. Pour into a buttered 8-inch square pan (or into muffin pans—the recipe will make eight 2-inch muffins).

Bake 40 to 45 minutes, or until the bread is set and beginning to brown. Serve hot with butter.

Serves 6 to 8.

Definitely one of the best of our cornbreads—this is moist, rich, and with the extra flavor of fresh corn. You might wish to substitute canned or frozen corn, but I wait and save it for the summer months when fresh corn is available.

GEORGIA SPOONBREAD

<table>
<tr><td>1</td><td>cup stone-ground cornmeal (or ¾ cup regular cornmeal and ¼ cup masa harina— see page 401)</td><td>1</td><td>teaspoon salt</td></tr>
<tr><td></td><td></td><td>1</td><td>teaspoon sugar</td></tr>
<tr><td></td><td></td><td>1</td><td>tablespoon bacon fat (or butter)</td></tr>
<tr><td>3</td><td>cups milk, scalded</td><td>3</td><td>eggs, separated</td></tr>
</table>

*P*reheat the oven to 375°F.

Sprinkle the cornmeal over the scalded milk and cook over low heat for 5 minutes, stirring to make sure there are no lumps and the "mush" doesn't stick to the bottom. (Cornmeals vary, and it takes less of some to make a good mush than others, so the first time you try this recipe use the above amount, and adjust next time if necessary—the mush should be thick, but not so thick that folding in the egg whites later is difficult.)

Stir in the salt, sugar, and half the fat. Remove from the fire and let cool a bit. Put the rest of the fat in a soufflé dish or casserole and place in the oven till it nearly smokes (or only to heat and sizzle, if using butter).

Beat the egg yolks into the mush. Beat the egg whites till stiff but not dry, then fold them lightly into the mush. Spoon into the hot dish and bake for 45 minutes, or until the bread is puffed and golden.

Serve immediately, to be spooned out at table and topped with butter or meat sauce.

Serves 4 to 6.

This cornmeal soufflé—for that is exactly what it is—makes one of the glorious triumphs of U.S. cookery. There is probably no other dish I would invariably serve a foreign visitor to impress and delight. Light and crusty, it can be served with almost any meal, simply buttered. But I also like to use it as the Italians would polenta, as a side dish to hearty braised meats with plenty of rich sauce. The next day, any left over can be sliced and sautéed lightly in butter for a side dish to eggs, bacon, or sausage.

HUSH PUPPIES

1	cup stone-ground cornmeal (or ¾ cup regular meal and ¼ cup masa harina— see page 401)		Freshly ground pepper
		2	green onions, minced with part of tops
½	teaspoon baking power	1	egg
½	teaspoon salt	¼	cup milk
			Fat for deep frying

*C*ombine the cornmeal, baking powder, and salt and pepper. Beat the green onions and egg into the milk. Let both sit until you are ready to fry the hush puppies.

After you have fried fish in the fat (heated to about 370°F), mix the egg-milk mixture into the dry ingredients. Drop by teaspoonfuls into the hot fat.

Let fry 3 to 4 minutes, or until they are golden brown on both sides. Place on absorbent paper as each batch is done, to drain. Serve with Tartar Sauce (page 292).

Serves 4 to 6.

Frankly a campfire dish for fishermen, long since tamed for the kitchen. Often they are flat and greasy, but done with care to proper temperature they are the perfect accompaniment to fresh-caught fish flipped over the fire in a lacy cornmeal crust. I like to serve three or four of them as a side to fresh sizzled trout, with a garnish of watercress, a cruet of fine vinegar, and good home-made tartar sauce.

WILD RICE
AND CORNMEAL GRIDDLE CAKES

2	tablespoons wild rice	¼	teaspoon baking soda
	Salt	¼	teaspoon salt
½	cup cornmeal (preferably stone-ground)	1	cup water
			Vegetable oil
¼	cup flour		

Cook the wild rice in plenty of salted water 45 minutes, then drain in a sieve. While the rice cooks, stir together the cornmeal, flour, soda, salt, and water in a bowl, and let sit. Stir the rice into the batter.

Drop the batter by the tablespoonful onto a well-greased griddle set over medium-high heat. Cook the cakes about a minute per side. Stir the batter each time you make a batch, and make sure the pan is well oiled.

Makes 20.

These delicious lacy cakes have a variety of uses. They can, of course, be served with maple syrup in the grand old tradition of native pancakes, but they are equally welcome as a side dish for meat dishes such as Thomas Jefferson's Salmi of Duck (page 162).

HAPPY VALLEY BISCUITS

1½ cups flour	¼ cup cornmeal (preferably
1 teaspoon salt	stone-ground)
2 teaspoons sugar	¼ cup lard (or butter)
1 teaspoon baking powder	1 cup buttermilk
½ teaspoon baking soda	

*P*reheat the oven to 450°F.

Sift the flour, salt, sugar, baking powder, and soda into the bowl of a food processor fitted with the steel blade. Twitch a few times to mix, then add the cornmeal and the lard or butter. Twitch several times more, until the mixture has the texture of cornmeal.

Add the buttermilk and turn on and off a time or two only until it seems well mixed. (This can also be done pretty quickly in a bowl as well, cutting in the fat first, then stirring the buttermilk in quickly with several strokes.)

Grease muffin tins, and sprinkle with a little cornmeal in each cup. Shake to coat the sides and bottoms of the pan. Drop the dough from a spoon, filling the cups about two-thirds full. Sprinkle a little more cornmeal over the tops and bake 12 to 15 minutes, or until golden and crusty.

Makes 12.

A few years ago I came on a recipe for biscuits, hid in a small farm magazine collection importing Gugelhupf and blintzes to Omaha, which called for a measure of cornmeal in a rich buttermilk mixture. I set to with their recipe during two dispiriting batches, until I went to Irma Rombauer for general guidance. In one try it became a favorite, still called "Happy Valley," pretty and of crusty character enough to become called for by family, worthy of any company when there's no time for yeast, toasted split with butter the next day. The next best thing about them is they take about as little time as a packaged mix.

SUMMER CLOUD BISCUITS

2 cups presifted flour	½ teaspoon salt
1 teaspoon sugar	4 teaspoons baking powder

¼   cup minced parsley and/or   1   egg
        watercress, chives,   ⅔   cup milk
        tarragon, basil, etc.
½   cup cold butter (lard or
        vegetable shortening)

*P*reheat the oven to 450°F.

Sift the dry ingredients into a bowl, add the herbs, and cut in the fat with two knives or a pastry blender until it is the consistency of coarse meal. (This can also be done with a couple of twitches of a food processor.)

Whisk the egg till frothy, beat in the milk, then add them all at once to the flour mixture. Stir only until moistened.

Turn onto a lightly floured board, knead gently and quickly a few times, and roll out ¾ inch thick. Cut with a biscuit cutter dipped in flour, place in an ungreased baking pan (preferably glass), brush the tops with milk, and bake 12 to 15 minutes.

Makes 24.

These biscuits seem to rise sky-high for everyone. They are fine in winter, when only parsley or watercress is available, but they are a wonder when you have the summer herb patch to choose from—even without herbs they are superb.

WHIPPED CREAM BISCUITS

1   cup heavy cream   ¾   teaspoon salt
2   cups presifted cake flour   Pinch of sugar
2¼ teaspoons baking powder

*P*reheat the oven to 450°F.

In a good-sized bowl, whip the cream till it just holds soft peaks—do not overbeat. Sift the dry ingredients over it, and quickly fold together until the dry ingredients are just moistened.

Turn onto a lightly floured board and knead gently and quickly a few times. Roll out ¼ inch thick, and cut straight down with a biscuit cutter dipped in flour.

Bake on an ungreased baking dish (preferably glass) 10 to 12 minutes.
Makes 24.

When you have the cream and cake flour on hand, these make the lightest, most delicate biscuit of all. Those who associate biscuits only with coarse country cooking might do well to try these rather than yeast rolls at their next dinner party.

HELENE'S DROP SHORTCAKES

1	cup buttermilk		Pinch of salt
½	teaspoon baking soda	1	teaspoon baking powder
1½	cups flour	6	tablespoons butter
3	tablespoons sugar		

*P*reheat the oven to 450°F.

Mix the buttermilk and soda in a small bowl (it will puff up like a yeast as you mix the other ingredients). Sift the flour, sugar, salt, and baking powder into a medium bowl. Cut the butter into this with a pastry cutter or two knives until the mixture resembles coarse cornmeal. Lightly stir in the buttermilk just until there are no floury lumps. (This is the traditional way, but if you have a food processor, just flick the dry ingredients a little without sifting them, cut in the butter in a few more flicks, and then pour in the buttermilk and mix very lightly.)

Drop about ¼ cup of the dough onto an ungreased baking sheet—do this with a fork, and smooth the dough out a bit to make a 3-inch circle. Repeat to make 6 cakes. On top of each of these drop a dollop of dough, dividing it evenly among the cakes. With the fork tines lightly prick up the tops of the cakes so there are little peaks. (This later will make crispy nuggets to hold the juices, and making the drop in two processes insures easily divided shortcakes.)

Bake 12 to 15 minutes, or until crusty and beginning to brown. Remove from the oven and let cool. To serve, split the cakes open, cover the bottoms with sweetened juicy fruit, place the top on, pour cream over and around the cakes, and place a few more pieces of fruit on top.

Serves 6.

These delights are a specialty of Helene Sharpless from Bloomington, Indiana. The buttermilk gives them a good delicate crumb, and dropping them with a fork makes for a much better cake than the usual rolled variety. (To make shortcakes for a savory filling rather than a sweet, put in 1 teaspoon of salt, rather than a pinch, and substitute a pinch of sugar for the 3 talbespoons.)

WHOLE-WHEAT BISCUITS

1	cup presifted all-purpose flour	4	teaspoons baking powder
1	cup presifted whole-wheat flour	½	cup cold butter (or lard or shortening)
½	teaspoon salt	1	egg
		⅔	cup milk

*P*reheat the oven to 450°F.

Sift the dry ingredients into a bowl and cut in the fat with two knives or a pastry blender until it is the consistency of coarse meal. (A food processor is fine here.)

Whisk the egg until frothy, beat with the milk, and pour all at once into the flour mixture, stirring only until moistened.

Turn onto a lightly floured board, knead gently and quickly several times, and roll out ¾ inch thick. Cut straight down with a biscuit cutter dipped in flour. Brush the tops with more milk and bake on an ungreased baking sheet 12 to 15 minutes.

Makes 24.

Biscuits with whole-wheat flour never rise as delicately as white flour biscuits, but these are light enough and much more savory than most plain biscuits. Since there is more flavor to the flour, I don't feel it necessary to add sugar here, but you may wish to—or brown sugar, or honey.

PARSLEY DUMPLINGS

1½	cups presifted flour	½	teaspoon minced fresh rosemary, thyme, or basil
2	teaspoons baking powder		
¾	teaspoon salt	3	tablespoons butter (or lard or shortening)
2	tablespoons minced parsley		
		¾	cup milk (approximately)

*S*ift the flour with baking powder and salt. Add the parsley and rosemary (or other herb). Chop the fat (with two forks, knives, or a pastry blender) into the flour until the mixture resembles coarse cornmeal.

Add enough milk, while tossing lightly with a fork, to make a batter that can be dropped from a spoon.

Cook the dumplings in a stew (or steamed in a colander), tightly covered, for 15 minutes—or until a toothpick inserted comes out clean.

Makes 12.

Because they happen at the last minute, I am usually mistrustful of dumpling recipes. Sure-fire cornmeal dumplings can fall to pieces over a pot of good greens, turning them into an unsavory mush as well as not, or you may have a succulent sauce suddenly pulled up by leaden cloudings. I have never had these fail, however, and they are splendid with any of the fricassees.

PENNSYLVANIA POTATO MUFFINS

2	eggs, separated, plus 1 egg white	½	cup flour
		¾	teaspoon baking powder
2½	cups finely grated potatoes	1	teaspoon salt
3	tablespoons finely grated onion	4	tablespoons butter, melted

*P*reheat the oven to 400°F.

Mix the egg yolks into the potatoes and onion in a medium-sized bowl. Sift the flour with baking powder and salt over the potatoes, and mix in lightly. Stir in the melted butter.

Beat the 3 egg whites in another bowl until stiff but not dry, then fold them into the mixture very gently. Grease muffin tins and spoon in the batter, filling no more than two-thirds full.

Bake for 20 to 25 minutes, or until the muffins puff up and are golden. Serve immediately with butter.

Makes 12.

My fellow countrymen have a great liking for sweet and even fruited muffins with their meat. In this I cannot share, though I can imagine they would be excellent with coffee for breakfast, or for an afternoon tea. These old-style potato muffins with a hint of onion, however, are to my taste a successful substitute for the starch in many a meal—try them.

BEATEN BISCUITS

2 cups flour	4 tablespoons butter
1 teaspoon salt	½ cup ice water
¼ cup lard	

*P*reheat the oven to 350°F.

Place the flour and salt in a food processor fitted with the steel blade. Turn on and off a few times, then add the lard and butter cut into small pieces. Process with a few more turns until the mixture resembles a coarse meal.

Turn the processor on. Pour ice water through the tube and process until the whole forms a ball. Continue for 2 to 3 minutes, or until the dough is quite smooth and elastic.

Roll out very thin on a lightly floured board, then fold the sheet of dough over on itself. Cut with a 1½-inch biscuit cutter dipped in flour and place on an ungreased cookie sheet.

Prick the tops of the biscuits three times with the tines of a fork. Bake 25 to 30 minutes, or until browned and puffed up.

Makes 48.

These distinctive unleavened biscuits have not been prepared for some years, even in the South, for their lightness depends on the cook (usually a black one) who had the wrist and time to hammer the dough with a mallet for 30 minutes or more, until it "blistered." With the advent of the food processor, however, these are brought within the range of the modern cook, for it takes only a few minutes to achieve this lovely crisp accompaniment to delicate soups.

CHARLESTON BENNE WAFERS

¼ cup sesame seeds	½ teaspoon salt
1 cup flour	¼ teaspoon cayenne (optional)
1 teaspoon baking powder	4 tablespoons butter (or lard)
¼ teaspoon baking soda	½ cup buttermilk

*P*reheat the oven to 400°F.

While the oven heats, toast the sesame seeds in a pie plate or cake pan, stirring now and again, until they turn pale amber. This will take about 10 minutes.

Sift the dry ingredients together, then cut in the fat till the mixture is the consistency of coarse meal. (This can also be done in a food processor.) Add the sesame seeds, then stir in buttermilk until the dough just holds together.

Turn out onto a lightly floured board and knead gently 5 or 6 times. Roll out about ¼ inch thick and cut in 1 inch rounds (if you don't have a cutter that small, some bottle caps are that size, and do nicely).

Place on an ungreased baking sheet and bake 10 to 15 minutes, or until the wafers are gold and crisp.

Makes 48.

Benne (or sesame) seeds are grown extensively in South Carolina, and are used in many of the local cookies and candies, as well as in this lovely biscuit. They are usually served as a cocktail tidbit, but as I like my cocktails unadorned, I make these to accompany soups for a dinner's first course. They can be made ahead, and last several days in a tin.

MY GRANDMOTHER'S GOOEY BUTTER ROLLS

1¾	cups presifted flour	1	cup sugar
2	teaspoons baking powder	5	tablespoons butter, at room
½	teaspoon baking soda		temperature
¼	teaspoon salt	⅓	cup milk
¼	cup lard (or butter)	½	teaspoon vanilla
¾	cup buttermilk		

*P*reheat the oven to 450°F.

Sift the flour, baking powder, soda, and salt into a bowl. Cut in the fat until the mixture resembles coarse meal, then add the buttermilk and stir to mix. (Both these steps can be adapted to a food processor.)

Knead lightly on a floured board just until you have a smooth dough. Shape it into a rectangle and roll out with a rolling pin to a rectangle approximately 13 × 9 inches.

Mix ½ cup of the sugar and 4 tablespoons of the butter together in a bowl—they don't have to be "creamed," but just to hold together. Spread this over the dough, then roll up into a long jelly roll. Grease an 8 × 8-inch square baking pan. Slice the roll into 16 sections and place the sections in the pan, cut side up.

Bake the biscuits for 10 to 12 minutes, or until they are lightly golden. As they bake, combine the milk, remaining ½ cup sugar, and remaining 1 tablespoon butter in a saucepan. Cook over high heat, stirring, for several minutes, until the mixture has thickened slightly. Let cool a bit, then stir in the vanilla.

When the biscuits look done, pour the sauce over them and put back into the oven for 2 more minutes. Remove and let cool.

Makes 16.

Everyone knows those glorious sticky buns made from yeast rolls, sprinkled with sugar, butter, and cinnamon, then cooked on a nutty caramel base. These are similar, take no time at all as yeast rolls must, and are, I think, every bit as good when you want to turn out a hasty sweet treat for the family. I like the simplicity of the basic vanilla version my grandmother made, though often as not I make one of the following variations I evolved: (1) Orange Butter Rolls: *Before rolling up the dough, sprinkle the butter-sugar mixture with grated rind of 1 orange and a little cinnamon. Substitute orange juice for milk in the final sauce, and omit the vanilla. (2)* Caramel Nut Butter Rolls: *Substitute brown sugar (either light or dark) for all the sugar in the recipe. Before rolling up the dough, sprinkle the butter-sugar mixture with chopped nuts and cinnamon. When you cook the final sauce, the milk will be likely to clot up, but don't worry—just keep stirring and it will smooth out as it cooks.*

Yeast Breads

*T*hese are everyone's memory of what a fragrance can be, whose mothers or grandmothers baked the daily loaf. Nothing is so sweet and cleanly in its smell, unless a meadow just cut for hay. Every cook who bakes bread will also remind you there is nothing near as liberating to the soul as kneading yeast dough, and anyone who has eaten bread just out of the oven will understand nothing else tastes quite as good. Economists point out how cheap it can be, and dieticians how wholesome—this "staff of life." So why do so few make bread? I can't answer this, but I know it's possible to put a batch together in the time it takes to watch one television program (addicted, you can manage both), and it can be set to rise in the refrigerator overnight. The next day it takes 10 minutes to punch down and form into loaves, and you can do anything else while it rises and bakes. Why not?

PARKER HOUSE ROLLS

1 tablespoon sugar	2 tablespoons warm water
3 tablespoons butter	1 egg
½ teaspoon salt	2 ⅔ cups flour, sifted
1 cup milk, scalded	Melted butter
½ cake yeast (or ½ package active dry)	

Add the sugar, 3 tablespoons butter, and the salt to the scalded milk, and stir off the fire till the sugar is dissolved. Cool till lukewarm. Dissolve the yeast in the warm water and let sit 10 minutes to "proof" and puff up.

Combine the milk mixture and yeast in a good-sized bowl. Beat in the egg, then the flour in batches. Add enough additional flour to make a dough that can be handled easily.

Turn the dough out onto a lightly floured board and knead until it is smooth and elastic. Put in a lightly buttered warm bowl and turn to coat the entire surface with butter. Cover with a towel and let rise in a warm place until doubled in bulk—about 2 hours.

Punch the dough down and form into rolls. This may be done by filling greased muffin tins with 3 small balls, and brushing with melted butter. (Or, by rolling out the dough, cutting it with a biscuit cutter, and creasing each across the middle with a knife. These are then brushed with butter, and folded over—pressing the edges tightly together—and placed on a baking sheet to rise. The latter method is the classic Parker House shape, but more often these days the "cloverleaf" roll is thought prettier.)

Whichever you prefer, let the formed rolls rise again until doubled, covered again with a towel. It will take about 30 minutes.

Preheat the oven to 400°F.

Bake for 15 to 20 minutes, or until golden on top.

Makes 24.

No native holiday feast is complete without these delicate yeasty rolls, and in many a home they still grace any company, at any formal or informal meal. Though there are many recipes, the one from the Parker House in Boston has circulated most widely, and it seems a sound base on which all other rolls might be compared.

SHAKER ROSE GERANIUM ROLLS

1	recipe Parker House Rolls (see preceding recipe)	2	tablespoons sugar
		6	rose geranium leaves

Make the preceding recipe with an extra 2 tablespoons sugar, and when forming rolls make one ball the size of your muffin cups, with a small piece of geranium leaf in the center of each. Let rise and bake as for Parker House rolls.

Another Shaker delectable. Rose geraniums are grown for their sweet-scented leaves rather than their flowers, and if you chance to have a plant available you can be blessed (as were the Shakers) with the most fragrant bread imaginable.

LIGHT SESAME ROLLS

¼	cup warm water	2	tablespoons sugar
1	package active dry yeast	1	cup water (or milk)
4	tablespoons butter (or vegetable shortening)	1	egg
		3	cups unbleached white flour
1¼	teaspoons salt		Sesame seeds

These are refrigerator rolls. Early in the day, or the night before, pour warm water over the yeast, stir, and let sit to "proof" and puff up. Heat the butter, salt, and sugar in a saucepan with a cup of water or milk until the butter melts. Let sit till lukewarm, then stir in yeast and egg well, then the flour. This will make a rather sticky batter, which need not be kneaded.

Plop the batter into a greased bowl, oil your hands, and pat the top smooth. Cover the bowl with plastic wrap or foil and refrigerate. This dough kneads itself, as it were, while it sits.

About 2 hours before baking the rolls, punch down the dough and grease muffin pans. Sprinkle the bottoms and edges of the pans with sesame seed, shaking out what doesn't cling. Take the dough up (with oiled hands, if necessary, for it is a very soft dough) and drop about 2 tablespoonfuls of it into each muffin cup. The rolls will be nicest looking if you stretch the dough smooth and tuck the rest under as you go.

Sprinkle the tops with more sesame seeds, and let rise about 2 hours covered with a damp towel or plastic wrap. The dough should really fill the muffin cups.

Preheat the oven to 425°F.

Bake the rolls about 15 minutes—or until roundly brown. Shake out into a basket or bowl immediately, and serve warm with butter.

Makes 18.

Light, North Carolina, no-nonsense, no-knead rolls prepared well ahead of any kitchen rush, with a superior hard crust. They are so easy to make anyone with about 10 minutes forethought in the morning can serve up magnificent evening breads equal to any occasion. To make them cover two evenings, use half the dough. Oil the top of the rest and wrap again, then refrigerate for the next night.

CHILD'S FAMOUS BUTTER CAKES

2	packages active dry yeast	2	tablespoons soft butter
1¼	cups lukewarm water	2	teaspoons salt
1	teaspoon sugar	3½	cups flour

*P*ut the yeast in a large mixing bowl, stir in ¼ cup of the warm water, and the sugar, and let "proof" for 10 minutes—or until quite bubbly.

Add the remaining 1 cup warm water, the soft butter, salt, and 1 cup of the flour. Beat until smooth, and continue adding flour in batches as you stir. By the time all the flour is added the dough will start to come away from the sides of the bowl and form a ball.

Put dough in a warm buttered bowl and turn to coat all sides well with butter. Let rise, covered with a towel, in a warm place for 1 hour, or until doubled in bulk.

Punch the dough down and roll out ¾ inch thick on a lightly floured board. Cover with a towel, and let rise 30 more minutes.

Cut the dough in rounds with a 3-inch cutter or glass, then cook the cakes in a greased large frying pan over medium-low heat, 3 to 5 minutes on each side, or until golden brown.

Serve hot, or the next day split and toasted with butter.

These cakes have been known to make a strong New Yorker come all over goosebumps with memory. Though not widely known outside that city, and no one else I know—even there—makes them at home, I make them often. Reminiscent of English muffins, they are at the same time yeastier, more delicate, and certainly less expensive (unless you make your own muffins). I also believe they make a superior roll for hamburgers—a use Child's never put them to. They last several days in the refrigerator, and need only to be split like an English muffin, spread with butter, and toasted under the broiler.

MY WHITE BUTTERMILK BREAD

1	package active dry yeast (or 1 cake)	1¼ cups buttermilk
¾	cup warm water	4½ to 5 cups unbleached white flour
2	tablespoons sugar	¼ cup lard, melted
		2 teaspoons salt

*D*issolve the yeast with the warm water and sugar. Stir it, and let sit till puffy. Combine this with the buttermilk, 2½ cups of the flour, melted lard, and salt in a bowl—an electric mixer of some kind is best. Beat it for several minutes on medium speed in the mixer, or by hand. Then beat in by hand the rest of the white flour. Add only enough so the dough no longer clings to the sides of the bowl.

Dump the dough onto a floured board and knead about 5 minutes. Place in a greased bowl and roll to cover with grease all over. Place a damp towel or plastic wrap over the bowl, place in a warm spot, and let rise till doubled in bulk.

Punch the dough down, knead a few times, then roll out with a rolling pin to get out the bubbles.

Divide in 2 pieces and shape into 2 loaves. Place these in greased bread pans, grease the tops of the loaves, and cover again with a damp towel or plastic wrap. Let rise about an hour in a warm place—or until doubled and filling out the pans.

When risen, place in a cold oven, turn the heat to 400°F, and bake about 40 minutes, or until the tops are brown, the loaves have separated from the sides of the pans, and they ring out when tapped with a knuckle.

Makes 2 loaves.

It took me some time to fix on this as my favorite white bread recipe, but the looking and cooking was worth it. All the loaves piled up month by fragrant month, from the kitchens of Lady Bird Johnson and James Beard, and more anonymous ovens, but I like the moist crumb this bread is given from its buttermilk, and I seem to like lard better than butter for a reason I can't put a name to. The sugar and salt are, to my mind, perfectly balanced (even if Lady Bird did go up to ½ cup of sugar in hers—a bread the former President was said to trot from the ends of the ranch for by nose—and many of the regular farm recipes from the past contained up to ½ cup). I don't budge far as L.B.J. while making this bread, certainly, but its sweet smell would carry on those wide Texas winds.

HOMEMADE GARLIC BREAD

	White-flour bread dough for 1 loaf	1	teaspoon minced garlic
4	tablespoons butter, at room temperature	1	egg yolk
		2	tablespoons heavy cream

When you make a two-loaf recipe for white bread, it's nice to make one plain and one garlic. Let the dough rise in the usual manner, punch it down, and roll out on a lightly floured board to a rectangle about 15 x 9 inches.

Mix the butter and garlic well, then spread it on the dough. Roll the dough up (starting with the short side) and seal the ends by pinching. Place in a well-buttered loaf pan. Cover and let rise until doubled in a warm place.

Preheat the oven to 350°F.

Brush the top of the loaf with the egg yolk mixed with the cream, and bake 35 to 45 minutes, or until well browned. (If you use My White Buttermilk Bread, bake it as in that recipe, on page 334.) Remove from the oven and cool on a rack.

A bread ever so much more subtle than the usual French bread split and slathered with garlic butter, then warmed in the oven.

SHAKER DILL BREAD

1	package active dry yeast	1	tablespoon minced chives (or green onions)
¼	cup lukewarm water	1	teaspoon salt
1	cup cottage cheese, at room temperature	¼	teaspoon baking soda
1	teaspoon sugar	1	tablespoon butter, melted
1	egg	2½	cups (or more) flour
2	teaspoons dried dill (or dill seeds)		

Combine the yeast and warm water, and let sit to "proof" and bubble up. Put all the other ingredients, except the flour, in a large bowl. Stir well, then stir in the yeast.

Add the flour gradually, stirring all the while, until you have achieved a stiff dough. Knead on a floured board for 10 minutes at least, or until the dough is smooth and elastic. (This whole procedure will take no time in a food processor.)

Place the dough in a buttered bowl and turn to coat evenly with butter. Cover with a towel or plastic wrap, and let rise for an hour in a warm place— or until doubled in bulk.

Preheat the oven to 350°F.

Punch down and shape into a loaf. Place in a buttered loaf pan, cover, and let rise again until doubled—about 30 minutes. Bake 30 to 40 minutes in the oven, or until golden brown and the top is hard when you rap it. Remove from the oven and brush the top with butter. Cool on a rack.

A remarkably modern-sounding bread (because it seems to have been copied again and again) that is another fine creation of the Shakers. If any is left the next day, it makes excellent toast or sandwiches. I don't know why, but I always think of eating it outside, with an outdoor barbecue, or spread with butter and lettuce leaves to accompany cold fried chicken on picnics.

ANADAMA BREAD

2 cups water	1 teaspoon salt
½ cup cornmeal	1 package active dry yeast
2 tablespoons butter	½ cup lukewarm water
½ cup molasses	5 cups (approximately) flour

*I*n a saucepan bring the water to a boil, then turn off the flame. Add the cornmeal slowly, stirring with a whisk to make sure there are no lumps. Turn the fire back on, bring to a boil, and let simmer gently for 5 minutes. Add the butter, molasses, and salt and allow to cool to lukewarm.

Dissolve the yeast in warm water till it "proofs" and puffs up, then add it to the meal. Beat in enough flour to make a stiff dough. Turn out onto a lightly floured board and knead well till elastic and smooth.

Put in a well-buttered warm bowl and turn to coat completely with butter. Cover and let rise for 1½ hours, or until doubled in bulk.

Punch down, shape into 2 loaves, and place in buttered loaf pans. Cover and let rise again until double—about 30 minutes.

Preheat the oven to 400°F.

Bake the loaves for 1 hour, or until golden brown.

Despite the fact that it appears in all the books of U.S. cookery, I know only a handful of people who actually bake this bread besides me. I first tasted it over twenty years ago, and it has been ever a friend to my kitchen since.

MISS DOROTHY'S BROWN BREAD

1 tablespoon plus 1 teaspoon granulated sugar	2 cups boiling water
2 tablespoons brown sugar	2 packages active dry yeast
3 tablespoons lard	½ cup lukewarm water
2 teaspoons salt	2½ cups white flour
1 cup oatmeal	2½ cups (approximately) whole- wheat flour

*P*ut the 1 tablespoon granulated sugar, the brown sugar, lard, salt, and oatmeal in a bowl. Add the boiling water, stir until the sugar is dissolved, then let sit till lukewarm.

Add the ½ cup lukewarm water to the yeast, and stir in the 1 teaspoon granulated sugar. Let sit till it "proofs" and puffs up, about 5 minutes. Add to the oatmeal mixture, stir, then stir in the white flour. Add enough whole-wheat flour to make a stiff dough, then turn out onto a lightly floured board and knead 10 minutes, or until smooth and elastic.

Divide into 2 loaves, and place in buttered loaf pans. Cover and let rise until nearly doubled in bulk—about 30 minutes.

Preheat the oven to 350°F.

Bake the loaves for 50 minutes, or until slightly golden on top and springy. Cool on a wire rack.

Truly a daily loaf, with both a superior texture and taste—some wheat germ, also, can be added as part of the whole wheat flour.

EMILY DICKINSON'S RYE AND INDIAN BREAD

½	cup cooked pumpkin or sweet potato	2	packages active dry yeast
⅓	cup molasses	⅓	cup lukewarm water
5	tablespoons butter	¼	teaspoon sugar
1	teaspoon salt	2	cups rye flour
1	cup cornmeal	1½ to 2	cups white flour
1	cup boiling water		

Combine the pumpkin, molasses, butter, salt, and cornmeal in a large bowl. Pour the boiling water over, stir, and let stand 10 minutes.

Mix the yeast with the warm water and sugar and let sit till it bubbles up. Add the yeast to the bowl, then stir in the rye flour and 1 cup of the white flour. Mix well, then add enough additional white flour to make a stiff dough.

Turn out onto a lightly floured board and knead 10 minutes, or until the dough is smooth and elastic. Put in a well-greased bowl, and turn a few times to coat completely with grease. Let rise, covered, in a warm place for 1½ hours, or until doubled in bulk.

Punch the dough down, halve, and form each half into a ball. Place each ball in a greased 8-inch pie plate or cake pan and let rise, covered, for another hour, or until doubled again.

Preheat the oven to 375°F.

Cut a cross with a razor blade on the top of each loaf and bake for 15 minutes. Reduce the heat to 325°F and bake 45 minutes to 1 hour longer, or until browned and the bottoms sound hollow when tapped. Cool in a wire rack.

Of homegrown poets, only Emily Dickinson seems to have taken an active pride in cooking. She constituted a whole family's active baker till infirm, and if her gingerbreads were more well known than her poems to the neighborhood, that seems to be the way of the world. I used to balk at being introduced as "This is Ronald Johnson—he writes cookbooks," but since there are more people who read cookbooks than poems, I now just shrug my shoulders.

SALT RISING BREAD

2	potatoes, peeled and thinly sliced	2	cups boiling water
2	tablespoons stone-ground cornmeal	2	cups milk
2	tablespoons sugar	9 to 10	cups flour
	Baking soda	1	tablespoon salt
		¼	cup shortening, melted
			Melted butter

*P*ut the sliced potatoes, cornmeal, 1 tablespoon sugar, 1 teaspoon salt, and a pinch of soda in a quart jar and add boiling water to cover. Screw on the top and shake several times, or until sugar and soda look dissolved. Unscrew the top of the jar and put it back on the jar loosely (it needs bacteria to get in). Let stand in a warm place, out of drafts, for 24 hours, or until there appears to be about an inch of foam on top and it has a yeasty smell.

Scald the milk, add another pinch of soda, and cool to lukewarm. Strain a cup of liquid from the potato jar and add it to the milk. Stir in, cup by cup, enough flour to make a stiff dough.

Place in a greased bowl and turn to coat all sides. Cover and let stand in a warm place about 2 hours, or until doubled in bulk. Punch down, and knead in salt, the remaining 1 tablespoon sugar, and the melted shortening, making an elastic ball but never letting the dough get cold.

Return to the greased bowl, turning until the entire surface is coated, cover again, and let rise again until doubled.

Punch down again and shape into 3 loaves. Place the loaves in greased loaf pans and brush with butter. Let rise again, covered, until doubled.

Preheat the oven to 350°F.

Bake the loaves for 1 hour.

Even after living in San Francisco for some years, with its truly famed sour-dough breads available, this settler's found-yeast bread is one of my favorite white breads. There may be other crusts and ingeniously shaped loaves, but the strong fragrance and subtle taste of this is my undoing. I eat the first loaf, and the rest I bake in small individual loaf pans and freeze in plastic bags. They can then be taken out, wrapped in foil, and heated in a hot oven for 15 to 20 minutes, for guests.

SOURDOUGH BREADS

*I*n the Old West, where what we know as yeast was hard come by, most breads were either made from baking powder or from natural yeasts floating through the air. This was a tricky process, since the "starter" didn't always work, or its taste wasn't quite right, so that starters were often traded, jour-neyed for, handed down—as the ones for the famous San Francisco sourdoughs (these guarded closely as pots of gold). In fact, even with a good sourdough starter, it is impossible to reproduce these famed breads made in special ovens with hard-wheat flour. I know, I've tried, using all the methods Julia Child can summon up, and with pans of steaming water, hot tiles, etc. It's good, but just not good enough when you can get the real thing. However, there are other ways to use this unique leaven with a tangy savor.

If you wish to try your hand at making your own starter, stir a package of active dry yeast together with 2 cups hot water from the top and 2 cups white flour. Put the mixture in a warmed bowl, cover with plastic wrap, and let it sit at room temperature for 2 days or more. When and if ready, it will be bubbly and have some yellowish liquid on top. Store in the refrigerator in a covered container when it has "taken." It improves with age, but you will need to use it about once every 2 weeks or it gets very sour indeed.

To use your starter, remove from the refrigerator early in the day and place in a warm spot for an hour, or until it starts to bubble again. A cup of starter will approximate a package of yeast, though it will rise more slowly than yeast. For this reason many users, and most bakeries, often add a package of yeast as well as the starter—the sourdough being more for flavor than leaven.

Every time you use part of the starter for a bread, it will need to be re-plenished with a cup of flour and a cup of warm water for every cup used. Simply stir it in well, let bubble up again in a warm place, cover, and refrig-erate once more till needed.

The first time I tried this process I got a pretty good starter, but then I tasted a friend's sourdough that had been originally begun from commercial sourdough starter. It was so superior I went out and bought a packet. I recommend you do the same, if you want to make daily breads. Anyway, next to a good backrub, the process of rising, punching down, kneading, rising, and baking finally is probably the most soothing thing possible. The rest, Mae West could only comment gracefully on.

SOURDOUGH WHITE BREAD

½	cup milk	1	cup sourdough starter
1	teaspoon sugar	3¼	cups (approximately)
1	teaspoon salt		unbleached white flour
2	tablespoons butter (or lard or vegetable shortening)		

Scald the milk with the sugar, salt, and butter. Let cool to lukewarm. Place in a warm mixing bowl with the sourdough starter, then stir in the flour. Turn out onto a floured board and knead 5 to 6 minutes, adding any extra flour needed to achieve a nonsticky, elastic dough.

Place in a lightly greased bowl and turn to coat the surface all over with the fat. Cover with a towel or plastic wrap and let rise in a warm spot till doubled in bulk—this will take about 3 hours.

Punch the dough down, turn it out onto the board, cover with a towel, and let rest for 15 to 20 minutes. Then shape into a loaf and place in a greased bread pan. Cover and let rise until doubled again in bulk.

Preheat the oven to 375°F.

Bake for about 50 minutes, or until the crust is brown, the loaf is shrunk away from the pan, and it sounds hollow when tapped. Remove from the pan and cool on a wire rack. (Note: This can also be prepared as any basic white bread recipe for the food processor. I like to knead it, but you may not.)

The best easy first loaf to make with sourdough starter. You get all the flavor undiluted at once. You can speed up the process by cutting the milk down by 2 tablespoons, and adding half a package of active dry yeast dissolved in 2 tablespoons of warm water. Made alternately with the following Cracked Wheat Bread, and frozen, you will always have the soundest white and brown breads available.

SOURDOUGH CRACKED-WHEAT BREAD

1	cup milk	1	package active dry yeast
2	tablespoons shortening	2	cups sourdough starter
2	teaspoons salt	1	cup rye flour
2	tablespoons molasses	1	cup cracked wheat
½	cup warm water	5 to 6	cups unbleached white flour

*S*cald the milk with the shortening, salt, and molasses and let cool to luke-warm. Dissolve the yeast in the warm water till it bubbles up. Place both, with the sourdough starter, in a warm bowl. Add the rye flour, cracked wheat, and enough white flour to make a smooth, nonsticky, elastic dough as you knead it. (About 10 minutes of kneading will do the trick.)

Place in a lightly greased bowl, turning to coat the entire surface of the dough with grease. Cover with a towel or plastic wrap and let rise in a warm place until doubled in bulk.

Punch down and let rise till doubled again. Punch down once more, and let rest, covered, for 10 minutes.

Divide the dough in half, shape into loaves, and place in 2 greased bread pans. Cover and let rise till doubled again. Preheat the oven to 375°F.

Bake the loaves for 40 to 45 minutes, or until crusty brown on top and shrinking away from the sides of the pans. Turn onto wire racks to cool.

Makes 2 loaves (one can be frozen for freshness).

My alltime favorite for everyday eating, and I make it on schedule every 2 weeks to keep my sourdough starter alive.

OLD-TIME SOURDOUGH BISCUITS

1½	cups sifted flour	½	teaspoon salt
2	teaspoons baking powder	4	tablespoons butter (or lard)
¼	teaspoon baking soda	1	cup sourdough starter (page 341)

*S*ift the dry ingredients together, then cut in butter or lard with two knives or a pastry cutter until the mixture resembles coarse meal. Stir in the starter. Turn the dough out on a lightly floured board and knead—have a deft hand, and only knead until the dough seems smooth. Roll out ½ inch thick and cut with a glass or biscuit cutter about 2 to 2½ inches round.

Grease a baking pan and place the biscuits in it. Brush with melted butter and let rise for about an hour in a warm spot.

Preheat the oven to 425°F.

Bake the biscuits for 20 minutes. Serve piping hot, with plenty of butter. Makes 10 to 12.

Truly a biscuit like no other, light but rich and tangy—they become rather a habit, I find.

DESSERTS

The dessert reminded me of a postcard Virgil Thompson once sent us from the Côte d'Azur, delightfully situated within sight of the sea, pine woods, nightingales, all cooked in butter.

—*Alice B. Toklas,* The Alice B. Toklas Cook Book

Summer and Winter Pies

*P*ies were my mother's great specialty. When she sailed in to church suppers, every eye was nailed on that pie, and each succulent bit would be scooped up before we got to it. Fortunately, she always made one for us to eat later at home, or she would have had a bunch of savages on her hands. I think pies, out of all possible dishes, are our national glory. No one makes such delicate pastry, made to crumble at the poke of a fork: the French consider it a container, while we expect it to be as good as the filling itself. And an English woman I attempted once to talk pie crust with could not even conceive of what I meant by "flaky." Everyone knows the apple and berry and fruit pies of summer, but now that we get fruit the year long, many have forgotten the "winter pies" that used to be turned out—since most homes were never found pieless. These are some of the very best of all.

MY MOTHER'S PIE CRUST

2¼ cups flour	¾ cup cold lard (or vegetable
¾ teaspoon salt	shortening)
	6 tablespoons ice water

*P*ut the flour and salt in a medium bowl and cut lard into it with two knives or a pastry blender until no piece is larger than a small pea.

Sprinkle ice water over—preferably from a sprinkle top bottle (my mother uses a commercial sprinkler top used to cork pop bottles for wetting laundry, while I use an ordinary glass kitchen salt shaker that holds just 6 tablespoons ice water and needs only to be put in the freezer before crust-making).

As you sprinkle, turn with a fork until the meal is evenly covered and starts to compose a mass. If it looks too dry, don't worry, and don't add any more water because that will make it tough.

Dump the dough on a sheet of waxed paper and twist into a ball with the corners. Place in the refrigerator several hours, or overnight. (It needs this time for the particles of flour to absorb the water.)

To roll out, divide the mixture in two and make a ball of each. On a lightly floured board, or pastry cloth, flatten each and roll out to a 12-inch round (as the books say). In practice, you have to be pretty deft, and the dough is liable not to hold together, but if you pinch and patch, a round that can be attained the first roll is best. If not, fold the dough and start a second time.

Making sure the dough is loose from the floured board beneath, fold over in half and lift into a pie plate. Unfold. When the pie is filled, repeat the process for your top half.

Trim the crust—the bottom for a single-crust pie and top and bottom for a double-crust—to about a ½-inch overhang around. Fold under, and crimp the edges in scallops with the forefinger of one hand and the forefinger and thumb of the other meeting in an arrow—or by simply pressing all around with the tines of a fork to seal the pie.

The top crust should be pierced in some way for steam to escape, and each cook used to have a distinctive pattern. My favorite pattern among many is the old-fashioned "moon and stars": a crescent knifed out with fork pricks all over for the stars.

A lattice top is made with ½-inch-wide strips cut from the second crust, and it is sealed in the same way. Any top crust may be brushed with milk before cooking, or sprinkled with sugar after.

All easier done than said.

Makes 2 individual crusts, or top and bottom crust for 1 pie.

Of course, this can all be done in a whisk or three of a food processor, and rolled out in a trice, but the result is never so flakily tender. There are several good tools to make it go easier, however: a pastry blender to knife the flour and fat, and a pastry cloth kept floured to roll out on, along with a pastry sock or "sleeve" for the rolling pin. These make for assurance and speed in any pastry work. In the general alchemy of it all, one ought to remember the rule that everything ought to be kept as cold as possible.

This recipe makes a little more than is actually necessary for two crusts— most recipes call only for 2 cups flour. But actually this makes it easier for a beginner, as there is more leeway in rolling out your circle. The scraps that are left over may also be used. My mother gathered them all together, then rolled them out again. This she sprinkled with sugar, cinnamon, and dribbled a bit of butter over. It was then baked along with the pies for us kids. (It was a kind of sop thrown us so we wouldn't stick our fingers in the pie, I imagine.) Another thing to do is to cut out tiny rounds with a cutter, and spread them with anchovy paste, or as they do in the Carolinas, with sesame seeds and a little cayenne. These make fine cocktail nibbles.

If you are going to use a recipe which calls for only half the dough, you have two choices: you can either make two pies, or you can make half a recipe. The flour is easy to divide, as you will need 1 cup plus 2 tablespoons. The lard has to be played by eye. Since you measure lard by putting it in a cup measure with ¼ cup cold water, just put enough lard in to make the water level come up to between the ½- and ⅔-cup mark—don't worry, if it's a little more or a little less, it will still be fine.

UPSIDE-DOWN APPLE PIE

⅔ cup plus ½ cup (packed) brown sugar

⅔ cup whole pecans

4 tablespoons butter, melted
Pastry for a 2-crust pie (page 348)

2 pounds tart apples (about 5 or 6)

Pinch of salt

1 tablespoon flour

½ teaspoon ground cinnamon
Freshly grated nutmeg (or ¼ teaspoon ground cloves)

3 tablespoons butter
Juice of ½ lemon (or a whole one if apples are sweet)

*P*reheat the oven to 450°F.

Press the ⅔ cup brown sugar over the bottom and sides of a pie plate, and arrange the pecans over it in a decorative manner. Press the pecans into the sugar, and dribble melted butter over. Roll out the bottom crust and lay it in over the pecans.

Peel, core, and slice the apples into a bowl. Toss them with the ½ cup brown sugar, the salt, flour, and spices. Arrange them in the crust, dot with the butter, and squeeze the lemon juice over. Roll out and place the top crust over, but instead of folding the crust edge under, fold it up from the bottom before you crimp the edges.

Prick the top of the pie several times with a fork, place in oven and bake at 450°F 10 minutes, then turn the heat down to 350°F and bake 45 minutes to 1 hour longer, or until the crust is golden and the insides bubbly.

Remove the pie from the oven and cool 15 minutes, then loosen the edges with a knife all around, place a plate over the top of the pie, and invert so the pie falls upside down on the plate.

Serves 6 to 8.

Reminiscent of the famous tarte Tatin, *this is perhaps even more luscious. It makes a beautiful presentation to be shown to your guests before slicing at table.*

PARADISE PIE

1 cup cranberries	3 large cooking apples (1½ pounds), peeled, cored, and sliced
¾ cup plus 2 tablespoons sugar	
Pastry for a 2-crust pie (page 348)	
	2 tablespoons flour
1 large quince (about ¾ pound), peeled and cored	Juice of ½ lemon
	6 tablespoons butter
3 tablespoons honey	

*P*lace the cranberries in a blender or food processor with some of the ¾ cup sugar, and whirl until as fine as possible. Add the rest of the ¾ cup sugar, stir well, cover, and let sit in the refrigerator for an hour or more. (This can be done at the time you make the pie crust, and they can be put to chill together.)

Preheat the oven to 450°F.

Roll out the bottom crust and fit it into the pie plate. Refrigerate while you prepare the fruit. Grate the quince into a bowl (making sure all the hard core is well removed) and toss it with the honey. Toss the apple slices in another bowl with the flour and lemon juice, then toss fruits both together. Mix in half the cranberry mixture and put the fruit in the pie shell.

Pour the rest of the cranberry mixture over the fruit and dot with 4 tablespoons of the butter. Melt the other 2 tablespoons butter and set aside while you roll out the top crust and place it on the pie. Brush with the melted butter and sprinkle with the 2 tablespoons sugar. Bake at 450°F 10 minutes, then reduce the heat and bake at 350°F for 45 to 50 minutes longer—or until crisp and golden on top. Remove from the oven and cool.

Paradise Pie is named after that ineffable combination of apple, quince, and cranberry known as "Paradise jelly." Both live up to the name—from color to taste, all Paradisaical. Quinces somehow need other fruit to bring out their best perfume, and then they become a kind of catalyst flavor, sparking and perking and expanding their partner (usually apple). Quince trees are less common than they used to be, and they seldom come to market, and when they do it is usually not at cranberry time. For this reason I usually put up batches of sugared cranberry purée in season, freeze them, then keep an eagle eye out for the first golden, fragrant quinces.

SHAKER RHUBARB CUSTARD PIE

1½	cups granulated sugar	3	cups rhubarb, cut in 1-inch
3	tablespoons flour		pieces
½	teaspoon freshly grated		Pastry for a 2-crust pie (page
	nutmeg		348)
2	tablespoons butter, melted		Confectioners sugar
2	eggs		

*P*reheat the oven to 450°F.

Put sugar, flour, nutmeg, butter, and eggs in a bowl, and beat till smooth.

Roll out the pastry for the bottom crust; line a pie plate. Arrange the rhubarb evenly over the pastry lined plate, then pour the sugar-egg mixture over. Make a lattice topping with the rest of the pastry.

Crimp the edges of the pie and bake at 450°F for 10 minutes, then reduce the heat to 350°F and bake 30 minutes longer, or till golden brown and bubbly.

Remove from the oven and sprinkle confectioners sugar through a flour sifter over the top of the pie. Let cool.

Serves 6 to 8.

"Pie plant" is the old-fashioned name for rhubarb, and though these tart, tonic red stalks can be used in many ways, they shine in a pie. The Shaker method rather than gilding the lily seems simply better than the standard recipe in which all too often the sugar remains granular on the bottom rather than making juice. The nutmeg custard gives just the proper balance to the sour rhubarb, the balance and proportion the Shakers are famed for. After discovering this recipe, I seldom cook rhubarb any other way, and I find it is also a fine rule to follow for many a fruit—with a bit less sugar and nutmeg, and lemon juice and grated peel to make up for the sourness of the rhubarb. Particularly fine are sour cherries, green apples, and blueberries.

FRESH PEACH PIE

	Pastry for a 2-crust pie (page 348)		Pinch of salt
4	ripe peaches	2	tablespoons butter, melted
1	cup sugar	2	eggs
		⅛	teaspoon almond extract

*P*reheat the oven to 450°F.

Drop the peaches in a pot of boiling water for a minute or so, take out with a slotted spoon, and slip the skins off. Cut in half and remove the pits.

Roll out the pastry for the bottom crust; fit into a pie plate.

Place the peach halves, cut side up, decoratively in the pastry-lined plate (if they are large you will most likely only be able to use seven halves, so you can eat the other as you bake the pie).

Beat the sugar, salt, butter, eggs, and almond extract together, and pour over the peach halves. Make a lattice crust with the remaining pastry, place over the top, and crimp the edges.

Bake at 450°F for 10 minutes, or until beginning to brown, then turn the heat down to 350°F and bake 30 minutes more, or until brown and bubbly. Remove from the oven and cool.

Serves 6 to 8.

The almond-flavored custard in this recipe perfectly complements fresh peaches— and it is an extremely pretty pie to contemplate, or eat. If you like, it can also be sprinkled with slivered toasted almonds.

PLANTATION LEMON MERINGUE PIE

4	eggs, at room temperature	2	teaspoons grated lemon rind
½	teaspoon cream of tartar	3	tablespoons lemon juice
1½	cups sugar	2	cups heavy cream

*P*reheat the oven to 300°F.

Separate the eggs, and beat the whites until they foam up, then add the cream of tartar and beat until they hold stiff peaks. Add 1 cup of the sugar gradually, a tablespoon at a time, beating after each addition. The meringue should be thick, stiff, and glossy.

Spread it in a lightly greased pie plate so that the rim comes up higher than the center, and so will make a "crust" for the filling. Bake for 40 minutes. Remove and set on a wire rack to cool.

Beat the egg yolks until they are thick and light colored, then beat in the lemon rind and juice and remaining ½ cup sugar. Cook this in the top of a double boiler over simmering water 15 to 20 minutes, or until the mixture thickens. Cool.

Whip 1 cup of the cream and fold it into the cooled lemon mixture. Fill the center of the meringue with it and place in the refrigerator overnight—it should sit at least 12 hours before serving.

To serve, whip the other cup of cream and frost the top of the pie with it. Serves 6 to 8.

The most ethereal of lemon pies. It will last in the refrigerator for several days, getting even better, if possible.

SHAKER LEMON PIE

	Pastry for a 1-crust pie (page 348)	5	eggs
		½	cup butter, melted
3	lemons		Pinch of salt
2	cups sugar		Whipped cream

*P*eel 2 of the lemons thinly with a vegetable peeler, and cut the strips of peel with a sharp knife into very small slivers, the size of toothpicks. Simmer in water 10 minutes, then drain and run cold water over. Place on paper toweling to dry.

Squeeze the lemons—there should be ⅔ cup of juice—and put in a saucepan with the sugar. Bring to a boil, add the peel, and cook slowly 5 minutes, or until the peel is transparent. Remove from the heat and let stand 30 minutes.

Preheat the oven to 450°F.

Roll out the pastry and fit into a pie plate; crimp the edges. Beat the eggs, then add the sugared peel, melted butter, and salt. Pour into the pastry lined plate and bake at 450°F for 10 minutes, then turn the heat down to 350°F and bake 30 minutes longer. Cool, then serve with dollops of plain whipped cream.

Serves 6 to 8.

The other side of the coin to Plantation Lemon Meringue Pie (see preceding recipe)—this is dense, rich, and about as delicious as any pie could hope to be. This pie was served at the Pleasant Hill, Kentucky, Shaker community, open to the public now as a museum, the first time I went there. It became an instant favorite that I have continued to serve over the years. The Shakers made it a little differently. They sliced lemons thin, and let them sit for several hours in sugar, before beating in the eggs and butter. But I was attempting this pie at someone's home one day, only to find out there wasn't a knife sharp enough to cut them. So I tried this method, which I think is even better.

TALLAHASSEE LIME
PIE WITH PECAN CRUST

1	cup flour	2	eggs
	Confectioners sugar	5	tablespoons lime juice
¼	teaspoon salt	1	teaspoon grated lime peel
½	cup cold butter	½	teaspoon baking powder
⅓	cup finely chopped pecans		Whipped cream flavored with
1	cup granulated sugar		rum

*P*reheat the oven to 350°F.

Sift the flour, ¼ cup confectioners sugar, and salt into a bowl. Cut in the butter with a pastry blender (or with a whirl or two in a food processor) until the mixture resembles coarse meal. Add the pecans (they do not have to be ground, but a food processor is excellent for chopping them very fine).

Press the mixture into the bottom and sides of a pie plate and bake for 25 minutes, or until the crust is pale gold. Remove from the oven (keep it at 350°F) and let cool while you prepare the filling.

To do this, beat the granulated sugar, eggs, lime juice and peel, baking powder, and a pinch of salt until smooth. Pour the mixture into the pie shell and bake another 25 minutes. Remove from the oven and let cool. When cool, sprinkle the top with powdered sugar put through a flour sifter, and serve with dollops of rum-flavored whipped cream.

Serves 8.

Another rich confection with a dense consistency, lovely crunchy crust, and the unexpected tartness of lime. A little goes a long fine way.

GREAT AUNT HESTER'S ORANGE PIE

	Recipe for a 1-crust pie (page 348)	Pinch of salt
		Grated rind of 1 orange
2	tablespoons butter	Juice of two oranges (½ cup)
¾	cup sugar	1 cup heavy cream
4	eggs	Confectioners sugar

*P*reheat the oven to 450°F.

Roll out the crust and fit it in a pie plate; crimp the edges. Prick the bottom of the crust with a fork at about 1-inch intervals and bake for 10 minutes. Remove to a rack to cool while you make the filling, and turn the oven down to 350°F.

Beat the butter until it softens, then beat in the granulated sugar bit by bit (it won't really "cream," as there's not enough butter). Beat in the eggs, one by one, then the salt and orange rind and juice. Whip the cream till it holds a peak, then fold into the orange mixture. Do this delicately and carefully.

Pour the mixture into the pie shell—you'll have a bit left over, as a 9-inch shell can't quite hold it all. Bake for 30 minutes—or until a toothpick inserted in the middle comes out clean. Let cool on a rack, then dust lightly with confectioners sugar before cutting.

Serves 6 to 8.

A delicately flavored heirloom pie from Bob, Rose, and Cora Brown's 1940 America Cooks—*an enormous treasury of regional cooking long out of print. It was submitted by a great-niece who found the pie in a diary dated 1801, and she says of it: "I have no idea how old this family recipe is, but my great-grandmother sold copies of it to help raise money for her Dutch Reformed Church in Manhattan."*

I knew Bob Brown (his wife and mother were by then both dead) when I went to college in New York City. He was one of the legendary writers who attended the Gertrude Stein circle in Paris in the twenties, and had delightful tales to tell of everyone who was anyone, and some who were not. His own books from the period have been forgotten, except for a lovely book of picture poems reprinted by Jonathan Williams' Jargon Press. But you could go to his apartment in the Village and find the likes of Marcel Duchamp or Djuna Barnes leaning on a shelf, still talking of Alice, and Gertrude, and Pablo, and Ernest—no one, to my joy, ever had a last name.

My secretest joy, though, were the bookshelves that went up to every ceiling in the place. There were thousands of cookbooks crammed everywhere! How I would have liked to take a semester off from Columbia, and simply read and read them, but of course it was impossible, and an imposition, so the chance was lost. I often wonder where they all ended up, and if they are all together still. . . .

MY ORANGE PECAN PIE

2	small oranges	¼	cup butter, melted
1½	cups sugar		Pinch of salt
	Pastry for a 1-crust pie (page 348)	1	cup pecan halves
			Whipped cream
3	eggs		

*P*eel the oranges thinly with a vegetable peeler, and cut the strips of peel with a sharp knife into very small slivers, the size of toothpicks. Simmer in water 10 minutes, then drain and run cold water over. Place on paper toweling to dry.

Squeeze the oranges (there should be ½ cup juice), and add with the sugar to a saucepan. Bring to a boil, add the peel, and cook slowly 5 minutes, or until the peel is transparent. Remove from the heat and let stand 30 minutes to cool.

Preheat the oven to 450°F.

Roll out the pastry and fit into a pie plate; crimp the edges. Beat the eggs, then add the sugared peel, melted butter, and salt. Place the pecans in the bottom of the pastry-lined plate and pour the egg-orange mixture over. Bake at 450°F for 10 minutes, then turn the heat down to 325°F and bake 30 minutes longer. Serve topped with plain whipped cream.

Serves 8.

Anyone who likes sweets at all admires that most enduring of our winter pies— the Southern pecan pie. My version uses a homemade fresh orange syrup rather than the usual bottled dark "Karo," and has a lively zing not often found in this dark rich confection.

BURNT SUGAR WALNUT PIE

2 cups sugar	½ teaspoon vanilla
¼ cup hot water	Pinch of salt
¾ cup heavy cream	4 tablespoons butter, melted
Pastry for a 1 crust pie (page 348)	1 cup walnut halves
3 eggs	Whipped cream flavored with vanilla (optional)

*P*ut the sugar in a heavy saucepan, and stir over a medium flame until it melts to a golden syrup. The flame should not be so hot that the sugar becomes dark brown.

When there are no more undissolved bits of sugar, carefully pour in, drop by drop, the hot water. (The sugar will boil up violently, so be careful not to add too much water at a time.) Let this syrup cool slightly and then stir in the cream.

Preheat the oven to 450°F.

Roll out the pastry and fit into a pie plate; crimp the edges.

Beat the eggs till frothy with the salt and vanilla, then beat in the melted butter and lastly the burnt sugar syrup. Arrange the nuts in the bottom of the pastry-lined plate, then pour over the sugar-egg mixture.

Bake at 450°F for 10 minutes, then turn the oven down to 325°F and bake 30 minutes longer. Serve, if you wish, with whipped cream flavored with vanilla.

Serves 8.

A jewel of a pie—darker than the darkest pecan pie, and less sweet, since a lot of the sugar is lost in the burning process.

BUTTERMILK CHESS PIE

Pastry for a 1-crust pie (page
   348)
3   eggs
1   cup buttermilk
1   cup sugar
1   tablespoon flour
6   tablespoons sweet butter,
      melted

½   teaspoon vanilla
    Pinch of salt
2 to 3   tablespoons rum
      Whipped cream flavored
         with rum (optional)

*P*reheat the oven to 425°F.

In a mixing bowl, beat the eggs till frothy, then add the buttermilk and mix completely. Add the sugar, flour, melted butter, vanilla, and salt. Mix well and stir in the rum.

Roll out the pastry and fit into a pie plate, crimp the edges. Pour the filling into the pastry-lined plate and bake at 425°F 10 minutes, then turn the heat down to 350°F and bake 20 to 25 minutes longer. A knife should come out clean in the center when it is done.

Remove from the oven and cool. Serve, if you wish, with unsweetened whipped cream flavored with a hint of rum.

Serves 6 to 8.

There are a wide variety of "chess" pies in our past. All were true winter pies, baked up when there was no fruit, and usually consisting of eggs, sugar, and butter, with some flavoring such as nutmeg, etc. They were called "chess" pies because they were kept in pie chests—a screened box to keep the flies out before the days of refrigeration. This is an unearthly version, with a complex subtle flavor I find irresistible. I use sweet butter for its extra flavor here, but if you have only regular butter, use it and omit the pinch of salt.

MY MOTHER'S
TRIPLE LAYER CHEESE PIE

1¼   cups vanilla wafer crumbs
 2   tablespoons unsweetened
         cocoa powder

5   tablespoons butter, melted
8   ounces cream cheese, at
       room temperature

2   eggs
¼   cup plus 3 tablespoons sugar
3   tablespoons light rum
1   cup sour cream

¼   teaspoon vanilla
1   cup heavy cream
    Chocolate curls

*P*reheat the oven to 350°F.

Combine the vanilla wafer crumbs with the cocoa and melted butter, then press onto the bottom and sides of a pie plate. Bake 10 minutes, then remove and cool. Keep the oven heat at 350°F.

Cream the softened cheese with the eggs, the ¼ cup sugar, and 2 tablespoons of the rum. (This can be done by hand, or in a blender or food processor.) When smooth, pour into the pie shell and bake another 15 minutes. Remove from the oven, keeping the oven heat at 350°F, and cool 10 minutes, or until the top is firm.

Mix the sour cream with the 3 tablespoons sugar and the vanilla, then spread on top of the cream cheese mixture. Bake another 10 minutes. Remove, and chill in the refrigerator.

Before serving, whip the cream and mix with the remaining 1 tablespoon rum, then spread lightly over the pie. Top with chocolate curls made by paring slightly warm semisweet baking chocolate with a vegetable peeler (or sharp knife).

Serves 8.

An incredible pie, better I think than any cheesecake—and like cheesecake, rich but not too sweet. It is also a tour de force dessert for those who feel shaky about preparing pie crust.

MY SOUR CREAM RUM-RAISIN PIE

Pastry for a 1-crust pie (page 348)
½   cup raisins
⅓   cup plus 1 to 2 tablespoons rum (dark, if possible)
4   eggs, separated

¾   cup sugar
    Salt
1½ cups milk, scalded
1   cup sour cream
1   tablespoon lemon juice

*P*reheat the oven to 450°F.

Roll out the pastry and fit into a pie plate; crimp the edges. Prick the pie shell with a fork, cover the bottom with aluminum foil weighted with a few dry beans, and bake 10 minutes. Remove the foil and bake another 2 to 3 minutes, or until the bottom has browned. Remove and let cool. Keep the oven heat at 450°F.

Cook the raisins a few minutes with the ⅓ cup rum in a covered pan, then remove from the fire and let sit, covered, to plump up and absorb the rum.

In the top of a double boiler, beat the egg yolks with ¼ cup of the sugar and a pinch of salt, then pour in the hot milk and stir over simmering water till the sauce thickens slightly and coats the spoon. Let this cool, then add 1 to 2 tablespoons of rum to taste, cover, and refrigerate.

To make the filling, beat the egg whites till stiff, then add the remaining ½ cup sugar, bit by bit, as you continue beating—as you would for a meringue. When all the sugar is added and the whites are silken and glossy, fold in the sour cream, lemon juice, a pinch of salt, and the raisins. (If the raisins haven't absorbed all the rum, drain them first.)

Mound the egg white–sour cream mixture into the cooked pie shell and swirl it decoratively on top with a knife. Bake 10 minutes, or until the top is golden brown and the meringue has set. Cool the pie and serve sliced in sections, with the rum custard poured over.

Serves 6 to 8.

Fond as I have always been of the regular sour cream raisin pie—an old-fashioned winter pie served from New England through the Midwest—I think this recipe improves an already fine thing. I came upon a strange pie, in an old flimsy "Alumnae" spiral-bound cookbook given me by friends, that consisted of simply egg whites beaten with a cup of sugar and then with sour cream folded in. I tried it, and though it seemed much too sugary and had not much flavor, it seemed a fine process. So the next try I added rum raisins, toned the sugar way down, and made a custard sauce with the leftover egg yolks. I've been cooking my sour cream raisin pies this way since, and they are always a delight for family or guests.

DERBY PIE

	Pastry for a 1-crust pie (page 348)	1½	tablespoons cornstarch
1	envelope gelatin	1½	cups milk
¼	cup plus ⅓ cup bourbon	1½	squares unsweetened chocolate, coarsely grated
4	eggs, separated	½	teaspoon vanilla
½	cup (packed) brown sugar	¼	teaspoon cream of tartar

½   cup granulated sugar   Finely grated semisweet
½   cup heavy cream (optional)   chocolate

*P*reheat the oven to 450°F.

Roll out the pastry and fit into a pie plate; crimp the edges. Prick the bottom with a fork all around, then bake for 12 to 15 minutes, or until golden. Remove and let cool.

Sprinkle the gelatin into the ¼ cup bourbon to soften. In the top of a double boiler, over hot but not boiling water, beat the egg yolks with the brown sugar and cornstarch. Gradually stir in the milk and the ⅓ cup bourbon, then cook, stirring constantly, until the custard is thickened and smooth. Remove from the heat and pour half the mixture into a bowl. Stir the dissolved gelatin into the mixture in the bowl and reserve.

Add the grated unsweetened chocolate to the custard remaining in the pan and place back over the heat. Stir till the chocolate has melted. Pour this into the pie shell and let cool.

Beat the egg whites with the cream of tartar until they hold a soft peak. Gradually add the granulated sugar until the mixture becomes a satiny meringue. Fold this into the gelatin custard, and spoon over the chocolate custard in the pie shell.

Chill in the refrigerator until firm. Whip the cream, if you use it, and pipe through a pastry bag around the rim of the pie. Sprinkle with finely grated chocolate.

Serves 8.

This Kentucky pie, served up during Derby time, is not only beautiful to look at, it is a gastronomical treasure in its combination of flavors and textures.

Cakes, Tortes, and a Cookie

I am frankly a pie man rather than a cake man, but there are some cakes I like in the way I like pie—in the old Yankee mode, at breakfast, with coffee. Midwesterners share this yen with them, and hanker after last night's pie for starters. So any cake I put out has to be one that gets only better for sitting awhile, promising moist slices from the refrigerator. And what gems turn up out of our sources: Raw Apple Cake (page 363) for an instant picnic, Shaker Carolina Cake (page 366) for breakfast or tea, Texas Long Cake (page 367) better than brownies for a crowd, Tennessee Jam Cake (page 372) for holidays. All enjoyable to the last crumb. I've also put in a few glorious tortes in lieu of Boston cream pie, and recovered a lost cookie.

RAW APPLE CAKE

1	cup butter, at room temperature	½	teaspoon salt
2	cups sugar	2	cups flour
2	eggs	1	teaspoon vanilla
2	teaspoons baking soda	4	cups peeled, cored, and chopped apples
2	teaspoons ground cinnamon	1	cup chopped pecans

*P*reheat the oven to 350°F.

Cream the butter and sugar together till light and fluffy. Beat in the eggs, one at time. Sift the flour with soda, cinnamon, and salt, and add it gradually to the butter mixture as you beat.

Stir in the vanilla, chopped apples, and nuts, then spoon the batter into a greased tube or Bundt pan. Bake 1 hour, or until the sides of the cake begin to come away from the pan. Cool in the pan.

This simple recipe makes a rich, moist cake, dense with apples. Apples, in fact, supply the only liquid in it. Like old-fashioned applesauce cakes, it slowly grows better covered with foil in the refrigerator. It is better the second week than the first (in fact it probably should age at least a week before cutting), so it is the perfect cake for a small family—or one person. I squirrel some away after the first serving and eat a slice with my morning coffee.

MY MOTHER'S ORANGE PEEL CAKE

2	oranges	1	teaspoon baking soda
1	cup golden raisins	¾	cup buttermilk
1½	cups sugar	2	cups flour, sifted
½	cup butter, at room temperature	½	cup finely chopped walnuts (optional)
2	eggs		

*P*reheat the oven to 350°F.

Halve the oranges and juice them. Save the juice. Take the peels and re-move the white inside pith with a spoon. Cut the peel up and chop it fine with the raisins by whirling it a few times in a food processor (or by putting through a food grinder).

In a bowl, cream 1 cup of the sugar and the butter till light and fluffy. Add the eggs, beating in one by one. Dissolve the soda in the buttermilk. Add the flour and buttermilk alternately, beating well after each addition. Add the nuts (if used), and the chopped peel and raisins.

Pour into a buttered tube or Bundt pan, and bake 45 to 50 minutes, or until the cake shrinks from the sides of the pan and a toothpick inserted comes out clean. Remove and cool on a wire rack.

While the cake is baking, dissolve the remaining ½ cup sugar in the reserved orange juice. Pour this over the cake while it is still hot, over and down the edges.

To serve, flip out onto a plate, and sprinkle granulated sugar over it evenly with a flour sifter or sieve.

Another cake that grows better over the days. It is at its peak always at the time the last slice is served.

MISSISSIPPI MUD CAKE

1¾	cups strong brewed coffee		Pinch of salt
¼	cup bourbon	2	cups sugar
5	ounce unsweetened chocolate	2	eggs
		1	teaspoon vanilla
1	cup butter		Unsweetened cocoa powder
2	cups flour		Sweetened whipped cream
1	teaspoon baking soda		flavored with rosewater

*P*reheat the oven to 275°F.

Put the coffee, bourbon, chocolate, and butter in a double boiler set over simmering water. Let the chocolate melt, stirring now and then to keep smooth. Meanwhile, sift the flour with the soda and salt into a bowl.

When the chocolate mixture is melded, pour into the bowl of an electric mixer. At low speed, add the sugar, bit by bit. Beat until the sugar is dissolved. Add the sifted flour, bit by bit, to make a batter. Beat in the eggs and vanilla until smooth.

Butter a tube or Bundt pan, and sift unsweetened cocoa in to completely dust the pan. Pour in the batter. Bake for 1½ hours, or until the cake shrinks away from the sides of the pan and a toothpick inserted in the middle comes out clean.

Let the cake cool completely on a rack before turning it out onto a serving plate. Dust with more cocoa, so that the cake is an even velvety brown all over.

Serve with whipped cream, flavored if possible with a few drops of rosewater. If you cook the cake in a Bundt pan, it is attractive to completely fill the middle hole with the fragrant cream.

I don't remember where I picked this recipe up, but I can certainly remember the times I've eaten it. It is rich enough to keep well, wrapped in foil in the refrigerator, for any chocoholic in the family.

OMAHA FEATHER RUM CAKE

1	cup vegetable shortening	1	teaspoon baking powder
2¼	cups granulated sugar	½	teaspoon baking soda
2	teaspoons vanilla	1	teaspoon salt
1	tablespoon lemon juice	¾	cup buttermilk
1	teaspoon grated lemon rind	¼	cup dark rum
6	eggs, separated		Confectioners sugar
3	cups cake flour, sifted before measuring		

*P*reheat the oven to 350°F.

Beat the shortening until creamy in a large bowl. Beat in 1½ cups of the granulated sugar until the mixture turns almost fluffy. Add the vanilla and lemon juice and peel, then beat in the egg yolks, one by one.

Sift the flour with the other dry ingredients, then add it, alternately with the buttermilk, to the shortening mixture, beating soundly after each addition. Finally beat the egg whites in a clean bowl with clean beaters until they hold a peak. Gradually beat in the remaining ¾ cup granulated sugar until the whites take on a satiny, meringuelike sheen. Stir some of this into the batter, then lightly fold the rest in.

Pour into a greased and floured Bundt or tube pan and bake for 1¼ hours. The cake is done when it is lightly springy on top and a toothpick inserted comes out clean.

Let the cake cool 15 minutes, then pour the rum over it in the pan. Cover with foil and let rest for several hours before unmolding. Sprinkle with a little sifted confectioners sugar before slicing.

An enormous, light, simply flavored cake perfect to serve large company or family gatherings—perhaps with sliced strawberries or a scoop of ice cream. If you wish, you could make a rum glaze with powdered sugar and dark rum to dribble over the cake. That might make it look prettier, but nothing is needed to improve the flavor of this lovely cake with a texture just this side of angel food. Also, kept well covered, it lasts for several days, and if it starts to dry a bit, some more rum may be sprinkled on as you go.

SHAKER CAROLINA CAKE

1	cup finely chopped nuts	2	eggs
	Grated rind of 1 small orange	1	teaspoon vanilla
⅓	cup (packed) brown sugar	2	cups flour, presifted
1½	cups granulated sugar	1	teaspoon baking powder
1	teaspoon ground cinnamon	1	teaspoon baking soda
1	teaspoon ground ginger	½	teaspoon salt
1	cup butter, at room temperature	1	cup sour cream

*P*reheat the oven to 350°F.

Grease a 12 × 9-inch baking pan.

Combine the nuts, orange rind, brown sugar, ½ cup of the granulated sugar, and spices in a bowl, and mix thoroughly. (Or whirl briefly in a food processor.)

Beat the butter and remaining 1 cup granulated sugar in a large bowl until light and fluffy. Beat in the eggs, one by one, then the vanilla. Sift the flour with the baking powder, soda, and salt. Add it, alternately with the sour cream, to the butter mixture, beating well and soundly after each addition.

Spread half the batter in the greased baking pan, then sprinkle half the nut mixture over. Spread on the rest of the batter, and sprinkle the top with the rest of the nuts. Bake for 35 minutes, or until the cake is springy and a test toothpick comes out clean in the center.

Carolina cake, though constructed like a coffee cake, is as rich and light as any good butter cake. It can be served to company with a bit of whipped cream for dessert, and be even better the next morning with coffee. It keeps moist for several days, though with a family of cake eaters in and out of the kitchen it will not last them—or even one.

TEXAS LONG CAKE

1½	cups butter	2	eggs
1	cup water	1	cup sour cream
¼	cup plus 6 tablespoons unsweetened cocoa powder	6	tablespoons milk
		4	tablespoons unsweetened cocoa
2	cups flour	1	pound confectioners sugar, sifted
2	cups granulated sugar		
½	teaspoon salt	1	teaspoon vanilla
1	teaspoon baking soda	1	cup chopped nuts

*P*reheat oven to 350°F.

In a saucepan, melt 1 cup of the butter, then add the water and the 6 tablespoons unsweetened cocoa, stir until smooth. Bring just to a boil, then remove from the heat. Pour into a bowl.

Sift together the flour, granulated sugar, salt, and soda. Add, alternately with eggs and sour cream, to the butter mixture, beating after each addition. Grease and flour a jelly-roll pan or rimmed cookie sheet (17 × 12 inches), pour the batter in, and bake for 20 to 22 minutes, or until the cake is springy and starts to leave the edges of the pan. Let cool.

To make the icing, melt the remaining ½ cup butter in a saucepan. Add the milk and the ¼ cup cocoa and stir until the mixture comes to a boil. Remove from the heat and beat in the confectioners sugar. Stir in the vanilla and nuts, then spread with a spatula over the cake while it is still warm. Cool to cut.

Makes 24 squares.

Everything about this ample cake smacks of Texas. It can serve a party of 12 at least, and it is particularly good with plain vanilla ice cream.

PENNSYLVANIA DUTCH PLUM CAKE

1	cup flour	¼	cup milk
1½	teaspoons baking powder	15	fresh ripe Italian plums
½	teaspoon salt	1	teaspoon ground cinnamon
6	tablespoons sugar	¼	teaspoon greshly grated
¼	cup vegetable shortening (or		nutmeg
	butter)	3	tablespoons butter, melted
1	egg	⅓	cup current jelly
		1	tablespoon water (or brandy)

*P*reheat the oven to 450°F.

Sift the flour, baking powder, salt, and 3 tablespoons of the sugar into a bowl. Cut the fat in with two knives or a pastry blender until the mixture resembles coarse meal. Beat the egg and milk together, then stir into the flour mixture.

Spread this batter evenly in a greased 12 × 8-inch pan. (It will have to spread very thinly, and a spatula will help.) Cut the plums in half and remove the seeds, and place them, cut side up, in rows over the batter. Sprinkle with the cinnamon, nutmeg, and remaining 3 tablespoons sugar, then dribble the melted butter over the top.

Bake 35 minutes, or until the cake is puffed up slightly between the plums and it begins to brown. Remove from the oven to cool. Heat the jelly with water or brandy until it is smooth, and glaze the top of the cake with it.

A particularly fine cake when Italian prunes come on the market. If you like it cakier it may be baked in a square pan, but I like it spread out thin so there is little cake and lots of prunes.

NANTUCKET GLAZED LEMON CAKES

1½	cups sugar	1	teaspoon baking powder
5	tablespoons butter	⅓	cup sour cream
2	eggs	2½	tablespoons milk
1½	cups flour, sifted	⅓	cup chopped walnuts
½	teaspoon salt		Juice and pulp of 1 lemon

*P*reheat the oven to 350°F.

In a bowl, beat 1 cup of the sugar, the butter, and eggs till thoroughly mixed. Sift the flour, salt, and baking powder into a second bowl. Add it, alternately with sour cream and milk, to the batter mixture, beating the batter till smooth between. Fold in the nuts.

Pour into buttered cupcake pans, filling each about ⅓ full. Bake 25 to 30 minutes, or until the cakes are gold and springy.

While the cakes are baking, mix the lemon juice and pulp with the remaining ½ cup sugar. When the cakes are done, remove them from oven and spoon the lemon sugar over them until they are glazed. Let them cool in their pans.

Makes 30.

These are very good little glazed cakes, not too sweet and with a tart lemon glaze that makes them even better next day. A treat both for adults and children, and particularly good for picnics.

GINGERBREAD

½	cup vegetable shortening (or butter)	1	teaspoon ground ginger
½	cup (packed) brown sugar	½	teaspoon ground cinnamon
1	cup molasses	¼	teaspoon ground cloves
1	egg	½	teaspoon salt
1½	cups flour, sifted	1	teaspoon baking soda
		1	cup hot water

*P*reheat the oven to 350°F.

Grease and flour an 8-inch square baking pan.

Cream the shortening and brown sugar in a bowl. When they are light and fluffy, beat in the molasses and egg.

Sift the flour and spices over the mixture, then beat in. Dissolve the baking soda in hot water, then gradually stir it into the batter—the mixture will be very thin.

Pour into the baking pan and bake for 40 to 45 minutes, or until a toothpick inserted in the center comes out clean and the cake is light and springy.

Gingerbread remains our most characteristic simple cake, synonymous with our scarlet autumns, but shared through all the tucked-up long winters. Like

*any staple, it reaches from the gingery glazed cakes Emily Dickinson was fa-
mous in her neighborhood for, through New Hampshire Election Day cake—
a rather dour bread—to the above very soft and richly spiced cake. Often it is
eaten still warm with some whipped cream or homemade applesauce, but it
really needs no accompaniment, fresh from the pan.*

WASHINGTON PIE

1	gingerbread, fresh from the oven	2	tablespoons cornstarch
2	teaspoons unflavored gelatin	¼	cup milk
¼	cup plus 2 tablespoons water	¾	cup heavy cream, scalded
1	grapefruit	1	egg
½	cup granulated sugar	1	tablespoon rum
			Confectioners sugar

While gingerbread cools, soak the gelatin in the 2 tablespoons water. Set aside. Peel a grapefruit thinly with a vegetable peeler or sharp knife. Chop the peel very fine (this is easiest accomplished in a food processor).

In a saucepan set over medium heat, combine the granulated sugar, the ¼ cup water, and the grapefruit peel. Cook slowly for 15 minutes, or until the peel is candied. Pour the mixture into a sieve set over a glass measure. Measure the syrup and place ⅓ cup of it in the top of a double boiler. Set the candied peel aside.

Dissolve the cornstarch in the milk and stir into the syrup. Add the scalded cream and mix. Cook over hot water for 10 minutes, stirring until the mixture begins to thicken.

Beat the egg with the rum, then add it to the cream mixture along with the grapefruit peel. Cook a few minutes longer, still stirring, then remove from the heat. Stir in the softened gelatin and cool till firm in the refrigerator (or in a bowl of ice water). Stir now and again to ensure smoothness.

To assemble, split the gingerbread into two even layers. Spread the grapefruit cream between the layers, and sift powdered sugar over the top.

This recipe appears to be chef-writer Louis De Gouy's answer to Boston cream pie, and a very fine answer it is, too. His version reads for assorted candied fruit, but I like the simplicity of this candied grapefruit cream with the spicy ginger.

TENNESSEE JAM CAKE

1	cup sugar	1	tablespoon ground cinnamon
1	cup butter, at room temperature	1	teaspoon ground allspice
		½	teaspoon ground cloves
5	eggs, separated	1	teaspoon baking soda
1	cup seedless blackberry jam	1	cup buttermilk
1	cup strawberry preserves	1	cup chopped nuts (preferably
1	cup apricot preserves		black walnuts, or hickory)
3	cups flour		

*P*reheat the oven to 350°F.

Butter three 9-inch round cake pans, then line with buttered waxed paper.

In a large bowl, cream the sugar and butter till light and fluffy. Add the egg yolks, then the jams, stirring well after each addition.

Sift the flour with the spices. Add the soda to the buttermilk and stir to dissolve. Beat the flour and buttermilk alternately into the batter, making sure it is always light. Stir in the nuts. In another bowl beat the whites till they hold a peak, then fold them lightly into the batter.

Divide the batter among the prepared cake pans. Bake for 50 to 60 minutes, or until a toothpick inserted in their centers comes out clean and the sides have begun to shrink from the pans.

This great purply cake is my candidate for all the mincemeat and fruitcake you can trundle out for holidays. In the South it is customary to frost it needlessly with a caramel cream frosting. I simply fill the layers with two different kinds of jam between, and top it with a glaze spooned over the top and dribbled down the sides. For a glaze, I stir together 1 cup confectioners sugar, 1 tablespoon hot milk, and ½ teaspoon vanilla (or kirsch). Kept covered and chilled, this cake will outlast most anything but the traditional aged fruitcake. I keep one in the back of the refrigerator from Thanksgiving to Christmas, to slice thin for any visitor.

FUDGE CREAM TORTE

¾	cup butter	1	cup flour, sifted
6	ounces unsweetened chocolate	½	cup chopped nuts
		1	tablespoon hot water
5	eggs	½	cup plus 2 tablespoons confectioners sugar
¼	teaspoon salt		
2	cups granulated sugar	1	cup heavy cream
1¼	teaspoons vanilla		

Melt ½ cup of the butter and 4 ounces of the chocolate in the top of a double boiler over simmering water and let cool to room temperature. At the same time, remove the eggs from the refrigerator to come to room temperature.

Butter two 8-inch round cake pans, then line with buttered waxed paper. Preheat the oven to 350°F.

Separate 4 of the eggs; beat the egg yolks in a bowl with salt until they are foamy. Add the granulated sugar bit by bit, as you beat. When well creamed, add 1 teaspoon of the vanilla. Fold in the chocolate butter, then the flour, nuts, and lastly the egg whites, beaten stiff.

Divide the mixture between the prepared cake pans. Bake for 25 minutes, or until a toothpick inserted in the centers comes out clean. Let the layers cool on a rack.

Melt the remaining 2 ounces chocolate in the top of a double boiler over simmering water, add the hot water, and stir off the heat with the remaining egg, beaten, and the ½ cup confectioners sugar. When smooth, add the remaining ¼ cup butter, bit by bit, beating until it is very smooth. Cool till slightly thick, in the refrigerator.

To assemble the cake, whip the cream till it holds peaks, and flavor with the 2 tablespoons confectioners sugar and the remaining ¼ teaspoon vanilla. Turn the fudge layers out onto a board. Frost each equally with the whipped cream. Place one layer on a cake server, and dribble some of the chocolate glaze over it. Place the other layer on top (if it wobbles a bit you can secure it with toothpicks till it chills). Dribble the rest of the glaze over the whole cake. Refrigerate till firm.

The ultimate American brownie. Also an example of what can be learned from Irma Rombauer's Joy of Cooking. *She tells of a cake there made by simply whipping egg whites into brownies, and adds it might be garnished with whipped cream. This is what I came up with. It is only for chocoholics, and should be consumed in small portions. I must confess it is the birthday cake I'd like most.*

PLANTATION NUT TORTE

3	cups pecans, walnuts, or black walnuts	6	eggs, at room temperature, separated
2	tablespoons cake flour	1½	cups granulated sugar
2	teaspoons baking powder	2	cups heavy cream
	Pinch of salt	¼	cup confectioners sugar
		1	teaspoon vanilla

*P*reheat the oven to 350°F.

Grease two 8-inch round cake pans, and lay in rounds of greased waxed paper to fit.

Chop the nuts very fine in a food processor (or you might be able to manage it slowly in a blender. The result should be like coarse meal.) Add the flour, baking powder, and salt to the ground nuts.

Separate the eggs. Beat the whites till stiff, and fold into the nuts. Beat the yolks with the granulated sugar until light and foaming. Fold this into the nut mixture.

Pour into the prepared cake pans and bake for 20 to 25 minutes, or until the tops of the layers are slightly golden and the edges are beginning to shrink from the pan. Remove from the oven and let cool on a rack for 30 minutes.

To assemble the torte, loosen the edges of the layers from the pan and flip the first layer onto a cake server. Whip the cream till it holds a peak, and add the confectioners sugar and vanilla. Spread half this on the first layer, top with the other layer and spread the rest of the cream on top of that. The torte should sit for at least an hour, in the refrigerator, before serving.

Whenever I come upon a bargain in fresh crop nuts, I think of this—worth throwing a party for. It is of a lightness that only grows better for being kept a few days in the refrigerator, so it can also be made a day in advance if need be. The original recipe called for Southern pecans, of course, but it is fine with walnuts, and ineffable with black walnuts if you can find any.

SNICKERDOODLES

1	cup vegetable shortening	2	teaspoons cream of tartar
1¾	cups sugar	1½	teaspoons baking soda
2	eggs	½	teaspoon salt
2½	cups flour	½	teaspoon ground cinnamon

*P*reheat the oven to 400°F.

Cream the shortening and 1½ cups of the sugar till light and fluffy. Beat in the eggs till creamy. Sift the flour with cream of tartar, soda, and salt, then beat into the shortening mixture till smooth. The dough will be quite stiff.

Roll into balls the size of a thumb tip. Roll them in the remaining ¼ cup sugar mixed with the cinnamon, and place on greased baking sheets. Bake for only 5 to 6 minutes, or until the cookies flatten and start to crinkle on top.

Makes 100.

We are great ones for cookies, and I have a file full of recipes for them. Snickerdoodles are, however, a lost classic that could stand beside the greats like chocolate chip, peanut butter, and oatmeal cookies. If you can keep your fingers out of it, they last in a tin for several weeks. A simple cookie, they well accompany ice creams and fruits as crisp chewy complement.

Puddings, Ice Creams, and Fruits

*E*arly on, most cookbooks spread a good bulk of their space over desserts. I resolved not to do this, from the beginning, but good sweets accumulate even when you only serve them to company. My apologies to all the family of grunts, slumps, crumbs, bettys, and cobblers—baked down here to only one state fair prize winner. Two other prize winners are included, never near a state fair: Mrs. Truman's Pudding (page 377), and Roanoke Rum Cream (page 382), both of which can be put together out of nothing, in no time, to general applause. Homemade ice cream used to be a national summer pastime, and should be again, so these could not be avoided, and besides we now have electric machines that do all of the work and spare us none of the wonders. And then certainly everyone needs a few delightful ways to vary fruit. But to each good thing there comes, even so, an end.

MRS. TRUMAN'S PUDDING

1	egg	½	cup peeled, cored, and grated
¾	cup sugar		apple
2	tablespoons flour	½	cup chopped walnuts (or
⅛	teaspoon salt		pecans)
1¼	teaspoons baking powder	1	teaspoon vanilla
			Whipped cream

*P*reheat the oven to 325°F.

Beat the egg and sugar well together until light and satiny. Sift the flour, salt, and baking powder over, then fold in. Mix in the apples, nuts, and vanilla.

Spread in a greased pie plate and bake for 30 minutes, or until puffed up and browned. Serve slightly warm, scooped out into dessert plates, with whipped cream (slightly sweetened and flavored with vanilla, if you wish).

Serves 4.

The former first lady's dessert is so simple that at first it is not credible how it could taste so sumptuous. I have served it for years, and neither I nor my guests tire of its levels of texture—from rather gelatinous to crispy light—and its honest flavors. On research, it seems to be an Arkansas pudding loosely modeled on something called a "Huguenot torte," but to me it will always be Mrs. Truman's Pudding.

BLUE RIBBON PEACH COBBLER

½	cup butter	⅛	teaspoon freshly grated
¾	cup flour		nutmeg
2	teaspoons baking powder	¾	cup milk
	Pinch of salt	2	cups peeled and sliced fresh
2	cups sugar		peaches

*P*reheat the oven to 350°F.

Put the butter in an 8-inch square baking pan, and place in the oven to melt as it heats. Mix the flour, baking powder, salt, 1 cup of the sugar, the nutmeg, and milk to a batter. Mix the fruit with the remaining 1 cup sugar.

Pour batter over the melted butter, then drop the peaches evenly over the surface. Bake for 1 hour. Serve warm, with a pitcher of cream.

Serves 6 to 8.

You were right if you looked twice at this state fair–winning recipe—it has more sugar and butter than anyone would expect, and cobbler tradition has been thrown to the winds. It is also better than any cobbler you've ever eaten, as all that butter and sugar combine to make a great beautiful crusty exterior with the fruit lusciously syrupy within. I've tried cutting the total of sugar down to 1½ cups, and it was good, but not as good. Any tart fruit or berry may be substituted for (or added to) the peaches, I've found. Some of the best of these are peach with boysenberries, apples with rhubarb, or rhubarb alone (really the best!)

COTTAGE CARAMEL PUDDING

2	cups (packed) light brown sugar	2	tablespoons butter, melted
1½	cups milk	1	cup flour
3	tablespoons cold butter	1	teaspoon baking powder
1	egg	1	teaspoon vanilla
3	tablespoons granulated sugar	½	cup chopped nuts (optional)

*P*reheat the oven to 350°F.

In a soufflé dish, or a 1½-quart baking dish, mix the brown sugar and 1 cup of the milk together. Cut the cold butter into bits over the top of the mixture.

In a mixing bowl, whisk the egg lightly, then beat in the remaining ½ cup milk, the granulated sugar, and melted butter. Sift the flour and baking powder over, beat well, and stir in the vanilla and nuts. Pour this batter over the brown sugar–milk mixture—it will float on top. Smooth it out with a large spoon or spatula.

Bake for 45 to 50 minutes, or until the top is puffed and golden. Serve still warm, spooning out portions onto dessert plates with caramel sauce from the bottom poured over each serving. If you wish, heavy cream in a pitcher, or even sour cream, may accompany it.

Serves 6.

Children dote on this golden pudding, and even adults who sniff they don't care for sweets I notice never leave a scrap on their plates. Perhaps we are all reduced to childhood before its generosity. As it is very simply prepared, it might well become a family favorite on chill autumn evenings.

DENVER PUDDING

1 cup granulated sugar	2 tablespoons butter, melted
1 cup flour	2 ounces unsweetened
½ teaspoon salt	chocolate
2 teaspoons baking powder	½ cup (packed) dark brown
½ cup milk	sugar
½ cup chopped black walnuts	1 teaspoon cornstarch
(or walnuts)	1½ cups boiling water
1 teaspoon vanilla	2 tablespoons bourbon or rum
	(optional)

*P*reheat the oven to 350°F.

Butter a soufflé dish.

Put 1 cup of the sugar in a bowl. Sift the flour, salt, and baking powder over it. Mix in the milk, nuts, vanilla, and melted butter.

Melt the chocolate in the top of a double boiler over simmering water. Add about three fourths of it to the above batter, and stir in. Into the remaining chocolate stir the remaining ½ cup granulated sugar, the brown sugar and cornstarch; stir in boiling water until the mixture is smoothly thickened. Add bourbon or rum, if you wish.

Pour the chocolate sauce in the bottom of the soufflé dish and spread the nut batter over it. Bake at 350°F for 45 minutes, or until a good puffed cake has formed on top of a bubbly sauce. To serve, spoon out and dribble some of the sauce over each serving. Pass cream, or serve with whipped cream.

Serves 6.

Another splendid pudding which makes its own ample sauce. It is similar to Cottage Caramel Pudding, but not so sweet.

MY PERSIMMON PUDDING

4	tablespoons butter	¾	cup milk
¾	cup granulatd sugar	1½	cups ripe persimmon pulp
1	egg		(either American or
1	cup flour		Japanese)
1	teaspoon baking powder	½	cup chopped walnuts
1	teaspoon baking soda		Confectioners sugar
½	teaspoon ground ginger	1½	cups heavy cream
¼	teaspoon salt	1	teaspoon lemon juice
		⅛	teaspoon ground ginger

*P*reheat the oven to 325°F.

Grease and flour a 9-inch round cake pan.

Cream the butter and granulated sugar until light and fluffy. Beat in the egg. Sift the flour with the baking powder, soda, ginger, and salt and add it, alternately with milk, to the butter mixture, stirring after each addition. Sieve 1 cup of the persimmon, or whirl it in a blender or food processor. Fold it into the batter, along with the walnuts.

Pour the persimmon mixture into the cake pan. Sift confectioners sugar over the top. Bake for 1 hour. Remove from the oven and let cool.

To serve, whip the cream until it holds a peak. Fold in the remaining ½ cup persimmon pulp, 2 tablespoons confectioners sugar, the lemon juice, and ginger. Place a dollop on each serving of pudding.

Serves 8.

This is my holiday pudding. Japanese persimmons are now very common in the markets, but this kind of pudding used to be made from the native persimmon, which is only edible after frost, the settlers found. They can pucker the tastebuds for hours, if eaten before then, but ripe they are the very tropics.

NEW ORLEANS BREAD
PUDDING WITH BOURBON SAUCE

3	cups sliced leftover French bread	5	eggs
3	cups milk	2	cups sugar
		¾	cup raisins (optional)

2 teaspoons vanilla	¼ cup heavy cream
Salt	¼ cup bourbon
½ cup butter	

*T*rim the bread of crusts or not as you wish. Cover with the milk, and let sit several hours or overnight.

Preheat the oven to 350°F.

Crumble the soaked bread with your hands. Beat 4 of the eggs with 1 cup of the sugar, then stir, along with the raisins, vanilla, and a pinch of salt, into the bread.

Pour into a buttered 8-inch square baking dish. Place in a larger pan containing about 1 inch hot water. Bake for 35 to 45 minutes, or until the top is slightly crusty. Remove and cool.

While the pudding cooks, make the sauce. Melt the butter in the top of a double boiler over simmering water. Stir in the remaining 1 cup sugar and a pinch of salt, and cook until the sugar dissolves. Beat the cream with the remaining egg, and whisk into the sauce until it thickens slightly. Remove from the fire and cool. Add the bourbon.

To serve, cut portions of the pudding and ladle bourbon sauce over each generously.

Serves 9.

Bread puddings are synonymous with thrift, and though everyone likes them, most cooks hesitate to serve one to company. I go right ahead, and use the best aged bourbon in this spectacular sauce. The recipe solves the problem of what, besides making bread crumbs, one does with a leftover French loaf from a small dinner party—you transform it into the simplest of puddings topped by a spiked sauce.

SHAKER LEMON
MERINGUE BREAD PUDDING

1 cup very fine fresh bread crumbs	½ cup plus 1 tablespoon sugar
2 cups milk	2 eggs, separated, plus 1 egg white
2 tablespoons butter	Juice and grated rind of 1 lemon

*T*he best way to prepare this fine pudding is to take 6 or 7 slices of decent white bread and put them in a low oven early in the day, then turn the heat off and forget about them. By dinner you have perfect fodder for a blender or food processor, and also the delicate beginning of your pudding.

Preheat the oven to 350°F.

Warm the milk, remove from fire, add the crumbs, cover, and let sit while you assemble the pudding.

Melt the butter, and use some of it to grease a soufflé dish. Beat the rest with the ½ cup sugar, the egg yolks, and grated lemon rind. Stir into the bread crumbs, and scoop into the soufflé dish.

Set in a larger pan containing 1 inch of hot water and bake for 30 minutes, then remove from the oven. Beat the 3 egg whites stiff, add the 1 tablespoon sugar, and beat until silky. Dribble the lemon juice in as you beat. Spread this meringue over the pudding and bake another 10 minutes, or until slightly golden on top.

Serves 6.

This dish is all balance and proportion—there is Shaker about it everywhere. It is, as the sisters report, of excellence either hot or cold, and needs no cream. They do not tell you that with very little time and money you have achieved a pudding to delight anyone, anywhere, anytime. Its base is the purest possible pudding, with a topping of nigh unbelievable sour meringue.

ROANOKE RUM CREAM

3 egg yolks	3 tablespoons rum
¼ cup sugar	1 cup cream, stiffly whipped
1 tablespoon lemon juice	

*B*eat the egg yolks with the sugar until they are thick and light colored. Add the lemon juice and rum in a stream while continuing to beat. Fold in the stiffly whipped cream and ladle into stemmed glasses. Chill. If you wish, these may be topped with extra plain whipped cream.

Serves 4.

What a friend this pudding is! With a good electric mixer or food processor you have a suave light dessert in minutes—one you could proffer Julia Child. Everyone needs at least one recipe like this as the perfect simple end to a complex meal.

BIG MOMMA'S FLOATING ISLAND

3	eggs, separated		Pinch of salt
½	cup sugar	1	teaspoon vanilla
3 to 4	cups milk	2	tablespoons aged bourbon

Whip the egg whites till stiff, then beat in ¼ cup of the sugar a tablespoon at a time. Scald 3 cups milk in a large frying pan. When it starts making little bubbles around the edges, turn the heat low and drop the meringue from a large spoon to make 4 to 6 large mounds on the milk. Poach, without letting the milk boil, 2 minutes on each side, turning with a skimmer or slotted spoon. Lift out onto a dry towel to cool.

The meringues will have absorbed about a cup of the milk. Measure to make sure, and add enough if necessary to make 2 cups milk. Place in the top of a double boiler set over simmering water. Beat the egg yolks. Add some of the hot milk to the yolks and beat in, then stir the mixture into the remaining milk. Add the remaining ¼ cup sugar and salt, and stir constantly over very low heat until the custard coats your spoon. Immediately remove from heat and add the vanilla and bourbon.

To serve, place the custard in a serving dish and place the meringues on top. Chill thoroughly.

Serves 4 to 6.

Big Momma was not named for her girth, but, in Atlanta gentility style, for her grandmotherhood. Indeed, I remember her, straight as a cameo profile, and as transparent and delicate, serving this pudding some twenty years ago now. On being complimented, she showed me her secret stash of Jack Daniels in the cupboard, used only for this company dish, as she "didn't touch a drop!" herself.

FLORIDA ORANGE FLAN

¾	cup sugar	3	eggs
1	tablespoon orange juice	1½	cups heavy cream, scalded
3	tablespoons bitter orange marmalade	1	teaspoon grated orange rind
			Orange slices

*P*reheat the oven to 350°F.

Combine ½ cup of the sugar, the orange juice, and marmalade (use the best dark marmalade you can find, or add a few drops of Angostura bitters). Boil over a medium flame until the mixture is slightly reduced and coats a spoon—about 5 minutes.

Pour two thirds of the mixture into the bottom of a baking dish—a soufflé dish is about the right size for this. Turn the dish to coat the bottom and sides, and place in the refrigerator to harden the glaze.

Beat the eggs with the remaining ¼ cup sugar. Add the scalded cream, bit by bit, whisking. Pour through a fine sieve and add the orange rind. Pour into the baking dish. Place it in a larger dish with about 1 inch of hot water in it.

Bake for 1 hour, or until a knife inserted in the center comes out clean. Remove, let cool, and refrigerate, covered, several hours or overnight.

Unmold on a platter. Heat up the reserved glaze till it is liquid. Slip thin peeled orange slices in the glaze and decorate the top of the flan with them.

Serves 6 to 8.

The bittersweet sauce from this richest of flans makes the most beautiful glaze. The result is a tour-de-force presentation to apex a company dinner.

WHITE WINE SNOW

1	tablespoon unflavored gelatin	3	tablespoons lemon juice
¼	cup water	3	egg whites
1	cup dry white wine (or		Pinch of cream of tartar
	champagne)		Green grapes
⅔	cup sugar		

*S*prinkle the gelatin on the water and allow to soften for 10 minutes. Mix the wine, sugar, and lemon juice in a stainless-steel or enameled saucepan. Bring to a boil, then lower the heat and stir till the sugar is dissolved. Put in a bowl, stir in gelatin, and refrigerate until the mixture begins to set.

Beat the mixture with an egg beater or electric mixer until light and frothy. In another bowl, beat the egg whites with the cream of tartar until they hold stiff peaks. Fold the two mixtures gently together. Mound into 6 individual dessert cups, decorate with halves of seedless green grapes, and chill for an hour or more.

Serves 6.

In summer, or after any rich meal, often only a very light end is possible. The usual answer is to serve a refreshing ice or sherbet, but this delicate desert is an unusual answer. The better the wine used, of course, the more exquisite the final product. If you have the end of a fine bottle of champagne gone flat, that is best.

PHILADELPHIA VANILLA ICE CREAM

6	cups light cream	1½	vanilla beans, split
1½	cups sugar		lengthwise

*P*lace 2 cups of the cream, the sugar, and split vanilla beans in the top of a double boiler over boiling water. Stir 10 minutes, or until the cream is scalded. Remove from the heat.

Take the beans out and scrape the inner pulp and seeds back into the cream. Cool, add the rest of the cream, and freeze in an ice-cream freezer according to the manufacturer's directions.

Serves 6 to 8.

If ice cream did not originate here, it is certain that in this country it reached its widest appeal. As many of our foods, ice cream has suffered a decline till that bought in stores, nowadays, is little more than pig fat, sugar, and air. The bowls of our childhood, on a summer's dusk, seem to have vanished along with back porches, fireflies, and extra elbows to turn the crank. There are new small electric freezers on the market, however, that are the boon of small families with an appetite for the real thing again.

GEORGIA GINGER PEACH ICE CREAM

4	cups heavy cream	1½	teaspoons vanilla
1	cup sugar	6	ripe peaches
	Pinch of salt	½	cup chopped crystallized ginger

*H*eat 1 cup of the cream, with ½ cup of the sugar and a pinch of salt, in the top of a double boiler over simmering water. Stir until the sugar is dissolved and the cream is scalded—about 10 minutes. Pour into a bowl, add the vanilla and the rest of the cream, and chill in the refrigerator.

Drop the peaches in boiling water, then remove and slip off the skins. Take out the peach stones and chop the peaches coarsely. Put in a bowl, add the remaining ½ cup sugar and the ginger, and stir well. Let sit in the refrigerator to accumulate juices.

Freeze the cream mixture in an ice-cream freezer according to the manufacturer's directions. When the cream is nearly done, add the peaches and ginger and freeze for 10 to 15 minutes more.

Serves 6 to 8.

No ice cream to me is quite as good as pure vanilla, but this comes a shave close.

MY FROZEN DARK CHOCOLATE MOUSSE

1½	cups sugar	1	cup water
2	cups water	4	ounces unsweetened chocolate
1	vanilla bean, split lengthwise	¼	teaspoon salt
		2	tablespoons brandy
1	envelope unflavored gelatin		

*C*ombine the sugar, water, and vanilla bean in a saucepan and cook over a medium flame 10 minutes, stirring to dissolve the sugar. Remove the bean, and when cool enough to handle scrape all the seeds out and return them to the sugar mixture.

Soften the gelatin in a cup of water for 5 minutes. Melt the chocolate in the top of a double boiler over simmering water. When melted, combine all the ingredients (except the brandy) and place in the refrigerator to cool. Freeze in an ice-cream freezer according to the manufacturer's directions, and when nearly done add the brandy.

Serves 6.

This has no cream or milk, so it is technically an ice, I suppose—but whatever you call it it is rich, and dark, and very smooth. I first made it as an attempt to duplicate a very dark chocolate ice sold by one of the better ice cream chains, and which I admired over all their flavors. Mine turned out smoother and subtler, so there seemed to be no reason to attempt exactitude.

CHARLESTON BUTTERMILK
RUM-RAISIN ICE CREAM

½	cup raisins		Pinch of salt
⅓	cup dark rum	2	cups buttermilk
2	egg yolks	1	cup heavy cream
½	cup sugar	2	teaspoons vanilla

*P*lace the raisins with the rum in a small saucepan. Bring to a boil and simmer gently 5 minutes. Turn off the heat, cover, and let sit for 1 hour.

Beat the egg yolks, sugar, and salt together. Bring the buttermilk and cream to a boil in a saucepan, then turn the heat down low and add the egg-sugar mixture bit by bit while whisking the cream. Cook over low heat, stirring constantly, until slightly thickened—about 5 to 6 minutes. Stir in the vanilla and cool in the refrigerator.

Freeze in an ice-cream freezer according to the manufacturer's directions. When the mixture begins to thicken, add the raisins, and any rum they have not absorbed, and freeze until firm.

Serves 6.

Sometimes it is necessary to wonder why one likes a thing that strikes all minor notes, as in this ice cream in which three things are an "off" flavor—buttermilk, rum, and raisins. Not in the eating, however.

PINK GRAPEFRUIT ICE

2	teaspoons unflavored gelatin	2	cups pink grapefruit juice
1½	cups water	¼	cup lemon juice
1	cup sugar	⅓	cup orange juice
	Rind from 1 grapefruit, peeled with a vegetable peeler and cut into tiny julienne strips	¼	teaspoon salt
		2	egg whites, beaten stiff

*D*issolve the gelatin in ½ cup of the water. Combine the sugar and remaining 1 cup water in a saucepan and bring to a boil. Add the grapefruit peel and simmer 10 minutes. Add the gelatin and stir until dissolved. Chill in the refrigerator.

When cool, add the fruit juices and salt, and fold in the egg whites. Freeze in an ice-cream freezer according to the manufacturer's directions.
Serves 6.

The fine slivers of candied grapefruit peel lift this ice into another category altogether.

CRANBERRY ICE IN ORANGE SHELLS

1	quart cranberries	2	teaspoons gelatin
2	cups water	2	egg whites
1¾	cups sugar	12	large half orange shells
1	cup orange juice		

*P*ick over the berries, discarding any that are spoiled. Cook them in 1¾ cups of the water till they pop. Sieve them (or whirl in a blender or food processor). Put the sugar and orange juice in a saucepan, add the cranberry pulp, and cook over low heat 5 minutes. Remove from the fire.

Soak the gelatine in ¼ cup of the water, then beat into the cranberries. Chill in the refrigerator until the mixture begins to thicken. Beat the egg whites stiff and fold them in.

Pour the mixture into ice-cube trays and freeze until mushy. Beat till smooth in a blender or food processor, then scoop into the orange shells. Freeze until just hardened—2 to 3 hours.
Serves 6 (or 12 as a side dish).

These are wonderful as a relish to holiday goose, but they also make an attractive, tart dessert any time.

SHAKER ROSEWATER ICE CREAM

4	egg yolks	3	cups heavy cream, scalded
1	cup sugar	1	tablespoon rosewater
	Pinch of salt	1	cup milk

*B*eat the egg yolks with sugar and salt until frothy. Mix a little of the scalded cream into them, then whisk all back into the cream. Reduce the heat to low, then cook, stirring constantly, until the custard is slightly thickened—about 6 minutes.

Remove from the heat and add the rosewater and milk. Set in the refrigerator to cool, then freeze in an ice-cream freezer according to the manufacturer's directions.

Serves 6.

The Shakers put even their roses to work.

STRAWBERRY SHORTCAKE

Nothing could be a more typical, totally American, dessert than strawberry shortcake. It consists simply of a slightly sweetened biscuit—sometimes with a bit more fat cut in to insure richness (see Helene's Drop Shortcakes, page 324)—strawberries sliced and set to macerate in sugar to assure plenty of juice, and slightly sweetened whipped cream. What could be simpler—yet nowadays it has become lazily usual to use commercially packaged "Mary Ann" cakes, both overly sweet and artificially flavored. And perfectly awful. With only a biscuit standing between you and the pure real thing, then learn how easy it is to pop biscuits from the oven. Your family and friends deserve it.

STRAWBERRIES WITH STRAWBERRY SAUCE

| 1 | pint strawberries | 1 | tablespoon brandy (or kirsch) |
| | Sugar | | |

Wash and stem the berries. Take about two thirds of the best ones and slice in half into a bowl. Sprinkle with a tablespoon of sugar and reserve in the refrigerator.

Sieve the remaining berries. Measure the pulp and add equal parts of sugar. Cook this over low heat, stirring now and again, till it thickens slightly—10 to 15 minutes. Add the brandy or kirsch off the fire, and put to chill in the refrigerator.

To serve, ladle the strawberries into cups or dessert plates and pour the sauce over them.

Serves 2 to 3.

Every strawberry has just so much taste, from tiniest, wild scarlet-tucked zests, to pretty (but tasteless) giants. This, and the following recipe, put back some of the essence lost to size.

WHITE STRAWBERRIES

1	egg yolk	½	cup heavy cream, whipped
2	tablespoons butter, melted	1	pint strawberries, stemmed
1	tablespoon brandy (or kirsch)		and washed
½	cup confectioners sugar		

*B*eat the egg with butter and brandy, then the sugar. Fold this into the whipped cream and chill in the refrigerator for several hours, or until the butter has firmed it so that a spoon placed in the mixture will come out completely coated.

Toss the whole berries in the sauce, place in a large bowl or individual dessert cups, and chill until serving time.

Serves 4.

Not only would the superb sauce described here make nearly anything taste better, it completely coats the berries so no red shows through—a culinary conceit almost worthy of the Shakers. The berries look particularly lovely in a cut-glass bowl on a candlelit buffet table.

BANANAS IN RUM

4	bananas	⅓	cup sugar
2	tablespoons butter	⅓	cup rum (preferably dark)

*B*ananas for this dish should be ripe, but not so ripe they have started getting a speckle on their skins. Peel them, cut in half, then cut each half lengthwise, making 16 finger-shaped slices.

Heat the butter in a large frying pan set over low heat. When it begins to sizzle, put the bananas in, cut side down. Cook 3 minutes, then turn and cook another 3 minutes. Lift out into a shallow casserole large enough to hold them in one layer.

Add the sugar and rum to the pan and cook, stirring, until the sugar dissolves. Pour over the bananas, then cover and refrigerate several hours.

At serving time, lift the bananas out and arrange in a fan on plates. Put the sauce in a saucepan and cook over high heat until it bubbles brightly, then pour over the cold bananas.

Serves 4.

A recipe from my book Southwestern Cooking, *evolved over the years to suit any meal at all—from a fine touch for a simple supper, to a French repast with all the trimmings. To serve the bananas cold in a hot sauce is their real surprise, but in a push they can come straight out of the pan, so long as the sauce is reduced slightly. I used to serve them always with a dollop of whipped cream at the base of the fan, but fine as they are they don't really need it.*

ICED PINEAPPLE MADAME BÉGUÉ

At the turn of the century all New Orleans and Yankee beyond were lining up for Madame Bégué's "second breakfasts," long leisurely eleven o'clock repasts of six or so courses, from turtle or crayfish soups, light savory omelets (she was known to wield her long-handled skillet like a scepter, as her deft husband settled guests in the plain low-ceilinged room), such ducks and daubes, such artichokes and peppery snails, gumbos pungent with plump oysters, such rare beefsteak brightened on the plain linen by the stuffed tomatoes of Provence and local watercress, on to mostly simple heightened fruits, brandy, coffee, and cigars—all originally presented to please the hardy butchers and stall keepers of the French Market, after morning bustle with only a dawn cup of milky chicory coffee to last the stretch.

Long ago, in a high flat off London's Hampstead Heath, I first sat up to read Elizabeth David describing, as an elasticity of French cuisine, a Creole daube cooked with local home rum rather than the usual wine, all studded with olives, and culled from what my new-found author tantalizingly called "a little book of New Orleans cookery . . ." Later I was lucky to find a copy of a rare, browned *Mme. Bégué's Recipes of Old New Orleans Creole Cookery,* marked 50 cents on the cover. Though now her rules may seem too fuzzy and general, through the passing of time and modern temperament for quick exactitude, simple honesty in every mouthwatering example is undenied. Take her "recipe" for pineapple with white wine . . .

"Pare and slice a nice ripe pineapple. Place in a crystal dish a layer of pineapple and a layer of white sugar until all is used. Pour over this half a quart

FOURTH OF JULY
WATERMELON WITH SNICKERDOODLES

atermelon   Snickerdoodles (page 375)
ight rum

plug in a watermelon and add as much rum as the melon will absorb
he period of half an hour or so (a small melon should absorb at least ½
Replug the melon and let it chill overnight, turning it once or twice to
e sure the rum permeates the whole.
To serve, slice the melon in rounds, and accompany with Snickerdoodles.

um seems here to produce simply a more melony melon, without leaving
much more than a ghost of itself. Snickerdoodles compliment it so well that
give a feast of both on our national Day of Independence.

AMBROSIA

6   seedless oranges   Juice of ½ lemon
3   cups shredded fresh coconut   ⅓   cup sugar
    Grated peel of 1 orange

*P*eel the oranges, making sure to remove all the white pith. Slice into a bowl,
then add the coconut, orange peel, lemon juice, and sugar and toss lightly.
Refrigerate at least 2 hours before serving. Toss now and again as it sits to
distribute flavors.
   Serves 6 to 8.

Traditional Christmas fare in many Southern homes, where the dessert is served
in the best cut-glass bowl from the sideboard. It makes sense to have a light
end to all the rich heavy foods of the day, but it is a dessert anytime, any-
where, a delight.

of white wine and let it stand two hou
ready to serve stir well; pound a large pie
whole."

The recipe writer can tell at once that w
crystal bowl, glittering with a topping of ice,
a whole string of "buts" and "what-ifs" and "ho\
not to mention that he must have enough savvy
ripe enough, and to know it must be cut with a st.
simple recipe can sometimes make for choices all dow

I go about this by choosing at the market a beauti
from green to gold in the globe, with an arched powder}
put to look at as a centerpiece of fierce beauty in the kitch
The day it has turned all gold, I go look for a suitable dis
wine.

The wine poses the most choices of all, but since sweetness
tion here, one can be a bit more reckless than usual about choo\
and so chance on a new bouquet fit to sip while relaxing before din\
the thing is simple (remembering always the stainless knife)—it o\
be done well and roundly, cutting out any of the brown tucks, the\
into ½-inch slabs.

At this point, another question turns up. Should the cook leave the w\
centers in, for a diner to deal with, or should they be made less pretty
coring and quartering? Let's leave them whole, as this is to be a pretty dis\
by hook or crook. Now comes the sugar, left quite up in the air by La Bégué,
but pineapple is a sweet fruit, so better too little than too much—more can
be added later. Let us add ½ cup. When the fruit is sugared in our bowl (not
cut crystal, but yet nicely glass) only 1½ cups of wine is needed to brim it—
leaving just enough for two glasses for the cook.

After the dinner the final question looms: How to make the ice shine and
glitter for this chilly tropic of a dish? Cubes from the tray, certainly not, and
the clattering of a Cuisinart breaking ice is nerve-racking enough, even if there
were not guests. So the cook remembers ice being chipped from a block on a
back porch years ago, to feed the hand-cranked ice cream machine, and dumps
a tray of cubes into a clean dish cloth, twists it into a compact ball to be hit
lightly but well with a rolling pin, and brings the dish with good show to
table.

Such are the trials and delights of the questing recipe hunter.

METHODS & INGREDIENTS

With cooking on our own home ground there are fortunately few esoteric ingredients, and almost all methods are self-explanatory. There are a few fine points, however, that would clutter the recipes if repeated every time.

Almonds

The general use for these in the recipes is "slivered and toasted." This process is simple enough. To remove the brown husk and blanch the nuts, simply drop them in boiling water about half a minute. Slip the husks off by hand, and dry on paper toweling. Cut lengthwise into ⅛-inch slivers. Heat a mixture of half vegetable oil and half butter in a saucepan—about 1 tablespoon each for ½ cup nuts. Sauté over medium heat, stirring, until they are an even deep gold. This will take 4 to 5 minutes. Drain them on paper toweling to absorb the grease.

Baking Powder

Any baking powder has limited shelf life, particularly if any moisture gets to it. If you seldom bake, always test it before using, to see if it still has zip. Put a teaspoon in ⅓ cup hot water, and make sure it bubbles with some enthusiasm.

Beans (dried)

I've usually indicated the overnight soaking method for beans, but there is nothing wrong with the quick-soak method. This involves bringing beans to a boil in plenty of water, letting them cook 5 minutes or so, then they should sit covered off the fire for an hour or more—or until they plump up. These can then be cooked as any recipe indicates.

Bread crumbs

Not being an admirer of store-bought bread crumbs, I always make them myself. I use every scrap of leftover white bread, first cutting it and letting it dry out in a slow oven, then whirling it in a food processor—though a rolling pin does just as well. These crumbs can then be kept in a refrigerator jar, for any use.

Butter

For convenience I've just listed butter in recipes, but unsalted butter is always of a higher quality and superior flavor. It is particularly good in a buttery sauce, and in delicate baking. Of course the best thing would be to have churned butter as it was made with unpasturized cream, where bacteria could actually be tasted swimming on the tastebuds, but that would be the best of all possible worlds.

Buttermilk

I'm always surprised when people claim they don't like to drink buttermilk, and so never have it on hand. Drinking it aside (and I like it every bit as much as yogurt) buttermilk gives a certain tang to many dishes that used to be made with unpasteurized cream or milk, and it urges baked breads or cakes to a lighter, fluffier texture. I always keep it on hand. A bottle keeps a couple of weeks or more in the refrigerator, and tempts to new uses.

Cheese

Long gone are the days when only processed cheese foods were available, with maybe a slab cut off a green "longhorn." Not only cheese shops, but most large markets sell natural cheeses, aged and sharp or creamy and mild, of a wide variety. Always try to avoid large packagers in favor of local, and if possible buy from a store that cuts their own. Cheese should be brought to room temperature before serving.

Chicken

It's always cheaper to make a habit of buying a whole chicken and cutting it up yourself. I like to use breasts for one meal, then the legs and thighs for another, since the two cook at slightly different times for maximum succulence anyway. It also provides some variety. Cutting up a chicken is relatively simple, and doesn't require anything but a good knife. You can bend the leg back so the hip joint is easily seen. Cut there. The same applies for the joint between leg and thigh, if you want them in two pieces. Wings can be cut off by the same process of bending at the joint and cutting. Then you cut out the back in one fell swoop, or by cutting the first half off and cracking it back, then cutting the part out around the breast. The whole breast should be flattened with your fist, then cut up the middle bone from the back. The back and wings and giblets (minus the liver, which should be reserved for another meal) can be used to make stock (see *Stocks*).

Corn

It is a cliché that corn should have its pot put on the fire before picking, but it is true. Market corn is never as sweet or tender or flavorful—however, what ears you find in your market are preferable to frozen or canned any day. Choose ones with tiniest kernels, and that have their husk still on. Husk them, slip off the silk by rubbing your hand up and down the ear, knife the kernels into a bowl, then drag the dull edge of the knife down the ears to extract any juices.

Cornmeal

For those who have never tasted it, real stone-ground cornmeal with the germ still in it will be a revelation. Unfortunately, since it has a briefer shelf life, this is seldom found outside the South. There it is treasured, and constantly used. As I've never found any reliable mail-order source, I have friends send it to me. Even "gourmet" stores haven't caught on to this delicacy yet, though it can be found in some enlightened health food shops. But even there beware if it's not labeled from a Southern source. If you do find it, buy in bulk and keep in the refrigerator. A way to put some of the lost savor back is indicated in any recipe that depends on this meal to be completely successful. (See also *Masa harina.*)

Cream

Where cream is mentioned in a recipe, what I used was ordinary whipping cream. Except where the cream is actually whipped, however, a lighter cream may be used for a less rich dish.

Eggs

For convenience, I've used the size called "large eggs" in all the recipes. Whatever you have on hand is fine, though, except in the case of cakes—where the difference between small and jumbo eggs can seriously affect the outcome.

Egg whites

These ought to be at room temperature to whip to highest volume. They should not have any hint of yolk in them, and should be beaten in a grease-free bowl (neither plastic nor aluminum). By hand, you need a wire whisk and a steady rhythmic stroke, and in an electric mixer you must watch carefully. They should rise 3 to 4 times the volume, be firm, airy, glossy, and stand as a peak with a curl on top when you lift the beater from them. Folding these into a batter should be done quickly but gently as bathing a baby.

Fats

Everywhere I've indicated which fat is to my taste in a recipe. Often this runs to lard, butter, or bacon fat, but if for dietary reasons you must use vegetable "shortening," go right ahead, though do not expect flavor to accompany it. Lard especially has fallen out of favor, though it makes a shorter pastry than butter, and is excellent for baking and frying. My theory is that if you don't overdo fats, you should use the real right one when you do.

Fish

Almost all frozen foods are less tasty than fresh, but fish is a special case. When it thaws, delicate cells rupture and flavor runs out. This can be minimized by thawing slowly in the refrigerator, but never eliminated. I try to steer clear of frozen, in favor of the fresh catch with a shiny eye.

Frying

Frying technically means in some depth of fat, though I've been guilty of sometimes using it in its American sense of "pan-frying" or sauté. Any recipe that depends on deep frying either includes a thermometer reading, or tells you how the process should look and act. A thermometer is advised. 375°F is satisfactory for frying most foods. A way to test for this without a thermometer is a bread cube dropped in the fat: it should brown in 60 seconds. Never let the oil start to smoke, for it begins to break down at that temperature. Unless you are cooking some strongly flavored food, such as onions, oil can be cooled and strained and stored in the refrigerator for re-use. New oil should be added when this is done, and the oil should be thrown away if it becomes dark.

Garlic

Never ever use garlic powder or garlic salt. They have a flavor detectable as cheap scent across the room. Also, a garlic press is a useless instrument that tends to draw out unpleasant oils. Just go ahead and chop it. Smash the cloves slightly with the side of your knife, and slip the skins off. Mincing it with a little salt helps the garlic not to cling to the knife, if you like. Never let garlic cook to more than golden in a recipe, or it will lend a bitter taste to the dish. Finally—who knows what size a garlic clove is? They come in different sizes even from the same head, so use your own taste as judge, when it comes to measure.

Green peppers

Here and there are recipes that indicate green peppers grated without their skins. To do this, cut the pepper in quarters, remove the seed sections, then grate flesh forward on the coarse side of a grater. The skin will be too tough to grate, so just discard it.

Ham

Most these days are pumped with water and have little flavor but salt. They are never bargains. One good ham available everywhere is Hormel's Cure 81, of a fine flavor, boneless, ready to eat, and though more expensive, worth every penny.

Herbs

Except where fresh herbs seemed essential to a dish, I've indicated dried herbs. But if you grow your own, substitute at the rate of 1 tablespoon fresh for every teaspoon dried.

Knives

Any good cook knows that a knife is his closest friend. A whole battery is not needed, either. One fine small paring knife with a sharp point, a fairly large chef's knife, and perhaps a boning knife (all made of carbon steel) and you're in business. A serrated knife for slicing is also fine to have, but it needn't be carbon steel. Good knives last a lifetime, so don't be cheap, and while you're at it buy a sharpening steel to keep them razor edged.

Masa harina

This is found in any Hispanic market, for it is the flour tortillas are made with. (Don't ever attempt that, though—even so-called "tortilla presses" make a mess. Tortillas take years to learn to make.) Masa is useful, however, for making batters for the top of tamale pies, and since it has so much flavor I advise it as a help (if not a true substitute) in putting some back into ordinary cornmeal. When you can't get stone-ground meal, masa can take the place of regular flour in any cornbread recipe, and if only cornmeal is used let some of the meal be masa. Not only is flavor provided, but some of the smooth flour-iness natural to stone-ground meal is put back.

Nuts

Why buy small expensive packages of nuts in the market, when you can look around and find fresh crop nuts sold in bulk? Most health food stores stock them, if you haven't a grove near. These can be kept frozen for long periods, and not only have a fresh taste but are inexpensive enough to use lavishly.

Oils

I use olive oil a lot in these recipes, but then I also buy it in a Greek store around the corner that sells it for less than corn oil at the supermarket. Veg-etable oils can always be substituted if that is what you have, though they contribute no flavor.

Onions

I generally just go ahead and use the common yellow onion for cooking. But remember the white onions are milder and a bit more tasty, if more expensive. Any time you come on the really sweet varieties like Walla Walla or Maui, snap them up for eating raw—they are wonderful. Green onions are also called scallions (and, confusingly, in the South, shallots). The green tops are as tasty as the bulbs, so I always use at least an inch or two of the green when cooking a dish.

Paprika

Most Americans have a dried-out can or jar of this on the spice shelf, used to give a bit of color to a dull dish. But it ought to be a genial, living part of the kitchen, and definitely Hungarian. The Hungarians produce a range of paprikas from hot to sweet, but the sweet is the one to have for general purposes. Not only will color blush, but so will savor.

Pepper (black)

Everywhere this has been left up to taste, along with the personal choice in salt. Dishes that should be rather peppery are indicated in the text as such— these are almost always from New Orleans, or thereabouts. I always use a pepper grinder to get the liveliest flavor.

Portions

Where practicable, I've adjusted recipes to serve around four. However, almost any—except for pies and cakes and breads—can be halved or doubled at need. The exception is halving an egg, a process which the novice may find a boggle. It's possible, though. Beat the whole egg, then measure it—2 tablespoons is about right for half.

Potatoes

"Mealy" and "waxy" are about the only things to say about potatoes. Mealy are best for baking, while the waxy hold together better for sauté or salads. Except for the recipes that call explicitly for baking potatoes, I've used the ordinary market bag known simply as "potatoes." They work, but they're not the best—after all, something makes them cheaper. Spots have to be cut out, and sometimes they have not been stored properly, so have a layer of green under the skin. If so, they must be peeled before using, since the green part is slightly poisonous. Always make a test poke to see, unless you are using the absolutely top-notch spud.

Rice

I know some good cooks who swear by processed rice, but I see no reason for it (and certainly not for instant). With the fine texture and flavor of regular long-grain rice, what's a minute or so, when the difference is so evident?

Rum

Unless a recipe calls for light rum, dark is always preferable for deep flavor.

Get a good brand (these are of course more expensive) and keep it stored for cooking. Jamaica produces the best, and it will say so on the label.

Salt

Except where it must be measured to some exactness, I've left this also up to the cook. Everyone has a different taste for it. I've been told by those on a salt-free diet for a time, that the tastebud is assaulted by even a little, for sugar and salt are the most overpowering seasonings of all. A taste for more and more of it can amount to an addiction, so that some diners salt even before tasting. With this in mind, I usually undersalt rather than oversalt—it can always be added later. Kosher salt is preferable to ordinary salt, both for cooking and at the table, and it contains no additives.

Sauté

In English we seem only to have the term "pan-fry" for this process, and that is a little ambiguous, since frying usually means a certain depth of fat. Sauté is a process where something is cooked with a small amount of fat, preferably in a heavy-bottomed pan, over heat just high enough so you can cook quickly without burning the fat.

Spices

These have a limited shelf life. If possible, they should be stored in the cool and dark, rather than perched on a fancy shelf above the stove. I know, I keep mine there as you probably do, but I also go through them pretty quickly. Don't let any label get yellow, certainly, and when possible buy them whole, and grind in a coffee grinder kept for the purpose. Nutmeg is the perfect one to buy whole, for they are easy to grate, and have ten times the flavor.

Stock (beef)

Most home cooks find this stock too much of a chore to bother with. In a restaurant, not only are there lots of meat scraps and ends of vegetables, the stocks are a kind of by-product of everything that goes on. Certainly this kind of stock is the secret of the best sauces and soups, and the very best cook will not be deterred by the expense and fuss of keeping a stock pot on, now and again, and clarifying, and boiling down the result to a delectable brown essence for easy storage, but if you don't you don't. Rather than use bouillon cubes, however, I think canned beef bouillon has a better taste.

Stock (chicken)

This is easy for anyone to make. It's always cheaper to buy a whole chicken, anyway, and so one is provided with the back, wings, and giblets (not the liver, save that for another purpose) to make stock. The easiest is to put all these in a pressure cooker with an onion, a carrot, a stalk of celery, some parsley, a bay leaf, some thyme, a few peppercorns, and cook about an hour. This

404   METHODS AND INGREDIENTS

can then be strained and cooked down to an essence which keeps well in the freezer.

Stock (fish)
Many recipes say you can use bottled clam juice for this, but if you do remember it is very salty. I have used it when in a hurry, but I prefer to dilute it half with water. It is easy to pick up fish scraps now and again, and cook them with the same things as the chicken stock above, and have some on hand in the freezer.

Temperature
All ovens vary. The only way to be exact is to purchase an oven thermometer. I've tried to indicate how things should look and feel in any recipe, but when in doubt pay attention to sizzle, sputter, and—above all—smell. Any dish about done will also start to smell good, except for bread, which smells good all the way through. The stovetop is another matter. I prefer the flexible heats that gas offers, and have always cooked with it, except in other people's homes. So with an electric stove, do not always take my instructions of things like "medium high" as gospel for a dial setting—use your knowledge of the instrument, and how it responds for you alone.

Tomatoes
Grow your own, is my advice. They no longer exist in an edible form in markets. There, they are picked green and sprayed with a gas to make them turn reddish: I boycott these out of principle, for what is better than a vine-ripened tomato? For this reason I've recommended canned tomatoes everywhere possible—these are at least picked ripe. The best of these are Italian plum tomatoes, and the best of the best are ones with an Italian label. By all means, if you garden, use fresh peeled tomatoes. I envy you.

Tomato Paste
When a recipe calls for only a little tomato paste, there's no sense wasting the rest of the can. Measure what is left by the tablespoon onto waxed paper, and freeze the sheet. When hard, remove from the paper and put in a container. That way you'll always have them, already measured, on hand.

Vanilla
Always use pure vanilla extract. Artificial vanilla has smell but not taste. Better yet, buy the beans and put one split in a canister of sugar. This can then be used in any sweet recipe calling for vanilla (the British use this for sprinkling on melon, a lovely idea). You can also split an inch of bean, and scrape out the tiny seeds, for a glorious substitute for vanilla extract in any recipe.

Vinegar

Vinegars are not expensive when you consider that even the fanciest are used so sparingly they last a long while. So when you come on any fine one, buy it, and keep a shelf in proud array. They pay for themselves again and again on the daily salad alone.

Wine

There are no hard and set rules about what wine should be eaten with any American dish. So many varieties come out of California these days, it's hard to sort them all out anyway. Follow your own nose, tastes, and pocketbook. If a novice, remember that, for drinking with food, any dry is better than a sweetish wine, and a decliate dish needs a delicate wine. Sherry and Madeira, even in cooking, need be the best you can afford, and always dry. There is no such thing as a "cooking sherry."

Yeast

A package of active yeast is equivalent to 6 ounces fresh yeast, and the only difference is that fresh yeast should be dissolved in lukewarm water, while the dry can take water up to 115°F. There is always a date on the package telling when the yeast might deteriorate, but any recipe also indicates the process of putting it in some liquid to puff up and "proof." This is "proof" it works.

Zests

The zest of oranges, lemons, limes, and even grapefruits—which I refer to as "rind" or "peel" in these recipes—are marvelous flavoring agents, but remember to use only the colored part of the skin, since the white beneath is bitter. It's also best to have a light touch with them, so in a recipe that calls for them you might want to decrease the amount I have given—which tends toward the maximum rather than the minimum.

Index

Acorn squash soufflés, 244
Alabama fried chicken with milk gravy and fried
    biscuits, 147–148
Alda's chili meat sauce, 186–187
Alfred Lunt's meat loaf, 92
Almond(s)
    chicken Creole, 153–154
    general data about, 397
    ham slices with, 118
    rack of lamb with, 126–127
    soft-shelled crabs with, 61
Ambrosia, 394
American fried, 253
Anadama bread, 338
Ancestral turkey rice soup, 22
Anchovy cream, crisp sole with, 43
Apple(s)
    cake, 363
    chicken stuffed with sauerkraut and, 145–146
    crab, chicken stuffed with, 144–145
    fried rings, 220
    gratin of sweet potatoes, rutabagas, and, 220–221
    pie
        paradise, 350–351
        upside-down, 349–350
    pippins, ham, yams, and chestnuts baked with,
        119–120
Apple cider, see Cider
Applesauce, Shaker, 310
Apricot catsup, curried, 290–291
Artichokes
    à la neige, 222
    stuffed, 221
Asparagus
    "ragoo" of lamb and, 129
    San Francisco, 222–223

Aspic, cucumber, with shrimp, 71
Avocado(s)
    cream soup, 7
    guacamole, 190–191
    slices, marinated in rum, 191
Aztec pie, 197

Bacon
    buttermilk cornbread, 318
    and parsley pudding, 208
Baking powder, 397
Baltimore fries, 254
Bananas in rum, 391–392
B & O Railroad clam pot pie, 209–210
Barbecue
    beef, 83
    Georgia spareribs, 110
    lamb
        leg of, butterflied, 124
        riblets, 128
    oysters, 66
Barbecue sauces, 294–296
    composite, 296–297
    Pendennis Club, 296
Bean(s)
    four bean salad, 272
    general data about, 397
    soup, Senate, 20
    See also names of beans
Beef, 77–93
    barbecue, 83
    chipped, creamed, 211
    corned beef hash, with eggs, 84–85
    fillet of, 79–80

ground
  picadillo, 195, 200–201
  smoked oyster burgers, 92–93
Joe's special, 91
liver
  with herbs, 135
  Maryland, 136
meat loaf, Alfred Lunt's, 92
New England boiled dinner, 83–84
oxtail
  braised, with mushrooms, 90
  soup, 22–23
pot roast
  Madeira, 81–82
  Savoy Plaza, 82
ragoût of, 86
roast, with Yorkshire pudding and horseradish ice
    cream, 78–79
short ribs, braised, with celery, 89
sirloin Clemenceau, 80–81
steak pudding, 88
stock, 403
winter soup, 85
Beets
  with their greens in sour cream, 224–225
  "vichyssoise" of beet greens, 4–5
  Yale, 224
Benne wafers, 327–328
Beverly Hills Rangoon Racquet Club championship
    chili, 26–28
Big Momma's floating island, 383
Biscuits
  beaten, 327
  fried, fried chicken with milk gravy and, 147–
    148
  Happy Valley, 322
  sourdough, 343–344
  summer cloud, 322–323
  whipped cream, 323–324
  whole-wheat, 325
Bisque
  salmon, chilled, 8
  summer squash, 10
Black bean(s)
  soup, 21
  tostadas, with sour cream, 200
Black-eyed pea(s)
  hopping John, 183
  salad, 279–280
  soup, 23–25
Blueberry rhubarb relish, 311–312
Blue ribbon peach cobbler, 378–379
Bottled sauces, 297–298
Bouillon, court-, Creole, 36–37
Boulette de saucisson, 207–208
Bourbon
  Derby pie, 360–361
  sauce, bread pudding with, 380–381
Brabant potatoes, 253–254

Bread and butter pickles, 304–305
Bread crumb(s)
  -caper sauce, lamb chops with, 127
  general data about, 398
Bread pudding
  with bourbon sauce, 380–381
  lemon meringue, 381–382
Breads, 315–344
  anadama, 338
  benne wafers, 327–328
  biscuits
    beaten, 327
    fried, 147–148
    Happy Valley, 322
    sourdough, 343–344
    summer cloud, 322–323
    whipped cream, 323–324
    whole-wheat, 325
  brown, 338–339
  butter cakes, 333–334
  cornbread
    bacon buttermilk, 318
    jalapeño cheese, 318–319
    Shaker, 319
  cornpones, 316–317
  dill, 337
  dumplings, parsley, 325–326
  garlic, 335
  griddle cakes, wild rice and cornmeal, 321
  hush puppies, 36, 320–321
  maple toast, 216
  muffins, potato, 326
  rolls
    butter, 328–329
    Parker House, 331
    rose geranium, 332
    sesame, 332–333
  rye and Indian, 339–340
  salt rising, 340–341
  shortcakes, drop, 324
  sourdough, 341–344
    biscuits, 343–344
    cracked-wheat, 343
    white, 342
  spoonbread, 319–320
  white buttermilk, 334–335
  zephyrs, 317
Brown bread, 338–339
Burritos, simple, 202
Butter, 398
  cucumber, 42
  shad roe poached in, 51–52
Butter cakes, 333–334
Buttermilk
  bacon cornbread, 318
  chess pie, 358
  fried chicken and, 146–147
  general data about, 398
  mashed potato soufflé with, 251–252

Buttermilk *(continued)*
  rum-raisin ice cream with, 388
  white bread with, 334–335
Butter rolls, 328–329

Cabbage
  in caraway cream, 226
  cole slaw, 273, 276
    Grison's Steak House, 274
    old-fashioned, 274–276
    oyster pan roast with, 63
    wilted, with sour cream, 276–277
  fricassee of, 225
  sauerkraut
    chicken stuffed with apples and, 145–146
    spareribs and, 111–112
Cajun rabbit with orange rice, 165–166
Cakes, 362–370
  apple, 363
  butter, 333–334
  gingerbread, 370–371
  glazed lemon, 369–370
  jam, 372
  Mississippi mud, 364–365
  orange peel, 363–364
  plum, 369
  rum, 365–366
  Shaker Carolina, 366–367
  Texas long, 367
  See also Shortcake(s)
Calves' liver
  with French-fried sweet potatoes, 134–135
  with onions, 133
Caper(s)
  -bread crumb sauce, lamb chops with, 127
  turnip slaw with, 284–285
Capitol Hill soft-shelled crab sandwich, 60
Caramel pudding, 378–379
Caraway seeds, cabbage in caraway cream, 226
Carnitas, 192–193
Carolina okra salad, 279
Carolina parsnip soufflé, 238–239
Carrot(s)
  Draper Morrow, 226–227
  Golden Gate soup, 9–10
  slaw, 277
Casserole, pork, 109
Catsup
  apricot, curried, 290–291
  gourmet, 290
Cauliflower
  purée of, 228–229
  with sour cream, 228
Celery
  braised short ribs and, 89
  salad, Victor, 278
Charleston benne wafers, 327–328
Charleston buttermilk rum-raisin ice cream, 388
Charleston chicken, 152

Charleston cucumbers, 233
Charleston she-crab soup, 18
Charleston smothered veal with chestnuts, 100
Chaurice, 113
Cheddar cheese and jalapeño cornbread, 318–319
Cheese
  general data about, 398
  and green onion enchiladas, 195–196
  quesadillas
    Gordon Baldwin's, 201–202
    simple, 201
  See also types of cheese
Cherry tomatoes, herbed, 244–245
Chess pie, buttermilk, 358
Chestnut(s)
  with ham and yams, baked with pippins, 119–
    120
  purée, 229
  smothered veal with, 100
  soup, 16–17
Chicken, 143–158
  breast of
    cutlets, Nebraska, 157–158
    Delta-style, 158
    Maitland, 156–157
  Charleston, 152
  in cider cream, 150
  Creole, with almonds, 153–154
  fricassee, 154
  fried
    buttermilk, 146–147
    with milk gravy and fried biscuits, 147–148
  general data about, 398–399
  in green corn, 152–153
  livers, in Madeira cream, 137
  pie, chili verde tamale, 155–156
  pudding, Colonial, 149–150
  and shrimp *étoufée*, 73–74
  with Smithfield ham, 148–149
  spring, baked, 144
  stock, 403–404
  stuffed
    with crab apples, 144–145
    with sauerkraut and apples, 145–146
  tacos, with green chilies and sour cream, 198–
    199
Child's famous butter cakes, 333–334
Chili, Beverly Hills Rangoon Racquet Club cham-
    pionship, 26–28
Chilies, *see* Green chili(es); Red chili sauce
Chimichangas, 202–203
Chipped beef, creamed, 211
Chives, spinach with cream cheese and, 242–243
Chocolate mousse, 386
Chorizo, 192
Chowchow, 302–303
Chowder
  clam, New England, 30
  fish, 31

Chutney
  mock mango, 301
  Putney, 300
Cider
  cream, chicken in, 150
  pork chops with, 105–106
Cioppino, 37
Clam(s)
  chowder, New England, 30
  fritter, 56
  hash, 209
  Philly, 55
  pot pie, 209–210
  soup, Delaware, 17–18
Coach House four bean salad, 272
Cobbler, peach, 378–379
Cod fillets, chilled, 44–45
Cole slaw, 273, 276
  Grison's Steak House, 274
  old-fashioned, 274–276
  oyster pan roast with, 63
  wilted, with sour cream, 276–277
Colonial beef steak pudding, 88
Colonial chicken pudding, 149–150
Colonial corn pudding, 230
Colonial fricassee of cabbage, 225
Colonial green beans with mace, 223
Cookies, snickerdoodles, 375, 394
Corn
  on the cob, 230
  general data about, 399
  green, chicken in, 152–153
  okra, tomatoes, and, 231–232
  pudding, 230
  relish, 303
  Shaker yellow velvet, 232
  and shrimp pie, 70
  soup, 13–14
  succotash, 231
  Zuñi lamb stew with green chilies and, 125–126
Cornbread
  bacon buttermilk, 318
  jalapeño cheese, 318–319
  Shaker, 319
Corned beef
  hash, with eggs, 84–85
  New England boiled dinner, 83–84
Cornmeal
  general data about, 399
  hush puppies, 46, 320–321
  and wild rice griddle cakes, 321
Cornpones, Duchess of Windsor's, 316–317
Cottage caramel pudding, 378–379
Cottage roasted Jerusalem artichokes, 235–236
Country green beans, 223
Country tomato salad, 283
Court-bouillon, Creole, 36–37
Crab(s)
  eggplant stuffed with, 58–59

  green cracker, 57–58
  gumbo, cold, 9
  mustard ring, 59–60
  pie, 56–57
  she-crab soup, 18
  soft-shelled
    with almonds, 61
    sandwich, 60
Crab apples
  chicken stuffed with, 144–145
  spiced, 306
Cracked-wheat bread, sourdough, 343
Crackers, green cracker crabs, 57–58
Cranberry
  ice, in orange shells, 163–164, 389
  orange relish, 311
Cream(ed)
  anchovy, crisp sole with, 43
  avocado soup, 7
  baked fish with, 46–47
  caraway, cabbage in, 226
  chipped beef, 211
  cider, chicken in, 150
  dilly bean salad with, 270–271
  fudge torte, 373–374
  general data about, 399
  Madeira, chicken livers in, 137
  potatoes, 256
  pumpkin soup, chilled, 5–6
  rum, 382–383
  spring peas and new potatoes, 241
  tomato salad with, 284
  whipped, biscuits, 323–324
Cream cheese
  pickled jalapeños stuffed with walnuts and, 191–192
  pie, triple layer, 358–359
  spinach with chives and, 242–243
Creole almond chicken, 153–154
Creole court-bouillon, 36–37
Creole jambalaya, 178–179
Creole stuffed shoulder of lamb, 124–125
Cucumber(s)
  aspic, with shrimp, 71
  braised peas with, 239
  bread and butter pickles, 304–305
  butter, 42
  Charleston, 233
  icicle pickles, 305
  jade sticks, 278–279
  and potato soup, cold, 6–7
  triple pickles, 305–306
Curry(ied)
  apricot catsup, 290–291
  green tomatoes, gratin of, 246
Custard pie, rhubarb, 351–352

Delaware clam soup, 17–18
Delmonico scallops, 68–69

Delta crab pie, 56–57
Denver omelet, 214
Denver pudding, 379
Derby pie, 360–361
Desserts, 345–394
  bananas in rum, 391–392
  cakes, 362–370
    apple, 363
    butter, 333–334
    glazed lemon, 369–370
    jam, 372
    Mississippi mud, 364–365
    orange peel, 363–364
    plum, 369
    rum, 365–366
    Shaker Carolina, 366–367
    Texas long, 367
  chocolate mousse, 386
  cookies, 375, 394
  floating island, 383
  gingerbread, 370–371
  ice creams
    buttermilk rum-raisin, 388
    ginger peach, 385–386
    rosewater, 389–390
    vanilla, 385
  ices
    cranberry, 389
    pink grapefruit, 388–389
  nantillas, 204
  orange flan, 383–384
  peach cobbler, 378–379
  pie crust, 348–349
  pies, 347–361
    apple upside-down, 349–350
    burnt sugar walnut, 357
    buttermilk chess, 358
    Derby, 360–361
    lemon, 353–354
    lemon meringue, 353
    lime, with pecan crust, 354–355
    orange, 355–356
    orange pecan, 356–357
    paradise, 350–351
    peach, 357
    rhubarb custard, 351–352
    sour cream rum-raisin, 359–360
    triple layer cream cheese, 358–359
    Washington, 371
  pineapple, iced, Madame Bégué, 392–393
  puddings
    bread, with bourbon sauce, 380–381
    bread, lemon meringue, 381–382
    caramel, 378–379
    Denver, 379
    Mrs. Truman's, 377
    persimmon, 380
  rum cream, 382–383
  snickerdoodles, 375, 394

strawberries with strawberry sauce, 390–391
strawberry shortcake, 390
tortes
  fudge cream, 373–374
  nut, 374
white strawberries, 391
white wine snow, 384–385
Dill
  bread, 337
  green beans with, 306–307
Dilly bean salad, 270–271
Dixie pickled peaches, 309–310
Domestic game, see Duck; Goose; Rabbit; Turkey
Downeast turkey oyster shortcake, 170
Dried beans, 397
Duchess of Windsor's cornpones, 316–317
Duck (duckling)
  roast, 160–161
    with sauce paradis, 161–162
  salmi of, 162–163
Dumplings, parsley, 325–326

Egg(s)
  corned beef hash with, 84–85
  general data about, 399
  goldenrod, 215
  huevos rancheros, 203
  New Orleans, 216
  noodles with, 213–214
  omelets
    Denver, 214
    potato, 212–213
  and onion sandwich, 214–215
Eggplant
  deep fried, 233–234
  and ham pilau, 177
  stuffed with crab (or shrimp), 58–59
Egg whites, 399
Emily Dickinson's rye and Indian bread, 339–340
Enchiladas
  cheese and green onion, 195–196
  green chili, 196–197
Ephraim Donor's poor man's chilled salmon
    bisque, 8

Fairmont Hotel crab mustard ring, 59–60
Farmhouse ham hock boiled dinner, 121
Farmhouse onion pie, 210
Farmhouse skillet creamed potatoes, 256
Fats, 400
Feathered rice, 267
Fish
  baked, with cream, 46–47
  chowder, 31
  cioppino, 37
  fillets of
    pan-fried, with French Quarter sauce, 44
    tarragon, with cucumber butter, 42
  fried, with hush puppies, 46

general data about, 400
stock, 404
See also names of fish and shellfish
Flan, orange, 383–384
Floating island, 383
Florida orange flan, 383–384
Florida orange snapper, 45
Four Seasons ground lamb, 131
Fourth of July watermelon with snickerdoodles, 394
Frances Parkinson Keyes' cucumber aspic with shrimp, 71
Frances Sommer's jalapeño salsa, 188
French Quarter sauce, 44, 293
Fritters
    clam, 56
    zucchini, 248
Fruits, *see* names of fruits
Frying, 400
Fudge cream torte, 373–374

Galatoire's eggplant stuffed with crab (or shrimp), 58–59
Game, domestic, *see* Duck; Goose; Rabbit; Turkey
Garlic
    bread, 335
    general data about, 400
Georgia barbecue spareribs, 110
Georgia ginger peach ice cream, 385–386
Georgia spoonbread, 319–320
Georgia summer squash soufflé, 243
Gilded lily soup, 12
Gingerbread, 370–371
Ginger peach ice cream, 385–386
Glaze (glazed)
    for ham, 117–118
    lemon cakes, 369–370
    red currant-horseradish, ham loaf with, 102
Golden Gate soup, 9–10
Goose, stuffed roast, with cranberry ice in orange shells, 163–164
Gordon Baldwin's quesadillas, 201–202
Gourmet catsup, 290
Gourmet spareribs, 111
Grapefruit
    pink, ice, 388–389
    zest of, 405
Gravy
    milk, fried chicken with fried biscuits and, 147–148
    red-eye, country ham with, 116
Great Aunt Hester's orange pie, 355–356
Great Northern bean salad, 272–273
Green bean(s)
    country, 223
    dilled, 306–307
    with mace, 223
Green chili(es)
    Aztec pie, 197
    chicken tacos with sour cream and, 198–199
chicken tamale pie with, 155–156
chili meat sauce, 186–187
enchiladas, 196–197
salsa, 187–188
and tomatillo sauce, 185–186
Zuñi lamb stew with corn and, 125–126
Green corn
    chicken in, 152–153
    soup, 13–14
Green Goddess dressing, 294
Green peppers, 400
Greens, 235
Green tomato(es)
    caramelized, 245
    curried, gratin of, 246
    sauce, veal steaks with, 95
Griddle cakes, wild rice and cornmeal, 321
Grison's Steak House slaw, 274
Grits
    grillades and, 96
    Pontchartrain, 261–262
    soufflé, 262–263
Guacamole, 190–191
Gumbo
    crab, cold, 9
    ideal, 32–34
    turkey oyster, 34
    z'herbes, 35–36

Ham
    baked, stuffed, 115–116
    and eggplant pilau, 177
    general data about, 401
    glaze for, 117–118
    hocks, farmhouse boiled dinner, 121
    with hominy and peaches, 118–119
    loaf, with red currant-horseradish glaze, 120
    with red-eye gravy, 116
    slices, with almonds, 118
    Smithfield, chicken and, 148–149
    sweetbreads with mushrooms and, 141–142
    with yams and chestnuts, baked with pippins, 119–120
Hamburgers, smoked oyster, 92–93
Happy Valley biscuits, 322
Hash
    clam, 209
    corned beef, with eggs, 84–85
Hearts, lamb, lemon-braised, 140
Helene's drop shortcakes, 324
Herbs (herbed)
    cherry tomatoes, 244–245
    country liver with, 135
    general data about, 401
    gumbo with, 35–36
    soup, Shaker, 14
    See also names of herbs
Hominy, ham platter with peaches and, 118–119
Hopping John, 183

Horseradish
   ice cream, 78–79
   -red currant glaze, ham loaf with, 120
Huevos rancheros, 203
Hunt Club creamed chipped beef, 211
Huntsville deviled kidneys, 137–138
Hush puppies, 46, 320–321
Hyannis cod fillets, chilled, 44–45
Hyannis fish chowder, 31

Iceberg lettuce for garnish, 190
Ice creams
   buttermilk rum-raisin, 388
   ginger peach, 385–386
   horseradish, 78–79
   rosewater, 389–390
   vanilla, 385
Ices
   cranberry, in orange shells, 163–164, 389
   pink grapefruit, 388–389
Icicle pickles, 305
Iowa lemon-braised lamb hearts, 140

Jalapeño peppers
   and cheese cornbread, 318–319
   pickled, stuffed with walnut cheese, 191–192
   salsa, 188
Jambalaya
   Creole, 178–179
   rabbit, 180
   shrimp, 179–180
au Valois, 207
Jam cake, 372
James Beard's turnips with mushrooms, 246–247
Jerusalem artichoke(s)
   roasted, 235–236
   salad, 270
Joe's special, 91

Kentucky black bean soup, 21
Kentucky red rice, 265–266
Kidneys, lamb
   deviled, 137–138
   stuffed, 138
Knives, 401

Ladybird's fillet of beef, 79–80
Lamb, 122–131
   breast of
      barbecued riblets, 128
      epigram of, 127–128
   chops, with caper-bread crumb sauce, 127
   ground, Four Seasons, 131
   hearts, lemon-braised, 140
   kidneys
      deviled, 137–138
      stuffed, 138

leg of
   butterflied, barbecued, 124
   with Parmesan potatoes, 123
rack of, almondine, 126–127
"ragoo," with asparagus, 129
shoulder of
   Creole stuffed, 124–125
   Zuñi stew with corn and green chilies, 125–126
Lemon
   -braised lamb hearts, 140
   cakes, glazed, 369–370
   meringue
      bread pudding, 381–382
      pie, 353
   pie, 353–354
   zest of, 405
Le Ruth's sauce *à la neige,* 52–53
Lettuce, iceberg, for garnish, 190
Liederkranz cheese, McSorley's Tavern lunch, 211–212
Lima beans, succotash, 231
Lime
   pie, with pecan crust, 354–355
   zest of, 405
Liver(s)
   calves'
      with French-fried sweet potatoes, 134–135
      and onions, 133
   chicken, in Madeira cream, 137
   with herbs, 135
   Maryland, 136
Lobster
   Newburg, 61–62
   stew, 28–29
Long Island oyster stew, 28
Louis Diat's vichyssoise, 4
Louisiana breast of turkey en daube, 166–168
Louisiana ratatouille, 234
Lyle's black-eyed pea salad, 279–280

Mace, green beans with, 223
McSorley's Tavern lunch, 211–212
Madeira
   cream, chicken livers in, 137
   pot roast with, 81–82
Mango chutney, mock, 301
Maple syrup, Shaker maple toast, 216
Maryland baked fish with cream, 46–47
Maryland pot roast Madeira, 81–82
Masa harina, 401
Massachusetts braised short ribs and celery, 89
Maum Nancy's scalloped oysters, 62–63
Mayonnaise, blender, 292
Meals in a bowl, 19–37
   ancestral turkey rice soup, 22
   Beverly Hills Rangoon Racquet Club champion-ship chili, 26–28

blackeyed pea soup, 23–25
ciopinno, 37
Creole court-bouillon, 36–37
gumbo z'herbes, 35–36
Hyannis fish chowder, 31
ideal gumbo, 32–34
Kentucky black bean soup, 21
lobster stew, 28–29
Long Island oyster stew, 28
New England clam chowder, 30
oxtail soup, 22–23
posole, 25–26
Senate bean soup, 20
sweet scallop stew, 29–30
turkey oyster gumbo, 34
Meat loaf
  Alfred Lunt's, 92
  ham, with red currant-horseradish glaze, 120
Meat sauce, chili, 186–187
Milk gravy, fried chicken with fried biscuits and,
  147–148
Miss Dorothy's brown bread, 338–339
Miss Dorothy's mashed potatoes, 250–251
Miss Dorothy's stuffed pork chops, 107–108
Miss Emily's perloo, 176
Mississippi mud cake, 364–365
Mole sauce, turkey in, 170–171
Mousse, chocolate, 386
Mrs. Truman's pudding, 377
Muffins
  potato, 326
  Shaker, 319
Mushroom(s)
  braised oxtails with, 90
  and spinach salad, 282
  sweetbreads with ham and, 141–142
  turnips with, 246–247
Mustard
  crab ring with, 59–60
  homemade, French-style, 291
My buttermilk fried chicken, 146–147
My frozen dark chocolate mousse, 386
My grandmother's drop noodles, 263–264
My grandmother's gooey butter rolls, 328–329
My liver and onions, 133
My mashed potatoes, 250–251
My mashed potato salad, 281
My mother's ham platter with hominy and peaches,
  118–119
My mother's orange peel cake, 363–364
My mother's pie crust, 348–349
My mother's sour cream peaked cauliflower, 228
My mother's triple layer cheese pie, 358–359
My nested potatoes, 252
My orange pecan pie, 356–357
My persimmon pudding, 380
My slaw, 276
My sour cream rum-raisin pie, 359–360
My white buttermilk bread, 334–335

Nantucket firemen's supper, 108–109
Nantucket glazed lemon cakes, 369–370
Natchez shrimp jambalaya, 179–180
Natillas, 204
Nebraska chicken cutlets, 157–158
New England baked spring chicken, 144
New England boiled dinner three ways, 83–84
New England clam chowder, 30
New England clam hash, 209
New Orleans bread pudding with bourbon sauce,
  380–381
New Orleans epigram of lamb, 127–128
New Orleans roast duck with sauce paradis, 161–
  162
New Orleans summer fast day soup, 15
New York egg and onion sandwich, 214–215
Noodle(s)
  drop, 263–264
  with eggs, 213–214
  pancake, 263
Northwestern scalloped potatoes and smoked salmon,
  51
Nut(s)
  general data about, 401
  torte, 374
  See also names of nuts

Ohio buttermilk mashed potato soufflé, 251–252
Oils, 401
Okra
  corn, tomatoes, and, 231–232
  fried, Kentucky-style, 236
  pickled, 307
  salad, 279
Omaha feather rum cake, 365–366
Omelets
  Denver, 214
  potato, 212–213
Onion(s)
  braised, French Quarter-style, 237–238
  and cheese enchiladas, 195–196
  and egg sandwich, 214–215
  general data about, 401–402
  gilded lily soup, 12
  liver and, 133
  pie, 210
  rings, French-fried, 237
  scalloped, 238
  stuffed, pork roast with, 103–104
Orange(s)
  ambrosia, 394
  cranberry relish, 311
  flan, 383–384
  pie, 355–356
    with pecans, 356–357
  red snapper with, 45
  shells, cranberry ice in, 163–164, 389
  yams, rum and, 261
  zest of, 405

Orange peel
  cake, 363–364
  green salad with walnuts and, 269–270
Orange rice, 265
  rabbit with, 165–166
Oxtail(s)
  braised, with mushrooms, 90
  soup, 22–23
Oyster(s)
  barbecued, 66
  Bienville, 67–68
  under glass, 64–65
  loaf, 65–66
  pan roast with cole slaw, 63
  Rockefeller, 66–67
  scalloped, 62–63
  smoked, burgers, 92–93
  stew, 28
  turkey gumbo, 34
  turkey shortcake with, 170

Pancake, noodle, 263
Paprika, 402
  veal with, 98
Paradise pie, 350–351
Paradis sauce, roast duck with, 161–162
Parker House rolls, 331
Parmesan potatoes, leg of lamb with, 123
Parsley
  and bacon pudding, 208
  dumplings, 325–326
  and piñon sauce, 293–294
Parsnip soufflé, 238–239
Paste, shrimp, 72–73
Peach(es) 77 – 78
  cobbler, 378–379
  ginger ice cream, 385–386
  ham platter with hominy and, 118–119
  mock mango chutney, 301
  pickled, 309–310
  pie, 352
Peas
  braised, with cucumbers, 239
  and new potatoes, creamed, 241
Pecan
  orange pie, 356–357
  pie crust, lime pie with, 354–355
  soup, 15–16
Pendennis Club barbecue sauce, 296
Pennsylvania chicken stuffed with sauerkraut and
    apples, 145–146
Pennsylvania Dutch noodles with eggs, 213–214
Pennyslvania Dutch paprika veal, 98
Pennsylvania Dutch plum cake, 369
Pennsylvania grated rutabagas, 242
Pennsylvania noodle pancake, 263
Pennsylvania potato muffins, 326
Pepper (black), 402
Pepper relish, 304

Persimmon pudding, 380
Philadelphia vanilla ice cream, 385
Picadillo, 195
  tostadas, 200–201
Piccalilli, 302
Pickles (pickled)
  bread and butter, 304–305
  icicle, 305
  okra, 307
  peaches, 309–310
  triple, 305–306
  watermelon rind, 309
Pie crust, 348–349
  pecan, lime pie with, 354–355
Pies, 347–361
  apple
    paradise, 350–351
    upside-down, 349–350
  Aztec, 197
  buttermilk chess, 358
  clam pot pie, 209–210
  crab, 56–57
  cream cheese, triple layer, 358–359
  Derby, 360–361
  lemon, 353–354
    meringue, 353
  lime, with pecan crust, 354–355
  onion, 210
  orange, 355–356
    with pecans, 356–357
  peach, 352
  rhubarb custard, 351–352
  shrimp and corn, 70
  sour cream rum-raisin, 359–360
  tamale, chicken chile verde, 155–156
  walnut, burnt sugar, 357
  Washington, 371
Pineapple, iced, Madame Bégué, 392–393
Pine nuts (piñon) and parsley sauce, 293–294
Pink grapefruit ice, 388–389
Pinto beans, refried, 189–190
Pippins, ham, yams, and chestnuts baked with, 119–
    120
Plantation lemon meringue pie, 353
Plantation nut torte, 374
Plantation stuffed loin of pork with rum prunes,
    104–105
Plum(s)
  cake, 369
  wild, roast veal with, 101
Podrilla à la Creole, 182
Pompano en papillote, Antoine, 47–48
Pompion, 241–242
Pork
  bacon
    buttermilk cornbread, 318
    and parsley pudding, 208
  carnitas, 192–193
  casserole, 109

chops
    with apple cider, 105–106
    braised, with quinces, 106
    Nantucket firemen's supper, 108–109
    with scallions and sour cream, 106–107
    stuffed, 107–108
chorizo, 192
ham
    baked, stuffed, 115–116
    and eggplant pilau, 177
    general data about, 401
    glaze for, 117–118
    hocks, farmhouse boiled dinner, 121
    with hominy and peaches, 118–119
    loaf, with red currant-horseradish glaze, 120
    with red-eye gravy, 116
    slices, with almonds, 118
    Smithfield, chicken and, 148–149
    sweetbreads with mushrooms and, 141–142
    with yams and chestnuts, baked with pippins,
        119–120
loin, stuffed, with rum prunes, 104–105
posole, 25–26
roast, with stuffed onions, 103–104
spareribs
    Georgia barbecue, 110
    gourmet, 110–111
    and sauerkraut, 111–112
See also Sausage
Portions, 402
Portland potatoes, 259–260
Posole, 25–26
Potato(es)
    baked, 258
        zucchini-stuffed, 258–259
    creamed, 256
    and cucumber soup, cold, 6–7
    fried
        American, 253
        Baltimore, 254
        Brabant, 253–254
        Saratoga, 254–255
    general data about, 402
    mashed, 250–251
        buttermilk soufflé, 251–252
        salad, 281
    muffins, 326
    nested, 252
    new
        salad, 280
        and spring peas, creamed, 241
    omelet, 212–213
    Parmesan, leg of lamb with, 123
    Portland, 259–260
    Russian Hill, 255–256
    scalloped, smoked salmon and, 51
    Shaker alabaster, 247
    thing, 212
    See also Sweet potatoes; Yams

Prawns Marin, 72
Prunes, rum, stuffed loin of pork with, 104–105
Puddings
    bacon and parsley, 208
    beef steak, 88
    bread
        with bourbon, 380–381
        lemon meringue, 381–382
    caramel, 378–379
    chicken, Colonial, 149–150
    corn, 230
    Denver, 379
    Mrs. Truman's, 377
    persimmon, 380
    root, 227
    turkey, 168
    Yorkshire, 78–79
Pumpkin
    cream soup, chilled, 5–6
    pompion, 241–242
Purée
    cauliflower, 228–229
    chestnut, 229
Putney chutney, 300

Quesadillas
    Gordon Baldwin's, 201–202
    simple, 201
Quinces, pork chops braised with, 106

Rabbit
    jambalaya, 180
    with orange rice, 165–166
    tarragon, 164–165
"Ragoo" of lamb and asparagus, 129
Raisin, rum-,
    ice cream, with buttermilk, 388
    pie, with sour cream, 359–361
Ratatouille, Louisiana, 234
Red beans and rice, 181–182
Red chili sauce, 185
Red currant-horseradish glaze, ham loaf with, 120
Red-eye gravy, country ham with, 116
Red kidney beans, podrilla à la Creole, 182
Red snapper, Florida orange snapper, 45
Refried beans, 189–190
Relishes
    blueberry rhubarb, 311–312
    chowchow, 302–303
    corn, 303
    cranberry orange, 311
    pepper, 304
    piccalilli, 302
    turnip, 310
Rhubarb
    blueberry relish, 311–312
    custard pie, 351–352
Rice
    dry, 264
    feathered, 267

Rice *(continued)*
general data about, 402
— jambalaya
    Creole, 178–179
    rabbit, 180
    shrimp, 179–180
    — au Valois, 207 ✓
Miss Emily's perloo, 176
orange, 265
    rabbit with, 165–166
pilau
    ham and eggplant, 177
    Thomas Jefferson's, 266
    turkey, with walnuts, 177–178
podrilla à la Creole, 182
red, 265–266
red beans and, 181–182
turkey soup with, 22
wild, and cornmeal griddle cakes, 321
Roanoke rum cream, 382–383
Rolls
    butter, 328–329
    Parker House, 331
    rose geranium, 332
    sesame, 332–333
Root pudding, 227
Rosewater ice cream, 389–390
Rum
    avocado slices marinated in, 191
    bananas in, 391–392
    cake, 365–366
    cream, 382–383
    general data about, 402–403
    and orange yams, 261
    prunes, stuffed loin of pork with, 104–105
    -raisin
        ice cream, with buttermilk, 388
        pie, with sour cream, 359–360
Russian Hill potatoes, 255–256
Rutabagas
    grated, 242
    gratin of apples, sweet potatoes, and, 220–221
Rye and Indian bread, 339–340

Salad dressings
    Green Goddess, 294
    for a green salad, 269
Salads
    Carolina okra, 279
    carrot slaw, 277
    celery Victor, 278
    cream dilly bean, 270–271
    four bean, 272
    Great Northern bean, 272–273
    green
        dressing for, 269
        with walnuts and orange peel, 269–270
    jade cucumber sticks, 278–279
    Jerusalem artichoke, 270

Lyle's black-eyed pea, 279–280
potato
    mashed, 281
    new, 280
spinach
    and mushroom, 282
    and watercress, 282–283
string bean, 271
tomato
    country, 283
    with cream, 284
turnip slaw with capers, 284–285
watercress à la Germaine, 285
zucchini slaw, 286
    See also Cole slaw
Salem lamb chops with caper-bread crumb sauce, 127
Salmi of duck, 162–163
Salmon
    bisque, chilled, 8
    George Washington, 49
    smoked, scalloped potatoes and, 51
Salsa, *see* Sauces
Salt, 403
Salt rising bread, 340–341
Sandwiches
    egg and onion, 214–215
    soft-shelled crab, 60
San Francisco green salad with walnuts and orange
    peel, 269–270
Saratoga chips, 254–255
Sauces, 289–298
    apple, Shaker, 310
    barbecue, 294–296
        composite, 296–297
        Pendennis Club, 296
    bottled, 297–298
    bourbon, bread pudding with, 380–381
    caper-bread crumb, lamb chops with, 127
    catsup
        curried apricot, 290–291
        gourmet, 290
    chili meat, 186–187
    French Quarter, 44, 293
    green chili salsa, 187–188
    green chili tomatillo, 185–186
    green tomato, veal steaks with, 95
    jalapeño salsa, 188
    mayonnaise, blender, 292
    mole, turkey in, 170–171
    mustard, homemade French-style, 291
    à la neige, Le Ruth's, 52–53
    paradis, roast duck with, 161–162
    piñon and parsley, 293–294
    red chili, 185
    strawberry, 390–391
    tartar, 292–293
Sauerkraut
    chicken stuffed with apples and, 145–146
    spareribs and, 111–112

Sausage
boulette de saucisson, 207–208
chaurice, 113
homemade country, 112–113
jambalaya au Valois, 207
Sautéing, 403
Savoy Plaza pot roast, 82
Scallions, pork chops with sour cream and, 106–107
Scallop(s)
Delmonico, 68–69
stew, 29–30
Senate bean soup, 20
Sesame seed(s)
benne wafers, 327–328
rolls, 332–333
Shad roe poached in butter, 51–52
Shaker alabaster, 247
Shaker apple cider pork chops, 105–106
Shaker applesauce, 310
Shaker cabbage in caraway cream, 226
Shaker Carolina cake, 366–367
Shaker chicken in cider cream, 150
Shaker cornbread (or muffins), 319
Shaker dill bread, 337
Shaker herb soup, 14
Shaker lemon meringue bread pudding, 381–382
Shaker lemon pie, 353–354
Shaker maple toast, 216
Shaker rhubarb custard pie, 351–352
Shaker rose geranium rolls, 332
Shaker rosewater ice cream, 389–390
Shaker string bean salad, 271
Shaker veal fricassee, 98–99
Shaker yellow velvet, 232
Shellfish
cioppino, 37
See also names of shellfish
Shortcake(s)
drop, 324
strawberry, 390
turkey oyster, 170
Shrimp
and chicken *étouffée,* 73–74
and corn pie, 70
cucumber aspic with, 71
eggplant stuffed with, 58–59
jambalaya, 179–180
paste, 72–73
prawns Marin, 72
scalloped, 69–70
Slaws
carrot, 277
cole, 273–276
Grison's Steak House, 274
old-fashioned, 274–276
oyster pan roast with, 63
wilted, with sour cream, 276–277
turnip, with capers, 284–285
zucchini, 286

Smithfield ham, chicken and, 148–149
Smoked salmon, scalloped potatoes and, 51
Snickerdoodles, 375
with watermelon, 394
Soft-shelled crab(s)
with almonds, 61
sandwich, 60
Sole, crisp, with anchovy cream, 43
Soufflés
acorn squash, 244
buttermilk mashed potato, 251–252
grits, 262–263
parsnip, 238–239
summer squash, 243
Soups, 1–37
ancestral turkey rice, 22
avocado cream, 7
Beverly Hills Rangoon Racquet Club championship chili, 26–28
blackeyed pea, 23–25
Charleston she-crab, 18
chestnut, 16–17
chilled pumpkin cream, 5–6
chilled salmon bisque, 8
ciopinno, 37
cold crab gumbo, 9
cold cucumber and potato, 6–7
Creole court-bouillon, 36–37
Delaware clam, 17–18
gilded lily, 12
Golden Gate, 9–10
green corn, 13–14
gumbo z'herbes, 35–36
Hyannis fish chowder, 31
ideal gumbo, 32–34
Kentucky black bean, 21
lobster stew, 28–29
Long Island oyster stew, 28
New England clam chowder, 30
New Orleans summer fast day, 15
oxtail, 22–23
pecan, 15–16
posole, 25–26
Senate bean, 20
Shaker herb, 14–15
summer squash bisque, 10
sweet scallop stew, 29–30
tomato, with tarragon, 12–13
turkey oyster gumbo, 34
vichyssoise
of beet greens, 4–5
Louis Diat's, 4
winter, 85
Sour cream
beets with their greens in, 224–225
black bean tostadas with, 200
cauliflower with, 228
chicken tacos with green chilies and, 198–199

Sour cream (continued)
  pork chops with scallions and, 106–107
  rum-raisin pie with, 359–360
  wilted slaw with, 276–277
Sourdough breads, 341–344
  biscuits, 343–344
  cracked-wheat, 343
  white, 342
Southern dry rice, 264
Southwestern foods, 184–204
  Aldo's chili meat sauce, 186–187
  avocado slices marinated in rum, 191
  Aztec pie, 197
  burritos, 202
  carnitas, 192–193
  chimichangas, 202–203
  chorizo, 192
  enchiladas
    cheese and green onion, 195–196
    green chili, 196–197
  Frances Sommer's jalapeño salsa, 188
  green chili salsa, 187–188
  green chili tomatillo sauce, 185–186
  guacamole, 190
  huevos rancheros, 203
  natillas, 204
  picadillo, 195
  pickled jalapeños stuffed with walnut and cheese,
    191–192
  quesadillas
    Gordon Baldwin's, 201–202
    simple, 201
  red chili sauce, 185
  refried beans, 189–190
  tacos
    chicken, with green chilies and sour cream,
      198–199
    simple, 198
  tinga, 193
  tortilla chips, 188–189
  tostadas
    black bean, with sour cream, 200
    picadillo, 200–201
    simple, 199
Spareribs
  Georgia barbecue, 110
  gourmet, 110–111
  and sauerkraut, 111–112
Spices (spiced)
  crab apples, 306
  general data about, 403
Spinach
  with cream cheese and chives, 242–243
  and mushroom salad, 282
  and watercress salad, 282–283
Spokane scalloped onions, 238
Spoonbread, Georgia, 319–320
Squash
  acorn, soufflés, 244

summer
  bisque, 10
  Shaker yellow velvet, 232
  soufflé, 243
State Fair corn relish, 303
Stew
  lamb, with corn and green chilies, 125–126
  lobster, 28–29
  oyster, 28
  sweet scallop, 29–30
Stock
  beef, 403
  chicken, 403–404
  fish, 404
Strawberry(ies)
  sauce, 390–391
  shortcake, 390
    with strawberry sauce, 390–391
    white, 391
Succotash, 231
Sugar, burnt, walnut pie, 357
Summer cloud biscuits, 322–323
Summer squash
  bisque, 10
  Shaker yellow velvet, 232
  soufflé, 243
Sweetbreads
  country-style, 140–141
  with ham and mushrooms, 141–142
Sweet potatoes
  deep-fried, 260
  French-fried, liver with, 134–135
  gratin of apples, rutabagas, and, 220–221

Tacos
  chicken, with green chilies and sour cream, 198–
    199
  simple, 198
Talahassee lime pie with pecan crust, 354–355
Tarragon
  rabbit with, 164–165
  tomato soup with, 12–13
  vinegar, fish fillets in, 42
Tartar sauce, 292–293
Temperature, 404
Tennessee jam cake, 372
Texas jalapeño cheese cornbread, 318–319
Texas long cake, 367
Thing, 212
Thomas Jefferson's pilau, 266
Thomas Jefferson's ragoût of beef, 86
Thomas Jefferson's salmi of duck, 162–163
Tidewater scalloped shrimp, 69–70
Tinga, 193
Toast, Shaker maple, 216
Tomatillo and green chili sauce, 185–186
Tomato(es)
  cherry, herbed, 244–245
  corn, okra, and, 231–232

general data about, 404
green
    caramelized, 245
    gratin of, curried, 246
    sauce, veal steaks with, 95
salad, 283
    with cream, 284
    soup, with tarragon, 12–13
Tomato paste, 404
Tony's highway barbecue oysters, 66
Tortes
    fudge cream, 373–374
    nut, 374
Tortilla chips, 188–189
Tostadas
    black bean, with sour cream, 200
    picadillo, 200–201
    simple, 199
Trout with Le Ruth's sauce à la neige, 52–53
Turkey
    breast of, en daube, 166–168
    in mole sauce, 170–171
    oyster gumbo, 34
    oyster shortcake, 170
    pilau, with walnuts, 177–178
    pudding, 168
    soup, with rice, 22
Turnip(s)
    with mushrooms, 246–247
    relish, 310
    Shaker alabaster, 247
    slaw, with capers, 284–285

Vanilla
    general data about, 404
    ice cream, 385
Variety meats, 132–142
    hearts, lemon-braised, 140
    kidneys
        deviled, 137–138
        stuffed, 138
    liver, beef
        with herbs, 135
        Maryland, 136
    liver, calves'
        with French-fried sweet potatoes, 134–135
        and onions, 133
    liver, chicken, in Madeira cream, 137
    sweetbreads
        country-style, 140–141
        with ham and mushrooms, 141–142
Veal, 94–101
    fricassee, 98–99
    grillades and grits, 96
    roast, with wild plums, 101
    smothered, with chestnuts, 100
    steaks
        with green tomato sauce, 95
        paprika, 98

sweetbreads
    country-style, 140–141
    with ham and mushrooms, 141–142
Vegetables
    ratatouille, 234
    root pudding, 227
    See also names of vegetables
Vichyssoise
    of beet greens, 4–5
    Louis Diat's, 4
Vinegar, 405
    tarragon, fish fillets in, 42
Virginia shrimp paste, 72–73
Virginia sweetbreads with ham and mushrooms,
    141–142

Walnut(s)
    burnt sugar pie, 357
    green salad with orange peel and, 269–270
    pickled jalapeños stuffed with cream cheese and,
        191–192
    turkey pilau with, 177–178
Washington pie, 371
Watercress salad
    à la Germaine, 285
    with spinach, 282–283
Watermelon
    rind pickles, 309
    with snickerdoodles, 394
White bread
    with buttermilk, 334–335
    sourdough, 342
White wine snow, 384–385
Whole-wheat biscuits, 325
Wild plums, roast veal with, 101
Wild rice and cornmeal griddle cakes, 321
Williamsburg oysters under glass, 64–65
Wine
    general data about, 405
    white snow, 384–385
Winter soup, 85
Wyoming turkey pudding, 168

Yale beets, 224
Yams
    baked, 260–261
    with ham and chestnuts, baked with pippins,
        119–120
    orange, rum and, 261
Yeast, 405
Yorkshire pudding, 78–79

Zephyrs, 317
Zests, 405
Zucchini
    baked potatoes stuffed with, 258–259
    fritters, 248
    slaw, 286
Zuñi lamb stew with corn and green chilies, 125–
    126

About the Author

*R*onald Johnson was born November 25th, 1935, in the small, ordinary, artless, meat-and-two-veg town of Ashland, in southwestern Kansas. Some of the names of places in that part of the prairie make them more exotic than is the truth: Buttermilk, Bloom, Protection, Acres, Moscow, Ulysses, Liberal, Kismet. Kismet, Kansas — it's hard to beat.

I met Ron Johnson in Washington, DC at the beginning of 1958. He was handsome, red-haired, feisty, ebullient, and clearly very bright. The friendship was immediate and we joined forces. I became his mentor, just enough older for that relationship to work. We moved to New York and I worked at the famous 8th Street Bookshop in Greenwich Village, while RJ completed a B.A. degree at Columbia College. We hung out at the Cedar Tavern on University Place with friends like Joel Oppenheimer, Franz Kline, Dan Rice, Fielding Dawson, Gilbert Sorrentino, Esteban Vicente, many of whom I'd known from my earlier days at Black Mountain College. And we visited non-bar-type writers like William Carlos Williams, Louis Zukofsky, and Edward Dahlberg.

In the summer of 1961, RJ and I hiked the Appalachian Trail from Springer Mountain, Georgia to the Hudson River in New York, some 1447 miles. Perfect training for poets: learning to attend the names of birds and plants and stars and trees and stones. The summer of 1962 I was a writer-in-residence at the Aspen Institute of Humanistic Studies in Colorado; and RJ had his first culinary job, at *The Copper Kettle Restaurant*. In the autumn of 1962 we headed for England and walked five weeks in the Lake District. On the Sunday of the weekend of the Cuban Missile Crisis the poets spent the day trying to locate the graves of Beatrix Potter in Near Sawrey and Kurt Schwitters in Ambleside — and found neither.

In 1965-66 we were again in Britain doing a lot of walking, looking for all things, as RJ said, "most rich, most glittering, most strange." Jane Grigson cooked us Welsh gridle cakes for breakfast. Delicious! RJ made a Shaker lemon for the evening that we invited Buckminster Fuller and William Burroughs to supper. (Neither knew who the other was.) Fortunately two pies were made, since Burroughs ate an entire one. The Fourth of July, 1966, we had lunch at Fernand Point's *Restaurant de la Pyramide* in Vienne, the best food either of us had ever tasted.

The peripatetic life continued. I was again at the Aspen Institute. RJ decided one winter's day in 1968 that the rustic life was just plain tiresome. I didn't agree, so I stayed put and he headed for San Francisco. He lived there over twenty years, cooking and writing. Suffering from melanoma, he returned to Topeka Kansas, where he died in his father's house on March 4, 1998.

A good introduction to Ronald Johnson's poetry would be the recently published *To Do As Adam Did*, a selection from seven books, including *ARK*, a huge architectonic poem in 99 sections, published by Talisman House. It is very special.

RJ's excellent cookbooks include *Simple Fare, Company Fare, New & Old Southwestern Cooking*, and *The American Table*. This latter is a classic work, the prose right up there with M.F.K. Fisher and Richard Olney.

—Jonathan Williams
Skywinding Farm,
Scaly Mountain, North Carolina